The Achievement of
WILLIAM STYRON

Revised Edition

Edited by

Robert K. Morris

with Irving Malin

The University of Georgia Press

Athens

Copyright © 1975, 1981 by the University of Georgia Press

Athens, Georgia 30602

All rights reserved

Design by Martyn Hitchcock

Set in 11 on 13 Monticello

Printed in the United States of America

Library of Congress Cataloging in Publication Data
Main entry under title:

The Achievement of William Styron.

  Bibliography: p.
  1. Styron, William, 1925–   —Criticism and interpre-
tation—Addresses, essays, lectures. 2. Styron, William,
1925–   —Bibiliography. I. Styron, William, 1925–
II. Morris, Robert K. III. Malin, Irving.
PS3569.T9Z56   1981   813'.54   81-984
ISBN 0-8203-0567-7   AACR2
ISBN 0-8203-0569-3 (pbk.)

Contents

CONTENTS

Acknowledgments

Excerpts from the work of William Styron are reprinted with the kind permission of Random House and Bobbs-Merrill. Acknowledgments are also made to the following, who have granted permission for the reprinting of copyrighted material from the periodicals and books that are here listed.

"Notes on a Southern Writer in Our Time" by Louis D. Rubin, Jr., originally appeared as chapter 8, "William Styron: Notes on a Southern Writer in Our Time," in his *The Faraway Country: Writers of the Modern South* (Seattle: University of Washington Press, 1963).

"William Styron's Southern Myth" by Jane Flanders originally appeared in *Louisiana Studies* [now *Southern Studies: An Interdisciplinary Journal of the South*] (Fall 1976).

"*The Confessions of Nat Turner* and the Burden of the Past" by George Core originally appeared in the *Southern Literary Journal* (Spring 1970).

"The Recollective Structure of *The Confessions of Nat Turner*" by Ardner R. Cheshire, Jr., originally appeared in the *Southern Review* (1976).

"*The Confessions of Nat Turner*: Styron's 'Meditation on History' as Rhetorical Act" by Mary S. Strine originally appeared in the *Quarterly Journal of Speech* (1978).

"William Styron: A Bibliography" by Jackson R. Bryer updates and supplements previous listings by Harold W. Schneider in *Critique* (Summer 1960); David D. Galloway in *The Absurd Hero in American Fiction* (Austin: University of Texas Press, 1966); August J. Nigro in *William Styron*, edited by Melvin J. Friedman and Nigro (Paris: Lettres modernes, 1967); Bryer and Marc Newman in *William Styron's "The Confessions of Nat Turner"—A Critical Handbook*, edited by Melvin J. Friedman and Irving Malin (Belmont, Calif.: Wadsworth, 1970); and Professor Bryer's bibliography published in the first edition of this book.

The editor wishes to thank William Styron for granting the three interviews published in this collection.

Preface to Second Edition

In the six years since *The Achievement of William Styron* first appeared, critical and—if such a term is remotely applicable to sales of scholarly studies—commercial response has been most gratifying. That and the advent in 1979 of *Sophie's Choice* have generated the need for further reevaluation of an indisputably major American talent who grows with each novel written.

For the most part, we have revised the second edition of *The Achievement of William Styron* in light of the formidable and passionate canvas of the Holocaust. The amplified introduction attempts to place *Sophie's Choice* in the Styron canon; a new, long interview with the author—supplementing the two previous interviews—revolves primarily around it; a newly commissioned essay focuses on its central meaning; and the comprehensive bibliography is expanded to include it.

We have not, however, confined revisions to account solely for *Sophie's Choice*. Two essays on *The Confessions of Nat Turner* are new to this edition. Two new overviews of Styron's work—one (reprinted) dealing with a number of his major themes, the other (commissioned) dealing with his narrative technique—enlarge upon the overview found in our introduction and in Louis D. Rubin's classic essay.

With all the additions and deletions—some calculated, some unavoidable—we hope the second edition not only sustains the continuity of the first, but improves upon it, helping both the general reader and scholar to better understand William Styron's vision and value as an artist.

ROBERT K. MORRIS
IRVING MALIN

Abbreviations

LDD   *Lie Down in Darkness* (Indianapolis: Bobbs-Merrill, 1951)

LM   *The Long March* (New York: Random House, 1956)

SHF   *Set This House on Fire* (New York: Random House, 1960)

NT   *The Confessions of Nat Turner* (New York: Random House, 1967)

CS   *In the Clap Shack* (New York: Random House, 1973)

SC   *Sophie's Choice* (New York: Random House, 1979)

THE ACHIEVEMENT OF WILLIAM STYRON

ROBERT K. MORRIS & IRVING MALIN

Vision and Value: The Achievement of William Styron

A quarter of a century has passed since the heroine of a remarkable first novel flung herself and a dubious heritage from the twelfth story of a dingy Harlem tenement, shocking a silent and almost unshockable generation, and rocketing a young southern writer to fame. Peyton Loftis was the fated, tragic girl; *Lie Down in Darkness* the novel; and the writer William Styron: an expatriate intellectual from Virginia's Tidewater, to whom it must have seemed unlikely (though not undeserved) that his novel of southern generations would have spoken so eloquently to the entire generation of the fifties, and that his own place among important contemporary writers should have been so quickly secured.

It was, of course, something other than chance that accounted for Styron's immediate popularity, indeed notoriety; for he had labored over the book with conflicting emotions for nearly five years, honing each sentence to such perfection that his paragraphs could defend themselves by their cutting edge alone. But there was no denying chance had a good deal to do with it. Styron had caught in a precise and lucky way the spirit of time and place. The postwar world sagged with weariness, disbelief, acedia, and guilt. Naturally prepared to find its own conscience trapped in the psychic rifts of one like Peyton—possessed and dispossessed, haunted, alienated, desolate—it was equally willing to universalize the neuroses destroying the Loftises: to see their "nothingness" both as moral sanction and symbol for what remained for so many after Belsen and Buchenwald and Auschwitz, Hiroshima and Nagasaki and Dresden. Everything about *Lie Down in Darkness*—whose very title spoke of the metaphysical uncertainty of eternal certainties—proved that the sins of the fathers (both nouns damning whether capitalized or not) had been visited on the children; and showed it by way of instinct and art. For Styron seemed to be grappling with the big problems of the ethos: seeking to make more explicable and coherent what was easily absurd and incoherent; striving to unravel the gross and unreasonable confusion attending the change and destruction that operated in one small part of the South, but, spreading tentaclelike, were becoming symptomatic of America as a whole.

What we can see today, thirty years later, is that the now classic *Lie Down in Darkness* was not only in part a parable of and for the fifties, not only in part an incantatory prophecy of middle-class confusion and breakup in the New South following hard upon the breakdown of the Old, but a model for the fictional world Styron was to re-create in subsequent novels. That world, as he articulated in a letter to the *Paris Review* in 1953, was one of "disorder, defeat, despair," in which men and women search for "love, joy, hope— qualities which, as in the act of life itself, are best when they have to be struggled for, and are not commonly come by with much ease."[1] In the best way that writers "repeat" themselves in order to fathom and expand as profoundly as they can those very ideas that have initially committed them to art, so Styron continually drives his protagonists to the very edge of the abyss; lets them peer into deep, empty, nihilistic spaces before, in tragic recognition of themselves, they pull back, renewed, to carry on their search, or ecstatically transformed embrace their death. Such a theme—metaphysical, existential, overwhelming—is by no means original. Modern man's encounter with the abyss—his confrontation with being and nothingness, his agonizing over free will, his apprehensive acceptance of fear and trembling, his search for his soul—has, in one way or another since Dostoevski, been at the center of the modern novel. And no one would rest claims for Styron's originality or importance or achievement on this all-too solid, if worn, surface.

What makes him unique is that he has created characters who, despite their realization of the abyss, are willing, out of the sense of an ultimate motive and purpose in life, to challenge it. This is much of the reason why Peyton commits suicide; why Cass Kinsolving plunges into the gaping hell of Sambuco and Nat Turner into the horrendous, inevitable blood bath in Southampton County; why Captain Mannix and Private Magruder persist in their small, marvelous, unnoticed martyrdoms; why Sophie Zawistowska, after surviving the "absolute evil" of Auschwitz, though psychically dying there, endures further the demonic relationship with the schizophrenic Nathan Landau as a temporary recall to life. To be sure, much of this movement comes from sheer drive and energy alone. Styron's people are compulsive, intense, made of a human fiber both elastic and tough. It comes as well because in some ideal way each does aspire to "love, joy, hope," does (in Frederick J. Hoffman's words) "struggle just to *assert* one's humanness, to get over the barriers of understanding, to clear one's personality of obsessions."[2] But they are not impelled by intellectual, physical, even emotional kinesis alone. They are equally galvanized by a higher intuition, by the belief that the abyss, all too ready to claim and damn them, can be transcended, and some "impossible state"[3] (where pride, dignity, nobility become the final measure of man) achieved. Their quest is for nothing less than a kind of grail: buried within the darker divisions of a world of conflicting change and lost value, to which they are drawn by its fitful incandescence, as by their own burning, ecstatic, and often tragic visions.

To speak, first of all, of vision in Styron's characters is to realize at the outset a formidable play of perceptions among them: ranging from the realist to the mystic, from the supernormal to the lunatic, from the secular to the divine, from the private to the apocalyptic. It is to realize further that any and all such visions are spun out of a novelist who himself happens to tack close to becoming considered a "visionary": one, as Northrop Frye has defined the type elsewhere, "who creates a higher spiritual world in which the objects of perception in this one have become transfigured and charged with a new intensity of symbolism."[4] Unlike other visionary writers, though, who depart from parabolic or abstract figures of reality (we think of Dante and Milton, Blake and Yeats), Styron creates his personae's visions from metaphors of reality. His characters' yearning for the "impossible state," for (on their terms) a finer, more desirable world, even for some glorious surcease from the anxieties and pressures of this one, are always built upon what is concrete, mundane, ordinary: as though their symbolic imagination need root itself in the solid stuff of life.

Styron's visionary esthetic emerges almost entire in his first

[3]

novel. The Loftises' progress through private purgatories to attain some ultimate, untroubled heaven where mind and spirit and body are at peace proves a series of doomed encounters with a reality each tries to shape according to his own distorted, disoriented, self-serving and self-seeking yet solipsistically "true" vision. But such journeys become more. In Milton Loftis one senses something other than the merely fallen, aging, middle-class male at climacteric who seeks, but never finds, refuge and salvation in adultery and alcohol. Beyond the stereotype looms an archetype: that of the failed quester who has hoped to transform a common mistress into a divine Beatrice, and drink into the ambrosia that preserves to the last the dregs of mortality, shields him against age, despair, loss, inadequacy, pain, failure, and impotence; the quester who has found life a depressing recurrence of half-open doors through which he followed a dream, hoping to open the final door and look upon a beatitude instead, as he does, of peering into the horror and nothingness.

Like Milton, Helen is equally the victim and agent of her fate. Her effete, sentimentalized religion (the obvious foil to the vitalistic faith of La Ruth) is no less a dangerous construct of reality and of living in the world than her husband's sex and drink. She too hoped, through transcendental longing, for a "timeless, unaltered" state in which to knit crippling despair into wholeness. But if Milton is pulled down by his materialism and sensuality, Helen is damned by her obsessive piety and Puritanism: by her having traded this life for one of spiritual emasculation. Like certain fanatics who lose touch with the flesh-and-blood world, Helen treads the fragile line between mystic and catatonic.

And there is the incomprehensibleness and complexity of Peyton herself, whose neurotic, inspired madness and hallucinatory excess lead her to an end that is, as much as a reaction to her parents' conflicts, the consequence of their (and Sir Thomas Browne's) insights that life irretrievably slips away, evanesces. Peyton's hypersensitivity to love, hope, and joy, and her rejection of the cold, cheerless mechanisms making life run on as best it can, bespeak a prelapsarian idealism. But her answer to life is no truer than Milton's or Helen's. Her suicide, while partially a tragic expiation by doomed youth of sins committed by its fathers, at the same time evades all responsibility for harnessing one's strengths—instead of agonizing

[4]

over one's weaknesses—and working for stability and order. It takes neither intelligence nor guts to surrender to chaos; in retrospect, her death has perhaps more retaliative than retributive value. Indeed, her final vision—antimechanistic, falsely liberating, purgative, death-yearning—accompanying her fall from the highest rung of perverted innocence and her flight from paradise through a wilderness of tangled literary allusions, has almost no place in Styron's later work. Had she, in her final soliloquy, her *Liebestod*, brooded upon Camus rather than upon Aeschylus and Dante and the Bible, she might have understood that embracing the cosmos is meaningless without first having gained mastery over one's self. For as Styron implies, the man-made holocaust at Hiroshima and Nagasaki enacted synchronously with Peyton's suicide should give the lie to our ever taking the random, unthinking cosmos as hostile. Man alone is capable of evil; man creates; man destroys; man surrenders; man endures. In the most important way, their failure to conceive man's inward, latent power on all these counts permits the easy submission to fate by the three protagonists of *Lie Down in Darkness*. The lack of stoicism allows the self to be swallowed up by fate, victory in death, and nothingness.

Just how primary the affirmation of self is to Styron becomes apparent in his next novel, where the vision of recovery preempts this vision of extinction. Death gives the impetus and occasion to both books; but where the funeral in *Lie Down in Darkness* travels an inexorable route to pessimism and a kind of suspended nihilism (we are left at the end, however ambiguously, with the stoicism of the Negroes), the eight corpses strewn about the Carolina countryside at the opening of *The Long March*—transmitting an anonymous, but imagistically as potent a sense of capricious destruction as the single crushed body of Peyton Loftis—are calculated foils to the life-affirming purpose and sense of survival harbored in the themes and shaping vision of that novel.

It is Culver, the central intelligence of *The Long March*, who establishes from the first the novel's concern with vision. He ordains those subjective inventions of reality shared among the trio comprising himself, Mannix, and Templeton: inventions, however disparate and conflicting, that are psychologically and morally necessary for anyone who believes life is a matter of design rather than

[5]

accident. Consequently, *The Long March* becomes—after the grim, offstage misfiring of mortar shells—a series of small, resonating human explosions set off by charged psyches and volatile imagination. The world of the novel is scarcely rendered objectively at all, but through its progressive transfigurations of reality by each of its three principal actors.

When, for example, Culver stares at the "slick nude litter of intestine and shattered blue bones, among which forks and spoons peeked out like so many pathetic metal flowers," he transfigures the particular scene as well as the total setting of the novel by at once mediating and juxtaposing its two planes: the grim regimentation of barracks life and forced marches, and the world of nature whose order has been disturbed and violated. Even in the underplayed simile we find a jarring irony—one finds something almost identical in Henry Reed's magnificent poem, "Naming of Parts"—on the use (or misuse) of such vision. What we learn from *Lie Down in Darkness* is that the transfiguration of reality not only heightens the real world but makes it more tolerable to contemplate; what we learn from *The Long March* is that the passion of Styron's characters to transform the ordinary enables them to see things more clearly, and, however erroneously, more cohesively. This is much less of a paradox than it seems. Even so deadly and inimical an artifact as Templeton's .38 becomes for him a totem which substantiates his identity and helps transform *his* world. By owning this "emblematic prerogative"—an extension of himself, one of those concrete metaphors of reality alluded to above—he demonstrates to himself that he is "authority." As Templeton shapes his quite literal revolver into a symbol of existence, so Mannix shapes Templeton and the march into mythic quanta of fiend and trial to which he as the rebel hero must give battle.

This is by no means all *The Long March* has to say. But once we see how the various themes of *Lie Down in Darkness* have been heightened (and even defined) through visions induced by alcohol, religion, neuroses, and how through natural and mythic orderings of experience such visions have swelled to touch on additional themes of "will" and "power," we may better understand how Styron's material crescendoes and fuses in his next two novels, *Set This*

[6]

House on Fire and *The Confessions of Nat Turner*: the one dealing with the artist's, the other with the revolutionary's vision.

Suggesting that Styron is writer qua visionary is not to imply either directly or indirectly that his work shows a preponderance of content over form. The content of art qualitatively inheres because of the form imposed upon it: the "fancy" of the artist, the "aggregating or associative vision" as Coleridge (who has never been bettered in the esthetics of the creative principle) called it, is only completed through the act of "imagination" or "shaping vision." Exactly to what degree any artist must absorb the stuff of reality—the fixed objects of the real world that become his vision—before transmuting that vision into art, is a problem he must face sooner or later in his creative evolution; generally, with a writer, the problem itself provides a theme to be written about. Styron sought to face it (among other things) in *Set This House on Fire*, to question the force and responsibility of artistic visions as they tamper with life: not as Mann or Joyce or even Hesse did through surrogates of mature or ab ovo genius, but through three fallible visions by "artists" of sorts who themselves are subjected to tampering by life.

The first of such is Cass Kinsolving, a *peintre manqué* who views the world in bizarre, nightmarish ways, and who is dangerously overwhelmed by such visions, be they "good" or "bad." Here, for example, is one of the "good" visions: an epiphany of Paris:

It wasn't just the *scene*, you see—it was the sense, the bleeding *essence* of the thing. It was as if I had been given for an instant the capacity to understand not just beauty itself by its outward signs, but the other—the elseness in beauty; this continuity of beauty in the scheme of all life which triumphs even to the point of taking in sordidness and shabbiness and ugliness, which goes on and on and on, and of which this was only a moment, I guess, divinely crystallized. (SHF, p. 257)

And here is one of the "bad": not an autistic inspiration, this time, but one of a plethora of recurring

wild Manichean dreams, dreams that told him that God was not even a lie, but worse, that He was weaker even than the evil he created and allowed to reside in the soul of man, that God Himself was doomed, and the landscape of heaven was not gold and singing but a space of terror which stretched in darkness from horizon to horizon. (SHF, pp. 275–276)

[7]

Here, and throughout the novel, Cass's visions—alternatingly bea-tific and apocalyptic—are almost textbook examples of his sub-limating the art that fails to get put down on canvas and a budding schizophrenia exacerbated by drink and illness. Such visions sup-port, on several counts, his Dostoevskian plunge into sin and dam-nation (one recalls in *The Brothers Karamazov* Dmitri's paradoxical reconciliation of the Madonna and Sodom) before the Dantean as-cension through grace to salvation. Yet while the novel is concerned with Cass's redemption, with his phoenixlike rise from a wrecked bone-house near consumed by literal and symbolic fires, it does more than spontaneously generate an eschatology from the dunghill of psychopathology. Despite the novel's "Christian" overlay—the epigraph from Donne, however gloomy and portentous, neverthe-less augurs resurrection—Cass's "aggregating visions" have not readied him for last or otherworldly things; rather, his fanciful, privileged *Augenblicke* have returned him to the things of this world. That Cass comes by way of these eternal moments to reject the fatal, narcissistic longings of mystic, martyr, potential suicide, shows how even the imagination of a failed painter can reshape the imperfections of life in something like (as he calls it at the very end of the novel) ecstasy.

There is, in quite a different vein, the vision of Mason Flagg, who transfigures reality through his own peculiar artistry: sex. "Sex," he sees, combining his idée fixe into Krafft-Ebing objectivity and de Sade delirium, "is the last frontier." He wants an eternal "explora-tion of sex," one which will enable him to get free of his body and his oppressive feelings of oncoming impotence and weakness. But Mason as an artist—he claims that sex at its greatest is "nurtured and refined like any other high art"—fails to thrive either on vision or experience; he is too conscious or too *self*-conscious to mature in the throes of one or the other. Unlike Cass, who is overpowered by his visions to the point that each endows him with a "presentiment of selflessness," Mason is always in control: a *mechanical* man who manipulates any sensation to further perfect the lie that ultimately destroys him.

If, as would appear from this discussion thus far, Styron has so structured *Set This House on Fire* to suggest that through one kind of vision his protagonist is saved, and through another his antagonist is damned, then somewhere in the scheme of things we must account for the novel's third significant vision: that of its narrator, Peter Leverett. To say simply, as too many have, that Peter is the man between, impoverishes the book's scope. Clearly, Peter—square, normal, cool, solid, *l'homme moyen sensuel*—is a mediator of sorts; he comes to us initially as a bundle of fragile sensibilities which, like so many iron filings, are alternately attracted and repelled by the magnetism of Cass and of Mason. Yet just as clearly Peter is more than an absorbed, poetic shuttlecock. Like the Marlowe of *Heart of Darkness* whose rawness has been refined, his ego purged in the black vortex of Africa and Kurtz's hell, Peter struggles to cut through the chaos and illusion of personalities (his own included) and detail the fantasies, aberrancies, truths, lies into an intelligible if not always explicable pattern: what, in fact, by way of theme and structure, becomes the novel's design.

Unless we should perversely insist on reading *Set This House on Fire* (as one might read Ford's *The Good Soldier*) as some incredibly tenuous and ironic byplay among author, narrator, and reader, then we must trust Peter to exercise the "shaping vision" of the novel. His imagination comes as close to being Styron's artistic voice as Cass's articulation of visions comes to being his spiritual one. It is probably even safer and less suspect to conjecture the former. To a degree greater than *Lie Down in Darkness* and only slightly less than *The Confessions of Nat Turner*, *Set This House on Fire* imposes the present upon the past, experience—in the Blakean sense of the term—upon innocence. Almost from the beginning of the novel, the intensity of Peter's perceptions, and the magnitude, are established in a striking way as he recalls a pond in which he almost drowned when a boy, his furtive returns there despite the incident, and its "obliteration," its "stupendous unmaking" to accommodate a suburban development:

For now everything about the place . . . seemed to be informed by a sense of mysteriousness and brevity. . . . Here there had been taken away from me that child's notion that I would live forever; here I had learned the fragility not so much as of my own as of all being, and for that reason if it seemed a cruel scary place it also possessed a new and fathomable beauty. . . . in that stillness . . . I shivered with the knowledge of mortality. . . . Yet here on the identical spot, years later . . . everything was gone. Not just altered or changed or modified, not just a place whose outlines may have shifted and blurred . . . but were still recognizable, dependable, fixed—my marsh had vanished, a puff into thin air, and nothing of it remained. (SHF, p. 17)

Yet beyond mere nostalgia, beyond a set piece of purple narrative, beyond the fantasia on the theme of ubi sunt, Peter's remembrance inspires the more urgent reflection on the devastating possibilities of the past interacting with the present:

Perhaps one of the reasons we Americans are so exceptionally nervous and driven is that our past is effaced almost before it is made present; in our search for old avatars to contemplate we find only ghosts, whispers, shadows: almost nothing remains for us to feel or see, or to absorb our longings. . . . Estranged from myself and from my time, dwelling neither in the destroyed past nor in the fantastic and incomprehensible present, I knew that I must find the answer to at least several things before taking hold of myself: (SHF, pp. 18–19)

Here, antecedent to everything that happens in the novel, is almost its logical coda. For if the past cannot be recaptured, nor the present returned to the past, then the human imagination must, like the artistic vision itself, try to reconcile both phases of irredeemable time: must try, as Peter's imagination does, to understand life shorn of its "illusions and innocence." By acknowledging the "destroyed past" and the "fantastic and incomprehensible present," but by refusing to be enslaved by them, Peter fuses the visions of Cass and Mason—and surpasses them. The narrator, like the novelist, transfigures and shapes experience to understand his continuous and changing world, and ultimately to see it "steadily and whole."

Through such a synthesis of author and narrator's voice in *Set This House on Fire*, Styron enlarges its visionary mode. *The Confessions of Nat Turner* pushes voice and vision still further. As critical (both over and under) reactions attest, the novel is Styron's most notorious experiment; generally it is acknowledged an incredible success. Styron has gotten inside *a* black mind, not *the* white one; he has deserted the expatriate world of middle-class sophisticates to reconstruct the antebellum ethos through the eyes of an inspired revolutionary; and he has turned aside from esthetic or psychological speculations on time to treat it obsessionally, intuitively, symbolically, even four-dimensionally. Time in *The Con-fessions*—together with space—flows on two levels at once, the horizontal and the vertical, and carries Nat with it. Unlike Peter, he is not merely intellectually enslaved by past and present; he is liter-ally enslaved by them. The literal, however, leaps into the meta-physical. For as Nat tries to escape finite time—that is, historicity and the shameful history of his people—he converges toward a point and instant in infinite time. Styron's "meditation on history" becomes as well a meditation on timelessness.

The Confessions transforms the potentially lethal interplay of past and present—so keenly felt by Peyton and Peter—into the whirl of the future. As Styron's previous novels flow toward the anticipated awareness and epiphany, this novel, defying anticipation, startles us at the opening with a glimpse of Revelation, only just as suddenly to move backward through time. No longer will epigraphs from Sir Thomas Browne or John Donne—both meditations, broodings on eternity—serve to frame the temporal scheme. Now the novel must create—must *become*—its own metaphor for eternity. In part, Sty-ron achieves this through his exacting choice of superscription. John 21:4 is summoned out of Isaiah 26:21; the Christian belief in the final judgment at the end of an age supersedes with quiet ven-geance and nostalgia for transient, ephemeral, sinful man the Ju-daic belief in periodic judgments at times of historic crises. History (Isaiah) and apocalypse (John) are welded in a single vision, as fearful as it is benign.

But the true art of *The Confessions* rests on the primacy and flu-idity of the vision itself, flowing through a human vessel who is grand, though not grand enough to contain all of it, yet who has come the closest of any of Styron's creations to embodying the eter-nal moment in the mundane. It is for this reason that the beginning of a novel treating a man, a revolutionary, the major link in the new-forged consciousness of a race, holds eternity in the balance: for this reason that Genesis mirrors forth Judgment Day. Nat has judged, has been judged, and will, after enduring the judgment of his so-ciety, be called to the final judgment by his God. Judgment is the omega of existence toward which Nat has been yearning without being able to fathom or articulate it. Presentiments come to him only by way of a strange, recurrent dream filled with cliffs and seas and mazes. The dream is a "contemplation of a great mystery" that he is still unable, even on the eve of his execution, to discover. It is, of course, a vision of the apocalypse, wrapped up with his own death and resurrection and the call of the Lord: all only fulfilled shortly before the Southampton massacre in his most terrifying vision of the black destroying angel, the image of the holocaust to precede apocalypse.

Styron, however, has done more than impose the apocalyptic on the historic. In Nat, he has given us historic man's encounter with apocalypse, while paradoxically freeing him from the shackles of history. *The Confessions* is a novel of man's becoming and completion in time: of a life plunging linearly toward an end, changing the world as it does so, and controverting in its gallop toward apocalypse the archetypal entrapment in grinding, historical cycles. Nat shatters the cycle that seems overwhelming and ineluctable, and escapes to "freedom" through rebellion. And as with all revolutionaries—particularly with mystical, prophetic, religious revolutionaries—it scarcely matters whether the vision creates the age, or whether the spirit of the age generates the vision. It is a symbiotic, coalescing force catapulting the undistinguished, the obscure to a fame that may be as tragic as it is great; yet the phenomenon of such greatness is its inability to be otherwise. Nat—like the "young Luther" of a study that strongly influenced *The Confessions*—accedes to the acme of Erik Erickson's eight stages of man, where ego integrity champions over despair:

Although aware of the relativity of all the various life styles which have given meaning to human striving, the possessor of [ego] integrity is ready to defend the dignity of his own life style against all physical and economic threats. For he knows that an individual life is the accidental coincidence of but one life cycle with but one segment of history; and that for him all human integrity stands or falls with the one style of integrity of which he partakes. The style of integrity developed by his culture or civilization thus becomes the "patrimony of his soul," the seal of his moral paternity of himself. . . . In such final consolidation, death loses its sting.[5]

Where, but to apotheosis, could such a vision lead Nat Turner!

In an astounding way, *The Confessions* is Styron's declaration of the power of the human imagination to rebel against a world enslaving it, to make over through the act of creation such a world in its own image, and, just as inexorably, to go on to destroy itself and all that it created. The South could never be the same after Nat Turner's rebellion; and in a similar way our feelings about the South could never be the same after *The Confessions*. One may (like Cass Kinsolving) return from the abyss and begin anew; one cannot, after a vision of the apocalypse, return (like Nat) without experiencing some significant transformation.

Over the next decade, however, Styron seemed to realize that *The Confessions*, though it appeared to be the culmination of all those transfiguration patterns in his fiction, left an immense question unanswered: What transformation could be undergone by those who were enslaved and *unable* to rebel; those who sustained the horrors and evils as momentous as any connected with slavery in the Old South; those who suffered minute by minute, day by day, the dehumanization of the Nazi concentration camps; those, in short, who not only viewed the apocalypse, but lived through and beyond it? Haunted by the question, he took to reading dozens of books in the literature of the Holocaust, and under a mandate he himself finds hard to explain, wrote *Sophie's Choice*.[6]

Like *The Confessions*, *Sophie* is a "meditation on history," but on an event so ungraspable in its dimensions, as it is close to us in time, that its monstrous scars are still branded on our memories. Yet, one wonders, for how long? The black American, by his presence alone, will forever bear witness to the shameful history of his servitude. His existence provides continual proof of his hundreds of years' journey from slavery to emancipation, nominal and true freedom, victory: a journey mirrored in the progress of Styron's pilgrim, Nat, who escapes the prison of the body, mind and soul to celebrate apotheosis. This is Nat's (and every black's) triumph over the place-name Southampton. But what of Treblinka, Belsen, Dachau, Buchenwald, Auschwitz: a litany of place-names that evokes nightmarish visions of inhuman worlds, beside which the Dantean Inferno and the Miltonic Hell—spawned always in the sight of Paradiso or Heaven—are comprehensible and endurable? What was the triumph of those living dead who were "emancipated" from them? Who will stand as living testimony to the Nazi atrocities committed there once the ashes of their last survivors mingle with the ashes of

[13]

the cremated millions? Even today—a mere thirty-five years after *Endlösung*, or "the final solution"—the "wailing and weeping and gnashing of teeth" of Jew, Gypsy, and Slav alike are passing into the sob, whisper, and finally silence of history. One of the most sensitive critics of the Holocaust, George Steiner, believes this silence to be fitting: its language, he argues, is the only sane response to what occurred, for what is unspeakable is best left unspoken.

Against such a belief Styron vociferously rebels. Perhaps the visionary writer cannot retreat into the purlieus of philosophy or the peripheries of imagination: he can only move forward. At any rate, there is for Styron no language of silence. No more than slavery in the Old South must the Holocaust be forgotten. "*Someday I will understand Auschwitz*. This was a brave statement but innocently absurd. No one will ever understand Auschwitz. What I might have set down with more accuracy would have been: *Someday I will write about Sophie's life and death, and thereby help demonstrate how absolute evil is never extinguished from the world*. Auschwitz itself remains inexplicable." So writes Stingo, the narrator, on the last pages of *Sophie's Choice*, having completed a remembrance of things past that we hope will never be forgotten in things future. Thus *Sophie* is a memorial for the living as well as the dead. Out of the domination and enslavement and mass murders of the concentration camps, Styron has envisioned a tale so incomprehensible to our humanity that no language but the experience itself can ever help us to wrestle with the atrocities perpetrated by the Nazi Angels of Death, or lead us to an understanding of history's most diabolical horror.

How Styron orders this experience is the art of *Sophie's Choice*. No other novel of his so intimately allies the shaping imagination with narrative technique. For *Sophie* grows to fullness and power with Stingo's development as man and artist, both brought about through the gradual expansion of his vision. From his insulated, middle-class innocence in Virginia's Tidewater, he is cast into the world of Yetta Zimmerman's rooming house: a world in which the brilliant and certifiably mad Nathan Landau and the lovely, enigmatic Sophie begin intimating the little evils springing from human passions. Drawn into their tortured relationship, Stingo's vision is enlarged. Eventually, he is able to look longer and harder on the evils of his own heritage—slavery. Ultimately, through Sophie's concatenation of lies, truths, confidences, tales, he is wrenched from the present and thrust vicariously into the "Auschwitz experience,"[7] there to look on the cold, logical face of absolute evil, crystallized in that pure and hideous moment of absolute evil when Sophie must choose which one of her children should live, which should die.

With that choice comes her own "death," foreshadowed some hundreds of pages before, when she first realizes that she is losing touch with herself as a human being. Typing in the commandant's (Höss's) office, she is suddenly aware of fragments of an oratorio issuing from a phonograph notorious for blaring schmalz.

> *Die Himmel erzählen die Ehre Gottes,*
> *und seiner Hände Werk*
> *zeigt an das Firmament!*

The Elysian chorus, thrusting itself up through the muttering chatter of Höss and his aide below, stabbed her with such astonished exaltation that she rose spontaneously from her seat at the typewriter, as if in homage, faintly trembling. . . . the ecstatic hosanna moved across her skin like divine hands, touching her with ecstatic ice; chill after chill coursed through her flesh; for long seconds the fog and night of her existence, through which she had stumbled like a sleepwalker, evaporated as if melted by the burning sun. She stepped to the window. . . . She glimpsed the magical white horse again, grazing now, the meadow, the sheep beyond, and further still, as if at the very edge of the world, the rim of the drab gray autumnal woods, transmuted by the music's incandescence into a towering frieze of withering but majestic foliage, implausibly beautiful, aglow with some immanent grace. "Our Father . . ." she began in German. Half drowned, borne utterly away by the anthem, she closed her eyes while the archangelic trio chanted its mysterious praise to the whirling earth:

> *Dem kommenden Tage sagt es der Tag.*
> *Die Nacht, die verschwand*
> *der folgenden Nacht . . .*

"It stopped then, the music," Sophie said to me. . . . "It just stopped suddenly, this music, and I felt a complete emptiness. I never finished the paternoster, the prayer I begun. I don't know any more, I think maybe it was that moment that I begun to lose my faith. But I don't know any more, about *when* God leave me. Or I left Him. Anyway, I felt this emptiness." (SC, pp. 231–232)

[15]

When the music begins again it is not Haydn's *Creation;* it is the Beer Barrel Polka. But the complexity of the passage and its magnificence do not come merely from Styron's depicting the rape of the sacred by the banal. The resonances go far beyond this. For Auschwitz and the entire concentration camp universe were themselves unique and hideous creations, giving the great cosmic lie to the creation of God, their business being, as it was, *Vernichtung*—extermination. And, indeed, Sophie's psyche is destroyed, then her soul, then her child. Under these circumstances, these horrors, the death of the body must—to return to Erickson—lose its sting, but for reasons different from those in *The Confessions*. In a universe geared toward death, death soon loses its meaning. The tragedy of *Sophie's Choice* is that for many who survived the Holocaust, life lost its meaning as well.

The metaphysics and eschatology of the novel are Sophie's, but the book belongs to Stingo. In his journey from Eden to Apocalypse and beyond, as his visions of comparatively safe, slightly paranoid America expand to embrace those pictures of Europe's death universe, he learns that he must one day reckon with the absolute evil in the world. Stingo is the real survivor of Sophie's history. Physically freed from Auschwitz, but never from the guilt of being freed, dead to the marrow of her being, Sophie may be transfigured, but she can never be reborn. Only Stingo can.

And he is. In an entirely new key, the image of the creation returns in the last paragraph of the novel: not, this time, the musical *Creation*, but the natural one; not inspired by God's will, but born out of man's hope; not a creation wrought out of raw darkness and chaos, night and fog, but out of the bright day of the spirit:

When I awoke it was early morning. I lay looking straight up at the blue-green sky with its translucent shawl of mist; like a tiny orb of crystal, solitary and serene, Venus shone through the haze above the quiet ocean. I heard children chattering nearby. . . . Blessing my resurrection, I realized that the children had covered me with sand, protectively, and that I lay as safe as a mummy beneath this fine, enveloping overcoat. It was then that in my mind I inscribed the words: *'Neath cold sand I dreamed of death / but woke at dawn to see / in glory, the bright, morning star.*

This was not judgment day—only morning. Morning: excellent and fair.

[16]

Waking, morning, Venus, children, resurrection. They are all here—images evoking a new and wondrous life, reborn to speak out against the absolute evil so heedless of all life. We can, must, says Styron, always begin again. Even as *The Confessions* moves from creation to judgment to apocalypse, or *Sophie* from creation to holocaust—moves toward those ends awful in their finality, but tragically validated by history—Styron can still envision in the whirling configurations of determinism the possibility of a grander pattern: the movement from creation to a re-creation that is artistic, personal, singularly American, yet ultimately universal. "The light which puts out our eyes is darkness to us," wrote Thoreau. "Only that day dawns to which we are awake. There is more day to dawn. The sun is but a morning star." Styron's morning star—transcendental and transfiguring—is no less.

Powerful and compelling as they are, *The Confessions* and *Sophie* raise some disturbing and fundamental questions about Styron as a visionary novelist. What, in the particular sense, is one left with after the painful, final vision of Nat's and the hopeful, even optimistic vision of Stingo's have been recorded? What more can we take away from all of Styron's work after the numerous, sometimes even abstruse visions have been collated? Have we, that is, throughout all his novels and his single play anything apart from the visions themselves?

Before answering these questions, we should like to carry the consideration of the visionary novelist a bit further. Modern literature's invasion by the apocalypse, and the American novelist's particular (though not exclusive) acquiescence to it, have made it progressively more difficult to wrest from the intense fictions of writers like James Purdy, Thomas Pynchon, Joseph Heller, and John Barth social or metaphysical values that only several decades earlier were at least clearly demonstrable in the apocalyptic world of crumbling centers and windswept wastelands. Lawrence could evoke his dark, savage gods; Yeats could look to the ether for his "widening gyres"; and Eliot could eventually claim that in the end was his beginning. Now we only wait for the end. As Frank Kermode has pointed out in his brilliant study, the "sense of an ending" has progressively become the conditioned response of writers who have come to distrust the temporal, historic framework, *chronos*, and must consequently seek inspiration from the mythic super-structures, *kairos*. Apocalypse has superseded Henry Adams's dynamo as the integrating archetype of our disintegration.

One may rightly ask what sense there is in attempting to define values in a world so clearly tending toward entropy, or in seeking oases of permanence beyond the borders of wastelands, where novelists have sent weary heroes hungering after illusive beasts of revelation and corroded grails; and where, as an inevitable consequence, many ill-equipped critics have gone in quest of the questers. One may answer no sense at all. Perhaps there may be relief, if no comfort, in steeling ourselves for ultimate hopelessness: buying tickets of admission to watch the approaching spinoff; and, as corollary to this, perhaps the critical imagination, in its desire to expose, refine, explain, should not dare vie with the apocalyptic one.

On the other hand, even with apocalypse imminent and immanent, one may feel that the quest after values, though dubious and vain, is preferable to paralysis. There is, too, the nagging suspicion that however poetic and revelatory and fierce and deterministic the apocalyptic imagination is, it begs a rather basic question about apocalypse: for once it *is*, we are *not*. Putting aside for a moment the perdurability of the human spirit—since Pollyanna generally seems to wither before Cassandra—we would call attention to the cartoon in which in the first panel an Elijah type sports a sandwich board reading "The World Will End Tomorrow" and in which in the second panel, nothing has been changed save the phrase, now reading: "The World Ended Yesterday." We do not offer the analogy to blur a vision that has produced some of the most original and vital literature of the past decade: merely to suggest that equally original and vital fiction has also come by way of alternatives. We have, of course, Styron's work in mind, and that element of his work in particular which embraces the apocalyptic vision surrendering to its hysteria and confusion and nihilism. New values may spring fully armed from old ones. But those of Styron's characters who find some measure of love and hope and joy do so not by ascending a growing mountain of corpses thrust up by the past, but by hewing holds in whatever is concrete, stable, viable in the present.

Admittedly it might seem disastrous to determine from Styron's first novel that anything viable could emerge from the world as he then felt and knew it. *Lie Down in Darkness* reflects almost perfect disintegration. As in *King Lear* "nothing" cracks open a world and a universe; "nothing" echoes through the widening death-rictus of an ethos; almost complete in rendering personal despair, the novel is even more complete in catching the resonances of communal negation. Class fails; love fails; sex fails; religion fails; tradition fails; psychotherapy fails; history fails—or rather succeeds in effecting one of the greatest syntheses of all negations at Hiroshima. Even the Negroes' exultant cry after Daddy Faith is a whimper lost amidst the agonizing cry of Milton and Helen's "nothing," amidst "the whistle, roar, gigantic sound . . . like the clatter of the opening of everlasting gates and doors" as the train rushes north into the eternal blackness of "oncoming night."

But—as we suggested above in discussing the visionary aspects of the novel—such total negation was ancillary to a young novelist's sweeping away all debris of a culture he could, would, no longer accept. *Lie Down in Darkness* seems opulent in disclaiming any values whatever, in its generational inbreeding of melancholia, introversion, hysteria, neuroses, Puritanism, sin, and guilt. All this, we say, seems clear enough. Yet by way of paradox—a paradox that Styron was reasonably unaware of at twenty-five when he wrote *Lie Down in Darkness*—the novel, for all its despair, goads us into sloughing off our stifled sensibilities, liberating ourselves from the paralysis, shaking ourselves free of narcissistic brooding over how lost and damned we are, and beginning reassessment of ourselves somewhere—anywhere. By showing his generation where he felt it went wrong, Styron was indicating how it might go right. We spoke of *Lie Down in Darkness* as part parable; and it is just possible its moral is this, a faint hopeful light encroaching on the dark center of irony and ambiguity.

There is, however, a still further reading of the novel that expands its contexts somewhat. At its most general, the book has been taken as a tragedy enacted within three circles of meaning—private, domestic, social—all calculated to enclose and destroy the principal actors. In view of Styron's subsequent fictions, we are less inclined to see these circles linking, so much as overlaying each other—forming a cohesive, multifaceted *relievo* of the institutional or collective mind of the New South. Such a mind, at its most enfeebled, can be no more than a mute barrier to change and progress; at its most dangerous it can set in motion profligate forces to engineer its own humiliation, defeat, and self-destruction.

Because it is immune, indeed resistant to new problems, because it is conditioned to solve old problems only through ritualistic, aimless gestures, the world of the Loftises and Cartwrights and Carrs falls away at both center and peripheries; the sap dries up; the roots wither; the stock atrophies. Styron's white, middle-class, Protestant South is almost exclusively a choked world of the collective—country clubs, churches, fraternity and cocktail parties, socials and smokers—where being alone even for a moment becomes synonymous with loneliness, and where this loneliness immediately summons some crutch like drink or sex or God as support against anxiety and fear. To live within a framework where one scarcely knows oneself until it is too late is to be damned; yet to escape from it (as Peyton thinks she can) is to be equally damned. For in *Lie Down in Darkness* the collective mind is not endemic to the South. Harry's clique of northern liberal-progressive intellectuals operates differently, but no less depressingly. Peyton is trapped—trapped just as the South is—between tradition and change; in this way she adumbrates Styron's future heroes, is linked to Cass, Mannix, Nat Turner and Stingo: individuals questing for truth, longing for perfection and completion, who must escape the organized, rigid, ritualistic snares of the collective mind.

Or do battle with them: which in this way makes Styron's heroes rare in contemporary American fiction. They are not in the grain of those naive picaros who bungle their quests and end up as violated innocents. Styron's questers are rebels, though less out of choice than occasion and necessity. For to rebel is to endure, just as to endure is to rebel: a syllogism we offer without any design of mad tea party logomachy or solipsism or tautology, but as an entire construct of values that provides the Styron hero a reason of being as well as a reason for being. Those like Cass and Mannix who are lucky—if being alive at the end of a novel constitutes luck—may "last" as well as "endure." But Styron seldom guarantees much value beyond the self-defining act of rebellion.

This at least appears to be the case in his two treatments of the theme within military settings: *The Long March* and *In the Clap Shack*.[8] Styron wrote these works twenty years apart; one is a psychological novel, the other a stage comedy; yet their focus and conclusion (in places even their tone) are consistent enough to suggest his continuing fascination with the irrationality spawned by this particular breed of the collective mind. In one sense, these works are his most compressed studies of an institution trying to usurp identity by imposing conformity on the individual: attempting, that is, to absorb personal values in collective ones.

Yet like other of Styron's collectives, the United States Marines is not overtly hostile; it is an entity beyond feeling or involvement, and perhaps this is what makes it—and organizations like it—more insidious. It creates, by the very nature of its collective existence as opposed to private existence, a world outlook (such as we would find in the New South of *Lie Down in Darkness*, the Old in *The Confessions*, the expatriate world in *Set This House on Fire*) that can scarcely fathom anyone's desiring to go against it. What such organizations—incredibly inured, it would seem, to history and to meditations upon history—fail to learn is that the more they would impress obedience and anonymity on the individual, the more they would demand his surrender, the more forcefully he rebels.

As for the rebellion in the two works at hand, it is valued as more than quixotic tilts at power or emblems of power or a chain of endless command. Reason dictates that bucking the system is unreasonable; yet intuition makes demands beyond reason. Mannix and Magruder refuse to be stripped of the remnants of value left them, or to be desensitized to their belief in themselves as more than rank and serial number. Each rebels to affirm an identity in the face of an encroaching paranoia, symbolized in *The Long March* by the chaotic figure of Templeton, and *In the Clap Shack* by the comically monomaniacal Budwinkle. One should recall that *The Long March* was written in 1953: considerably before tremors of paranoia (sounded, for example, in *The Naked and the Dead* and *Invisible Man*) swelled into the literary shock wave exploited with considerable brilliance by writers like Heller and Purdy, and elevated to genius by Pynchon in *Gravity's Rainbow*. Styron's novella anticipates what is by now a nearly universal suspicion: that our rampant para-

noia is scarcely an orderly deviation from "norms," but a logical
response to conditioning under systems that have surpassed in ambiguity those perfect, though inexplicable worlds of Gogol and
Kafka.

Templeton's delusions of grandeur are volatile and potentially
tragic; but ironically it is the persecuted Mannix who, as war hero,
is responsible for sustaining the glory of the corps that fires men
like Templeton on. In another, only explicitly comic way, Magruder's hypochondria has already prepared the ground for the psycho-
somatic burrowing which in turn tunnels into the paranoid maze.
We are, Styron suggests, haunted by the bizarre ghosts and grotesque fancies we ourselves have created. Thus, though visions and
illusions might momentarily sustain our metaphysical health, they
are in the long run just as surely responsible for our metaphysical
ills. Being so divided, so—more profoundly than the cant sense of
the word admits—insecure, we cannot affirm values without first
understanding what they are. Our fear of what we might discover
prevents us from knowing or defining ourselves, yet the fear of non-
discovery paralyzes us further still. To be forced to crisis—like
Mannix in the gung-ho march, like Magruder with his falsely diagnosed syphilis—is perhaps the sole means of unearthing the values
we have, through one means or another, buried with our humanity.

It is this awaited impulse to find what is quintessentially human
in all of us that makes the quest in Styron valuable in itself. Its object is almost without importance; to endure in it is all. Were it otherwise, it would be difficult to assess values in a novel like *Set This
House on Fire* which is almost pure quest, and in which the act of
questing performs its own art of healing, transforms what is fragmented into what is whole. The search to know and explore oneself
is not, however, carried on in isolation—the book shows how impossible isolation is; Port Warwick and Sambuco are, as states of
the mind, one and the same place—but in terms of people, and,
most emphatically in the novel, in terms of avatars.

For *Set This House on Fire* marks a departure from Styron's creating character of pure Being, since without regeneration of the self,
Being has very little value at all. Rather, it is a novel of Becoming, of
emergence out of a past that has shaped us, and which we must
learn to reshape instead of reject. The book reaches out to embrace

nothing less than America itself: not the America of the jingoist or sentimentalist, but the America creative and destructive of our personalities and psyches, formulative of our feelings of love and hate toward her. The novel is both challenge and response to our culture. It is elliptical about many things, but almost transparent in its moral assertion of what it means to flee blindly or scrap mechanically the visible manifestations of our roots and origins. Thomas Wolfe said we were all lost in America; Styron says we are probably more lost anywhere else. To find America is to find the parts of ourselves we have lost. Thus a novel ostensibly concerned with expatriation becomes one of repatriation. It is not only Cass's continuing quest, but his continual questioning, his dialogue of self and self, self and soul—a dialogue in which Peter shares, and in which Mason, cinematically frozen in his static mask, does not share—that defines his, as well as the book's, Becoming.

The way stations reflecting Cass's progress from frantic visionary to one ready to wrestle with doubtful values and ambiguities about America are raised in much of his dialogue, though we think the substance of his change can be gathered from three short quotations. The first comes as a response to Poppy's question "Oh *why* are you so anti-U.S.A.?"

Because it's the land where the soul gets poisoned out of pure ugliness. It's because in the U.S.A. everything looks like a side street near the bus station in Poughkeepsie, New York. . . . It's because whenever I think of stateside I can't picture nothing else but a side street in Poughkeepsie, New York, where I got lost one night when I came to see you, and whenever I think of it I get consumed with such despair over its sheer ugliness that I feel great waves of anguish rolling over me. . . . Whatever I've said in—in *mitigation* of the horror America afflicts me with, strike it out. Strike it out! I was just being sentimental. (SHF, p. 282)

The second is reflected in his journal entry, some hundred pages later:

And I suppose its true, some twisted connection or crossed up circuit between love & hate in me is the secret of it all, . . . I am my own soul diviner & I do not hope to dredge up out of the depths anything but that which would momentarily solace me. And the blame is my own to bear. So that whenever I dream as I have done of old Uncle standing there as my own executioner I do not place the horror in his hands. . . . It's not old Uncle's

fault any more than it was Cape Gloucester. . . . Nor when I look into my
heart of hearts is it the U.S. I can blame at all though many times I would
like to & do, a bleeding expatriate that would put a bowery bum to shame.
Because though say even somebody like Poppy don't know it there are
times when just the thought of one single pine tree at home, in the sand, &
a negro church in a grove I knew as a boy & the sound of the negroes singing In Bright Mansions Above (?)—then I feel or know rather that all I
would need is that one trembling word to be whispered or spoken into my
ear. AMERICA. And I could hold myself back no longer and blubber like a
baby. (SHF, pp. 363–364)

And the last comes in the "Epilogue" in the short letter Peter receives from Cass after his return to the "whole smart-Alex, soft-
headed, baby-faced, predigested, cellophane wrapped, doomed,
beauty-hating, land":

Charleston will never become the Florence of the New World Im afraid
but the Sunday amateurs are keeping me busy & Im up to my ears in
work. Also, another trauma. Overpopulation. Race-suicide. Poppy is having another baby next June & Ive been walking around Charleston like a
wounded elephant, staggering with the usual pride and despair. Kinsey
was distinctly wrong. A man doesnt even get started until he moves in
toward il mezzo del camin. . . . Who was it in Lear who said ripeness is all.
I forget, but he was right. (SHF, pp. 505–506)

Cass's allusions to the opening lines of *The Divine Comedy* and to
Edgar's urgent moral to the blinded Gloucester (with, on Styron's
part, we suspect, a muted symbolic echo of Cass's traumatic experience on the Cape) underscore his dissent from nightmare and surrender and his assent to growing lucidity and acceptance. It is,
indeed, ascent after descent. As Dante's vision of Beatrice on the
Ponte Vecchio inspired such a descent into the Inferno that led to
Paradise, as Gloucester's false tumble from the Dover Cliffs brought
about the eleventh hour rescue of lost, interior vision, so Cass's sink-
ing into the dissipation, sensuality, and imprisonment of Sambuco
prepares for the "new birth" in Charleston. An exile like Dante and
Gloucester, Cass has learned that "Men must endure / Their going
hence, even as their coming hither." But he returns to America as
more than an exile; he returns as a human being.

Toward this condition, this value, *Set This House on Fire* tends
from the opening. But it is clear from the opening, too, that we are

still in the world of the white and the privileged. All barriers to be-coming human are raised after plans laid down by the grotesque or unsteady architecture of the self. As charged as Styron's first three novels are with man's struggle to locate and define his humanity, possibly none does nor could measure the scope of the struggle so eloquently as *The Confessions* and *Sophie's Choice*. Not one man nor two, not a half-dozen men come under scrutiny; not the Old nor the New South; not the alienated nor expatriated; not the soul damned nor in revolt, but—through their history, myth, atavisms, and ava-tars—all men, all times. *The Confessions* is a novel about humanity. Through Nat—the activating force in Styron's spent, doomed world—we watch the desperate and impossible struggle of a man wanting to assert his humanity, the realization of how improbable the recognition of it is, and the glorious, insane attempt to generate chaos in thrusting beyond both impossibility and improbability. Like Styron, we are compelled to meditate on the historicized myth *and* the mythicized history, though finally we must abolish the dis-tinctions that have brought as much articulate denunciation of the novel as applause for it. The compulsion is an imperative dictate be-cause *The Confessions* is, before being either myth or history, art; it is an archetypal tragedy; and Nat is the archetypal tragic hero, here torn between dream and reality by the disparity between promise and fulfillment. Nat's struggle was, as with others it now is and chances are with others to come will be, the timeless, universal struggle to achieve, no matter how horrendous existence becomes, his essential humanity.

Sophie's Choice—at least in the Auschwitz sections, which might well be called Sophie's confessions—is a novel of inhumanity. Even in the rigorously closed and codified slave society of the Old South, there were masters—Turner and Moore, for example—who con-ceded Nat's having feelings and intelligence, who acknowledged him as a human being. The concentration camps, whose horrors and finality were without antecedents in our history, were other-wise. Here, "men," "women," "children," "human being," "hu-manity" never applied, and so to aspire to any of these states was logically absurd. A world so totally inhuman and evil had never be-fore existed; brought into being, it abolished the vocabulary of hu-manity. Dehumanizing as slavery in the Old South was, it was, like all previously comprehensible slave societies, an economic institution (self-serving and self-perpetuating), whose very survival depended on the survival of its slaves.

Such was not the case with Auschwitz, Dachau, Belsen, Buchenwald, Birkenau. As Richard Rubenstein points out in *The Cunning of History*—a book whose thesis much influenced Styron—the concentration camps were more than places of execution. They were a radically unique kind of slave society, "a world of the living dead," based on ruthless domination and "the absolute expendability of human life." Finely honed, beautifully efficient, the Nazi *Vernichtungslagers* were genocidal juggernauts geared to enslavement and extermination—but not of Jews alone. Styron has made his heroine a Pole and a Catholic to expand our consciousness of the Holocaust, to make us mindful that millions of non-Jews—Gypsies, Serbs, Poles, Russians—also perished during "the final solution." To have value as history, history must accommodate as much truth as it can. Here, Styron would have us know, guilt and responsibility of murderers and survivors alike—for, ironically, many of those Gentiles annihilated in the camps were anti-Semitic—have universal dominion. Not to understand this "reveals a deficiency of moral responsibility and a dangerous insensitivity to those forces in contemporary life that might spawn new Holocausts."[9] We, like Stingo, must vicariously and repeatedly experience what Conrad called "the fascination of the abomination"; repeatedly reexamine the history of *l'univers concentrationnaire*, for while the whole truth about it may never be known, what truths we do know will die if we surrender to silence.

To drill into our consciousness, as well as to preserve in our conscience, the ultimate values of *The Confessions* and *Sophie's Choice* is surely the finest achievement of any writer. What makes *The Confessions* grand in design is that Styron's agon of man against himself, against society, even against his God goes beyond being a confession of aspiration to become a testament of affirmation. What makes *Sophie's Choice* equally grand is that Styron has shunned the popular or sensationalistic or existential approaches to the Holocaust in order to shoulder its overwhelming burden as history. We may never understand the Holocaust, yet to understand its univer-

[26]

sality is to measure somewhat its enormous scope. The Holocaust is behind us; but once such a hideous evil was born, the idea of it could never really die; its second coming, with all the horrors of the first, is ever imminent.

To dwell so on absolute evil as *The Confessions* and *Sophie* do is Styron's first step to the resurrection of the good. Certainly horror, shame, guilt, madness, and death brood over these novels, but only because they brood over much of human history concerned with struggles like Nat's to be free and like Sophie's to survive. Apart from merely acknowledging their dark presence and grim persistence, the novels try to show how man transcends them. That is why Nat's bitter negation and rebellion cannot finally be envisioned as blind alleys into solipsism, but as prime movers of self-definition; and why one cannot read the novel closely without finding it more hopeful than ambiguous. That is why Stingo's awakening to "morning: excellent and fair" tells us that even the most enormous of past crimes can be redeemed by our desire to remember and our will to act. *The Confessions* and *Sophie* hold out the promise that joy may come out of anger, justice out of injustice, quietude out of fear, redemption out of damnation, good out of evil, freedom out of enslavement, charity out of brutality and vengeance. Despite the deprivation of physical and spiritual love, Nat in the end still comes to love, still vindicates his rights as a human being even after committing those senseless and terrible acts that not only seem but are monstrous. Sophie, a survivor of acts more monstrous still, spiritually empty and drifting towards welcome death after her "life in death," can still inspire, perhaps empower Stingo to fight against the horrors that made her the way she is. A century apart in history, a hairsbreadth away from each other in ideology, *The Confessions* and *Sophie* argue that something akin to blood-brotherhood can arise out of the nightmare of bloodbaths and mass annihilations; something to signify that inhuman theories and the dehumanizing collective can never destroy man's intrinsic, instinctive sense of his own worth and dignity.

Such beliefs are Styron's chief legacy to literature and the times. His two great novels of transformation crown his achievement as a writer. It is fitting that they should. For they demonstrate how the

[27]

insurrection and survival of the human spirit lead to the resurrection of the artist's soul. This transformation is what any great writer undergoes in wedding his own private vision with enduring values; it is, we think, a transformation William Styron has undergone. Few achievements could be more desirable—or more lasting.[10]

Notes

1. *Paris Review* 1 (1953): 13.

2. "William Styron: The Metaphysical Hurt" from *The Art of Southern Fiction: A Study of Some Modern Novelists* (Carbondale, Ill., 1967), pp. 145–146.

3. See "Interviews with William Styron" in this collection.

4. *Fearful Symmetry* (Princeton, 1947), p. 8.

5. *Young Man Luther: A Study in Psychoanalysis and History* (New York, 1958), pp. 260–261.

6. "Interviews."

7. Ibid.

8. It would appear that this theme will be further amplified in his forthcoming novel, *The Way of the Warrior*, which is concerned with "the military mind in America." See ibid.

9. Quoted in Pearl K. Bell's review of *Sophie's Choice*, "Evil and William Styron." *Commentary* 68 (August 1979): 57–59.

10. This essay was revised in 1980 by Robert K. Morris.

ROBERT K. MORRIS

Interviews with William Styron

The following interviews with William Styron were conducted in part during the summer of 1972 at Mr. Styron's home on Martha's Vineyard, in part during the subsequent summer at his home in Roxbury, Connecticut, and in part on the Vineyard once again during the summer of 1979.

Q. In the last twenty years material about you and your work has appeared in some forty books, seven doctoral dissertations, about two hundred or more critical articles, and countless book reviews. Would you care to comment on how it feels to be, if you'll forgive the blatant phrase, "an American classic"?

A. That's a very good way to start the interview, especially inasmuch as I do not consider myself an American classic. I don't have any illusions, really, about what literature is. I think one generation's classic is another generation's corpse; and it's a chancy thing to talk about being a classic in your time. There's a book I haven't read written by the emeritus head of Duke University's English Department, Jay Hubbell, that has to do with just such matters: who are the acclaimed writers of their time. One of the interesting things I recall reading in a review of Hubbell's book is that in 1920 or 1921 there was a list drawn up of the sure-to-live immortals of that particular time. And heading the list, I *believe*, was Joseph Hergesheimer, followed closely by Booth Tarkington (or maybe it was the other way around); and Dreiser was something like number fourteen. This was a reputable poll, too, taken among serious critics. And so things like that make me a little itchy and nervous about answering what it is to be a classic.

Q. But by the same token there hasn't been that much written about Hergesheimer and Tarkington. Why do you think so many people are writing about you?

A. This is probably the time when people write things about writers to a degree they did not before. I think had the critical and academic apparatus been as lively and vigorous as it is now, Hergesheimer and the others would have had similar activities surrounding their work. Of course, it's nice to know you're alive and kicking, that you have a readership of some sort, that people are involved in your work, and that there is interest in it throughout various fields; but whether you are an American classic or not is still up to ol' posterity!

Q. Have you any feelings or reactions, one way or the other, about having your novels taught in the university?

A. I'm pleased when my work is taught there, very pleased. As I've said before, I really don't know how much validity can be given to the idea of the writer as a cult figure—and I'm thinking of the cult writers dating back to Salinger and Golding and moving on up through to Vonnegut. Yet at the same time to have the feeling one is being read by young people is a very inspiriting and happy state.

Q. You don't feel—even after *Nat Turner*—that you're a cult writer?

A. No, I don't; that is, I haven't any evidence pointing to it. But I do get enough responses to know that I am taught with some frequency and some currency at a large number of universities—and that pleases me.

Q. Is there any rough estimate you could make to the number of letters you receive from the people who read and like your books: letters not necessarily from those in the university?

A. It depends. When a book of mine comes out, all of a sudden I am inundated; and then it peters out to a sort of steady trickle of appreciative letters: sometimes several a day, but certainly several a week.

Q. Does receiving these letters gratify you?

A. Well, most of the time, yes. Most of them are "unsolicited testimonials" to the work, and that's pleasing; it makes you feel that what you've done has touched someone.

Q. Do you get any negative letters?

A. Yes, some. I got many, of course, after *Nat Turner*. But on the whole I get surprisingly few. Most people don't seem to want to sit down and write a negative letter.

Q. Do you think that the longer scholarly and critical pieces about your novels have been, in general, sound in evaluating your work? I mean, has what you considered the best of such criticism come closer to the mark than not on what you were planning to do?

A. I would say that, by and large, there has been a great deal of mediocre criticism which doesn't seem to get anywhere near the mark. On the other hand, you get really extraordinary insights by certain critics, who seem to smell absolutely, exactly what you're up to. They're in the distinct minority, however; but perhaps you can't expect any more than that!

Q. When you were interviewed for the *Paris Review* in 1952, immediately after the publication of *Lie Down in Darkness*, you remarked that bad notices always give you a "sense of humility, or perhaps humiliation . . . but they don't help [you] much." Do you still find that true?

A. Yes, substantially. Except I would now amend that to say that I don't know if they give me a sense of either at all.

Q. You've become hardened to criticism?

A. Yes. I think I've become as inured to criticism as it is possible for a writer to be.

Q. Has any salient criticism about an earlier book made you change or ponder direction in the writing of a later one?

A. No, unequivocally. I can't say there's been any connection between them.

Q. What kind of criticism, if any, do you find at least helpful, or is it all one?

A. I don't imagine a writer really finds any criticism helpful when his career is in full swing. I think possibly when he's young some criticism could be useful; but certainly by the time he is going full blast he should be aware of what his direction is, and there is very little profit I can see that he could derive from criticism. He's got his own voice, his own style, and I just don't see what the critic could tell or teach him.

Q. How do you feel about your books once they are published?

A. I feel a tremendous sense of fulfillment and gratification in terms of completion. Rightly or wrongly, you've done the best that

[31]

you can do—or you *think* you've done the best that you can do—and all you can have is a sense of achievement.

Q. In that same *Paris Review* interview you also disclaimed being a southern writer, yet you've continued to write about the South. Is there any inconsistency there?

A. Well, I wouldn't stand irrevocably on what I said twenty years ago, because I was in no position to know what I really meant. I think, probably, I had an honest impulse in saying what I did then about *not* being a southern writer, and in disclaiming southern roots. But as I go along I do understand there is still a strong pull in my work toward trying to explain or express certain southern biases, certain southern sympathies, certain southern apprehensions. And therefore I would amend that to say I was wrong. I do not consider myself a southern writer in the sense that, let us say, Eudora Welty might consider herself one. She is, and Flannery O'Connor is another, an almost perfect example of a fine "regional" southern novelist. Basically, I guess, I am trying to make a distinction between southern regionalism (which can be a very strong, fine thrust in literature), and my own work, which is southern, but perhaps not regionally southern.

Q. Has your living in New England for the past twenty years changed your emotional or intellectual responses to the South?

A. I would say distinctly so. But even before that I resolved to remove myself from the South because I simply did not find it compatible with what my moods and aims and ambitions were.

Q. Did you feel you were too much dogging the footsteps of the well-known southern writers—regional or otherwise? I'm thinking in particular, of course, of Faulkner.

A. Yes, surely. I think I perhaps also anticipated—and I don't mean to sound smart-ass—the fact that southern regional writing was about to become a thing of the past. And, generally speaking, I think it has. I felt a far more cosmopolitan sense of direction, and I needed to get out of the South because it was no longer a deeply involved part of my psychic nature.

Q. Are there any young southern writers today whom you feel have suffered by aligning themselves with this regionalism?

A. I would say that you have to be an exceptionally *good* writer to still set up shop as a "southern writer." One very good writer who has done well in this mode is Reynolds Price, but I don't know of many others. It's not to denigrate his talent to say that I think those writers very rare who claim in a strong and aggressive way that they are, with a capital *S*, Southern. I do not. Though to answer your earlier question I find to my surprise that I am never quite able to divest myself of southern thought.

Q. Do you align yourself with *any* school of writing?

A. No.

Q. With the exception of *The Long March*, each of your three major novels runs close to several hundred thousand words. Is there any particular reason why you write long novels?

A. Certainly *Set This House on Fire* is a very long book, but *Nat Turner* and *Lie Down in Darkness* were of more graspable dimensions—in terms of pure length. I don't think they're extraordinarily long, either one of them.

Q. Is there any reason why *Set This House on Fire* was longer, then?

A. In retrospect I think it's overly long. I wish I'd cut it down by a lot. But that's one of those mistakes you make that you can't repair. But even it, by certain standards—compared to the length of *The Brothers Karamazov*, say—is not long. My own feeling is that if you sit down to write a novel you need space to move around in—and a lot of space, in order to give this sense of movement and life to people in the book. Therefore I have always thought of the novel as being a commodious vehicle, one that would take tens of thousands of words, hundreds of thousands if necessary, to tell a story in.

Q. Then why did you make *The Long March* as short as you did?

A. It seemed to have its own length. I don't think there was any quarrel in my mind or any problem as to how long it would be. It just seemed to tell itself. As a matter of fact it started out as a short story. I was going to try to do it in 4,000 words, but it became something in between a short story and a novel.

Q. Did any of your other novels originate as short stories?

A. *Lie Down in Darkness* and *Set This House on Fire* started as novels, *Nat Turner* as a novella. I thought it was going to be something I could clean up in about eight months. Of course I realized fairly early on in its writing that it could not possibly be a short novel; it had to involve the whole time-space concept.

Q. You're intensely occupied with the dimensions of time and space in your novels, aren't you?

A. It seems to me *the* problem a novelist has to conquer, and to do it in a way that pleases his own esthetic and his own demands upon himself as an artist.

Q. It's been mentioned on several occasions that you don't go on with a succeeding chapter until the previous one has been polished to your satisfaction. Does that mean you really do little revision once the novel is completed?

A. Yes. The only place where I did any lengthy revisions was in *Set This House on Fire*. For some reason there was a lot of pruning to be done there, but I'm glad it *was* done. I would say with everything else I've written, including essays and reviews and reportage, that, with minor exceptions, when it's done, it's done.

Q. Were these revisions your idea or your editor's?

A. My editor, Bob Loomis at Random House, has a very "light hand," I'm glad to say; but with *Set This House on Fire* we mutually saw there was a great deal that could be peeled away, and it was.

Q. Can you remember what the revisions were?

A. Not exactly, because I'm not that close to the book any longer. But I do recall that great stretches of dialogue were made more concise through editing: long stretches, which even now are a bit long, were much longer, and they were simply pulled out. Also in Peter Leverett's descriptions of himself there are a lot of things he overly described—self-conscious reflections about himself—and I remember distinctly (though not exactly where) Bob Loomis and I got them out of there.

Q. You told me earlier today that your play, *In the Clap Shack*, underwent "endless revisions." Why?

A. Well, I *think* I know, but I'm not sure. Quite frankly, a play is simply a strange thing for a novelist to write. Its structure is different entirely: more like a poem, in that there is a direct line of mood that should be maintained from beginning to end, and there is a subtlety of expression that has to be—though this is not quite the best way to describe it—"formalized." A novel, almost by definition, is a form in which you can pour four extra paragraphs that seem to work, and do work: literally, because the novel is a kind of broad, marvelous, expansive form which allows for such latitude. There are flights one can take which to some degree seem, and may even be, extraneous. But in a play this doesn't apply. That single mood must be sustained. And when I discovered—as I did in this play—that I had mixed my moods, I was forced to go back and tear away all the superfluous detail.

Q. Of the four novels you've written, have you a particular preference for any one of them?

A. Most writers seem to be partial to the novel they've last completed. Whether that's a good thing or not I don't know. I think I've put most of my mature thinking into *Nat Turner* and I believe it's the one that says the most. But over the past few years I've gone back to *Set This House on Fire*; and though it's a somewhat less perfectly formed work than the others, at the same time it has some of my most passionate and best stuff, and I'm proud to have written it.

Q. Would you call *Nat Turner* a work of maturity and *Lie Down in Darkness* a work of youth? Could that account for your strong feelings about *Nat Turner's* place as your favorite?

A. I think it is my favorite only because I am so close to it. It still has resonances in my mind because of its nearness.

Q. I take it these resonances go beyond the social implications and critical reception of the novel?

A. Yes. It has nothing to do with these: just personal feelings. At the same time, I don't think I'll ever get over the sense of commitment and involvement and passion I experienced in writing *Lie Down in Darkness*, which was almost my life's blood when it came out. I think it's impossible to ever relive that first lyrical outburst (so poignant really) which every writer has in his twenties: when whole arteries and veins are pumping away.

Q. Was the creative process involved in writing your other novels different, then, from that in writing *Lie Down in Darkness*?

A. All the novels I've written were very difficult for me to write. I would say that once I got into *Lie Down in Darkness*—after the initial problems of composition—that it was the easiest to write. It seemed to pour out of me in a curious way; *The Long March*, too,

[35]

but to a somewhat lesser degree. *Set This House on Fire* and *Nat Turner* were terribly difficult to write, and for some diabolical reason it seems to get more and more this way than the other way around.

Q. Critics seem to feel there is a more "objective intensity" in the books after *Lie Down in Darkness*. Has the process of writing become more intense for you, would you say?

A. Really, the sense of intellectual responsibility has come down upon me. The novel I'm writing now—one I've tentatively called *The Way of the Warrior*—seems to be almost insuperably difficult to write because I want to say things which are intellectually and morally important to me, and I think important to say. And the telling of these things in an artful way has become a wretchedly difficult thing for me to do.

Q. Do you look upon novel writing as Dylan Thomas did upon poetry, as a "sullen craft and art": tremendously alone, private, agonizing?

A. Yes, absolutely; in spades. And sometimes almost hopeless!

Q. You mentioned somewhere that the actual technique of *Lie Down in Darkness* stumped you for a whole year. Did you have equal difficulty with the technique of your other novels?

A. Not so much in *The Long March*. That seemed to come with some ease, as I recollect. It took, for me, almost a negligible length of time to write: about six weeks, in Paris, in the summer of 1952, hot as it is now, in a little hotel room on the Left Bank. But with *Set This House on Fire* and *Nat Turner* the technique was very, very difficult.

Q. Why?

A. I think it was a matter of finding the true voice and rhythm of the narrative: programming the narrative so the voice merged with it in time and space, and so that there was a credibility at work. At one point in *Nat Turner* I stopped dead in my tracks for a long time. Months. Where it was was at the beginning of "Part Two," the flashback into Nat's past. I didn't have the momentum after "Part One" to just plunge ahead into this very, very tricky area in which I was trying to do a lot of things at once: among other things, to try and define what it must have been to be a slave growing up as a child, in that day and in that place. I finally, suddenly seized upon the idea that I must (as I did) meticulously outline the boy's life so that his subsequent actions would be credible.

Q. Was that flashback originally *conceived* as a flashback?

A. No, not originally. It just came; and had to become a flashback: a long flashback of 45,000 words.

Q. Do you generally find imagination dictating technique as you go along?

A. I think you could say that. The two really intermingle.

Q. Concerning the matter of technique, your novels tend to develop elaborate symbols and motifs. Have you any set idea of how these symbols are to work in your novels? Do you at all formulate them before you begin, or do they evolve in the creative process?

A. It depends on what you mean by symbols. I know "they" are there; but my own feeling is that they tend to spring up out of the soil of the work, to arise naturally from the narrative. Most of the time they simply seem to work. I just don't really know. I think it's an unanswerable question.

Q. Along those lines, your three major novels all seem preoccupied with dreams. Is there any particular reason for this?

A. Yes, I think so. I think if there's any reason at all, it is because dreams are a very impressive part of my subconscious. They linger with me (as I'm sure they do with many people) and *seem* to be teaching me something. I don't know if they do or not, but they are a momentous part of life for me, and therefore they must have their own significance somewhere: where and how, exactly, I'm not prepared to say.

Q. Have you ever incorporated your own dreams in your novels?

A. Yes, I think I have; in fact, I know I have.

Q. You have in your novels a penchant for long descriptions, many of them pertaining to nature. Do such descriptions always serve an integral function, or are they sometimes a flexing of technique?

A. I think they serve a very important funtion: at least in my work. I know that other writers tend to ignore nature completely; it doesn't seem to have any effect on them at all. But it's an important thing for me because I see it as an important component of the way

[37]

people drift through existence. At this moment, for example, we're sitting on a porch on Martha's Vineyard. I'm enormously conscious not only of sitting here talking to you, but of being hot, of the water being out there, of hearing birds. These are components that I think we're never free of; and therefore I've always felt them a very important aspect of my work. For the same reason, I'd like to add that there is no extraneous nature writing in my novels. One critic came down rather heavily on its being extraneous in *Nat Turner*. But every bit of that writing about nature is crucial. Many critics— urban critics in particular—are probably not aware that a little black boy and a slave growing up in Virginia in 1831 had nothing *but* the presence of nature; and that nature, in fact, is where most of the black southern legends and myths derive from.

Q. All of your three longer novels are framed by epigraphs of a religious nature; yet in the novels themselves religion, per se, or at least Christian ritual, comes in for hard knocks. Is this intended simply as a controlling irony, or something more?

A. I think I've always been partially intent on contrasting the spiritual impulse as it is defined by Christianity with the hypocritical ritual and hypocritical shallowness and thought that surround much of the manifestations in life. So I consider the use of epigraphs an important device of irony.

Q. Why did you choose epigraphs from seventeenth-century writings: Thomas Browne for *Lie Down in Darkness*, John Donne for *Set This House on Fire*, the King James Bible for *Nat Turner*?

A. With *Nat Turner*, of course, it had to be. With the others I was, at the time I wrote them, still very much steeped in seventeenth-century poetry and prose; and I seemed to want to strike chords that were common both to that time and ours.

Q. Can you explain why your protagonists tend to be visionaries, often of an apocalyptic sort?

A. That's an interesting question. I never quite thought of it that way. Perhaps I'm grounded in some manner of unconscious transcendentalism that makes me believe people really are striving for some impossible state. Perhaps they're all hopelessly romantic. (I don't know if that's the word, but perhaps it's as likely that as something else.) Anyway, this is an impulse I see in myself, and therefore it may take over these characters.

Q. In your novels any display of heroism is attended by a tragic outcome. Do you believe that "our age [to quote Lawrence] is essentially tragic"?

A. I think all ages are tragic, that heroism is always succeeded by tragic outcome, and that this is the human condition.

Q. Do you mean that all ages are tragic for the people involved in the age, or for the writer who transmits its vision?

A. I would say the two go hand in hand, and that they're inseparable in a way. If they are tragic for one, they're tragic for the other.

Q. In *Set This House on Fire* Cass Kinsolving is torn by, among other things, feelings of ambivalence about America: now loathing it, now longing for it. Were those your own feelings at the time, and have they changed any in the thirteen years since the novel was written?

A. I would say that if my feelings were validly expressed in the character of Cass, they're about the same now as they were then; perhaps even more so in both directions. You can't separate love-hate relationships; in fact, maybe this is what gives rise to viable and interesting literature.

Q. You realize, of course, that many contemporary American writers avoid writing about "America" as a concept. But you don't; you seem to engage it wholly.

A. Yes. I continue to and I don't know why. It's not particularly a value situation; it's certainly not a necessary component of good writing to have this awareness. I just simply happen to have it to the point of preoccupation, and I imagine I always will in whatever I happen to write.

Q. Another concept, sex, seems a cosmically destructive rather than a personally renewing force in your work: motivating in many instances the tragic outcome of your characters. Why?

A. I suppose you're being fairly accurate about that as a function in my work. I've often felt that what Freud called "this mighty urge" was, in the scheme of things, and in the contexts of things I've been writing about—the time, the place, the ethos—more destructive than constructive because of the prevalent morality. *Lie Down in Darkness* is a good example of what I believe you mean: the time and place being the thirties and forties in America, which was still very restrictive, especially in the South. Sex was the thing which one kept buried, I think unhealthily. I rejoice, really, in the new freedom of today, but in that time I believe it was a destructive force.

Q. Do you feel that if Nat Turner had "found his woman" the slave revolt would not have come about?

A. I don't think you can pose the question that way, but I'll try answering it by citing an example I've used before. Other revolutionaries—I'm thinking specifically of Martin Luther—consciously eschewed this matter because they believed that women, sex, etc., got in the way. And I think this has been demonstrated over and over again. Nat wasn't sophisticated enough to look at it in that fashion; but probably the reason he did *not* have a woman—and I still stick to my guns in saying that the historical record is, at the very least, obscure about the matter—was because he unconsciously felt this would obstruct his own revolutionary impulse and idealism: that the cause had to be served by steadfast asceticism.

Q. Several critics have noted in your novels recurrent motifs of master-slave relationships: e.g., Dolly and Milton in *Lie Down in Darkness*; Mason Flagg and Cass Kinsolving in *Set This House on Fire*; Nat and his owner, Hark and Nat. Is there any special reason for this, or is it purely fortuitous?

A. I've noted it myself. I suppose life is probably that way to a degree. Maybe I tend to focus on it more than other writers; but perhaps for me life is a demonstration of oppression and submission, and variations upon them.

Q. Has this anything to do with your southern origins?

A. I think it does, to some degree, yes.

Q. Since I'm asking about recurring patterns, can you explain why your heroes all happen to be thirty? Fitzgerald said that after thirty a man can't lie to himself anymore. Is thirty the age for "the moment of truth"?

A. I wish I knew. I would say that maybe it's fifty or fifty-five. But really, you can't ever lie to yourself. Actually, I hadn't thought of thirty as recurring as often as you say, but I guess it is a kind of crucial age in that you're no longer a youth; you're an adult. I think you could say it's an arbitrary age. There was a time when I was under thirty that I thought things would float along; and when I hit thirty, all of a sudden I had to get hold of myself. I don't know if that was the exact age or not, but when I turned thirty I was kind of glum. I see in retrospect how stupid the whole thing was.

Q. Your first full-length play, *In the Clap Shack*, was presented on December 15, 1972, at the Yale Repertory Theatre in New Haven, Connecticut. What decided you on play writing?

A. This particular theme, this episode seemed (like nothing else I've ever written) to outline itself as a play. The two acts, the setting, everything literally seemed to form itself in my mind as a play. And it did come very easily. Whatever the merits or demerits of the work, I certainly think it's a very theatrical piece.

Q. Did you find it easier to write than fiction?

A. Much, much easier. Let me qualify that. Harder in a curious way, but not harder in a more important way: harder in a kind of nit-picking way.

Q. Did you approach the writing of the play in the same way as you approached the writing of your novels?

A. More or less, yes. I sat down and did those four or five pages a day. I found they went very rapidly, and that it took me only two and a half months to write the play. Of course the revisions took a lot longer: and that's the big difference, for me, between play writing and novel writing. There's a lot of work to be done after the first draft is laid out.

Q. *In the Clap Shack* is a comedy. Isn't the writing of comedy something of a departure from your normal mode of writing?

A. Put it this way. I would like to think that all my work has some humor in it, and I think it does. But you're basically right. The comic mode has not been my . . . dodge! But I do think the irony that's necessary to both tragedy and comedy is in me. And it was easy to switch to comedy as long as I understood that the play was going to be a satire—which it is: a satire on a lot of things.

Q. What were the critics' reactions to the play?

A. *The* critic, namely Clive Barnes, saw no value in it at all. Too bad that he's *the* critic, because that destroyed, at least immediately, any chance of its going on to better things. However a lot of the other critics liked it. In places like the Hartford papers and *Variety* it got rather good reviews. Brendan Gill, a man of taste I think, saw it and liked it very much, though he saw it too late for a *New Yorker* review. In fact he wrote me a letter and put down Barnes rather severely for having failed to see anything in the play.

Q. Even more importantly, I was wondering what your reactions were to the initial production in New Haven.

A. I thought there were good and bad things. I thought there was bad casting in several instances, namely in the Magruder part. But also I thought the play had some very strong casting in the parts of Schwartz (Eugene Troobnick) and Clark (Hannibal Penney, Jr.). I thought they superbly fleshed out the characters. As I look back on it, I think the production probably lacked imagination. I think it was done too conventionally. It needed an element of extravaganza about it. The whole thing needed to be done more surrealistically to have given it bite, and to have removed it from the rather conventional sort of setting.

Q. Do you think (since you *are* a playwright now) that a playwright can or deserves to be satisfied with a production of his play?

A. I think so. I'm not knocking the production I got. I was very glad to have a production. I was pleased, above all, that though the audiences in New Haven are variable, they almost universally enjoyed the play.

Q. Do you feel, now that the play has been published, as close to it as to your novels?

A. No, absolutely not. At the same time I don't mean to sound as though I'm trivializing my relationship to it. I put much work and effort into it, and I respect what I achieved in it; but I don't have the same commitment to it emotionally, in any sense, as I do to my novels, nor even to some of the essays I've done.

Q. Robert Brustein, dean of the Yale Drama School, helped you in the revision of the play. Could you tell me what his most valuable contributions were to the final script?

A. He saw the unity I was trying to achieve but not achieving. The play was diffuse in its tone. It was a tragicomedy, whereas the comic tone should have been ascendent. So he made me, in effect, and I gladly did, cut out the extraneous things which tended to be grim and morbid in favor of the humorous elements.

Q. I would scarcely have called these other elements "grim and morbid." I remember them from the first drafts as memories or reveries, mostly Magruder's. Would you say those elements, whatever we might call them, were the novelist intruding on the playwright?

A. Yes, I would definitely say they were a hangover from novel writing.

Q. As a novelist, then, would you like to see the earlier drafts published with the "cuts" restored: to see the play, I mean, published not necessarily as a drama in the acting version but solely as a piece of writing?

A. I don't think it would serve any purpose. I'm happy with it the way it evolved. It's my belief, among other things, that of all art forms, of all literary art forms, play writing is the only one that's really collaborative. And that it allows for collaboration without compromising the integrity of the original creator. If an editor had taken the manuscript of a novel of mine and done as much changing as Bob Brustein suggested I do in this play, I would have felt compromised. But in terms of the play I don't feel that at all. I feel that's one of the aspects of play writing which is constant: that it lends itself so readily to a collaborative point of view.

Q. How did you "see" the play while you were writing it, and how did your vision of it change (if it did) when it went into the final production?

A. Very little. I think the two coincided very well. But from *this* vantage point, that is now, retrospectively, I still think it could have been transformed into something more exciting by the use of some experimental stagecraft, lighting, stage effects, and so on. I don't have all the theatrical jargon down, but what I'm trying to say is I think it could have been more exciting.

Q. I'd like to ask you a question about the acting itself. Would you respond to how you felt the actors supported, distorted, or changed your meaning as *you* wrote the play?

A. Let me be specific. I think that the actor who played the doctor, Glanz (Jeremy Geidt), is an excellent actor, and I wouldn't fault him for a moment, but I thought he was miscast in this particular role. He's an Englishman and he has an English gloss. In fact, we had to add things in the script to give his accent credibility. When he announces his pedigree to Magruder he says things like medical training at the University of Budapest, and Guy's Hospital, London. This was done in order to establish a foreign background.

But even that wasn't enough to keep from distorting the role. I visualize, and I think he's central to the play, a very important figure in the play, a kind of mid-Western efficiency expert. I always saw someone very deadpan, getting his laughs out of the lines. Jeremy got a lot of laughs out of the way he played it, which is O.K., it's legitimate. But ideally I saw someone like Hume Cronyn: a combination of malevolence and illness, on the order of Queeg from *Caine Mutiny*, though much funnier. For me the role fell far short of what it should have been.

The role of Magruder, too, I thought was miscast. The part needs a young stud instead of the round, pink-cheeked, little innocent it got.

On the other hand, the ensemble playing was excellent; and, as I said before, so were the actors who played Clark and Schwartz. Also there were some very imaginative minor roles.

For instance the Catholic chaplain, in his one little scene, did a marvelous job. As a matter of fact I remember Bob Brustein or Alvin Epstein (the director) thinking about taking that whole scene out because it seemed to interrupt the tempo of the play. But in the acting it "worked"; he got a hand every night. In fact, to give an example of the collaborative aspect of play writing I mentioned before, the actor (Bill Gearhart) changed some of the lines during one rehearsal, and changed them beautifully. At one point, you remember, he's arguing about whether it's a Protestant or Catholic who's dying, and he pulls out a very official paper. Now I had the line reading, "I have a message from Battalion Headquarters saying that a Catholic *is* dying on D Ward." And he changed the tense to say "a Catholic *will be* dying." I think that's a nice piece of imaginative ad-libbing on the part of an actor. And of course we left it in because it turned out to be a funny, funny line.

Q. There is a difference, of course, in seeing a play on paper before it goes into production, and even in realizing what the actors are doing by way of bringing the written play to life. But an equally important dimension in the theater is the audience. Do you think the audiences' reactions influenced your original conceptions of the themes and characters? I mean, you created them one way; the audiences responded to them in another way. Or did they?

A. Well, that's curious, because I never realized before I'd writ-

[44]

ten a play the way that audiences vary. For example, I was supposed to go—but I missed a plane somewhere and couldn't—on the night Phillip Roth went, and apparently I missed a fantastic evening. Apparently there was continuous laughter, according to Phil, who's tried play writing himself and is a very tough guy to please. He couldn't contain his enthusiasm for the way the play went *that* evening. And then Howard Stein, who knows theater as well as anyone, I guess, said it had been a marvelous audience; he said there had been a chemistry. After the show there were "Bravos" and a standing ovation—just one of those incredible theatrical exchanges between actors and audience. Then I went on several occasions after this. One evening there was a rather small audience; the house was about two-thirds full and there was a kind of intimacy in the theater. The audience responded (I thought) happily to the way *I* saw the play. And then I went to another production with a much larger audience—it was a performance toward the end of the run— and this audience was taking it as a straight play. Lines which had universally cracked people up (including the famous night Phil Roth went) fell dead! Now this is an indication for me of a very important thing about the theater. Audiences vary of course. Everyone "in theater" knows it. But *I* didn't know it until I became a playwright.

Q. Were the production to be done again, say on Broadway, what changes if any would you make?

A. I think that would be up to the director. I think it needs a different, more imaginative setting. That's one criticism Clive Barnes made that I would agree with, where he said that it was adequate and what else can you do with a hospital ward. Well, I think a set designer can do a lot of things with a hospital ward. It needs a new concept.

Q. I'd like to ask you something slightly more "literary." Dialogue in novels may have as many connotations as there are readers to interpret it. In a play, though, the audience is chained to the director's and actors' interpretations. Do you find this adds a significant limitation to the dramatic form?

A. I think it can work both ways. Obviously if the actor is inadequate to the dialogue he's going to convey that inadequacy. On the other hand, if an actor sees depth in a role he can often bring to the dialogue a new dimension. And I think within the framework of this play I had good examples of both possibilities. Many of the lines delivered by Glanz lacked the irony and bite they should have had because of the failure of the actor to fulfill that role. It just wasn't his part. The lines did not have the resonance and abrasiveness that I saw. Conversely, I thought the two best actors, who played Clark and Schwartz, brought, surprisingly to me, dimensions to the lines I had given them. Penney's marvelous laugh, for example, that seemed to encompass the audience at many points in the play was just superb. I had not visualized, in the writing of the play, that kind of range and effectiveness.

Q. Even were scenes like these to be found in a novel, you couldn't really imagine them being enriched in any way by the sensitive interpretations of readers themselves? What you're saying, it seems to me, is that in many cases it was *the* way you wanted a scene, though you didn't conceive all its possibilities in the writing!

A. Yes. And that's a salient difference between novels and plays. If I had wanted to write about this black man's evil laugh I would have had to describe it in that way, glossing the whole thing. But what happened here is that Hannibal Penney (who I think is a promising actor and someday will be a fine one) brought it all off automatically. It was part of *his* concept. And that's the great difference between these two literary forms.

Q. Do you have in mind any real limitations of the novel form over the dramatic form?

A. Basically I'm still a novelist and partisan to the novel. To put it the other way round, one of the things that makes writing plays so pleasant is their length: the fact that you can dispense with those endless descriptions, those sunsets, those entrances and exits, all that furniture and nuance which is part of the tedium to me of novel writing. This gives play writing a basic attraction.

Q. Then you do plan to write more plays.

A. I think so. Not immediately, but I do intend to.

Q. You're presently at work on a novel, *The Way of the Warrior*, about the marines. One chapter of it, as a matter of fact, appeared in *Esquire* for September 1971 and was called "Mariott the Marine." Will this be a long novel, too, and have you been working on it for long?

A. It's going to be longish: shorter than the other three long novels, but of reasonable length. I've had stops, many hung-up moments, but I've been working fairly steadily off and on.

Q. Do you feel that after *From Here to Eternity*, *The Naked and the Dead*, *Catch 22*, and *Slaughterhouse Five* there still might be interest in a war novel?

A. I think it depends entirely on the approach. What I'm writing about is very unusual. It's not in the "war novel" tradition. It's becoming, I think, a rather thickly textured examination of the professional military mind in America.

Q. That last is a very intriguing phrase. Can you elaborate on it, or would that be giving away a good portion of the novel?

A. The phrase, really, has become in *my* mind a symbolic representation of what America has been up to for many years. The hero is an idealistic military man. He is a man who joins this primitive, militaristic organization called the Marine Corps as it was forty years ago, at the end of the twenties and thirties when it was simply an arm of American imperialism, a kind of police or enforcing arm for the First National City Bank. The man comes of age through World War II and becomes someone who sees the necessity for civilizing military life in order for us to proceed as a civilized nation. An idealistic point of view, but nonetheless one based on a very real and tragic apprehension of existence: namely, that war is an absolute component of life, one that will never vanish so far as we can tell from the human condition. In other words, he's a kind of Fifth Columnist for the "good": a man who has almost some quixotic notion that if he can change the way that military people live, he will change the face of life.

Q. Isn't it paradoxical to bring the idea of civilization into the military?

A. Of course it is. That's one of the points of the book. This is what makes the man, I think, a rather splendidly unique sort of character.

Q. Does the military mind, per se, frighten you personally? Are you obsessed by it in any particular way, or only as a vehicle for the novel?

A. It doesn't frighten me as an abstraction, no. I think the military mind has been badly misunderstood in this country, mainly be-

[47]

cause we have a unique military establishment. It doesn't follow the patterns of the professional military establishments in other nations. It's a product of democracy after all; whereas, generally speaking, the military establishments of other Western nations have been the product of an aristocracy. It takes a different form. It's a reflection really of what we are as a nation. But it's a far more complex thing than many people envision it. The cliché of the "dumb military man" is simply not true.

Q. Is the novel in any way a roman à clef?

A. In no way, no way at all.

Q. What decided your turning to military subjects for your last two works? *In the Clap Shack* has a military setting; so does *The Way of the Warrior*. Was there any direct inspiration for writing it?

A. I'm like Edmund Wilson in this respect. I'm fascinated by the Marine Corps: its traditional glamor, the fact that it's an elite and dedicated establishment within an Establishment, and that it very distinctly has in our time involved men of courage and action. I'm fascinated by a sort of amalgam of personality about it. Perhaps like so much of what one writes it's a working out of one's fantasies. And who knows but whether this character I'm writing about is not a kind of projection of my own fantasies: the idea of a man who is at once a man of incredible physical courage, yet a man of learning and culture, a man who is, in addition, an idealist who wants to put an end to war: at least to bring civilization to the art and science of warfare.

Q. But the inspiration for this character wasn't pulled out of thin air. There were, are people who may have served as models.

A. Like everybody one writes about there is a figment here. There is a man who crossed my life at one point or another who resembled the character I'm writing about; but basically he is an imaginative projection.

Q. *The Long March* and *In the Clap Shack* are based on actual marine experiences. Is this true of *The Way of the Warrior*?

A. No. Well, I'm only being partly accurate. There is a lot in the book that's semiautobiographical.

Q. *Set This House on Fire* is written in the first person. *Nat Turner* is written in the first person. Long and substantial sections of *Lie Down in Darkness* are monologues, which can almost be considered first person narrative. And even *The Long March* might qualify for a first person narrative considering its "central intelligence" as James called him. Why do you prefer this voice, or something akin to it?

A. I tend to gravitate toward it because of its immediacy. It lends a kind of authenticity to a narrative that is sometimes quite lacking when you're describing a third person situation.

Q. It doesn't make the writing of the novel any easier, does it?

A. It certainly doesn't. It often makes it quite harder because it tends to start limiting your point of view, and you've got to find a way to get into the other peoples' heads. You trust to luck or skill that that happens.

Q. Is it still luck, at this point in your career? Don't you know what you're doing at every moment in the writing of a novel?

A. Obviously if it works it works. I've been criticized for many things but rarely for not being convincing.

Q. In *Nat Turner* you ingeniously devise a separation and synthesis of biography, history, and fiction. From what one gathers from the excerpt from *The Way of the Warrior* in *Esquire* it seems that your point of departure for that novel is autobiography: which means you are working this separation and synthesis between *autobiography*, history, and fiction. Are there any new techniques (new to you, that is) you had to adopt or invent in achieving this fusion?

A. No. Again it's a matter of tone, I think. Clearly, I have to gain the reader's confidence and credulity; and in order to do this I've had to say at certain points: "Look, I don't know what this man is thinking, but I'm trusting you, the reader, to go along with me in an imaginative exploration of this man's mind."

Q. Is it significant in any way that the narrator is a novelist who is almost or quasi-William Styron?

A. That's another thing. I wanted definitely to leave the impression that it was I, William Styron, telling this story, though I never refer to myself by name nor is my name ever mentioned. But this is the impression I want to establish. Again, I don't claim by any means to have invented this technique, because it's been done before. But I don't believe it's been done terribly successfully or very much: this writing in the form of a fictional memoir. In other words, a fusion of two forms, in which you start off distinctly giving the reader that it is you, William Styron, writing, and yet merge this into fiction. It gives the impression of autobiography but in reality it's not. It's something much different.

Q. The autobiography is there to establish the credulity only?

A. As in a court, yes, so you'll have an unimpeachable witness to things.

Q. Of course we're talking about a work in progress. I mention this because I wonder if current events, relating not only to the military, but to the government to which it is subordinate, changed the direction of the novel since you began writing it?

A. Yes. Well, I would think that events in Vietnam have illuminated things a lot. I think that through the evolution of recent history I have been able to see insights into this man that I am writing about which I did not have before. This has been a slow evolution for me because I did not realize what the philosophic center of this book was until pretty recently. And it is just what I've described to you a few minutes ago: a kind of symbolic rendition of what is very much part of the American spirit and embedded in it, this kind of blind, almost puerile groping for a national identity, part of it taking the form of wanton imperialism. It is a chapter about twentieth-century American history which has never really been fully written yet.

The fact is that we have, for example, been criminally involved in Latin America. Of course everyone who is sophisticated knows this, but hardly the extent of it. And that ever since the turn of the century, ever since the Spanish-American War, we have been involved in these criminal activities which have been mini-Vietnams. We had no business there, torturing civilians, fighting guerillas, and so on. It prefigured this war we are still ostensibly, despite what passes for a truce, fighting.

And what I want to do is show how a man is able to come to a moral consciousness, even as he has been engaged in these things. He starts out, you see, as a young, cultured, hothead Virginian of the old-fashioned type, VMI graduate, but brought up partially in France, with a great flair for languages and a great appetite for life. He's a young lieutenant of twenty-three or twenty-four, commissioned into the regular Marine Corps, in Nicaragua on patrol, and he hates these Communists. He comes from an anti-Communist background (what could be more anti-Communist than Virginia?). Well, three Nicaraguan guerillas are captured, and he cheerfully presides over cutting their throats with a bayonet. He does it himself. So I'm trying to show how this man evolves through a career in the Marine Corps up through the Second World War and the Korean War into by this time a colonel who sees his mission in life as a man who is going to pacify the military: a man who *knows* through his sense of destiny that he's going to become commandant of the Marine Corps. The book begins with a fantasy where, now a general and in his fifties, in the year 1963, he persuades John F. Kennedy to get out of Vietnam. I think you'll have to wait for publication to see how it ends.

Q. The novel does seem to depend a lot on history. Would you call it, like *Nat Turner*, another "meditation on history"?

A. No. I wish it were; it would be easier to write; I'm having to invent it all.

Q. In any case you are consciously avoiding writing a war novel after the accepted style.

A. Yes. And when I reflect on this book it has many of the themes you brought up today—master-slave relationships, destruction by sex, America, and other of those various motifs.

Q. I read sometime back that *Nat Turner* was going to be made into a movie. Have they begun filming it yet?

A. It's been bought and paid for—thank God—but that's all. It hasn't been produced, though the production came close to being started. I went to Hollywood for a week and stayed at very posh quarters and wrote a "treatment" which was never used because the producers began to get very upset over the black reaction. And that became a stumbling block. Finally for that reason, and probably for financial reasons, they postponed it or put it on the shelf, or whatever they call it out there.

Q. Had you ever written for the films before you did this treatment?

A. I collaborated on a screenplay just recently which was bought—or rather an option was taken on it. It's a screenplay based on a 1927 murder in New York (quite famous in its day) called the Snyder-Gray murder case, which was an especially gory triangle murder having to do with a woman, her paramour, and her hus-

[51]

band. It was a big cause célèbre and ended up in the double execution of the woman and her husband. It's called *Dead! A Love Story* and was sold to Paul Newman and his production company who've recently renewed the option.

Q. Would you like to see your work filmed?

A. Well, this I would. It's something that grabbed me and also my collaborator who is John Phillips (the son of John Marquand). We had great fun doing it; but I doubt very seriously that I'd care to make script writing a career.

Q. I think what I meant was did you ever want to see your novels turned into films?

A. Every one of them has been optioned at one time or another; scripts have been made for all of them, with the exception of *The Long March*, which had a disastrous run on television in the fifties: the last live broadcast on *Playhouse 90*. With the exception of that, everything has fallen through for one reason or another. The only novel that *I* think would possibly make a good movie is *Nat Turner* because it has an exterior scope. The others are too interior. Not that *Nat* isn't interior to some degree, but I can visualize it as a panorama more readily than the others.

Q. Along rather different lines again. I recall that you taught a seminar in creative writing at Yale.

A. Yes. Just for a semester. Several years ago.

Q. Did you like teaching?

A. I enjoyed it, yes.

Q. Did you have any luck teaching people to write?

A. I *think* I did; in a funny way. Unless I'm terribly mistaken I think the students improved. I had thirteen students. Most of their things looked awfully poor at first, and then at the end they looked better. And I attribute *some* of that to my guidance.

Q. Do you have any particular tack you take in teaching people to write, besides just criticizing their writing? Do you emphasize certain things?

A. I think I pointed out to them certain important things about language that they were vague about: the specific choice of words. I tried to point out that language, after all, is behind all this, and that many of them had great visions but not much linguistic capability, and that was because they were not being very careful about how they wrote. I pointed out rather primitive things at first. For example, if you sprinkle too many sentences with adverbs they're clumsy sentences, mostly if not always.

Q. What did you deal with after language, which I think we would all agree is the primary thing in teaching writing?

A. A combination of things. The students were college sophomores and juniors, so they were not very old, and so far as writing went not very experienced. I tried to point them toward a fusion of vision and language, emphasizing that subject matter was important, that they should avoid cliché situations, that there were certain mechanical hurdles to get over. Another thing I tried to get them to do was a lot of reading, because many of them had not. I had a suggested reading list and most of them went along with that. And I think profited from it, because at an early age writers profitably imitate.

Q. Was this a short-story writing course?

A. More or less.

Q. You yourself don't write many short stories. Do you feel in any way that the short story is a dead form?

A. No, I don't think it's a dead form. I'm not attracted to it very much because I think it's a limiting form, and that I work better in a larger medium. I remember the ones I've tried always restricted me; I felt the need to expand. As the case with *Nat* which, as I mentioned, started out as a novella.

Q. Would you care to express your feelings about the younger writers, thirty-five and under, of today? Have you any particular favorites?

A. There *are* two writers whose careers I've followed. One is a writer named Donald Harrington, who's very clever, and who's written several novels: none of which has gotten the attention it deserves. The other is Michael Mewshaw who went to the University of Virginia, and who, I think, is an awfully talented writer.

Q. How about the writers of your own generation: Capote, Salinger, Mailer, Bellow? Have they in your opinion come through or fallen off?

A. I don't like to comment on other writers too much. I used to,

[53]

but I don't like to any longer because I don't feel competent in doing so. The writers you've mentioned are all good writers, worthy of our attention. I think it's a very various and lively gathering of writers we have in America and have always had. Today is a very vital, good, fruitful time; and I think it's clear that this is where the major voices are and where the action is.

Q. What are your feelings about critical collections such as the present one?

A. I don't think they do any harm; they might do some good. I think as an introduction to a writer's work it can be useful; and it can also be useful as a guidepost for the time when, if your work is fortunate enough to last, it will be a thing for people to consult.

Q. You've never, to my knowledge, expressed positive disdain for critics, as some of your contemporaries have.

A. Actually I think I have, but *when* I have I haven't really been sincere. I think I value the critical function very highly; it's ridiculous not to. I think it only becomes unfortunate when the critical faculty is esteemed over the creative faculty, which it was for some time—ten, fifteen, twenty years ago. There was a time when it was thought that to be a critic was to be superior to a writer of prose fiction. It was, fortunately, a passing phase, and criticism today when good is very valuable.

Q. If it's all right with you, I'd like to take up where I left off seven years ago. You said then that you were pretty much inured to criticism. But, really, don't your feelings run high about the critical disparagement of novels you've taken so long to write? Are you really hardened to reviewers who are in no way novelists themselves, who have scarcely written anything significant, who pontificate and carp and dismiss ten years of sweat, blood, and tears with a nod and a wink and a clever phrase or two?

A. Well, first, I don't think it's necessary for anyone who sets himself or herself up as a professional critic to have written anything major to make that person competent as a critic. I don't think that literary achievement itself is a necessary component of the critical function, so I would tend to regard that part of your question as somewhat irrelevant. As for the other part, I think I am even more inured now to criticism than when we first talked seven years ago.

[54]

Sophie's Choice, for instance, received an *extremely* enthusiastic critical reception. I was pleased by it. You can't help but be. Any writer who says he's totally oblivious to that sort of reaction is not telling the truth.

Q. But what about those terribly disparaging reviews: those implying—indeed saying—that you couldn't write, you couldn't think, you couldn't . . .

A. Oh, sure. Of course there were those. There were extremely vicious reviews—mainly by academics! But I've come to expect that. Yet there were many—more—appreciative reviews, mainly by professional writers of one sort or another and journalists. The ones who attacked the book were, as I've said, almost exclusively professors of English, a breed of critic which I distrust in general.

Q. Why do you think they were so hostile?

A. I don't know, honestly. Perhaps the fact that I write independently; that I'm not a "post-Modernist" writer who demands that critics get out their little tool kits and dissect me, as they do with such loving glee for John Barth and Thomas Pynchon and people like that. I think that because I'm a different kind of writer it annoys some of them. I don't really know. I don't really care. My books are there. I'm fully conscious that all of them will be read fifty years from now.

Q. Writing so much as they do about you, critics and reviewers naturally fall into academic or journalistic clichés: "neo-Wolfian," "post-Faulknerian," "Southern Gothic," "WASP novelist," etc., etc. Have you a particular aversion to any of these epithets, or are they all pretty much anathema?

A. I'm tired of all of them. It's strange, you know, this desperate need to find safety in a convenient categorization. It's become part of the academic critics' stock-in-trade. Most have no daring, so they have to fall back on shibboleths, which they do with regularity; a book which does not correspond to preconceived notions of what writing is, is a terrible bother to them—or an embarrassment. And that's why, I repeat, I have very little regard (and certainly very little interest) in what they say. To say that I have not *read* these reviews would not be frank. But I read them largely with more amusement than anything else.

[55]

Q. One of the more balanced reviews of *Sophie* refers to your advance into the "mortal hell of Auschwitz." Considering the progress of your big novels—that is, *Lie Down in Darkness*, *Set This House on Fire, Nat Turner*—would you say that they show an increasing concern with this "mortal hell"?

A. Well, I would think my concerns are by now pretty obvious. They involve, as I've said before, human institutions: humanly contrived situations which cause people to live in wretched unhappiness. And this seems to be the largest mystery of human existence. Why we here on earth—we fellow human beings, theoretically a family—should find ourselves in such constant and universal discord: not supportive of each other, not sympathetic, not loving, but filled with hate and revenge and the desire to annihilate our own kind. This seems to be the aspect of the human condition that never disappears, and I suppose all my work has been an effort to try to understand why.

Q. Are you conscious of your books' showing this human conditioning as worsening, each time you do a big novel?

A. No, I don't think so. I don't think I've in any way furthered the feeling of its getting worse. My themes simply seem to demonstrate this absolute proclivity on the part of human beings to dominate each other, and the consequent need on the part of human beings not only to understand why this domination occurs, but why the way to counteract it may be only through love, or something like it.

Q. Is that why your books over the years seem to end more optimistically? The end of *Sophie* seems to me by far the most optimistic ending of all the books you've written. Maybe I'm wrong and maybe you don't feel that way yourself.

A. I think I see what you mean. Indeed, Stingo wakes to the dawning of a new day. This is certainly as honest a way as any of ending a book as profoundly despairing in nature as *Sophie's Choice*. Life did go on after Auschwitz. People did see hope, did see redemption. Again, by the very nature of writing, we are affirming something optimistic, it seems to me. Only a man with a very demented vision of life—someone like the Marquis de Sade, say—can come up with a totally negative view of any human experience.

Q. Am I being overly simplistic if I suggest that one of the major philosophical constructs of *Sophie* is that if you understand what the greatest evil is in the world, then you may understand what is the greatest good in the world?

A. It may not be quite as simple as that, but, yes. I have felt a sort of mandate as a writer (I don't know where it comes from; inner necessity, perhaps) to probe evil of the worst order in order to discover what makes people tick, what makes society tick, what makes human beings in their constant confrontation with each other tick. And because it seems that evil itself is a very illustrative value—even when as a writer, and certainly as a human being, I'm unsuccessful in fully understanding it—I feel that I'm able to discover ways toward good by that exploration.

Q. A corollary. So many of your major characters come to this conclusion at one point or another: that there is no guiding purpose governing human life; that man is doomed to a kind of mindless suffering in a godless universe. And yet you can end your books with a tremendous optimism that actually exhilarates people. Your works seem to me almost classically purgative.

A. You might be right. To me, the universe is benign or indifferent. We don't know why we're here; at least *I* don't. And yet the possibilities of life are limitless. We exist capable of great joy, ecstasy even. And these make the whole trip worthwhile. But the fly in the ointment, what pollutes the whole thing, is this evil which human beings alone are capable of. Animals aren't capable of evil. A meadow's not capable of evil; the sky is not; nor is the water. Human beings are the only vehicles through which the whole order is overturned. We ourselves are the agents of our own destruction, and this is what makes human existence so desperately perilous. Our beautiful opportunities which we have as human beings are absolutely destroyed because of our proclivity toward hatred and toward massive domination of each other. That is slavery and Auschwitz!

Q. In rereading all your novels recently, I came upon what appears an increasing concern—over thirty years—with the theme of deception. It seems that your major and greatest characters get through life by deceiving themselves or others as a way of surviving. Are you suggesting that this kind of deception is *needed* to survive in the world, that it is the only way one *can* survive? It happens with Peyton, with Nat, with Sophie. And when they say to themselves, "I'm not going to lie any longer," they are done for.

A. I think I see what you mean. Sophie is a perfect example of that. Maybe I'm not demonstrating anything in particular other than the need on the part of people to maintain their illusions in order to survive. This seems to me a very constant aspect of human behavior. The very act of living and surviving is so tough and often so nearly unendurable that we have to surround ourselves with a smoke screen of lies in order to tolerate what we're doing. And I suppose in the totally severe and extreme cases, life *doesn't* go on once the illusion is shattered. One might be, as you say, "done for."

Q. Would you say that all fiction—even when dealing with fact and truth and philosophy—is concerned with illusion?

A. Very definitely. At least it's been at the heart of my work since the beginning.

Q. John Gardner in his review of *Sophie* remarked—and I paraphrase—that northern readers don't seem to be tuned in entirely to the sensibilities of the southern novelist; that we wince or squirm or blush when the characters are listening in painful joy to classical music or always talking poetry. In short, that the northern sensibility is different from the southern sensibility. I wondered if this might account for other reviewers' reacting as they did to Stingo, the narrator.

A. Of course. John Gardner has every right to his own feeling, but I think this line of criticism shows a failure of *his* sensibility. I believe he was the only major reviewer who said the book has no sense of humor. Now the one thing the book does have, the one thing that keeps it going, the thing that saved it, is a strain of comedy that should be recognized by northern and southern sensibilities alike. The subject of *Sophie* is the most somber subject one can treat in our time. But my strategy all along was to maintain, sustain this vein of humor, and most of the more thoughtful reviewers felt that that's what makes the book work.

Q. The book struck me as a conscious *alternation* of the somber and the humorous: along the lines of some large musical form—a suite, say, or symphony. I mean not only slow and fast movements, but things like *scherzos* alternating with *marches funèbres*, *bourrées* with *graves*, or some such.

A. That's a wonderfully astute observation, I think, and one that I haven't seen made directly before. But, you know, the book is filled with music. One of its major points of sensibility *is* music, and people who fail to understand that may well fail to grasp the book on one of its most important levels. I'm not saying the book can't be read by people who have no response to classical music, but it's more than helpful to have one to get at some of the underlying levels of *Sophie*.

Q. Did you spend more time in researching *Sophie* than you did *Nat Turner*?

A. No. Considerably less.

Q. Did you read everything about the Holocaust, make notes, and then write, or did you constantly interrupt yourself for more research?

A. I've always had a theory that one of the most dangerous things that can happen to a novelist writing a specific novel having to do with history—and I think you can say Auschwitz is now history—is to overresearch. Heavy research may be useful to scholars, but not to novelists. On the other hand, I think it's dangerous to enter into a subject as intimidating to one's moral responsibility as Auschwitz and not be faithful to the facts. As a consequence, I read a great deal of literature on Auschwitz; yet compared to Jewish scholars on the Holocaust, I'm sure even my range of knowledge was rudimentary. Still, I have not to date seen a single criticism attacking me on a substantive point.

Q. You call *Nat Turner* a "meditation on history." *Sophie* is a similar meditation, is it not?

A. Yes, certainly. As with Nat's rebellion, I wanted to deal with the Auschwitz experience as a big moment in history. If I may get parenthetical for a moment, I'd like to say that I much prefer the term "Auschwitz experience" to "Holocaust" because I find the latter too parochial for what I was attempting. Recently, in the *New York Review of Books*, Neil Asherson reviewed a book on the Holocaust by a man named Rosenfeld, who, in the course of his book, Asherson points out, comments on *Sophie's Choice*. Rosenfeld was irritated because Sophie is a Catholic, and enraged because Nathan is a Jew who epitomizes all the Christian fears of the demonic Jew. He was further incensed that I tried to universalize the experience by making it clear that it touched other people and was not entirely a Jewish victimization, which the term *Holocaust* immediately sets off.

The Auschwitz experience, like Nat Turner's experience, seems to me a central event treating of that evil I alluded to earlier. Writers like myself, who wish to plumb profound human events, *have* to seize on one of these single moments in history. Tolstoy felt the same about the Napoleonic Wars, to cite the most famous example. Over and over again, it's been not only the right but the necessity, the obsession, of writers to seize these big moments and try to analyze them. For centuries writers have been feeding upon these moments: not to capitalize on them or exploit them, but to artistically develop them as paradigms of human existence. Slavery and Auschwitz are two such paradigms, and in my books I tried to master everything I had learned about these moments.

Q. Would you dare say that the Auschwitz experience looms more significantly in world history than does slavery in the South?

A. No. I think the two are intertwined. I think that they represent variations of each other. Plainly there are very large differences. Slavery did *not* involve mass annihilation: quite the opposite. Very rarely did European/American slavery involve genocide. It was antipathetic to the whole idea. What makes Auschwitz so bewildering and nonunderstandable still is why a civilized nation should want to annihilate another race, either by working them to death or by gas chambers. One way or another, annihilation came by way of enslavement, but neither evil makes any sense.

Q. Was it because the Auschwitz experience was so incredible, horrible, without sense that you adopted the narrative tack you did? Did you feel that five hundred pages of a single narrative view of Sophie would have been unbearable to take?

A. I hope that anyone critically perceptive in the broad sense can see that my strategy was quite plain, that I was trying to do something new. It was not to go over old ground, even remotely connected as I was to the Holocaust or concentration camps, but, at the start, to get as far away as possible. Young southern boy comes to

New York with nothing on his mind but to get laid and write a book, and finally, through the auspices of this beautiful girl, is sucked further and further into this terrible event. This seemed the only way to really make my book work, and I think it has worked on a very special and distinct level because I distanced myself the way I did.

Q. Yet many critics found it hard not to criticize *Sophie* ad hominem, saying you didn't fully understand the Holocaust (which Stingo of course says himself). How much should a writer understand his material before he writes about it? Doesn't the writing help him understand, though fiction is, I should hope, more than a purging?

A. You're absolutely right in underlining the fact that I have my narrator say "I will never understand Auschwitz"; that it was an incomprehensible event. The critics who attacked me ad hominem for not fully understanding are missing that point. It's not in the "understanding" of Auschwitz that the book has its greatest meaning, but in the attempt to understand, which is all I intended from the very beginning: to look at the concentration camp phenomenon from an entirely different perspective, to complexify it, to show how it affected not just Jews but other nationalities and races, to ultimately deal with aspects of the thing that had not been dealt with before.

Q. Is that the case with your other books: the *attempt* to understand the Zeitgeist of the late forties in *Lie Down in Darkness*; the *attempt* to understand slavery in *Nat*; the *attempt* to understand the demonic/artistic experience in *Set This House on Fire*?

A. What else can a writer do *but* attempt to understand? He's not God. He's a man trying to deal with materials as best he can, to bring new light upon old subjects.

Q. I ask this because I was thinking of when Zola, say, sat down to write one of his books, he seemed to have all the materials and facts at his command; he seemed to have mastered them all. But you feel differently about such a method.

A. Zola, remember, was writing a hundred years ago, laying the foundation for a different kind of novel—the naturalistic novel—at a time when this genre was in its heyday, and he had every right to use the materials at his disposal and to write the way he did. We no longer live in the nineteenth century; the novel has gone through many mutations as an art form. So to write a naturalistic novel about slavery or Auschwitz would be totally out of the question. Both *Nat Turner* and *Sophie* are intentionally very personal, impressionistic books, approaching the subjects from original points of view. Literature's become a different ball game. It's no longer dealing in the old abstract naturalistic forms but in something else.

Q. Then you would say that after writing *Nat Turner* you understood more about slavery and the black man and his attitude toward slavery and rebellion than before you started writing it.

A. Oh, absolutely. And I understood more about Auschwitz after I finished *Sophie*. In that sense, both books were voyages of self-exploration. If they did nothing else—even if they had become total failures as literature—I would have learned much about the question I addressed myself to.

Q. Much more than just by reading the dozens of books you did about Auschwitz?

A. Much, much more.

Q. Can you explain why?

A. From the simple act of creating a character whom I could identify with, of creating in Sophie a totally flesh and blood human being.

Q. And it was indeed through creating the character that you understood the experience.

A. Yes. Taking this theoretical but symbolic moment—the moment when a young and innocent woman is asked to make a choice between her two children—was in itself a statement about Auschwitz which was, I think, original artistically, though based on fact. Using that moment, I created what thousands of letters have told me is a memorable human being.

Q. Was the model for Sophie the same woman you *really* knew in that Brooklyn rooming house, or someone else, a composite, or what?

A. The girl I knew in the rooming house—the original Sophie—did not have the experience of having to choose between her children. I linked her with another woman who *did* have to choose. As you say, Sophie is a composite.

Q. Your intertwined narratives strike me that way, too. Would

[62]

you say that *Sophie* demonstrates your most complex narrative technique to date?

A. I *think* so. One of my favorite reviews refers to the narrative as "seamless," and that's what I like to think it is. If the book succeeds on the narrative level, it's because it doesn't show any fissures or cracks, and because the complexity of the narrative worked: compressed in many ways, but loose in many ways, so that one enters spheres of experience without feeling any jolt.

Q. There seem to be three spheres in the book: Stingo's coming of age as man and writer, Sophie's relationship with Nathan and at the end with Stingo, and Sophie's narrative about her past and Auschwitz: all "seamless," as you say. But how does one come to grapple with the larger dimensions of the book—the Auschwitz experience, Sophie's narrative—with the aid of the other two plots, so complex in themselves?

A. I think all the lines in the novel are interdependent and that none would actually work independently as a novel. The most important thing was of course to find the central narrative voice that (with wry and comic overtones) would first engage the reader in a completely straightforward way. That is Stingo. "Look," he says. "I'm the narrator. I'm going to tell you an interesting story about myself when I was a young man, living in New York, having a lot of trouble, and so on." This goes on for much of the way. It's not really until the reader is a quarter of the way through the novel that Auschwitz is even mentioned—and that as a sort of throwaway. My strategy was, well, the oldest story teller's strategy: to pull the reader in on the most basic level and then, by hook or crook, carry him to another level, and then another—to ascend vertically, so to speak.

Q. How about horizontally, too? When I think of *Sophie* I think of concentric circles being set up in a still pond. There's Stingo at the center, alive, young, thinking of love and sex and art, gradually discovering these other things, and carried at last to the complete horror of Auschwitz, all ripples going at once.

A. Yes, that's a good image. The book was certainly meant to radiate outwards.

Q. Many critics had trouble deciding whether your central narrator was meant to be you, a self-parody, a person purely fictional. If there is any ambiguity in the character, are you conscious of it, was it intentional, can you set the record straight, or am I being impertinent?

A. Plainly I had to go in and out of all those modes. Sometimes Stingo's myself, sometimes an invented person, sometimes a combination of the two. I wrote as the whim seized me. Obviously he was intentionally me at times, but most of the things that happened to him were totally made up, totally products of the imagination and had no connection with me whatsoever. But I wouldn't be able to give you a scene-by-scene breakdown as to when Stingo was who or what.

Q. A related question, if I may. You recall, I imagine, how vulnerable you were after *Nat Turner*. But with all your trying to get inside Nat's mind it was not actually William Styron narrating Nat's history. In *Sophie*, the narrator *seems* glaringly to be you. You don't even appear to wear the mask of a narrator.

A. Well, I intended it that way. I didn't necessarily want to have a mask. I wanted at any moment to become as autobiographical as I chose to be—with all the stops pulled out. On the other hand, there were moments in which I totally dissembled and told fibs, created situations which either didn't happen to me or couldn't have happened to me, and had nothing to do with me as a person. But I intended to be as loose about that as possible, completely relaxed, without any constraints about truth or accuracy in terms of me or my persona.

Q. Believe it or not, I'm leading up to something. I was wondering, you see, about later critics who come to write about *Sophie*. They might say: "There's so much in Stingo that's apparently William Styron. But the other characters—Nathan, Sophie, Höss— are obviously composites." There would seem to be some difficulty in writing considered criticism about a narrator that may be authentic and other characters that are indisputably fictional.

A. I'm perfectly satisfied to have people bewildered by that very thing. One early, intelligent, appreciative review (Jonathan Yardley in the *Washington Star*) said that because we, the reader, know that this happened to Styron, the immediacy of it all is staggering. Now the point was well taken, and I appreciate his feeling that the book did this to him, but of course these things did not really happen to *me*. None of that having to do with Sophie, the story of Nathan and

Sophie and Stingo—absolutely none of that happened. But here's a man of fine intelligence and good critical sense responding as though I'd written an autobiography in which every word was supposed to be true; and I was frankly tickled by it because it revealed the power of what I felt I had achieved in terms of "immediacy," as Yardley called it.

Q. Speaking of immediacy, did you choose to write a novel with a heroine rather than hero because of the initial inspiration: that woman in the boarding house? Or was there more to it than that?

A. I was actually seized by the metaphor which I mentioned before: that awful moment of choice that is inherent in the title.

Q. In other words, Sophie as heroine is there to lead up to the impact of that choice.

A. Of course. But she serves her own function on dozens of other levels, too: as an object for Stingo's love and passion; as a channel through which to learn something about Poland before World War II; as a reflector on anti-Semitism in Poland; that sort of thing. I just wanted to create a totally complex human being.

Q. Is this the first novel that deals with a heroine in Nazi concentration camps?

A. As far as I know, it's the first book dealing with concentration camps in which a single figure, female *or* male epitomizes all. There have been many fine autobiographical works like Tadeusz Borowski's and Elie Wiesel's, and then there's the classic *The Last of the Just*. All of these and dozens like them are outstanding works, but I think Sophie is the first character in the so-called Holocaust literature who is indistinguishable from the concentration camp experience and totally identified with it.

Q. Critics have already begun comparing Sophie with Anna Karenina, Sue Bridehead, and other tragic heroines, as a way of suggesting that she is a symbol of a society and an era. You pulled the same sort of masterstroke with Peyton Loftis in the fifties. Where did you get that insight into female psychology?

A. I don't know. I wonder if any writer knows. I've been reading Troyat's biography of Tolstoy, and Troyat, interestingly enough, was puzzling over the same thing. I just have a feeling that writers of fiction—and this is an off-the-top-of-my-head speculation—almost demonstrate their virtuosity if they're able to do women.

Tolstoy, Flaubert, Balzac, Hardy, Faulkner. They were all able to do women supremely. It's almost a demonstration of this mysterious thing which Jung (I think it was) stated accurately: that we all have this component of femininity or this dual sexual nature. The femaleness in the male and the maleness in the female is part of nature's mechanics which allow each of us to relate to, without being sexually involved with, both sexes. The femaleness in me allows me to truly understand the femaleness in the female, the maleness (if not carried too far) in the male. As a consequence, if a writer is able to balance equitably the sexual affinity he has, he should be able to feel certain female emotions with the same intensity that he feels the male. Anyway, I've always found this to be true. I've never had any trouble at all in works I've written in relating or describing women or feeling their emotions. I simply don't know what causes it, except that I seem to have a sort of balance that way.

Q. So you don't set about writing about women differently from the way you go about writing about men. You merely write about women, and it appears.

A. Yes, it appears. And with good women writers, too. Virginia Woolf was able to write about men. So were Jane Austen and George Eliot. One of the most dismal aspects of women's writing today is that they *can't* seem to write about men.

Q. The brilliance of your depiction of Sophie notwithstanding, one critic mentioned that you hadn't said anything new about experiences in concentration camps, but resorted to the "literature of the Holocaust"—Hannah Arendt, Bruno Bettleheim, George Steiner and others—for parallels and commentaries on Sophie's case. Why did you feel that this supportive documentation was necessary if you were writing fiction?

A. Actually, I think it was mentioned by several reviewers, as though it were some kind of felony to draw as much as one *wants* on the actual sociological/historical commentary on the Holocaust or concentration camps. People who have written about them have in general provided valuable insights. When I mention Simone Weil or Hannah Arendt or George Steiner, it's not as if I were screaming for help, but merely doing what Tolstoy and other writers greater than I by far have done over and over again: to constantly quote former and contemporary authorities. Take *War and Peace*.

It's a compendium of other writers. We can all name dozens of books that are, too. And so such criticism to my mind seems fussy and pedantic. Sophie plainly has faults—I know what they are; I have a little catalog of them—but they do not include such preposterous cavils to the effect that I'm not allowed to quote from other writers. It's a time-honored custom for a writer of fiction to bring in anything he wants in support of his own search for truth. And if it includes writers of and on the Holocaust, well, it's Bill's book, isn't it? Since when does a writer have to have original ideas anyway? It's usually worked to the writer's disadvantage more than the other way around. Writers are not supposed to be original philosophers; they're supposed to be delvers into human nature. And if they can, as they often do, use authorities to support their speculations, then they *should* use them. There should be no embarrassment by it; nor should it be a demonstration that the writer has a poverty of ideas.

Q. The novel's subject, if one can put it baldly and horribly, seems to be absolute evil: "gloomy, monotonous, barren and boring" as you quote Simone Weil as saying. What, if bared to the bones, would your definition of "absolute evil" be?

A. Total domination of human beings by others up to the point of extermination seems to me to come as close as one can to the notion of absolute evil. Because if you take the corollary—What is the greatest good?—it would be freedom. Therfore the corollary to *that* is the greatest evil: the absolute lack of freedom, the totally irrational, unjustified lack of freedom. Now there are, of course, relative lacks of freedom. A man who has committed a crime is put in prison and deprived of his freedom for a good reason. You can—and this is totally aside from what you feel about penology and punishment—at least say there is a case to be made for the restriction of his freedom. But to take innocent people and enforce against them, en masse, absolute lack of freedom in the form of extermination seems to me about as close to absolute evil as you can get.

Q. This next may seem very flagrant, but I remember reading some years ago your "Life in Death of Benjamin Reid," an essay against capital punishment. Would you condemn a person like Höss to death?

A. Oh yes. No question about it. But that's an entirely different thing. There's absolutely no question that you can make exceptions about capital punishment. I make them all the time. Yet even for the most loathsome, atrocious civil crimes there is absolutely no justification, in my mind, for capital punishment. But on the level of the Nazi phenomenon, I don't think we can talk about capital punishment in the same way. It would have been a delicious pleasure to have seen Höss and Hitler and all that gang hanged: without qualification.

Q. Another one that might be a bit flagrant. It's about the character of Nathan, who strikes me as a genius, beast, madman, controlled by a murderous and suicidal idée fixe. In short, he seems an obvious parallel to the Nazis themselves. Is that way off base?

A. Not at all. He was an agent of destruction, just as single-mindedly in many ways as the Nazis were.

Q. Then he is parabolic in a sense? I mean if *anyone* is controlled by an idée fixe like that, then violence and horror are going to follow.

A. Yes. But of course in Nathan's case there is a snapper. The qualification has to be held out all the time that he was (and I made it quite explicit) certifiably insane. So that one must have, I think, certain moral reservations about his evil. I think that if a man is nuts, this is one of the paradoxes of nature we can't really cope with in terms of pure morality. Nathan was nuts.

Q. But the Nazis were nuts, too, weren't they?

A. No, no; they were not. That's the most awful part of it. They were *not* nuts. There were some crazy Nazis, no doubt, but the truly terrifying thing about Nazism is how calculated, rational, logical its agents were. A battery of totally impartial psychiatrists did Eichmann up and down and they were astonished at his rationality. I think that this sanity is the single most terrible touchstone of the Nazis.

Q. So Nathan's evil is mitigated because he's certifiable?

A. To my mind, yes. The Nazis were sane and evil; he was crazy and evil. But, you know, evil can come from both directions; and remember, too, Nathan had a good side, a loving side.

Q. One of the epigrams to *Sophie* reads: "I seek that essential region of the soul where absolute evil confronts brotherhood." Would you be kind enough to gloss that?

A. The moment when the doctor tells Sophie she has to choose;

when an innocent young woman and her two children—representing brotherhood—is told by this personification of total domination that she must choose death for one of her children: that seems to me the juxtaposition of brotherhood and absolute evil.

Q. Would you say that's the thrust of the novel?

A. That's what the novel is seeking, yes. And that is that essential region of the soul where humanity is at its most mysterious.

Q. Innocence, benevolence, brotherhood. Aren't they always destroyed in that essential region?

A. I'm afraid they are, in one way.

Q. But *Sophie* also suggests they are renewed in another way.

A. Yes. The book is about that as well.

Q. *Sophie* is being filmed, is it not?

A. Yes.

Q. Are you writing the script for it?

A. Definitely not.

Q. Why?

A. Well, there's an old, ugly phrase of some writer (I forget who it was) who said that writing a script from his own novel would be like a dog eating its own vomit. I don't feel quite that vividly about it, but it would be like going over terribly old ground. I wanted to be free of it entirely for the movie. I can't be 100 percent certain about the movie, but I have a great deal of confidence in Alan Pakula, who's directing and writing the script, and who has a marvelous sensibility. And of course he does consult with me often.

Q. Last question. Is *The Way of the Warrior,* which you interrupted to write *Sophie,* still next on your list, or something else?

A. I'm definitely going back to *The Way of the Warrior,* yes.

Q. And it's still much as you talked about it in our last interview?

A. Yes. Absolutely the same. There are the inevitable changes, but I know where I'm going.

LOUIS D. RUBIN, JR.

Notes on a Southern Writer in Our Time

In 1952 a young Virginian, William Styron, published his first novel. Entitled *Lie Down in Darkness*, it was the story of a young woman whose existence grew increasingly desperate until finally she took her own life. The novel was received with considerable acclaim, and reviewers prophesied a distinguished future for its author.

In an interview with David Dempsey, Styron readily admitted that he had first begun *Lie Down in Darkness* immediately following an intense reading of the novels of William Faulkner. And indeed, there were more than a few obvious similarities to Faulkner's fiction, notably with *The Sound and the Fury*. Both novels were set in the South. In both there were a family with an alcoholic father, a selfish mother, and several children, one of them mentally retarded. Both had protagonists who wandered about a city far away from home, clutching a timepiece, before jumping to their deaths. Both had faithful Negro servants who went to church to mourn the disintegration of their white folks. Another Faulkner novel, *As I Lay Dying*, was built about a family's journey to inter a coffin. In *Lie Down in Darkness* a family's trip to the cemetery to inter a coffin provides the frame for the novel. And so on.

All the same, Styron's novel was not simply warmed-over Faulkner. For one thing, it had a contemporaneity to it, a sense of dealing with moderns in the modern world, that is not present in Faulkner. For Faulkner's attempts to use the contemporary urban milieu to create fiction, notably in the last two volumes of the Snopes trilogy, have been melodramatic and unsatisfactory. By contrast, Styron's novel was set convincingly in a contemporary setting, and was fully of the present moment in its concerns and attitudes. Where so much fiction by younger southern writers seemed like inferior

Faulkner, Styron's talent was recognizably his own; and as with the better Faulkner novels, it had the sense of *mattering*, of dealing with characters who definitely stood for something as human beings. Nor was it composed with the terse understatement typical of so much present-day American fiction. It had the high rhetoric, the sounding language, of the best fiction of Faulkner, Wolfe, and Warren.

Here, then, was a novelist who seemed to write squarely within the southern tradition, and yet was definitely his own man. He was, furthermore, quite young—only twenty-five when his first novel appeared—and he obviously possessed the kind of stylistic mastery emblematic of the truly gifted writer. There was no apprehension of his first novel's having been a fluke, depending for its impact on a lucky combination of topical subject matter and the author's momentary psychological attitude, as was true of a novel such as James Jones's *From Here to Eternity*. The novelist who could write *Lie Down in Darkness*, one felt, could and probably would follow it with other novels of similar or higher caliber. This opinion was confirmed a year later when Styron published a novella, *The Long March*, a vigorous tale of Marine reservists called back to duty. It too bore the mark of the writer thoroughly in control of his craft.

What happened then was very strange. For almost a full decade, William Styron did not publish another novel. Though rumors of a new work in progress recurred, year after year went by with no new fiction by Styron. Yet paradoxically, instead of gradually dropping from sight in public reputation as novels by other good writers were published and achieved recognition, as one might expect to happen to the author of a good first novel who did not produce additional work, William Styron's stock kept right on rising. On the strength of that one novel and the novella, he came to enjoy the kind of literary prestige that few other writers commanded. Critics habitually referred to him as one of the handful of really distinguished novelists of his generation. He was interviewed, quoted, repeatedly cited, and discussed. For the better part of ten years he possessed a reputation that the author of a half-dozen good novels might well envy.

Lie Down in Darkness was a good book, and everything that was said about it in the way of the augury it held was justified. But good as it was, one is hard put to explain the extraordinary growth of

Styron's reputation in terms of it. It was no *Look Homeward, Angel* or *The Sound and the Fury*. It was surely not, for its time and place, the kind of novel that *Sister Carrie* had been during the 1900s. To an extent it was derivative. It had flaws aplenty. Though it thoroughly warranted its author's being marked as a man to watch, a potentially important novelist, it was after all only a single, well-written, medium-length novel, and not a sustained body of literary work. So that one might ask why its author, during the 1950s, gained the astonishing reputation he enjoyed. Was it something else besides the book itself? One of Styron's contemporaries, Norman Mailer, jealously hinted as much in *Advertisements for Myself*, suggesting that it was Styron's own doing. "Styron has spent years oiling every literary lever and power which could help him on his way, and there are medals waiting for him in the mass-media," Mailer wrote. Exactly how Styron managed this feat Mailer did not bother to explain.

In any event, the reputation was there, and it outran the novel, with the result that when in 1960 Styron did bring out a second novel, what happened might have been expected. *Set This House on Fire* was treated to a torrent of critical abuse the like of which has seldom been seen in our time. On all sides it was roundly condemned. If one believed most of the review media, it was almost inconceivable that any novelist could have produced as bad a work as William Styron had done in his second try. The Most Promising Young Novelist Of His Generation was thoroughly denounced. The popular critics and the academic reviewers seemed to compete in the rage and intensity of their abuse, and not content with demolishing *Set This House on Fire*, some went back and decided that *Lie Down in Darkness* was not really so good, either.

Was *Set This House on Fire* really so bad as everybody said it was? Not at all, I think. In fact, it was quite a good book. Like its predecessor it had flaws, perhaps more vulnerable ones, but in almost every way it was a more ambitious, more deeply perceptive work. It was a novel such as no other writer of Styron's generation could have produced; it contained some of the best writing of its day. But if this is so, then what explains its devastatingly hostile reception? Why was it singled out for such a barrage?

The answer, I think, is to be found in the *kind* of book that *Lie*

[72]

Down in Darkness was, and the reasons why that novel, in contrast to the second book, enjoyed such a stunning success. It has to do with the difference between the kind of book that *Lie Down in Darkness* seemed to be, and the kind of book it really was. For when it first appeared it seemed to be something very different, and much more familiar, than what it actually was; and the reasons for this have to do in large part with southern literature from Faulkner onward. The history of Styron's two novels is closely tied in with what southern writing has been during the past several decades, and what it can and might be in the future. I want now to discuss Styron's work in this light. For what is involved, I believe, is not only the history of one young novelist's career and reputation, but the whole question of the continuation of a literary mode into a new generation. I am not talking about "influences," nor am I concerned importantly with cultural history as such. Rather I shall seek to deal, by inference at least, with the deepest and most elementary relationships between a book and its times, between art and culture, between one writer who comes from a particular region and the writers of that region who preceded him. And without claiming for a moment that the concerns I shall be examining are the *conscious* concerns either of writer, or region, or reader, I shall seek to show what, in William Styron's own time, which is ours as well, it means to be a "southern" writer.

The central character in *Lie Down in Darkness* is a young woman, Peyton Loftis. Born of a well-to-do Tidewater Virginia family, she grows up in the seaport city of Port Warwick. Her father, Milton Loftis, is a lawyer. Once he had political ambitions, but over the years he has become much more interested in his golf game and in social drinking. Helen Loftis, Peyton's mother, is the child of a sadistic, puritanical army officer, who has left her a substantial fortune. Peyton is the older of two daughters; the second child, Maudie, is mentally defective. Milton Loftis is inordinately fond of Peyton, and far too indulgent. He cannot bear to jeopardize her affection for him, even momentarily, by denying her anything she demands. By contrast, Helen Loftis is highly resentful of her daughter's hold over Milton, and at crucial moments her jealousy is revealed in words and acts of great cruelty. The older Helen grows,

[73]

the harder her personality becomes. Milton, meanwhile, becomes infatuated with another woman, Dollie Bonner, who gives him the idolatry and the softness that his wife will not provide.

After a violent scene with her mother, Peyton goes off to school at a fashionable Virginia women's college, and never really returns home to live, though several times she tries and fails. Her life becomes increasingly unhappy. At crucial junctures Milton fails to provide her with the guidance and firmness she needs in a parent, while Helen denies her the motherly affection she craves. When Maudie sickens and dies, Helen accuses Peyton of causing her death. Several times a reconciliation between mother and daughter is attempted, but Helen's insane jealousy always wrecks it, despite the advice and encouragement that an Episcopal minister, Carey Carr, attempts to give to Helen.

Finally Peyton goes to live in New York, where she falls in love with a Jewish painter, Harry Miller. In a final effort to gain her mother's love, she comes home to Port Warwick for the wedding ceremony, but just when all seems to be going well, the mother's obsession and hatred are viciously reasserted, and the day ends in bitterness and misery. Peyton and her husband return to New York, and Peyton thereupon steadily destroys her own marriage by continually "testing" Harry's love through acts of selfishness and cruelty. At length she begins to sleep with other men, whereupon the tormented Harry forces himself to leave her; and, when a final, pathetic attempt at reconciling him fails, Peyton commits suicide by leaping from a building. Her body is brought home to Port Warwick and buried. Thus the plot of *Lie Down in Darkness*.

First let it be reiterated that it is a *good* novel; there is no doubt of that. Styron's sense of psychological complication is such that the descent of Peyton Loftis into darkness is convincingly motivated. Just as in Faulkner's *The Sound and the Fury*, the novel is an account of the failure of love. Had Milton Loftis's love for his daughter been less selfish, so that the father had been willing to incur his daughter's momentary displeasure by insisting that she do what was right rather than what she wished to do; had Helen Loftis's firmness been the product of genuine love and understanding for Peyton and not a hypocritical mask for jealousy and hostility; then Peyton might have grown up into someone who is able to love in her turn. But Milton sought in Peyton the affection that Helen did not provide him, and Helen struck out at Peyton in order to punish Milton. Thus Peyton has known for love only indulgence on the one hand and poorly masked jealousy on the other; and when she marries, she seeks a relationship on just those terms. She demands and must have continual forgiveness, and the acts she commits in her quest for proof of such forgiveness are too reprehensible for her husband to condone. Along with this goes an insane jealousy, in which she magnifies small failures on her husband's part into evidence of monstrous unfaithfulness; no sooner does she feel that Harry has forgiven her for her own misdeeds than she begins at once to berate him unreasonably and psychotically for imaginary infidelities. Thus Harry must play the part of forgiving father on the one hand, and erring husband on the other, neither of which roles he merits. In psychiatric terms, Peyton must first reenact her relationship with her father, and then her mother's relationship with her father. It is too much, finally, for Harry to accept, if he is to retain his own sanity. Whereupon, denied the only kind of love that she can recognize, Peyton takes her own life. A father's weakness, a mother's cruelty have brought about a daughter's destruction.

Set against a background of upper-middle-class, urban, southern society, the story is one of real dramatic tension. Peyton's struggle to save herself (more rending because of her own recognition of her plight) deeply engages the reader's sympathies. Intelligent, compassionate, with a great capacity for loving and being loved, she is doomed to frustration and pain, and when finally she succumbs to the forces that are dragging her downward, there is a genuine tragedy in her fall. Similarly, the characterization of Milton Loftis is a moving picture of weakness and ineffectual love. Milton too is aware of his plight, and his efforts to save himself and his family are pathetically moving. Helen Loftis, I think, is somewhat less effectively drawn; the psychological motivations for her conduct are never fully apparent, and must only be conjectured. The role of the family's Negro servants is too obviously contrived. Unlike Dilsey and her family in Faulkner's *The Sound and the Fury*, Ella and La Ruth in *Lie Down in Darkness* do not fill the dramatic position in the fortunes of the Loftis family that would justify Styron's use of them as tragic chorus.

Despite such flaws, however, *Lie Down in Darkness* is a successful, well-written work of art. As a first novel it surely justified those who saw in its author a writer of much promise, who might be expected to produce other works of distinguished fiction. To begin with, it was decidedly moving, and had genuinely tragic overtones; and it was the first novel to appear in the postwar period by a young writer of whom that could be said. Not one of the other postwar writers had been able to produce such a book. The best of their novels were ponderous, naturalistic works such as Mailer's *The Naked and the Dead*, and Jones's *From Here to Eternity*, both the products of writers of obvious passion, but written, I think, somewhat crudely. Both were war novels. Of the two Mailer's was the better written, but much of its power came out of its author's, and its readers', detestation of war and military life. In Jones's case that was about *all* that could be said for his book. In each instance a sense of civilized outrage, on the part of novelist and reader, contributed much to the success of the work.

By contrast, Styron's book was not a war novel. Its intensity was attained by the author's fictional craftsmanship, his talent at characterization, his insight into the tension and desperation of a modern, godforsaken urban existence. Such a novel had not appeared in some time, and the public was hungry for a writer who could produce more. It was thus quick to hail *Lie Down in Darkness*, and to hope and expect that Styron would be able to follow with other and even better books. Furthermore, in the decade that followed its publication, no other competitor appeared in sight. Good as Saul Bellow's *The Adventures of Augie March*, J. D. Salinger's *The Catcher in the Rye*, and other novels by writers such as Nelson Algren, Bernard Malamud, and Herbert Gold were, their works seemed infinitely more private, less public in their dimensions than Styron's one novel did. There was not the sense of any of these authors speaking so directly to the experience of his time as Styron did in *Lie Down in Darkness*. Peyton Loftis's downfall seemed to say something about the day and age that the more limited predicaments of the heroes of other novels did not. Styron alone seemed capable some day of producing really important literary work, novels that could stand up to the best books of the prewar novelists.

More specifically, *Lie Down in Darkness* seemed very much in the Faulknerian mode. Not that it was derivative; quite the contrary. There had been and would continue to be numerous southern novels that *were* derivative, that seemed to be imitation Faulkner. William Humphrey's *Home from the Hill*, for example, was almost a parody of the Yoknapatawpha novels, until halfway through when it left the primitive milieu of such stories as "The Bear" and descended into modern melodrama. The thing about Styron's novel was that, while it seemed to come out of the same literary and cultural tradition that had made Faulkner's fiction so profoundly moving, it created its own kind of tragedy, and did not rely on the secondhand insights of Faulkner and his contemporaries. Styron, in other words, seemed to be doing what good writers have always done: he used his tradition, rather than let himself be used by it.

That literary mode, it must be emphasized, had produced much of the finest American fiction of the twentieth century. It had avoided the sodden determinism of the naturalistic school of Dreiser, Dos Passos, Steinbeck, and Farrell, and had been able to achieve fiction in which human beings could be made to behave as free agents, able to pit their wills against their society and the limitations of their mortality in meaningful dispute. It had been able, too, to depict men in a necessary and inescapable relationship to society, so that the conflict between the private conscience and public circumstance could seem real. The characters of Faulkner, Wolfe, Warren, Lytle, and the others were not in arbitrary, casual contact with the world around them; they were inescapably a part of society, and any lasting isolation from society constituted a tragic condition. If society was hostile, it was never indifferent. Furthermore, these men's characters were not creatures of the moment; they existed in time, and the past affected them in crucial ways. Finally, the basis of their morality and the sources of their behavior were not only social and biological but religious as well; their transgressions were not ultimately against men, but through men against God.

When *Lie Down in Darkness* appeared, the southern literary mode had been the productive force of distinguished fiction for almost three decades. It had set up certain expectations on the part of the reading public. The reader had become, as it were, habituated to conceiving of tragedy along certain lines. When Styron's novel came along, therefore, it fell heir to a by-then familiar literary tradi-

[77]

tion, and was read in terms of that tradition. Here was another fine southern novel, with the implied promise that the author would be able to sustain and develop his talent within the accepted mode. The southern literary tradition was thus manifestly continuing into the postwar generation.

This seemed all the more important since, up until then, and in the years immediately following the publication of *Lie Down in Darkness* as well, no other southern novel by a younger writer seemed to hold out such promise. Truman Capote's *Other Voices, Other Rooms* had been too exotic, too private to allow one to feel that its author would be able to produce major work. Carson McCullers's fiction, interesting though it was, seemed limited in its scope; it stopped short of the tragic, contenting itself with a poignant exploration of surfaces. Flannery O'Connor's decidedly promising talent was limited in range and breadth; it seemed to fulfill itself adequately only in the short story form. Certainly James Agee's *A Death in the Family* was an excellent and quite original work, containing passages of great beauty and force; but its mode was not that of high tragedy, and besides, Agee had been dead for two years when his novel appeared. To be sure, Robert Penn Warren was obviously of major stature, even though he never seemed to repeat the achievement of *All the King's Men*; while Andrew Lytle's *The Velvet Horn* was both its author's best work to date and as good a novel as almost any written by a southern writer. But these two, like Faulkner, were members of the previous generation of southern writers, the generation of the high renascence. So for that matter were Eudora Welty and Caroline Gordon; both had been publishing fiction since before the Second World War.

In the post–World War II generation of Southern writers, then, Styron stood alone in his achievement, and in the nature of that achievement. If the southern literary mode was to retain its importance in contemporary American literature, William Styron seemed to be the writer who would lead the way.

Assuredly, I do not mean that the average reader was aware of all this when he encountered *Lie Down in Darkness*, though I suspect that many reviewers were, and to a greater extent than they perhaps realized. But I do think that when Styron's novel was published, it appeared to fit into a literary mode that a generation of excellent novelists had educated the reading public to understand, so that the reader was able to bring to *Lie Down in Darkness* an expectation and a frame of reference that the novel seemed to fill. This made possible a kind of cumulative public response that, at the time of publication and during the decade that followed, helped to give the novel its vogue, and contributed greatly to the nature and extent of Styron's reputation. Here, one felt, was another first-rate writer in the familiar southern style, one seemingly able to create genuine literary tragedy. And that it *was* tragedy he had managed, there could be no doubt; had not Faulkner, Warren, and the others already done just that, and in the same way?

Let me quote from one of Styron's more perceptive critics, John W. Aldridge. Writing in 1956, Aldridge spoke of the "Southern elements of the novel—particularly the elements of fundamentalist religion, regional guilt, and the contrast of races," as being "so powerful that if anything they seem excessive to the motives of the characters and perpetually to overcome them." He noted Helen Loftis's "Southern gentlewoman madness" and "the whole Southern blood-guilt." He remarked that "it is significant that it is after she marries and goes North that Peyton becomes overtly psychotic." Or lest I appear to single out Mr. Aldridge, who I believe has somewhat different thoughts on the matter now, let me quote from a review that I wrote of *Lie Down in Darkness* shortly after it appeared in 1951. I find, rather to my astonishment, that I did not have much to say about Styron's southernness as such, but even so the criteria I used for the evaluation were clearly taken out of the familiar experience of the southern novel. I remarked that "the Loftises want something, and none of them knows what it is. What they want is a purpose, a reason for being. In the final chapter Mr. Styron contrasts their aimlessness with the happy faith of their Negro servant, who is untroubled by acedia. The servant believes, and on the foundations of that belief is able to conduct a satisfying life." Note that this is an accurate description of the role of Dilsey in *The Sound and the Fury*—but not at all, as I shall try to show, of the servants in Styron's novel.

The question I should like to propose now, a decade after *Lie Down in Darkness* was first published, and with the hindsight that comes of having observed the progress of Styron's literary fortunes

[79]

over ten years, is whether such inferences as Mr. Aldridge and I made, and those of many another critic as well, were accurate. Was *Lie Down in Darkness* a novel of originality, but one written essentially within the accustomed southern mode, achieving its tragic force in approximately the same manner as the novels of Faulkner, Warren, and others in the southern tradition? Or did the "southernness" only *appear* to be important, and was *Lie Down in Darkness* in important and vital respects quite another *kind* of novel than those of Faulkner and the others, significantly different in its version of human experience, its conception of society and of people, so that the familiar southern motifs were considerably less important than had seemed true at first reading? In other words, had Mr. Aldridge and I and various other critics reviewed William Styron's novel, or had we in effect reviewed a new novel by William Faulkner?

Earlier I noted some obvious resemblances between *Lie Down in Darkness* and Faulkner's *The Sound and the Fury*. Since the latter novel is one of its author's two or three greatest works, and since the dimensions of the tragedy of the Compson family are so central to the southern mode—were instrumental, indeed, in fashioning that very mode—I want to compare the manner in which that novel realizes its tragic potentialities with the way in which Styron's novel does.

The Sound and the Fury is concerned with the collapse of the Compson dynasty in the modern world. Once great, the family has fallen upon evil days, and the novel describes its death throes and final spiritual extinction. The failures of the fathers have been visited upon the children. Jason Compson III drowns his days in alcoholic futility; his wife is a self-pitying hypochondriac who prattles about her past while failing to give her children the love they need. Quentin Compson holds forlornly to an outmoded concept of Compson honor, and when its inadequacy becomes apparent, commits suicide by drowning. Candace Compson seeks to find in promiscuity the affection denied her by her mother. Jason IV survives by abandoning all pretense of Compson honor and becoming a Snopes in everything but name, a vicious, embittered, small-time speculator and defrauder. The degradation of the family is symbolized by Benjy, whose helpless imbecility represents the dead end of a century of family tradition.

[80]

At first glance *Lie Down in Darkness* would seem to involve a greatly similar situation. Milton Loftis is a father who numbs his futility in alcoholism; indeed, his own father had a way of talking that was much like Jason Compson III's manner of addressing Quentin. Like Mrs. Compson, Helen Loftis is self-pitying and selfish, and takes out her frustration on her daughter. Peyton Loftis, like Candace Compson, turns to promiscuity in her need for affection, and like Quentin Compson she walks about a northern city carrying a timepiece before seeking the oblivion of suicide. And the mentally defective Maudie is surely the Loftis counterpart of Benjy Compson. In both families, too, there are faithful Negro retainers who mourn the downfall of their white families.

Yet are the situations really similar? Like the Compsons, the Loftises are the modern descendants of a once-distinguished southern family. But the implications of this in *Lie Down in Darkness* are very different. The Loftises exist entirely *in the present*. Milton Loftis's alcoholic stupor is not importantly the result of changed times. There is no outdated concept of Loftis honor, no heritage of former leadership to be lived down. Milton is not the sot he is because of the impossible burden of the past; his failure is entirely the result of personal weakness. His spinelessness must be blamed on his own character, not on the decadence of a fallen dynasty. Likewise, Helen Loftis is no Mrs. Compson; she is no morose worshiper of her family's past, but a twisted psychotic, whose sin is not hypochondria but insane jealousy. And her daughter Peyton's tragedy is not the result of a massively decadent family past, but of the personal failure of her parents. Though both Peyton Loftis and the young Compsons seek hopelessly for love and strength, the causes of the absence of those commodities are very different; with Peyton they lie in her parents' personal shortcomings, while with Quentin and Candace they are the result of the degradation of a dynasty in their time. They are *dynastic*, not personal. They are caused by *history*.

The difference is all important. For where the downfall of the Compson family symbolizes the crash of formerly great dynasties in time, and the central tragedy consists of the downfall of a once-great family, the death of Peyton Loftis in *Lie Down in Darkness* involves no such sense of the collapse of generations, no important implication that the sins of the dynastic past have caused the debacle of the present. In other words, in Styron's novel the historical dimension is almost entirely absent. Peyton is not the product of a family's and a region's history; she is a young woman whose own parents' failures rob her of the hope of happiness. What she is and is not can be blamed on Milton and Helen, and, in any important respect, no further back than that. Where Faulkner created a Greek-like tragedy, reminiscent of the fall of the House of Atreus, Styron produced a domestic tragedy that had no element of fated dynastic downfall about it.

We can see this clearly if we compare Maudie Loftis and Benjy Compson. The idiot Compson child is the proof of a family's downfall and disgrace, the barren fruit of exhausted loins; Maudie Loftis is only an unfortunately marred child. We do not see in her plight the judgment of fate on a dynastic collapse; she is not symbolic of the guilt of generations. She is a poor, pathetic little girl, bereft of her faculties, and nothing more. Missing entirely is any kind of implied commentary on family ambition and ancestral failures; Maudie's idiocy is the chance result of a biological freak. Not history, but biology, is to blame.

If we think upon the meaning of all this, we will recognize, I think, something essential about *Lie Down in Darkness*. And that is, that it is not a community tragedy but a private one. The relationship of the Loftises to the city in which they reside is vastly different from that of the Compsons to the county of Yoknapatawpha. Upper-class Port Warwick society, as seen in the occasions upon which it gathers in *Lie Down in Darkness*, is pleasure-seeking, decadent, even dissolute. But it is not anachronistic. It is not a holdover from a better day. There is little sense that what has happened to Milton, Helen, and Peyton Loftis is symbolic of the historic decline and fall of the Tidewater Virginia gentry. Port Warwick society is urban, cosmopolitan; it clings to no historical image of itself and its role. We can, if we wish, *infer* the death of the aristocratic tradition from its present condition, but any such inference will be based on our extraliterary historical knowledge, not on the manner in which Styron actually builds his tragedy. There is no concept of a Loftis role within the community, no presumption of leadership that is no longer respected. Milton Loftis had political ambitions at one time, but not because he felt a sense of an expected family role, of habitual function of command. It is entirely a matter of personal ambition with him. And when he fails to act on those ambitions, there is no feeling of his having betrayed a public trust, but only of his personal inability to make something of himself.

In short, the Loftises live in Port Warwick, but they are not and were not Port Warwick, in the way that the Compsons once *were* Yoknapatawpha County. If their decadence mirrors that of the community's upper social stratum, it is not the decadence of a historical tradition gone to seed, but that of a very modern, hedonistic segment of urban rich society living without faith and purpose. In *The Sound and the Fury* the emphasis is on an aristocratic family's abandonment of historical role; in *Lie Down in Darkness* it is on the general immorality of modern society. How the society got that way is, whether explicitly or by implication, not part of the story.

Contrast, for example, the description of Quentin Compson's last day at Harvard with Peyton Loftis's last day in New York City. Both are far from the country of their origins. Both are doomed souls. But how different are the implications! Quentin's estrangement from his home *constitutes* his tragedy. His alienation from Yoknapatawpha County is emblematic of his failure to cope with the modern world; he is the ineffective oldest son and heir of the once mighty Compson dynasty, and his isolation is not only one of place, but of time. What Quentin is estranged from is the role of the Compsons as leaders of the community, a role that is vanished in time. Cut off from his tradition, he wanders aimlessly about Cambridge, meditating on his plight, until finally he weights his clothes with lead window sashes and dives from a bridge into nothingness.

With Peyton Loftis, by contrast, we have no sense that her tragedy consists in her isolation from Port Warwick, no feeling that she belongs not in New York but in the community into which she was born, and that she is walking forlornly about the city because of her family's failure to fill its accustomed historical role back home. John W. Aldridge, as we have seen, noted that "it is significant that it is after she marries and goes North that Peyton becomes overtly psychotic." But is this really significant, in any important dramatic sense? It is not because Peyton is unable to go home to Port Warwick that we are distressed; on the contrary, we were rather relieved when we learned that she had departed, and our distress is at her isolation *in* the metropolis, from the husband she loves and who loves her. Is it a matter of New York's having *caused* the appearance of the psychosis in overt form, or was the psychosis already all but present, and was the move to New York only a futile attempt to postpone its imminent onset? Peyton's flight is her one last chance to retrieve her life; and her destruction is fated because of what her parents have been and have failed to be to her, not because of her estrangement from the society into which she was born.

In both novels the cause of the isolation is ultimately spiritual. Both tragedies symbolize the plight of human beings in the modern world. But where Faulkner saw it in historical terms, involving the blood-guilt of generations, Styron saw it in social terms, an indictment of modern society as symbolized by the selfishness and weakness of the Loftis family. In *The Sound and the Fury* a dynasty collapses; in *Lie Down in Darkness* a family breaks up.

Much has been made of the religious implications of Styron's novel. In my review of the novel, as already mentioned, I contrasted the aimlessness of the Loftises with the sturdy faith of their Negro servants, and remarked, rather clumsily, that "the servant believes, and on the foundations of that belief is able to conduct a satisfying life." To be sure, the religious implications are there, but is it as simple a matter as I proposed, that of a mere "contrast of races," to use Mr. Aldridge's phrase? I think not. For Styron does *not* neatly juxtapose the futility of the Episcopal minister Carey Carr's attempt to lead Helen Loftis to true repentance on the one hand, with the magnetic efficacy of Daddy Faith's healing spiritual balm for the Negroes at the riverside in the final chapter. Instead the contrast is much more complicated, and considerably more ironic. For while it is true that Carey Carr's gentle, benevolent brand of modern theology is so lacking in moral force, so watered down in precept, that it cannot persuade Helen Loftis to overcome her jealousy, is Styron actually proposing in its stead the kind of primitive fundamentalism displayed by Daddy Faith and his constituency? Hardly. For Daddy Faith, effectiveness is clearly attributable entirely to the ignorance, the lack of sophistication, the love of flashy showmanship and weakness for dubious hocus-pocus of his audience; Daddy Faith is a faker, a false prophet. "Who loves you, my people?" he asks. "You,

Daddy! Daddy Faith! You loves us! You, Daddy!" they shout back. "You, Daddy! Yes, Jesus, you loves us!"

But Daddy Faith certainly is not Jesus Christ; he is in no sense divine; indeed, his establishment is a gaudy parody of all known religions. He is effective in his charlatanry because of the gullibility of his audience. The idea, then, that Styron was criticizing the diluted intellectualism of Carey Carr's religion and its inability to provide ethical guidance for Carey's white parishioners by tellingly contrasting it with the primitive soundness of Daddy Faith's fundamentalism, is a misrepresentation of Styron's attitude. If anything, he seems to be making a much bleaker pessimistic observation, which is that the moral usefulness of religious truth decreases in direct proportion to the increase in the intelligence and sophistication of the believer. The implication is that religion can function effectively as a morality *only* when its communicants are ignorant and superstitious.

Here again the difference between *Lie Down in Darkness* and the comparable occurrence in *The Sound and the Fury* is revealing. The scene in Faulkner's novel in which Dilsey momentarily leaves the Compson household in the throes of its disintegration and takes Benjy to the Negro church to hear the preacher from St. Louis is one of the most dramatic in the novel. But contrast the two preachers. Daddy Faith is a flashy, gaudy showman. The preacher in *The Sound and the Fury*, though no mean performer in the pulpit, has nothing of the humbug about him. Though primitive and untutored, his sermon rings with sincerity, and his congregation is deeply moved. The minister's words speak directly to Dilsey, and she is moved to utter her simple but rending summation of all that has happened to the Compsons:

"I've seed de first en de last," Dilsey said. "Never you mind me."
"First en last whut?" Frony said.
"Never you mind," Dilsey said. "I seed de beginnin, en now I sees de endin."

The point is that Faulkner's presentation of the Negroes at church, though written in dialect and presented in a kind of pastoral simplification, is deadly serious. There is no sense of ironic qualification, no element of condescension involved. The variety of religion is simple, but not ignorant. Unlike Styron, it seems to me, Faulkner *is* contrasting, directly and dramatically, the formless chaos of the white folks with the unlettered but deeply felt faith of Dilsey, and this quality of belief in Dilsey enables her to give to the Compsons some of the love and strength that they themselves cannot attain. In her loyalty, her compassion and faith, Dilsey is clearly superior to her white employers. Dilsey believes, and can act on her belief; believing, she endures, while the Compsons, who have no such firm theological conviction, are doomed to perish.

To recapitulate, then, the apparent resemblance of Styron to Faulkner in respect to certain important aspects of experience is only a surface similarity. Upon closer examination Styron turns out to have a significantly different attitude toward many things. Where Faulkner envisions the disintegration of a leading southern family as something dynastic, the result of the spiritual and moral exhaustion of generations of aristocratic southern life, Styron portrays it as being psychological, the result of the personal weaknesses and sins of a father and mother. Faulkner's tragedy is historical; Styron's has no important basis in the past. The failure of the Compsons is the failure of the southern aristocracy; that of the Loftises is the failure of the effete rich. Faulkner's tragedy is deeply rooted in a region and its history; Styron's takes place in a recognizable place, but its dramatic causes lie almost entirely in the present. For Faulkner the fatal consequence of the breakdown of traditional southern leadership is to isolate its heirs from their heritage; in Quentin's and Candace Compson's separation from Yoknapatawpha lies the tragedy. In Styron the isolation is not from an accustomed heritage and role, but from society in general, whether in Port Warwick or New York. Thus, while both writers see isolation from human society as tragic, the older writer's conception of society is of something involving a particular locale and region, with a known history, while the younger writer conceives of society in much more general terms. Quentin as a character could properly exist only in Yoknapatawpha County; Peyton might have done as well, if not better, in the metropolis.

In other words, each writer's attitude toward society is the same—each sees a man's isolation from it as a violation of his human position; but with Styron this is only an attitude, while for Faulkner the attitude is inextricably connected with a particular society and a particular history, and the very nature of the man is inseparable from the man's historical role within his society. And while, as with Faulkner, Styron's attitude likely is the product of a particular kind of society and a particular history, the specific circumstances and the specific occasion that brought about the attitude are largely missing in Styron's work, while in Faulkner the attitude goes hand in hand with the circumstances that produced it.

That this is an important difference is clear: for the difference, it seems to me, is precisely that between the South in which William Faulkner grew up and that in which William Styron grew up. It is the difference between two separate generations of southern writers and of southern life. For the South of the 1900s and 1910s was painfully caught up in the process of breaking away from the old concept of community, the old, fixed patterns of life in a society in which inherited beliefs and accustomed roles played a central part in the conduct of life, in which the individual's identity was supposedly still defined within the community. Faulkner's novels, and in differing ways those of the other writers of his generation, record the breakdown of this older South before the onset of modern urban life. The attitudes toward society, toward history, toward theological and ethical values had been clearly embodied in specific institutions: a particular society with established roles and customs, a specific history, an accepted theology with a revealed ethic. In the growing failure of these specific and concrete institutions to provide order and authority for the human beings who sought to live within and through them, there lay either tragedy or comedy, depending upon the literary imagination concerned with them.

In Styron's South, however, that of the 1920s and 1930s, the process of social dissolution had proceeded much further, and the institutions had ceased importantly to embody the attitudes any more: no longer were there accepted and established roles. The history was no longer a living and concrete reality. And the particular theology could no longer be accepted as gospel truth. To an important degree the attitudes that grew out of these institutions still remained valid, and still do so: a belief that the individual belongs in society, that he is not a creature of the moment, that he needs the authority of religious conviction to guide his conduct. These are in-

[87]

deed present in Styron's novel. They are, however, no more than attitudes; they are not embodied in tangible institutions. And if Styron, as I think, is the leading southern writer of his generation, and if he is in any important sense representative of his generation, then there would seem to be a significant change in the southern literary imagination in the present generation, those writers who were born during or shortly after the First World War, growing up in the changing South during the 1920s and 1930s and writing their novels in the years after the Second World War. They would appear to constitute a generation that is much further removed than its predecessors from the concepts of a particular kind of community, of man as a creature of a particular history, and as a creature whose life is ordered by a particular scheme of theological belief.

For Styron's generation of southern writers, who grew up in a greatly changed South, only the general attitudes, the general ways of looking at human experience, remain real. And what we might expect from these writers, then, is a literature that involves the examination of these attitudes as they survive, or fail to survive, in a very different kind of experience. That, I believe, is what we have in *Lie Down in Darkness*: not a Faulknerian tragedy at all, but a literary exploration of the potentialities of certain surviving attitudes for imparting meaning and order to modern human experience, an experience that by no means is identical with traditional southern life as described and assumed in the work of the earlier writers.

If all this seems far removed from the accustomed concerns of fiction, think of it in specific terms. What, once again, is the difference between Dilsey at church on the one hand, and the contrast between Carey Carr and Daddy Faith on the other? Is the difference not that Faulkner assumes the reality of the theology, and measures the decadent Compsons against it, while Styron does not assume the theological reality, but instead explores its validity, showing both its failure to possess any meaning for the Loftises, and in the case of their servants, the charlatanry that must accompany the religion for it to succeed? Faulkner is not examining the validity of the theology; Styron is doing precisely that, and his implication that theological conviction would be desirable for the Loftises is the product of an attitude toward religion and society, not because of the theological validity of the particular religion itself.

What Faulkner *is* questioning is the validity of the historical tradition of aristocratic Compson leadership in the twentieth-century South. But here, by contrast, Styron conducts no such examination. He cannot even take such a tradition seriously; what little he presents of it is mouthed by Milton Loftis's aged father, long before the events that constitute the central tragedy of the novel. And Milton's memories of his father bear little dramatic relevance to the condition in which Milton finds himself as an adult. The theme of decline and fall, so far as it relates to a particular historical tradition, does not importantly exist in Styron's novel. By implication he may be said to show the results of the failure of such a tradition, but if we reach such a conclusion it is because of what we know about southern literature and southern history, and because of Styron's attitude, but not because Styron gave any dramatic embodiment to the theme of historical decline and fall in his novel, and thus attested to its concrete reality.

And, finally, consider again the inescapability of Quentin's relationship to Yoknapatawpha County in *The Sound and the Fury*, as compared with Peyton's to Port Warwick in *Lie Down in Darkness*. Faulkner, it seems to me, *assumes* that Quentin should have a role in the community of his birth, and in Quentin's inability to discover such a role Faulkner sees a commentary on Quentin and on the times. But Styron does not make that assumption at all. He examines Port Warwick, finds it wanting; whereupon he sends Peyton northward. There is no sense of a killing estrangement, no sense that Peyton's failure to find a meaning for her life in the metropolis is due to the fact that she does not belong there, but in Port Warwick. Either kind of community would do for her, New York perhaps better than Port Warwick—and neither kind will do. The trouble is in Peyton, and in her parents' failure, and in crass modern times in general. We do not feel that because Peyton cannot live in Port Warwick there has been a historical betrayal of what the community should have been and what Peyton should have been. What we do feel is that Peyton belongs somewhere, a part of some society. And once again, this is because of the author's attitude toward the individual in society, not because of any inference that there ought to be a community such as Port Warwick presumably used to be and that Peyton ought to have been able to find a role and a meaning for her life within that particular kind of community. Styron's imagination is not wedded to that kind of community, and that kind of person. He does not see the disappearance of either as fated, and therefore tragic.

So far as southern writing in our time is concerned, then, the question that William Styron's fiction occasions is the whole problem of continuity. If there has been developed over the course of several decades a kind of southern literary mode, a tradition as it were, then, on the evidence of Styron's books, how is it surviving today? Just what is the relationship between southern literature as we have hitherto know it, and a southern writer of a new generation who does not assume the inevitability of a relationship between his characters and the kind of historical community that we think of as southern, who cannot take seriously the importance of the continuation of a tradition of leadership in the modern South, and who does not measure his characters' ethical and spiritual conviction by their obedience to the authority of a particular kind of Protestant theology?

We should have to conclude, I think, that such a writer's relationship to that tradition is significantly different from that of any of the older writers within that mode. We should have to conclude that he is joined to them, insofar as those things are important, principally by his attitude—an assumption on his part that a community role is desirable, that a traditional basis for experience is a good thing, that men without theological conviction live fragmented, chaotic lives— but an assumption not embodied in concrete institutions and shared experiences.

And, if, then, it is only a matter of the survival of an attitude, not of the embodiment of the attitude in particular institutions, is not the next order of business the examination of the *assumptions themselves?* Not the institutions, but the assumptions. And insofar as a specific southern literary tradition is concerned, where does that leave us?

It leaves us, I think, with William Styron's second novel, *Set This House on Fire.* For almost a decade preceding its publication, and on the strength of one good, medium-length novel, Styron was widely held to be America's Most Promising Younger Novelist. I have conjectured as to why this came about—the particular state of the American novel at the time of the appearance of *Lie Down in Darkness*; the emergence of a novelist who could *write*, and not merely relate; the inherited prestige of a particular literary mode into which it seemed to fit so well, a mode that had been notably proficient in producing distinguished fiction, so that the reading public had been educated to respond to the dimensions of that mode. And I suggested that because *Lie Down in Darkness* seemed to fit into that mode, and yet to possess an originality of its own, reviewers and readers were quick to recognize Styron as potentially a very important writer.

In short, it was as if the appearance of *Lie Down in Darkness* constituted an assurance that the kind of contribution Faulkner, Wolfe, Warren, Welty, and the others had been making to American fiction for two decades and more was not going to dwindle and die, but could flourish for another entire literary generation.

Nine years elapsed, during which time a new novel by Styron was often rumored and once even announced, but without its appearing. Then, in the late spring of 1960, finally came *Set This House on Fire*. Unlike its predecessor, there was nothing tidy and portable about it; it was a big, hulking affair, two hundred thousand words long, the size of *Look Homeward, Angel* almost. It did not take place in Port Warwick, though the narrator came from there. In fact, though it was remembered and related by two men while fishing and reminiscing in Charleston, South Carolina, it did not importantly take place in the South at all, but in New York, Paris, and a small Italian coastal town. None of the customary trappings of the southern novel was present: there were no Negroes, no First Families, no church services, no blood-guilt of generations, no over-sexed southern matrons. It was thoroughly, completely modern, even cosmopolitan. There were expatriate artists, Italian peasants, Greenwich Village cocktail parties, pornographic orgies, American tourists in European cities and towns, movie making, Army PX's, philosophical Fascist policemen, and so forth. People quoted Ortega y Gasset and Wilhelm Reich, listened to Buxtehude and *Don Giovanni*, preferred Frankie Lane to Johnny Ray, worried about the decline of American capitalism. And—quite unlike most southern novels—the protagonists engaged in long, probing psychological analyses of their inner souls, after the manner of Proust and

Dostoevski. The story told was not at all Faulknerian; it was about a young artist who after a frightening stay in the lower depths won his way back to sanity. It was as if Eugene Gant had gone through the kind of furnace experience that Jack Burden underwent in *All the King's Men*, perhaps—but in Europe, not in Louisiana, and politics and the South were not involved. But to say that is to say very little, for Jack Burden never really ceased to take seriously all manner of verities that Styron's Cass Kinsolving not only flouted but even ignored. Styron's new novel was simply not a "southern" novel at all, in the way that southern novels had been written by his predecessors.

The new novel, as I have noted, was straightaway treated to a hostile critical barrage such as few other important works of fiction in our time have received. It was called romantic, melodramatic, pompous, sentimental, inflated, chaotic; it was self-pitying; it was even un-American. To repeat, the Most Promising Younger Novelist of his generation had fallen flat on his face.

The question I asked before was why, if *Set This House on Fire* was as I think a quite respectable novel, it came in for so hostile a reception. And the answer I proposed had to do with the nature of Styron's first novel, *Lie Down in Darkness*. That book had earned its author an impressive reputation, partly on the strength of the kind of novel it had seemed to be. To repeat, it seemed to be "southern," Faulknerian; it seemed an extension, into our own day, of the southern tragic mode, to fit into the mode even while giving it an original twist. But in reality Styron's first novel was significantly different; the specific experience that it related was not handled in the traditional way; only the attitudes remained close to the tradition, without their accompanying embodiment in concrete experience.

Set This House on Fire confirmed that break. And this time, there could be no mistaking the difference. By all rights, Styron should have produced in his second book another "typical" southern tragedy. But he did not. He did not write the kind of book he was supposed to write at all. The novel that he brought forth after nine years of silence was far removed from the familiar mode of southern fiction. And this, I think, caused a tremendous disappointment.

The nature of that disappointment was all too obvious: this

young, talented novelist, so heralded, so praised, had failed to do what was expected of him. He had not continued the literary mode of Faulkner, Wolfe, and the others into the new generation. Seemingly he had veered off in another direction. And the new direction did not permit the familiar kind of tidy, smoothly formed tragedy that *Lie Down in Darkness* had seemed to be. By its very nature it demanded the groping, restless, searching type of novel that Styron produced.

What I am suggesting is that, just as readers and reviewers read *Lie Down in Darkness* as if it were automatically a novel in the Faulknerian mode, and praised it highly for that, they read *Set This House on Fire* with precisely the same expectation, and since this time the novel did not remotely fit the mode at all, they denounced it. Styron, the apparent heir to the best of the southern literary tradition, had seemingly betrayed that tradition.

Yet had he? I am not so sure of it. It seems to me, rather, that Styron's second novel *was* an extension of the southern literary imagination into a new generation, was in fact perhaps *the only possible way that the mode could be made to stay alive*. And I believe that, when we look back in retrospect at the first novel, we can see that *Set This House on Fire* was exactly the kind of novel we might have expected Styron to write, if what we took to be his major stature was true; it grows squarely out of the implications of the first novel, and represents a coming-to-grips with the true concerns of the author's experience—an experience, I believe, that is still very much southern, but in significant respects not that of the previous generation of southern writers. To illustrate what I mean, I must first review the plot of *Set This House on Fire*.

There are three main characters in the novel: Mason Flagg, a would-be playwright, Cass Kinsolving, a painter, and Peter Leverett, a lawyer. Flagg is a wealthy, clever, bedeviled young man, who is always "going to write" a play but never does. Handsome, conversant in the arts, a brilliant talker, he spends his days and nights in quest of some ultimate sensation, usually sexual. Sex, he keeps insisting, is the only frontier left to modern man. Essentially Flagg is a fraud, a poseur, in some ways reminiscent of the character Starwick in Thomas Wolfe's *Of Time and the River*.

Cass Kinsolving is a painter who cannot paint. A southern boy, he is wedded to a sweet and not very intelligent woman named Poppy, and they have several children. A considerable portion of his time is spent in getting and remaining drunk.

Peter Leverett, through whom much of the story is related, is a boyhood friend of Mason Flagg's, who goes to visit Flagg in the Italian coastal town of Sambuco, where the major events of the novel take place. Peter is from Port Warwick, Virginia, the scene of *Lie Down in Darkness*. The new novel begins when Peter travels to Charleston, South Carolina, where a now-regenerate Cass Kinsolving is living and painting, and together they piece out the details of what happened in Sambuco, where a young peasant girl had been raped and Mason Flagg killed.

We see Mason Flagg, in other words, through the eyes of two persons—Peter Leverett, who knew him as a youth and as a young man, and Cass Kinsolving, who knew him in Sambuco just before his death. It is here that the chief structural flaw of the novel lies. For if this novel were primarily a study of Mason Flagg, what made him into the harried and driven creature he was, what drove him to his death, then the structural scheme that Styron chose to give his story might have sufficed.

But important though the character of Mason Flagg is in this novel, it is not in him that the chief meaning of the story is to be found. Rather, the central figure is the painter Cass Kinsolving.

For most of the novel, Cass is a man in bondage. In Paris, before he goes to Sambuco, he lives in an alcoholic daze, tortured by his inability to paint, spending his time drinking, wandering about, pitying himself, doing everything but confronting his talent. At length he moves his family down to Italy, where he comes under the sway of Mason Flagg. At one point Flagg even forces him, in exchange for his largesse, to paint a pornographic picture for his collection. Cass also becomes enamored of an Italian peasant girl and steals medicines in a hopeless attempt to save the life of her father, an old man in the last stages of tuberculosis.

Peter Leverett, about to leave Rome for the United States, drives over to Sambuco to visit Mason Flagg, arriving in time to witness the cataclysmic events that end the novel. The peasant girl is raped by Mason Flagg, then brutally murdered. Flagg is found dead at the foot of a cliff. The solution to these crimes is discovered by a philosophical young Italian policeman, who allows the culprits to go unpunished by the law.

The meaning of these events exists, as I have said, not in Mason Flagg's life but in Cass Kinsolving's. When Peter Leverett and Cass meet several years later to analyze what happened at Sambuco, Cass is well again, doing the painting he could not do in Europe, earning a living, caring for his wife and family. And though this novel is a murder mystery, the principal question it proposes is why Cass was for so long in bondage, unable to paint the pictures he wanted to paint and unable to receive and return the love of his wife and children.

In the events that come to a climax at Sambuco, I think, we do find out why. Cass was unwilling to accept the responsibility of his own talent, unwilling to face up to the fact that it alone could accomplish its own perfection. He wanted to find a form for his art outside of himself, when he alone it was who could give his art, and therefore his life, reason for being. He could not put up with his creative limitations and work his way out of them. He looked outside of himself, to the society, the people, the institutions surrounding him, for what could be found only within himself.

This was the hold that Mason Flagg had on him. For Mason could provide wealth, afford the glamor and excitement of "life," "experience"—or so Cass tried to pretend. Throughout the novel Cass attempted to deny the personal responsibility of his talent, attempted to substitute external experience for the dedication to artistic creativity that for him could be the only true account. He sought escape into "life," in alcohol, in false visions of Wordsworthian "ecstasy" that gave him the illusion of beauty, in Mason Flagg's largesse and phony dilettantism, in an insubstantial, idyllic romance with the peasant girl, in a quixotic and forlorn attempt to doctor an old man back to health. All these activities were ways of avoiding his own true mission and refuge—the remorseless requirements of discovering how to paint the pictures he wanted to paint. And because he was an artist, all these false externalizations of his need failed.

The attainment of this realization, through grief and pain, constitutes the development of the novel, and though it requires five hundred pages and two hundred thousand words, as a story it is dramatically and artistically convincing. When at last we put down this novel, we have witnessed the resolution of a rending conflict within a man.

Why, however, is Cass so constituted that it takes him so long to find out what at last he learns? We accept the reality of his bondage to "life"—but how, we may ask, did it come to be? The answer is there, but—and this, I think, is the major structural defect of *Set This House on Fire*—it does not lie in the experience of Cass Kinsolving. Instead, it is found in the characterization of Peter Leverett.

For it was Peter, not Cass, who grew up with Mason Flagg, who through him was exposed to the delusion of self-fulfillment through external "experience," instead of through personal creativity, who was progressively tempted by Mason Flagg's advocacy of false gods. The spiritual duel between Mason Flagg and Cass Kinsolving that constitutes the dramatic struggle of *Set This House on Fire* was begun long before Cass went to Sambuco and encountered Mason Flagg. It commenced in Virginia, when Mason and Peter were students in preparatory school together. As Peter wrote of his attitude toward Mason then, "his wealth, his glamorous connections, his premature ease with the things of the flesh—they worked on me a profound fascination." It is this attitude that is transferred, as it were, by the author to Cass Kinsolving, a Cass who has been miserably wasting his time in Paris trying to be an artist without painting, and who wanders down to Sambuco when even the opportunities for self-delusion possible to him in a city such as Paris begin to fail.

Mason's last, despairing attempt to "own" Cass Kinsolving by raping Cass's girl friend was the culmination of a long battle. Why did Mason try to dominate first Peter Leverett and then Cass Kinsolving? Because he knew that they alone, of all those who comprised his acquaintanceship, could judge him as an artist. Tempted though they both were, they alone did not confuse what Mason did with the true artistic responsibility. At one point, early in the novel, one of Mason's admirers praised him to Cass in these words: "That

Mason. Now there's a boy for you. A genius. Figure everything he's got. The eyes. The nose. The *expression*. Everything. It's uncanny, I tell you. Just like his dad." "You've read his play?" Peter asks him. No, the man replies, "but he's told me about it. It can't miss, I tell you. It's a natural. The boy has genius." But genius is a matter of plays written, not plays talked about, and Peter and Cass know it. Mason could bribe others, but he could not bribe them. They would not be owned.

But what is Cass Kinsolving's relationship to Peter Leverett? In the novel ostensibly both are friends of Mason Flagg, and that is all. Dramatically, psychologically, however, they are more than that. *They are one and the same person.* We meet Cass Kinsolving in mid-passage, a painter who cannot paint, a created, believable character. It is Peter Leverett's past history, not Cass's, that explains why Cass cannot paint. Peter Leverett, in other words, *becomes Cass Kinsolving.*

Now from a strictly logical point of view, that ought certainly to compromise Styron's novel. How can the experience of one character serve to create the characterization of another and entirely different man? But I want to emphasize that nevertheless we *do* believe in Cass Kinsolving. As a character he is convincing, and the events that give the novel its conflict and its resolution happen to him, not to Peter Leverett. So perceptive and imaginative is the characterization of Cass that the explanation of how he got that way, though interesting, is not finally of primary importance. Though logically we know that the early experience happened not to Cass but to Peter Leverett, dramatically and psychologically the development of the characterization is so secure that as readers we do what in terms of plot logic we should not be able to do: we give Peter Leverett's experience to Cass. We accept him, when he turns up in Paris, for what he is on the basis of what we know about Peter Leverett.

Building upon it, Styron succeeds in making Cass emerge as a formidable characterization, a figure that almost anyone who has ever attempted to paint or write or otherwise create artistic work can recognize. Cass Kinsolving is a familiar and crucial figure of our time, the artist seeking reality, confusing it with "life," struggling to locate it in his work. And coming as Cass Kinsolving does to us, the heir, so to speak, to a generation of fictional protagonists by southern novelists, it seems to me that his plight thoroughly mirrors the situation that confronts the southern writer of Styron's generation—a generation for whom the traditional institutions and embodiments of values have been so seriously modified that a new relationship between attitudes and values on the one hand, and "real life" on the other, must be created. To do that, the values and attitudes themselves must be examined. And what Styron makes his fictional artist learn is what Allen Tate once said about the poet Hart Crane. Crane, he declared, "is betrayed, not by a defect in his own nature, but by the external world; he asks of nature, perfection—requiring only of himself, intensity." The poet, says Tate, did not face up to the obligation "to define the limits of his personality and to objectify its moral implications in an appropriate symbolism." The Cass Kinsolving whom Peter Leverett visits in Charleston several years after the events of Sambuco has accepted that obligation, though he never speaks of such things at all. Wrongly constructed or not, the characterization is there.

Why, one asks, did Styron separate his characterization in this way? My own notion is that Styron himself did not fully recognize the essential connection between Peter Leverett's experience and Cass Kinsolving's. The actual origins he gives for Cass are not important to the novel. Cass was a boy from a small coastal town in North Carolina, the son of an Episcopal minister, who was left an orphan at the age of ten and brought up by a Methodist uncle and aunt. During the Second World War he landed in an army psychiatric ward, took up painting as therapy, was later married, and went to Europe to live and paint. It is interesting, though, that when Cass wins his way to sanity and takes his family back home to America to live, he goes not to North Carolina, but to Charleston, South Carolina, a seaport city—precisely what Port Warwick, Peter Leverett's home, was.

As for Peter Leverett, he too goes home in the novel, but early in the story, before he visits Cass in Charleston and they recall the events of Sambuco. When Peter stops by at Port Warwick there is a moving scene in which his father takes him driving about the city, and he is greatly struck by the changes that have taken place. Port Warwick now

had grown vaster and more streamlined and clownish-looking than I thought a decent southern town could ever become. To be sure, it had always been a ship-building city and a seaport (visualize Tampa, Pensacola, or the rusty waterfront of Galveston; if you've never seen these, Perth Amboy will do), and in official propaganda it had never been listed as one of the ornaments of the commonwealth, but as a boy I had known its gentle seaside charm, and had smelled the ocean wind, and had lolled underneath giant magnolias and had watched streaked and dingy freighters putting out to sea and, in short, had shaken loose for myself the town's own peculiar romance. Now the magnolias had been hacked down to make room for a highway along the shore; there were noisy shopping plazas everywhere, blue with exhaust and rimmed with supermarkets; television roosted upon acre after acre of split-level rooftops and, almost worst of all, the ferryboats to Norfolk, those low-slung smoke-belching tubs which had always possessed their own incomparable dumpy glamour, were gone, replaced by a Yankee-built vehicular tunnel which poked its foul white snout two miles beneath the mud of Hampton Roads.

Port Warwick, that is, is the *New South*—the South of modern times, in which the comfortable, sleepy old landscape is hardly recognizable. Peter and his father stop at a service station, and while there, Peter suddenly divines that almost on the very spot of reclaimed land where the gasoline pump now stands, there had once been a marsh creek where he had almost drowned and had been rescued by a Negro crab fisherman. Awed at the thought of the change that had taken place, in himself above all, he thinks that

perhaps one of the reasons that we Americans are so exceptionally nervous and driven is that our past is effaced almost before it is made present; in our search for old avatars to contemplate we find only ghosts, whispers, shadows; almost nothing remains for us to feel or see, or to absorb our longing. That evening I was touched to the heart; by my father's old sweetness and decency and rage, but also by whatever it was within me— within life itself, it seemed so intense—that I knew to be irretrievably lost. Estranged from myself and from my time, dwelling neither in the destroyed past nor in the fantastic and incomprehensible present, I knew that I must find the answer to at least several things before taking hold of myself and getting on with the job.

[99]

But what does Peter find out, in the ensuing story? He finds out what happened to Cass, not to himself. So if, as I have suggested, the young Peter Leverett is the young Cass Kinsolving, then several things are obvious. Peter's (and therefore Cass's) past is, figuratively and literally, buried in time. The creek where he almost died is covered by acres of fill dirt, upon which the properties of the new industrial South have been constructed. He cannot, as he says, dwell in the "destroyed past." When Cass Kinsolving, in effect the adult Peter Leverett, goes home, it is to a city which in many ways is like Port Warwick, but which is not Port Warwick. Charleston resembles Port Warwick in that both are seaports, both are on tidewater, both are surrounded by salt marsh; but except for the fact that both are seaports, their particular histories are quite different. There is thus, so far as Cass is concerned, no continuity of community, of history, of family role. But in Charleston, to a much greater extent than in Port Warwick (which is Newport News, Virginia), the evidence of the past does survive into the present. It is very much more a historical town, much more leisurely and quaint, in its waterfront areas at least, than Port Warwick. In other words, the general climate of everyday life in the older, less-industrialized South remains for Cass, but *without any personal, institutional ties to it on his part.* He lives there, but he is not of it.

Before Cass comes to Charleston, he is adrift, homeless, cut off from his past. He wants to paint; he cannot. He is married, with children; he wants to love them and care for them, but he cannot. He cannot discern any order and meaning to his experience. What he finally learns, in the frenzied chaos that produces the catastrophe at Sambuco, is that only through respect for his own personal integrity, as a human being and as an artist, can he give his life the order he seeks. He cannot look for his order and purpose in "life," in the institutions of the exterior world, in his environment, but only within himself. He must face his responsibilities, paint his own pictures. Then, and not until then, can he go home, to America, to the South.

What Cass had to know, before he could go home, was what Peter Leverett knew, about his childhood, about the place where he grew up—that it was, in Peter's words, "irretrievably lost." But also, as Cass finds out, that for a man to live and create, it must be replaced by order and purpose within oneself. For a world without order and purpose, without the values of love, self-respect, compassion, and responsibility for one's fellow human beings, is a world of chaos and fragmentation, ending in the blind destructiveness of Cass at Sambuco. The results of what Peter Leverett has known produce the condition in which Cass finds himself in Paris and Sambuco. From this condition Cass manages finally to extricate himself.

In effect, Cass Kinsolving completes the symbolic journey begun by Peyton Loftis in *Lie Down in Darkness*. In the first novel Styron's protagonist left Port Warwick. In the second novel Cass Kinsolving comes home to Charleston. Earlier I sought to demonstrate how Peyton's background, society, and tradition had failed, not in terms of directly producing her own dramatic plight, but through their absence, their failure to be importantly present at all. Peyton dies in New York, estranged not only from Port Warwick but from human society as well. Now Cass Kinsolving comes back to the South, but not until he can furnish within himself the order, stability, and continuity he needs to exist, to live with other human beings.

What I am getting at is that *Set This House on Fire* is, among other things, an examination of the validity of certain precepts by which people live: an examination conducted on *southern* terms. Cass Kinsolving's particular past is dead, forgotten, inoperative—but Cass as Styron describes him is nevertheless a man who requires the stability of belonging to a place that is anchored in time and that possesses order and stability. As Cass tells Peter Leverett in Charleston,

"Funny thing, you know, in Europe there sometimes, when everything got as low as it can get for me, and I was hating America so much that I couldn't even contain my hatred—why even then I'd get to thinking about Charleston. About how I'd like to go back there and live. It almost never was in North Carolina, or the pinewoods up there in Columbus County where I was brought up. I didn't want to go back there and I sure as hell didn't want to go back to New York. It was Charleston I remembered, straight out of these memories I had when I was a boy. And here I am." He pointed across the wide harbor, radiant and gray-green and still as glass, then in an arc around the lower edge of the town where the old homes, deep in shade, in hollyhock and trumpet vine and bumblebees, had been defiled by no modish alteration, no capricious change. "You'll search a long way for that kind of purity," he said. "Look at that brickwork. Why, one of those houses is worth every cantilevered, picture-windowed doghouse in the state of New Jersey."

What Styron has done has been to describe the terms on which a man such as Cass Kinsolving can find such order and tranquillity for his life. It is emphatically made clear that Cass is unable to do without these commodities, but equally there is no intimation that he can find them in the life and institutions lying outside of himself. He must do it on his own. Cass can finally live in Charleston, when Peyton was unable to live in Port Warwick or New York and he himself in Paris and Sambuco, because he is creating—which is to say he is drawing his spiritual sustenance from within himself. Until he can do this, the environment makes no difference and the past is of no help. Cass himself is an orphan; Peter Leverett's Port Warwick is buried beneath the fill dirt; the traditional southern circumstance, with its historical notion of role, its institutions, its community order, means nothing anymore.

We remember Faulkner's Quentin Compson in Cambridge; for him too the southern past no longer enabled him to define himself as a man. The difference is that Quentin's failure to discover his role was inextricably connected with his failure to embody the values of a Yoknapatawpha County that no longer existed; while, contrariwise, Cass's eventual success in finding his place comes *before* he joins the community. Quentin left the stability behind him, geographically and in time; Cass brings to the community his own stability. Cass is in effect a new man, prepared to sink down roots in the community—but a different kind of a community for him, one in which there are no historical and social links with his past. Quentin's hope for stability and sanity rested in institutions, traditions, concepts of role, theological authority that no longer existed. Cass Kinsolving knows nothing about such things; he creates his own salvation.

The stability and order he finds cannot be dissociated from religious values—the ability to love, to care for one's loved ones, to act justly and responsibly, to be kind and generous. And these things Cass has learned to do, through realizing his own private integrity as a human being. "A man cannot live without a focus," Cass remarks at one point. "Without some kind of faith, if you want to call it that. I didn't have any more faith than a tomcat. Nothing. Nothing! . . . I was blind from booze two thirds of the time. Stone-blind in this condition I created for myself, in this sweaty hot and hopeless attempt to get out of life, be shut of it, find some kind of woolly and comforting darkness I could lie in without thought for myself or my children or anyone else." But let it be noted that if Cass has acquired such faith, it is personal, and apart from any revealed theology. We recall that his father was an Episcopal minister, and that he was brought up by Methodists. At one point, too, Cass describes his first sexual experience, with a female member of the Jehovah's Witnesses sect, who comically remarks to him that "that's one thing you'll find out about us Witnesses. We're right liberal as concerns social contacts." If we wish finally to describe Cass's attitude as being essentially religious, there is certainly no hint that its basis lies in any of the theological systems of his childhood. In describing Cass at Sambuco, Styron examined what Cass needed to do in order to achieve order, integrity, and tranquillity and showed Cass living in hell on earth when he tried to do without spiritual conviction and moral responsibility. The redemption was from within.

I have spoken of Styron's fiction as embodying the traditional southern attitudes toward man's place in society, his need for order and stability, his desire for the love and responsibility that come from the authority of religious conviction, but without the institutions, the experience of life that embody those attitudes. I have said that *Lie Down in Darkness* possessed those attitudes, but without their fictional grounding in the traditional southern institutions. In *Set This House on Fire* Styron may be said to have proceeded with an examination, inherent in the fictional process, of the terms by which such attitudes can survive and flourish in modern life—how Cass Kinsolving, a southerner of our time and place, can live and cherish and create. It is as if, where the hell of *Lie Down in Darkness* lamented their absence, the purgatory of *Set This House on Fire* described their reacquisition. But the conditions whereby they

[103]

could be regained necessarily involved a complete alienation from the time and place in which they had once existed, and from which they had disappeared. Cass Kinsolving's entire separation from the South was, in effect, a severance from all lingering institutions and traditions that once might have, however inadequately, embodied those attitudes. He was indeed a man without a country. So that for Styron, *Set This House on Fire* represented a clearing away of the debris, as it were, of the southern fictional texture—all the accustomed embodiments of setting, history, community that for so long have provided the experience from which southern literature has been created, now swept away, like Peter Leverett's memories of the past, in the fill dirt upon which a new and modern experience was erected. Not in Port Warwick, but in Paris and Sambuco, was Cass Kinsolving's full initiation in the cauldron of modern experience conducted. All his surviving attitudes, his ideals, his emotions were there examined and tested and finally made to depend for their reality on his own inward and personal acceptance of them.

Whereupon he returned home. What, though, of Cass's alter ego, Peter Leverett? It may be noted that Peter Leverett no longer lives in the South. At the end of the novel, Cass writes to him that he "wanted to tell you how glad I am that N.Y. goes O.K. for you now." And there is no reason to suppose that Peter Leverett will be any more or any less happy living in New York than Cass seems to be in the South. To each one, "home" means something different. It is involved more importantly with what is going on inside them than with the place in which they have settled down to live and to work. For both these fictional characters live in a faraway country now, and that country, bound though it is to the "real world" by the pinions of time and memory, is finally a country of the mind.

Even so, it still bears a notable resemblance to a particular American region. Thus Cass Kinsolving, seated with Peter Leverett in a boat, fishing:

He rebaited his hook and cast out the line again, squinting against the light. The river shores were immensities of shade—water oak and cypress and cedar; the heat and the stillness were like a narcotic. "September's a good month for this kind of fishing," he said after a long spell of silence.

"Look over there, over those trees there. Look at that sky. Did you ever see anything so *clean* and beautiful?"

For Cass, who has come back, there is still the marshland, the water, the fishing, the sun. Changed and altered almost beyond recognition in many respects, it is even so the South.

JANE FLANDERS

William Styron's Southern Myth

Although William Styron's fiction develops themes basic to all twentieth-century writing, a broad pattern of meaning in Styron's work is defined by his use of southern characters, settings, and themes, and by his relation to the southern literary tradition. Just as Faulkner found in his "little postage-stamp of native soil" universal meaning, Styron uses southern materials to construct his great drama of rebellion, despair, and the search for order. It is a developing vision. As one novel follows another, after Peyton's suicide in *Lie Down in Darkness*, Styron's protagonists seem to confront their adversaries and themselves with increasing dignity and power. Each work presents with growing effectiveness the traditional southern themes: the curse of racism, the influence of the past, the power of the social environment over individual will. In each novel there is greater understanding of the intimate relation between the black and white experience in southern history. A closer look at these themes as they are advanced in Styron's three long works of fiction—*Lie Down in Darkness* (1951), *Set This House on Fire* (1960), and *The Confessions of Nat Turner* (1967)—suggests that over the years Styron has been moving toward a coherent view of southern history, a kind of "myth."[1]

To designate an author as "southern" is not merely to make a geographical reference; the term has come to refer to a whole complex of themes and attitudes identified with the southern milieu, particularly traditional attitudes of southern people about themselves and their destiny. Southern writing often looks to the past, is deeply concerned with race relations and class differences, the force of superstition and religious belief over the rational mind. It is often described as grotesque (and "southern Gothic" is a favorite critical epithet) because southern literature is obsessed by disorder, psychological disturbance, defeat, and unnaturalness, so much so that it almost seems to convey a radical pessimism. It presents, says John L. Stewart, "an image of man . . . stoutly anti-progressive, anti-rationalist, and anti-humanist, for it insists on the irreducible mystery in life, the all-pervasiveness of evil in human affairs, and the limitations of a man's capacity to understand and control his own nature."[2] Louis D. Rubin describes the southern literary attitude as a way of looking at human experience with "the assumption that to maintain order and stability the individual must be part of a social community, yet that the ultimate authority that underlies his conduct is not social but moral. It is, in short, a religious attitude."[3] A religious attitude, insistently aware of irrationality and evil, yet clinging to an ideal of moral harmony: in these two descriptions of the southern literary quality are reflected the two moods in Styron's own thinking.

Although a somber and negative view of humanity is evident in Styron's fiction, it would be inaccurate to call him a pessimist. Throughout his career Styron has grappled with conflicting beliefs—debating between the possibility of moral order and human dignity, and the folly of believing in such a possibility. The search for order in his works is undercut by recurring threats of disintegration, annihilation, and absurdity. This is Styron's fundamental debate, and its terms extend beyond "southern" limits. Nevertheless, Styron's choice of southern characters and themes, his lifelong interest in antebellum history (especially that of Virginia), his open imitation of Faulkner and Wolfe, and his rhetorical gifts enable him to work in a tradition congenial to his imagination. It is a tradition rich in implications about the nature of human experience, but Styron uses it in his own way, and over the years has struggled to his own conclusions.

Styron has not always been read as a southern writer, nor has he been eager to claim membership in the "southern school." The young Styron was especially nettled by questions about his debt to other southern authors (notably Faulkner), by the widespread criticism of his first novel as too closely imitative of *The Sound and the Fury*, and by the critical clichés about southern literature which were immediately applied to his work.[4] He protested that *Lie Down in Darkness* was not merely a regional novel, that its characters "would have behaved the way they did anywhere," that "the old idea of wreckage and defeat" was more than a southern phenomenon, and remarked in 1954 that he did not care if he never wrote about the South again.[5] At the same time he admitted that Faulkner had made a powerful impression on him, that he had rewritten large sections of *Lie Down in Darkness* to reduce Faulkner's influence.[6] More recently Styron has pointed to the influence of Thomas Wolfe, whose example inspired him at eighteen to become a writer.[7] In the last few years Styron has spoken less defensively of his debt to the southern tradition, having established in *The Confessions of Nat Turner* that he can work with native materials with some independence.

A survey of Styron's protagonists will suggest the outlines of what may be called his "southern myth." The first protagonist is female, beautiful and doomed, a representative of the corrupt white "aristocracy" whose abdication of moral leadership has been responsible for so much evil in southern history. For Peyton Loftis, there is no salvation, not even understanding; she dies insane. In his second novel Styron chooses a lower-class white southerner to dramatize man's power to rise above guilt and to discover significant values. Styron's third major protagonist is a black slave, a tragic and violent figure whose disastrous rebellion altered the course of history; yet Nat Turner surpasses his predecessors in the breadth of his final vision and his spiritual victory.

Thus the myth suggests a hierarchy of moral value among the levels of southern society in reverse proportion to their worldly standing. First, the effete white ruling class is most to be pitied and condemned; second, the country poor-whites, though tainted by race-prejudice and misguided religiosity, still possess the seeds of vitality and a kind of innocence; third, the blacks—especially the slaves—oppressed, denied all hope or self-respect, are paradoxically most capable of emerging from despair to find a basis for faith. All of Styron's protagonists confront despair. Peyton Loftis commits suicide. Cass Kinsolving is plagued by self-hate and despair until his almost miraculous deliverance, conquering himself as he defeats his enemy. Nat Turner, who experiences a trial by ordeal more desperate than anything experienced by his predecessors, convinced for a time that even God has abandoned him, achieves the fullest liberation and triumph. In this concept of a moral hierarchy we recognize elements of Faulkner's myth, particularly his view of black people as purified by suffering, saved by lowliness from the sin of pride, and thereby capable of a higher moral vision than white people can ever achieve. This view of racial differences, with its Christian overtones, is also related to the larger concept of the South as laboring under a curse since the days of slavery (evident in the blighted land and the grotesque creatures inhabiting it) and longing for release. White people are enfeebled by guilt, whereas the blacks, having learned to endure, will lead the way to wisdom and, possibly, deliverance. Variations on these themes are found throughout southern writing, and although Styron has forged his ideas from his own experience, his work reflects this now almost traditional view of southern history.

Styron's southern myth begins in despair. The primary victim of *Lie Down in Darkness*—Peyton is not really a "heroine"—represents the wealthy WASP elite whom Styron knew so well; the young Styron had apparently found the most damaged and hopeless people he had known to be of his own social group. By focusing on a female, moreover, Styron exploits the special absurdities of a young girl's preparations for southern womanhood. Peyton is confused by hypocritical values concerning sexual morality, religion, and family, the importance of money and social privilege—false values to which her parents have sacrificed everything meaningful in their lives, including their children. Less obvious, but latent, is the effect of white racism, which touches Peyton with unconscious guilt and which is obliquely responsible for her own ostracism because of her marriage to a Jew. The anti-Semitism unmasked by her marriage, crystallized in her mother's behavior, manifests the community's rejection of outsiders and any of its members who transcend its exclusive barriers. Such a society finally attacks its own. Peyton's extreme need for affection, which eventually destroys her marriage and her sanity, reflects her emotional starvation in an inverted, hate-filled home and community. Suicide can be her only response to an uninhabitable world.

Lie Down in Darkness exemplifies the southern Gothic mode in its emphasis on psychological disorder and its atmosphere of indefinable fear. The destruction of time achieved by its jumbled chronology creates a sense of entrapment, of experience as inescapably determined, a living hell. The Gothic mood is further enhanced by the unnatural family relationships described in Oedipal terms: Milton Loftis's incestuous attachment to his daughter Peyton and Helen's rejection of both of them as she turns to her other child, feebleminded Maudie. Unable to survive in such an atmosphere, Maudie dies young. Peyton attempts to escape, but she is dead on the first page; the entire action of the novel is organized by the slow progress of her coffin to the cemetery. Her defeat, and that of all the characters, was determined from the earliest time described in the story.

The Oedipal theme is a paradigm of the larger theme of the death-grip of the past which occupies so many southern writers. Despite its claustrophobic focus on a single family, *Lie Down in Darkness* says much about the racist, snobbish white society surrounding it, dominated by the hollow values inherited from the "aristocratic" past. The virulent inner disorders of the characters are directly linked to the community's enslavement to these values. The sense of stagnation and the breakdown of cause and effect conveyed through the complexity of the narrative imply the futility of any hope for change.

One of the most urgent of all southern themes—racial antagonism—seems curiously absent from the novel; but in this absence there is significance. *Lie Down in Darkness* is a "white folks'" novel in which blacks receive little attention. It would have been difficult in 1951 to predict how Styron would develop in his concern with matters which later become central to his work: the experience of southern blacks, white guilt and fear of retribution inherited from the slave-owning past and exacerbated by contemporary racism, and the need to recognize human brotherhood. But the novel's very lopsidedness is symptomatic of the blindness to immediate reality which destroys its characters. As Styron has said concerning southern segregation: to ignore the presence of black people, to deny their very reality, while living in daily contact with them, has made the white southerner violent and crazy in his responses.[8] In his first novel Styron is only half-conscious of the damage resulting from this separation between the races—it had hitherto been a fact of life for him—but the guilt is there, its impact on whites undeniable.

His white characters become hysterical and monstrous, driven by alcoholism, hypochondria, psychosis. Blacks appear only in the background, chiefly as servants. Like Faulkner's Dilsey, they are indispensable, and saved from the pride and ennui of white people by the exigencies of toil, but they are invisible. As in Faulkner, the moral decadence of whites is dramatized by their unthinking dependence on their black attendants and indifference to their humanity. But unlike Faulkner, Styron does not idealize the Negro's religious faith. While the novel's final scene—a religious revival—echoes the end of *The Sound and the Fury*, the effect is ironic. Styron's blacks are the dupes of a charlatan whose promises are as hollow as is the hope of redemption for whites in such a world; the poison of white society seems to have penetrated even the black community. Styron's main attention, then, is given to the degradation of his white characters, only hinting at the relation between their suffering and the repression of the Negro. In succeeding works Styron will pursue the themes of white self-loathing and black defiance, the need for release from the curse of separateness. But his first novel begins and ends in despair.

In *Set This House on Fire* Styron continues to focus on the horrors of entrapment and psychological disorder, but in a new key and in new surroundings. Perhaps in an effort to shake off his southern heritage, he locates much of the action in Europe and takes his inspiration from contemporary European fiction and Existentialist thought. He characterizes his hero as afflicted by a "sickness unto death,"[9] who finally chooses "being" over "nothingness" (SHF, p. 475). Nevertheless, *Set This House on Fire* is still a southern novel. All three of its major characters are southerners; their conflict, though it takes place in Italy, is rooted in their southern past; the novel opens and closes in the South, and crucial sections of the hero's narrative are located there. Most important, its basic issues are those of the southern tradition. Styron apparently found it difficult to work outside the familiar southern environment, which was for him both a physical and moral context.[10]

Styron first presents his existentialist hero, Cass Kinsolving, as a "man of despair";[11] however, Cass triumphs over his personal afflictions, defeats a deadly enemy, and at the end finds a new life—the first of Styron's protagonists to do so. As a painter seeking refuge in

Europe from the ugliness of American culture, he illustrates the plight of the artist in a soulless and materialistic world. But he has found no relief from the inner conflicts which are destroying him. The novel centers on his encounter, one which assumes symbolic meaning, with a wealthy American film producer, Mason Flagg. Flagg (whose name identifies him with his country) stands for everything meretricious in American society which Cass has tried to escape. For his part, Cass is seeking to recover what that society has lost; as his surname suggests, he attempts to solve the question of his kinship with others and their common relation to God. His battle with Flagg, in which Cass emerges the victor, releases him from despair.

Set This House on Fire, so heavy with universal significance, can also be approached as a second stage in Styron's southern myth. Styron's ideas have developed since his first novel; now there is an element of hope. Interestingly, Styron softens his attack on the southern gentility and now directs his scorn toward the encroachments of alien commercialism and vulgarity into the South, in contrast to which the old tradition is to be preferred. But as is already implied in *Lie Down in Darkness*, though in harsher terms, the old values belong to a departing tradition; it must be from plebeian stock—raw, vital, and closer to the realities of life—that the new southern hero shall be derived.

Cass Kinsolving is a North Carolina redneck, a poor-white hillbilly, torn by conflicts traceable to his southern heritage of class inferiority, religious anxiety, and racist guilt. Like Huckleberry Finn, whom he resembles in a number of ways, the young Cass—poor, orphaned and half-educated—had unthinkingly absorbed the racist views of his community. At the same time he had been terrified by the strictures of an uncompromising religion. As a youth he had participated in an ugly episode of nigger-baiting, vividly described in retrospect, which frightened him by revealing the depth of his unconscious hatred of black people. Convinced of his sinfulness, Cass is filled with fear of divine vengeance. His paranoia follows him to Europe, drives him to dissipation and makes him easy prey for Flagg's perverted need to torment him until, unexpectedly spurred to violence, Cass murders his persecutor.

Mason Flagg brings in another dimension to Styron's view of the

[112]

contemporary South. He is an "ugly American," so identified by his connections with Madison Avenue and Hollywood, his hedonism, wastefulness, and dishonesty. But he is a southerner too, an adoptive one, having moved to Virginia after his millionaire parents bought a colonial estate, placed their son in a select private school, and set themselves up in society. In this way Flagg represents the corruption of the South by alien sophistication and materialism which, in the form of rapid urbanization and commercialism, threaten to undermine the values of the plain people and what remains of an already weakened social tradition.[12]

The established tradition is represented by the narrator Peter Leverett (whose name means Peter Rabbit), an ineffectual character reminiscent of Faulkner's melancholy patricians. Though weak, he comes of good stock: Leverett's father is an old-fashioned southern liberal whose stalwart ideals serve as a measure for the chaos related in his son's narrative. Leverett's emotional paralysis, his susceptibility—despite himself—to the allure of Flagg's money, suggest the extent of the weakness afflicting the South. He is powerless; it is Cass who saves him. Cass's defeat of Flagg asserts the power of the native southerner—albeit one painfully marked by the intolerance and poverty of his childhood, guilt-torn and prey to corruption—to extricate himself and reaffirm the positive lessons of his upbringing. Perhaps, it is implied, the South can resist the commercial despoliation and moral shabbiness of the mid-twentieth century, can preserve the best of the old tradition as it finds the basis for a new morality.

The circumstances leading to the crisis—Flagg's murder—are significant, and indicate that even in a novel without a single black character, Styron is again advancing ideas about racism. Here the Italian peasants are the "niggers," and Flagg's cruelty, his arrogant refusal to see them as human beings, suggest southern racism, and Cass sees the parallel. Cass kills Flagg in vengeance for the rape and alleged murder of one of his servants—a peasant girl named Francesca whom Cass had loved and whose dying father, Michele, he had attempted to save with stolen drugs and amateur "doctoring." With each visit to Michele's hovel, whose "stink of wretchedness reminds him painfully of the black sharecropper's cabin he had once vandalized" (SHF, p. 396), Cass grew more determined to help

[113]

these degraded people, as though seeking atonement for his sins and those of his kind against black people. At the same time, he also sees the peasantry as analogous to the poorest southern white caste; in defending them, he is also asserting himself. Thus his sympathy with the peasants brings his awakening, drives him to the desperate deed which caused him to perceive the identity of peoples he always had thought to be separate. But, obsessed by guilt, Cass is slow to accept the healing forgiveness accompanying this recognition. Having lived in a racially divided, class-divided society, Cass has known poverty and humiliation; he has himself been a victim. Yet he had also been a racist. He had been taught hate, while religion had taught him guilt. The resulting contradictions have nearly torn him apart. Finally accepting his freedom, Cass makes a hesitant choice to "be what [he] could be for a time," (SHF, p. 477) and returns to the South—but not home, to a new place, a new beginning. In keeping with the novel's criticism of urban life, Cass takes his family to a remote place in the South Carolina tidewater, finds work, and settles down to a new life.

The hope conveyed in Styron's picture of his raw, bumptious, innocent southern hero and his triumph is offset by the novel's chaotic structure, its changes in direction and point of view, its strained rhetoric, its often forced symbolism, its reminders of the capriciousness of events and the weakness of the will which until the very last threaten to defeat all Cass's efforts at self-control. These dark undercurrents, conveyed in the hysterical pitch of Cass's narrative and Leverett's somber reflections, reveal qualities typical of southern literature, and echo the major themes of Styron's first novel. Cass's self-destructive drinking, his remorse and temptation to despair, evoke the sense of entrapment of *Lie Down in Darkness*. The "satanic" aura surrounding Flagg—"the man is a devil," says Leverett[13]—and his sinister power over Cass creates a lurid, Gothic atmosphere. Like the earlier novel, *Set This House on Fire* is concerned with racism and class-consciousness; but, as before, racial issues are kept below the surface and the damaging separation between peoples is only implied through symptoms or analogous situations. Styron is still not ready to confront racial matters directly in his fiction, though Cass's liberation from tyranny is also a release from the old sin of separateness—so often seen as the original curse

[114]

on the South. *Set This House on Fire* affirms the power of a hero to lift the curse, exorcise the devil and master himself—and in so doing, it ventures an optimistic prediction for the future of southern society.

Like all of Styron's fiction, *The Confessions of Nat Turner* is concerned with great questions going beyond regional limitation: the quest for freedom and self-knowledge, the effects of tyranny, the torments of isolation and despair. At the same time these universal themes are dramatized in a novel exploiting the major themes of southern writing: race relations, the legacy of guilt from the past, the power of fear, indoctrination, and religious mania—all played out by a variety of tortured characters against a blighted Virginia landscape. And *Nat Turner* exhibits a third stage in the evolution of Styron's southern myth, and a new kind of southern hero. This time a slave recapitulates the persecution, entrapment, and despair of Styron's earlier protagonists; and although the rebellion fails and he dies, Nat Turner goes beyond any of Styron's white southerners in spiritual growth.

The Confessions of Nat Turner demonstrates with new power the corrupting force of the social environment—an expression of the entrapment theme which has always interested Styron. *Lie Down in Darkness* relates the perversion of its characters to the false values of their social milieu, while the psychic destruction caused by a youth's upbringing in a racist and stratified southern community is portrayed in *Set This House on Fire*. In writing about slavery, of course, Styron adds to psychological entrapment the literal chains of bondage. Styron can imagine no more crippling experience than to be treated as property, reduced to a thing. Nat Turner's capacity to rise above the degradation forced upon him affirms the possibility of human freedom more forcefully than anything Styron had previously written.

In *Nat Turner* Styron faces directly the disturbing themes of racial injustice, vengeance, and white guilt which are only obliquely referred to in previous works. In addition to displaying Styron's continuing interest in the effect of southern social and racial taboos on the individual, *Nat Turner* presents a panoramic view of a whole society, adding historical dimension to his understanding of the contemporary South. The slave economy of antebellum Virginia is covered in considerable detail; the novel examines social patterns, legal and religious sanctions for slavery, and the impact of slavery on all members of the community. Thus Styron confronts that period of the past and the original crime which invoked the curse plaguing the South ever since. He seems to have decided that by exhibiting slavery in all its horror—yet not shirking "what must have been after all the tolerable aspects of the situation"[14]—by entering into the slave's experience as it might be understood in contemporary terms, he might somehow overcome the curse and transcend the barriers of fear, guilt, and ignorance blocking the white's understanding of black people, and perhaps help people of both races to know one another.

Styron's concern with contemporary race relations, particularly the racial attitudes of white southerners, always lay behind his interest in the slave hero. In an article describing his research into the Turner legend, Styron recalls his amazement at the discovery that when he visited the scene of the rebellion, the legendary slave had all but vanished from local memory. People did not want to remember Nat Turner. For Styron this exemplified the schizoid attitude of many white southerners: denying the humanity, almost the very existence, of blacks, yet regarding them with "unending concern." While ignored by white people, says Styron, "Negroes impinge upon their collective subconscious to such a degree that it may be rightly said that they become the focus of an incessant preoccupation, somewhat like a monstrous recurring dream populated by identical faces wearing expressions of inquietude and vague reproach."[15] One of Styron's motives in writing his slave novel was to deal with this anxiety. He was aware of the psychological damage he had himself suffered as a privileged white youth growing up in segregated Virginia; he could only wonder at, and present in fictional form, the experience of the whites living in slave times—the ministers, the women, and the poor-whites, the planters and lawyers and judges who fill the novel. The importance of white characters in Nat Turner has often been overlooked in the furor aroused by its portrait of a black hero.

In addition to presenting a merciless scrutiny of the ways in which white people accommodated themselves to slavery, Styron also undertook to re-create the slave's "psychic and moral devastation"[16] by telling the story in the slave's own words. By writing "inside a black man's skin" Styron erases racial distinctions, at least in his own imagination; he wanted to take on a black persona and to learn as he wrote "what it must have been to be a slave . . . in a manner of self-discovery."[17] Thus like Cass Kinsolving, to whom the unity of all suffering humanity is revealed, Styron himself seeks the same vision by adopting a first-person narrative stance. He then traces a similar enlightenment in his hero: Nat Turner, dehumanized almost to insanity, masters himself and forgives his oppressors, moving from a hatred so absolute that he attributes to it divine sanction, to a final vision of union and love.

To accept as Styron's purpose the glorification of his black hero has not been easy for all readers, many of whom—despite Styron's efforts to transcend racial barriers—were still thinking in racial stereotypes. Black critics especially were offended by *Nat Turner*, and denounced Styron as a southern "racist," charging him with distorting history and belittling his hero for the purpose of discrediting all black revolutionaries.[18] Styron was dismayed at these interpretations, pointing in vain to the lack of real evidence about Turner, the faithfulness of much of his account to the actual "Confessions" published in 1831, and the right of the artist to reshape history. But his novel came into conflict with attitudes deeply engrained in our society, and the hostility it aroused could have been predicted. The explanation for such a response may be found in the novel itself, which sensitively portrays the blindness engulfing those isolated by suspicion and hate. Styron dared to make an assault on those attitudes by evoking the experience of a slave who is more than a black hero, one who represents all humanity.

Styron does not make Nat Turner a hero because he organized the only sustained slave uprising, nor is it his purpose merely to present a field commander in action.[19] A paradox hangs over the doomed rebellion; justified as resistance may have been, the insurrection led to a series of bloody reprisals—countless innocent blacks were murdered—and repressive laws which fostered a new intensity of race-hatred and defeated the cause of abolition in Virginia, and thus made the Civil War inevitable. Moreover, the rebellion occupies only forty pages at the novel's conclusion, while Nat's early experience, the people, ideas, and events which shaped him, demand most of our attention. Nat Turner's greatness, in Styron's conception, lies not in his courage to kill, but in the courage to believe in his own dignity—for a slave, an astonishing feat of imagination and self-creation. But the creative impulse, in bondage, is perverted to destructive ends; Nat can exercise his will only in rebellion. His vision falters for a long despairing time as he questions both the means he had chosen and his right to the freedom he had so desperately sought, until he is finally delivered by the vision which comes to him moments before death. To delineate his hero's spiritual odyssey is Styron's difficult purpose in writing the novel.

Nat Turner rises against more than slavery. Like all of Styron's characters, he is afflicted by fear, apparently confirmed by his experience, that no guiding purpose governs human life, that man is doomed to mindless suffering in a godless universe. The minister Richard Whitehead preaches from his pulpit that the slave's condition is ordained by heaven itself. In innumerable ways the slave is encouraged to think of himself as subhuman, a thing to be bought and sold. Ugly comparisons with animals and insects abound. Early in the novel the lawyer Thomas Gray expounds on the definition of the slave as "animate chattel," and Jeremiah Cobb bitterly observes that most white people would regard an educated slave like Nat Turner as a "mammoth rat, six feet long."[20] Perhaps the most devastating blow Nat sustained was the betrayal of his own master, who had promised him freedom.

Blacks even have contempt for themselves. Nat is distressed by the self-loathing of his fellow slaves: "You is *men*, brothers, *men* not beasts of the field! You ain't no four-legged dogs!" (NT, p. 295). But Nat too has known the effects of bone-breaking labor, has himself felt reduced to a creature "half-man, half-mule" (NT, p. 234), and realizes that such is the constant condition of most slaves. In his darkest moments Nat thinks of himself as a "wriggling insect" (NT, p. 24), meditates whether he is like a fly, like "one of God's supreme outcasts" living out the horror of "an existence in which there was no act of will, no choice" (NT, p. 38). In his despair it seems that his "black shit-eating people were surely like flies . . . lacking even that will to destroy by their own hand their unending anguish" (NT, p. 39). At least the rebellion, which Nat must have felt to be suicidal, was an expression of conscious will, an act repudiating forever the condition of the slave.

Eventually, rejecting the yoke of tyranny comes to mean for Nat Turner the affirmation of faith in God. The insurrection is the culmination of all he has striven to do in his life: to prove to himself that not absurdity nor purposeless evil, but some kind of order prevails in the universe. Thus his growing religious fanaticism, his yearning to hear the voice of God and learn His will. But alienated as he is—neither free, nor willing to be a slave—he must seek his way in isolation.[21] His obsessive study of Scripture leads him to identify himself and his fellow slaves with the Israelites in bondage and to cast himself in the role of an Old Testament prophet carrying out the will of a vengeful God. To acquiesce in his condition was to deny God, or—like his friend Hark—to see God as the special tormentor of the slave: "'Hit do seem to me, Nat,' he said in a measured voice, 'dat de Lawd sho must be a white man. On'y a God dat was white could figger out how to make niggers so lonesome.' He paused, then said: 'On'y maybe he's a big black driver. An' if de Lawd is black he sho is de meanest black nigger bastid ever was born'" (NT, p. 278). Rejecting bondage through violence came to mean for Nat Turner the affirmation of a righteous God and the dignity owing to one of His creatures.

As he studied the 1831 "Confessions," Styron was struck by a problem which, as a novelist, he had to work out: that is, Nat Turner's perplexing behavior during the insurrection, his apparent distaste for the violence he had set in motion, as suggested by his late arrival at the scenes of murder and his inability to strike a death-blow. Despite his conviction that the uprising was commanded by God, Nat killed only one victim himself. Styron builds his entire novel around an explanation for this paradoxical behavior: it was not weakness, but the expression of a complex and heroic spirit.

Styron postulates what must have been Nat's contradictory feelings toward white people, particularly his master. As a youth he had been a favorite of the Turner family, and had been encouraged to nurture great hopes for his future. His own black father only a memory, Nat came to love his master (whose surname he bore) like a father. But this "father" betrayed him when his fortunes changed. Abandoned, Nat Turner banished his master from his mind and turned to the perfection of that "exquisitely sharpened hatred" of white people (NT, p. 249) which ended in the insurrection.

This master-slave relationship, with its Oedipal overtones,[22] offers a parallel to Nat's relation to Margaret Whitehead, the young white girl who had respected him, perhaps loved him, and who becomes Nat's only murder victim. Like Samuel Turner, obliterated from memory and destroyed indirectly in the uprising, Margaret is both loved and destroyed by Nat Turner. Love for a white girl is denied the slave—proscribed by unimaginably powerful taboos— as is love for a white "father." The impulse is to kill.[23] It seems like a coincidence; as the mutinous Will challenges Nat to shed white blood as proof of his right to leadership, Margaret is the fleeing victim: "Does you want her, preacher man, or she fo' me?" (NT, p. 391). Although the deed is the logical end of all Nat had worked for, in murdering Margaret—the act described in the most ironically lyrical passage in the novel—he realizes with horror what he had become. From that time, he cannot sustain his faith in the uprising. Margaret's death reveals to Nat the absurdity in which he had trapped himself; his vengeance had destroyed the one person who had looked through the barriers separating them and, in her limited way, had loved him. The evil he had suffered had only bred evil in himself.

Such is the evil of slavery, Styron concludes: a man reduced to a thing can only retaliate by denying the humanity of those who violate him. Bondage creates in the slave a maddened desire for freedom so intense that he believes that he wants nothing, no law, no one above him—nothing shall stand in the way of his will. Isolated in the terrifying conviction that no order or responsibility binds together the human community, Nat Turner responds to this vision of nothingness by committing himself desperately to annihilation. Then, for the first time in his life, he loses contact with God, not emerging from this state until moments before his death. He is illumined by a vision of wholeness as he acknowledges his love for Margaret. His decision at the end that he would have spared her marks the beginning of an acceptance of human frailty and a God of love. Turning "in surrender" to the voice which "commands" him (NT, p. 404), Nat does not give up his freedom. He emerges from the isolation of the terrible freedom which had threatened like the abyss, to submit willingly to the bonds of humanity which alone make men free.

Combining Oedipal and existentialist themes, Styron conceives of Nat Turner as a tragic figure locked in conflict with authority, struggling with a vision of nothingness, purged through violence, and, possibly, finally transfigured. This pattern of conflict is basic to all Styron's fiction, and Nat Turner's plight, until his resistance, resembles that of Styron's earlier protagonists. However, there are important differences. Never before has Styron invested a main character with such dignity and stature. Never has he portrayed such tyranny and such justification for violent resistance—for the slave, the only way out. Yet in *Nat Turner* Styron comes to a new conclusion regarding the tragic necessity of violence in the struggle for freedom. Cass's murder of Flagg is inevitable, even right; and violence for Cass is the key to purgation and release. However, Nat's murder of Margaret Whitehead brings release of another kind. Recognizing in her the embodiment of love and sacrifice, admitting his desire for her, Nat Turner reaches a vision of wholeness which no barriers can restrain.

Nat Turner's disastrous career is tragic, and on the surface Styron's slave novel does not project a hopeful future of racial harmony or human understanding. But out of the slave's suffering comes a revelation; his story enlarges the possibilities for mankind. Nat Turner is the culmination of Styron's developing southern myth, and overall his three major works of fiction point to a tentative but growing optimism. *Lie Down in Darkness* reflects the young Styron's shame and despair for his own class and people; in *Set This House on Fire*, a different kind of hero—while nearly engulfed by the trials which test him—discovers the moral consistency and courage to survive in a chaotic world. *The Confessions of Nat Turner* presents a slave-hero's rebellion, defeat, and despair; yet it ends with spiritual resolution. Styron acknowledges the martyrdom which drove Nat Turner to violence; but in attributing to him a transfiguring final vision which qualifies all he had done, Styron affirms the resiliency of the oppressed spirit and his hope for the reconciliation of peoples whose separation has blighted southern history.

Notes

1. Critics have often noted that Styron's novels center on a few basic themes following a consistent line of development. Louis D. Rubin, who readily identifies Styron as belonging to the southern literary tradition, points to the coherence of Styron's fundamental attitudes ("William Styron and Human Bondage," in Melvin J. Friedman and Irving Malin, eds., *The Confessions of Nat Turner: A Critical Handbook* [Belmont, California, 1970], pp. 73–76). In "William Styron's *Divine Comedy*" (in Friedman and Malin, pp. 164–175), Karl Malkoff also argues for the unity of Styron's work, observing in it a synthesis of Freudian psychology and Existentialist ideas. Malkoff argues that Styron's protagonists' conflicts with authority—variations on the Oedipal conflict—are each resolved by a greater triumph, a greater affirmation of "being." These readings lend authority to the approach which I explore in this essay.

2. *The Burden of Time: The Fugitives and Agrarians* (Princeton, N.J., 1965), p. 42.

3. In Friedman and Malin, p. 75.

4. This pattern was established by Malcolm Cowley's review of *Lie Down in Darkness*, "The Faulkner Pattern," *New Republic* 125 (8 October 1951): 19.

5. Peter Matthiessen and George Plimpton, "The Art of Fiction V: Interview with Styron," *Paris Review*, Spring 1954, p. 47.

6. David Dempsey, "Talk with William Styron," *New York Times Book Review*, 9 September 1951, p. 27.

7. "The Shade of Thomas Wolfe," *Harper's*, April 1968, pp. 96 f.

8. "This Quiet Dust," *Harper's*, April 1965, p. 138.

9. *Set This House on Fire* (New York, 1961), p. 267. Subsequent references are in the text.

10. Louis D. Rubin in *The Faraway Country: Writers of the Modern South* (Seattle, 1963), pp. 211–230, develops at length the idea that *Set This House on Fire* represents a new extension of the southern literary imagination—not so much concerned with southern institutions as with the underlying assumptions on which they are built.

11. See Lewis Lawson, "Cass Kinsolving: Kierkegaardian Man of Despair," *Wisconsin Studies in Contemporary Literature* 3 (Fall 1962): 54–66.

12. The "pillaged town" of Port Warwick, Virginia (Leverett's home town) exhibits the effects of the "go-getting commercialism" again referred to in "This Quiet Dust."

13. P. 228. The violated Francesca also says, "he is a devil," p. 414, and during the rape scene a recording of *Don Giovanni* is played on the phonograph.

14. Interview with George Plimpton, "William Styron: A Shared Ordeal," in Friedman and Malin, p. 38.

15. "This Quiet Dust," p. 136.

16. "New Editions," Review of Frank Tannenbaum, *Slave and Citizen, New York Review of Books* 1 (Special Issue, 1963): 43.

17. R. W. B. Lewis and C. Vann Woodward, "Slavery in the First Person," in Friedman and Malin, p. 53.

18. See John Henrick Clarke, ed., *Ten Black Writers Respond* (Boston, 1968).

19. Lerone Bennett, "Nat's Last White Man," in ibid., p. 14.

20. *The Confessions of Nat Turner* (New York, 1967), p. 75. All further references are in the text.

21. Nat's anomalous position and his enforced role-playing is sensitively discussed in Louis D. Rubin, "Nat Turner and Human Bondage," in Friedman and Malin, pp. 79–82.

22. See Malkoff, "William Styron's *Divine Comedy*," in Friedman and Malin, pp. 169 f.

23. This point is discussed both by Rubin and by Malkoff, in Friedman and Malin, pp. 31, 171.

PHILIP W. LEON

Styron's Fiction: Narrative as Idea

Flannery O'Connor mastered the device of using secondary characters to counterbalance and reveal central figures, as we can see in *Wise Blood* (1952), when Enoch Emery's bewildered search for a messianic friend becomes coterminous with Hazel Motes's search for the Church Without Christ. Robert Penn Warren's fiction thrusts a central figure into situations requiring illuminating interaction with others; thus in *All the King's Men* (1946) Willie Stark's story is bonded to Jack Burden's brooding introspections on power and loyalty. Writers of this caliber surpass authors who depend too heavily upon a one-dimensional character on whom the reader must focus. But fiction with twists and turns—unless contrived in vain pursuit of profundity—can delight with ultimate understanding. From the special mix of complex characters in believably difficult circumstances comes a distillate that satisfies intellectually and vicariously.

Over the last thirty years William Styron has assembled a canon of fiction which places him clearly in the ranks of such thinking writers as O'Connor and Warren who are capable of telling us a good story about the complexities and difficulties inherent in the Age of Anxiety. From *Lie Down in Darkness* (1951) to *Sophie's Choice* (1979), Styron's characters confront these adversities, a testimony to man's endurance that Faulkner in particular would approve of. Doubtless much of Styron's success, both critical and popular, can be attributed to his manipulation of narrative point of view to convey the *idea* of the novels. What I call the idea can mean variously the central metaphor, the controlling image, or, as in the case of *The Confessions of Nat Turner* (1967) and of *Sophie's Choice*, the amorphous *Angst* of a generation struggling against cultural undertows that seek to draw us into the vastness of anarchy and bondage. Styron expresses ideas through narrators—not necessarily the "main" character—whose inextricable relationships with others lead to a depiction of the sometimes hellish emotional labyrinths from which modern man seeks emancipation.

Sophie's Choice represents a confluence of the best ideas of Styron's earlier novels. Expressing those ideas through dual narrators, *Sophie's Choice* is at once consistent with the narrative technique of the previous works and individual in the central idea it proffers. Sophie's suicide is not Peyton Loftis's suicide updated and retold; that is not the sort of connection I wish to make. Here I seek to establish a bond between all of Styron's novels as they consistently employ an artistically complex narrative method to reveal the author's central idea.

When *Lie Down in Darkness* appeared, critics were quick to recognize this new talent, automatically ascribing to Styron the role of "southern writer," a label Styron does not cultivate but which he has largely been unable to avoid. The story is set, for the most part, in the South, but it is the industrial New South, not a Faulknerian Mississippi hinterland. The novel shows noteworthy craftsmanship and is still praised as a remarkable first work.[1] Styron's debt to Faulkner's *The Sound and the Fury* for characters and basic plot has already received ample attention from a number of critics; most find in these parallels a creditable adherence to the southern tradition rather than a mere derivation from Faulkner. Peyton Loftis, however much she resembles Candace Compson, remains her own character, penned from Styron's imagination. That the real name of Faulkner's idiot Ben is Maury and that Styron's retarded child is Maudie might show that same influence. But the tone of modernity, the rendering of setting, of dialogue, of action, is Styron's own worthy writing.

Styron's use of the omniscient third person gives great latitude for description, and Styron excels in description. There are finer illustrative passages, but the opening paragraph of the novel reveals a control of tone and image that tells the reader his time will be well spent:

Riding down to Port Warwick from Richmond, the train begins to pick up speed on the outskirts of the city, past the tobacco factories with their ever-present haze of acrid, sweetish dust and past the rows of uniformly brown clapboard houses which stretch down the hilly streets for miles, it seems, the hundreds of rooftops all reflecting the pale light of dawn; past the suburban roads still sluggish and sleepy with early morning traffic, and rattling swiftly now over the bridge which separates the last two hills where in the valley below you can see the James River winding beneath its acid-green crust of scum out beside the chemical plants and more rows of clapboard houses and into the woods beyond.[2]

The "Port Warwick" of the novel is Styron's native Newport News, and the train we see in this opening paragraph bears the body of Peyton Loftis, the doomed daughter of Milton Loftis, who awaits her body at the train depot. After a tumultuous adolescence, much of it spent both teasing and avoiding her incestuous-minded father, Peyton goes to New York City where an unhappy marriage to Harry Miller, a destructive love affair, and a life gone awry lead her to plunge to her death from the rooftop of a tenement. Now, the device of having the reader work back through these and other events is not particularly original, and it does make ambiguous the use of phrases such as "time-present" and "time-past," but it remains a valid device which can be effective.[3]

Each chapter of *Lie Down in Darkness* has its dominant persona, thus giving Styron a double narrative: he can render descriptions through the omniscient third person, and he can enter into the consciousness of these dominant characters with ease, rendering their thoughts in a quasi-first-person voice. Some representative passages will illustrate this technique. In chapter one, as Milton waits at the train station for Peyton's body to arrive,

Dust sifted down, enveloping the dock like a fog; down the tracks two lone redcaps, hauling baggage from the station, trundled along, disappeared like phantoms, and Loftis, watching them, thought: I won't think too much about this. I'll try to occupy my mind with the water instead. On the ship a solitary figure, brick-red, trailing a cable, hopped along a catwalk and yelled into the hold, "Easy!" Perhaps, he thought, if I only think of this second, this moment, the train won't come at all. (LDD, p. 13)

Notice the structure of this passage. The omniscient third person narrator is free to describe details, using two similes which the otherwise preoccupied Milton would likely not use, slipping easily by the use of a colon instead of quotation marks into Milton's thoughts, then picking up the narrative thread of detail and metaphor, until finally we return to Milton's first-person thoughts.

Similarly, here is a complete paragraph from chapter two in which the dominant character is Dolly Bonner, Milton's mistress, who accompanies him in the limousine escorting Peyton's body:

> She turned and stared miserably out of her window: He's that way not just because he's grieving for Peyton, but because he's rejecting me. I can tell. Two buzzards flapped soundlessly up from a junk heap, swooped toward the weeds, were gone. (LDD, p. 70)

Again, in this second typical example, Styron has a confluence of narration from two persons, the third and the first. Usually Styron is able to blend the two so skillfully that neither narrative stance disrupts the other, but rather complements it and sustains the tone of that particular passage. A good example occurs in chapter four, in which the dominant character is the Reverend Carey Carr, a source of religious solace for Milton's wife, Helen, as she struggles with Milton's infidelity and with her own jealousy of Peyton's beauty and wantonness. Carey Carr muses as he drives in his automobile to comfort Helen on this day that Peyton's body arrives at Port Warwick:

> She had come to him six years ago, he remembered, on a rainy Sunday night in October when the leaves of sycamores lay upon the rectory lawn in drenched disordered piles and a gathering wind, blowing in chill and premonitory gusts from the river, had made him think wistfully of a new furnace and despairingly of his God who, he had prayed, would reveal Himself finally this year and preferably before Advent. (LDD, p. 109)

The descriptions such as the "rainy Sunday night" are stylistically effective only through the third person; the "irreverent" poke at Carey Carr's insecurity in his calling comes at once from within the character himself and from the third person narrator. Styron has it both ways in passages such as this one, and they abound throughout the novel. The reader need not prescind the two narrative stances; indeed, Styron's artistry is such that the blend is unobtrusive.

There remains in *Lie Down in Darkness* one further noteworthy narrative device, and that, of course, is Peyton's long (fifty pages!) interior monologue presaging her suicidal plunge. Peyton's monologue resembles Molly Bloom's in Joyce's *Ulysses* and has the same stream-of-consciousness tone of disorientation as Ben's section of *The Sound and the Fury*. With the exception of a denouement consisting of two brief scenes (Milton violently taking his leave of Helen, Dolly, and Carey Carr, and Daddy Faith, the black evangelist, leading a mystical prayer meeting), Peyton's long monologue concludes the novel. By turning over to Peyton this large corpus of information, Styron surrenders his authorial third person to Peyton's first person. She becomes the primary teller, even recounting dialogue both directly and indirectly as she stumbles incoherently toward her death. We watch the disintegration of this once-beautiful girl, now beset by alcohol, guilt over her love affairs, and a confusion of longings for life and death. No summary of this superbly crafted monologue with its complex set of symbols such as the impotency of flightless birds, can do it justice, but look briefly at the final moments, at the embedded parental dialogue in Styron's italics and Peyton's visual fall into death:

And so it happens: treading past to touch my boiling skin—one whisper of feathers is all—and so I see them go—oh my Christ!—one by one ascending my flightless birds through the suffocating night, toward paradise. I am dying, Bunny, dying. *But you must be proper.* I say, oh pooh. Oh pooh. Most be proper. Oh most proper. Powerful.

Oh most Powerful

Oh must (LDD, p. 386)

The interior monologue, a wide-ranging, effective technique, provides the reader with Peyton's own version of the shaping events of her life and the occasions which led to her death. Her private symbols, such as clocks, moths, flightless birds, become associated with characters, thereby providing insight into people and events. Peyton feels that she can find refuge inside an alarm clock which she carries with her on her final journey. There in the clock she thinks she can escape the birds which follow her. She says, "Guilt is the thing with feathers, they came back with a secret rustle, preening their flightless wings and I didn't want to think" (LDD, p. 352). Though the birds themselves are guiltless, they haunt her, they represent her guilt. Emily Dickinson's poem "Hope is the Thing with Feathers" probably informs Peyton's statement, "Guilt is the thing with feathers." The only hope for Peyton is in death, which her feelings of guilt—the birds—bring about. She divests herself of her protective symbol by throwing the clock into a drain shortly before she throws herself from the twelfth story of a Harlem building. These symbolic touches are more effective in the sections written as stream of consciousness than in the more straightforward narration.

Thus the reasons for Peyton's death, the reasons for the arrival of the train in Port Warwick at the first of the novel, are made clear by the use of an omniscient observer who allows the various focal characters to assist in the role of narrator. Though the critical and popular success of *Lie Down in Darkness* demonstrates Styron's skill in the use of both omniscient and limited narration, he is not content to write by formula. His second novel, *The Long March* (1952), uses third-person narration modified to convey simultaneous views—those of participant and observer—of a challenge to human will and persistence.

The Long March reflects a personal experience, Styron's recall to the Marine Corps as a reserve lieutenant during the Korean War. At Camp Lejeune, North Carolina, Styron experienced a forced night road march, the basic frame for the interaction of the three primary characters in the novel. Colonel Templeton, the battalion commander, orders a thirty-six-mile road march at night to test his unit's combat effectiveness. One of his men is Lieutenant Culver, Styron's fictive persona, though not a first-person narrator. Captain Mannix, a thirty-year-old Jew—the central figure of the novel—hates himself for remaining in the reserves and hates the Marines for subjecting him to degrading experiences such as the march.

Styron's resentment of the military in general informs almost every page of the novel. *Lie Down in Darkness* was barely turned over to his publisher when Styron packed his bags for Camp Lejeune and possible shipment to the war zone in Korea. Having served honorably in the South Pacific during World War II, Styron, like many others, experienced a bitter disillusionment with the military during the Korean "police action." Styron has written that the "true military man is a mercenary . . . and it is within the world of soldiering that he finds his only home."[4] This sense of the military man's separation from the "real world" pervades the novel.

Colonel Templeton, who is not an evil man, displays no emotion upon hearing of the accidental death by mortar fire of eight Marines. To react emotionally would violate the impersonality of the system to which Templeton belongs. When the radioman, Hobbs, excitedly tells him of the mishap he "said nothing at first. The brief flicker of uneasiness in his eyes had fled, and when he put down his messkit and looked up at Hobbs it was only to wipe his hands on his handkerchief" (LM, p. 13). I find a similarity between Templeton in this scene and Pilate at the trial of Christ: "When Pilate saw that he could prevail nothing, but rather that a tumult was made, he took water, and washed his hands before the multitude, saying, I am innocent of the blood of this just person" (*Matt.* 27:24).

Both Styron's and Culver's lives are shattered by their recall to duty. Just as the young Styron had recently finished his first novel and was beginning to receive critical acclaim, so had Culver begun to achieve success "as one of the brightest juniors in a good New York law firm" (LM, p. 7). Lest there be any doubt about Styron's antipathy for the military, his feelings can be clearly seen through the juxtaposition of two of his writings, one from his unfinished novel *The Way of the Warrior* and the other from his review of Douglas MacArthur's *Reminiscences*, written some years ago. A selection from the unfinished novel describes military life as

the truly vicious, intolerable waiting—then the indecent hustle, the offensive food, the sweat and the flies, the lousy pay, the anxiety and fear, the fruitless jabber, the racket of rifle fire, the degrading celibacy, the trivial, evanescent friendships, the whole humiliating baggage of a caste system calculated to bring out in men their basest vanities: I am capable of brooding on such matters with self-punishing persistence, with mixed anguish and pleasure, as one relives so often some ugly ordeal successfully endured.[5]

In his review of *Reminiscences*, Styron writes that

the world that MacArthur thrills to makes most of his fellow Americans choke with horror. It is training manuals and twenty-mile hikes, stupefying lectures on platoon tactics and terrain and the use of the Lister bag, mountains of administrative paperwork, compulsive neatness and hideous barracks in Missouri and Texas, sexual deprivation, hot asphalt drillfields and deafening rifle ranges, daily tedium unparalleled in its ferocity, awful food, bad pay, ignorant people, and a ritualistic demand for ass-kissing almost unique in the quality of its humiliation.

Styron perhaps felt that Culver's first-person narrative could become too strident if Culver were to remain the central figure of the novel. Thus Styron's theme of antimilitarism must be conveyed by Mannix indirectly through Culver. Irving Malin correctly identifies Culver as Styron's "center of consciousness"[6] in the novel; I find that an apt phrase. Mannix is the "center of action," for his determined efforts to finish the march become the "rebellion in reverse" (LM, p. 73) that is the novel's prevailing image. Mannix, though he hates Templeton and the Marine Corps, insists that his men finish the march to show their defiance. Culver's thoughts tell the reader that Mannix's rebellion is futile and ironically tragic, for in determining to finish the march, Mannix, creating his own Catch-22, does precisely what Templeton wants him to do anyway.

Though Styron ostensibly uses the third-person omniscient narrator because it is the best way to tell this story, it is clear that we are to view Mannix through Culver's thoughts, as in this representative passage:

But underneath his rebellion, Culver finally knew, Mannix—like all of them—was really resigned. Born into a generation of conformists, even Mannix (so Culver sensed) was aware that his gestures were not symbolic, but individual, therefore hopeless, maybe even absurd, and that he was trapped like all of them in a predicament which one personal insurrection could, if anything, only make worse. (LM, p. 56)

There is little doubt that Mannix, the heroic man of action, symbolizes all who are trapped in a system which brooks no disobedience, while Culver is the contemplative observer-participant. Culver sees what is happening to Mannix, and he understands Colonel Templeton; still he is unable to do anything but acquiesce and follow "behind the Colonel, like a ewe who follows the slaughterhouse ram, dumb and doubting, too panicked by the general chaos to hate its leader, or care" (LM, p. 85).

Through Culver we watch as Mannix stumbles painfully along

until the seemingly interminable march concludes. Culver observes the final scene in which Mannix makes his way toward the shower room. The Negro maid who sees him says, "Oh my, you poor man. What have you been doin'? Do it hurt?" (LM, p. 109). This scene recalls Milton Loftis of *Lie Down in Darkness*, at his lowest depths in the drainage ditch in Charlottesville, when a Negro man asks him, "Do it hurt much?" (LDD, p. 214). Mannix drops his towel, leaving him "naked as the day he emerged from his mother's womb" (LM, p. 119). Though Mannix speaks the final words of the novel, "Deed it does," we know that the witness Culver has a clear understanding of the kind of hurt that Mannix means, the soul-defeating anguish of a victim. Culver's thoughts set the tone for us when we read that he "felt that he had hardly ever known a time in his life when he was not marching or sick with loneliness or afraid" (LM, p. 117). And Culver's thoughts, revealed to us by the third person, extend beyond his immediate military situation. Culver sees that Mannix's spirit, his drive, cannot be beaten, even if the system can punish him for insubordination with a court-martial, as Templeton tells him it will. Mannix illustrates the indomitable human will which enables us to try to endure our individual long marches. As Styron's spokesman, Culver shows us his admiration of the character strong enough to attempt to establish the individual in a world of oppressive systems.

Set This House on Fire (1960), Styron's existential novel of debauchery in postwar Italy, bulges with individual incidents, many of which could stand alone as short stories. Reviewers and critics disparaged Styron's book as having too many seemingly unrelated episodes. John Aldridge typifies the critics' reactions when he deplores Styron's "piling scene on scene, the intricate system of flashbacks, the self-obsessed excavation and examination of nuance, the sheer intensive 'working' of the medium."[7] In an interview at Styron's home on 23 June 1973, we talked about the generally unfavorable reception of his book. I asked him what he thought were some good aspects which were overlooked by the critics. Styron avoided answering the question directly, confessing to a certain discomfort when talking about what is good in his work, but he said he would, if he were writing the book now, make it shorter and leave out some of the episodes.

Clearly the novel is complex; it is long, and critics have noted how difficult the novel is to read if the reader looks for a single-line plot development. But I contend that most critics fail to see that the narrative structure is the meaning of this novel. The idea of the book concerns an existential problem, centering on Cass Kinsolving's decision to *be*. Structurally the novel becomes a series of bits of knowledge in the form of dreams, stories, and flashbacks which enable the characters to know themselves and therefore to be. Part one, in which Peter tells Cass of his early days with Mason, serves mainly to establish the fact that Mason has for all of his life been self-serving. Despite his bad qualities Mason holds an attraction for both Peter and Cass which they themselves do not fully understand. Much of their dialogue is given over to solving this strange attraction. Part two, in which Mason's evil is positively demonstrated, is largely composed of Cass's talking to Peter at such length that Cass effectively becomes the narrator.

In a letter to *Publisher's Weekly*, 30 May 1960, Styron says he respects the first-person narrative because credibility is readily achieved, but he recognizes that the first-person narrator is handicapped in dealing with

the complexities of any character aside from himself. In writing *Set This House on Fire*, from the very outset I was determined to beat this problem, to write a long complex book which would allow me to say all I wanted to about American life, but which at the same time would be written in the first person and the third person—two apparently irreconcilable points of view. . . . I had never seen a narrator who, beginning in the first person, could convincingly end up in the third person, the story so merging and mingling that one might accept without hesitation the fact the narrator himself knew the uttermost nuances of another man's thought.

The structural division using two narrators allows both Peter and Cass to attempt to discover their identities through each other; their quest must deal with Mason's identity and with his evil. Peter and Cass, though they recognize Mason's evil, somehow feel that they contributed to Mason's wickedness in Sambuco.

There is ample evidence in the novel that Mason represents evil, perhaps the evil which is in all of our beings and which, when it becomes the dominating force in our lives, requires excision. The novel, however, is not a "Good vs. Evil" dilemma with Peter and Cass opposing Mason. Rather, the novel gradually brings the reader to the realization that each of us, to one degree or another, embodies some of the qualities of each of the central characters. Like Peter, a lawyer, we want a sense of propriety, of things being right in the world. At one point in the story a hillbilly song, "What's the Matter with This World?" booms out over Mason's villa in Sambuco. Like Cass, the unproductive artist who plays the hillbilly record, we sometimes stumble, drunken, confused, infatuated, hoping to attain high goals. Like Mason, each of us has an evil nature which, according to the Judeo-Christian tradition, keeps us sinners in constant need of the grace and salvation that Cass, in some measure, obtains. Not only does Mason represent evil, but he represents it in the extreme, and sins in myriad ways: lying, adultery, salacious obsession with pornography, cunning, extortion, and rape. Because Peter and Cass are involved with Mason, they are involved with his evil.

When Cass begins part two and takes over the narration he assumes some of the blame for what takes place in Sambuco: "How can you ever know where the blame lies? What part was Mason's and what part was mine and what part was God's?" (SHF, p. 239). Cass says sometimes he thinks he, not Mason, was "the evilest man who ever walked" (SHF, p. 239). He says something forced him to go to Sambuco, but the answer to his problem does not begin in Sambuco with Mason: "It started in me early, way back. . . . But it really started in Paris the year before, when I was sick and these here nightmares began to come upon me. It began *then*, and without knowing about that you couldn't know how and why it ended with Mason" (SHF, p. 239). So Cass begins his journey into the past, relating experiences from his youth and from Paris which he attempts to link with his nightmarish existence with Mason.

The meaning of *Set This House on Fire* can be clear, despite the fact that the events do not move logically from beginning to end throughout the novel. To arrive with Styron at the end of his novel with an existential resolution, we must allow the narrative structure to reflect the causes that change Peter and Cass into the characters they become. Only the retrospection of Peter and Cass, working together in complementary narratives, can help them understand the significance of past events in shaping their lives, in making them the people they are in the present.

This complementary, balanced structure of the novel may be illustrated by presenting some important episodes from Peter's narration juxtaposed with events from Cass's life:

1. Peter wonders, "What am I doing? Where am I going?" (p. 11).
Cass wants to know "who and what I was and had been and was to be" (p. 379).

2. Peter's father says the country needs "something terrible to happen to it" (p. 18) in order to recover its soul.
Cass undergoes "something terrible" in Sambuco which enables him to cleanse himself of the "paralyzing death of the soul" (p. 12).

3. Mason brings out in Peter his "willingness to be owned" (p. 146) at prep school and in New York.
Mason "owns" Cass in Sambuco, degrading, insulting, and manipulating him.

4. Peter's car hits Luciano di Lieto on his motorscooter as Peter goes to Sambuco (p. 32).
Cass first enters Sambuco riding drunkenly on a motorscooter, miraculously, he says, not having been killed "beneath the wheels of some truck or bus" (p. 300).

As the structure of the novel deepens and becomes more complex, Cass takes over as narrator, and there are parallel scenes in his part too:

1. Cass sees a vision of loveliness in a Paris street; he is "sick with desire and yearning for what I saw" (p. 247). The vision fades and he despairs once more.
Cass remembers seeing Vernelle Satterfield, a "palpitatingly carnal reality" (p. 250). Her "virginity and innocence" are a sham; she betrays him and causes him misery.

2. Cass blasphemously recites the Mass for the Dead over his children's dead parrot (p. 275).
Cass's children are stricken with streptococcal meningitis—a further suffering and torment for Cass (p. 276).

3. The ostensibly devout McCabes accompany Poppy home from celebrating Holy Week in Rome (p. 287). Cass tries to fleece them in a poker game, but loses badly (p. 293).

Like Vernelle Satterfield, the McCabes are not what they appear to be. Like Cass's fraud in his priestlike posture at the parrot's funeral, the McCabes are in reality grasping, greedy, uncharitable tourists rather than devout Catholic supplicants.

4. Cass recalls the day he and Lonnie destroy the Negro cabin in Virginia. He speaks of the "stench" of "poverty naked and horrid and unremitting" (p. 357).

Cass describes Michele's hut near Sambuco as "the bleeding stink of wretchedness" (p. 396). Michele's illness gives Cass a chance to atone for his destruction of the Negro cabin years before.

5. In Sambuco Cass performs lewd acts for the entertainment of Mason and his friends in return for liquor. Cass vows to pay Mason back, refusing to be owned by him.

Peter told Cass earlier that he was Mason's only friend at prep school because Mason "entertains" him while also making him feel superior (p. 133).

6. The guests at Mason's villa demonstrate the evil which pervades the place when they appear as "three little Oriental apes, mute, deaf, and blind to all evil" (p. 101).

Cass tells Peter that when he met Mason, "I was still in the dark, see— deaf, dumb, and blind" (p. 364). Cass means he fell under Mason's evil spell.

7. Mason rapes Francesca but does not love her. She represents another aspect of Mason's control over Cass.

Cass loves Francesca, has many opportunities to make love to her, but refrains. Cass says that when Mason raped Francesca he "was raping me" (p. 421).

8. Cass, the real murderer, gives himself up to Luigi, the policeman.

Luigi refuses to do justice under the law, but insists that Cass go free in order to suffer for his guilt.

9. Cass takes Luigi's advice and "considers the good" in himself rather than tormenting himself with his own evil. He recovers and decides to exist, to be.

Peter feels that he at last understands the events in Sambuco and that his life now has direction and meaning. Luciano di Lieto miraculously recovers from his accident with Peter.

The events of the second part of the narrative appear chaotically unrelated, joined only by the fact that they happen to the same man,

Cass Kinsolving. But Cass knows these events have meaning for him and his existential decision. He continues his life of art, but he no longer aspires to be a great painter. He returns to his native South to draw political cartoons. Thus art and politics merge; the aesthetic and the real are united, and it is in this union that Cass's soul finds its freedom.

Peter Leverett achieves freedom at the end of the novel, too, because he vicariously experiences the suffering Cass underwent in Sambuco. He finds the answers to the questions of "What am I doing? Where am I going?" The problem of identity is solved by dealing directly with the problem of evil. To survive in a world of evil and suffering first requires a recognition of that evil. We can expel evil by cutting it out, as Cass does by murdering Mason, but then we kill part of ourselves. Or, better, we can, as Luigi finally enables Cass to see, recognize the good in ourselves. Cass and Peter, who were once "mute, deaf, and blind" to evil, finally opened their eyes. It is in that clear vision of themselves, their discovery of identity, that they are able to exist. They are no longer "Oriental apes" (p. 101), but men.

A person's life is episodic, with events occuring chronologically, not logically. If an existential conclusion, such as Cass's decision, is to be based upon past experiences, it must depend upon a sorting out of experiences, an ordering of them into a comprehensible and discernible pattern from which to make reasonable judgments.

Cass's chaotic life finally makes sense when he and Peter reinforce each other's experiences. The two-narrator device controls the basic parallelism of the novel's structure, and Cass, as the more important narrator, takes the parallelism to more complex and profound experiences. The structural looseness which many critics have disparaged actually has a balanced parallelism which permits Cass to put his "house" in order.

In *Set This House on Fire*, Cass Kinsolving's subservience to Mason Flagg causes Cass to become the *famulus* of the Sambucan villa; in *The Confessions of Nat Turner*, Nat is a true house slave who seeks to satisfy his masters. When Cass can no longer suffer Mason's indignities, he erupts in a violent retaliation and murders Mason;

similarly, when Nat cannot bear to see his knowledge and sophistication abused by mindless whites, he leads other blacks on a retributive rampage. There are not many similarities between Styron's third and fourth novel except that thematically they both show an individual who seeks to assert himself in a repressive world. Captain Mannix of *The Long March* shares this theme with Cass and Nat.

Nat Turner must be several people at once. Raised as a privileged house slave, he learns to read, in violation of the law of the time. He absorbs table manners, art, music, literature, scripture; he enters a white world which mystifies the field hands. Too educated to be a simple laborer, Nat is unalterably a slave, an emasculated black man in a rigid white society. Sociologists would term Nat a "marginal man," having qualities of two cultures, belonging to or identifying with neither. Nat tells us, "Not for my soft pink palms—accustomed to the touch of silver and crystal, of pewter and glossy oiled oak—was the grimy feel of the hoe handle and the sickle and the ax. Not for me was the summer heat of the blacksmith shop or the steaming, gnat-mad fields of corn or the bone-cracking labor of the woods" (NT, p. 167). Further, he describes himself as "a pet, the darling, the little black jewel of Turner's Mill. Pampered, fondled, nudged, pinched, I was the household's spoiled child, a grinning elf who gazed at himself in mirrors, witlessly preoccupied with his own ability to charm" (NT, p. 169).

When Nat leaves the beneficent opulence of Marse Samuel and comes under the guidance of the Reverend Eppes—that he is a minister is significant—Nat experiences the labor and degradation he had so haughtily disdained when he was part of the mansion staff. He says, "It seemed to me that I had been plunged into a hallucination in which I had parted from all familiar existence and was suddenly transformed into a different living creature altogether— half-man, half-mule, exhausted and without speech, given over to dumb and reasonless toil from the hours before dawn until the dead of night" (NT, p. 234). Nat's ordered, comfortable life becomes a sieve of emotions through which flow his chances for a return to his former carefree life as Marse Samuel's noble experiment.

George Core writes convincingly that Styron gives Nat two voices—"the one is a received, standard nineteenth-century southern rhetoric . . . the other is plantation Negro dialect of the same period."[8] How Styron handles these two languages, making Nat a paradoxically unified dual narrator, provides much of the novel's richness and conveys its idea. Nat's "bilingual" utterances mark his progress toward his famous insurrection.

In Nat's first words in the novel the reader sees how he has learned to use his bilingual ability. In his prison cell awaiting execution, Nat speaks to a young white man: "'Marse Kitchen,' I said, 'I'm hungry. Please. I wonder if you could fetch me a little bite to eat. Kindly please, young mastah'" (NT, pp. 22–23). Then in the narrative and thus in private fashion to the reader, Nat confides, "Big talk will fetch you nothing but nigger talk might work" (NT, p. 23).

In another instance Nat and his companion Hark speak to Judge Jeremiah Cobb, whom Hark directs to the cider barrel for a drink: "'Red bar'l, massah. Dat's de bar'l fo' a gennleman, massah.' When the desire to play the obsequious coon came over him, Hark's voice became so plump and sweet that it was downright unctuous" (NT, p. 64). Nat becomes "seized by rage" over Hark's groveling manner, and, when Cobb is out of earshot, says to Hark: "'Black toadeater,' I said. 'Snivelin' black toadeatin' white man's bootlickin' scum! You, Hark! Black *scum*!'" (NT, p. 65). Nat then gives Hark a lecture in terms he can understand:

You just got to *learn*, man. You got to learn the difference. I don't mean you got to risk a beatin'. I don't mean you got to be uppity and smart. But they is some kind of limit. And you ain't a *man* when you act like that. You ain't a man, you is a fool! And you do this all the time, over and over again, with Travis and Miss Maria and Lord help you even with them two *kids*. You don't learn nothin'. You a fool! *As a dog returneth to his vomit so a fool returneth to his folly.* You a *fool*, Hark. How'm I goin' to teach you? (NT, p. 66)

Nat's emphasis on being a man illustrates the degree to which his education allows him to see clearly the condition of emasculation which slavery imposes. When Hark uses the language of a slave he admits to his servility and denies the fact of his own manhood. Nat's need to rebel fulfills his need to be a man.

Nat comes to see himself as an Old Testament prophet. As a young boy, his exposure to such ministers as the Reverend Eppes disillusions him about the nature of men who claim to have received the call to the ministry. While Nat basks in the adoring eyes of the Turner women, the Reverend Dr. Ballard, an Episcopal minister, visits Turner's Mill. Debating with Marse Samuel over the education of slaves, Dr. Ballard maintains, "I'll swear to you that if you show me a little darky whom you've taught to read the complete works of Julius Caesar forward and backward in the original Latin tongue, I will show you a darky who is *still* an animal with the brain of a human child that will never get wise nor learn honesty nor acquire any human ethics though that darky live to a ripe old age. A darky, gentlemen, is basically as unteachable as a chicken, and that is the simple fact of the matter" (pp. 164–165). Eppes and Ballard represent the abuses done in the name of religious righteousness, echoes of which occur in *Sophie's Choice.*

Nat's own call to the ministry appears more sincere than any of the white ministers' calls, though his guilt over his imagined sins prods him into seeking God's grace. His venial homosexual encounter with Willis fills him with feelings of impurity until he determines, "Difficult as it might become, I must bend every effort toward purity of mind and body so as to unloose my thoughts in the direction of theological studies and Christian preaching" (NT, p. 203).

Another minister, a Baptist at a camp meeting in Gates County, North Carolina, unwittingly provides Nat with the date for his insurrection. The preacher says his camp meeting will last, "From Friday the nineteenth of August until Tuesday, guess that's the twenty-third" (NT, p. 339). Nat says he "understood that the date of my great mission, emanating from those ecclesiastical lips, had just then been revealed to me as vividly as the fire of the Lord that showered down at the feet of Elijah" (NT, p. 339). That Nat's rebellion results from a complex association of servitude, sex, and religion indicates the psychological contrarieties which form the character. Religion and sex, in particular, commingle.

In one instance, Nat and the other slaves go to the Methodist church on Mission Sunday to hear the Reverend Richard Whitehead justify the institution of slavery by citing appropriate Scripture. Nat sits in the hot balcony with the other slaves and watches them "picking their noses and scratching, sweat streaming off their

[140]

black backs in shiny torrents, the lot of them stinking to heaven" (NT, p. 102). Then Nat describes the slaves as "a score of faces popeyed with black nigger credulity, jaws agape, delicious shudders of fright coursing through their bodies as they murmur soft *Amens*" (NT, p. 103). In the congregation is Margaret Whitehead, Richard's sister, for whom Nat feels mingled love, lust, and hatred. When the service draws to a close Nat looks at the slaves around him, then looks down and sees Margaret in the congregation below, then looks once more at the slaves. When he looks first at his fellow slaves, he says, "They seem to me as meaningless and as stupid as a barn full of mules, and I hate them one and all." But after seeing the angelic Margaret, "a radiance like daybreak on her serene young face," he sees the slaves with "a kind of wild, desperate love" (NT, p. 109), an ambivalence that reveals his marginality and his confusion of emotions.

Ironically, just as the Reverend Whitehead quotes Scripture as proof of the propriety of the slaves' bondage and the holy requirement of their subservience, so does Nat manipulate appropriate passages of Scripture to justify his insurrection against the whites.

Nat's dual narration takes us from standard English into the slave dialect as he preaches his first sermon to the slaves gathered at the market in Jerusalem, Virginia. He says, "My language was theirs, I spoke it as if it were a second tongue" (NT, p. 295). He tells the slaves: "White man make you sing an' dance, make you shuffle, do the buck-an'-wing, play 'Ole Zip Coon' on the banjo and the fiddle. . . . You is men! You is *men*, my dear brothers, look at yo' selves, look to yo' *pride!*" (NT, p. 297). Nat learns to use every weapon at his disposal; that he understands both languages and the power each can wield is a debt to his white masters that will be repaid in violence.

The narrative method of *The Confessions of Nat Turner* gives us Nat as confessor, who provides the overall view of the story of his insurrection, and Nat as participant, the leader in the slave rebellion. Nat the participant is further divided into Nat the refined, intelligent imitator of his white masters and Nat the slave-talking, fundamentalist preacher exhorting his flock to change from lambs into tigers. The dual narrative device effectively and appropriately conveys the marginality of the divided Nat. As in *Set This House on*

Fire, the narrative structure both reflects and sustains the novel's theme.

Styron's most recent novel, *Sophie's Choice*, brings together several elements from earlier works and further develops the intricate narrative pattern thus far observed. As in *Lie Down in Darkness*, the focus is on a troubled young woman who ends her life in suicide, the victim of a series of misfortunes. As in *The Long March*, war provides an unobtrusive but undeniably important backdrop against which is set the dramatic interplay of characters with whom we sympathize. As in *Set This House on Fire*, we see a relatively naive narrator who discovers some measure of eye-opening maturity by hearing someone else's story. And, too, as in *The Confessions of Nat Turner*, we witness the wholesale persecution of a people who seek merely to survive.

These shared themes—guilt, coming of age, the sometimes mindless military state, the acquisition of a sense of identity, and the essence of evil gone to unspeakable extremes—make *Sophie's Choice* emblematic of Styron's depiction of humanity. In a 1968 interview in *Le Figaro littéraire*, Styron says, "I admit now that my books revolve around the persecuted, the failure, the commoner, slaves, those who suffer, those who are on the bad side of the fence. It is sometimes hard to bear: the novelist assumes his characters, sharing their trials, takes their burdens for his own. It is very much for one man."

From Peyton Loftis to Sophie Zawistowska, Styron's central characters are entrapped by events from which they must deliver themselves. Peyton, unable to live with a man who refuses to be a father to her, commits suicide. Captain Mannix, unable to conform to the military system, becomes insubordinate and faces court-martial. Cass Kinsolving achieves a measure of resolution and freedom only after he murders Mason Flagg. Nat Turner, unable to live a marginal existence as an educated black man in a white world, brings death upon others and upon himself. Sophie's suicide with her lover-tormentor Nathan completes the circle begun by Peyton Loftis, both women's deaths resulting not from evil inherent in them, but from an external malevolence of a fiercely incisive nature.

Styron's use of his autobiographical persona Stingo to tell Sophie's story causes some discomfort among critics, and while I do not want to dwell on the similarities and differences which can be drawn between Styron the author and Stingo the character in Styron's novel, Styron most probably adopted such a narrative stance in order to convey a heightened verisimilitude and to unburden himself of what he perceives to be a longstanding debt in the name of humanity. The autobiographical elements do not artistically disrupt; they rather establish a consistent theme of guilt which incrementally shifts from Stingo to Sophie and back to Stingo as the narrative point of view changes.

Here is a passage illustrating an autobiographical reference and the establishment of Stingo's sense of guilt. Having reflected upon an inheritance he receives from the sale, long ago, of a family slave, Stingo says,

Years later I thought that if I had tithed a good part of my proceeds of Ariste's sale to the N.A.A.C.P. instead of keeping it, I might have shriven myself of my own guilt, besides being able to offer evidence that even as a young man I had enough concern for the plight of the Negro as to make a sacrifice. But in the end I'm rather glad I kept it. For these many years afterward, as accusations from black people became more cranky and insistent that as a writer—a lying writer at that—I had turned to my own profit and advantage the miseries of slavery, I succumbed to a kind of masochistic resignation. (SC, p. 32)

In the context of Styron's *The Confessions of Nat Turner* this passage receives added import.

We see other examples of Stingo's capacity to feel guilt, including a poignant episode in which he neglects his cancer-ridden mother. Stingo "speculated with dread on the notion that my abandonment that day had sent her into the long decline from which she never recovered. Guilt. Hateful guilt. Guilt, corrosive as brine. Like typhoid, one can harbor for a lifetime the toxin of guilt" (SC, p. 298). Similarly, in *Set This House on Fire*, Cass Kinsolving makes repeated references to his sense of guilt about what happened in Sambuco. And even though Mason Flagg seems to deserve retribution, Cass suffers further from that violent act. Mason's death, Cass tells Peter, increases "the guilt and shame half-smothering me . . . adding such a burden to the guilt and shame I already felt" (SHF, p. 361). Luigi, the policeman who knows Cass murdered Mason, sets Cass free—literally and symbolically—by saying, "Simply consider your guilt itself—your other guilt, the abominable guilt you have carried with you so long, this sinful guilt which has made you a drunkard, and caused you to wallow in your self-pity, and made you fail in your art. Consider this guilt which has poisoned you to your roots" (SHF, p. 475). Cass's guilt "poisons" him and Stingo bears the "toxin of guilt"; both characters need to be cleansed or, as Stingo says, "shriven."

In *Set This House on Fire*—the novel in Styron's canon most closely related thematically and structurally to *Sophie's Choice*—Peter says of Cass, "Deep down and for reasons I couldn't fathom, he had his own private riddles to solve and untangle. And just as I thought that he could clear up my oppressive mysteries, so he saw in me the key to his own" (SHF, p. 53). Similarly, in *Sophie's Choice*, Stingo comes to understand guilt in its "poisonous" extremity when he learns of Sophie's unbearably miserable life. The thematic bond between *Set This House on Fire* and *Sophie's Choice* is apparent from several views of both novels, but let me furnish a brief example. In one of the earliest moments in *Sophie's Choice*, when Sophie confides in Stingo, she tells him of her "very, very strong guilt" and of the ineffable sadness she feels upon hearing Handel's "I know that my Redeemer liveth" because, as she says in her uncertain English, "I know that my Redeemer don't live and my body will be destroyed by worms and my eyes will never, never again see God" (SC, pp. 87–88). Here Styron makes what is perhaps an unconscious connection to *Set This House on Fire*. That earlier novel, it will be remembered, bore a theme-setting epigraph from Dionne's "To the Earle of Carlile, and his Company, at Sion," which says, in part, "what gnawing of the worme is not a tickling, what torment is not a marriage bed to this damnation, to be secluded eternally, eternally, eternally, from the sight of God?"

Again and again in the novel we hear Sophie talking about her guilt—a guilt rooted primarily in the loss of her children and in her unsuccessful efforts to save them. We also see her demented lover Nathan alternating between tenderness and abuse, increasing her guilt by asking her how she could live through Auschwitz when so many others, particularly Jews such as himself, were gassed.

I want to suggest that the idea of *Sophie's Choice* is not to show us Sophie's guilt; she merely did the things she could do to try to survive. The idea of the novel is instead to show us Stingo's guilt. By extension, since Stingo reflects the naiveté of America, the novel further seeks to reveal the guilt of all who are indifferent to the slaughter of millions.

When Styron, the Reconstructed Virginian, tried to express a creative homiletic about slavery, he aroused a vicious backlash of resentment. His personal outrage over the Nazi death camps is a matter of record and is clear from the novel. How, then, should this outrage be expressed? Directly from a Jewish survivor? Certainly that is one way; but Styron's subtle narrative technique presents Sophie, a Catholic—do not forget that the word means universal—who tells her guilt to Stingo, a WASP from the American South. As Stingo hears of the significant days of her life—the day her husband and father are killed, the day she is arrested, the day she chooses which of her children will live—he remembers where he was and what he was doing. His life, vapid and carefree, mocks Sophie's suffering. Transcending even his lust for her, Stingo's guilt becomes the abiding theme of the novel. The suffering and guilt that Sophie experiences directly, Stingo experiences indirectly; her suffering, filtered through his own adolescent insouciance, magnifies his guilt. Having heard the story of her life, Stingo must make her a part of his life as well. Sophie's narration, a counterpoint to Stingo's first-person narrative, provides a balance between the lusty humor of Stingo and the unutterable despair of Sophie.

In all of his novels, Styron achieves description and dialogue, characterization and meaning through a complex narrative structure. In *Lie Down in Darkness* the shifting narrative focus allows a latitude that conveys through several viewpoints a powerful story of a doomed girl. In *The Long March* the narrative focus moves from Lieutenant Culver to Captain Mannix while retaining Lieutenant Culver's consciousness. In *Set This House on Fire* Peter Leverett surrenders the narration to Cass Kinsolving. In *The Confessions of Nat Turner*, Nat divides himself into narrator and actor with diction appropriate to each role. And in *Sophie's Choice* Stingo lets Sophie tell her story, but he, the survivor, will live with his new cathartic knowledge of true suffering, thus enabling him to understand his smothering guilt and wake to a new day of hope.

Notes

1. "Southern Occasions," *The Sewanee Review* (Spring 1980), p. xlix, calls *Lie Down in Darkness* the "best first novel ever written by a writer from the United States."

2. P. 9. I have used the following editions of Styron's novels: *Lie Down in Darkness* (New York, 1951); *The Long March* (New York, 1952); *Set This House on Fire* (New York, 1960); *The Confessions of Nat Turner* (New York, 1967); *Sophie's Choice* (New York, 1979). Pagination appears in the text.

3. With the exception of *The Long March*, all of Styron's novels use this discontinuous time structure. Peter Leverett seeks to discover the facts about the events of Mason Flagg's murder in Sambuco long after he returns to America; Nat Turner's insurrection is over when he delivers his confessions; and Sophie's Auschwitz experiences, including her agonizing choice, must be recounted to Stingo in America.

4. "MacArthur," *New York Review of Books*, 8 October 1964, p. 4.

5. Part of the unfinished novel *The Way of the Warrior* appeared as a short story in *Esquire* (September 1971) as "Marriott, the Marine." The excerpt quoted here is found on page 101 of that issue.

6. "The Symbolic March," in this volume.

7. *The Devil in the Fire* (New York, 1972), p. 212.

8. "*The Confessions of Nat Turner* and the Burden of the Past," in this volume.

JOHN O. LYONS

On *Lie Down in Darkness*

It is sad that Peyton Loftis cannot love another as herself. It is sad that her father Milton loves her to excess in compensation for the love that his wife Helen lavishes on their crippled and moronic daughter Maudie. And it is sad that Helen cocoons herself in the memory of her father's sterile world. But it is not tragic. Much of the commentary of the novel insists on its tragic mold, but I think that Styron depicts a world which is beneath tragedy. This is not just a matter of our age's being unsuited to tragedy, although many have insisted that man is now too diminished for Aristotelian pre-scriptions. It is more a matter of the emotional level on which the characters in *Lie Down in Darkness* experience their lives. Styron, through allusion and symbol, attempts to impose a weighty signifi-cance on these events, but the characters tend only to blubber un-der the burden of their lives. Even the admiring critics allow the work tragic dimension with one hand, and then take it away with the other. Jonathan Baumbach, for example, speaks of the novel as echoing the fall of the house of Atreus and sees Peyton as Electra, "(also Orestes)," but finally says that the work "may fail ulti-mately."[1] This is the hedging tone often taken with impressive first novels, but in the past two decades *Lie Down in Darkness* has re-ceived more plaudits than pummelings. It may seem uncavalier to raise a dissenting voice now, but Styron's reputation is secure and will survive my animadversions. I also believe that my comments may be instructive in the matters of the risks of ambitious first nov-els, Styron's style, and perhaps the novel of generational crisis in general.

The derivativeness of the novel is invariably commented upon. Even the casual reader notes traces of Wolfe, Joyce, and of course Faulkner. Baumbach calls this indebtedness "unassimilated,"[2] but David Galloway writes:

That Styron is able to succeed so well and so personally with techniques that are associated with Faulkner and Joyce is in part, of course, a tribute to his enormous skill as a writer, but in part, too, the result of historical accident; for Styron is not essentially an experimenter, and therefore does not run the dangers which Joyce and Faulkner often ran of becoming overwhelmed by technique itself. Character and story are of immense importance to Styron, and his intense fully drawn characters give the novel concentration and unity, just as such characters give substance to Faulkner's best work.[3]

Perhaps in this Galloway is also saying that Styron's indebtedness is unassimilated, for he could be saying that the techniques of Faulkner and Joyce are used as ornaments to the narrative. No matter how certain passages of the work are read, it seems to me that we not only read the passage for what it says, but we read it with an ear open to the way that the young Styron manipulates his literary enthusiasms. This is not the case when we read Joyce in which the spore of Ibsen, say, is virtually indetectable, or when we consider in turn Faulkner's use of Joycean fictional time in *Light in August* or the interior monologue in *As I Lay Dying*. When a writer has assimilated his sources he creates an artifact that stands—even in literature—almost independently of the referent. I think this is a case with Joyce and Faulkner, and even Wolfe, but in *Lie Down in Darkness* the fine writing proposes to make the reader see and feel the action as clearly as possible—but through its gauze.

There are many novels (I think of those of Hardy or Lawrence, for example) that have their roots deep in the journalistic tradition. In them the narrative is the end, and so the often plodding prose does not stand in the reader's way for it does not pretend to do other than narrate, and its infelicities make little difference. Styron has chosen to be a different kind of writer, and his way is a demanding one for he wishes to make us both see a scene and the process of seeing it. There are some extraordinary passages in the work that are brilliant in their subject and technique. When, for example, Milton Loftis is called to Charlottesville where Maudie has been hospitalized he finds Helen in the solarium trying to control her anguish.

Below, Halloween horns blew amid a garland of cowbells, a football sound, and the old invalid suddenly strangled behind them, horribly and obscenely, with a noise like the last gurgle of water sliding down a drain. They both turned; the man looked up, perfectly composed. He had a huge scimitar of a nose from which the skin had begun to peel away in flakes, eyes pressed so deep in his head that they seemed, to Loftis, like billiard balls sunk in their pockets. With a shock Loftis realized that the man had no hair on his body at all. And with the disregard for convention which is the privilege of lonely old people, he made no introduction but stared at the two of them from the caves of his skull and stretched a skinny, hairless arm toward the hills.

"Might as well be frank," he said. "I came up here to die. I came up to die near Mr. Jefferson. There he is—" he pointed toward Monticello— "there he is, up on the hill. On clear days you can see it from here. Yes sir, I sit here in the afternoon and look up at the hills and it takes a lot of the pain away to know you're near Mr. Jefferson when it comes time to shuffle off this mortal coil." His voice rose, thin, tremulous and old; Loftis saw a tiny flake of skin fall from his nose, but now there was a touch of color, too, on his cheeks, somehow rather dangerous. "I came all the way from the Eastern Shore to spend my last days here and Mr. Jefferson, if he was alive he'd appreciate it, I think. He was a gentleman. He was—." (LDD, pp. 191–192)

The passage does much with unusual economy, for the flaking man suggests not only the way Milton feels his life to be flaking away in what appears to be wholesome sunshine, but the lost human dignity of a Thomas Jefferson is soon to be echoed in Milton's memory of his own father's meeting with the angelic Lincoln. Yet even here the simile of the "billiard balls sunk in their pockets" is a little strained and self-conscious. Much too often the reader is invited to admire the process of narration, and this turns into a contemplation of Styron's sources. Early in the work we have a coal car making a "wild descending lisp of steel on steel," and a few pages later a locust making a sound, "shrill, ascending then, like something sliding up a wire." The metaphors are descriptive of the sounds, but one might wonder if language was carried fresh to the experience or if Styron had heard them through Whitman's "the carpenter dresses his plank, the tongue of his foreplane whistles its wild ascending lisp" from section 15 of "Song of Myself." The result of such as this is a kind of pastiche in which images are dragged in by the heels. When we get to Peyton's own narrative just before her suicide (which must be thought of as read over the omniscient author's shoulder) her style is astonishingly like that used by Styron in the rest of the work, except that it is liberally sprinkled with allusions to writers and painters she was exposed to at Sweet Briar and thick with images of clocks, drowning, and wingless birds.

It is the Faulknerian ghosts that are most often remarked in *Lie Down in Darkness*. Louise Gossett points out the likenesses between Peyton and Caddy Compson and Maudie and Benjy in *The Sound and the Fury*.[4] One could add the likeness between the use of the small dark juggler who amazes Maudie and Faulkner's mysterious dark vessels of magic and ritual, such as Sam Fathers or the unnamed father of Joe Christmas. But more important, I think, is Styron's use of Faulkner's rhetoric. He loves the Faulknerian negative prefix which gives the world he describes a dying Gothic beauty, beautiful because it is sepulchered and motionless. This can be seen in "by the dahlias light fell upon the figurine dresser lamps, upon those beribboned eighteenth-century lords and ladies frozen timeless and unaltered in some grave and mannered dance, the light and the heat and the silence in the house suddenly all becoming one, with form, it seemed, and with substance, inert and unyielding," or "yes, perhaps now it will be upturned, the chalice he has borne of whatever immeasurable self-love, not mean, yet not quite so strong as sin." In this passage the chalice and the circumstances under which it is borne suggest the chalice borne through a throng of foes by the romantic little boy in Joyce's "Araby." In the first passage there is also Faulkner's use of the suspended adjective, which can be seen again and again—"Milton who, fascinated, tries vainly." Styron also employs Faulkner's characters' sense of a doomed prescience, as in "committing himself, he somehow knew, with foreknowledge and awareness, as if to an exciting and perilous journey." "Was this part of the plan, the nightmare?" Milton thinks later. And as the old Packard hearse of the undertaker, Llewellan Casper, repeatedly breaks down under its burden (shades of *As I Lay Dying*—but updated) so that the characters can mull upon their past, the Faulknerian formulae are used to introduce their meditations. Carey Carr reflects, "She had come to him six years ago, he remembered, on a rainy Sunday night in October," which requires our being reminded ten pages later of the narrative situation: "Here Helen paused, Carey remembered, and had turned away." This process of remembering is refined: "But later he was able to reconstruct the scene in his mind." This all makes Carey Carr sound like a younger sibling of Gail Hightower, whom he also resembles in his narrative function as confessor. At the end of the work he is like that Tennessee furniture dealer (but without the humor) at the end of *Light in August:* "Then Carey saw something take place which he could never have predicted—much less, he later said to Adrienne, thought ever could happen at all, among civilized people of a certain maturity." Faulkner had read his Joyce and Conrad with care, but in his works the stylistic turns become part of a machine of his own design, and the reader properly takes delight in his delight at the invention. But here Styron seems to be riding another's bicycle, and although it is impressive how well he makes it work, it is still another's.

John Aldridge takes issue with Styron when he contends that the world of Port Warwick is a world that could be anywhere, that its events are universal.[5] Aldridge (perhaps because he is writing on southern literature) insists that the world is peculiarly southern with its militarism, its bourbon drinking, its strange combination of frigidity and sexuality, and its racial fears. Aldridge may be right, but Styron's world is certainly not Faulkner's—it is more suburban and upper middle class. This may be what makes the characters often sound distressingly like the soap operas they listen to on the radio or the Warner Brothers movies of domestic mayhem they see. Carey Carr even states his awareness of this likeness: "And after coffee and a talk full of stupid (he knew) reservations about a woman's right to happiness, all of which sounded vaguely like a soap opera." Milton has a similar thought: "And when Helen talked like this, just as they do in the movies, with such conviction." This may be a way in which Styron pillories—or at least characterizes—Helen. But most of the characters have this tendency. And, once more, this is possibly Styron's point—that the essential lovelessness of these people is a result of the watered gruel of their popular culture. The result, however, is to make the novel a series of case studies—of narcissism, self-indulgence, frigidity—so that the screeching is sad, but not tragic.[6]

[151]

When Styron's prose is on its own it tends to attribute thoughts in cadences that we have little reason to suspect the characters of possessing, and without the Faulknerian "he thought, or would have thought. . . ." Through the haze of champagne toward the end of the wedding reception, Milton reflects on his loss of Peyton:

He drinks. The bells toll on through his memory. Seawardborne, they strike reefs of recollection, shatter and recover, come back to smother his soul like something heavy and outrageous. *Time! Time!* he thinks. *My God has it finally come to this, do I finally know?* And lost in memory, thinking not of Peyton but of this final knowledge—this irrevocable loss of her—he recalls the incessant tolling bells. With a steady, brazen certainty they had struck off the passing hours, marched through the house night and day forever. It seems that he had heard them for the first time, though they are silent now, motionless in their yokes. The guests reel giddily before his eyes, on his arm the dentist's clutch is raw and painful. *Those bells,* he thinks, *those bells.* Why now did they return to afflict him with such despair? *Count off twenty years.* The light in the room deepens toward gold, sending sandy threads through Peyton's hair. (LDD, p. 289)

If he is as bleary at this point as we are led to believe, it is hard to imagine him assembling these echoes from *King Lear*, Poe, Meredith, and of course Faulkner, ending with the maudlin "sandy threads through Peyton's hair." But then the prose often gets out of hand and metaphors sometimes turn upon their heels and march the other way ("a knot of sailors on the deck—she could see them, far out, as tiny as pins—scattered away like a broken cluster of pearls"), or the blacks—who appear to carry some of the burden of hope in their belief—sound like something from "Amos 'n' Andy";

"He gonna make de 'Pearance now."
"He sho' is. I kin always tell."
"How come *you* know?"
"I kin always tell. When de elder goes in, it's almos' time."
"De band gotta come yet."
"Dat's right. Wonder where dey is?"

(LDD, p. 393)

Even stranger is this comment on La Ruth, after she has given an astute reply to the Marse. Milton reflects, "If you were to peel back her skull, he thought, you'd find no convolutions at all on the brain, only a round, thoughtless, shiny sphere." From the passage it would seem that Styron is not trying to characterize Milton or that there is any sort of irony intended. Or could it possibly be that La Ruth is a black Maudie?

In his *Paris Review* interview Styron says that the greatest problem he had with *Lie Down in Darkness* was in handling "the progression of time."[7] He also says, of his indebtedness to Faulkner, that "I'm all for the complexity of Faulkner, but not for the confusion."[8] This novel tries very sincerely to combine the sense of the few hours that it takes to convey the body of Peyton from the train station to the cemetery with the memories of Milton, Helen, Dolly, and Carey which review the past that led to this day. Behind this scheme are the models of *As I Lay Dying* and *Ulysses*—and perhaps especially the "Hades" section of *Ulysses*. The chronology is very important to the novel if Styron is to keep the events and the motives clear to the reader, but he also wishes to present that chronology through the tormented jumble of the present moment. Styron establishes his "real" world through his allusions to historical events and people, and this creates a base on which the experiences and emotions of his characters play a kind of obbligato. This use of public events would seem to be mainly indebted to Joyce; the use of family history to Faulkner.

Yet Styron offers the reader a few quandaries where the dates are concerned. In one passage Helen has a memory of a visit to her brother Edward in Pennsylvania. She is twenty-four, which would place the scene in 1922 as Helen was born about 1898.[9] In this scene Maudie is talking—precociously for someone with her defects—as she appears to have been born just about this time, and Peyton is going for a walk with her uncle even though she wasn't born until 31 August 1923. This we know because she is nine the spring of 1933, and her sixteenth birthday is 31 August 1939, "the day before the war began." But here the trouble with dates deepens. Milton has a letter from Peyton which he carries at the funeral and which begins, "Dearest Bunny, today I was 22." But Peyton's twenty-second birthday would be on 31 August 1945, and her suicide was on 7 August, the day after the atomic bombing of Hiroshima, and so she would have been dead for three weeks. On this day when we have Peyton's account of her life in New York she hears someone speak of Nagasaki—someone who must know what only the inner circle of the Pentagon knows, for Nagasaki was not bombed until 9 August. There is also a problem about what happened between these two significant dates. Peyton plunges naked from the washroom of a Harlem loft on 7 August. Since her body is unclaimed, she is buried in Potter's Field on Hart Island until she is claimed by Harry Miller, her estranged husband. The body is then shipped by train to Port Warwick for burial, but there is still enough time for it to show up there for the bombing of Nagasaki two days later on 9 August. Such matters, I think, rarely move so swiftly, but it appears that Styron wishes to sacrifice chronology for dramatic impact and larger significance.

His major purpose would appear to be to document the spiritual and emotional malaise of the Loftis family in these generations. He often suggests that theirs is a universal situation, but the characters themselves see their predicament as unique to the time and place and so they look to some past time as a time of happiness. For Helen it is a memory of her girlhood at Fort Myer where her stern and patriotic father, mounted on horse back, reviewed his troops. For Milton it is also his youth, thirty years ago, which he remembers as "a finer, more tranquil age." For him, however, it is a mixed memory, for he hates his father who dominated that age, who spoiled him and favored him with orotund homilies on prudence. One condemnation of this age comes from Milton's father as a result of meeting, when a little boy, Lincoln in Richmond shortly before the assassination.[10] It was as "if he had looked into the eyes of Christ, like he said: the last angel, the last great man who ever walked on earth." He adds that "we are a race of toads," and when Dolly accuses him of bitterness he says that he is not bitter, but that "we have lost our lovewords." Such passages appear to be taken seriously by the author as well as the characters, without that tinge of irony when, for example, Faulkner writes of the antebellum South or Joyce has Bloom ask himself if he were happier in former days. And I gather that we are to take seriously the sodden Weltschmerz of an old grad at Charlottesville who asks Milton, "I guess this generation's just lost the goddam Cavalier spirit don't you?"

It is in Peyton's relationship to her father and mother that the issues of what I have called the novel of generational crisis must rest. In the nineteenth century (I have in mind the way in which this subject is treated by Balzac or Turgenev) the youth are often hotheaded, mistaken, and invariably selfish, but there is an impressive vigor about their ideals even when these are nihilistic. This is not the case with Peyton. She seems so completely wrapped up in herself that she is more a case study than an adequate vessel of the larger issues. In New York she is asked flippantly if her psychiatrist said she was "dangerously abstracted or . . . psychogenically incapable of sexual fidelity." Either way the prospects are dim for her being a clear mirror of her age. If she is dangerously abstracted she might serve as an aloof commentator on the events of the novel and make the author's intent clearer, but this she does not do. If her problem is a Messalina complex which might reflect the gnawing hungers of the time this might serve, but Styron more often presents us with images of her flawless beauty than her unsatisfied lasciviousness. Her husband tells her that she is "absolutely incapable of love," that she "just can't love," and all the evidence indicates he is right. In these scenes on her last day she sounds dangerously like her mother, although Helen's syntax is more believable: "Then, Harry, I would say, why are you like this to me? Not for your defection so small, really, did I do my petty vengeance, but just because always you've failed to understand. Me." This is petty narcissism given the circumstances so that when she leaps to her death it is not our ills she is curing—the ravages of Time, the Bomb, and so forth—it is her own ills.

We are still offered some light in this gloom. First there is the character of Harry Miller. It appears to be in his favor that he is polite, his parents are dead, he is Jewish, he fought in Spain, and he is a painter who feels he has something to express. But (and here most of the critics agree) we are shown too little of him and, one could add, he turns the final deaf ear to Peyton in her distress.[11] Another reason for optimism might be found in the placid wisdom of Maudie who loves everyone in her dependence and refuses to be cast down although a cripple and prisoned in her child's mind. Helen insists that Maudie knows more than all of them, and this

[155]

knowledge seems to be how to love selflessly. Helen reflects that "strange things make her happy," and this is true, but Helen herself is as mad as a hatter and an odd person to be allowed this testimony since Maudie cannot testify for herself.[12] The third glimmer of hope often remarked is the recurring figure of Daddy Faith (probably modeled on Daddy Grace), the black Baltimore revivalist who comes to Port Warwick every August to save lost souls. His gathering followers force the hearse to detour at one point, and in the epilogue there is a full account of a sunlit baptismal service which contrasts with the Gothic squalls that have gone before. There is certainly an impressive contrast here between the hysteria of the crypt and that by the water's edge, but the intellectual leap from an account of a sick white society to a wholesome black one is difficult. Perhaps the faith of these simple souls has to be more fully documented throughout the novel. But even if it were it still might not successfully imply resurrection for Peyton, for the contrasts between her life and that of the white gowned at the water's edge is remarkable. Cooper Mackin's comments on the novel end with the significance of the title from Sir Thomas Browne and the lines from Henry Vaughan's "they are all gone into the world of light" which Peyton trades with Dr. Holcomb at the wedding reception.[13] His point is that both passages emphasize that there is resurrection "one short sleep past," and he suggests that this is what we are to expect for Peyton. This could well have been Styron's intent, but the passages (especially that from Vaughan) are oddly imported. And if this is the intent I am still troubled by the wingless birds ("dodos and penguins and cassowaries, ostriches," "the emus and dodos and ostriches and moas") in Peyton's final meditations. All of this makes it difficult to see the epilogue implying resurrection for Peyton.

But the main difficulty with *Lie Down in Darkness* is in the style. This has been much lauded and it is certainly a remarkable performance for a writer of twenty-six, but I think that it tends to obscure where it proposes to make clear. This is probably the most awesome trap that first novelists encounter, for their style is almost of necessity gleaned from their literary enthusiasms, and when their matter runs counter to the style, very difficult choices must be made. When the work is ambitious—in style and subject—those choices are virtually impossible.

[156]

Notes

1. Jonathan Baumbach, *The Landscape of Nightmare* (New York, 1965), pp. 130, 133. Ihab H. Hassan calls the novel "a vision of tragic ambiguities and ironic necessities, of human experience spanning the abyss," but ends his essay saying that "the reader's mind is purified without recourse to a genuinely tragic catharsis." "Encounter with Necessity," in *On Contemporary Literature*, ed. Richard Kostelanetz (New York, 1964), pp. 603, 606.

2. Baumbach, p. 123.

3. David D. Galloway, *The Absurd Hero in American Fiction* (Austin, Tex., 1966), p. 54.

4. Louise Y. Gossett, *Violence in Recent Southern Fiction* (Durham, N.C., 1965), p. 126.

5. John Aldridge, *In Search of Heresy* (New York, 1956), p. 146.

6. Hassan writes, "For Peyton's darkness, however 'clinical' it may seem—and there is no doubt that it is more dramatic than clinical—must still illumine the universal urge of human beings to clutch some impossible idea of eternal childhood or innocence, must illumine and expiate that urge" (p. 599). Here I do not agree and feel that Hassan himself uses *must* in a very delicate way.

7. Peter Matthiessen and George Plimpton, eds., "William Styron," in *Writers at Work: The Paris Review Interviews* (New York, 1958), p. 280.

8. Matthiessen and Plimpton, p. 275.

9. Helen might have been born about 1900, which would place the scene in 1924, but this still creates problems.

10. Lincoln visited the ravaged Richmond 4–5 April 1865.

11. Galloway, p. 61, for example.

12. On Maudie see Cooper R. Mackin, *William Styron*, Southern Writers Series (Austin, Tex., 1969), pp. 6–9.

13. Mackin, p. 11.

JAN B. GORDON

Permutations of Death: A Reading of *Lie Down in Darkness*

> Riding down to Port Warwick from Richmond, the train begins to pick up speed on the outskirts of the city, past the tobacco factories with their ever-present haze of acrid, sweetish dust and past the rows of uniformly brown clapboard houses which stretch down the hilly streets for miles.   (LDD, p. 9)

> The train came on with a clatter, shading the trestle, and its whistle went off full-blast in a spreading plume of steam. "Yeah! Yeah!" Another blast from the whistle, a roar, a gigantic sound; and it seemed to soar into the dusk beyond and above them forever, with a noise, perhaps, like the clatter of the opening of everlasting gates and doors—passed swiftly on—toward Richmond, the North, the oncoming night.   (LDD, p. 400)

Like the Tidewater which serves as its setting, the predominant movement of William Styron's *Lie Down in Darkness* is the slow rhythm of sedimentation and withdrawal. If the novel's first paragraph places the reader aboard a train homeward bound from "Columbus or Detroit or wherever," its final page places the potential passenger back aboard an outbound train highballing it for the night of the eternal snow, the North. The excursion period which separates the two segments of this unique round trip is in effect the novel itself. The reader is a stranger, trapped between inbound and outbound trips in a novel that moves almost imperceptibly when it moves at all. That is to say that the narrative serves to fill in those interstices of character and motive rather than to develop a plot. It is not that Styron's novel is written backward, as is say, *Wuthering Heights* or Faulkner's *Absalom! Absalom!* where we know the events of the novel and read in order to discover causes and motives, but rather that the action seems to eddy. *Lie Down in Darkness* circles about Peyton's funeral, accumulating details of fragmented lives

[158]

rather than giving us a fragmented picture of lives which we must piece together through narrative disjunction.

All of this is to say that the action of the novel is structurally analogous to those estuaries that dot the coastline north of Cape Hatteras; neither all sea, nor all river, nor all land, but a curious hybrid geography. Its stillness is perhaps the closest one might come to that other cycle of growth and decay—the great Dismal Swamp which flanks the Tidewater on the lee side of the coast. That bit of primeval America is, of course, the place where life and death meet insofar as it is an arena where the processes of decay yield to new energy. The swampland south of Port Warwick, like the worship of the black revivalist, Daddy Faith, is an intersection of growth and decay where denizens on the verge of extinction are making a last stand of sorts, and whose space remains almost impenetrable. The epigraph to the novel is drawn from Sir Thomas Browne's *Urn Burial:*

And since death must be the Lucina of life, and even Pagans could doubt, whether thus to live were to die; since our longest sun sets at right descensions, and makes but winter arches, and therefore it cannot be long before we lie down in darkness and have our light in ashes; since the brother of death daily haunts us with dying mementos, and time that grows old in itself, bids us hope no long duration;—diuturnity is a dream and folly of expectation.[1]

Like Keats's urn later, Browne's is a repository where the relationship between a civilization's ruins and its ceremonies are the occasion for a discourse upon the nature of immortality. Among the questions posed by Browne's inquiry upon the discovery and disinterment of the ancient graves (which parallels the exhuming of Peyton's body from Potter's Field in *Lie Down in Darkness*), is the nature of death and immortality. And Styron's novel really explores the same themes, notably the relationship between death-in-life and life-in-death in a civilization which is itself trapped between the two, the cavalier coast of a Virginia where all that remains of the life of southern aristocracy are the empty forms of a way of life, perhaps best symbolized in the label from the Jack Daniels bottle that slips off into Milton Loftis's perspiring palms.

One of the primary objections raised over the years by critics of Styron's achievement is the derivative nature of his style and the-

matic interests. Inevitably, comparisons with Faulkner or Eudora
Welty or Robert Penn Warren are used to the detriment of Styron's
reputation. Yet, in the largest sense, Styron is a "second generation"
southern writer whose stylistic interests and thematic concerns set
him apart from the mainstream of southern fiction. In the first
place, Styron does not imagine himself as a member of some larger
agrarian brotherhood, but rather as part of a different world:

> Much of the power of a writer like Faulkner, for instance, or Flannery
> O'Connor, derived from their ability to see the bizarre connotations of this
> *difference* of the South, to perceive the ironies and contradictions involved
> when people inheriting so directly the manners and mores of a nineteenth-
> century feudal, agrarian society collided head-on with the necessities of an
> industrial civilization. . . . Yet now as this difference is erased and the con-
> tradictions smoothed out, now that the South to everyone's amazement
> proves to accommodate itself to racial integration far more gracefully than
> the North . . . now that the difference has gone, and no one save a few
> antiquarians and scholars and readers of Faulkner can know what the Old
> South really was; now, in short, as the South is truly absorbed into the
> substance of the rest of the nation, I think that Southern writing, if it
> doesn't fade away altogether, will certainly no longer correspond to any-
> thing we recall from its illustrious past. Possibly the works of Walker
> Percy give a clue.[2]

Interestingly, Styron seems to believe that the South is in the process of being "absorbed"—that is losing its separate sense of identity. Somewhat later, in the same interview, he speaks of southern
writing having entered a "grey" area, almost as if, like the "emerging majority," the nation would take its strength from those border
kingdoms, geographic and psychic. William Styron does not create
a separate fictional region, like Faulkner's Yoknapatawpha or Conrad's Costaguana, but rather makes use of the local geography as it
is. There is no effort to recapture as fictional space something that
has been lost, and the corollary to such an attempt at reclamation,
the pervasive myth of the fall of the Old South, is seldom a part of
his imagination. In short, Styron's South deserves special attention
precisely because it is so radically different from what we might expect: the lawyer has replaced the farmer; shopping in Washington,
D.C., is a habit among the respectable middle class and the stern
Calvinism that was part of the land's curse in earlier southern writing has been relaxed into the mannered and more socially accept-

able Episcopalian mutterings of Carey. It is a world different in both kind and degree from that of all, save perhaps the late Faulkner. It is the Faulkner of *The Reivers* with its wild ride to a Memphis racetrack that is closest to the emotions of *Lie Down in Darkness*, emotions that are part of a newer urban South where some ancient curse upon the land is replaced by some similarly ill-defined neurosis which afflicts the collective psyche.

A large part of the final one-third of *Lie Down in Darkness* is set in New York where Peyton lives with her husband, Harry Miller, a Jewish painter with somewhat radical politics. Although Miller is not a well-drawn character, the reason for his sketchiness is clearly related to the very functional role that he plays in the novel. He is always on the periphery of a group of metropolitan intellectuals and pseudointellectuals who engage each other with all the fads: orgone boxes, oriental mysticism, and such neohumanistic bombast as the generalization, "the evil in man is both beautiful and preordained." This realm is one of almost incredible pretense, where a psychiatrist named Dr. Irving Strassman can tell Peyton she is "hopelessly abstracted" without recognizing that in the mere use of such phrases he is more abstracted than she. Her final soliloquy, as a matter of fact, is filled not with abstractions, but with the most concrete memories of her childhood in Virginia: the sea gulls, picking flowers, and the sound of guns—all of which we have read about earlier in the novel. But the conversations at Albert Berger's house *are* hopelessly abstracted and the names that swallow up Peyton provide some insight into the nature of the allegory that Styron has constructed: Gould, Fischer, Liebowitz, Freeman. In a sense, her journey north and into the darkness, like that of the train at the conclusion of *Lie Down in Darkness*, is the saga of the South being absorbed into the life of the growing urban areas of the country, complete with the conversations of spoiled Jewish intellectuals. All that is missing from Berger's gathering, alas, is poor Portnoy, and he lurks, fictionally at least, just around the corner. Several years ago, Norman Mailer severely criticized Styron as one of those "uncircumcised dogs" whose values were antithetical to the "arrival" of Jewish fiction in the early sixties. And more than once, Styron has been accused of antisemitism in his fiction and in his public pronouncements. Yet, Miller is drawn with considerable sympathy, and Peyton is surely as spoiled by her father as the various Jews at Berger's apartment have been spoiled by their mothers. The tragic last pages of *Lie Down in Darkness* are much more complicated than such easy interpretations will allow. Surely, these last pages are an allegory of southern fiction in the process of being supplanted by other values, of the shift of a fictional generation. If the last chapter ends with the baptismal party of the black revivalist, Daddy Faith, the penultimate section concludes with a glimpse of Harry Miller's painting, showing a rabbi with upraised arms and eyes walking through a desolated city. The IRT local runs beside one and the Port Warwick–Richmond express runs beside the other, but both represent some attempt at life triumphing over death. Thus each image is undoubtedly symbolic of various fictions common to their respective regions: the dying faith of the Old South and the dying martyrdom of the urban rabbi who must cross a desolated landscape. Perhaps *Lie Down in Darkness* will someday be read not as the last gasp of southern fiction, but rather as a self-reflexive commentary upon the history of the nation as well as the history of her fiction.

Perhaps the one feature, however, above all, that sets William Styron apart from the mainstream of twentieth-century southern writing is his emphasis upon *nostalgia* as opposed to *memory*. Were one to attempt to locate a common denominator in the development of an American literature, the pervasive influence of memory manifested as some ancestral curse would loom large. Almost inevitably some sin, usually sexual in nature, exerts an influence upon later generations as they struggle to do penance for acts which now exist only as a part of history. Hawthorne's *The House of the Seven Gables*, Ahab's wound in *Moby Dick*, the visit of those ghosts upon a governess in James's *The Turn of the Screw*, the mixture of incest and miscegenation in Faulkner's *The Sound and the Fury*—all share in the American penchant for a literature of atonement. It is perhaps what we might expect from a nation of vagabonds who successfully mounted a rebellion against their colonial master long before the rest of the children fled the imperial household in the nineteenth century. Perhaps a civilization which sees itself as the naughty child invents a sin for which it might legitimately feel guilty. But if the typical orphan of nineteenth-century British fiction felt himself duty bound at some point to reclaim the ancestral family estate (whose names—*Mansfield Park*, *Wuthering Heights*, *Bleak House*, and *Howard's End*—provide the titles for major Victorian novels), his American counterpart seems to revel in his outcast state. Rather than the pattern of departure and return which J. Hillis Miller sees as a central structural motif of the nineteenth-century British novel,[3] the American rogue seems intent upon authenticating his illegitimacy a la Huck Finn. Instead of affirming legitimacy by acknowledging his inheritance (and thereby being cut into all those disputed wills that pervade deathbed scenes in Victorian fiction), the outlaw of American fiction typically becomes a combination explorer, confidence man, and purveyor of folk wisdom. He creates his own space rather than returning to that of his father. But memory always haunts him, as if somehow civilization were indistinguishable from history. It is when history itself is called into question that memory is replaced by nostalgia. Although the precise relationship between the two is often difficult to establish, memory is generally a function of our ability to recapture either traumatic or highly pleasurable moments. By contrast nostalgia tends to screen those traumatic aspects of memory in favor of an aestheticization which takes a segment of time and spatializes it, so that say, the late fifties return on our "rock" radio stations as "greaser days." As its root would suggest, nostalgia is a collective experience—an attempt, often sentimental, by a civilization to write its own history.

Unlike most southern fiction where memory is often represented as the product of some elder white or black sage/prophet, there are few such old people with clairvoyance in *Lie Down in Darkness*. And the absence of such a figure tells us something. Rather than being trapped in its own unique history, the country surrounding Port Warwick is forever unable to recapture any part of its collective past, except as nostalgia. Lyrics from songs popular at the time recur throughout the novel: "Try Me One More Time," "Saturday Night (Is the Loneliest Night in the Week)," and "Deep Purple." These are all tunes that were popular during and immediately after the Second World War, but, more importantly, they are all songs whose lyrics speak to a certain decadence of romance, of a desire to recapture the golden age of love: "'Member, Helen? 'Member how we used to drive up to Connellsville in the summer? Marion and Eddie's? 'Member the time when Peyton almost got stung by the bees?" We have entered a realm once removed from memory through the vehicle of self-consciousness. As part of the attempt to recapture an idyll (perhaps something like the fateful summer of '42?), these words participate in the nostalgia that they attempt to describe. Although *Lie Down in Darkness* was first published in 1951, the events of the novel are set back six years to August 1945, since the newspaper headlines during Peyton's last days read of Hiroshima and of the hopes for a quick truce. Then six years before 1945, in August 1939, Milton Loftis and his mistress, Dolly Bonner, had first made love during the celebration surrounding Peyton's sixteenth birthday. That, we also know to have been "to call back ancient history . . . the day before the war began." On that day, there was, we are told, "talk about a Corridor." This chronological scheme which seems always to involve intervals of six years accomplishes something else, notably a synchrony between the human events and international circumstance. What is happening among the nations of the world parallels the events that afflict the Loftis family. It would seem that Styron, like George Eliot in *Middlemarch*, has set his novel back as a way of talking about disjunction in time. The people who walk through the pages of *Lie Down in Darkness* are literally dispossessed; like the orphans of Victorian fiction, they have no knowledge of their origins. There is a certain organic rhythm that links Peyton's death with the deaths of thousands of Japanese and Milton's attempts at a truce with his estranged wife to the global effort to seek peace between the Allies and the Axis powers. Yet, somehow, it all seems too late for that. In this novel, history is never determined a priori by blood lines, nor is it a part of some rigid Calvinistic eschatology, but rather history is made by humans and human interaction. There is little suggestion of regional uniqueness in *Lie Down in Darkness*, but rather the complaint of Mrs. La Farge that "the international Jewish bankers are conspiring to send my Charlie into war" floats above a Virginia cocktail party much as it floated around the earth on the eve of

World War II. The mysterious "corridor" could as easily apply to the strip of Tidewater as to the devastated finger of Poland. The struggle between colonial-suburban Hellenism and urban Hebraism is seen as part of the systoles and diastoles of the civilization. It impacts the largest kingdom as well as the smallest person, this collective guilt which prompts Peyton to marry Harry Miller. And for that reason, *Lie Down in Darkness* is a great panoramic novel of the order of, though finally a lesser achievement than, say *Middlemarch* or *War and Peace*.

Yet, because they make their own history, none of the figures of Styron's novel can ever rise above these events. The "world" of Styron's novel is a world where no resolution is possible, and it must be read with that proviso in mind. The question that the novel poses on 9 August 1945, the day of Peyton's funeral, is no less than, "How did we get here?" It is a question to be applied to the Loftises, Dolly Bonner, the blacks of the household, and to a nation— all of which find themselves looking death in the face after a long struggle. It may also represent, at least allegorically, the history of the American novel looking at its own death. Throughout the sixties, critics like Leslie Fiedler and Richard Poirier were speaking of the demise of the "traditional" American novel with its various existential outlaws: Dimmesdale, Ahab, Huckleberry Finn, and the Snopeses. Although the argument varied in its details, there was a sort of Turner Thesis applied to the development of our fiction: as the frontier filled, there was simply no more new territory to which one might "light out," and the image of the populist rogue, that combination "Confidence-Man" and "Rifleman," that has permeated our literature and our politics was transformed. With the advent of "beat" fiction in the late fifties and sixties, the "road" of Jack Kerouac and the circuitous path of Richard Fariña have led neither into the future nor the past, but only into a world that lives in an eternal present. Lacking both history and prophecy, the hero of this new fiction quickly became the perpetrator of "instant history," the persona of a new naturalism who marched with the *Armies of the Night*. If the "old" American novel was dominated by the individual of strong will, the new fictional antihero tended to be among the "beautiful losers" tossed about by events whose causality was in-

[165]

determinate. Although not the outcast from society, these urban dwellers felt alienated from themselves, and any terror stemmed not from the unknown and the unsettled, but rather from some mirror image: the encounter with an alternative self. History, when it appears at all as an influence, is invariably a psychologized history, so that vague guilt tends to be a substitute for a definable evil that has been watered by relativism. Peyton's plight in *Lie Down in Darkness* is not unlike the plight of the American novel in the fifties and sixties: having depleted her existential spaces, she becomes unable to complete any act save that of a morbid fascination upon her own genesis.

Not so of Helen Loftis. Whatever else we might say of her, a fixation upon the past is her most noticeable trait. Combined with a sense of languor and infirmity, she is the modern day descendant of Dickens's Miss Havisham whose every effort is part of some colossal attempt to return to a prior state of which the reader is only dimly aware:

Now she did something that she had done many times before. She pulled the skin of her face taut over the cheekbones so that the web of lines and wrinkles vanished as if it had been touched by a miraculous and restorative wand; squinting convergently into the glass, she watched the foolish and lovely change: transfigured, she saw smooth skin as glassy white as the petal of gardenia, lips which seemed but sixteen or twenty, and as unblemished by any trouble as those she had held up to another mirror thirty years before, whispering "Dearest" to an invisible and quite imaginary lover. (LDD, p. 24)

Her entire life has had the same psychic dimension as that exhibited in the revelatory scene during which we first meet her. Between glances at the morning paper announcing the possibility of a truce with the Japanese, she looks in the mirror at a face artificially, albeit magically, transformed. Her husband, Milton, has already telephoned the paper requesting that the announcement of Peyton's suicide be deleted. In both of her glances then, Helen faces a profound absence. It is almost as if one could successfully transform that which has happened into that which has not simply by living a lie. The look into the mirror involves the refusal to accept the scandal of time, and the reading of the newspaper involves a similar doctoring of events to avoid a more social scandal. Both involve the need for repair by excision, and more than once in the novel, Helen Loftis expresses the desire to actually live the death that has been her existence for a quarter century:

"Don't try," she said sighing. "Oh, it's so hot!" And thought, *Indeed if I consider Charlottesville that will be all. Which is worse, past or future? Neither. I will fold up my mind like a leaf and drift on this stream over the brink.* (LDD, p. 149)

This desire to fold oneself up is, stated another way, a wish for a life that is all boundary, that walls oneself up behind identifiable barriers. And that condition is perilously close to the nothingness of death. As R. D. Laing has suggested in his astute examination of the defensive personality, *The Divided Self*, such individuals come to imagine themselves as being disconnected, quite literally out of touch. From another perspective, they are all outer wall or surface which implies that the interior or "inner" self is all emptiness, a word which occurs with increasing frequency as we read through *Lie Down in Darkness*. We inevitably see Helen alone within some confined existential space. Neither the look in the mirror nor the cursory reading of carefully edited news is a look outside the self. For most of the novel, Helen Loftis's life alternates between the bedroom where she weeps herself to sleep under the influence of tranquilizers and another interior chamber, that of the boozy country club where everyday is an Old Forester kind of day. The bright glare of a funereal sun on the day of Peyton's last return home to Port Warwick blinds her. Helen's light, when it does exist at all, is always reflected or refracted—the light of the mirror, the muted Japanese lanterns at the country club, the twilight cocktail parties, or the wild summer moon out of whose dim glare she arrives at the home of the Reverend Carr to seek marital advice.

In every way Helen Loftis leads a derivative existence; having little sense of her own selfhood, she attempts to contain it by erecting barriers that compartmentalize both her physical being and her soul while creating a similar distinction between self and other: "'Just a minute, Milton. I'm not finished. Let me tell you, too. Let me tell you. I know what sin is,' she repeated, and the word *sin* was like the cold edge of a blade sunk deep somewhere in his body. 'I do. I do. In knowing that I'll always be superior to you.'" For Helen

[167]

Loftis, knowledge is the equivalent of mental property insofar as it is to be hoarded. As her Virginia ancestors imagined a relationship between the ownership of land and personal salvation, so she believes that her knowledge of sin places her just outside the domain of the devil. For her, all knowledge of sin in the world represents a bit of the soul's space reclaimed from the Kingdom of Death. But Helen's speech reveals as much about her as her Protestant fundamentalism, for hers is the language of an incredible emptiness for which the personal pronouns *I* and *me* provide the fiction of a center. Actually, in the ensuing discussions with her pastor, the reader discovers that Helen Loftis really has very little knowledge of sin. It is truly one of those "hopeless abstractions" of which Peyton is later diagnosed by Dr. Strassman. Helen's is virtually a satellite existence; forever on the periphery, always attempting to claim some space of her own, she manipulates and is in turn manipulated by others. Their daughter, Peyton, can use her body to manipulate her father into granting whatever she wants. Helen Loftis's temptation, then, is a representation of Milton's rejection of her body, internalized as the self-hatred of her own body, and then reprojected (mirrored) as envy upon her daughter's relationship with her husband. The love triangle involving Dolly Bonner is no different from the triangle which exists in her own family; two women vie for the love of a single man.

If Helen Loftis's words in *Lie Down in Darkness* are only barely memorable, Milton Loftis speaks far too much. His excessive verbosity is a complement to her weary silence. If her lie is the assumption of knowledge where none exists in order that the self might thereby be more effectively buttressed ("her only hope . . . was to supply her soul each day with new attitudes, new bulwarks"), Milton blurs the boundaries between self and other by the alcoholic's diffusion of being. In his physical appearance, spreading middle age means that all of those limits to being are exceeded, and the proper metaphor for such a condition is the hangover:

At the age of fifty he was beginning to discover, with a sense of panic, that his whole life had been in the nature of a hangover, with faintly unpleasant pleasures being atoned for by the dull alleviated pain of guilt. Had he the solace of knowing that he was an alcoholic, things would have been brighter, because he had read somewhere that alcoholism was a disease, but he was not, he assured himself, alcoholic, only self-indulgent, and his disease, whatever it was, resided in shadier corners of his soul—where decisions were reached not through reason but by rationalization and where a thin membranous growth of selfishness always seemed to prevent his decent motives from becoming happy actions. (LDD, p. 153)

Milton Loftis had been told by his cavalier father that love and passion have an inverse relationship, one with the other. As the flames of passion are extinguished by the sands of time, love ripens and endures. It is the everlasting light that matters rather than the witches' bonfire: "*My son, never let passion be a guide. Nurture hope like a flower in the most barren ground of trouble. If love has fed the flame of your brightest imaginings, then passion will perish in that flame and only love endure.*" Of course, such a vision is merely another way of saying that love is the reward for having conquered passion, legitimizing a frightening double standard. Milton Loftis, having lost one, seeks the other in Dolly Bonner. His relationship to his mistress is symbolically represented by the peculiar syntax that is vehicle for the expression of that "love." The use of the spider web and of the word *entanglement* is a perfect representation of Milton Loftis's speech:

The eccentric manner of twisting words into grotesque parodies of themselves, his supplications—"Oh, God" or "Oh, Jesus" when something went wrong—uttered with such profound and comical intensity to the heavens; and his own particular wit, the subtleties of which she often did not get: to listen to that steady flow of words, the fine enthusiasms and the wry, damning accusation of things in general. (LDD, p. 71)

Milton Loftis is the ringmaster of a linguistic circus, and most of his utterances are the verbal equivalent of the "shambling procession of lies and excuses" which stroll through his mind. Milton's problem, like that of most wandering men, is that he must be in too many places at the same time. Covering his tracks while meeting Dolly in Washington or Richmond, he must always account for time spent, and there are the inevitable overlaps that short-circuit one-on-one relationships with a kind of verbal overkill, the oratorical equivalent of rationalization. After a few drinks, he is always tongue-tied, the internal correlative to the "knots" that comprise his pseudo-affections. Although his excess is the other side of Helen's empty silences, both live a perpetual lie. Milton is no more in touch with Dolly Bonner than he is with his wife. Although he and Dolly occasionally share a bed, the net result is not much different from that love which stems from the separate bedrooms inhabited by him and his wife:

> In the darkness, taking his hand, with nothing troubling her secret glow of triumph, she lay down next to him on Helen's bed. Soon, "Have you?" she said.
> "Not yet."
> "Have you?"
> "No. I can't," he groaned.
> "Now?"
> "Yes, yes," he said.
> It was a lie but she couldn't tell. (LDD, p. 187)

Clearly, his parody of lovemaking parallels the parody of the language, that other form of communication. Although Milton continually alleges that Dolly's hips drive him wild, it is quite clear that he is driven wild only from a distance. That the hand redeems—one of the aphorisms of Carey Carr—is never fully recognized. Milton Loftis, unable to get both sides together, must forever live with distance providing the basis for desire. In other words, Milton Loftis is a voyeur *manqué:*

> "I wish I had been a poet."
> "Oh, you could do it, Milton," she burst out, forgetful of his slight.
> "You keep saying that. Why don't you do it? What would you start writing now?"
> "Pornography. As befits a dirty old man. The way we make love, that's what I'd write about. The way I love it. The way—." (LDD, p. 179)

May the good Lord protect his readers! The blank in this dialogue is the visible emblem of the absence at the heart of his life. Whenever that which he desires enters the range of possibility, Milton Loftis must use a flood of oral or written verbiage in order to defeat the possibility. His desire to write pornography is but another excuse, yet another apologia for failed connections.

The two children share the attributes of each parent. The crippled Maudie, a study in arrested development, inhabits the spaces of silence. Unable to move or to comprehend anything beyond the most immediate family relationships, she passes her life folded up in a heap. Peyton is her opposite; flirtatious, gregarious, highly verbal, she, like her father, is all excess—too much liquor, too many false expectations, too many lovers, and too many midnight travels away from home. And, like Milton, she does not approve of nor enjoy sex. She is called "the body" at the Kappa Alpha dance after a University of Virginia football game, but it is a body she does not really possess. Whenever the young Cartwright wishes to embrace her gratuitously, she pulls away. Her desire is closely related to want (as in the episode where she kisses her father in return for the promise of a new red auto for graduation), and, of course, that is precisely the point. Since the other side of "want" is "lack," it must be expected that, serially, desire-as-want is easily transformed into *wanton* behavior. Unable to gain satisfaction, Peyton must move from lover to lover until her suicide. Just as Helen and Milton Loftis lead lives that border on death, so the two children who share in those lives both die—one by shrinking up into nothingness in a Charlottesville hospital, and the other by falling between New York skyscrapers, thereby filling up the abyss between structures.

In *Lie Down in Darkness* love is seldom freely given, since there is simply too much demand for reciprocity. Several times in the novel, *love* is equated with *need*, and the two abstractions are used interchangeably. Helen greets Milton's return following Maudie's death with a perfect instance of such a confusion: "'Darling,' she said that afternoon, 'darling, darling, you have learned, haven't you? You have learned what I need, haven't you? You have learned. I believe you. Oh, yes, together we can never die!'" Peyton gets caught in the same bind, for at the onset of her honeymoon, she bases the connection on a mutual dependency, using almost the same language as her mother, while she and Harry cross on the night ferry:

"I'm sorry for what I said, darling. I married you because I need you."
He looked into her eyes. "Need?"
"I mean—" She struggled to say something.
"Need?" he repeated.
"I mean—"
"Need? Love?" (LDD, p. 320)

This identification of love and need has a number of consequences, not the least of which is addiction. We need those people whom we cannot do without, so that relationships based upon some love-need dynamic are usually strongly determined. In addiction need is the middle term in a dialectic which links love to hate. One fears absence so much that he cannot do with and he cannot do without. Even as love binds the two, the possibility of the "want-lack" permutation enters the relationship. We wish not for the presence of the other, but instead come to define the relationship negatively— as *not* wishing for the absence of the other owing to that which accrues to self. We feign affection for the other only as a way of avoiding any self-confrontation. This deceit is doubtlessly part of the lie by which love comes to be regarded as a need. The second manifestation of the equation of love and need is the growth of something akin to rescue-fantasy. Unable to love the other unconditionally, we imagine ourselves as rescuers of those in trouble so that we might disguise desire within the garb of salvation, thereby achieving the sharing of distance and desire once again. It is clear that Peyton does not love Harry Miller, and just as clear that what she does love is *not* to be abandoned. She loves a nothingness that is perilously close to suicide, even from the beginning of her saga. She desires not Harry at all, but rather she desires his desire of her and only then is she authenticated. She lives a double lie, once removed from the inauthenticity of her parents. In order to command his desire, she must always reenforce his role as a redeemer by threatening to live her own absence. She must make Harry chase her just as she made Milton chase her through the fraternity parties at Charlottesville: "You could have done something. But you weren't there. You left me just like you always do. When I needed you. Why didn't you come and rescue me? Didn't you see—." The elder Virginia gentlemen had enacted the ritual of courtship by the moonlight elopement on a horse. But Peyton Loftis is the decadence of such a romanticism; in her contrived parodies of rescue, she gives the lie to history. Only when she is in the extreme defensive posture can she love. Of course, as inevitably happens, one of the rescues fails or the signal is refused by the knight, and she is left only with the nothingness of her own death.[4] The relationship of *love, need, want* (as lack or absence), and the necessity of *salvation* in *Lie Down in Darkness* reads as practically a concordance to southern puritanism.

[172]

The final, and perhaps the worst aspect of the equation of love and need, is in effect a symptomatology. By the end of the novel, practically every white person is suffering the effects of some illness whose symptoms suggest the desire to reject some deep-seated evil. As Helen and Maudie fold themselves up in a defense against exterior pain, so Milton Loftis vomits bile and his daughter Peyton feels her selfhood draining away in menstruation. Vague trips to doctors are mentioned with increasing frequency, and the revelry of the football game is paired with a visit to the deteriorating Maudie in the hospital. Everyone seems to be afflicted with illness, either spiritual or physical, so that the entire novel comes to resemble a hospital room. The last stage in the evolution of this metaphor is the group therapy scene in Berger's house, where the only hope for community stems from the recognition that all the guests are sick. When love is made a companion to need, then every act of communion must be masked as therapy. Calvinistic notions of salvation are transformed into a dependency upon the psychiatrist or some other facilitator-mediator. And Peyton's last letter to Daddy, which is a sort of suicide note that says "please save me," resembles in its broken syntax, the halting speech of Helen Loftis when she seeks out the Reverend Carr for her own midnight confession:

Oh, Daddy, I don't know what's wrong. I've tried to grow up—to be a good little girl, as you would say, but everywhere I turn I seem to walk deeper and deeper into some terrible despair. What's wrong, Daddy? What's wrong? Why is happiness such a precious thing? What have we done with our lives so that everywhere we turn—no matter how hard we try not to—we cause other people sorrow? (LDD, p. 38)

The novel itself might be considered as a survey of the various types of families and, long before social scientists were detailing its deterioration, William Styron was exploring the theme. Most family rituals in the novel conclude with some act of violence: Peyton's birthday celebration at the country club; the Christmas dinner when Peyton returns from Sweet Briar; or the ill-fated wedding ceremony. Love, whenever it does exist, is always the accompaniment to threatened absence, whether it be Peyton's flight from home or Milton's flight back to his wife from Dolly's arms. Physical embrace and caress occur upon arrivals and departures, but never in the ordinary course of events. Even the embrace which briefly unifies Milton and Helen after the death of the crippled Maudie occurs only in response to a new absence in their lives. There is, of course, one family which is not deteriorating into a sick bay, and that is the family over which La Ruth and Ella Swan rule. Although this family is a stereotyped black family whose father has long since departed, love and the physical touch that is always an integral part of the deepest love, flourish. Even rebuke, such as that which occurs at Peyton's wedding when one of the children spills the tiny hot dogs being used as hors d'oeuvres, is always directed physically. Children are kissed as well as struck. Peyton's neurosis fits the standard Freudian definition as some "abnormal attachment to the past," and in her last days, she carries about the alarm clock that will enable her to know of time in the present. But La Ruth has a kind of internal clock that always tells her when someone will be late for dinner or at precisely what moment to bring on the next course. Her "family" is the entourage of Daddy Faith, whose witchcraft is of the same order as that of the shrink who is the spiritual father to the group of Jewish intellectuals with whom Peyton keeps company. Both find the necessity for constructing a fictional "origin" as the substitute for an absent father.

In order to find life in this Kingdom of Death, one must reconstruct his "origins" even if he must disguise it as a fiction taken on faith. In this decaying world about to enter the September of its life, the real fathers act upon a shared faith. They touch by immersing themselves in the life of the other. Once, in her yard, Maudie meets such a playmate who does not love out of a fear of rejection. And before her death she participates in a "mysterious communion":

Then he turned and came toward Maudie. Up went the balls again; each vanished as he caught it: his hands were empty. They stood there looking at each other, and again there seemed to be something sad and mysterious in his gaze; he was like the old magician, old artificer from another country, and his eyes were black and tender: it was as if he had many secrets and somehow knew everything there was to know: not just those dancing balls, but the earth and sky, leaves and wind and falling rain; he knew their sorcery, knew their mysteries, and knew the secret heart of this girl he'd never spoken to. Bennie. Could he talk? He never said a word. There was something in him that understood love and death, entwined forever,

[174]

and the hollow space of mindlessness: he gazed at Maudie and didn't smile, only reached out his hand and made a ball come out of her ear, another from her hair. (LDD, p. 223)

Bennie is a real magician, not a transformed image in the mirror of Helen Loftis's soul. His cheeks bulge, we are told, like those of a rabbit, and clearly identify him as the real father to Maudie whose surrogate is Milton Loftis, called "bunny" by Peyton. He is a real father because, like Daddy Faith, he both plays with and protects his children. Bennie is a variant of the harlequin who graced so much of the literature of the fin de siècle and emerges in Picasso and Miro as the Pierrot figure. Combining life and art, Bennie lives his mask rather than uses it as a disguise. And like Daddy Faith, he recognizes that "love and death" are "entwined forever," as he enters the preverbal world of the child in the same way that the black preacher participates in the phylogenetic primitivity of his flock on the banks of the stream. Both have a freedom that is associated with "play." Early in his life, Milton Loftis's father had told him of those who have freedom: "*My son, most people, whether they know it or not . . . get on through life by a sophomoric fatalism. Only poets and thieves can exercise free will, and most of them die young.*" Bennie, as a magician who makes juggled balls appear and disappear without getting entangled, is a combination of poet and thief. Daddy Faith takes four hundred dollars in contributions from the black domestics who run the Loftis household, and also speaks in the stentorian tones of a black Demosthenes—perfectly balancing the occupations of poet and thief. In keeping with the dichotomy of *Lie Down in Darkness*, one is the poet of silence and the other, the poet of excess.

To recognize that love, life, and death are all inextricably related is to recognize the nature of seasonal rhythms. Amidst all of the infidelities of this novel, only the truth of the earth remains constant. Helen Loftis sees her garden as the only constant in a world where changes mystify her:

She wished she could tell Carey how much her garden meant to her. Whenever the dreadful depression came back, she would fly toward her garden as one dying of thirst runs toward water. She'd pluck and weed and pick, and as she knelt on the cool ground she felt, she said, absolutely rooted to something firm and substantial, no longer a part of the family. (LDD, p. 21)

[175]

Lie Down in Darkness has all the trappings of one of the ancient fertility myths, with everyone asking the same question, namely what will restore fertility to the kingdom of sterility. Except for the blacks, there are no children born in this novel, nor is there the prospect of any in the Loftis line. Everyone is afraid of giving birth; even for Helen Loftis the voices of children intrude into her dreams as a nightmare. If this novel is patterned upon the structure of ancient fertility rituals, then each person must ask of his oracle a painful question. All oracles, even from the beginning of time, have given the same answer: we can restore fertility only by being reborn, and that involves a confrontation with our own death. That would take place only if the funeral cortege bringing Peyton to her final resting place would encounter the baptismal raft of Daddy Faith. But it does not, instead opting for the detour—one more example of the circuitousness that pervades the lives of wanderers and travelers in the novel. All of the trappings of the fertility myths are there, including the beggar fisherman whom Peyton meets on her last walk, trying to catch coins out of a subway grate with a string attached to a pole. But there is no renewal for these people, because they cannot imagine death and life as part of the natural order of things, as Sir Thomas Browne well knew. Nor is there any cool, lifegiving shower, save for those blacks who immerse themselves in the stream's spray. The glare that has produced a spiritual desert continues to blind and suffocate the Loftises.

Peyton's last letter to Port Warwick, which arrives just before the news of her suicide, represents one last attempt to construct an individualized history of one who has no origins. For Peyton's letter is a sort of pseudoautobiography, a last confession. And it transforms us readers into would-be psychoanalysts who must listen with sadness and nod. In a world like that of Port Warwick at the end of World War II, in the process of transformation, there is no longer a "given" history, but each person must aestheticize his own past. Nostalgia is to memory as Peyton's last letter home is to the rest of the novel. Everyone in the novel—Dolly Bonner, Helen Loftis, Milton Loftis, the Reverend Carr, and Peyton—are confessing that they have been wrong. And yet, no one has been wrong. Peyton Loftis moves from the rural countryside to the city and discovers death. Daddy Faith at the end of each summer moves out from the city and into the countryside, imitating the journey of the Apostles in bringing life. Port Warwick is both beginning and ending for two attempts at revival. But the people there are in an interlude between summer and winter, life and death, collective history and autobiography, in this August of 1945. As the train which moves through Whitman's "When Lilacs Last in the Dooryard Bloom'd" links Lincoln's death with the spring lilacs of rebirth, so Styron's novel is an elegy for a civilization that is a season, where trains at the beginning and ending link life, death, and love in a trilogy that is bound to the love of nostalgia:

Perhaps now, upon reflection, it was only the season that had made her unhappy: this tail end of summer, the September midpassage when the year seems sallow and emaciated like a worn out, middle-age countrywoman pausing for breath, and all the leaves are mildly, unsatisfactorily green. Everything then is waiting, expecting, and there is something in the air that promises smoke and burning and dissolution. One's flowers bloom gaily for a little while, but September is a quick, hectic month, bearing on the air seeds for burial and making people feel tired and a little frantic, as in a station just before the train pulls out. (LDD, p. 131)

Notes

1. *The Works of Sir Thomas Browne*, ed. Geoffrey Keynes (Chicago, University of Chicago Press, 1964), 1: 167–168. In the same paragraph Browne was to write that "the number of dead long exceedeth all that shall live." The significance of the epigraph is extensive, since in his five-chapter discourse, Browne attempted to show the folly of a civilization in attempting to participate in immortality while still on earth. As a survey of the various habits and customs of burial among the peoples of the world, it is a sort of parody of the ancient "Book of the Dead."

2. "The Editor Interviews William Styron," *Modern Occasions* 1 (1971): 503–504.

3. J. Hillis Miller, *The Form of Victorian Fiction* (Notre Dame, Ind., 1968), pp. 67–68.

4. This tendency of the so-called schizoid individual to participate in these patterns of potential or real rescue is a fruitful topic for further study. In *The Savage God* A. Alvarez has posed the question in the course of examining the history of suicide. Alvarez finds that a number of suicides actually wish to be saved and construct elaborate ruses in order to effect a rescue. Yet, he too falls into the trap when he suggests that the late Sylvia Plath really did not want to commit suicide and hence labels her death "almost accidental." In a somewhat

similar way Peyton Loftis tempts the inauthenticity of others by demanding rescue or affection as a way of insuring the maintenance of a fragile self. It is a way of enforcing love, even where none exists, so that the other cannot refuse. Again, it is the equation of love and need which prompts a bond sealed by negatives and double negatives rather than genuine affection.

IRVING MALIN

The Symbolic March

The opening paragraph of *The Long March* tells us much about the symbols, themes, and characters of the entire novelette. Styron begins with "noon," the hottest part of the day; the heat is as intense and extreme as the events—and the reactions to these events—he will eventually describe. (Even *noon* is intensified by the word *blaze*.) Then Styron introduces the human element: "eight dead boys are thrown apart among the poison ivy and the pine needles and loblolly saplings." The contrasts are vivid—the boys are dead, wasted, "strewn"; the noon burns with energy. Several questions leap to mind. How do men face extinction? What is the role of accident or design? Can death be meaningful?

We would expect Styron to give us more information about the *causes* of death, but he maintains the suspense. He simply informs us in the next sentence that the boys, only "shreds of bone, gut, and dangling tissue," look as if they had *always* been dead. Their past lives have disappeared. The continuity between past and present is shattered. (This theme is one of Styron's characteristic ones.) But we do know that the accident occurs in the early 1950s under "a Carolina sun" as the Marines train for service during the Korean War.

The mystery continues, but we now meet Lieutenant Culver, the "center of consciousness." He is an alert, thoughtful observer—he, like us, will have to put the pieces into some pattern—if only to *survive*. It is interesting that his sentence is the longest one so far; it contains so many qualifications, so many turns of syntax, because he does not know how to get to the heart of the situation. He cannot act simply; he must reflect at length. Thus his "how? why?"— which occur at midpoint in the sentence—seem to capture his thoughts. His question is said to buzz furiously; it is as active as the "noontime heat" which is again mentioned. Culver identifies with the "fifteen or so surviving marines" who barely escaped death;

his questions are theirs as well. His initial response to the entire scene—to the "eight·dead boys" and to the survivors—is perfectly natural: he vomits. And his vomiting, like his questioning, establishes our sympathy with him.

Styron tells us more about Culver. He gives us many details which demonstrate that our guide (through the "underbrush") is both a man of action and feeling. He is not a career officer; he is, on the contrary, an ironic commentator. He has the intelligence to ask the right questions about the causes of the training accident, even though he is "pulsing" with excitement. He does not, in other words, simply react without thinking about his reactions. His age clearly demonstrates that he is "no longer an eager kid just out of Quantico with a knife between his teeth." He is a tired thirty-year-old who seems to be out of place, having been called back for service during the Korean War.

There are many images which suggest the "unreality" of the entire situation. Culver sees among the "slick nude litter of intestine and shattered blue bones" some spoons—the survivors had been eating—which peek out "like so many pathetic metal flowers." What a strange description! We don't usually expect flowers to be metallic and, of course, we don't expect them to be "pathetic." Metal, abstract emotion, and nature—the three things are thrown together. It is up to Culver to define each, or better yet, to explore what is *truly human*. The description is metaphorically precise, but it also suggests that the lieutenant is a kind of visionary. He makes "odd," poetic connections.

I want to express the visionary qualities of Culver (which, by the way, make him an even more interesting guide). We are told that before he was called back to service during the Korean crisis, he experienced an "odd distress." He was dream-ridden; he was baffled by peace. But he enjoyed one recurrent vision of Sunday strolls in the park—he saw nature then as kind and calm (in contrast to the present "noon"). When Culver remembers peacetime, he thinks of the calm city heartbeat, the "pink-cheeked" people, the "sooty white tatters" of a recent snow, and these various images contrast sharply with the explosive, fragmented, and violent scene before his eyes. And in sharp contrast to the "pathetic metal flowers," he remembers two lovely little girls "like tumbling flowers." It is significant that the first part of the novelette ends with Culver's feeling that his last day before his return to service had been an "evil" one. He had to relinquish carefully defined pleasures for the renewed uncertainty of wartime service. The last sentence stresses blurring vision—he will have to see things differently; he enters strange coasts. He is adrift.

By the end of the first part, Styron has indicated the contrasts which he will develop throughout his narrative: peace and war; thought and action; "vision" and "reality"; design and accident; humanity and nonhumanity. It is Culver's fate to see distinctions clearly and to confront, if not artistically shape, them for his future well-being.

Part two begins again with the immediate past before the explosion and this time the warning signals are emphasized: a rustling of leaves; a "*crump crump*" noise. The contrasts between the "earth-shaking sound" and the relative silence of mealtime, between almost-cosmic interruption and daily routine, are vividly suggestive. They remind us of Culver's anxiety in the midst of peacetime—war always shatters things. And when Styron introduces the unease of a "clownish" radio corporal who is said to be usually "whimsical," we feel an "added dread."

Now we meet the colonel. His name is not mentioned at first; his rank (power) is all that is important. We are surprised that he receives the news of the explosion as if it were the most "routine of messages." He cannot feel dread. Although Culver recognizes that Colonel Templeton is probably "acting," he is irritated by the neat performance. Perhaps he would like to share the colonel's calm. (His own suspense throbs "inside him like a heart-beat.") We are not told. We sense, however, the growing conflict between them.

At this point Captain Mannix is introduced. His first word is "Jesus." This is the beginning of a later symbolic identification of the captain and Christ. (When we learn that he is a dark Jew aged thirty, we are not surprised.) Mannix is outraged by the meaningless explosion, but unlike Culver, he says something. He demands to know and to punish the agents of destruction. What will Congress do about such accidents? He seeks meaningful authority

[181]

which he can understand. Thus he will be able to fight "the sons of bitches" responsible for such accidents.

The stage is set for a close view of the three men. There is tension among them because they react so differently. Culver, still the "center of consciousness," stands in awe of the others. He observes; he passively notes things. He regards Templeton ironically as a prematurely aged "ecclesiastic," but he is afraid of the man's voice "which expected to be obeyed." The colonel represents "absolute and unquestioned authority." In Freudian terms Templeton is the father as lawgiver; surely his name and the religious metaphors (like "ecclesiastic") suggest an Old Testament wrath.

Culver is "in a constant state of half amusement, half terror," not knowing how to work out his tensions. He is a weak son. (We are never informed about psychological reasons for his attitudes.) He would like to be as rebellious as Mannix, but he cannot. Thus he thinks of him not as his "sibling" or partner but as another kind of superior being. Mannix is *man* as rebel against authoritarian commands; he is, oddly, as mysterious as Templeton (despite all his vocal complaints).

Culver wants to sleep—to retreat from choosing between the alternatives of Mannix and Templeton. He dreams "fitfully" of home. But sleep, peace, and home no longer exist for a marine. And when the sergeant announces a "long walk tonight," we share his anxiety and gloom. Culver is trapped, recognizing that the long march may be as explosive as the real explosion, and he resents the sergeant. He pictures him "grafted to the system as any piece of flesh surgically laid on to arm or thigh." (Culver continually thinks of the body; he is keenly aware of mortality.)

Now Culver remembers that he heard of the march the night before. There is a flashback. He recalls Mannix and Templeton acting out their psychologically determined roles. Templeton is "solitary," aloof, and amused by Mannix's hot complaints. Both men (and also Culver) seem to be puppets. Culver is "the only one in the tent who could see, at the same instant, both of their expressions. In the morbid, comfortless light they were like classical Greek masks, made of chrome or tin, reflecting an almost theatrical disharmony." These lines are important. Culver is pictured again as solitary observer; he is caught between the two men. He sees more than either one, but he cannot forcefully act. He regards himself as audience. The irony is that he is "doomed" to his role as spectator—as much as the heroes on stage. By performing their habitual roles, Templeton and Mannix are nonhuman masks. They have lost some sense of choice; they apparently *must* act as they do. They are made out of "chrome or tin"; they perform mechanically. This is not to say that Culver fails to admire them. Using such words as *devout* and *religious*, he tries to be ironic—to shield himself from commitment (running up on stage)—but his admiration shines through his own ironic mask: he is oddly in awe of these extreme, godlike figures.

Mannix wears a mask of rebellion. He smiles toughly; he curses, saying "Christ on a crutch!" His gestures and remarks are "exaggerated." We are not told why. Does he choose his part? Or is it an overcompensation for chores forced upon him? The questions are important, but Styron does not answer them, except to suggest that Mannix is not a "regular."

Mannix, however, makes Culver squirm. Culver can no longer regard the march as an "abstraction"; he surrenders his theoretical view of life—at least for the time being. The imagery is significant here. Again Culver is the symbolist, finding that his surroundings "had shifted, ever so imperceptibly, into another dimension of space and time." He scrutinizes things in a dreamlike, lurid light: Mannix's "shadow cast brutishly against the impermeable walls by a lantern so sinister that its raging noise had the sound of a typhoon at sea"; he is in a "dazzling, windowless box"; he is upon a "dark and compassless ocean." The emphasis is upon exaggerated, neurotic visions of immobility and, strangely, movement. Culver lies *between* his superiors, between *all* the opposites of life. He dangles.

Culver may be an abstractionist, but he is controlled by his body. Indeed, he is afraid of it—he would like to get out of it (another windowless box?) and fly away or back in time—and we can recognize that the opening explosion is also a traumatic symbol of his psychological needs. There is a subtle interaction between the external event and the internal interpretation, a field of action. It is almost possible to say that the explosion would have to be "invented" (if it had not occurred) to satisfy Culver's imagination. He courts it as a reflection of his inner being.

Culver gradually becomes less of the careful observer we had

[183]

taken him to be—he is a kind of sick symbolist, unaware of his resemblance to either Mannix or Templeton. As he broods about the forthcoming march—we are still in the lengthy flashback—he hears noises; he sees things; and he discovers meaning in the wails. The radio noises seem "like the cries of souls in the anguish of hell." We have once more the religious metaphors, but we don't know how to respond precisely to them. Why does Culver see (or hear) hell? Does he *believe* in an *actual* hell? Why should he use the word? Styron has not given us enough of Culver's background to establish the religious frame of reference. We are tempted to take the earlier words as ironic. Irony has given way—to what? Despite these questions, we are moved by the curious linkage of private and cosmic symbols, especially when Culver thinks of himself in a contained "universe" of sound.

One long paragraph makes his symbolist universe especially clear. Culver thinks of the captain as a fellow symbolist. Mannix is said to be a code maker, a creator of a different kind of language from the "secret language" of the military. In this respect he destroys such words as *hero*, which means different things for marine and civilian. Mannix yearns for "pure" meanings. He tries to find these in his body scars. He is down-to-earth. What is fascinating for us, if not to either man, is that although both are symbolists, one is conscious (Culver) and the other unaware of his imaginative creations (Mannix).

There is a flashback *within* the flashback. Styron insists upon the "pastness" of events; he pictures time as an ever-receding point. The marines have to cope with a never-ending (indeed, always beginning) universe which can never escape from symbolic meanings.

We meet Mannix, Culver, and Templeton five months earlier— just after the reserves have been called back. They are slaves to a "horde of cunningly designed, and therefore often treacherous machines." *Peonage, renewed bondage*, and *oppressive weather* are some descriptive words used by Styron. Mannix is, as usual, the rebel, falling asleep during orientation meetings. He irritates the lecturers, but he also "inspires" Culver. Culver is off the center stage; he sits down "during the darkness of a lantern slide." But he does not feel entirely comfortable. Styron makes much at this point of *space*. The lecture "hall" is contrasted to the "Heaven's Gate" of the officers. Culver feels trapped by both. Although he should feel at home in the latter "pleasure-dome ingeniously erected amid a tangle of alluvial swampland, and for officers only," he finds little joy in this "playground" and, of course, less joy in the dark hall. Both places—like the marines and the body itself—trap him. He would like to "burn down the place" and assert his freedom from necessity.

One incident reinforces these symbols of imprisonment. Mannix recalls a past event—notice how we move even more deeply into time; our movement is, appropriately enough, a "long march"—and we see him drunk in a hotel room in San Francisco. He emerges naked from a shower and suddenly finds himself pushed out of the window by his buddies: "Imagine being that high upside-down in space with two drunks holding onto your heels. . . . I just remember the cold wind blowing on my body and that dark, man, infinite darkness all around me." The incident is perhaps the most explosive one so far described—with the exception of the opening explosion—because it strips Mannix (and Culver, his listener) of everything. He is "less than human"; he is alone with the sense of mortality. He dangles in space; he is out of control. But there are ironies. He realizes then that he is "human" and that no other person can help him get out of his condition.

Culver does not know what to make of Mannix, the survivor; he stares at him, but he cannot completely understand him. The peaceful scene—they are near the sea—blurs before his eyes. Instead of the "promenade of waves"—so unlike the possible fall into space—he sees the "substanceless night" in which he, and all slaves, move. Blood rushes to his head.

Suddenly we are wrenched back to the "noon" of the explosion. Culver snaps awake. (But which is the dream? The past or the present?) He is, nevertheless, unable to tell where he is. Styron writes that "time seemed to have unspooled past him in a great spiral." Finally he realizes that he is listening not to Mannix but to the sergeant. He must still go on the forced march. In the jeep with Templeton and Mannix, he closes his eyes. He fights his visionary nature, not wanting to see the "ghosts of the bereaved and the departed" or the "motions without meaning." He longs for sleep.

The scene shifts. Styron moves from Culver's closed eyes to the closed eyes of one boy killed by the explosion. They are "brothers."

[185]

Perhaps Mannix senses this identification (and his own) when he says in the last words of this section: "Won't they ever let us alone?"

Part three begins at twilight "just before the beginning of the march"; the time is appropriate because Culver is very unsure of his motives. The "noon" intensity has given way to dim vision. Mannix finds a nail in his shoe. The nail is, of course, an omen of doom—it functions as an almost-Greek "curse"—but it also serves to inspire his rebellious nature. He needs this "pinpoint of torture" as a kind of muse and, consequently, he refuses to listen to Culver's common sense.

What are we to make of Mannix here? He is far from the classical hero. He courts death in a "nervous and touchy way." He is "at odds with his men, to whom he usually had shown the breeziest good will." He twitches. He is, to use Styron's phrase, a bundle of "raw nerves." (The body imagery is never omitted.) But Mannix is a modern "hero" because he accepts the absurdity of things. He laughs painfully. He goes to extremes in an already extreme situation. He obsessively defies the marine obsessions of Colonal Templeton. He considers the nail as his private symbol—of "lousy luck" and also the lust for survival.

Culver recognizes the symbolic thrust of Mannix. He also sees Templeton as symbolic. When the colonel appears "neat, almost jaunty, in new dungarees and boots," carrying a ".38 revolver," the gun becomes Templeton's "emblematic prerogative." Note the contrast between the nail and the .38. Both objects are imbued with "power" by their owners; they become unreal and huge, carrying abstract meanings. It is also interesting to consider their metallic qualities. By surrendering to their symbolic objects, the men act mechanically—like the puppets mentioned once before.

Culver cannot explain his feelings, but he emphasizes his fears. He thinks of "helpless children," puny houses of "straw," "cataleptic sleep"—the recurring symbols capture his descent into panic. Surely Culver knows that he is involved in the march; he can no longer be out of view.

The march begins. Culver stares at the colonel who pushes "ahead in front of him with absolute mechanical confidence of a wound-up, strutting tin soldier on a table top." He cannot laugh at the metallic man. He is hopelessly involved with his own body—

pains. The body, which had been pictured previously as a threatening, claustrophobic container, grows in symbolic importance. It is Culver's enemy. It forces him to do things he hates; he is thirsty; he is sweaty; he is faint. By insisting upon Culver's physical pains, Styron also makes us recognize that there is no way out of the body—symbolic meanings are physically earned: "And so it was that those first hours Culver recollected as being the most harrowing of all, even though the later hours brought more subtle refinements of pain. He reasoned that this was because during the first few miles or so he was at least in rough possession of his intellect, his mind lashing his spirit as pitilessly as his body." The "lashing," the "rough possession"—such words suggest that the master-slave relationship of Templeton and his men is mirrored privately in Culver. He cannot coexist with his body—except with great struggle. Thus before the "breather," he looks at Mannix and sees a "shape, a ghost, a horror—a wild and threatful face reflected from the glass." He identifies with him in this "absurd" universe of mirrors.

When they continue the march, Culver wonders how he will last. He is a fish under the sea—falling deeply (like Mannix in the hotel?). Then he is a "ewe who follows the slaughterhouse ram." His passivity asserts itself in such symbolic details. Consequently, when he sees Mannix limping, he shares his pain, and offers some advice. The Christ words are stressed here; both officers are in a state of communion, plagued by the crucifixions of the march (stations of the cross?).

Templeton appears to smile at them. He looks "like the priest in whom passion and faith had made an ally, at last, of only the purest good intentions; above meanness or petty spite, he was leading a march to some humorless salvation." He is the false father, hiding his intentions behind "solicitous words." He hopes to grind Mannix to dust with kindness. He tells him to *ride*, not to march any more: "Nothing could have been worse."

Culver hates Templeton not as Templeton but as "the Colonel, the marine." He considers him as the very symbol of all the "crazy, capricious punishment" imposed upon him. But he dimly understands that the colonel, like Mannix, is part of his own mind. The long march is within!

[187]

The march continues and becomes "disorganized." Styron plays with such notions as "organization" and "disorganization." One is as bad as the other. The former suggests Templeton, authoritarian principles, unquestioning allegiance; the latter hints at complete chaos. Styron apparently believes that one must be "loose," ironic, and aware of patterns or, better yet, able to shape patterns flexibly without yielding to either wildness or rigidity.

In the absence of Templeton (who has gone away in a truck), Mannix goes to extremes. He will endure the march; he will transform the pattern imposed upon him into his *own. He will create order.* What black comedy! The rebel becomes the complete organization man, despite his "terrible limp."

Styron is ambivalent about Mannix and his command. He admires—or at least Culver does—the captain's "perversity" and courage, but he suggests that he acts like a robot. (We find the same kind of situation in Ahab's "mad" march toward the whale, not knowing how to distinguish between "perversity" and "heroism.") Culver, like an Ishmael, wants to say to Mannix: "*you've lost; stop*": "Nothing could be worse than what Mannix was doing—adding to a disaster already ordained (Culver somehow sensed) the burden of his vicious fury." But he cannot vent his own rage.

Culver recognizes that he is less of a man than Mannix. He lacks the power to rebel against him (as the captain did against Templeton); he remains passive. Once more he thinks of "crazy cinematic tape, chaos, vagrant jigsaw images." He even dreams of cubed ice in a carnival tent. The machine, the performance, the box (tent)—all imply that Culver regards himself as an actor in someone else's confined script. He is no longer the reflective spectator watching classical masks; he is at center stage.

Templeton returns and demands that Mannix ride in the truck. Culver again recognizes the symbolic structure: when men cannot agree upon symbols (or words like *heroism, courage,* and *devotion*), they must battle. He tries vainly to separate the two men (and thereby act powerfully), recognizing that they have lost their manhood in loyalty to abstractions. And yet, in a perverse way, he is as rigid as they. All of them—not merely Mannix—are distorted, painted clowns.

The last line of this section is "What the hell," [Mannix] whispered, "we've made it." It is ambiguous. *Have they made anything?* Have they, on the contrary, been made? And "it"? What has Mannix won—except an insane, clownlike pattern? Styron does not permit Culver to respond here. The omission is especially interesting, suggesting that there are few final solutions or victories. Each man must believe that "he has made it"—if only to go on living—but he is finally alone without any listeners or critics. He is isolated in his symbolic universe.

Part five attempts to resolve the ambiguities. Culver lies in bed, trying to sleep. (Styron uses the contrast between the march and stasis.) He closes his eyes. But he cannot join the dead boys of the explosion because he is, after all, an aware survivor.

He keeps seeing visions—of open space and commingled "sunshine and darkness." These keep him in touch with reality; they will not permit him to drift away. The visions, like Styron's symbolic details, are full of commingled opposites. When Culver looks out of the window, he notices the officers' swimming pool ("grotto-blue") and "decorous" wives. (We think of their presence in contrast to the boys' strewn bodies.) But Culver moves beyond "Heaven's Gate"; he senses the "threatful beginnings of a storm." He knows that angry thunder lurks over "peace and civilization."

Culver feels a "deep vast hunger" for some transcendental vision which will *overarch* grottolike peace and threatening storm, dead boys and "lovely little girls with their ever joyful, ever sprightly dance." The vision finally eludes him because he is caught in time. He has seen too much—or not enough. Now he knows that as an anxious man—he has not been cured by the march—he can identify with all the others who must march to satisfy their symbolic longings. His hunger dies. He must live with the "hateful contraries"—with the "somber light" *and* thunderheads, with highs *and* lows (we see a "swan-dive" and a "skyward" glance), with war *and* peace.

It is fitting that Culver's victory, as tentative as it may be, should force him to move out of his room and meet Mannix. Both men have "won" victories; they "limp" to show their wounds. (Victory for Styron implies scars.) They are able to have one "unbroken minute of sympathy and understanding"—this is how long transcendental vision lasts—before their communication is destroyed.

[189]

Culver notices the Negro maid "employed in the place." She asks Mannix: "Do it hurt?" She senses his pain (and Culver's?); she has also lived in bondage. Before he can answer she says "Deed it does" (after the two of them share one "unspoken moment of sympathy and understanding").

It is at this point that Styron uses the symbolic device: Mannix's towel falls (he is going to shower); he is "naked as the day he emerged from his mother's womb." The nakedness is, of course, a comic "accident"—as opposed to the not-very-comic accident at the beginning—but it also reinforces Styron's insistence upon human frailty (mortality): man somehow dead (or at least dead tired) and alive, "clutching for support at the wall." Finally in the last words Mannix repeats: "Deed it does."

And Culver? He does not have the final word. He will, presumably, survive this scene to create his own pattern of meaning, to perform his solitary deeds. He will march again.

ROBERT PHILLIPS

Mask and Symbol in
Set This House on Fire

"We'll bring back tragedy to the land of the Pepsi-cola and the peanut brittle and the Modess," Cass Kinsolving, the hero of William
Styron's third novel, proclaims in a speech which could be said to
reveal the author's intentions as well. Certain critics have enjoyed
the exercise of comparing Styron's works to classical Greek tragedy.
Indeed in *Set This House on Fire* Styron appears to encourage such
comparison. In one scene Cass is shown reading *Oedipus at Colonus*
(a book he frequently quotes from within the novel, professing to be
"as blind-drunk off of Oedipus as I was off of booze") in a cafe on the
Boulevard Saint-Germain, and Styron skillfully contrasts Cass's
cultured and civilized mentality with that of the gross American
tourists at an adjacent table: "He was hemmed round by a sea of
camera lenses and sport shirts; the noise of his compatriots assailed
his ears like the fractious harangue of starlings on a fence." In this
scene at least Styron intends to pit the nobility of Greek drama
against the crassness which can turn even Paris into a Howard
Johnson's.

While it is tempting to inflict a generic tragic interpretation upon
the novel, such a reading strikes me as no more valid than some of
the psychological, allegorical, and analogical interpretations which
I shall also discuss before proceeding to my own. For Cass Kinsolving is surely no tragic hero. An artist of modest achievement, in his
lifetime he has assumed no heights from which to fall. If he has a
fatal flaw it is his solipsism, which leads him finally to the conclusion that hell is not giving of oneself. Yet his final encounter with
the ultimate selfish man, Mason Flagg, ends in a murder which is
more melodrama than a drama to inspire pity or fear. If there is a
potential Oedipus figure in the novel, in fact, it is Flagg, who at
least spiritually kills his father and loves his mother ("Wendy-

dear"). Flagg is a possibly acknowledged bisexual, all of whose women seem to resemble his mother.

Yet Mason Flagg is not the hero of this novel. Cass Kinsolving is, and an Oedipal reading of the book is unsatisfactory. There is, incidentally, just as much "evidence" to support an allegorical reading based on Homer's *Odyssey*—with Luciano, the one-eyed menace and the threat who almost prevents Cass's/Odysseus's passage serving as Polyphemus (the Cyclops); and Saverio as one of the swine from the Island of Circe, described by Styron as a "ragged figure that approached us with a husky snuffling noise—a series of rich, porcine grunts." Later in the novel the narrator, Peter Leverett, calls Flagg "a swine" as well, and at one point Americans are called swine.

A third possible approach is to compare the novel with Malcolm Lowry's *Under the Volcano* (1947), which it resembles in an uncanny number of ways. Both novels pit an alcoholic protagonist against a Dantesque universe; the action of both focuses ostensibly on the events of one fatal day; the settings of both are exotic, foreign lands to emphasize the hero's alienation; and, most important, the common theme of the fall of man shared by both novelists is depicted in intensity and with the grandeur of a Melville or a Faulkner. Both Lowry's Consul and Styron's Cass are potentially tragic figures isolated in their own hells.

Such readings are fascinating, but seem to me to distort Styron's meaning beyond the intention of the novel's dream. To discover such parallels is to champion a preconceived notion at the expense of its subject, to be genre-ridden or (in the narrowest sense) idea-ridden, to move through the novel arbitrarily rather than letting the work's form and texture dictate its own discussion. *Set This House on Fire* does not seem such a willful work. Rather, it purposefully lacks sequence and order, like our own memories and dreams. The novel is so rewarding because there are many levels of meaning attributed to many acts and symbols, rather than a strict adherence to one- or two-leveled meanings.

What I hope to achieve, instead, is to follow Cass Kinsolving's observation on his own dreams: "What you've got to do is get behind the mask and symbol." For I maintain that to weave his rich tapestry, Styron has consciously or unconsciously drawn upon threads of many ageless myths and works of the imagination. Because his allusions and parallels are drawn from such a range of literature and experience, for the critic to insist upon one specific interpretation is to shortchange the author and the reader.

Before examining these masks, these symbols, let us begin with a statement of what the novel seems to be "about," and then examine the materials which support such a meaning.

Essentially *Set This House on Fire* is one man's search for inner freedom and his regeneration. When Cass Kinsolving takes his family to the Amalfi coast, he hates himself as much as he hates the America he has fled. (Of anti-American invective in the novel one could compile a small anthology; such invective perhaps reaches its apogee in the description of the United States as "an ashheap of ignorance and sordid crappy materialism and ugliness!") This hatred is primarily focused against what American public life does to man's private life—and Cass being an artist feels the invasion of private life more keenly than most.

After seesawing between the alternatives of living or dying, Cass redeems himself through two acts—personal sacrifice in attempting to save the dying peasant Michele's life and personal regeneration in succeeding in taking the life of the degenerate Mason Flagg. Cass's personal hell has been caused by his own self-centeredness. In risking his own health to save that of Michele, he finally gives of himself and propitiates a guilt of many years' standing, dating back to his southern boyhood when he unwillingly helped a companion destroy the contents of a poor Negro's cabin—a supposed test of Cass's manhood which he at first "failed" by protesting, then later "passed" by saving face and helping destroy the humble home. He feels he has been running roughshod over the lives of others ever since. Michele dies, however, and Cass must assume more guilt in feeling the man did not live because he himself did not give enough. The man's death is felt just as if one of Cass's children had died, and when Cass hears of it he echoes Macduff's speech, "All, then? *All?*" In failing to save Michele, the attempt at salvation being Cass's one "creative" act for some months, Cass again experiences a failure of spirituality within himself. Yet the attempt to save the peasant was an act of life, not of death, and in doing so he directly defied the degenerate Flagg.

That guilt is minimal when compared to the burden Cass ultimately comes to feel over his unpunished murder of Flagg: "I've enough guilt about it to equip a regiment of Sumner's." Because the murder, allegedly in retribution for Flagg's rape of Michele's daughter, Francesca, in reality is a rationalization, a violent act intended to exorcise Cass's own evil. And when the police officer Luigi conceals Cass's crime from authorities, he robs the artist of the luxury of paying for it behind bars. ("You are a damnable romantic from the north," Luigi explains. "In jail you would wallow in your guilt.") Cass must instead accept the heavy burdens of freedom.

Cass's regeneration dates from this murder of his degenerate friend. It is a two-pronged salvation. In killing Flagg he has, first, struck a blow in defense of human dignity, which Flagg had violated in many ways: making Cass get down on all fours and perform like a seal is Flagg's symbolic mode of reducing man to the animal level, just as forcing Cass to paint pornography is an overt debasement of art. In the end Cass's commitment to humanity is greater than that to art; he steals pills from Flagg to save Michele, but it had never before occurred to him to steal back the pornographic painting till the search for the pills brings him inside Flagg's quarters. There is a paradox here. Cass has to remain tied to Mason in order to gain the financial means to save Michele and thereby free himself through achieving a state of selflessness. There is an additional irony in that the medicine which saves Michele is a product of and made possible by the American affluence Cass so disdains. More than even this, when Cass destroys Flagg's hold over him (achieved only by destroying Flagg), he attains the final triumph over self, which we know from one of Cass's Sambuco dreams "is to triumph over Death. It is to triumph over that beast which one's self interposes between one's soul and one's God."

The power of Flagg's hold over Cass cannot be overestimated. It is insidious and possibly homosexual in basis. (The Italian sergeant, Parrinello, makes a meaningful mispronunciation when he calls Flagg "Flogg.") Flagg is, as an individual, so totally unfulfilled that his only release can be achieved through violence, specifically the rape of Francesca. And since the peasant girl is Cass's beloved, Flagg in essence is raping Cass, either because he unconsciously wishes to do so through lust, or through revenge, since Cass is a true artist-figure and Flagg a mere pretender, a playwright who never wrote a play.

With Flagg eliminated, Cass's regeneration can be complete, and he returns to the America from which he had been alienated. In a way. In another way, the America to which he returns—the rural Carolinas—is the country of his childhood and not the noisy vulgar industrial nation he so despises. This leads to our first examination of Styron's use of names in the novel, the masks behind which his characters enact their roles. I suggest that when Cass strikes out against Flagg, he is also striking against the flag—the American flag. Early in the novel Styron gives us his epitome of American vulgarity, the so-called "palatial villa of Emilio Narduzzo of West Englewood, N.J., USA," which he describes as "a structure the size and shape of an Esso station," and which is "flaunting at its proud turreted roof half a dozen American flags." The flag here is a debased object, and Mason Flagg is a debasement of the American Dream. He is the man who apparently has everything—looks, money, women—and he is detestable. He is the embodiment of what Cass late in the novel calls

the man I had come to Europe to escape, the man in all those car advertisements—you know, the young guy waving there—he looks so beautiful and educated and everything, and he's got it *made*, Penn State and a blonde there, and a smile as big as a billboard. And he's *going* places. I mean electronics. Politics. What they call communications. Advertising. Saleshood. Outer space. God only knows. And he's as ignorant as an Albanian peasant. (SHF, p. 392)

(It is one of Styron's ironies that, while Cass so detests the capitalist system as being dishonest, he depends upon his wife's trust fund for living.)

Mason's first name also carries symbolic value. He lived north of the Mason-Dixon line. To Cass, who is a southerner and returned from Europe to become a southerner again, Mason Flagg is the paradigm of the slick Yankee who embodies even more of the crass characteristics of the modern America he so despises.

Cass Kinsolving's revolt, then, is against the American way of life, which is no way of life for an artist. (For "artist" read any sensitive soul.) Cass's failure as a painter and as an individual are intended to be emblematic of the artist's failure in our society today. Read in such a manner, *Set This House on Fire* is totally consistent with Styron's central theme: that of the individual's revolt and outrage against the system.

The theme was first posited in *Lie Down in Darkness*, in which the family was the institution against which the protagonist, Peyton Loftis, rebels. The theme was more overtly explored in *The Long March*. Here the military displaces the family as an odious system. Captain Mannix (representing Man) leads a protest against Templeton (the Temple, the Authority) and the latter's order of a thirty-six-mile forced march. Rather than dropping out of the system, as did Peyton in fleeing to New York and Cass by wandering across Europe, Mannix registers protest within the confines of the system. That is, he defies Templeton's expectations by having his men complete the long march. Mannix's injured foot is an outward and visible sign of his inner difference, his individuality, which in Cass the artist remains unseen. There is something to be said for Mannix's method of confronting the enemy head on. In fleeing, both Peyton and Cass seem not only to drop out of the system, but out of the human race as well. *The Confessions of Nat Turner* is of course Styron's most violent and outrageous dramatization of one individual's revolt.

There is a microcosm of the American macrocosm in each of these novels: the country club in *Lie Down in Darkness*; the officer's club in *The Long March*; the commissary in *Set This House on Fire*; and the plantation house in *Nat Turner*. These are all places in which false values are perpetuated (though some positive values are expressed and enacted at the Turner house, such as Samuel Turner's arguing against slavery, and Nat's being taught to read). Indeed, Flagg's endless trips to the commissary for steaks and whiskey function much as does Jay Gatsby's prideful display of his beautiful shirts in Fitzgerald's novel. Milton Loftis is as much a weak and self-indulgent American as Mason Flagg, however; both are men to be fled from. Both, pointedly, are alcoholics. Their excessive drinking is a manifestation of the American death wish. Cass Kinsolving's theory is that Americans drink so much because "drinking drowns the guilt over having more money than anybody in the world." Mannix's soldiers spending days uselessly chasing imaginary enemies also becomes a symbolic act for the way the majority of our countrymen waste their days pursuing an illusive American dream, whoring after false gods.[1]

Violation of the individual by the demands of institutions, then, is the heart of Styron's theme. Each of his books is a plea for man's dignity and individuality, a protest against the gradual deadening of conscience and sensibility to humane values for which we should all feel guilty. A good message for Americans to hear, in view of memorable official United States proclamations over the late Vietnam war: such as "In order to save the village we had to destroy it." Not that Styron had any particular political message to impart here; in his themes he manages to imagine deeply enough into human—and thereby national—characteristics that the subsequent manifestations of these ring true and strike a universal note. This universal theme of a national guilt is not restricted to recent events in *Set This House on Fire*: the narrator's father comprehends the enormity of our national guilt over slavery and ecological abuse. Peter Leverett himself evidences guilt over the Second World War ("I'm sorry, lady . . . I didn't bomb your home").

Nor is it an accident that Cass's last name is Kinsolving. On one level the name is the same as that of a famous patrician family of American Episcopal clergy, and thereby evokes spirituality. But more important, Styron implies that it is through reaching out to our kin—our fellow human beings—that we can solve our own problems. This is the very lesson Cass learns so late in life, and Michele's physical illness is but a parallel to Cass's spiritual one. Cass comes to perceive that if the one could be saved, both could. To save Michele through giving of himself would be his own salvation, through earned self-respect and faith. (Styron emphasizes that Michele is not much older than Cass; they are brothers in the flesh.)

One final word on Cass's name: several times in the novel Flagg calls him "Cassius." This is exactly the kind of pseudointellectual word play Styron's Flagg would relish. But, like so much else in the novel, it too may have its irony. The Cassius of Shakespeare's *Julius Caesar* was the instigator of a conspiracy which ended in the death

[197]

of a powerful dictator. It is easy to comprehend Flagg as a Caesar, Cass as Cassius, and the narrator Peter Leverett as Brutus. For several brief scenes, these are the masks the trio wears.

If the names Mason Flagg and Cass Kinsolving are so redolent with meaning, what of the symbolic implications of the others? I submit that Michele, the peasant gallantly dying, is a Saint Michael figure, one who must fight his personal dragon, tuberculosis. His daughter, Francesca Ricci, is possibly named after Francesca da Rimini, another unhappy and guilty Italian beloved. The family name of Ricci is cruelly ironic in view of Michele and Francesca's extreme poverty.

In contrast to the virginal Francesca is Vernelle Satterfield, a voluptuous figure from Cass's past who was quite literally vernal: springlike, youthfully fresh, and amazingly fecund and sexual. Fausto Windgasser's last name is farcical, his first classical, invoking the magus who sought worldly knowledge without help from God and who eventually sold his soul to the Devil. Of Styron's Faust, a hotel proprietor who thinks of nothing but revenue from the tourist trade, it is said, "on doomsday that guy will be scalping tickets for seats front and center, including his own." Fausto indeed. He is one of Styron's most pointedly archetypal characters.

Peter Leverett, the narrator, is a "square" who is repeatedly and significantly mistaken for a Levitt of the Levittown dynasty. Poppy, Cass's wife, is perhaps named for the associations of the flower by that name, which is said to be symbolic of consolation.[2] Then there is Luciano di Lieto, the indomitable victim, named not so much for Lucian, the second-century Greek satirist and wit, as Lucian, the chief character in *The Golden Ass* of Apuleius. In that early work Lucian is changed into an ass as a personification of the follies and vices of the age. Styron's Luciano has a similar function. His life is a triumph over blunders, and, as the director of nursing care says of him: "He will live to bury us all." Despite losing fingers and an eye, despite his streetcar and automobile accidents, his is the persistence of survival. He is like John Crowe Ransom's much beset Captain Carpenter and Lemuel Pitkin, the hero of Nathanael West's *A Cool Million*, both of whom are also disassembled in their daily contacts with what passes for reality. Luciano presents a near-comic spectacle of "the house" on fire: the human body plagued. After colliding with Cass, he is a mock *pieta* in the roadway, "flat on his back, asprawl in sacrificial repose . . . with his tangled sweet look of liberation and racking ecstasy." Like Styron's Ella Swan (the Loftises' black maid in *Lie Down in Darkness*), Luciano will prevail because he endures.

Finally, Styron peoples his novel with a cast of caricatures of recognizable American figures who have become types. Most notable are Burnsey, the tough-guy Hollywood actor (a ringer for "Bogey"), and the Reverend Dr. Ervin Franklin *Bell*, "the exemplary, prolific and optimistic Protestant clergyman" who is surely intended as a hit at Norman Vincent *Peale* and the demise of true spirituality. While these two caricatures further the novel's theme of degeneration, their presence somewhat jangles in the otherwise intense cast of characters. The scenes devoted to the Reverend Dr. Bell seem to be embarrassingly gratuitous flights of humor, and disturb, despite thematic relevance, the novel's tone.

The narrator encounters all these extraordinary people wearing masks from classical and contemporary mythologies. The mixed nature of their roles and symbolic intentions of their names deliberately add to the dreamlike quality of Sambuco, much in the way Tennessee Williams's mixed gathering of great romantics from all history—Casanova, Lord Byron, Don Quixote, even America's Kilroy—populate his drama enacted somewhere at earth's end, *Camino Real*. It is almost as if Leverett and Cass Kinsolving were projected into Hades and encountered there all the lost souls of the ages. Leverett's initial quest for knowledge of Flagg switches to a quest for knowledge of Cass, whom he originally saw as just another of Flagg's hangers-on, but whom he eventually comprehends, through his care of Michele, to be "this tormented, sad, extraordinary character." Cass's is the torment of hell on earth.

So much for personae. Styron gives Cass's torment symbolic dimension in several ways. The first is through the use of "psychescapes," interior and exterior landscapes as perceived by Cass in his confused and sickened state. A good example of the psychescape is Cass's encounter with "the sun, pitched close to its summit, [riding] like a heat-crazed van Gogh flower, infernal, wild, on the verge of explosion." Here we not only see the sun (flower) in the distorted way of Cass's hallucinating imagination, but we make a connection between him and the mind which first made such a sun tangible, the mad van Gogh. Elsewhere in the novel, the piazza of the town is said to be captured in "a dazzling noose of sunlight"— the noose shape summoning the menace everywhere attendant in Sambuco. Many of Styron's psychescapes are more subtle, as in the description of the "kind of shimmering jade light" which pervades Cass's Paris apartment. Symbolically, jade generally corresponds not only to the masculine yang principle, but to the dry element as well.[3] Paris was Cass's driest, most unproductive period. There is another paradox here: the more Cass drank, the drier he became.

The central symbol of the novel is that of the swallow which is trapped inside the palace, that bird "which swooped down among the fluted columns, then upward, and still beat its wings against the skylight in flight toward the inaccessible sun." This is, of course, a symbol for Cass's struggle to rise above the spiritual abyss into which he has fallen. Hindu tradition has it that birds represent the higher states of being, and folklore the world over generally interprets a bird as symbolic of the soul. (A more recent novel, *The Optimist's Daughter*, by Styron's fellow southerner Eudora Welty, makes very similar symbolic use of a bird trapped inside a house.)

It is significant that Styron's bird flails upward in rooms where there is a frieze of "dingy nymphs," a contrast between Cass's hoped-for spirituality and Flagg's carnality, which must be transcended. The swallow, specifically, was a bird sacred to both Isis and to Venus, and served as an allegorical figure for spring (or rebirth). This swallow (Cass) must escape Flagg's palace for such a rebirth to occur. Late in the novel the imprisoned bird is still seeking freedom, only less frantically. Like Cass, it has been worn down. But still it tries to escape through "the moonlit fleur-de-lis of glass." The shape of the window is also suggestive. As an emblem, the base of any fleur-de-lis is an inverted triangle, representing water; above it is a cross (expressing conjunctions and spiritual achievement), with two additional and symmetrical leaves wrapped around the horizontal arm. The central arm is straight and reaches heavenward.[4] The symbolism is self-evident: an emblem of salvation, of illumination, and indeed of the Lord. Later yet in the book, the poor bird is still fluttering. But when Cass fights Flagg, "one single pigeon shot toward them, then veered aslant in fright with the faintest snapping of its wings." The struggling swallow is displaced by the descending dove, a benediction of the Holy Spirit. Release is at last achieved.

Other cohering symbols in the text include the figure of the tom-cat with a mouse trapped between its paws (the mouse being at once both Cass and Francesca, whom Flagg has captured), and Poppy's symbolic act of donning a rain slicker indoors when it is not raining: an act which underscores her basic insecurity and need for protection. (Styron here echoes, perhaps purposefully, Temple Drake and her raincoat in *Sanctuary;* though both authors probably go back to Joyce's *The Dead.*) Another symbolic act is the death of Ursula, Poppy's Flemish-speaking parrot, which functions as a bad omen for Cass, as did the accident with Luciano for Leverett. The death of the bird is another death of the soul, like the trapped swallow. But why name the bird Ursula? And why have her die on the voyage to Sambuco? Of course, a part of Cass did die in Sambuco. But it is also perhaps not coincidental that in legend Saint Ursula was a Cornish princess, the course of whose voyage (and life) was utterly changed when shifted by adverse winds. She and her companions (and Cass traveled with family) were finally driven to Cologne, where they were destroyed by the Huns. As an omen, this legend is singularly appropriate. Instead of being undone at the hands of Huns, they meet their fate through an arch-representative of the "smart-Alex, soft-headed, baby-faced, predigested, cellophane-wrapped, doomed, beauty-hating, land."

To the catalog of masks, symbols, and symbolic acts which give meaning and dimension to this novel, one must add the many dreams which Cass and Cripps endure. As products of a character's fantasy—a mental process differing from that which supposedly governs their conscious thinking and behavior—they contain keys to their inner world. Yet I must state at the outset that I find the dream sequences to be one of the novel's failures. The dreams of Styron's characters seem all too literal, too much just another symbolic version of what already has been seen before. The Hollywood figure, Cripps, for instance, is said to dream that "a golf pro and a crooner and a drum majorette are all contesting for my soul." Cass's dreams are also too direct a transposition of his life's problems, as in the dream in which the face on a Polaroid portrait of a friend has been replaced by that of a monster. Of course Mason Flagg is a monster, a man who "would have sympathized with cancer if he thought it was à la mode." But this outward manifestation of his inner terribleness seems almost too facile. Flagg is more complex than that, and Styron is more to the point when he has the narrator, in full consciousness, declare:

All the time I spent with Mason, I felt I never knew him, never could put my hands on him. He was like a gorgeous silver fish in a still pond: make a grab for him, and he has slithered away, and there you are with a handful of water. But maybe that was just the thing about him, you see? He was like mercury. Smoke. Wind. It was as if he was hardly a man at all, but a creature from a different race. (SHF, p. 446)

Three dreams are worth examining. The first is Cass's repeated fantasy of the three struggling old women in rags. These could be Styron's representation of the Moirae (called the Parcae in Roman mythology), the three Fates (Clotho, Lachesis, and Atropos) with their spindles becoming sticks in Cass's dream. They are the traditional allegorical divinities for man's fate, and as Cass dreams of the wood-bearing women struggling and suffering, he sees before him the slow march of his own lot. Cass also dreams of beaten dogs, particularly of one whose body has been crushed yet whose head, miraculously, survives. In simplest terms this separation of body from head seems symbolic either of the split between the carnal and the spiritual which exists in Cass, or of his lack of feeling for others, which is not corrected till he begins to care for Michele. But Plato, in *Timaeus*, posited the thesis that "the human head is the image of the world." Thus, this graphic separation could also embody Cass as the body which has been crushed, with the surviving head being the reality which goes on without him, a symbolic alienation. (One is reminded of all the threats of decapitation in that masterpiece of alienation, Lewis Carroll's *Alice in Wonderland*.) Eventually the dream of the suffering dog and that of the downtrodden women with the sticks become one in Cass's mind. Then the dog being beaten by a pitying but incompetent doctor becomes an allegory for us mortals in the hands of God: "He is *beating* us, yet *mercifully*."

The third and less literal dream is that of Cass taking a shower in a stall in which giant spiders feast on struggling insects. This destructive act is related to the universal significance of spiders as symbols of the world of phenomena.[5] This significance, as explained by Marius Schneider, views spiders in their ceaseless killing and weaving, destroying and building, as symbolizing the endless alternation of forces on which the stability of the universe depends—and ultimately signifies the continuous sacrifice of man throughout his life. Cass sees himself as such a sacrifice, and Styron's vision is not unlike that of Ingmar Bergman's film *Through a Glass Darkly*, in which God is perceived as a giant spider. When Cass later suffers the DT's, it is a spider vision he sees.

One final device employed by Styron to add dimension to his novel is that of alternating narration (which in itself alternates between that of Leverett and Cass, between time present and time past) with Leverett's letters and quotations from Cass's journal. In the latter, Styron makes use of free association. A good example occurs in the entry in which Cass reports his son Timmy has just been bitten by a crab. Later in the same entry Cass writes: "I should have been brought up North in N.Y. suburbs Scarsdale or somewhere on that order, where I might never have learned the quality of desire or yearnings & would have ended up on Madison Avenue designing deodorant jars." For Cass, the pure artist, this is a vision of a very low estate to which one can sink. Is it, I wonder, all brought on by thoughts of Timmy's crab, a low creature, which leads to echoes of J. Alfred Prufrock's "I should have been a pair of ragged claws," which leads directly into Cass's "I should have been brought up North" and all that follows? This seems to reinforce our belief that Cass, and Styron, equate the North with insensitivity to true values. It is a possible free association. Styron echoes e. e. cummings earlier in the novel, stating Leverett's father "moved through dooms of love."

Poetic borrowings such as these, coupled with Styron's own considerable rhetorical gifts, sustain an emotional pitch seldom encountered in a novel of such length. Only occasionally does Styron flag (and the pun is intended), as when he persists in polysyllables such as *murmuration* instead of using the shorter *murmur*. Styron also allows his character Luigi to pontificate at excessive length about such good things as how "true justice must always somehow

live in the heart," and how "this existence itself is an imprisonment." The points have been made long before.

The virtues of course outweigh the faults, and *Set This House on
Fire* must be seen as a curiously neglected novel, one which was re-
maindered in hardback during its first year of publication and
which has not, I take it, found a great following since. This is all the
more curious because superficially read it could make a claim for
popularity greater than the best-selling *The Confessions of Nat
Turner*: for it is (nearly) a novel as mystery story. Constructed similarly to *Lie Down in Darkness*, it begins with a death the result of
violence, then proceeds to present a slow unraveling of the events
leading up to that death. By mystery story, of course, I am not implying the cheap thriller, or even the not-so-cheap thrillers of Ross
Macdonald, Raymond Chandler, or Dashiell Hammett. Styron's is,
unlike many others, a serious American literary novel with murder
at the core. (One thinks also of Dreiser's *An American Tragedy* and
Mailer's *An American Dream* and there the list seems to end.)
Styron's use of murder, if it resembles anyone's, is like Dostoevski's—murder employed ritualistically as well as symbolically. And
while early in this essay I rejected comparisons with Sophocles or
Homer or even Malcolm Lowry, I will invoke Dostoevski.

For like Raskolnikov in *Crime and Punishment*, Cass Kinsolving
is not morally hopeless, but merely tormented by his search for an
object equal to his endless rationalistic striving, for some meaning
to the world equal to his ceaseless tormented life of thought. Cass,
like Raskolnikov, can have hope for the future, but only after repentance. Styron and Dostoevski alike share great sympathy for the
poor and the defeated. (Some of Styron's best writing anywhere are
the descriptions of the contents and smells of the Negro cabin and
Michele's house, both in this novel.) Both writers are skillful in por-
traying abnormal states, and both write dramatic dialogues and
passages of intensest introspection. Yet the quality Styron most
shares with Dostoevski is his commitment to the novel of moral
responsibility. Published in a decade when the heroes of so many
novels were antiheroes—perverts and pushers, cowards and cads—
Styron's book deserves comparison with that of a great writer if for
no other reason than that he attempts something greater than most
of his contemporaries.

[204]

Art, according to Thomas Mann, is the fusion of suffering and the desire for form. More than in the works of Updike, Capote, or Barth, for instance, Styron assimilates human responsibility and moral suffering, and gives them shape we can recognize. While he has not yet accomplished a *Crime and Punishment*, through his fusion of mask, symbol, and dream into a theme of great suffering, Styron does achieve in *Set This House on Fire* high art. Cass Kinsolving's choice of being as opposed to nothingness, "not for the sake of being, or even the love of being much less the desire to be forever—but in the hope of being what I could be for a time," is a message for the decades.

Notes

1. For this and other observations I am indebted to Louise Y. Gossett's admirable chapter on Styron in *Violence in Recent Southern Fiction* (Durham, N.C., 1965), pp. 117–130.

2. See *The Language of Flowers* by "F. W. L." (London, 1968), p. 22.

3. J. E. Cirlot, *Dictionary of Symbols* (London, 1962), pp. 153–154.

4. Oswald Wirth, *Le tarot des imagiers du moyen age* (Paris, 1927), as quoted in Cirlot, *Dictionary of Symbols*, p. 103.

5. Marius Schneider, *La danza de espadas y la tarentela* (Barcelona, 1948), as quoted in Cirlot, *Dictionary of Symbols*, pp. 289–290.

GEORGE CORE

The Confessions of Nat Turner and the Burden of the Past

> We all have our simplifying image, our genius, and such hard bur-
> den does it lay upon us that, but for the praise of others, we would
> deride it and hunt it away.
> —W. B. Yeats, *The Trembling of the Veil*

The southern novelist must often awake, during the darkest hour of
the night, in a roil of tangled bedclothes and cold sweat. He is
haunted by a recurring nightmare—that he will be called *southern* by his critics and that his work will be defined as gothic and
grotesque—or that, worse still, the same fiction will be deemed a
historical novel. In this nightmare the ghost of Sir Walter Scott presides, the shade of William Gilmore Simms lingers nearby, and
Edgar Allan Poe's apparition laughs knowingly in the wings.

There is a long foreground to modern southern fiction, a foreground dense with folklore, myth, and history which twentieth-
century novelists have not hesitated to seize upon; yet at the same
time they have shrunk from being styled historical novelists as if *admittedly* using the form were the mark of Cain. Both Allen Tate and
Andrew Lytle have gone to incredible lengths to deny that they or
any other serious southern artists have written historical fiction: indeed Tate has said that *Gone With the Wind* is a historical novel and
that *None Shall Look Back*, *The Old Order*, and *The Velvet Horn* are
fiction as history, while Lytle has defined the historical novel as costume romance.

Part of this aversion no doubt dates from the inevitable and violent reaction to Walter Scott after his great popularity in the South.
Everyone remembers Mark Twain's famous indictment of Scott in
part 2 of *Life on the Mississippi*:

The South has not yet recovered from the debilitating influence of his books. . . . Sir Walter had so large a hand in making Southern character, as it existed before the war, that he is in great measure responsible for the war.

If this particular diatribe has escaped the memory, then I will recall for you the famous steamboat in *Huckleberry Finn*, a nesting place of thieves and murderers, which is named the *Walter Scott*; and when we last hear of the vessel it is rapidly heading downstream to certain destruction.

I am not here to praise or to bury Walter Scott, but I will say that although his example as novelist has been unfortunate in its effects, at least to the extent it has been followed by *American* imitators, Scott is a fine novelist, finer by far on the whole than Mark Twain. But we can readily sympathize, I think, with the novelists who have wanted to get out from Scott's long shadow, for they have seen his effect on the nineteenth-century novel. It has been persuasively argued that southern novelists today are trying to get out from under Faulkner; in times past they have attempted to move away from Scott's hegemony and the aura of Simms, Cooke, and Page.

The modern southern novelist has then adopted a defensive posture about the historical novel, having forgotten for the moment that a Russian count by the name of Tolstoy wrote a perfectly respectable historical novel entitled *War and Peace*. When a southern writer thinks of historical novels, he calls to mind Walter Edmonds, Kenneth Roberts, C. S. Forester (whom freshmen invariably think is E. M. Forster's famous brother), John Masters, and, especially, Margaret Mitchell. This habit of mind is by no means limited to the South: when Richard Hughes's *The Fox in the Attic* was published five or six years ago it was obvious most reviewers do not know a historical novel from an etiquette book. More recently Wilfrid Sheed has said that no historical novelist has ever done more than put his own experience into fancy dress and see how it works. The wonder is that the serious writer, in or out of the South, continues to create historical fiction.

Which brings me to the case of William Styron—after a long and circumlocutory introduction, for my allusion to Sheed is taken from his review of *The Confessions of Nat Turner*, a novel Mr. Styron has

[207]

called a meditation on history. Although it can technically be called that, I will say flatly that Nat Turner's story, as Styron presents it, is a historical novel. Now the misunderstanding of the historical novel is one reason for the furore which has surrounded this book within the last year or so—and especially after the release of a rebuttal by ten Negro writers. The most unfriendly critics have said, often and vociferously, that Styron's novel is neither historically accurate in its general outline, that is to say in its depiction of Virginia society and chattel slavery in the early 1800s—nor in its specific instance of Nat Turner as embodiment of a shadowy historical character. These reviewers believe that although Nat has a black skin, he has a white heart—and that he is a straw man set up by William Styron in a new but ultimately transparent defense of the Old South. For these critics the novel is therefore a racist tract, a spurious piece of propaganda, meretricious in its original promise.

If there is any way to isolate the fire of racial unpleasantness from the brimstone of other controversial matters (and I doubt this), I would say that much of the real grounds for argument resides in the old misconception of the differences between fiction and history, a distinction Aristotle drew sharply some twenty-three hundred years ago: "the one describes the thing that has been, and the other a kind of thing that might be." Sir Philip Sidney agreed with Aristotle that poetry is "something more philosophic and of graver import than history, since its statements are of the nature rather of universals, whereas those of history are singulars." As Sidney put it, the historian is "captived to the truth of a foolish world." Yet fiction and history have much in common, and Macaulay felicitously expressed one aspect of this connection: "History begins in novel and ends in essay." One might respond to Richard Gilman by quoting Macaulay. Gilman recently said, in a review of *Nat Turner*, that "literature, as literature, has nothing to do with history, other than being able to draw upon it as it is free to draw upon anything." Robert Penn Warren has observed that the historian and the fictionist are both dealing with imagined worlds, but that the historian wants the facts about and behind that world while the writer must know the inside of his world. Here history and fiction meet on the same ground, in a complementary, invariable kinship, far from the relation Gilman posits.

[208]

In *The Confessions of Nat Turner* William Styron is primarily concerned about depicting his characters fictively, from within—against a setting which must be at once historical and contemporaneous. Styron brings to life both the larger, encompassing action (Tidewater Virginia in the early nineteenth century) and the main action—the conflict of Nat Turner and the society of which he is a part. The conflict is characteristic of the historical novel, in that the action represents the collision of two worlds, the one dying, the other struggling to be born. (One might argue, with some justification, that the old world is today still in the agony of labor.) Nat as protagonist carries the seeds of this struggle within: it is reflected time and again in his innermost feelings, attitudes, and thoughts as well as his outward behavior. Indeed the very tensions within Nat—the discrepancy between what he believes and what he is forced to do—are representative of his society.

Whatever else may be said for and against the novel it must be granted, I think, that the enveloping action is beautifully rendered. By this I mean the whole ambience of the setting as Styron re-creates it for the reader through Nat is believable and moving. C. Vann Woodward has said that the novel "is informed by a respect for history, a sure feeling for the period, and a deep and precise sense of place and time." Even unfriendly critics have admitted this. Sheed, for instance, has said: "But if the book fails by default, as a novel, it does succeed in many places as a kind of historical tone poem. Styron's version of the old South is . . . place freshly imagined stone by stone." Quotations from the novel will not easily demonstrate this aspect: it is better to examine a representative scene and see what it will yield. The scene I choose is the visit at Turner's Mill by "a pair of traveling Episcopal clergymen—'the Bishop's visitants.'" The bishop is "awaiting some *providential wind* to guide us in the right direction," the priests intone solemnly. The providential wind must come from "the more *prosperous* landowners of the diocese," whom these unctuous henchmen have been detailed to poll. The ensuing conversation between Samuel Turner, his alcoholic brother Benjamin, and the priests throws the period attitudes toward slavery into a harsh, clear light: Samuel Turner's sane voice—slavery "is a cancer eating at our bowels, the source of all our misery, individual, political, and economic. It is the greatest curse a supposedly free and enlightened society has been saddled with in modern times, or any other time"—is drowned out by his brother's drunken, hilarious, and contemptible dogmatics: "A darky, gentlemen, is basically as unteachable as a chicken, and that is the simple fact of the matter."

So Styron begins his dramatic rendering of the failure of religion in the upcountry Tidewater. The society revealed in the early parts of the novel is what Allen Tate has called a "feudal society, without a feudal religion; hence only a semi-feudal society." As he has remarked, the Old South was incapable of creating an appropriate religion, appropriate for its way of life—the economy, politics, and culture of the region. One might go further and say, with Mr. Tate, that the god of the Old South was created by the New World merchants of the sixteenth century. The mythology of the Old South was therefore incomplete: the fabric of its life was fatally marred by the divergence between the secular and religious impulses. Religion cannot be perfunctory and formalistic in a traditional society, if that way of life is to survive.

The enveloping action of *The Confessions of Nat Turner* deals in large part with this failure of Protestantism, and Styron makes it perfectly clear the failure is principally due to the curse of slavery. In this respect—the comprehensiveness and credibility of the picture of decadent Protestantism—Styron has outstripped other southern novelists who have touched upon the same subject; and this, to my mind, may be the most important historical and social dimension to the novel—more so than its depiction of slavery.

Nat's masters are all religious in the trite mechanical sense, and Samuel Turner (who is significantly not a church-going man) is the most nearly Christian of them all. The mannered Episcopalianism which Turner half-heartedly professes is replaced in Nat's life by the backwoods fundamentalism of the Reverend Eppes. In church Eppes whips his parishioners into a frenzy, whereupon they strip to their underwear and ride "each other bareback up and down the aisles." Later Nat is exposed to the callous Methodism of Margaret Whitehead's brother. When we last see this divine—prior to the onset of the rebellion—he is joining the posse to track down Will, "his prim lips vengefully set." It is ironic that a Baptist camp meeting gives Nat the chance to put his tactical plan into motion, and it is a mark of Styron's sure craftsmanship that the immediate foreground of both great turning points in Nat's fortunes—his transfer from the Turners to Eppes—and his rebellion (which begins with the murder of his first kind master since Samuel Turner)—are preceded by camp meetings. Nat misses the first when he inadvertently delivers his friend Willis to a slave trader; the second gives him the opportunity for the vengeance against all that has gone before in his life, for all the wrongs, real and imagined, including the sale of Willis, which he has carried in his heart.

But this is of course only half the story. The greatest irony in Nat's confessions lies in the fact that he is a more religious man than any of his masters, indeed more than anyone else in the novel; and his primitive Christianity is purer, more orthodox, than the Protestantism of the region, taken singly by denomination or as a whole. Yet Nat is separated from his spirituality when the rebellion begins, and the redemptive moment at the end of the novel, immediately before his execution, is a little forced.

Styron has said that *The Confessions of Nat Turner* is "a sort of religious parable and a story of exculpation. . . . It should be apparent that the book expresses the idea of Old Testament savagery and revenge redeemed by New Testament charity and brotherhood—affirmation." This is admittedly one aspect of the novel; but in giving us an allegorical explanation the author is unnecessarily limiting the meaning of his fable. As Andrew Lytle has remarked, "Whenever a writer talks about a story or a novel he has done, he is not speaking in his true voice. That voice has already been heard in the rendition of the action."

The Confessions of Nat Turner is more than religious parable—what some critics might call a modern-day version of *Pilgrim's Progress*, with Nat as a negative hero caught in the throes of an existential agony like Camus's Stranger. Indeed Walter Sullivan has persuasively read the novel in terms not far removed from these. I believe, on the contrary, that the novel is generated by a deeply religious impulse which is not so simple as either Christian or existential parable would have it; for the story has that timeless, nonsectarian Christian dimension which one finds over and again in Hawthorne, Melville, Faulkner, and Warren. And it is all to Styron's credit that he has firmly resisted the perhaps strong desire to make his protagonist into a Christ-figure. The consequences of this almost-suicidal urge on the part of American novelists are too well known to bear repeating here, although I will ask rhetorically whether the appearance of a Christ-figure in any major piece of American literature since *Billy Budd* has been anything short of embarrassing to reader and author alike.

The point is relevant to my discussion because several critics have cited the historical Nat's retort to Thomas Gray's question about the failure of the rebellion: "Was not Christ crucified?" This piece of verbal heroics may be a "direct, simple and great flash" and "the most dramatic moment in the actual *Confessions*," as Herbert Aptheker has said; but a beginning student in fiction writing could tell Mr. Aptheker such a line doesn't belong in fiction. Judgment of this kind is unfortunately typical of the critics who have attacked Styron for his novel's lack of historicity. The critic who makes it— Stanley Kauffmann, Richard Gilman, Mike Thelwell, and Aptheker are typical—has no idea what George Saintsbury meant when he remarked, seventy-five years ago, that the great danger for the novelist is decanting too much history into his novel.

It is of course not enough for a novelist to be a good historian in order to make a fiction which will be read a century or even a decade after it is written. Were this so, Kenneth Roberts's work would not already be largely forgotten. Roberts is quite a good historian, but his talent for fiction is too limited for him to render novelistically the history he understands so well.

We come now to the vexed question of what a historical novel is—how it characteristically works—and why (a question that I do not intend to belabor). E. M. W. Tillyard has shrewdly argued that the historical novel is the lineal descendant of the epic—another literary form that is little understood today. In epic one is immediately confronted by the idea of myth and mythology—what the informing vision of a traditional society entails, as I have mentioned. In the epic and in the historical novel the dying traditional society has a shared way of looking at the world, a definite yet unstated ethic; and that ethic collapses in the face of pressures from within and without the society. The protagonist is of that society—yet apart from it, aware of change, and contending with change in the vortex of a historical crisis in which he is inescapably affected. The author uses history, then, as a frame for the central action, the inspiriting conflict which is his true subject; but the historical element is deliberately muted so far as particulars go: if it is not, then the novelist loses control and history takes over. In consequence the good novelist is careful not to put major historical figures in the center of the stage. In the same way, unless he is a superb craftsman who is utterly in control, he had best steer away from major historical events—from letting those events play too great a role in his fiction. That these dangers are real may be simply proven when we remember that a good novel has never been written about the American Civil War—or the Second World War.

There are two kinds of themes in the historical novel which the artist must seize and which he must bring together into firm unity: those that deal with the actual events and characters of the period he is writing about—the outer world—and those that concern the human life and its peculiar emotional gravity in this period and any other—the inner world. Since it is far easier to depict the outer world of fact as it can be historically reconstructed than it is to render the emotional life of the leading characters, the novelist must take pains to ensure that fiction is not subordinated to history; for otherwise what we get is history with a fictional subplot—the kind of work that Kenneth Roberts has characteristically written. The center of composition in a good historical novel, as in any other kind of significant fiction, is provided by the fable, which is nothing less than the central action in miniature—the particular recurring pattern of life the author chooses—which can only be abstractly expressed through theme.

The rich density of Styron's fable in *The Confessions of Nat Turner* may be measured in large part by Philip Rahv's praise. He finds that the novel's creative success has come from the author's having caught "a substantial theme central to the national experience." That theme is expressed in various and similar ways by Judge Cobb, Samuel Turner, Margaret Whitehead, and Nat himself. Cobb puts it best when he cries out about the wrecked old dominion—Virginia. He sees the wasteland around him as having been caused by economic greed which sprang from Virginia's success with tobacco. The land has been literally ravaged by the reckless planting of tobacco; it has been figuratively cursed by the presence of slavery which now takes its most ominous form since Virginia has become "a monstrous breeding farm to supply the sinew to gratify the maw of Eli Whitney's infernal machine," as Cobb shouts to Nat.

The historical crisis eventuates in the breakup of Tidewater plantation society, and the personal reflection of this great transformation is instanced in Nat Turner's struggle to achieve selfhood. And so the historical, objective, logical plane of the novel—the larger action—is joined to the human, subjective, psychological level—the fable—by the common theme of the curse of slavery. Slavery, as Styron sees it, is the primary reason for the social, economic, and political changes which take place in Nat's world; whereas the failure of religion to provide a mythology shows the hollowness of its values, values which are prudential and expedient. The collapse of this society, Styron implies, is caused by its arrogant commercialism—and its inhumanity. Nat, like any other slave, is affected on both counts.

By showing how slavery affects every department of life and every stratum of society in Virginia in the early 1800s, Styron not only gives human embodiment and concreteness to his themes, but he brings to us a sense of the society as a whole and the interaction of the individuals who make up that society; for we are shown both religion and class through representative characters and actions. For instance, Travis, Nat's last master, is a mountaineer whose origins are similar to Thomas Sutpen's; McBride, the overseer who rapes Nat's mother, is a shanty Irishman; and so forth. In these ways Styron gives his novel the continuity of what George Lukács calls popular life, the life of the common people and the way history (as we know it from the vantage point of the present) impinges upon them.

Nat himself is essential to the unfolding action since he tells the story from beginning to end; and in examining his importance as a literary creation we are touching upon the nerve center of William Styron's novel. It is by now a commonplace that Styron's most daring strategy in *The Confessions of Nat Turner* is to present the action from the standpoint of a Negro when the author is a white man. Certain Negro critics have argued—unconvincingly, I think—that a black man cannot be effectively rendered by a white author, especially a Virginian; by this reasoning we should throw out *Othello* and do away with any other work of literature in which an author of one race depicts the life of another race from within. (I know of no such cry from the Indians about *A Passage to India*.)

Technically, once Styron had "solved" the problem of his narrative point of view and of getting inside the mind and psyche of a complicated black human being, he really had little else to contend with. By this I mean that if you grant Styron his donnée and find it credible, you almost of necessity will find the novel convincing. Through this device the author has achieved a new simplicity which is not evident in his first two full-length novels, fictions which are enormously more complicated in a technical sense than *The Confessions of Nat Turner*. In his work Styron has exhibited the tendencies which Glenway Wescott sees as characteristic of contemporary fiction:

My conclusion is that brilliancy of ego, headstrong and headlong display of intellect, powers of elaboration, poetical afflatus, and that frenzied and exalted artistry which is like drunkenness, play an important part in literature; but as regularly as clockwork, most of the time, everything of that sort has to give way to a prosaic simplicity, to brevity and explicitness, and to traditional themes and immemorial symbols and images.

If I may be permitted to display an old chesnut, it is clear that William Styron has used "technique as discovery" in this novel more than most novelists can or will—and yet technique by no means becomes preeminent. He has followed the examples of Ford Madox Ford, Faulkner, Tate, and Warren in his strategies; and on the whole these have worked. The chief one involves point of view, as I have said; and here Styron has used a convention, one immediately recognizable to anyone who knows how to read fiction. The author invests Nat with a sensibility and intelligence and range of knowledge which are doubtless greater than he in fact possessed as historical personage, but this is possible because so little is known of the actual Nat Turner. If we knew more about him, the very recalcitrance of the facts that were the man might prevent his becoming an important fictive creation. This is true of Lee, for example. Warren once said of him: "Who cares about Robert E. Lee? Now there's a man who's smooth as an egg. Turn him around, this pri-

mordial perfection: you see, he has no story. . . . It's only the guy
who's angular, incomplete, and struggling who has a story."

Having given Nat Turner considerable complexity Styron must
render it; and he does so by providing Nat with two voices—the
one is a received, standard nineteenth-century southern rhetoric
which has much in common with the similar language of Faulkner,
Wolfe, and Warren; the other is plantation Negro dialect of the same
period, this last being more enduring and less literary, and it may
still be heard often today. The problem is how to account for two
radically different forms of speech coming from the same person.
The first voice approximates the written word, the way Nat would
have set down his story himself; it is stately rhetoric, one appropriate for the occasion of his confessions to Gray and the world—and a
form of speech in keeping with the language of the educated southerner. The second voice is that of the spoken word, caused by necessity—Nat's need not to antagonize his masters and his equal
need to communicate with his fellow Negroes. That such bifurca-
tion ordinarily exists between written and spoken language could
not be proven, not even by the histrionics of a transformational
grammarian; but there is a basic distinction between language as
we write it or otherwise employ it formally—and language as we
use it conversationally, especially with folk whom we presume to be
more ignorant than ourselves. Styron has grounded his convention
on that solid and indisputable foundation.

Some critics have objected that no one ever talked as Judge Cobb
and Thomas Gray and Nat Turner do in the course of the narrative.
To this argument one might answer that nobody (even Thomas
Wolfe himself) ever spoke the mellifluous idiom of Eugene Gant,
and that no one in conversation ever used the baroque periods of
Mr. Compson or Gavin Stevens. The related objection that Styron
has written the novel directly in his own voice will not stand inspec-
tion, even though Styron has testified against himself in this respect. The language of *The Confessions of Nat Turner* is not the
language of *Lie Down in Darkness* or *Set This House on Fire*, and
the difference is not simply a matter of artistic change and maturity.

Styron has deliberately fashioned a southern, biblical language
for Nat which is complemented by a level of definite Latinity, of
Miltonic sonorities, as George Steiner has remarked. The deeper

current of this prose, Steiner tells us, "relates the novel to other moments in American consciousness and prose in which the syntax of the Jacobean Bible, compressed by Puritan intensity or loosened and made florid by political rhetoric, served to define the new world. From Cotton Mather to Faulkner and James Baldwin, biblical speech has set a core of vision and public ornament inside the American language." The deliberately archaic quality of the language therefore has a range of powerful effects. The style reflects the religious themes, the sacramental dimension which is part and parcel of the novel.

We turn now to the character of William Styron's Nat Turner. Nat is haunted by three obsessions, each bound to the other: repressed sexuality, the possibility of escape from servitude through violent overthrow of his white masters, and religious fanaticism. It is the quality of his religiousness that gives Nat his deep humanity and complexity, not his sexual urges, which Styron has used quite plausibly as an alternative means for the modern reader to understand Nat and the condition of his servitude. Ultimately Nat's spirituality exceeds his religious fanaticism, and his sexuality is also sublimated. Stanley Kauffmann, in a perverse and brilliant misreading of the novel, has suggested that Styron left his religious parable unfinished by not presenting Nat as a Christ-figure but that, having so failed, he could have still "saved" his fiction by presenting the "psychosexual drama" in a more believable, less hackneyed fashion, rather than being "glib and reductive." Kauffmann really wants Freudian tragedy, I suspect. He misreads the character of Nat Turner as Styron reveals it: Nat is a sensitive man who is wholly possessed by his humanity and by his sacramental way of looking at the world: this in the end leads to his undoing as a revolutionary leader and to his redemption as a man. Indeed one might say that the tragedy of Nat Turner is caused by his humanity against the general inhumanity of his time, and that in the moment of crisis he was unable to stifle that humanity.

Now I would not argue that *The Confessions of Nat Turner* is a flawless novel in a technical or a substantive sense, as I will doubtless be accused of doing. I would only say that its critics have on the whole seriously misjudged its virtues and defects through a misreading not only of the novel but of southern history. For example,

Styron's slight departures from the text of the original *Confessions* are beside the point, because in a fictive sense and in the larger historical perspective it makes little or no difference who taught the actual Nat how to read, or whether he or his father ran away, or whether Will was a homicidal maniac, or whether slaves helped quell the rebellion. What is of essential importance is Nat's stature as a man as Styron renders it—and his place in the society which produced him. I wholly agree with Louis Rubin when he says, "It is my belief that when the smoke of controversy blows away . . . the best critics . . . will recognize how fine a characterization, and how great a man, William Styron's Nat Turner is."

The defects of the novel result principally from the author's use of a single, restricted post of observation and his decision to write a tour de force. Nat's presence becomes a little tedious at times, even though the shifts from panoramic summary to scenic presentation work well on the whole. His commentary on the natural setting as it reflects his own visions tends to strain our credulity, despite our awareness that the pathetic fallacy in such instances is part of the prophetic mode. What Styron sacrifices in his choice of point of view is typical of tragedy and epic—that quality which Yeats calls the emotion of the multitude—the choral effect. Styron's method lets us see life as a whole in the historical situation he has chosen to illuminate, but that method is necessarily a little too schematic in the treatment of slaveholders, as some critics have complained, and, to a lesser extent, in the anatomy of Protestantism. In limiting the action to one post of observation Styron has lost the advantage of the multiple point of view: greater comprehensiveness, objectivity, and credibility might have inhered in a different treatment; and I think it undeniable that more reflectors would have provided another analogy for the action. As it is the action has but two dimensions—the larger historical frame which may be called overplot, and the main action which embodies the fable. So *The Confessions of Nat Turner* lacks an underplot, and Nat's recurring dream of the mysterious "white building standing on its promontory high above the shore" is not a satisfactory alternative for a fully realized analogy to the action. An underplot would have given the kind of random, indeterminate quality of felt life itself, had it been used properly. If *Hamlet* and *Bleak House* and *War and Peace* are too stern in the examples they offer, one can cite appropriate instances from Faulkner and Warren. Lacking this dimension the plot seems a little contrived, too neat in short.

I have purposely been applying the highest standards, because even though *The Confessions of Nat Turner* does plainly fall short of greatness, it does not miss by much being a novel of the next rank— the place occupied by *The Sound and the Fury, Light in August,* and *Absalom, Absalom!* It will not be said, I hope, that my implication is that technique is everything—that by a mere change of strategy here and there Styron might have produced a masterpiece, a southern *War and Peace.* Certainly no one would argue this who knows anything about the historical development of the novel—nor would he agree with Richard Gilman that with a "'subject' such as Nat Turner . . . you either advance fictional art or set it back." (Gilman and Kauffmann both suggest that Styron needed to create a new novelistic form: to this the most appropriate answer is Dr. Johnson's—"Ignorance, sheer ignorance.") Technique in the end is merely a way of seeing the job at hand and getting at it; the informing vision of the artist and the spreading field of possibility it affords him and the reader are something else again. This brings us to a consideration of the most abiding aspects of the novel at hand—and indeed of any good historical novel about the South.

The balance sheet reveals that in *The Confessions of Nat Turner* William Styron has clearly and ably used those strategies which Scott made available for the historical novelist; but Styron has worked not so much deliberately as intuitively, I would think. He did not set out to write his novel along the lines of the classic formula I have sketched—quite the contrary. The book would seem to have come, as Warren tells us, out of a long and painful "brooding, an activity deep, personal and at any conscious level, aimless, the process of finding a self for the story and story in the self." That this is evident strikes me as unarguable: one need only look at Styron's response to Herbert Aptheker in the *Nation*, or to his opening remarks at a Southern Historical Association panel discussion. In both places he quotes at some length from George Lukács's brilliant study of the historical novel. Obviously Styron read this book after writing Nat Turner's story and getting embroiled with Aptheker and others in defending it. He encountered Lukács with a shock of recognition and realized his methods in the novel were classically correct. In speaking of Lukács rather selfconsciously, Styron is erecting a defense for his novel which is far more substantial than his earlier random remarks which I have alluded to on several occasions—remarks which have tended to undercut his art by oversimplification. Today Styron would not be embarrassed to admit that *The Confessions of Nat Turner* is a historical novel—and, having discovered this, he may now be content to let the novel stand on its own. There is an obvious moral to be drawn for the southern novelist, but I will spare you that; for I want to look once again at the novel—this time in a slightly different perspective.

"Things reveal themselves passing away," someone remarked to Yeats; and this comment holds not only the largest significance of *The Confessions of Nat Turner* but of the historical novel generally. In this novel we see the destruction of feudal society in Tidewater Virginia, and its death throes produce a Nat Turner, one of those specters who appear in the darkening gloom when a way of life is coming to an end. Nat as we know him historically is a symptom and little more: indeed Edmund Wilson is being metaphorical in calling him a black John Brown. In bringing Nat to life as a complex, deeply human person of tragic dimensions, Styron has given us what Lukács calls the sine qua non of the historical novel—a concrete prehistory of the present. Now this does not mean the past is simply a preliminary to the present, and that it is distorted from its proper shape to become congruent with the apparent configuration of the present: it is to say that Styron shows the transformations of history as the changes in common life—life not only in early nineteenth-century Virginia but in our own time, because these social disruptions and transitions are essentially alike: they always are. As Lukács says, "Without a felt relationship to the present, a portrayal of history is impossible." The trick is in "giving poetic life to those historical social and human forces which . . . have made our present-day life what it is," without distorting the past.

William Styron has dramatized a significant moment in the southern past—the Nat Turner rebellion, and in illuminating that moment through the informing power of fiction he has revealed to us what may be seen as the first important crossing of the ways that radically affected the established southern social fabric. The early decades of the nineteenth century in the upcountry Tidewater reveal a serious breach in the feudal complexion of southern society; and if the old squirearchy of Virginia is here passing away to be reincarnated in the plantations of the Deep South (a story told in *The Long Night* and *Absalom, Absalom!*), the same pattern of disruption and accommodation recurs in more obvious, cataclysmic proportions in the Civil War and its aftermath. It is not being too fanciful, I believe, to suggest that John Brown's raid as prologue to the war is a repetition of the Nat Turner rebellion in some respects: in this sense Wilson's analogy holds true. The later crossroads in southern history—the end of Reconstruction and the birth of the New South, the First World War, the depression years, and finally the decades since the Second World War (a period of which we are so much a part as to be partially blinded to whatever truth it may hold)—have a good deal in common with the 1820s and 30s in upcountry Virginia. To this extent, then, *The Confessions of Nat Turner* is a paradigm of the present: William Styron has used memory and imagination for a liberation—ours and his—from time future as well as time past. Nat's ultimate redemption, Styron suggests, is our own, since as Eliot says,

> A people without history
> Is not redeemed from time, for history is a pattern
> Of timeless moments.

Styron shows us the past in the present in this novel, but his fiction does not compress and refract all time to the eternally present. We are therefore redeemed from time, if only briefly, by our understanding of a moment in history as it bears upon the present and our own experience. In this sense *The Confessions of Nat Turner* is very much a novel of our day.

Through our understanding of the past, whether it is made possible by fiction or history—by a William Styron or a Vann Woodward, we are liberated from the old atavistic and disabling southern preoccupation with the past, but we are by no means freed entirely from it. On the contrary, we simply come to terms with the past and the present and therefore ourselves and the predicament of being human in a time of terrible stress and disrelation. The collective experience of the southern people, Woodward has shrewdly observed, is the most distinctive and enduring feature of the South—not the legends, shibboleths, and apologias which have derived from it. If we as southerners are ever entirely freed of our awareness of a common past—if we ever give up our attempts to understand that past in the light of all the knowledge and compassion which we can bring to bear on it, the South and the southern identity will no longer signify; and the region east of the Mississippi and south of Mason and Dixon's line will simply be a part of the national geography.

The southerner is uniquely himself by virtue of the South's history, his feeling for that history and the place which that history affords. For him, as Faulkner said, "The past is never dead. It is not even past." A novel such as *The Confessions of Nat Turner* reconciles past and present without confusing either. And in consequence of the renewed awareness of the southern experience which William Styron makes possible for us—an awareness that this experience is itself a great image of the human condition, we can more easily assume the burden of the past.

ARDNER R. CHESHIRE, JR.

The Recollective Structure of *The Confessions of Nat Turner*

In part 1 ("Judgment Day") of William Styron's *The Confessions of Nat Turner* (1967), Nat sits in his cell awaiting the hour when he will be brought to trial for his insurrection and summarily sentenced to die. Stripped of his belief in the absolute righteousness of his rebellion, all Nat can feel is "despair, despair so sickening" that he thinks it might drive him insane. He feels as if he has been cast by God "beneath the largest rock on earth, there to live in hideous, perpetual dark." In the quiet of the autumn afternoon, Nat raises his eyes skyward and asks: "*Then what I done was wrong, Lord? . . . And if what I done was wrong, is there no redemption?*" Receiving no answer from God, he returns in memory to "old times past" in an attempt to understand why he is trapped in such terrifying spiritual darkness.

A man on his judgment day, reflecting on his moral responsibility for past actions and the possibility of redemption—this is an important motif not only in *The Confessions of Nat Turner* but in Styron's two other novels as well. At the beginning of *Lie Down in Darkness* (1951), for example, Milton Loftis awaits the coffin which holds the body of his beloved daughter Peyton. For the first time in his life, he must confront and assess the "evidence of all his errors." As he waits for Peyton's body to arrive on the train, Loftis returns in his mind to time past, hoping to find answers to the questions which have been pushing their way into the forefront of his consciousness: What did I do wrong? What is my responsibility in Peyton's death? Is there any hope that I can transcend my sorrow and my guilt? Similarly, in *Set This House on Fire* (1960), both the narrator, Peter Leverett, and the hero of the novel, Cass Kinsolving, are drawn back in memory to Sambuco, Italy, because of Peter's feelings of sorrow, regret, and recrimination, and to those old questions: "*What am I doing? Where am I going?*"

Previous interpretations of Styron's work have not dealt with the significance of this recollective framework. Yet, particularly in *The Confessions of Nat Turner*, the recollective character of the hero's meditation on past experience provides the structural key to the novel. When *The Confessions of Nat Turner* is viewed from this perspective, the existential questions that Styron poses are placed in sharp focus, and the novel transcends the many heated arguments concerning the relationship between black characters and a white author and the institution of slavery in the Old South.

Nat's confession is much more than a series of flashbacks; it is a recollection of past experience. Although recollection has been significant in Western philosophic thought and literature since Plato's dialogues, Gabriel Marcel's *The Philosophy of Existence* (1949) and *The Mystery of Being* (1950) define the process in a way which best illuminates the meditative framework of Styron's last novel. This connection does not necessarily imply that Styron was a student of Marcel's philosophy, though in several interviews he has indicated his longstanding admiration of French literature and philosophy. The extent of his debt to Marcel or anyone else is not the concern of this study. It is simply that Marcel's philosophy helps us better understand the recollective structure of *The Confessions of Nat Turner*.

In all of his philosophical works, Marcel makes a distinction between primary reflection, which is analytical, and secondary reflection, or recollection, which is recuperative. In primary reflection, one views experience as a problem to be solved, as something which can be broken down and viewed objectively. In secondary reflection, on the other hand, one is involved in a very personal, sympathetic meditation of past experience. Marcel writes of the two processes in *The Mystery of Being:* "Roughly, we can say that where primary reflection tends to dissolve the unity of experience which is first put before it, the function of secondary reflection is essentially recuperative; it reconquers that unity." He defines recollection even more straightforwardly in *The Philosophy of Existence:* "The word means what it says—the act whereby I recollect myself as a unity."

What are the conditions necessary for recollection? In *The Mys-*

tery of Being Marcel indicates that recollection never occurs unless the individual feels that something important is at stake, unless he faces an experience or an obstacle which threatens his concept of self. There must be "an anxious self-questioning," Marcel says, "about the relationship that subsists between me and my life." In such a situation the individual feels that there has been a total break in the continuity of his experience, and he loses all sense of self-direction or destiny. Recollection results from the individual's attempt to pass from a state of ontological disorientation to a higher state of existence which recaptures a sense of personal wholeness and direction.

Through secondary reflection, the individual not only attempts to surmount the antinomies of personal experience and recover unity of being, he also tries to break down the barriers between himself and other human beings and between himself and Being. Ultimately, recollection moves an individual from the emptiness of isolation and estrangement to the plenitude of participation. When such barriers as ignorance, misplaced fidelity, and egoism in all its many forms are transcended, the individual is able to participate more fully in Being, to move from an I-It to an I-Thou relationship with the world. This ontological communion is essentially a religious experience that gives meaning to life. All being, Marcel thinks, experiences the need for communion. The individual is insufficient and frustrated if denied participation with others.

Nat's confession has all the distinguishing characteristics of a recollection as defined by Marcel. Faced with a spiritual discontinuity (his inability to pray or to feel the presence of God), and an existential discontinuity (his imminent death), Nat attempts, through recollection, to understand the fundamental orientation of his being and to establish a new relationship with God. He comes to see through his meditation that his redemption depends, and always has depended, not only on rebelling against and being free of the system of chattel slavery, but on participating in the fellowship of Being, on moving away from isolation and estrangement toward a loving relationship with another human being. The story of Nat Turner is one of a man in quest of himself and communion with others and with God, a quest that almost fails initially because of his misplaced fidelity to his white masters, and later, because of his inability to see the world in nonabstract, human terms.

In "Old Times Past: Visions, Dreams, Recollections," Nat is depicted as being unable to comprehend, much less to pursue, his own unique destiny. He has an unquestioning faith in his white masters instead of himself. Unaware that the very nature of the master-slave system precludes any real individual freedom or any loving relationship between whites and blacks, Nat thinks that Turner's Mill is Paradise and that "Marse Sam" is a wise and kind deity. "At this time," Nat says, "my regard for him is very close to the feeling one should bear only toward the Divinity." And if Marse Sam is Apollo to young Nat, Sam Turner's wife, Nell, is Athena. It is she, along with her oldest daughter, who teaches him to read, write, add, and subtract. The other goddess in the Turner household is Marse Sam's youngest daughter, Miss Emmeline. "I worshiped her," Nat remembers, "with the chaste, evangelical passion that could only be nurtured in the innocent heart of a boy like myself, reared in surroundings where women (at least white ladies) seemed to float like bubbles in an immaculate effulgence of purity and perfection."

For a time, the Turners do, in fact, appear to deserve Nat's worship of them, particularly after Sam Turner decides to give Nat his freedom when he becomes twenty-five. At first, the idea of freedom is quite unsettling to Nat. "But," he says, "my worst fears began to melt away . . . when like some blessed warmth there slowly crept over me an understanding of this gift of my own salvation, which only one in God knew how many thousands of Negroes could hope ever to receive, and was beyond all prizing." At this point in his life, Nat's devotion to Samuel Turner knows no bounds. His god has justified his faith with a promise of new life.

Somewhat later, Nat's faith in Sam Turner is severely shaken. The one close childhood friendship that Nat forms is abruptly broken when Sam Turner sells Nat's friend Willis in order to raise capital for the plantation. Nat never feels closer to anyone than he does to Willis, whom he comes to consider his brother. Working together in the carpenter shop and afterward reading the Bible and praying, they become inseparable companions. When Willis is sold,

Nat is crushed. He naïvely believed that Willis was only to be hired out to another Virginia plantation for two weeks. But as soon as he meets the white men who take Willis, Nat realizes that Sam Turner only used a ruse to sell a slave without an unpleasant scene. Nat is especially miserable because he himself delivered Willis in the dead of night to the slave trader. After sitting in the wagon for more than an hour after Willis is gone, he starts back to Turner's Mill "with an emptiness" that he had never felt before.

Nat's faith in the Turners is seriously undermined and finally destroyed when they are forced to sell the mill, and Nat is placed in the hands of the homosexual Reverend Eppes. Because Nat resists his advances, this fanatical, backwoods preacher treats him not like a pet but a field hand. From before sunup to after sundown, seven days a week, Nat hoes, chops, shells corn, empties chamber pots, and generally does for the first time what most of his fellow blacks had done from the time they were teenagers. Nat remembers that he "began to sense the world, the *true* world, in which a Negro moves and breathes. It was like being plunged into freezing water." He continues to stay with this crazed preacher only because of "the gloomy comfort of Ecclesiastes"—the book of the Bible which Camus used as a starting point for *The Myth of Sisyphus*, and which Nat undoubtedly uses as the starting point for his later belief in absolute, existential freedom.

Though Eppes is supposed to carry out Sam Turner's promise to make Nat a free man at age twenty-five, the preacher sells him instead to an illiterate small farmer named Tom Moore. The promise of freedom, which had so helped to sustain Nat, is taken away. He suddenly realizes that he exists, and always has existed, in a closed system which denies him the right to be an individual. On the winter day he is sold, Nat remembers: "I experienced a kind of disbelief which verged close upon madness, then a sense of betrayal, then fury such as I had never known before, then finally, to my dismay, hatred so bitter that I grew dizzy and thought I might get sick on the floor." Needless to say, Nat no longer sees Marse Sam as a benevolent deity. From the moment he is sold by Eppes, Nat banishes his first master from his mind "as one banishes the memory of any disgraced and downfallen prince." Nat's childlike faith in white authority is destroyed, but at this point he is unable to reflect on past experience in any philosophical way. He is too filled with hate. Not until he is in jail does he come to understand that his misplaced fidelity to white authority made it impossible for him to achieve an authentic identity or to enter into a loving relationship with another human being.

In part 3 of *The Confessions of Nat Turner,* "Study War," Nat swings from submission to violence and attempts to transcend the chaos of his existence through a quest for complete existential freedom. Having read and talked only about the Bible all his life, Nat understandably expresses his intense desire for freedom through Old Testament rhetoric, and he plans the details of his rebellion using the prophetic books of the Old Testament. The Old Testament God of retribution replaces Sam Turner in Nat's reordered world, and as Styron has stated in an interview in the *Yale Alumni Magazine* (November 1967), Nat sees himself as an "avenging Old Testament angel."

Underlying Nat's biblical rhetoric, however, is a philosophy of personal commitment, action, and choice rather than any reliance on authority. The decision to rebel against his white masters is his and his alone. Throughout "Study War," Styron undercuts the idea of Nat's being controlled by God. He clearly indicates that Nat's visions always occur when he is in a weakened condition from fasting or when he has been driven almost to a frenzy by punishment or sexual desire. For example, his most significant vision comes on the fifth day of one of these fasts when he sees a white and a black angel locked in celestial combat. The white angel strikes the black with his sword, but the sword breaks and the black angel is unharmed. As Nat continues to look skyward, he sees the black angel riding "triumphant among the clouds." He takes this as a sign from God, though he is unsure if the Lord really intends him literally to take up the sword against the whites. To his whispered question, "Lord . . . hast Thou truly called me to this?" Nat receives "no answer, no answer at all." It seems quite clear that Nat himself freely chooses to rebel against the condition of slavery; God does not command or guide him. Still, because of his religious sensibilities, Nat ascribes the inspiration for his rebellion to God, an Old Testament God of retribution.

Having chosen to fight for his freedom, Nat is now faced with a moral dilemma which becomes the central issue in the section "Study War": what to do about the few white people for whom he has sympathy. The success of his insurrection demands that they be killed, but something inside Nat recoils at the idea of such a completely heartless slaughter. Nat and the other slaves will be forced to kill both the cruel, such as Will's owner, Francis, and the basically kind, such as Nat's master, Travis. Women and children will also have to die. Despite Nat's hatred of the white man, his obsession with freedom, and the precedents for slaughter he finds in the Old Testament, he has misgivings about taking human life so indiscriminately.

Nat's moral aversion to murder is dramatized at the very outset of the rebellion, which he is supposed to inaugurate by killing Travis. However, when the time comes to slay his master, Nat misses him "by half a foot" with his broadaxe. On his second attempt, the axe blade glances harmlessly off Travis's shoulder. Before Nat can lift his weapon for the third time, Will bounds into the room and with one blow of his hatchet sends Travis's head rolling on the floor. Though Nat convinced his followers that murder was essential to their freedom, he cannot kill the very man who holds him as chattel. This is the case because in the seconds before he first raises his axe, Nat actually *sees* Travis for the first time. As Travis awakes, his eyes and Nat's meet, and Nat is aware that "beneath the perplexity, the film of sleep, his eyes were brown and rather melancholy, acquainted with hard toil, remote perhaps, somewhat inflexible but not at all unkind." Nat feels that he knows his master at last. Until this moment, Travis had been to Nat a "far-off abstract being." Now, Nat realizes that "whatever else he [Travis] was, he was a man."

Why, then, does Nat kill Margaret Whitehead? By his own admission, she was the only woman with whom he had "experienced even one moment of a warm and mysterious and mutual confluence of sympathy." There appear to be three plausible answers to this important question. First, Nat must kill Margaret if he is to maintain control of his followers. Challenged by the fanatic Will either to spill blood or to relinquish his command, Nat decides that the success of his rebellion hinges on slaying Margaret. Second, Nat kills her because of that very sympathy she had for him. With the exception of Jeremiah Cobb, when a white person in Southampton County sympathizes with or pities Nat or another black, it is obvious that he does so from a decided position of superiority. It is not the concern of one fellow human being for another; it is more like the concern of a human being for an injured animal. Margaret, for example, reacts to the half-crushed turtle in the road in much the same way she does to the plight of the "poor darkies" who are mistreated by their masters. Consequently, when pitied, Nat burns inside, believing that the person who pities him refuses to see him as a man with pride, as a man capable of acting with courage and dignity even in a losing cause.

Third, and perhaps most importantly, he murders Margaret because she is an innocent, beautiful, white girl. Most white southerners would have considered any serious mistreatment of a southern lady by a slave to be the ultimate crime a black could commit. Hence, when Nat runs his sword into Margaret's body and caves in her skull with a fence post, he is symbolically raping and destroying what southern white society held most dear. "*Die*, God damn your white soul," shouts Nat, "Die!" Here he is thinking of Margaret not as a person but as an abstraction, as a most treasured and holy part of the white man's imagination, which he, a slave all his life to the white man, defiles.

After killing Margaret, Nat is suddenly aware that his intense hatred for the white man and his burning desire for freedom have caused him to lose his humanity. Before the murder he saw the world only in terms of his quest for freedom, as an object that was real only insofar as he conceived of it as such. Now he sees for the first time that he is not morally autonomous. As he sits on a log after the murder, he finds himself "unaccountably thinking of ancient moments of childhood—warm rain, leaves, a whippoorwill, rushing mill wheels, jew's harp strumming—centuries before." Like all of Styron's major characters, Nat as a fallen man tries to recapture his lost innocence through a reverie of childhood days. It is his first attempt to recollect experience. But because recollection is much more than a dream of innocence, Nat cannot escape for long the reality of the present. He walks back toward Margaret's dead body and paces in sorrow around and around it as if on "a ceaseless pilgrimage."

Styron said in an interview with George Plimpton in the *New York Times Book Review* (8 October 1967) that after the murder Nat "was suddenly overtaken by his own humanity. It is partially why the revolt fails." This certainly appears to be true, for Nat lets escape into the woods at the Harpers Farm a young girl who alerts the farmers closer to Jerusalem. "I might have reached her in a twinkling," he says, "the work of half a minute—but I suddenly felt dispirited and overcome by fatigue, and was pursued by an obscure, unshakable grief. I shivered in the knowledge of the futility of all ambition. My mouth was sour with the yellow recollection of death and blood-smeared fields and walls. . . . I know nothing any longer. Nothing. Did I really wish to vouchsafe a life for the one that I had taken?" The answer to Nat's question seems to be yes. The reality of death has shown him the limits of his solipsistic rebellion.

In *The Mystery of Being* Marcel indicates that the process of recollection is always creative. He compares this reflective self-discovery to the "development of a musical composition; even if such a composition apparently ends with the same phrases that it started with, they are no longer felt as being the same—they are, as it were, coloured by all the vicissitudes they have gone through and by which their final recapture, in their first form, has been accompanied." The central question posed in both the first and last sections of Nat's confession is: "*Then what I done was wrong, Lord? . . . And if what I done was wrong, is there no redemption?*" After his recollection Nat can answer the first part of the question: "No . . . I have no remorse for anything. I would do it all again. Yet even a man without remorse, in the face of death, may have to save one hostage for his soul's ransom, so I say yes, I would destroy them all again, all— But for one . . ." This "one," of course, is Margaret Whitehead. With the exception of his murder of Margaret, Nat believes that what he did was not wrong. Given a choice between slavery and freedom again, he would choose freedom, even if that choice meant others would die. In this respect, Nat is much like Orestes in Sartre's *The Flies*. Both men not only choose freedom at the expense of human life, they also refuse to submit to the remorse which would doom them. Nat, though, is not simply a Sartrean existentialist. Despite his lack of remorse, he does feel a sense of loss and incompleteness. Through recollection, however, Nat comes to understand why he feels such emptiness: he realizes that he has never entered into the redemptive fellowship of Being. From his early adolescence at Turner's Mill until his capture by the whites after his insurrection, Nat remains a being apart.

Nat's isolation from both blacks and whites results not only from his own misplaced fidelity to authority and his later solipsism, but from his own unique position within the system of chattel slavery. At Turner's Mill Nat lives in the same house with his white gods, not in a shanty with other blacks. Naturally enough, because of his favored status, he begins to think of the field hands "as a lower order of people—ragtag mob, coarse, raucous, clownish, uncouth. For even as a child," Nat says, "I am contemptuous and aloof, filled with disdain for the black riffraff which dwells beyond the close perimeter of the big house." Also, because he can read like the whites, Nat makes a further distinction between himself and the slaves who work in the fields. "I began more and more," Nat remembers, "to regard the Negroes of the mill and field as creatures beneath contempt, so devoid of the attributes I had come to connect with the sheltered and respectable life that they were worth not even my derision." Moreover, with the exception of Wash for a brief time, Nat's age and education separate him from the house servants, for superior though they might be to the field hands, none are literate and none are young. Though surrounded by other blacks, Nat is really not a part of the Negro community at Turner's Mill. On the other hand, though he likes to identify himself with the Turners because of his education and his unusual household status, he is not a part of the white community either. Nat may be "the darling, the little black jewel of Turner's Mill," but he is an "experiment" to them and not a human being.

As we have seen, the one close relationship that Nat does form at Turner's Mill is severed when Sam Turner sells Willis to raise capital. The powerful effect on Nat of even this short, adolescent friendship is dramatized in a fishing scene at the mill pond one weekend. After wounding himself with a fish hook, Willis yells, "Fuckin'

Jesus!" Without thinking, Nat strikes his friend in the face, an action for which he is almost immediately sorry. As he reaches out to comfort Willis, they become tangled together and the end result is mutual masturbation. Feeling somewhat guilty after this sexual experience, Nat searches his mind for some justification. As he is to do so often in the future, he sees a precedent for his actions in the Bible: "*The soul of Jonathan was knit with the soul of David, and Jonathan loved him as his own soul. . . . They kissed one another, and wept one with another . . . until David exceeded.*"

The sacramental nature of this experience with his friend Willis makes Nat feel that the spirit of God is flowing through him and the surrounding countryside (much the same feeling he has at the end of the novel when he "communicates" with Margaret). "It was almost as if God hovered in the shimmering waves of heat above the trees," Nat thinks, "His tongue and His Almighty voice trembling at the edge of speech, ready to make known His actual presence to me as I stood penitent and prayerful with Willis ankle-deep in the muddy waters." Nat waits for God to speak, to give him a sign, but he hears nothing. Then a verse from the book of Paul enters his mind, and Nat consummates his new relationship with Willis the only way he knows—through baptism. Afterward, "loving him so much, loving him as a brother," he vows to do everything in his power to educate Willis in both biblical thought and in reading and writing. This experience with Willis is extremely important because it indicates the value Nat places on ontological communion. It adumbrates the kind of loving togetherness that Nat seeks all his life.

After he leaves Turner's Mill, Nat remains isolated from others. Certainly, the Reverend Eppes is no bosom companion of Nat's, though they eat, sleep, and frequently work side by side. Likewise, Nat obviously cannot talk seriously with the illiterate Moore or with his subsequent owner, Joseph Travis. Nor, because of his egoism, can he really communicate with his fellow worker and only adult friend, Hark. Even when they are alone together in the woods, Hark generally hunts or fishes while Nat reads the Bible. Nat says that "in certain ways he [Hark] was like a splendid dog, a young, beautiful, heedless, spirited dog who had, nonetheless, to be trained to behave with dignity." It is also symptomatic of Nat's egocentrism that he thinks of Hark as "a necessary and crucial experiment," the same view Sam Turner had of Nat. Filled with such arrogance, Nat cannot fully unburden himself to a man like Hark. Only with Margaret Whitehead does there seem to exist a possibility for real communication, but because of the immense social gulf that separates them, the idea of a true dialogue with Margaret does not even push its way into Nat's conscious thought until he is about to die. Only then can Nat break the taboos of his slave society and express love and passion for a white woman.

Nat's redemption as a man results from his awareness, through recollection, that he must enter into a loving relationship with another human being. At the very end of the novel, Styron dramatizes Nat's movement from a self-conscious I-It relationship with the world to a participatory I-Thou one. First, he is "flooded with swift shifting memories, too sweet to bear, of all distant childhood, of old time past." Then Nat's thoughts shift to Margaret Whitehead, and he hears her voice whispering, *"Beloved, let us love one another: for love is of God; and everyone that loveth is born of God, and knoweth God."* To Nat, this voice is so real and lovely that he searches for Margaret in the dark of his cell, "finds" her, and consummates their "marriage." Immediately afterward, Nat no longer feels the maddening despair which he experienced prior to his recollection. And because he no longer believes himself to be cast by God into perpetual darkness, Nat sees the morning star riding "in the heavens radiant and pure, set like crystal amid the still waters of eternity." Through recollection, he has broken down the barriers between himself and another person and moved to a higher level of participation where unity of being is recaptured. This loving experience with Margaret leads to a feeling of reconciliation with God. It is, paradoxically, a transcendence through immanence. Nat thinks that he reaches God (a Christian God of love and mercy) through his communion with another human being.

There are two main problems with this redemptive ending. First, it is autistic. Though Nat believes that he briefly fuses his spirit with Margaret's, she is, of course, quite dead. Though dramatically powerful, this redemptive moment is at first intellectually troubling. Second, as Alan Holder has pointed out, "Having built such a case against her, the book is asking too much of us to accept Margaret as an incarnation of Christly love and the agent of Nat's redemption. We are given a spiritual happy ending that is decidedly forced" ("Styron's Slave: *The Confessions of Nat Turner*," *The South Atlantic Quarterly* [Spring 1969], p. 177). Nevertheless, despite these objections, there is perhaps another, more satisfying way of viewing the end of the novel.

Nat's discovery of the necessity of ontological communion is dramatically and thematically valid enough. But given the fact that he is confined to a jail cell and is soon to die, the problem becomes how and with whom can he express this new awareness. Styron partially solves this dramatic dilemma in the short scene in which Hark is taken from his cell to be hanged. Having recaptured his humanity, Nat no longer thinks of his companion as an experiment, but as a friend whom he loves. He hammers at the walls and cries out wildly to the white men who are mistreating Hark. When Hark is carried by Nat's cell door, Nat tries desperately to reach out and touch his friend, but must be content with whispering in a loving voice, "*Good-bye, Hark, good-bye.*"

Of course, this brief gesture is not by itself a redemptive experience. Styron must find yet another way to dramatize Nat's understanding of the I-Thou world of relationship. Consequently, after Hark has been led away and Nat is once again alone, his thoughts turn to the one girl who in her naive, condescending way tried to communicate with him. It is true that Nat perhaps once hated Margaret because she was white, had sympathy for him, and unwittingly tormented him sexually. But it is also true that he always loved her, or at least was smitten by her, for much the same reasons. Nat remembers well the times when Margaret told him that he was the only person she could talk with. He likewise remembers Margaret telling him that she would feel lost without his companionship. Furthermore, he remembers vividly that when he and Margaret left the wagon one Sunday and walked to the creek for a drink of water, Margaret almost begged him through her actions to make love to her. Consequently, it seems quite natural that just before his death Nat would turn to Margaret—or more precisely to a vision of Margaret—in order to share with her his new awareness. From Nat's point of view, Margaret does appear worthy of being his

Thou in an I-Thou relationship. Through such an interpretation it becomes possible to accept the redemptive ending of the novel. It makes it possible for us to see Nat as Styron surely does—as an authentic human being who through recollection has transcended the voids of submission to authority and solipsism and achieved redemptive communion.

MARY S. STRINE

The Confessions of Nat Turner: Styron's "Meditation on History" as Rhetorical Act

In the foreword to his penetrating analysis of contemporary American cultural values, *The Crisis of Confidence*, Arthur M. Schlesinger, Jr., identifies the modern threat to the integrity of the national character: "We are in a double crisis—the crisis of our internal character as a nation and the crisis of the relationship between America and the world. After so many years of overweening confidence in our ability to fix up all the troubles of mankind, we are now suffering increasing doubt that we can even heal the ills of our own national community. The time has surely come for a reassessment of our institutions and values."[1] The radical reassessment of which Schlesinger speaks implies at least in part a resensitization of American historical consciousness, a cooperative effort to cope with the violent strain in American history—to recognize that "an impulse to destroy coexists with our impulse to create—that the destructive impulse is in us and that it springs from some dark intolerable tension in our history and our institutions."[2] Schlesinger identifies a major source of this tension as racial exploitation:

We began, after all, as a people who killed red men and enslaved black men. No doubt we often did this with a Bible and a prayerbook. But no nation, however righteous its professions, could act as we did without doing something fearful to itself—without burying deep in itself, in its customs, its institutions, its conditioned reflexes and its psyche, a propensity toward violence. However much we pretended that Indians and Negroes were subhumans, we really knew that they were God's children too. It is almost as if this initial experience fixed a primal curse on our nation—a curse which still shadows our life.[3]

[237]

Current cultural historians have noted that the residual problems of Negro slavery constitute a major cause of contemporary violence and intranational dissension.[4] Paradoxically, the mainstream of American historical scholarship, until recent years, has failed to relate individual instances and eras of racial oppression and exploitation to the decisive formation of the national American character. It has largely been left to the literary writers to record this crucial dimension of the American unconscious.[5] This essay examines *The Confessions of Nat Turner* by the contemporary American novelist William Styron as a strategic rhetorical response to the enduring problem of racism in the United States, a racism with far-ranging implications in American social and institutional history. The argument is that the novel's shaping vision both illuminates the ethical dilemma of the liberal humanist and explores the ramifications of violence for self-definition and social reform.

William Styron's enduring concern with the moral implications of racial tension and violence is clearly evident in his first three significant works of fiction.[6] With the publication of *The Confessions of Nat Turner* in 1967, Styron irrefutably establishes himself as a writer seriously engaged with this social issue of profound national consequence. Rahv begins his review essay of the novel with precisely this observation:

This is a first-rate novel, the best that William Styron has written and the best by an American writer that has appeared in some years. One reason at least for its creative success is that its author has got hold of a substantial theme central to the national experience. Moreover, he has been able to adapt it to his imaginative purposes without political or sectional bluster. It is a theme that relates mainly to the past but surely to the present as well, for it is obvious that we have by no means seen the last of the consequences of chattel slavery.[7]

A review of Styron's nonfictional writings between the publication of *Set This House on Fire* (1960) and the appearance of his latest novel supports Melvin J. Friedman's observation that "during the years when he was thinking through and writing *The Confessions of Nat Turner*, it is clear that most of his energies were directed toward analyzing the burdens of slavery and their implications for the black man living in the 1960's."[8] Among the most noteworthy of these are two sequentially related essays[9] concerning capital punishment in the case of Benjamin Reid, a young Negro who at the time of the writing of the first essay had spent four years and three months on death row in the Connecticut State Prison at Westerfield awaiting execution for murder.

In the first essay Styron stresses the dehumanizing aspects of blind retributive legal justice, compassionately examines the brutalizing socioeconomic conditions which led to Reid's crime, and persuasively argues that as a poor and subliterate black man of marginal intelligence Reid is "a kind of wretched archetype: the Totally Damned American."[10] The article aroused considerable public interest in the Reid case and was instrumental in having his death sentence commuted to life imprisonment.[11]

Styron attended Reid's hearing before the State Board of Pardons in June 1962. His account of that hearing, written largely from the point of view of the condemned man, extends his impassioned critique to the American judicial and penal systems in general, which, he finally contends, reflect a devastating inability of Americans generally to cope maturely with the full historical ramifications of the human condition. He concludes this argument as follows: "It may be said perhaps that in prison a man's identity cannot be much, but we who are on the outside looking in—we who are so prone to forget that all men must be given at least the possibility of redemption—are in no position to judge. Not only capital punishment, but all punishment in general, is one of our most crucial dilemmas; the death penalty is the wretched symbol of our inability to grapple with that dark part of our humanity which is crime."[12]

Several subsequent book reviews reflect not only Styron's interest in the relationship of slavery to contemporary social problems but indicate further the central thrust of that concern. In a discussion of the reprint edition of Frank Tannenbaum's *Slave and Citizen: The Negro in the Americas* (1946), Styron expresses a certain impatience with the enduring scholarly debate over the abstract moralistic issue of slavery, finds arguments that reflect either the Ulrich B. Phillips or the Kenneth M. Stampp positions hopelessly tautological,[13] and applauds Tannenbaum for addressing himself to the more important questions: "Why was American slavery the unique institution that it was? What was the tragic essence of this system which still casts its shadow not only over our daily life, but over the national destiny as well?"[14]

Tannenbaum, approaching the question through a comparative study of North and South American slavery, observes the essential differences in the contrasting attitudes toward the human potential of the slave: "There is in the history of slavery an important contribution to the theory of social change. Wherever the law accepted the doctrine of the moral personality of the slave and made possible the gradual achievement of freedom implicit in such a doctrine, the slave system was abolished peacefully. Where the slave was denied recognition as a moral person and was therefore considered incapable of freedom, the abolition of slavery was accomplished by force—that is, by revolution."[15] The Latins, he claims, irrespective of their treatment of the Negro in individual instances, acknowledged the inherent moral worth of the slaves as human beings, whereas North Americans, lacking historical precedents with the "peculiar institution," categorically denied the Negro such moral status. Styron, reflecting Tannenbaum, notes: "Neither the Protestant Church nor Anglo-American law was equipped to cope with the staggering problem of the status of the Negro: forced to choose between regarding him as a moral human being and as property, they chose the definition of property. The result was the utter degradation of a people."[16] Styron considers this "total dehumanization of a race" to be the most significant moral legacy of antebellum culture and the principal cause of racial tension today: "It was an oppression unparalleled in human history. In the end only a Civil War could try to rectify this outrage, and the war came too late. . . . That is the problem we are faced with today: *too many white Americans still deny the Negro his position as a moral human being.*"[17]

Styron's assiduous concern with the dehumanizing effects of racial stereotyping is further indicated in his objection to the extreme revisionist historiography of Herbert Aptheker. With *American Negro Slave Revolts* (1943), Aptheker attempts to prove the existence of a continuous and pervasive spirit of rebellion among the antebellum slaves. In so doing, according to Styron, he ironically reverses rather than eradicates the degrading Stepin Fetchit caricature. Styron argues that "in his eagerness to prove the actuality of what was practically non-existent, Aptheker, like those latter day zealots who demean the Negro's humanity by saddling him with mythical powers of eroticism or other attributes he neither wants nor needs, performs only a disservice to those who would understand American Negro slavery and the meaning it has for us."[18]

In sum, both images, the superior and the inferior, of the antebellum Negroes underrate their fundamental integrity as complex human beings and divert critical attention from the crucial moral issue of plantation culture, "a capitalist super-machine which swiftly managed to cow and humble an entire people with a ruthless efficiency unparalleled in history."[19] For this reason, Styron is particularly inspired by such nineteenth-century southern individualists as Lewis H. Blair, who in 1889 daringly published *Prosperity in the South Dependent on the Elevation of the Negro*. Republished as *A Southern Prophecy*, the book boldly confronts the devastating implications of racism for the socioeconomic culture as a whole and argues courageously and unequivocally for absolute racial equality in all aspects of society, northern as well as southern—a position which reminds us, Styron suggests, "that such passion is not bound by geography or time but remains, quite simply, the passion that binds us together as men."[20]

Such a passion clearly provides the underlying motivation for Styron's *The Confessions of Nat Turner*. Styron has indicated that his novel on the Southampton Insurrection was the first book that he wanted to write when he began his career in the late 1940s,[21] and that it represents the culminating moral vision of his earlier literary efforts.[22] Moreover, he directly relates his literary interest in the problem of slavery to his experiences as a contemporary American, specifically as a white liberal southerner faced with the psychological consequences of antebellum culture.

In "This Quiet Dust," his contribution to *Harper's* Civil War Centennial supplement entitled *The South Today*, Styron attributes the source of current racial tension and strife to the white's virtual ignorance of the Negro on interpersonal terms:

An unmarked paradox of Southern life is that its *racial animosity is really grounded* not upon friction and propinquity, but *upon an almost complete lack of contact*. Surrounded by a sea of Negroes, I cannot recall more than once—and then briefly, when I was five or six—ever having played with a

Negro child, or ever having spoken to a Negro, except in trifling talk with the cook, or in some forlorn and crippled conversation with a dotty old grandfather angling for hardshell crabs on a lonesome Sunday afternoon many years ago. Nor was I by any means uniquely sheltered. Whatever knowledge I gained in my youth about Negroes, I gained from a distance, as if I had been watching actors in an all-black puppet show.[23]

Despite this apparent racial insularity, Styron contends that the Negro is an indispensable part of the South's psychological setting—"a perpetual and immutable part of history itself"[24]—and, for the contemporary white southerner, "the focus of an incessant preoccupation, somewhat like a monstrous, recurring dream populated by identical faces wearing expressions of inquietude and vague reproach."[25] Thus, Styron reasons:

No wonder the white man so often grows cranky, fanciful, freakish, loony, violent: how else respond to a paradox which requires, with the full majesty of law behind it, that he deny the very reality of a people whose multitude approaches and often exceeds his own: that he disclaim the existence of those whose human presence has marked every acre of land, every hamlet and crossroad and city and town, and whose humanity, however inflexibly denied, is daily evidenced to him like a heartbeat in loyalty and wickedness, madness and hilarity and mayhem and pride and love? The Negro may feel that it is too late to be known, and that the desire to know him reeks of outrageous condescension. *But to break down the old law, to come to KNOW the Negro, has become the moral imperative of every white southerner.*[26]

He freely acknowledges this, then, as his primary and compelling motive in writing *The Confessions of Nat Turner:* "I suspect that my search for Nat Turner, my own private attempt as a novelist to re-create and bring alive that dim and prodigious black man, has been at least a partial fulfillment of this mandate [to know the Negro] although the problem has long since resolved itself into an artistic one—which is as it should be."[27]

In a prefatory note to the novel, Styron claims that he has written "less an 'historical novel' in conventional terms than a meditation on history," and thereby identifies the basic strategy of *The Confessions of Nat Turner.* Much of the subsequent controversy surrounding his purported departure from the established historical facts stems from a fundamental misunderstanding of the artistic ramifications of this underlying rhetorical intention.

There are clear indications that the novel's intentional design strategically incorporates the formal constraints of meditation, both as a distinctive poetic mode and as a public communicative genre. Martz provides a functional definition of the meditative poem that aptly describes the structure of *The Confessions of Nat Turner*. According to Martz, meditative poetry "creates an interior drama of the mind." He continues: "This dramatic action is usually (though not always) created by some form of self-address, in which the mind grasps firmly a problem or situation deliberately evoked by the memory, brings it forward toward the full light of consciousness, and concludes with a moment of illumination, where the speaker's self has, for a time, found an answer to its conflicts."[28] In a complementary vein, the *Oxford English Dictionary* includes among the various definitions of "meditation" its use as a rhetorical form: "A discourse, written or spoken, in which a subject (usually religious) is treated in a meditative manner, or which is *designed to guide the reader or hearer in meditation*."[29] Both senses of meditation, I shall argue, undergird the novel's communicative structure.

The novel deals specifically with the sociopsychological circumstances surrounding "the greatest of all American slave rebellions."[30] The Southampton Slave Revolt of 1831—planned, organized, and directed by Nat Turner, a prodigious thirty-one-year-old literate slave preacher of exceptional intelligence and singleminded purpose—brutally claimed the lives of fifty-five white citizens in the remote pastoral region of southeastern Virginia.[31] Severe reprisals on the part of the outraged white population followed. As one historian notes, the retaliatory "reign of terror" far exceeded the actual rebellion in unmitigated and wanton violence:

In a little more than one day 120 Negroes were killed. The newspapers of the times contained from day to day indignant protests against the cruelties perpetrated. One individual boasted that he himself had killed between ten and fifteen Negroes. Volunteer whites rode in all directions visiting plantations. Negroes were tortured to death, burned, maimed and subjected to nameless atrocities. Slaves who were distrusted were pointed out and if they endeavored to escape, they were ruthlessly shot down.[32]

[243]

The revolt also led to heated and urgent renewal of the legislative debates over the issue of slavery within the state of Virginia and "so as to provide for a more adequate supervision and rigid control of the slaves and free people of color,"[33] to a subsequent strengthening of the oppressive Black Codes. Finally, according to Styron, the insurrection was significantly instrumental in fomenting the social unrest which eventuated in the Civil War.[34]

Despite its emergent historical importance, the actual motivation for the revolt remains largely shrouded in mystery, for the only official account of the incident, a 5,000-word pamphlet purportedly dictated by Nat Turner to his court-appointed lawyer, Thomas R. Gray, clearly reflects the latter's polemical bias.[35] Thus, against the vitriolic charges of white racism and of capricious and arbitrary distortion of historical facts,[36] Styron has staunchly defended his right to the responsible exercise of artistic license in dealing with this historical incident. He argues against the imperviousness of historical interpretation to new insights and steadfastly contends that *The Confessions of Nat Turner* is "neither racist nor a tract but a *novel*, an essay of the imagination where the necessities of always questionable [empirical] 'fact' often become subsumed into a larger [sociopsychological] truth."[37]

Styron finds artistic justification for flexibility in dealing with purportedly historical "facts" in the literary theory of the Hungarian Marxist Georg Lukács and freely draws on Lukács's *The Historical Novel* for support. Quoting Lukács, Styron argues:

What matters in the novel is fidelity in the reproduction of the material foundations of the life of a given period, its manners and the feelings and thoughts deriving from these. This means that the novel is much more closely bound to the specifically historical, individual moments of a period, than is drama. But this never means being tied to particular historical facts. On the contrary, the novelist must be at liberty to treat these as he likes, if he is to reproduce the much more complex and ramifying totality with historical faithfulness.[38]

A second important strategy, coextensive with the first, involves Styron's decision to center the action in the reflective consciousness of the condemned man waiting execution and to relate the narrative exclusively from his point of view. Styron claims that this decision was motivated in part by a reading of Camus's *The Stranger* and in part by his close friendship with James Baldwin. Recalling his first reading of the Camus novel, in 1962, Styron notes:

There was something about the poignancy of the condemned man sitting in his jail cell on the day of his execution—the existential predicament of the man—that hit me. And so did the use of the first person, the book being told through the eye of the condemned. The effect of all this way so strong that I suddenly realized that my Nat Turner could be done the same way: that, like Camus, I would center the novel around a man facing his own death in a jail cell, which of course was true of Turner and how his life ended. And so there, suddenly provided, was the architecture of the book, its framework, along with the idea of telling the story in the first person.[39]

He freely acknowledges, also, that his relationship with Baldwin provided an essential inspiration in his conception of Turner:

I think Jimmy—this is the confession of William Styron now—I think that Jimmy broke down the last shred of whatever final hangup of Southern prejudice I might have had which was trying to tell me that a Negro was never really intelligent—a black Negro, not a, you know, white Negro, but a black, black homely Negro. Perhaps it was his diamond-bright intelligence which allowed me to say, "When I plunge into Nat Turner, it will be with no holds barred, and he will respond with as much intelligence as I can bring to his voice."[40]

Styron thus attempts to maximize the existential accuracy in his re-creation of Turner's world and to penetrate imaginatively the historical experience culminating in contemporary racial strife by vicariously sharing in the slave's point of view: "I wanted . . . to explore in some kind of depth this whole area of American life and history, to take on the lineaments as well as I could of a slave and, using that persona, walk myself through a time and a place in a manner of self-discovery. I was learning all along as I wrote about Nat what it must have been to be a slave."[41] Elsewhere, he acknowledges the use of the first person, major character point of view as his most difficult and challenging undertaking in his fictional approach to the Southampton Insurrection.[42]

Styron's "meditation on history," in summary, can be said to function as a meditation both on and through the confessions of Nat Turner and to show that "an event that took place in the South more than a century ago, is in a sense not only repeating itself in the

Detroits and Newarks of today but is analogous to still earlier events: that psychologically and spiritually, the past and present are one."[43] Significantly, Baldwin has applauded Styron's novel as both courageous and hopeful, claiming, "He has begun the common history—*ours*."[44]

The narrative development in *The Confessions of Nat Turner* comprises a series of self-disclosing, analytical meditations which occur during the final week of Nat Turner's life, between the day of his trial and that of his execution. These "confessions" cumulatively offer a dramatic corrective to those transcribed by Gray, his court-appointed lawyer, whose official analysis of the revolt has formed the basis of most subsequent writing on the subject.[45] In each of the novel's four sections, Nat reflectively concentrates on his experiences within the antebellum culture which relate to the Southampton Insurrection. In its most inclusive sense, the novel constitutes a sociopsychological exploration into the causes and consequences of racial violence as a primary impediment—past and present—to the realization of community in the United States.

In contrast to Gray's characterization of Turner as a remorseless villain and in dramatic counterstatement to his assessment of Nat's motives as inexplicably fanatical, Nat emerges in the act of narrating as a complex and sensitive human being. His destiny was so shaped by the unfulfilled promise of the "American Dream" as to imbue him and his self-defining act of rebellion against the depersonalizing institution of slavery with archetypal significance.[46] The historical situation, as developed in the novel, clearly follows the pattern of an Adamic self in quest.

Born and reared the property of Benjamin and later Samuel Turner in Southampton County (known as the "Black Belt" of southeastern Virginia) during the early decades of the nineteenth century, Nat from the first enjoyed a privileged status within the enlightened and liberal Turner household. His mother having established herself as a favored domestic servant, Nat escaped the anonymity of the common field hand. With the early discovery of his unusual intelligence and industriousness, Nat became the particular "project" of the Turner family, was taught to read, assiduously drilled in the Scriptures, and "became in short a pet, the darling, the little black jewel of Turner's Mill."[47]

The Turner family naturally functioned as the primary focus of social orientation for Nat. He came to regard his fatherly mentor, Samuel Turner, with "very close to the feeling one should bear only toward the Divinity" (NT, p. 126), and, since his association with the field Negroes was largely restricted, to regard them in their poverty and ignorance with aloof condescension. When Nat was eighteen years old, Samuel Turner outlined a plan for Nat's continued training in carpentry and for his eventual emancipation. Thus, Nat approached his majority with the burgeoning hope and promise of a latter-day American Adam: "It seemed to me that all that long while it was as if I had been mounting a winding and pleasant slope toward the distant hills of the Lord. . . . I had expected to pause at this lofty place and then go on, proceeding upward by gentle stages to the remote, free, glorious peaks where lay the satisfaction and fulfillment of my destiny" (NT, p. 208).

Shortly before his twenty-first birthday, Nat experienced the devastating trauma of having all hope destroyed. Thus began a brutal ten-year initiation into the dehumanizing reality of the slave's existence. A failure of the Virginia tobacco crop and the resultant recession in plantation economy forced Samuel Turner to abandon his "experiment" in Negro emancipation. The Arcadian community of Turner's Mill was disbanded and Nat passed through the hands of the Reverend Alexander Eppes, an unscrupulous Baptist preacher, into the debasing ownership of Thomas Moore, a rudely insensitive, illiterate, poor white farmer in the Southampton area. Upon Moore's death, Nat became the property of the more kindly Joseph Travis and spent the remainder of his life in this relatively permissive, though clearly subservient, role.

Although his lot during the final decade of his life was not altogether brutal, Nat brooded incessantly over his overwhelming sense of personal betrayal and unfulfilled promise. He progressively shifted his sociopsychological orientation from that of the oppressive white world to that of the Old Testament, fortifying himself and, through his preaching, his immediate followers with the righteous wrath of the vengeful prophets, especially Ezekiel, Daniel,

[247]

Isaiah, and Jeremiah. Observing increasingly clear analogies between the scenes of biblical bondage and the condition of the contemporary slaves, and finding further inspiration from recurring, fasting-induced visions, Nat strategically planned and executed a slave rebellion aimed at Negro emancipation and annihilation of the white population of Southampton County.

The historical pattern of events acquires existential significance within the narrative structure as centered in the reflective consciousness of the physically and psychologically defeated rebel leader awaiting sentence and execution.

Part 1, "Judgment Day," recounts a series of intimate and penetrating reflections through which Nat attempts to explain and clarify, ostensibly both for himself and his reader, not only the motivations prompting the Southampton revolt but also the psychological conditions leading to his feeling of abject social and spiritual desolation. By implication, his intention in publicly "confessing" is to offer a more thorough and personally accurate account of the circumstances surrounding the revolt than that published by the lawyer Gray, whose official commitment to defending the status quo precluded a true appreciation of the revolt's full psychological and social significance.

In part 2, "Old Times Past," Nat vividly reenacts scenes from his early childhood and young adulthood which specifically foreshadow the later racial tension. The pattern of his recollections traces his early bases of personal and social orientation at Turner's Mill through critical moments of initiation, into the moral complexities of antebellum culture, to an irreversible disillusionment with and alienation from the dominant white society in general.

With part 3, "Study War," Nat calculatedly retraces his ill-fated strategies for establishing an alternative to the oppressive white culture, following his radical shift in sociopsychological orientation from that of the futuristic dream of freedom within the existing social order to that of Old Testament vengeance and retribution against the dominant culture.

Part 4, "It is Done . . .," begins on the morning of Nat's final day and ends with the start of his execution. His reflections in this brief, though intense, section alternate with quotations from the final chapter of the Book of Revelation and thereby imbue this final meditation-confession with the aura of an apocalyptic litany.

During these final moments of Nat's life, his despair at being unable to pray becomes gradually allayed through a hope born of charity and love. The section culminates in an epiphanic act of redemption involving an inextricable fusion of sexual, social, and religious longing. Through a masturbatory fantasy, Nat repents of the single murder for which he was personally responsible, that of Margaret Whitehead. Recalling her simple unworldly philosophy of idealized Christian love not only between persons but also between races, he ecstatically envisions a social-sexual-spiritual transcendent union with her: "With tender stroking motions I pour out my love within her; pulsing flood; she arches against me, cries out, and the twain—black and white—are one" (NT, p. 426). The novel ends with Nat's power to pray restored, and with his repentant death-redemption.

The narrative action from Nat's point of view is framed by two contrasting pairs of excerpts taken from historical accounts of the insurrection and its aftermath and from the final book of the Bible which, taken together, function rhetorically as a further clarification of tone, of Styron's implied attitude toward the "meditation on history." Thomas R. Gray's legal preface to his 1831 transcription of Turner's original "confessions," reflecting the popular consensus of antebellum sentiment regarding the Turner revolt,[48] functions as the introductory frame and suggests that the reading public it so earnestly addresses is, in certain fundamental respects, transhistorical. Both in tone and content, Gray's introduction reveals a concentrated effort to rationalize the Southampton tragedy as the ill-fated "off-spring of gloomy fanaticism" and to defend the integrity of the dominant white culture. A slave-owning resident of Southampton County himself,[49] Gray claims that his rationale for publishing the record of Turner's confession was to satisfy "public curiosity" as to the "origin and progress of this dreadful conspiracy, and the motives which influenced its diabolical actors."

In a polemical description of this "first instance in our history of an open rebellion of the slaves" (NT, p. xiii), Gray stresses the innocence of the victims and the moral degradation of the rebels. He reassuringly advises his readers that the following confessions read as a self-indicting document and ultimate justification for the social structure built on Negro slavery:

It reads as an awful, and it is hoped, a useful lesson as to the operations of a mind like his, endeavoring to grapple with things beyond its reach. How it first became bewildered and confounded, and finally corrupted and led to the conception and perpetration of the most atrocious and heart-rending deeds. It is calculated also to demonstrate the policy of our laws in restraint of this class of our population, and to induce all those entrusted with their execution, as well as our citizens generally, to see that they are strictly and rigidly enforced. (NT, p. xv)

Gray's preface, followed by an official affidavit signed by six court magistrates, certifies that Nat, on hearing the confessions read, had nothing more to say. The preface, however, is followed by a hopefully prophetic excerpt from Revelation, anticipating divine resolution of all historical tension within apocalyptic time as a lead into the novel's first section.

Styron's hopeful attitude toward the far-ranging sociopsychological implications of his "meditation on history" is further mirrored in the closing juxtaposition of two markedly dissimilar accounts of the consequences of the revolt. An excerpt taken from the historian William S. Drewry's *The Southampton Insurrection* (1900) presents a detachedly factual record of the personally and historically effacing aftermath of the rebellion. Again, the historical statement is countered by the mystical vision of Christian hope reflected in Revelation. In light of the foregoing narrative action, the sociopsychological significance of the insurrection and its aftermath for Nat exists in a fusion of the two.

The reader also experiences the meaning of Nat's fictive confessions as a tensive synthesis of contingent social "fact" and transcendent psychological-spiritual "truth." As Styron through the novel suggests, the reality of this or any other historical event—its final significance in time—is fully understandable only in terms of this infinitely complex, tragically unresolvable tension between recorded fact and lived experience.

Stanley M. Elkins's definitive analysis of slavery as a problem in American institutional and intellectual life provides a useful theoretical basis for interpreting the sociopsychological implications of *The Confessions of Nat Turner* as rhetorical act.

Elkins traces the rise and legitimization of slavery in the United States during the nineteenth century to the rise of capitalism, which he perceives to be "the principal dynamic force in American society."[50] He argues that the agricultural economy of antebellum Virginia most clearly exemplified this force in operation: "Here a growing system of large-scale staple production for profit was free to develop in a society where no prior traditional institutions, with competing claims of their own, might interpose at any of a dozen points with sufficient power to retard or modify its progress."[51]

The plantation thus became the paradigmatic social structure and its planter the social structure's most influential figure. Furthermore, since the planter required absolute physical control over the plantation's labor forces in order to operate efficiently and to maximize agricultural production, slavery became a literal economic necessity. It was in light of such an economic imperative that Negro slavery in the United States attained social, legal, and religious sanction.

In an interview, Styron explicitly corroborates this thesis, claiming that "in Turner's time, the two institutions which sold the Negro down the river were the legal system and the church. Either, or both, could have at one time exerted their influence for the better. But they didn't, and it was perhaps the cruelest sell-out of all time."[52]

The Confessions of Nat Turner is a dramatic illustration of Elkins's argument. Nat's recollections make vividly clear the impact of economic determinism on the course of social, legal, and religious attitudes within the apartheid plantation culture and, more importantly, penetrate the burdensome, ultimately unresolvable moral dilemma of the would-be humanist confronted with this situation. Elkins characterizes this dilemma: "The man of reason and good will in the Jeffersonian and immediate post-Jeffersonian South tried again and again to balance within himself two conflicting sets of feelings about slavery. On the one hand was the sentiment . . . that the institution was uneconomic, morally dubious, and a burden on both the slaveholder and the community. That the Negro, on the other hand, lacked the capacity to care for himself as a free Ameri-

[251]

can was a conviction that slavery's strongest opponents . . . could seldom escape."[53]

Samuel Turner, Nat's fatherly mentor and the benevolent owner of Turner's Mill, epitomizes the aspiring social humanist whose frustrating inability to put into practice his abstract commitment to principles of racial equality provides the most significant and direct motivation for Nat's violent revolt. As Nat bitterly recalls, "During the dark years of my twenties . . . I spent a great deal of idle and useless time wondering what may have befallen my lot had I not been so unfortunate as to have become the beneficiary (or perhaps the victim) of my owner's zeal to tamper with a nigger's destiny" (NT, p. 154).

In contrast to his older brother Benjamin's pragmatic, economically based defense of slavery, Samuel Turner's social philosophy reflects a clear recognition of the evils of slavery and implies a responsible plan for gradual Negro emancipation. Both the specific nature of this family dissension as well as its social impact are vividly reflected in a friendly quarrel involving the brothers and two traveling Episcopalian clergymen, who deferentially consult the influential planter class in formulating their official positions on the moral issue of slavery. The Reverend Dr. Ballard discreetly indicates, "We are at the crossroads—that is the Bishop's own expression—we are at the crossroads, marking time, awaiting some *providential wind* to guide us in the right direction" (NT, pp. 158–159).

Fully cognizant of his privileged position, Benjamin Turner with forthright congeniality asserts his belief in the innate inferiority of the Negro race: "I do not believe in beating a darky. I do not believe, either, in beating a dog or a horse. If you wish my belief to take back to the Bishop, you can tell him that my belief is that a darky is an animal with the brain of a human child and his only value is the work you can get out of him by intimidation, cajolery, and threat" (NT, p. 161). The religious ambassadors solicitously respond in kind by suggesting that such a belief in the moral inferiority of the Negro has Biblical precedent:

Would it also be accurate to discern in what you have just said a conviction that perhaps the Negro lags so far behind the rest of us—I mean, the white race—in *moral* development that, well, for his own welfare it might be

[252]

best that he—well, be kept in a kind of benevolent subjection? I mean, is it not possible that slavery is perhaps—how shall we say?—the most *satis-factory* form of existence for such a people? . . . *Cursed be Canaan. A ser-vant of servants shall he be unto his bretheren.* Genesis, ninth chapter, twenty-fifth verse. Certainly the Bishop is not completely disinclined to take this viewpoint. (NT, p. 163)

Samuel Turner, however, makes his counter position equally clear and explicit:

I have long and do still steadfastly believe that slavery is the great cause of all the chief evils of our land. It is a cancer eating at our bowels, the source of all our misery, individual, political, and economic. It is the greatest curse a supposedly free and enlightened society has been saddled with in modern times, or any other time. I am not . . . the most religious of men, yet I am not without faith and I pray nightly for the miracle, for the divine guidance which will somehow show us the way out of this terrible con-dition. It is evil to keep these people in bondage, yet they cannot be freed. They must be educated! To free these people without education and with the prejudice that presently exists against them would be a ghastly crime. (NT, pp. 159–160)

However, the clergymen's response to his arguments are notably detached and evasive. Nat distinctly recalls: "Dr. Ballard did not immediately answer, but when he did *his voice was detached and in-distinct.* 'How interesting,' he murmured. 'Fascinating,' said the other minister, *sounding even more far away*" (NT, 160; emphasis added).

Upon Benjamin's sudden and untimely death, Nat becomes Sam-uel Turner's test case and as a consequence enjoys numerous social and educational opportunities denied the other slaves. Shortly after Nat's eighteenth birthday, Turner proudly informs him that his "experiment" has been remarkably successful and promises Nat fur-ther training in carpentry and eventually his freedom:

You have by no means acquired what is known as a liberal education. . . . But you seem to be equipped now with the best part of an elementary schooling. You can read and write, and you can count. You have the most amazing knowledge of the Good Book of anyone within my ken, and that includes several white ministers I know. . . . You are the walking proof of what I have tried so hard and usually so vainly to persuade white gentle-men, including my late beloved brother, namely, that young darkies like yourself *can* overcome the natural handicaps of their race and at least acquire such schooling as will allow them to enter into pursuits other than the lowest menial animal labor. (NT, pp. 190–191)

Yet, as Nat later reflects, "despite warmth and friendship, despite a kind of *love*, I began as surely an experiment as a lesson in pig-breeding or the broadcasting of a new kind of manure" (NT, p. 155). It is precisely the impersonal objectivity of Samuel Turner's concern, his ultimate evasion of responsibility for the interpersonal consequences of his human experimentation, that most disillusions Nat and leads to the turbulent reprisal against all white people.

When major economic reversals compel Samuel Turner gradually to sell his slaves to more prosperous plantations in the lower South, he does so surreptitiously in order to preserve the surface equanimity of Turner's Mill and to protect his delusively idealized version of plantation culture. Feeling the moral weight of his duplicity, the frustrated capitalist-humanist rails against the dehumanizing effects of the capitalistic social system and exclaims to Nat, "The duplicity! The masquerade! I should have done it in broad daylight with all the plantation as gaping onlookers to a plain and simple sale, with money changing hands in full view" (NT, p. 219).

Samuel Turner's ethical evasiveness reaches its nadir when, forced to relinquish the mill itself, he shifts the burden of Nat's future to the Reverend Alexander Eppes and thereby absolves himself of personal responsibilty for standing behind the consequences of his commitment. When Eppes finally sells Nat to slave traders for $460 and his last hope for emancipation is brutally destroyed, it is notably Samuel Turner who becomes the concentrated focus of Nat's wrath: "I experienced a kind of disbelief which verged close upon madness, then a sense of betrayal, then fury such as I had never known before, then finally, to my dismay, hatred so bitter that I grew dizzy and thought I might get sick on the floor. Nor was it hatred for the Reverend Eppes—who was really nothing but a simple old fool—but for Marse Samuel, and the rage rose and rose in my breast until I earnestly wished him dead, and in my mind's eye I saw him strangled by my own hands" (NT, pp. 246–247).

Legal humanism suffers a similar fate when confronted with the historical forces of capitalistic, slavery-dependent agrarianism. Judge Jeremiah Cobb, the presiding magistrate at Nat's trial, epitomizes the socially sensitive individual tragically torn between a personal sense of morality and a conflicting public and legal commitment to uphold a given social order. Nat's first contact with the judge occurs approximately one year prior to the insurrection, at which time Cobb's sickly and brandy-numbed physical condition mirrors his spiritual distress over the inherent evils of slavery. Nat recalls that "the face I beheld was one of the most unhappy faces I had ever seen. It was blighted, ravaged by sorrow, as if grief had laid actual hands on the face, wrenching and twisting it into an attitude of ineradicable pain" (NT, p. 49).

Once a prosperous Southampton merchant and banker as well as the leading county magistrate—and having within a short span of time endured Job-like reversals of fortune including the death of his family through typhoid fever, a major property loss through fire, and a permanent and painful physical infirmity through an accidental fall, Cobb becomes a personal metaphor for the once prosperous, now declining, Old Dominion. Like Samuel Turner before him, Cobb prophetically predicts the bitter self-destruction of the Virginia culture through the curse of slavery:

The fairest state of them all, this tranquil and beloved domain—what has it now become? A *nursery* for Mississippi, Alabama, Arkansas. A monstrous breeding farm to supply the sinew to gratify the maw of Eli Whitney's infernal machine, cursed be that blackguard's name! In such a way is our human decency brought down, when we pander all that is in us noble and just to the false god which goes by the vile name of *Capital!* Oh, Virginia, woe betide thee! Woe, thrice woe, and ever damned in memory be the day when poor black men in chains first trod upon thy sacred strand! (NT, p. 69)

Through cataclysmic rebellion, Nat becomes, in effect, the avenging angel of Cobb's prophecy.

At the time of Nat's trial, the lawyer Gray provides the anxious public with predictably reassuring rationalizations in support of the "genial institution of slavery." In his efforts to answer the disturbing questions, "How did it happen? From what dark wellspring did it flow? Will it ever happen again?" (NT, p. 83), he draws for support on the then popular theories of scientific racism and on his interpreta-

THE CONFESSIONS OF NAT TURNER

tion of the confession itself to prove that "all such rebellions are not only likely to be exceedingly rare in occurrence but are ultimately doomed to failure" because of "the basic weakness and inferiority, the moral deficiency of the Negro character" (NT, p. 84).

In his official capacity as presiding magistrate and functioning in the interest of legal justice, Judge Cobb administers the retributive death sentence. At the same time, however, he conveys a heartfelt compassion for Nat's position as a fellow human being. Nat realizes at this moment "that he too was close to death, very close, almost as close as I myself" and, sensing the old man's ethical turmoil, feels "a curious pang of pity and regret" (NT, p. 105). Immediately after the sentencing, Cobb and Nat share a silent moment of interpersonal understanding which transcends the racial divisiveness and political exigencies of the immediate situation. Nat remembers: "We gazed at each other from vast distances, yet close, awesomely close, as if sharing for the briefest instant some rare secret—unknown to other men—of all time, all mortality and sin and grief" (NT, p. 106).

The ultimate inability of religious humanism to alter significantly the depersonalizing socioeconomic forces of plantation culture is epitomized in the relationship between Nat and the young Margaret Whitehead. As the sheltered, totally dependent daughter of a relatively prosperous Southampton family, Margaret typifies the naïve spiritual idealist whose would-be effectiveness in promoting a community of Christian brotherhood is ironically countermined by a culturally enforced insensitivity to the depersonalizing reality of a slavery-based society.

On those occasions when Nat is temporarily "loaned" by Travis to the Whiteheads, Margaret relates to him with effusive personal warmth and kindness. She eagerly shares his interest in the Scriptures and, in general, innocently violates the sumptuary laws which prohibit even casual social intimacy between races. On one such occasion she remarks, "You're so good at remembering the Bible, Nat. And you have such a knowledge of, oh, spiritual things. I mean it's funny, you know, when I tell the girls at school they just don't believe me when I say I go home on weekends and the only person I can talk to is a—is a darky!" (NT, p. 91).

She is equally direct with him in sharing her disdain for the slave system and confides that her earnest desire is to see the Negroes improve their subservient condition: "I just don't know, Nat! I just don't know why darkies stay the way they do—I mean all ignorant and everything . . . and so many of them having people that own them that don't feed them properly or even clothe them so that they're warm enough. I mean so many living like animals. Oh, I *wish* there was some way that darkies could live decently and work for themselves and have—oh, real self-regard" (NT, p. 365).

Yet, throughout the time of their sporadic but close interaction, he as slave and she as mistress, her apparent failure to recognize the degrading reality as well as her tacit complicity in his condition of depersonalizing servitude fills Nat with bitter frustration and longing. Unwittingly, her incredible innocence serves to strengthen his resolve to destroy the social system which categorically denies his right to the full interpersonal relationship that her unconscious flirtations invite.

In summary, the moral dilemma of the liberal humanists resides in their full acknowledgment of the inherent evils of slavery coupled with their at least tacit complicity in the exploitative social structure supporting it. This painfully conscious capitulation of liberal tendencies—familial, legal, and religious—to the socioeconomic exigencies of agrarian capitalism, as exemplified in the ethical duplicity of Samuel Turner, Judge Jeremiah Cobb, and Margaret Whitehead, incisively contributes to Nat's profound sense of interpersonal betrayal and ultimately accounts for the violent course of his self-defining retribution.

The strategic function of violence in modern American fiction has received considerable attention by theorists and novelists alike. David Brian Davis emphasizes that "in twentieth-century literature, violence has come to be identified with the very quintessence of reality, as opposed to abstract ideals, myths, and institutions."[54] According to Flannery O'Connor, violence has a definite heuristic function for the fiction writer: "With the serious writer, *violence is never an end in itself. It is the extreme situation that best reveals what we are essentially.* . . . The man in the violent situation reveals those qualities least dispensable in his personality, those qualities which are all he will have to take into eternity wth him."[55] Styron himself considers Nat Turner's confrontation with the awesome responsibility for the use of violence to be central to his novel: "He found that he couldn't deal with the violence that he himself had ordained. . . . I think it's very central to the book—the idea of what happens when a man boldly proposes a course of total annihilation and starts to carry it out and finds to his dismay it's not working for him. I think it's unavoidable in an honest reading of Nat Turner's confessions that he himself was almost unable to grapple with violence, to carry it out successfully."[56]

Elkins's analysis of the reforming impulse in American intellectual life helps to account both for the violent form of Nat Turner's retributive design and the profound intrapersonal crisis that it provokes. Elkins identifies certain cultural conditions as common to American reform situations; each of these instigative elements is clearly present within the socioeconomic context of Nat's world.

The first distinguishing characteristic of the reform situation, according to Elkins, involves a "disruption of expectations, not necessarily connected with the actual objects of reform."[57] Clearly, Nat's sense of betrayal by the irresponsibly idealistic Samuel Turner not only brutally violates his expectations for personal freedom but provides the enduring incentive for his revenge against all whites.

A second, related feature, the presence of "*some* maneuvering space, an absence of *total* crisis conditions," also characterizes the social context within which Nat develops his apocalyptic scheme. Nat specifically acknowledges that the relatively humane and permissive atmosphere of early nineteenth-century Virginia—unique among the slave states at that time—allows him time for private meditation and reflection (NT, p. 267).

The third element, "the absence of clear institutional arrangements for channeling radical energy," manifests itself in a distinctive pattern for exercising this radical energy in social reform. Elkins observes that "this lack of channels seems to produce in the reformers a constant reconsideration of first principles, an urge to develop a great variety of new organizations, and an overwhelming illusion of the individual's power to change society." Nat's particular circumstances typify this situation, both in his social, religious, and legal disaffiliation as a powerless but culpable "animate chattel" and in his plan for establishing a "new" black society.

In preparing to establish his new community, Nat imitates certain strategies of the original American Experiment, sharing in its implacably optimistic spirit of radical social reorganization. Although his plans are later changed, he originally decides on Independence Day 1831 for the start of the rebellion. His choice of the Dismal Swamp as the isolated primordial setting for the new black community significantly parallels the North American continent for the first European settlers. He reflects: "It seemed to me . . . a perfect stronghold for a small band of resolute, woods-canny Negroes: though large, . . . trackless, forbidding, as wild as the dawn of creation, it was still profusely supplied with game and fish and springs of sweet water—all in all hospitable enough a place for a group of adventurous, hardy runaways to live there indefinitely, swallowed up in its green luxuriant fastness beyond the pursuit of white men" (NT, p. 335). And, like earlier white American colonists, Nat feels that his plan for revolution is blessed by divine sanction and guidance: "I knew that my cause was just and, being just, would in its strength overcome all obstacles, all hardships, all inclement turns of fortune. I knew too that because of the noble purpose of my mission even the most cowed and humbled of Negroes would divine its justice, and I foresaw legions of black men everywhere rising up to join me. Black men all over the South, all over America! A majestic black army of the Lord!" (NT, p. 361).

Thus, Nat himself emerges as the apotheosis of the fourth and final factor, the intellectual reformer "without connections," whose reforming zeal, or sense of social responsibility, grows out of "guilt" over social disaffiliation and at least a tacit desire to function in a meaningful social role. Elkins explains this peculiarly American phenomenon:

Contrasted with the civilizations of Europe, our Protestant culture with its strong secular inclinations has been conspicuous for its lack of institutions, religious or secular, among whose functions has been the absorption and transformation of guilt. Guilt must be borne as an individual burden to a degree not to be observed elsewhere. Guilt in a structured situation has formalized outlets, limits within which it may be expressed constructively and with effect. Otherwise, it has no such channels. It will thus accumulate, like static electricity; it becomes aggressive, unstable, hard to control, often destructive. Guilt may at this point be transformed into implacable moral aggression: hatred of both the sinner and the sin.

For Nat Turner, calculated retributive violence becomes the paradigmatic strategy for exercising this moral aggression.

Nat's ultimate decision to overthrow the white culture is strategically dependent on the support of a unified black community. Most disturbed by the obvious lack of social cohesiveness and communal identity among the Negroes, Nat senses in their low self-esteem and interpersonal disregard a tendency clearly in the interest of interminable white domination. His efforts to promote a vital black spirit of community begins with the discovery of his own persuasive potential. While addressing a shiftless crowd of self-effacing slaves one market day, he discovers his marked ability to communicate effectively in the slave language: "I began to realize, far back in the remotest corner of my mind, that I had commenced the first sermon I had ever preached. . . . My language was theirs, I spoke it as if it were a second tongue. My rage had captured them utterly, and I felt a thrill of power course out from myself to wrap them round, binding us for this moment as one" (NT, p. 308). He thus passionately urges his fellow blacks to reject the white supremacist propaganda of existing local religions. Bible in hand, he preaches black pride.

Alternating vivid descriptions of slavery conditions with Old Testament quotations and tales of bondage and deliverance, he makes an energetic, urgent plea for righteous anger borne of self-love:

"But oh, my brothers, black folk ain't never goin' to be led from bondage without they has *pride!* Black folk ain't goin' to be free, they ain't goin' to have no spoonbread an sweet cider less'n they studies to love they own *selves.* Only then will the first be last, and the last first. Black folk ain't never goin' to be no great nation until they studies to love they own black skin an' the beauty of that skin an' the beauty of them black hands that toils so hard and black feet that trods so weary on God's earth. And when white men in they hate an' wrath an' meanness fetches blood from that beautiful black skin then, oh *then,* my brothers, it is time not fo' laughing but fo' weeping an' rage an' lamentation! *Pride!*" I cried after a pause, and let my arms descend. "Pride, pride, *everlasting* pride, pride will make you free!" (NT, p. 311)

He further attempts to generate a black community spirit by fabricating Negro myths based on those of the Western cultural tradition—bolstering his trusting but ignorant followers with a fictitious sense of their own history by relating tales of the Biblical "Negro heroes" Joshua and David and relishing in the military grandeur of a "nigger Napolean" (NT, p. 331).

To assist in the rebellion, Nat selects as his "generals" and chief confidants fellow slaves who share his pure hatred of white men. These "inmost four"—Hark, Sam, Nelson, and Henry—are subject to Nat's absolute authority and function ultimately as metaphoric extensions or facets of his own complex personality. Hark epitomizes the spirit of loyalty and devotion; his supportive presence provides Nat with a necessary personal reassurance. Nat admits that Hark's "splendid good nature, his high spirits, his even-tempered and humorous acceptance of the absurd and, one might add, the terrifying—all of these things in Hark cheered me, easing my loneliness and causing me to feel that I had found a brother" (NT, p. 286). Sam, the "liveliest, pluckiest, certainly the most venturesome and resourceful" (NT, p. 333) of the group, is valued for his intelligence. Nelson, "as solid as a slab of seasoned oak," is the most trustworthy and disciplined (NT, p. 332). Finally, Henry, in compensation for physical deafness, exhibits uncanny sensitivity to physical surroundings and is known for his "religious ardor, infusing light and fantasy through the gravestone silence of his inner world" (NT, p. 332).

Will, another symbolically significant figure in the rebellion, represents the force of unrestrained violence. (Notably, Will and Henry—personifying violence and religious ardor—are among the few slave casualties during the revolt and account for Nat's dejected state of religious alienation during his incarceration.) Will appears just before the outbreak of the rebellion and demands to be included. Although Nat is initially hesitant and fearful of Will's demented hatred, he admits him to the group in the belief that Will's "brute fury" can be productively channeled in the interest of the revolt: "I was . . . fearful of him, afraid that I could not control him or bend him to my will; and it was this instinctive mistrust that had caused me months before to eliminate him from my plans. At the same time, it was clear now that if I could channel his brutal fury and somehow keep him in check he would make a potent addition to our striking force" (NT, pp. 377–378). Herein lie Nat's most profound personal turmoil and the central tension in terms of which his self-defining choices are made. Fully cognizant that the destructive energies which Will embodies are essential to the execution of his apocalyptic plan, he nonetheless becomes morally repulsed by the fact of violence itself. Upon entering the Travis home, the first stop on the cataclysmic march, Nat suddenly realizes his potential victim's manhood and runs from the savage scene in horrified revulsion (NT, p. 391). In his existential confrontation with a direct, premeditated act of violence, Nat feels ethically incapable of killing another man.

Throughout the rebellion, Nat's authority is jeopardized by his apparent inability to act on his abstract commitment to violent retribution. Nat's hesitancy in dealing the death blow, on four noted occasions, is intercepted by Will's bloodthirsty, insane fury. Will continuously challenges Nat's leadership and is significantly restrained from assuming control of the bloody revolt by Nelson, the voice of reasoned discipline. In a final, frantic effort to reassert his leadership, Nat pursues Margaret Whitehead, the young girl with whom he has shared a strangely intimate and loving relationship during the final years of his life.

The climactic scene of his final confrontation with Margaret marks not only Nat's single act of violence but constitutes a distorted consummation of his frustrated affection for her. He recalls the circumtances of that final chase, his intense desire for her, and the terrifying ambivalence with which he administers the death blows. The sword "hung like the weight of all the earth" (NT, p. 413) at his side and Margaret's scream echoes "like a far angelic cry" (NT, p. 414) in his ears. He painfully reflects on the heart-rending compassion, rather than impersonal hatred, which motivated the actual fatal stroke:

"I hurt so," I heard her whisper.
"Shut your eyes," I said. I reached down to search with my fingers for a

firm length of fence rail and I could sense once more her close girl smell and the fragrance of lavender, bitter in my nostrils, and sweet. "Shut your eyes," I told her quickly. Then *when I raised the rail above her head she gazed at me, as if past the imponderable vista of her anguish, with a grave and drowsy tenderness such as I had never known,* spoke some words too soft to hear and, saying no more, closed her eyes upon all madness, illusion, error, dream, and strife. So *I brought the timber down and she was swiftly gone and I hurled the hateful, shattered club far up into the weeds.* (NT, pp. 414–415, emphasis added)

Confronting his own imminent death, Nat reflectively faces his awesome personal responsibility not only for Margaret's death but also for the failure of the revolt as well. He concedes that a subconsciously retributive act of mercy in sparing another young girl on the day of Margaret's murder was at least in part responsible for his military defeat. As the section closes, Nat's reflection on that young girl causes him to pose the crucial question on which his self-definition and personal salvation ultimately hinge: "I might have reached her in a twinkling—the work of half a minute—but I suddenly felt dispirited and overcome by fatigue, and was pursued by an obscure, unshakable grief. . . . Who knows but whether we were not doomed to lose. I know nothing any longer. Nothing. Did I really wish to vouchsafe a life for the one that I had taken?" (NT, p. 417).

The viability of violence as a legitimate strategy for effecting meaningful social change has received increasingly widespread endorsement, both practical and theoretical, in recent years, particularly with regard to the pressing issue of civil rights reform. The devastating race riots of the late 1960s in Watts, Harlem, Chicago, Detroit, and Newark are indisputable testimony to the fact that seething resentment over the treacherous discrepancy between the promise and the fulfillment of racial equality will not go unexpressed. Hofstadter, in discussing the social impact of Fanon's *The Wretched of the Earth*, notes that the black Algerian psychiatrist's "full-throated defense of the therapeutic and liberating effects of violence has been one of the most widely read books of our time."[58] Fanon forcefully argues that under circumstances of racial oppression violence produces both social cohesiveness and self-esteem. He concludes that "for the colonized people this violence, because it constitutes their only work, invests their characters with positive and creative qualities. The practice of violence binds them together as a whole" and that, for the individual within such a situation, "violence is a cleansing force. It frees the native from his inferiority complex and from his despair and inaction; it makes him fearless and restores his self-respect."[59]

The purportedly positive social effects of violent protest advocated by certain militant Black Power leaders derive strong theoretical support from Fanon's argument. One articulate spokesman for Black Power specifically singles out the Nat Turner rebellion as a model for the revolutionary strategies of that movement during the 1960s: "Turner is important because he attempted to destroy an oppressive system totally; he saw himself always as one of the oppressed, and his actions were undertaken in the spirit of liberty for all, with the intent of bringing freedom to all. Turner demanded destruction of the oppressive apparatus not coexistence with it, realizing, as today's moderate Negro leaders do not, that coexistence (integration) is only another way of enabling many—though many more many—to oppress the few."[60]

Styron's fictional account of the Southampton Insurrection presents a dramatic counterstatement to the above arguments. His "meditation on history" constitutes not only an imaginative exploration into the enduring causes of racial violence as reflected in that historical event but also an incisive critique of the intrapersonal consequences of violence as a strategy for social reform. Nat's unendurable sense of personal betrayal and the absence of socially constructive channels for self-expression clearly account for the violent alternative he chose. However, his selfhood and ultimate salvation hinge precariously on the self-defining moral choices made in his dramatic confrontation with the fact of violence itself.

Styron, sympathetically acknowledging the significant parallels between Nat Turner's circumstances and those of the oppressed minorities of contemporary times, notes a similarity in their motivations for violent retributive action: "When Negroes, today as in Nat Turner's case, get a taste of freedom, are teased with it before it is jerked away or seems unattainable, there is an overwhelming sense of powerlessness. And perhaps at that point, under certain conditions, revolt becomes something of a psychic imperative."[61] Yet, central to the imaginative reconstruction of the sociopsychological circumstances surrounding the Turner revolt (as told through the reflective consciousness of the condemned rebel leader) is the fact that violence is ultimately and invariably self-destructive. Significantly, Nat's sense of profound alienation from the time of his capture to the day of his death is relieved only through repudiation of the violence that he had personally committed and a final act of interpersonal charity and love.

Broadly generalizable solutions are notably absent from Styron's fiction. His strengths as a socially engaged writer rest rather in his incisive illumination of immanent social problems and in his dramatization of strategies for coping with apparently unresolvable tensions in contemporary life. The social significance of *The Confessions of Nat Turner* rests precisely in the depth and penetration of its moral vision. That vision dramatically illuminates the causes and consequences of contemporary racial tension; it implicitly argues both *for* the responsibility of the liberal humanist to counter the depersonalizing forces of racial oppression and *against* violence as an inherently dehumanizing and self-defeating strategy for self-definition and social reform.

Notes

1. *The Crisis of Confidence* (Boston, 1969), p. xi.
2. Ibid., p. 10.
3. Ibid.
4. In their introduction to the report to the National Commission on the Causes and Prevention of Violence, June 1969, Hugh Davis Graham and Ted Robert Gurr include "the psychological residues of slavery" among the primary causes of "individual and collective violence that troubles contemporary America." *Violence in America: Historical and Comparative Perspectives* (Washington, D.C.), p. xi.
5. Schlesinger, p. 11.
6. The tragic failure of the Loftises to generate a viable community spirit in *Lie Down in Darkness* (1951) is at least in part a function of their inability to transcend the racial caste structure of Port Warwick and to establish a meaningful relationship with the fundamentally more cohesive and wholesome Negro community. Notably, Captain Mannix in *The Long March* (1952) finds his single identification figure in a Negro maid with whom he ostensibly shares a common long-suffering alienation from the dominant culture. Finally, Cass Kinsolving's self-destructive

obsession with personal guilt stems directly from his involvement in an irremediable act of racial violence in *Set This House on Fire* (1960).

7. Philip Rahv, "Through the Midst of Jerusalem," *New York Review of Books*, 26 October 1967, p. 6.

8. "William Styron," in *The Politics of Twentieth Century Novelists*, ed. George A. Panichas (New York, 1971), p. 342. See also, Melvin J. Friedman, *"The Confessions of Nat Turner*: The Convergence of 'Nonfiction Novel' and 'Meditation on History,'" *Journal of Popular Culture* 1 (1967): 166–175.

9. William Styron, "The Death-In-Life of Benjamin Reid," *Esquire*, February 1962, pp. 114, 141–145; rpt. in *An Approach to Literature*, ed. Cleanth Brooks et al., 4th ed. (New York, 1964), pp. 496–503; and William Styron, "The Aftermath of Benjamin Reid," *Esquire*, November 1962, pp. 79, 81, 158, 160, 164.

10. Styron in Brooks et al., p. 498.

11. Editor's note to William Styron, "The Aftermath of Benjamin Reid," *Esquire*, November 1962, p. 79.

12. Styron, "The Aftermath of Benjamin Reid," p. 164.

13. The Southern historian Ulrich B. Phillips's *American Negro Slavery: A Survey of the Supply, Employment and Control of Negro Labor as Determined by the Plantation Régime* (1918), the pioneer work of scholarship in this area, presents a generally benign and humane view of antebellum culture based on the assumed racial inferiority of the Negro. Kenneth M. Stampp's *The Peculiar Institution* (1956) epitomizes the anti-Phillips position. Contrary to Phillips's view, Stampp argues that the effects of slavery were totally devastating and brutal for its victims.

14. William Styron, "New Editions," review of *Slave and Citizen: The Negro in the Americas* by Frank Tannenbaum, *New York Review of Books* 1 (Special Issue, 1963): 43.

15. Frank Tannenbaum, *Slave and Citizen: The Negro in the Americas* (New York, 1946), p. viii.

16. Styron, "New Editions," p. 43.

17. Ibid. Emphasis added.

18. William Styron, "Overcome," review of *American Negro Slave Revolts* by Herbert Aptheker, *New York Review of Books*, 26 September 1963, p. 19.

19. Ibid.

20. William Styron, "A Southern Conscience," *New York Review of Books*, 2 April 1964, p. 3.

21. George Plimpton, "William Styron: A Shared Ordeal," *New York Times*, 8 October 1967, sec. 7, p. 2.

22. Raymond A. Sokolov, "Into the Mind of Nat Turner," *Newsweek*, 16 October 1967, p. 69.

23. William Styron, "This Quiet Dust," in *The South Today*, ed. Willie Morris (New York, 1965), pp. 17–18. Emphasis added.

24. Ibid., p. 20.

25. Ibid., p. 16.

26. Ibid., p. 20. Emphasis added.

27. Ibid., p. 21.

28. Louis L. Martz, *The Poetry of Meditation*, 2nd ed. (New Haven, 1962), p. 330.

29. *Oxford English Dictionary* (Oxford, 1961). Emphasis added.

30. Richard Maxwell Brown, "Historical Patterns of Violence in America," in Graham and Gurr, p. 39.

31. The actual revolt occurred 21–23 August 1831. With Turner in command, a small band of slaves wrought apocalyptic destruction over the Virginia countryside. The rebellion was finally subdued with the assistance of the state militia and, in part, through the complicity of recalcitrant slaves. Nat escaped, but was apprehended on 30 October, brought to trial in the county seat of Jerusalem on 5 November, and hanged on 11 November 1831. The original "confessions" were transcribed by Thomas R. Gray, Nat's court-appointed lawyer, during 1–3 November in the Southampton County Jail.

32. John W. Cromwell, "The Aftermath of Nat Turner's Insurrection," *Journal of Negro History*, 5 (1920): 208–234; rpt. in Henry Irving Tragle, *The Southampton Slave Revolt of 1831: A Compilation of Source Material* (Amherst, 1971), p. 374.

33. Ibid., p. 386.

34. Plimpton, sec. 7, p. 30.

35. Note esp. the preface "To the Public" in Thomas R. Gray, "The Confessions of Nat Turner (1831)" reprinted in Tragle, *Southampton Slave Revolt*, pp. 303–305.

36. Note esp. John Henrik Clarke, ed., *William Styron's Nat Turner: Ten Black Writers Respond* (Boston, 1968). For an incisive analysis of the black intellectual community's objections to Styron's novel, see Robert F. Durden, "William Styron and His Black Critics," *South Atlantic Quarterly*, 68 (1969): 181–187.

37. William Styron, "William Styron Replies," *Nation*, 22 April 1968, p. 545.

38. Georg Lukács, *The Historical Novel*, trans. Hannah and Stanley Mitchell (Boston, 1963), pp. 166–167; quoted in Styron, "William Styron Replies," p. 546.

39. Plimpton, sec. 7, p. 2.

40. Quoted by Sokolov, p. 67.

41. R. W. B. Lewis and C. Vann Woodward, "Slavery in the First Person," *Yale Alumni Magazine*, 31 (November 1967): 35.

42. Robert Canzoneri and Page Stegner, "An Interview with William Styron," *Per/Se*, 1 (Summer 1966): 39.

43. Robert H. Fossum, *William Styron* (Grand Rapids, Mi., 1968), p. 36.

44. Quoted by Sokolov, p. 69.

45. Tragle, *Southampton Slave Revolt*, p. 301.

46. Stanley M. Elkins, citing R. Jackson Wilson, *In Quest of Community: Social Philosophy in the United States, 1860–1920* (New York, 1968), p. 3 notes: "The 'liberation' of the individual from the perennial constraints of institutions was a process . . . that 'comes as close as anything can to constituting the relative distinctiveness of men's experience in America,'" in Elkins's "Slavery and Ideology," in *The Debate Over Slavery: Stanley Elkins and His Critics*, ed. Ann J. Lane (Urbana, 1971), pp. 365–366.

47. William Styron, *The Confessions of Nat Turner* (New York, 1967), p. 169. Page references for subsequent excerpts are indicated in parentheses.

48. Henry Irving Tragle, "Styron and His Sources," *Massachusetts Review* 11

(1970): 135–153, reprinted in Tragle, *The Southampton Slave Revolt*, p. 402.

49. Ibid.

50. Stanley M. Elkins, *Slavery: A Problem in American Institutional and Intellectual Life*, 2d ed. (Chicago, 1968), p. 43.

51. Ibid.

52. Plimpton, sec. 7, p. 34.

53. Elkins, p. 208.

54. "Violence in American Literature," in *Violence: Causes and Solutions*, ed. Renatus Hartogs and Eric Artzt (New York, 1970), p. 64.

55. "On Her Own Work," in *Flannery O'Connor: Mystery and Manners*, ed. Sally Fitzgerald and Robert Fitzgerald (New York, 1961), pp. 113–114. Emphasis added.

56. Canzoneri and Stegner, p. 39.

57. All the following quotations from Elkins are in *Slavery*, pp. 159–161.

58. Richard Hofstadter, "Reflections of Violence in the United States," in *American Violence: A Documentary History*, ed. Richard Hofstadter and Michael Wallace (New York, 1970), p. 29.

59. Frantz Fanon, *The Wretched of the Earth*, trans. Constance Farrington (New York, 1968), pp. 93 and 94.

60. Addison Gayle, Jr., *The Black Situation* (New York, 1970), p. 68.

61. Lewis and Woodward, p. 38.

ROBERT K. MORRIS

In the Clap Shack: Comedy in the Charnel House

In the Clap Shack, William Styron's first full-length play, seems on
the surface a rather surprising work to follow on the heels of *The
Confessions of Nat Turner*, or, for that matter, for the author of *Lie
Down in Darkness* or *Set This House on Fire* to have written at all.
To begin with, it is, quite in the classic sense, a comedy: a mode of
composition not normally associated with Styron, even though the
darkest stretches of his fiction have always been shot through with
timely and redeeming comic effects. Again, the play was conceived
(as Styron himself notes in the interview printed in this collection)
as a satire, suggesting even further an opening up of the interior,
particularized, frenetic worlds of those novels supersaturated with
tragedy and apocalypse, to a more palpable and universal realm: to
an art, in short, that works through common exposure, rather than
private disclosure. And most surprising of all is Styron's apparent
departure from those "biases, sympathies, apprehensions"[1] that
have sustained critics (predominantly urban and eastern, and often
more acerbic and capricious than accurate) in their mechanical slap-
ping on of the pre-pasted labels "southern" and "regional" writer.

I say "on the surface," for while the play must, almost by definition, be different from the novels, it is at the same time very much
like them. Despite Styron's shift in genre and mode, despite his excursion into obvious satire, despite his rigorous exclusion of southern problems—aren't such, really, *all* our problems now?—the play
balances the novels' passion, intensity and irony, takes on (in a way
deceptively simple for the textured novelist Styron is) many of their
patterns and overviews, and catches its hero up (as other of Styron's
heroes are caught up) in the "ghastly struggle just to assert [his]
humanness, to get over the barriers to understanding, to clear [his]
personality of obsessions."[2] Styron has not relaxed his probings into

[269]

the human condition, and he still ponders why (to paraphrase Hoffman) the human creature potentially capable of rising to dignity, even nobility, is "often the victim of accident and absurdity." But he has relaxed his tone and technique: moved out the furniture and fixtures of his novels—the solemnity, rhetoric, and lyricism—and left us with basic confrontations in a nearly naked room. One might almost believe that the superior exhaustion Styron experienced after the completion of *Nat Turner* demanded such relaxation, a new perspective, even, to emphasize the commonality rather than the eccentricity of human beings. And that instead of ripping and tearing back to expose the rawness of humanity's common wounds, Styron decided to probe them with the scalpel of the satirist, to make clean, direct incisions into human motives and actions.

The simile (if a trifle purple) is apposite to *In the Clap Shack*, for it is a play about disease—gonorrhea or "the clap" in particular—though Styron takes this common garden variety of venereal infection as the physical, solid center only, moving out through expanding and widening circles to operate on social, moral, psychological, even metaphysical disease. In a way that will not be strange to readers of *The Long March*, the urological ward of the naval hospital is a microcosm, peopled (as most American novels and plays about the war are conventionally peopled) with Negro, Pole, Jew, WASP, Irishman, Italian, southerner and northerner, officer and enlisted man, who share in their enforced isolation, in their taint, in their ostracism from the world outside, a kind of vulnerability that paradoxically unites and separates them.

Such a theme might appear unpromising for comic satire, especially since the play makes clear from the outset that its comedy is not to move via black, grotesque, or nihilistic routes. Somewhat eclectically, but with a fine intuitive sense for drama, Styron maneuvers freely among farce, set gags, and *shticks*, the comedy of situation, manners, humors even, in order to sustain the initial tone, to keep the pace up and the action fluid; yet no one of these devices can be singled out as the salient base of his comic method. For they all ultimately cohere in what I would call the comedy of dislocation or discontinuity: a type of dramatic irony dependent upon inversions of certain premises that must be accepted before the range of the satire and the thematic treatment of disease can be fitted together.

The first of these inversions evolves in a direct way from the ethics of illness: the very conception itself a parody of the normal. The venereal patients on the ward are viewed by their superiors—Dr. Glanz, the chief urologist, and Captain Budwinkle, the hospital commandant—as morally recalcitrant, antisocial beings; and their unfortunate but innocuous and totally human indiscretions are condemned as acts of "corrupt," "depraved," "licentious" voluptuaries. Enamored as each officer is with his professionalism, and the importance of his mission (one administrative, the other, supposedly, curative), neither the martinet Budwinkle nor the autocratic Glanz (who persists in speaking of himself in the first person plural) gives more than a mere nod to the most obvious of absolute truths: that the war is responsible for the conditions on the ward.

Glanz, with his strange, vintage puritanism—strange only until it is exposed as something more—and Budwinkle, with his idée fixe on efficiency and loyalty, both assume that any displays of emotion or feeling are signs of moral weakness and turpitude: conduct unbecoming a man and a marine. These prejudices extend to the sexual act itself and would make any marine who refuses to remain monkish in the performance of his duty—who, that is, falls prey to natural drives (and contracts VD)—a near criminal, at least by service standards. Reduced from its specious premises to its absurd conclusion, the argument suggests a man must keep himself incorruptible and inviolate for the heroic mission before him—so in the end he will be in tip-top condition to fight and kill and die.

A ludicrous instance of such endemic logic at work comes in a brief "bit" during the first act, when a minor character, McDaniel, reads a letter he has received from Rhonda Fleming's "personal secretary":

Dear Davy: Like all screen stars, Miss Fleming receives hundreds of fan letters every day, and she could not possibly answer them herself. But you write her so often that she's terribly impressed, and she wanted me to send you this personal message. She thinks marines like you are the finest, cleanest, bravest boys in America, and she hopes you'll be thinking of her when you go overseas and slap that Jap. (CS, 1. 2)

And later, when Glanz and Budwinkle are grilling the young southerner Wallace Magruder about the "betrayal" of his fiancée (Magruder, drunk and lustful one summer night when his betrothed was away, "had relations" with a middle-aged cotton mill worker), the captain pays lip service to those Boy Scout virtues that equate moral with physical health:

I may be dense, Magruder. Obtuse. Stupid even. Feel free to correct me if I don't make sense. But one of the important aspects of love between man and woman is *fidelity*, is it not? Decks clean fore and aft, and all squared away amidships? (*Pauses*) I won't blow the whistle on you for having premarital relations, although that to my mind is a poisonous business. What I truly can't abide—and I want you to hear it loud and clear—is the idea that you betrayed this girl during her summer vacation! (CS, 2. 2)

As a satirist interested in going beyond the mere attitudinizing of his characters, Styron is not concerned with extensive or profound analyses of this discouraging sort of thinking. Both the movie star and Budwinkle may be honest and aboveboard in their moral stance ("clean fore and aft and all squared away amidships"), may not be posturing at all, but the demands of both are exigent—and possibly dangerous. They are a foil to the way human beings really act. The important point, however, is that neither belief is "realistic" in the context of the times or in view of the tempers of men. War, Styron suggests from the very beginning of the play, breeds its own ineluctable illness—the cry of the dying Chalkey that opens the first act, "Pearl! Pearl!" is the name of his sister, but (hardly fortuitously) the name of the harbor as well—inverting, subsequently, all values of normalcy and health. And with illness as the norm, all "healthy" standards become suspect.

The second of these major inversions develops from the ethos of the war itself. It is 1943. As men are dying on the battlefield, so they are dying on the ward. Chalkey has pyelonephritis complicated by galloping hypertension; Schwartz has a fatal renal tuberculosis. But more than metaphorical, the stench of death is literal, for the Negro Clark in the late ulcerative stages of granuloma emits a "rancid, pungent odor" from his bed that every now and again elicits nauseous shudders from fellow patients and doctor alike. It is onto this "thoroughly discouraging and corrupt scene" (as Glanz calls it) that Styron thrusts Magruder. Diagnosed for syphilis because of a three plus on his Wassermann and Kahn tests, Magruder is received admiringly by the men (he is an "ass *and* tit man," Dedario tells Stancik) and, since the syphilitic can anticipate blindness, paralysis, and insanity—a point that Glanz makes cheerfully plain in his several interviews with the young marine—even as something of a hero.

Magruder, a would-be writer who is innocent and hypersensitive as well as hypochondriac, at first reacts with incredulity at the diagnosis. He has had sexual relations with only two women in his life—his fiancée and the factory worker—and never experienced any of the earlier indications of syphilis. But worked over by Glanz (in an attempt to reconstruct the patient's "sexual profile") and plagued by his own heightened romantic sense of doom, he soon overreacts. Mere disbelief becomes depression, then despair, and finally fear. A mild hypochondriac to begin with, Magruder whips himself into morbid melancholy and anxiety, is driven almost insane by Glanz's suggestion that the foulness and pollution have been transmitted to his fiancée, and, in the extreme terror of his neurotic imagination, sees himself as a walking corpse and the ward as a "charnel house."

Once it is understood how Styron must, for most of the play, enforce Magruder's brooding in order finally to affirm the vitality and comedy of life over the fact and horror of death—the charnel house atmosphere of the ward, though imagined by Magruder, is no less real for him; and indeed the world outside is already one huge, grim, universal charnel house—the slow raking of his hero over the coals becomes a thematic and dramatic necessity. For one thing it prepares for the comic catharsis galvanized by Styron's twist in plot: the discovery that Magruder's chronic trench mouth, not syphilis, was responsible for the high positive readings on his Wassermann and Kahn. For another it resolves (in a catharsis of another sort) the agon between Magruder and Glanz which, too comically and casually, has built up over the long two acts; it allows Magruder's stifled rage and helplessness in the face of medical and military authority to burst full-blown into violence and to free him of past and present obsessions. As Magruder, in his final speech, says to Schwartz:

I guess I am lucky. I guess anyone who gets out of here is lucky. You know, even going to the brig and all—a court-martial, prison, *anything* after this—I couldn't care less, really. It'll seem like being set free. . . . And you know another thing, Schwartz? Whatever else, I think I've gotten rid of my hypochondria. Breathe on me, Schwartz! . . . Fantastic. The breath of a babe! It was like a zephyr! (CS, 3. 3)

In the broadest way, however, Magruder's initiation and revelation together become the simple denial of the omnipresent death force wrought by war. With so many lines of life unlived, his true struggle is to overcome the absurd choices of death outlined calmly and logically by Lineweaver (the chief male nurse on the ward and a kind of choric voice), who tells him after the negative Wassermann report has come back: "You'll live to die a hero on a wonderful Pacific beach somewhere. That's a lot better, isn't it, than ending up with the blind staggers, or in the booby hatch? And if you really die with enough dash and style, they might even give you the Navy Cross." No less true for being absurd and more hopeless for appearing inescapable, the alternatives are annihilated, by Magruder at least, in his willfull, passionate, foolish, spontaneous, and very human aggression against Glanz. Practically, the bullying and humbling of the urologist is quixotic; but it might be the compulsive act of anyone who believes—and Styron seems to share the belief with his hero—that man's energies should be directed to the pursuit of living rather than the avoidance of dying: to the choices of life rather than of deaths.

Styron's attempt to invert these insidious, preconceived premises about illness and war is the groundwork for his satire. But his attack is not centered solely on men like Glanz and Budwinkle—mere cogs in the machinery set in motion by more virulent and dangerous minds—but on all those who suffer from destructive and self-destructive obsessions. I do not mean to apply this generalization rigidly. At the most unsophisticated (though perhaps funniest) level of the comedy, Styron introduces foils like Dedario and Stancik—happy warriors and habitual offenders who are regularly in and out with the "clap" and who have spent most of the war at short arm inspections, "skinning it back, squeezing it, milking it down." These characterizations show how comparatively benign a good, solid, healthy obsession with sex can be. For Styron the fact of disease is unfortunate but irrelevant, a matter of fate and chance. Certainly disease per se is not being satirized and is even disposed horizontally through the play in a hierarchy of gravity. Dedario and Stancik's gonorrhea is of minor consequence placed side by side with Schwartz's renal tuberculosis or Clark's nephritis, though potentially more serious (penicillin has not yet replaced sulfadiazine) than Magruder's trench mouth. What *is* being satirized is tied more directly to the play's concentric movement: one originating with varieties of physical illness, but becoming either destructive or self-destructive as the obsession with disease is transformed into the disease of obsession.

Budwinkle's obsession, for example, is too obvious and too patent (though nonetheless dangerous) to demand any but the broadest strokes. It is that of the prototypic administrator—eternally the same in or out of uniform—whose concern over the incidence and treatment of VD is unrelated to the health and welfare of the men and is focused solely on the administrative problems they present. A Navy captain—"imperious, patrician of carriage, aloof and proud," as Styron characterizes him—he is determined to set the hospital administratively shipshape and to run it on the order of a seagoing vessel. "One of my first and most urgent duties on assuming this command," he tells Glanz on a tour of the ward, "is to get an accurate bearing on our venereal situation. To get a clear view from the poop deck, that is, so we can navigate the rocks and shoals . . . we'd better batten down all ports and hatches and man the fire stations." Budwinkle's total lack of empathy with the VD patients—he finds their morals repugnant and their presence (as the presence of patients in a hospital thoughtlessly tends to be) the chief stumbling block to perfect administration—is further aggravated by his mechanism:

A splendid lab, Dr. Glanz, perfectly splendid. Great little gadgets! I especially am taken by those Kraft-Stekel monoprecipitators. . . . I'll bet they set the Navy back a pretty penny. . . . It is too bad, however, Doctor, that you don't have a Banghart twinspeed pressure pump for reverse catheterization. They're damned useful in a pinch. (CS, 1. 1)

This grim and bathetic fascination of Budwinkle's with things— an automaton's substitution for interest in people—resonates in act 2, when Glanz explains to him the wire recorder used for taking down the men's "sexual profiles." The machine is not freighted with the heavy symbolism it carries in a play like *Krapp's Last Tape*, but it is perhaps symbolic enough. As one of the smaller machines spawned by the grander mass machine—one of the "incalculable technological benefits" derived from war, as Glanz tells the captain—it ultimately functions as a replacement for the characters and personalities of the men themselves, who are taken by their superiors for little more than machines anyway. (Magruder, incidentally, is standing at strict attention outside the doctor's office while the explanation is going forward.) Implicit in Glanz's methods, greeted by Budwinkle with approbation, is the idea that in the last analysis a man can actually *become* his recording, fixed, exact, impersonal: "As you well know, sir, most venereal patients are inveterate liars, and the machine helps bend them in the direction of the truth. A patient will . . . choose his words more carefully . . . if he knows that his statements are . . . subject to scrutiny ex post facto." Such a technological tour de force could make the viability of the human mind and its freedom obsolete indeed!

Styron turns Budwinkle's indifference toward the men (except as VD cases and serial numbers) and his lack of sympathy or empathy with them into something appalling and ridiculous. But compared to Glanz's obliquity, his moral smugness and officiousness are straightforward. One expects scant humanity from the obsessive administrator, but one imagines the case to be quite different with a doctor of Glanz's training and experience. Normally it would be, I suppose, were it not that Glanz himself is psychologically ill. He is, to put it fairly directly, a megalomaniac, though the fact does not emerge until well toward the end of the play and is further complicated by his weird and novel "audiolagnia." For most of the play we think of him as a mere monomaniac. Styron has stacked the deck against Glanz, made him the whipping boy for what is deceitful and dangerous at any time and in any place. The satire against his toadying, egotism, blustering pomposity, spurious benignity, phony and patronizing solicitousness, against his gathering and culling of "sexual profiles," against his amateurish psychoanalyzing and mumbo jumbo, and finally against his sadism is unrelieved.

Budwinkle at least shows a kind of stupid wonder and curiosity in the things going on about him; Glanz displays not so much as a flicker of humanity.

Though I imagine most people will find Glanz's "humors" and actions ludicrous and laughable long before they interpret them as dangerous, Styron's line with him may seem unusually severe for a comic satirist to take. Like any imaginative satirist, however, who in the end is interested in truth—or even in truths that admit of ambiguities—Styron does not care whether the means suffer incredible distortions. (Dr. Johnson, one remembers, remarked of *Gulliver's Travels* that once you got the idea for big men and little men the rest was easy.) Glanz must be pernicious *and* absurd because both qualities uncomfortably go hand in glove with men who desire to play god in all matters including life and death. And one of the "big" questions Styron is asking in the course of the play—a question to which Glanz is but the mark of punctuation—is up to what point will we sheepishly submit and knuckle under to authority, up to what point will we allow those of supposed intelligence, integrity, diligence, and concern to exercise control over us? It is, in another way, the same question asked in *Nat Turner*.

One could almost excuse Glanz his personality and idiosyncracies, ignore his eonistic practices in privately auditioning the recorded "sexual profiles," even feel some pathos at his being a megalomaniac, did not his grandest delusion unite what might otherwise have been disparate and ineffectual aberrations into a syndrome that actually blinds him to his power to destroy, rather than to save life. "I am a *healer!* I have taken the Hippocratic oath," Glanz howls while Magruder pins him to the chair. To which Magruder retorts: "You're not a healer, Glanz! You're a ghoul! You feed off the very dregs of death!" If Styron feels the need to spell out the incipient destructiveness of such an obsession, it is to keep this most forceful irony of the play from becoming lost in the violence of its climax. For, though perhaps less melodramatically than Magruder sees it, Glanz is a kind of parasite whose own illness unfortunately finds its "objective correlative" on the VD ward. Like VD itself, Glanz's psychological disease is antisocial, infectious, possibly even fatal.

It is not difficult to see the satirist's dilemma in suiting this problem to comedy, for the play could just as easily have tipped over into tragedy. Glanz's "infallible" diagnosis of Magruder as a syphilitic might have driven him, were he other than he is, into madness and suicide. Healers, naturally, must have sickness about them before they can heal; ironically, their raison d'être is predicated on it. And a mind as twisted and perverse as Glanz's must, in order to continually reaffirm its existence, take the rationalizing, self-fulfilling, logically insane step of believing disease exists even though there is the remotest chance it does not. The patient, as Magruder discovers, is a loser both ways:

MAGRUDER (*Very loud now*) You could have—*told* me!

GLANZ (*Slightly rattled by his tone*) Told you what?

MAGRUDER (*His words very precise and measured in his rage, which is barely controlled now*) Told me what you just told me now.

GLANZ We don't quite understand—

MAGRUDER (*Frankly aggressive now, heedless of his subordinate position*) Then I'll try to *make* you understand. If what you say is true you could have given me some *hope*. You could have told me that I *might* have had some other disease. Latent trench mouth. Athlete's foot! Ringworm! Something else! Anything! You could have been less goddamned certain that I was going to *die* full of paresis and locomotor ataxia!

GLANZ (*Alarmed by Magruder's tone here, rises from his chair*) Mind your tone, Magruder. We're in authority here! The reason we failed to give you such information is because it is our firm policy never falsely to arouse a patient's expectations, his hopes—

MAGRUDER (*Fully exercised now, he advances in a fury on the doctor, circling the corner of his desk*) Hope! What do you know about hope and expectations, you wretched son of a bitch! Don't talk to me about hope and expectations! . . . Don't give me any more of this "we" shit, either! You're not Congress, or some goddamned corporation, or the King of Sweden! You're a loathsome little functionary with a dirty mind and a stethoscope, and, goddamn you, from now on I insist you say *I*—like niggers, Jews and syphilitics! (CS, 3. 2)

Absurd as it might be to suggest that Styron is serving up the warmed-over admonition of "physician, heal thyself"—I don't believe for a moment, that is, that the author has an abiding grievance against the AMA in general or urologists in particular—the universal implications of this entire violent, though comic exchange (the heavy and villain *is* given a physical and mental drubbing) tangentially works off the precept. Ideally, the remedy for any matter of ills should originate with those with knowledge and power to cure them; yet our truckling to both or either too often obviates the measures necessary for the cure. Indeed, authority uses our very weakness and submission, our ignorance and innocence to sustain its own delusions and obsessions. Most of us, in our day-to-day confrontations, are powerless to strike out as directly and satisfyingly, and in this case symbolically, as Magruder or to reach any moral or psychological equivalence to even his Pyrrhic victory. Magruder's catharsis, which delivers him from the fear of death and affirms his faith in life (the bleak anticipation of a court-martial and probable imprisonment notwithstanding) is won through Glanz's defeat and humiliation. Yet because this works for Magruder does not mean it will work for anyone else in quite the same way. Ironically, Magruder is able to heal himself *despite* "hope and expectations"—had he been given them earlier he would not have been able to sound his depths or experience the revitalizing changes—and Styron, no utopian, will not commit himself to the shallow fantasy and optimism that claims "hope and expectations" will sustain life when life is not there to begin with.

Too much else in the play controverts the idea. The most striking instances are the cases of Schwartz and Clark. Clark dies, and Schwartz, dying, will die: the Negro harboring to the end hate and anti-Semitism, the Jew holding on to tolerance and charity and forgiveness as if holding on to life itself. Styron's selection of these two apparently antipodal types runs the risk of plummeting into cliché and turning representatives of long-suffering minorities into caricatures; I imagine the play might be attacked on this very point. The assumption is perhaps viable given the rapid gloss of a theatrical production; but whether true or false, such an assumption must account for the qualifications and extensions of the characters, however close to types or stereotypes they might first seem.

Schwartz, to be sure, is more fully drawn than Clark; simply by virtue of being on stage longer and always in dialogue with Magruder he is a rounder character. We know little else about the southern Negro except his monolithic hatred of Jews, and we know why he hates them: not (as Magruder tries to elicit from him) because they crucified Christ, but because they "crucified niggers,"—the point of departure for Clark's harangue about a Jewish businessman in a small Tennessee town who reclaimed all the appliances and furniture from Clark's father because he was unable to meet payments. On the other hand, we know that Schwartz's wife is going to fat; that he likes poetry (he considers "Crossing the Bar" the acme of poetic inspiration), has dreams of managing a pet shop after the war, reads self-improving ethnic tracts like *Tolerance for Others; or, How to Develop Human Compassion*, and (in the face of an ulcer complicating his renal TB) delights in browsing through a Jewish cookbook called *Mazeltov*.

There is a great deal that is homespun and humane, pathetic, compassionate and comic about Schwartz and much that is odious and contemptible about Clark. Yet though the Negro is—in Schwartz's words—"evil" and "no good" and has elevated his hate of whitey and Jews to a kind of metaphysical disease, he, of all the others on the ward, has the truest, if grimmest, sense of reality: a visionary fatalism that comprehends the ultimate link among the men. And while no one else dares name it, Clark will: "I *do* stink and I *is* black, and I is po' as Job's turkey, and I isn't got any kinfolk to mou'n me to my grave. But one thing I does know is dat dere ain't no difference between a dead nigger and a dead Jew-boy when dey is both food for de worms. *Equal!*" Clark's fatalism, inspired by a searing, outraged sense of inequality and injustice and fed by his obsessional hatred is amplified with multiplying ironies in a later scene in which the Negro tries to explain to Magruder why he "likes" him and not Schwartz:

CLARK Because you is a *Southren* boy. I is Southren too. Born and reared in Bolivar, Tennessee. Us Southren boys got to stick together. Born together. Die together. Dat's *equality*. . . . You an' me—us Southren boys—us *knows* we gwine die. Jew-boy, he gwine die, too. He jus' skeered to own up to de nachel-born truth. . . .

MAGRUDER (*There is an edge of compassion in his voice, as if he were trying to cope with or understand the irrationality of this Negro*) Can't you see how wrong and stupid it is of you to feel this way? It's a tough spot we're all in here. We're all in a terrible situation. Why don't you try to like Schwartz too, Lorenzo? It won't do any of us any good if you keep on storing up this unreasonable hatred. Hatred for someone who's done you not the slightest bit of harm.

CLARK (*Feebly but with passion*) I'll like de Jew boy. I *will* like him! I'll like him on de day dat de Lawd make roses bloom in a pig's asshole. (CS, 2. 1)

As suspicious as he was of Magruder's appeal to "hope and expectations" of life when life is not there, so Styron is here distrustful of the appeal to reason when reason is not, cannot be there. As it should not be. Clark and his race had very little to be reasonable or rational about thirty years ago. His irrational hatred—which grows uglier and more obsessional before he dies and in its last-ditch effort even succeeds in momentarily turning Schwartz and Magruder against each other—can only be purged through some sort of miracle.

Styron's comedy, however, does not toady to miracles; the edge of satire is honed until the very end. For a further irony is that neither compassion nor pacification can counter Clark's kind of implacable, irrational hatred—as the times showed too well. (The zeitgeist as a matter of fact makes its own grisly advent in the form of a yellow "S" for syphilitic on Magruder's robe: an analogy with the yellow star that the European Jews were forced to display and one that does not escape Magruder or Schwartz.) We are caught up short in our sympathies with Schwartz's trying to reach Clark in extremis as soon as we realize that this attempt at connecting, at understanding and pacifying is a weakness in itself—I would go so far as to say a disease in itself: the terrible and fatal rationalization of many who were swept away in the holocaust:

Wally, as I got up and looked at him, looking at that fuckin' agony on his face, and watching him breathe in this tortured way, I said to myself, "Well, he's dying. . . ." Then I said to myself, "This hatred of his, it's only because of the hatred that we in turn—we whose skins are white—have poured out on *him*." I thought I should ask Lorenzo to forgive me—to forgive us—for all we've done to him. . . . And then I said, "Don't you understand, Lorenzo? Can't you forgive me?" And . . . I heard him say, "Forgiveness." And he . . . said again, "Forgiveness. Dat do grab my black ass. . . ." Wally, I was desperate! He was . . . dying right in front of my eyes. I felt that I just *couldn't* let him go with this hatred all bottled up inside him. . . . Then I . . . said: "Lorenzo, we mustn't live and die with this awful hate inside us. We must be brothers and love one another." Then at last I said, "I love you, Lorenzo. I love you as a brother. Please allow yourself to love me in return. . . ." And finally he spoke—so faint and weak—they must have been almost the last words he said. And you know what they were? . . . He said, "Yes, I'll love you . . . *Yes*, I'll love you! I will love you, Jew-boy. I will love you when the Lord makes roses bloom in a pig's asshole." (CS, 3. 2)

These dying words effectively foul the net of Judeo-Christian virtues that Schwartz casts out hoping to snare Clark's forgiveness and love. Schwartz has the right impulse toward love, but makes the wrong appeal for it; Clark has the proper hold on his hate, but the wrong outlet for it. As scapegoats of the ages, in degree and kind, both the Jew and the Negro are in some respects equal,[3] but their responses to persecution and slavery have been almost directly opposed: the one, even up until Nazi Germany, meeting these with suffering, the other with rebellion and revolution. Schwartz's grand but futile attempt at expunging in seconds hundreds of years of an inhuman and unbearable condition works out of a heritage that few southern Negroes would have then understood, just as Clark's last gasp of blasphemous contempt works out of one that would have been mystifying to most northeastern Jews. Thus, more than merely dynamiting the cliché of the deathbed scene, Styron is also piecing together fragments of ailing sensibilities that can never be whole again until the disease fostering hate and suffering—born and nurtured by the same institutions that created a Glanz and a Budwinkle—is eradicated.

I fear, however, that *In the Clap Shack* offers no remedy for this most persistent and recurrent disease. It is not a satire accommodating "hope and expectations," though it does manage tentatively to affirm the perdurability of man's spirit. The affirmation is found in Magruder's discovery—born out of wrath and indignation, a chastened sensitivity and sense of justice—that equality among men should not be gauged through suffering or disease or death, but through the joy and freedom in living. This is why, perhaps, in his farewell to Schwartz, he can inhale the dying man's fetid breath as "the breath of a babe . . . a zephyr." And why, too, this exaltation of his newly realized freedom hearkens back to a line from Wallace Stevens that he quoted earlier in the play, unconscious then of its ultimate connotation: "The body dies; the body's beauty lives." This would indeed be a strange message to take away from a charnel house had not Styron resurrected from the tragic fact of death the human comedy and purpose of life.

Notes

1. See the interview with William Styron in this collection.
2. This and the following quote are taken from Frederick J. Hoffman's article "William Styron: The Metaphysical Hurt," first printed in *The Art of Southern Fiction: A Study of Some Modern Novelists* (Carbondale, Ill., 1967), p. 145.
3. Schwartz's name symbolically links him with Clark in blackness.

RICHARD PEARCE

Sophie's Choices

Sophie Zawistowska, just beginning to recover from the horrors of Auschwitz, was returning home from work on the Brooklyn BMT. The subway was already hot and crowded when a group of young-sters dressed in baseball uniforms thrust aboard, shouting and pushing in all directions. Sophie was crushed between two sweat-ing shapes as the train shuddered to a halt and the lights went out—and, in the darkness with the noise making a scream impos-sible, she felt a hand rising between her thighs and then a finger, neither random nor clumsy but "working with surgical skill and haste." Simple panic turned to shock and "horrified disbelief." She "heard herself gasp 'Please,' certain of the banality, the stupidity of the word even as she uttered it." Nor had the atrocities she wit-nessed or the outrages suffered "numbed her to this gross insult." "A straightforward . . . rape would have done less violation to her spirit and identity."[1]

Sophie's Choice is filled with nightmares of both the daylight and nighttime worlds, but, except for the climactic incident which ex-plains the title, no scene is more harrowing. The dark, crowded subway is a nightmare, where the threat derives not from some de-monic power but the ordinary. Sophie is absolutely helpless and senselessly assaulted. Her assailant is anonymous; she can neither see his face nor sense his body. So she is isolated not only from the other passengers but from the assailant himself. She cannot make him know how she feels, "through a grimace or a hot level stare or even tears" (SC, p. 93). She is even cut off from her self by the disembodied finger "working with surgical skill," thoroughly depersonalized.

In this singular rape—with its terrifying banality, senseless ratio-nality, and impersonal threat that reaches from beyond the sightlines of the subway car—William Styron is leading toward the impos-sible subject of a novel that took him ten difficult years to write.[2]

True, Sophie is not a Jew, and the novel is designed to show how the Nazi threat extended beyond their primary victims. Moreover, it was surely Styron's purpose to show the Holocaust resulting from the cruel logic of history, as well as one nation's attempt to murder the Jewish people. Nonetheless *Sophie's Choice* is about that particular crime—or, I should say, about an American writer's attempt to approach what is beyond the limits of the human imagination.

Styron was willing to take on the black critics in *The Confessions of Nat Turner* and the Jewish critics in *Sophie's Choice* because he is one of the few major contemporary writers who believes in the power of the novel to grapple with historical reality, awaken consciousness, and achieve a kind of redemption. But from *The Confessions of Nat Turner* he seems to have learned a lesson about how to approach a subject that is so threatening. Rather than stepping into the center and identifying with the victim, he has built a bridge—with two spans. First, he has created a narrator with whom he could easily identify, reviving a technique he employed in his first two novels, and who is frankly like the aspiring writer he was when, living in Brooklyn, he began *Lie Down in Darkness*. Second, he has chosen as his narrator's link a woman who, though violated by the Nazis, was not a Jew, and who was indeed implicated in the Nazi crime. Sophie leads Stingo, and with him the reader, toward the novel's actual subject: the ultimate nightmare of history. But the novel never reaches its subject. By focusing on Sophie—who takes us no closer to "the heart of darkness" than did Conrad's Marlowe—he leaves the Holocaust unimaginable and unutterable. By identifying with Stingo, and limiting the reader to his point of view, he compels us to recognize the limitations of our imagination and language in dealing with the historical event we must nonetheless confront.

Stingo's postadolescent obsessions are embarrassing and incongruous. But they dramatize his innocence as well as the distance between his world and ours. The sexual revolution of the sixties, the decline of the novel, the neglect of history, and the displacement of crisis theology have made it hard to imagine a young man in his twenties who still sees sex as a mystery, models himself after Thomas Wolfe, and seeks redemption for his grandfather's sin as a slaveowner. Even more important, Stingo's obsessions exemplify what he learned from reading George Steiner: the problem of "time relation," or the impossibility of reconciling the Holocaust with any other order of simultaneous experience. Steiner describes two brutal deaths at the Treblinka extermination camp, and then points out, "Precisely at the same hour in which Mehring and Langner were being done to death, the overwhelming plurality of human beings, two miles away on the Polish farms, five thousand miles away in New York, were sleeping or eating or going to a film or making love or worrying about the dentist. This is where my imagination balks" (SC, p. 216). And so does Stingo's when he thinks that at the same moment Sophie was boarding the train to Auschwitz, he was gorging himself on bananas. Though he was stuffing himself to pass the physical exam for the Marine Corps, it was not to fight the Nazis (for, like millions of Americans, he had never even heard of the concentration camps); his racist imagination had focused all its animosity on the "Oriental foe" (SC, p. 217). Stingo's initiation, while not simultaneous with Sophie's experience at Auschwitz, is simultaneous with his discovery of her experience. Indeed, it is simultaneous with her first fully conscious confrontation with it. As her experience becomes part of his initiation, we come to understand their absolute irreconcilability.

Stingo begins with the normal fantasies of a young man his age in a period of sexual repression. Alone in New York, looking out of his apartment window onto the garden below, he imagines making love to a Mrs. Winston Hunnicutt on an Abercrombie & Fitch hammock, only to be interrupted by the arrival of Thornton Wilder, or E. E. Cummings, or Katherine Anne Porter, or John Hersey, or Malcolm Cowley, or John P. Marquand. But when he moves to the pink apartment in Flatbush, just below Nathan and Sophie, his dreaming takes on a darker side. He has just heard that Maria Hunt, whom he had "passionately but chastely adored" as a fifteen-year-old (SC, p. 43), had committed suicide (like Peyton Loftis) by leaping out of a window in New York. And he dreams of her standing before him "with the abandon of a strumpet stripping down to the flesh" (SC, p. 45). While this dream is partly comic—"she who had never removed in my presence so much as her bobbysocks"—it is more morbid and threatening. And when he awakes in "dire distress," the "primeval groan . . . wrenched from the nethermost dungeons of my soul" comes less from the frustrations of celibacy than deep feelings of guilt. Moreover, when the thumping of the mattress upstairs causes him to feel "another nail amplify my crucifixion," the language is only in part the hyperbole of an energetic youth drawn to gothic romance. Stingo tells us that his most memorable dreams have dealt with either sex or death (SC, p. 45); we see how the two are related. His dream of Maria has produced an impression only matched by one eight years before, when he saw his mother's "shrunken, cancer-ravaged face twist toward me in the satin vault" (SC, p. 46). He later recalls the cold winter day she was dying, and he selfishly forgot to bring wood for her fire.

Stingo's "crucifixion" ironically foreshadows the relationship into which he will soon be drawn. And this is reinforced by Sophie's distant resemblance to Maria, or, even more, by the look of despair like that "Maria surely must have worn . . . along with the premonitory, grieving shadows of someone hurtling headlong toward death" (SC, p. 46). Nonetheless, his dreams, as well as his self-absorption and self-dramatization, are incongruous with Sophie's living nightmares. They make her actual dream—which also connects sex and death—stand out in sharp relief.

Sophie is at Auschwitz, fortunate to be working as a secretary for the commandant, Rudolf Höss. She has just failed in a clumsy attempt to steal his daughter's radio, her first and only act in support of the Resistance. Exhausted, she falls asleep and dreams of walking on a beach, clothed in a transparent skirt, and followed by an attractive German she cannot quite recognize. "He smiled at her with clean white teeth, stroked her on the buttocks, uttered a few words that were at once barely comprehensible and flagrantly lewd, then disappeared." Soon she finds herself in a chapel, standing before a primitive altar, unclothed and giggling when the chapel is "suddenly suffused by the grief of a single contralto voice and the strains of [a] tragic cantata." The man from the beach reappears, now naked. "He was no longer smiling; a murderous scowl clouded his face and the threat embedded in his countenance excited her." He orders her to turn around and kneel at the altar. She "knelt on hands and knees, heard a clattering of hoofs on the floor, smelled smoke, cried out with delight as the hairy belly and groin swarmed around her" (SC, pp. 401–402).

Alvin H. Rosenfeld has written a sensitive, passionate, and persuasive book on the literature of the Holocaust. The judgments of *A Double Dying* are based on the undeniable singularity of the concentration camp, the irrevocable change it produced in human consciousness, the impossibility but necessity of finding a language to fit its form, the limits of the imagination in dealing with events that have already reached beyond its limits—and, therefore, the necessity of remaining true to the facts. For Rosenfeld, *Sophie's Choice* transposes "erotic and aesthetic motives onto a landscape of slaughter." At best, it "reveals all too clearly the literary imagination . . . seduced by the erotic underside of totalitarian terror," readily accepting it "as a metaphor for what exists just beneath the normal life of social and sexual behavior." At worst, he argues, "by reducing the war against the Jews to sexual combat" Styron "has misappropriated Auschwitz and used it as little more than the erotic centerpiece of a new Southern Gothic Novel."[3]

Rosenfeld is one of Styron's most formidable critics, and it is difficult to argue with the witnesses he summons. But he seems to overlook the need for a writer who is not a witness, trying in good faith to come to grips with the Holocaust over a distance of time and culture, to start somewhere in the world he knows. In *Sophie's Choice*, Auschwitz is not a metaphor for the dark underside of sexual experience, but this darkness may serve as a metaphor reaching toward a horror that must remain unimaginable and unutterable. I will not argue with what seems an incontrovertible fact, that in the camps "the central, most frustrated, and hence most abiding appetite was for food. Other passions were secondary and, it seems, for most were held in abeyance." Or that "Holocaust writings at their most authentic . . . are peculiarly and predominantly sexless" (Rosenfeld, p. 164). And I am fully aware of the dangers of taking liberties with the facts. But there are other facts—such as those associated with the psychology of submission and the guilt for even staying alive— that Sophie's dream can suggest for us to explore.

Sophie's guilt may stem from more than the accident of her survival, as might the guilt of any other survivor. In her case it also derives from her relationship with her father. For she did type and edit his manuscript, *Poland's Jewish Problem*, which dealt which "population transfer" and, finally, "total abolishment" (SC, p. 240).

Indeed, she admitted that "she may have even relished her virtually menial submission" (SC, p. 241). True, she came to hate her father when she realized that he was prescribing murder in his rational, circumspect way. But it is interesting that this hatred becomes most pronounced when she sees him in contrast to Walter Dürrfeld, the director of IG Farben, who stopped by during his brief visit to Cracow in 1937. Handsome, healthy for his years, well groomed and well mannered, Dürrfeld makes her father seem "hopelessly dowdy" (SC, p. 383), and a sycophant if not a buffoon. As he discreetly courts her during the conversation, she dismisses the almost certain knowledge that he is a Nazi and feels the erotic, "sweetly queasy sense of danger she once felt in Vienna years ago as a child at the very peak of the terrifying Prater Ferris wheel" (SC, p. 386). In liberating herself from her father and her husband, who is only a poor copy of him, Sophie transfers her feelings to another father figure, one with the same principles (though she will not admit this to herself) but more power. And in her dream, the demonic lover turns out to be this same man.

I do not mean to "explain" Sophie through a Freudian analysis of her dream. For the dream also serves to reinforce the inescapable nightmare through which Sophie has been living—where the actual source of terror, though familiar and pervasive, cannot be fixed, and where the father embodies just the kind of rational but banal evil that Stingo can only recount from his readings of Arendt, Weil, and Rubenstein. But Sophie's dream also expresses, in ways I have only begun to explore, her inability to separate voluptuousness from evil, desire from submission, freedom from guilt, procreation from death, the power of her father from the power of the Nazis, and the chronicle of her life from the history that culminated in the death camps. And her meeting with the swollen caricature of her *Liebestraum* the next day, when she was expecting to see her son, illuminates the reality beneath her idealization and will contribute to the helplessness, guilt, and terror she feels when she is violated on the subway.

Sophie's dream also helps us understand her self-destructive relationship with Nathan Landau. Nathan is Sophie's only source of hope and escape. Although he is fatherly in his caring as well as command, he seems a genuine alternative to Professor Zbigniew

Biegański, Distinguished Professor of Jurisprudence at the Ja-
giellonian University of Cracow and Doctor of Law *honoris causa*,
Universities of Karlova, Bucharest, Heidelberg, and Leipzig. For
Nathan is Jewish, vital, and mad. He can entertain Sophie and
Stingo as they walk along Flatbush Avenue and startle the win-
dowshopping Hadassah matrons by concocting "an entire southern
Appalachian scenario, a kind of darkling, concupiscent Dogpatch
in which Pappy Yokum was transformed into an incestuous old
farmer" (SC, p. 75). In the space of an hour, he can "with no gratuitous strain, weave together Lytton Strachey, *Alice in Wonderland*, Martin Luther's early celibacy, *A Midsummer Night's Dream*
and the mating habits of the Sumatran orangutan into a little jewel
box of a . . . lecture" (SC, p. 185). He can feed Sophie, restore her
to health, bring music back into her life and laughter into her
throat, make love to her day and night, rail at her for an imagined
infidelity, beat her, reduce her to despair by calling her an Irma
Griese who played footsie with the SS to get out of Auschwitz (SC,
p. 335). And he can cry out "in a tone that might have been deemed
a parody of existential anguish had it not possessed the resonances
of complete, unfeigned terror: 'Don't . . . you . . . see . . . Sophie
. . . we . . . are . . . dying!'" (SC, p. 77).

Nathan is not a realistic character. He is a life force. But he is also,
as Morris Fink says, "a golem," "a runaway fuckin' *monster*" (SC,
p. 60). That he is suffering from a degenerative disease does not
reduce him to a clinical case, but makes him all the more responsive—like an enormous sounding board—to the Holocaust as well
as to the change in human consciousness. His role in the novel is, on
the one hand, to symbolize this change and, on the other, to raise
Sophie to a character of tragic proportions. The young woman who
typed and edited her father's anti-Semitic pamphlet, the mother
who out of fear for her children would not join in the Resistance,
even the desperate secretary to Rudolf Höss was, after all, quite
ordinary. It is only after she commits herself to Nathan—and, dramatically, only in relation to Nathan—that Sophie develops the
thirst for life, the capacity for guilt, and the attraction to death
which give her such tragic stature. Nathan is an alternative to Sophie's father, indeed a substitute, as he brings her back to life in a

new world. But rather than allow her to escape, he compels her to face in full consciousness the living death she has escaped from. Granted, she tells her story to Stingo and hides the dark facts from Nathan. But she tells Stingo more and more only as her relationship with Nathan becomes more and more threatening.

Styron's use of suspense is only in part gothic. Through her relationship with Nathan, Sophie is driven to confront more and more of her experience. Nathan's developing madness drives her to consciously confront the madness of the Holocaust as well as her own involvement in it. One of the most powerful sections of the novel is generated by Nathan's "raging insistence . . . that she justify to his satisfaction the way in which she survived Auschwitz while 'the others' (as he put it) perished" (SC, p. 310). Styron amplifies the madness of this episode, and hence its effect on Sophie, first by suspending the story of her relationship with Höss, and then by fracturing the new storyline and leaping back and forth in space and time. Although the rest of the novel is relatively straightforward, alternating mainly between Stingo's present and Sophie's past, chapter eleven is broken into fifteen sections; indeed, there are actually twenty-two breaks in the continuity, each coming faster and more radically than the one before. The story cuts back and forth, leaps forward, digresses, or is arbitrarily broken by a space in the text—now recounting the visit of Stingo's father, now recalling the scene where Stingo fails to attend his dying mother, now taking us to the Maple Court where he pleads with Sophie to tell him about Nathan, now focusing on the suicide of Dr. Blackstock's alcoholic wife, on Dr. Blackstock embracing Sophie after the funeral while Nathan watches from the window, on Nathan telling Sophie about his breakthrough at the lab and listening to H. V. Kaltenborn's obituary of Hermann Göring, on the Danny Kaye movie and the newsreel of the Warsaw ghetto, the party where Nathan surprises Sophie with an announcement of their wedding, his frenzy the next morning over what he imagined was Sophie's infidelity with Dr. Blackstock, and—back and forth all out of sequence—the drive to Connecticut, as he calls her Irma Griese and kicks her in the ribs with his well-polished shoes and tries to urinate in her mouth, and the inn where they lie in bed and he wiggles a tiny cyanide capsule between his fingers and continues to taunt her about her prostitution while Mrs. Rylander knocks on their door to remind them of supper.

As we gradually learn, Nathan is not far off in his judgment of Sophie, though it may be wrongly based and intolerably severe. While Dr. Blackstock had other ideas, Sophie never entertained the thought of infidelity. Still, she had at least tried to prostitute herself in Auschwitz to save her son. And she had tried to use the anti-Semitic pamphlet that so disgusted her to save herself. What Styron does in the disorder of chapter eleven is to bring together a wide range of infidelities—Stingo's natural desire to play rather than chop wood for his mother, Sophie's innocent embrace of Dr. Blackstock, her selfless attempt to save her son, and her more ambiguous but no less desperate attempt to save herself. He also holds them up to an absolute though unreasonable standard of morality. It is indeed disturbing to see Nathan taking on the role of the God of the Old Testament, the stern Father and omniscient Judge, although it is in just this role that he compels Sophie to confront the actuality of her guilt and thus raises her from the level of ordinary woman to that of tragic heroine. And it is equally disturbing to recognize the Christ-like dimension of Nathan's character, for he is nonetheless compassionate; moreover, his madness reflects the human condition after the Holocaust, and his suffering may be seen as a propitiation for the sins of man. What makes these dimensions of his character so disturbing is, of course, the demonic role he plays in the novel.

For, while Nathan takes on the role of Sophie's father in the new world, he also takes on the role of a character who was far more threatening and destructive—the doctor Sophie encountered when arriving at Auschwitz, whom Stingo calls Jemand von Niemand. After all, despite the singular term in the novel's title, Sophie is compelled to make two impossible choices. The first choice is demanded by the Nazi officer who, while drunk and boorish, is nonetheless arrestingly handsome, aristocratic, "silkily feminine," and disturbingly attractive—whose first words are: "Ich möchte mit dir schlafen," or, as Stingo translates it, "I'd like to get you into bed with me" (SC, p. 481). This is the doctor assigned to choose who will go to the labor camps and who will be killed. And, after he frightens Sophie into lying that she is a believer in Christ, he asks "in a thick-tongued but oddly abstract voice, like that of a lecturer examining the delicately shaded facet of a proposition in logic, . . . 'Did He not say, "Suffer the little children to come unto me"? . . . You may keep one of your children. . . . The other one will have to go. Which one will you keep?'" (SC, p. 483).

The sexual invitation and ironic use of the Christian parable carry the theme of submission, infidelity, betrayal, and violation to its limit—especially as it is associated with Sophie's father and her *Liebestraum*. Moreover, through the inescapability of the situation, the nature of the choice, and the gratuitousness of the demand Styron can illuminate the innocent side of Sophie's choice. And he can also suggest an experience of total domination, depersonalization, senseless guilt, and horror that are beyond the power of the imagination to picture. But Styron is also aware that Sophie's choice at Auschwitz fails to convey the reality of the concentration camp for another reason. Stingo quotes Simone Weil: "Imaginary evil . . . is romantic and varied, while real evil is gloomy, monotonous, barren, boring" (SC, p. 149). Which is why Sophie's violation on the Flatbush subway, with its terrifying banality, is more telling. Styron's ambivalence between the power of imaginary evil and the demands of realistic fidelity is reflected in Stingo's need to fill out the character of Jemand von Niemand.

Stingo creates Jemand von Niemand from the clues in Sophie's story, some scraps of information she picked up later at Auschwitz, his readings on the Holocaust, and, no doubt, his reading in Dostoyevsky. The doctor had been a religious man; he had wanted to enter the ministry but was compelled by a mercenary father to go into medicine. But, "awaiting the arrival of countless trains from every corner of Europe, then winnowing out the fit and the healthy from the pathetic horde of cripples and the toothless and the blind, the feeble-minded and the spastic and the unending droves of helpless aged and helpless little children, he surely knew that the slave enterprise he served . . . was a mockery and a denial of God. Besides, he was at bottom a vassal of IG Farben. Surely he could not retain belief while passing time in such a place. He had to replace God with a sense of the omnipotence of business" (SC, p. 486). When Himmler sent down the order that all Jews must be exterminated it must have been a kind of relief, for the doctor would no longer be responsible for the selection. But when there was a new need for slave labor at IG Farben and selections had to begin again, Dr. Jemand von Niemand lost control. He drank, became sloppy, and wondered about the absence of God, and his sense of sin. "He had suffered boredom and anxiety, and even revulsion, but no sense of sin. . . . All had been unutterable monotony. All of his depravity had been enacted in a vacuum of sinless and businesslike godlessness, while his soul thirsted for beatitude" (SC, p. 486). So to restore his belief in God, he had to affirm his capacity for evil and commit the most intolerable sin he was able to conceive.

It is important to realize that Jemand von Niemand is Stingo's creation and fulfills Stingo's needs. He has learned from his readings about the "banality of evil" and has used this knowledge in motivating the doctor he calls Someone or Anyone from No one. But he has not assimilated his lesson and remains a romantic who needs to imagine an evil that still affirms the heroic possibilities of man, and still allows the possibility of redemption.

By making her choose one of her children for the gas chamber, the doctor initiates Sophie into the reality of Auschwitz and implicates her in the horror. Nathan brings Sophie back to life, awakens her consciousness, and offers her a second choice. But is this choice any different from the first? If the doctor at Auschwitz mocks the Christian parable, Nathan mocks the Trinity in his form of Father, Son, and Devil. If Nathan is a life force, he is also mad, and driven toward death. Sophie's final choice is between life and death. But if the only life force in the world of the novel is Nathan, where is the choice? Nor, at any time since Nathan took on the roles of her father and the doctor at Auschwitz, did he ever offer her any new hope. Sophie is too much of a realist to choose Stingo and the peanut plantation. So, ultimately, she has been reborn into a world that offers no escape from the past, and she has been twice led to a knowledge of its senseless logic.

Still, there is more to the novel than this double experience of despair. For in the end, Sophie and Nathan are seen lying atop the bright apricot bedspread, "as peaceful as two lovers who had gaily costumed themselves for an afternoon stroll, but on impulse had decided to lie down and nap, or kiss and make love, or merely whisper to each other of fond matters, and were frozen in this grave and tender embrace forever" (SC, p. 507). And Stingo, having emptied himself of tears, collapses on the sand of Coney Island, dreams of being split in two and drowned in a vortex and buried alive, and awakens to the chattering of children. *"'Izzy, he's awake!' 'G'wan, yah mutha's mustache!' 'Fuuu-ck you!'* Blessing my resurrection, I realized that the children had covered me with sand, protectively, and that I lay as safe as a mummy beneath this fine, enveloping overcoat. . . . This was not judgment day—only morning. Morning: excellent and fair" (SC, p. 515).

What are we to make of this ending after we have been lead through a novel that has honestly tried to approach if not confront the experience of Auschwitz? Stingo looks back at three lines he preserved from his youthful writing. One of them is "*Someday I will understand Auschwitz*"—which, thirty years later, he can see is "innocently absurd." Another is, "*Let your love flow out on all living things*." And now he wonders if love is possible "in a world which permitted the black edifice of Auschwitz to be built" (SC, pp. 513–514). But he does stand by his final line: "*'Neath cold sand I dreamed of death / but woke at dawn to see / in glory, the bright, the morning star*," an affirmation of his resurrection on Coney Island (SC, p. 515).

Though Styron's first novel was influenced by Fitzgerald and Faulkner, it is now clear that he soon found his mentors in Melville and Dostoyevsky. In the confrontation between Colonel Templeton and Captain Mannix, he imaginatively conflated the agons of "Billy Budd" and "The Grand Inquisitor." Cass Kinsolving is a modern Stavrogin. Nathan Landau and Jemand von Niemand stem from Raskolnikov, Rogozhin, and the Underground Man. Sophie takes some of her shape from Sonya, whom Raskolnikov calls Sofya (Stingo was reading *Crime and Punishment* at the time). And the narrator of *Sophie's Choice* greets us with "Call me Stingo" (SC, p. 4). What both Melville and Dostoyevsky offer, besides the tragic stature of their heroes, is a pattern of redemption—and their influence is most direct in *Sophie's Choice*. *Lie Down in Darkness* ends, after the suicide of Peyton Loftis, with a baptism presided over by Daddy Faith. *The Long March* ends, after the defeat of Captain Mannix, in a comic recognition scene that affirms Mannix as

"Christ on a crutch."[4] The apocalyptic *Set This House on Fire* ends with Cass Kinsolving being redeemed by the innocent Francesca. Nat Turner is redeemed by the voice of the murdered Margaret Whitehead speaking words of love from the New Testament. And now Sophie, who went through hell in Auschwitz and then again in Brooklyn, and whose nightmares of submission have been cruelly revived by Nathan's mad jealousy, ends her life on an apricot bedspread in the tender embrace of her lover—while Stingo, who has come not only to love but identify with her, is, like Ishmael, who identified with Ahab, reborn from the vortex.

The problem with *Sophie's Choice* is twofold, relating to both the Holocaust and the history of the last thirty years. Melville may have looked into the fires of hell and Dostoyevsky may have glimpsed the nethermost reaches of the human spirit, but both lived before the Holocaust. If Styron wants to affirm the possibility of redemption, he can no longer rely on them, but must work it out within the imaginative limits of either Sophie's world or the world that has evolved since her death. It is certainly difficult to imagine what, in the past thirty years, might have given Stingo the basis for new hope—at least as it is expressed in his novel. Indeed, it is surprising how untouched Stingo is by anything that has happened since 1947. Nothing in the novel suggests he has been in the least affected by the cold war, Korea, Vietnam, Watergate, or the end of the American expansion and the concomitant end of its messianic spirit.

Which still leaves one possibility: Stingo, though a reliable narrator, is not a reliable witness. The novel's point of view dramatically exemplifies George Steiner's problem of "time relation." Stingo has not learned from his experience and has not completely outgrown his postadolescent view of the world or self-conscious desire to write the Great American Novel. His sexual adventures with Leslie Lapidus and Mary Alice Grimball are incommensurate with Sophie's experience. The preoccupation with his own guilt as a southerner is incommensurate with the view that the Nazis introduced not only human extermination but a new and unparalleled form of slavery (SC, p. 235). So while the story of Sophie's choices leads us towards the inconceivable experience of the Holocaust, Stingo's voice places this story in sharp relief—demonstrating, to paraphrase Steiner, that this is where the imagination balks.

I do not mean to suggest that Styron designed his novel to demonstrate the incompatability of the Holocaust with any other order of experience, though, as I concluded in my earlier study, his imagination often leads him farther than his designs.[5] Clearly, Styron has not separated himself from Stingo; he identifies with the middle-aged author who views his youthful self with very little detachment. But to criticize him for this is presumptuous. For is the middle-aged Stingo that much more limited than most middle-aged American intellectuals—even if those more clearly affected by the events of the past thirty years have become more cynical, and even if other writers have invested their imaginative powers in subjects not limited by historical fact? By turning to the Holocaust, Styron insists that at least this historical fact should not be forgotten. By limiting us to Stingo's point of view, he may remind us of our limitations in dealing with this fact—or even with a character like Sophie, whose capacity for feeling and understanding are extraordinary, but who can only lead us to approach the reality of the Holocaust, not to understand or even imagine it.

Notes

1. William Styron, *Sophie's Choice* (New York, 1979), pp. 92–93. Subsequent page references will be made in the text.

2. Robert Brustein discusses Styron's difficulties in writing this novel in "The Novel of the Year: *Sophie's Choice* by William Styron," *Vogue* (July 1979), pp. 164–167.

3. Alvin H. Rosenfeld, *A Double Dying: Reflections on Holocaust Literature* (Bloomington, Indiana, 1980), pp. 165–166.

4. From the perspective of this novel, I have revised my assessment of redemption in Styron's first two works as I expressed it in *William Styron* (Minneapolis, 1971), reprinted in *American Writers: A Collection of Literary Biographies*, ed. Leonard Unger (New York, 1974), 4:97–119.

5. Ibid.

JACKSON R. BRYER

William Styron:
A Bibliography

This bibliography updates, corrects, and supplements the similar listing in the first edition of this collection. It does so principally drawing upon James L. W. West III's *William Styron: A Descriptive Bibliography* (1977) in its Works by Styron section and upon *William Styron: A Reference Guide* (1978), compiled by myself with the assistance of Mary Beth Hatem, in its Works about Styron section. For assistance in updating these two areas with material since 1977 and 1978, respectively, I am grateful to Professor West and to the Publicity Department of Random House, especially Calvin Curtis. William Styron has been supportive of my efforts in numerous important ways; Ruth M. Alvarez has helped with a myriad of essential research tasks. For reviews or articles which are only partially concerned with Styron, I have listed the page numbers of the full piece first and then, in brackets, listed the page or pages mentioning Styron. Throughout, I have, in annotations, abbreviated Styron's name to WS and abbreviated the titles of his books as follows: *Lie Down in Darkness* (LDD), *The Long March* (LM), *Set This House on Fire* (SHF), *The Confessions of Nat Turner* (NT), *Sophie's Choice* (SC), *In the Clap Shack* (CS). Where an author has written more than one piece within a section of the bibliography, the pieces are listed in chronological order. With the exception of interviews in French publications, a few critical essays in French or Italian, and an occasional review of a French translation of one of Styron's novels, no foreign-language material has been included. References to newspaper page numbers have been standardized.

I. Works by Styron

A. NOVELS

Lie Down in Darkness. Indianapolis and New York: Bobbs-Merrill, 1951; London: Hamish Hamilton, 1952.

The Long March. New York: Modern Library Paperback, 1956; London: Hamish Hamilton, 1962; New York: Random House, 1968.

Set This House on Fire. New York: Random House, 1960; London: Hamish Hamilton, 1961.

The Confessions of Nat Turner. New York: Random House, 1967; London: Jonathan Cape, 1968.

Sophie's Choice. New York: Random House, 1979; London: Jonathan Cape, 1979.

B. PLAY AND SCREENPLAY

In the Clap Shack. New York: Random House, 1973. [Play.]

"Dead!" *Esquire* 80 (December 1973): 161–168, 264, 266, 270, 274, 277–278, 280, 282, 286, 288, 290. [Screenplay by WS and John Phillips.]

C. SHORT FICTION

"Where the Spirit Is." *The Archive* (Duke University) 57 (January 1944): 2–3, 18–19.

"The Long Dark Road." *The Archive* (Duke University) 57 (March 1944): 2–4, 16–18. Reprinted in *One and Twenty: Duke Narrative and Verse, 1924–1945*, selected by William Blackburn. Durham, N.C.: Duke University Press, 1945. Pp. 266–280. And reprinted in *William Styron's "The Confessions of Nat Turner": A Critical Handbook*, edited by Friedman and Malin (see 2, A below). Pp. 117–125.

"Sun on the River." *The Archive* (Duke University) 58 (September 1944): 12–13.

"A Story about Christmas." *The Archive* (Duke University) 58 (December 1944): 6–7, 35, 38–39.

"Autumn." *The Archive* (Duke University) 58 (February 1945): 6–7, 13–16, 20. Reprinted in *One and Twenty: Duke Narrative and Verse, 1924–1945*, selected by William Blackburn (see above). Pp. 36–53.

"This Is My Daughter." *The Archive* (Duke University) 59 (May 1946): 6–7, 20, 22–24.

"The Ducks." *The Archive* (Duke University) 60 (October 1946): 8–10, 21, 23.

"A Moment in Trieste." In *American Vanguard*, edited by Don M. Wolfe, Ithaca and New York: Cornell University Press, 1948. Pp. 241–247. Reprinted in *New Voices: American Writing Today*, edited by Don M. Wolfe. Garden City, N.Y.: Permabooks, 1953. Pp. 347–352.

"The Enormous Window." In *1950 American Vanguard: A Collection of Short Stories*, edited by Charles I. Glicksberg. New York: Cambridge Publishing Co., 1950. Pp. 71–89.

"Long March." *Discovery* 1 (February 1953): 221–283. Collected as LM. Reprinted in *The Best Short Stories of World War II: An American Anthology*, edited by Charles A. Fenton. New York: Viking Press, 1957. Pp. 361–421. Reprinted in *Eight Great American Short Novels*, edited by Philip Rahv. New York: Berkley, 1963. Pp. 359–410. Reprinted in *The World of Modern Fiction*, edited by Steven Marcus. New York: Simon and Schuster, 1966. "American" Volume, pp. 295–344. Reprinted in *Fiction and Analysis: Seven Major Themes*, edited by Robert Canzoneri and Page Stegner. Glenview, Ill.: Scott, Foresman, 1970. Pp. 141–179. And reprinted in *Short Fiction: Shape and Substance*, edited by William Peden. Boston: Houghton Mifflin, 1971. Pp. 470–526.

"Set This House on Fire." *Esquire* 51 (June 1959): 128, 130, 132, 134, 136, 138–151. Incorporated into SHF.

"The McCabes." *Paris Review* 7 (Autumn–Winter 1959–1960): 12–28. Incorporated into SHF.

"Home from St. Andrews." *Esquire* 53 (May 1960): 147–148, 150–152, 154, 157, 160–162, 164. Incorporated into SHF.

"Runaway." *Partisan Review* 33 (Fall 1966): 574–582. Incorporated into NT.

"Virginia: 1831." *Paris Review* 9 (Winter 1966): 13–45. Incorporated into NT.

"The Confessions of Nat Turner." *Harper's Magazine* 235 (September 1967): 51–102. Incorporated into NT.

"Novel's Climax: The Night of the Honed Axes." *Life* 63 (13 October 1967): 54, 56–58, 60. Incorporated into NT.

"Marriott, the Marine." *Esquire* 76 (September 1971): 101–104, 196, 198, 200, 202, 204, 207–208, 210.

"The Suicide Run." *American Poetry Review* 3 (May/June 1974): 20–22.

"The Seduction of Leslie." *Esquire* 86 (September 1976): 92–97, 126, 128, 131–134, 136–138. Incorporated into SC.

"The Force of Her Happiness." *The Archive* (Duke University) 89 (Spring 1977): 94–114. Incorporated into SC.

"My Life as a Publisher." *Esquire* 89 (14 March 1978): 71–79. Incorporated into SC.

"Shadrach." *Esquire* 90 (21 November 1978): 85, 87, 88–90, 92–93, 95–96. See 1, H below.

D. ESSAYS AND ARTICLES

"Writer Tells of Confusion in Migration." *The Davidsonian* (Davidson College), 25 February 1943, p. 1. [Humorous news story.]

"Birdmen Get Fine Welcome by Local Mob." *The Davidsonian* (Davidson College), 11 March 1943, pp. 1, 3. [News story.]

"Salem, Queens Girls Frolic at 'Y' Party." *The Davidsonian* (Davidson College), 15 April 1943, p. 1. [News story.]

"Archie Speaks." *The Archive* (Duke University) 60 (September 1946): 5. [Editorial.]

"Sketches." *The Archive* (Duke University) 60 (October 1946): 16–17. [Character sketch of Newman Ivy White, Duke faculty member.]

"Sketches." *The Archive* (Duke University) 60 (December 1946): 12–13, 30. [Character sketch of Joseph Banks Rhine, Duke faculty member.]

"William Styron." *New York Herald Tribune Book Review*, 7 October 1951, p. 26. [Autobiographical statement.]

"The Prevalence of Wonders." *The Nation* 176 (2 May 1953): 370–371. [Contribution to a symposium.]

"The Paris Review." *Harper's Bazaar* 87 (August 1953): 122–123, 173.

"Novel, Far from Dead, Is Very Much Alive: Author William Styron Sees Fertile Field for Novelists Despite Growing Competition." *Richmond* (Va.) *Times-Dispatch*, 29 November 1953, p. 14.

"What's Wrong with the American Novel?" *American Scholar* 24 (Autumn 1955): 464–503. [Round-table discussion with Ralph Ellison, Hiram Haydn, et al.]

"Introduction." In *Best Short Stories from "The Paris Review."* New York: E. P. Dutton, 1959. Pp. 9–16.

"Southern Fried Chicken (with Giblet Gravy)." In *The Artists' & Writers' Cookbook*, edited by Beryl Barr and Barbara Turner Sachs. Sausalito, Calif.: Contact Editions, 1961. Pp. 87–92.

"Mrs. Aadland's Little Girl, Beverly." *Esquire* 56 (November 1961): 142, 189–191. [Humorous article.] Reprinted in *First Person Singular: Essays for the Sixties*, edited by Herbert Gold. New York: Dial Press, 1963. Pp. 209–216. Reprinted in *Esquire's World of Humor*. New York: Esquire, 1965. Pp. 210–212 (as "True Confessions"). And reprinted in *Smiling through the Apocalypse: Esquire's History of the Sixties*, edited by Harold Hayes. New York: McCall, 1969. Pp. 542–547.

"The Death-in-Life of Benjamin Reid." *Esquire* 57 (February 1962): 114, 141–145. Reprinted in *An Approach to Literature*, 4th ed., edited by Cleanth Brooks, John Thibaut Purser, and Robert Penn Warren. New York: Appleton-Century-Crofts, 1964. Pp. 496–503.

"Role of the Writer in America." *Michigan's Voices* 2 (Spring 1962): 3–26 [7–10].

"As He Lay Dead, a Bitter Grief." *Life* 53 (20 July 1962): 39–42.

"The Aftermath of Benjamin Reid." *Esquire* 58 (November 1962): 79, 81, 158, 160, 164.

"Writers under Twenty-five." In *Under Twenty-five: Duke Narrative and Verse, 1945–1962*, edited by William Blackburn. Durham, N.C.: Duke University Press, 1963. Pp. 3–8.

"Two Writers Talk It Over." *Esquire* 60 (July 1963): 57–59. [Discussion with James Jones.]

[Untitled introductory essay]. In *The Four Seasons* by Harold Altman. University Park: Pennsylvania State University Press, 1965. Pp. 2–3.

"This Quiet Dust." *Harper's Magazine* 230 (April 1965): 135–146. Reprinted in *The South Today: 100 Years after Appomattox*, edited by Willie Morris. New York: Harper & Row, 1965. Pp. 15–38. Reprinted in *Best Magazine Articles: 1966*, edited by Gerald Walker. New York: Crown, 1966. Pp. 1–19. Reprinted in *London Sunday Telegraph*, 3 May 1968, magazine, pp. 7–10. Reprinted in *Writers and Issues*, edited by Theodore Solotaroff. New York: New American Library/Signet, 1969. Pp. 220–240. Reprinted in *William Styron's "The Confessions of Nat Turner": A Critical Handbook*, edited by Friedman and Malin (see 2, A below). Pp. 18–35. Reprinted in *The Nat Turner Rebellion: The Historical Event and the Modern Controversy*, edited by Duff and Mitchell (see 2, A below). Pp. 120–140. And reprinted in *A Baker's Dozen: Thirteen Modern Essays of Excellence*, edited by Richard H. Haswell and John W. Ehrstine. Dubuque, Iowa: Kendall/Hunt, 1974. Pp. 53–69.

"Lillian Hellman." In *Double Exposure* by Roddy McDowell. New York: Delacorte, 1966. Pp. 190–193.

[Statement on Vietnam War]. In *Authors Take Sides on Vietnam*, edited by Cecil Woolf and John Bagguley. London: Peter Owen, 1967. P. 70. New York: Simon and Schuster, 1967. P. 72.

"Books to Send to a Distant Planet." *New York Times Book Review*, 3 December 1967, pp. 2, 96–97 [97].

"Violence in Literature." *American Scholar* 37 (Summer 1968): 482–496. [Round-table discussion with Robert Penn Warren, Theodore Solotaroff, and Robert Coles.] Reprinted in *The Writer's World*, edited by Elizabeth Janeway. New York: McGraw-Hill, 1969. Pp. 361–387.

"The Oldest America." *McCall's* 95 (July 1968): 94, 123.

"In the Jungle." *New York Review of Books* 11 (26 September

1968): 11–13. Reprinted in *Law & Disorder: The Chicago Convention and Its Aftermath*, edited by Donald Myrus. Chicago: Donald Myrus and Burton Joseph, 1968. Pp. 19–21 (as "Eyewitness: William Styron"). Reprinted in *Telling It Like It Was: The Chicago Riots*, edited by Walter Schneir. New York: New American Library/Signet, 1969. Pp. 32–42. Reprinted in *Crisis: A Contemporary Reader*, edited by Peter Collier. New York: Harcourt, Brace & World, 1969. Pp. 367–375. And reprinted in *Workshop: A Spontaneous Approach to Literature*, edited by Robert Crotty, Robert L. McRoberts, and Geoffrey Clark. Menlo Park, Calif.: Cummings, 1971. Pp. 4–12.

"My Generation." *Esquire* 70 (October 1968): 123–124. Reprinted in *Esquire* 80 (October 1973): 132–134. And reprinted in *"Esquire": The Best of Forty Years*. New York: David McKay, 1973. Pp. 13–15.

"On Creativity." *Playboy* 15 (December 1968): 136–139 [138].

"The Uses of History in Fiction." *Southern Literary Journal* 1 (Spring 1969): 57–90. [Discussion with Ralph Ellison, Robert Penn Warren, and C. Vann Woodward.]

"Acceptance by Mr. Styron." *Proceedings of the American Academy of Arts and Letters and the National Institute of Arts and Letters*, 2d series, no. 21 (1971): 30–32. [Acceptance speech for 1970 Howells Medal for Fiction.]

"Turner, Nat." In *Encyclopaedia Britannica*. Chicago: William Benton, 1972. Vol. 22, p. 413.

"Ralph Ginzburg Enters Prison Today." *New York Times*, 17 February 1972, p. 21. [Statements by WS and others.]

"Auschwitz's Message." *New York Times*, 25 June 1974, p. 37. [Editorial.] See 1, H below.

"William Styron's Afterword to *The Long March*." *Mississippi Quarterly* 28 (Spring 1975): 185–189.

Introduction to *A Death in Canaan* by Joan Barthel. New York: E. P. Dutton, 1976. Pp. vii–xii.

"Presentation to Thomas Pynchon of the Howells Medal for Fiction of the Academy." *Proceedings of the American Academy of Arts and Letters and the National Institute of Arts and Letters*, 2d series, no. 26 (1976): 43–46.

"An Indulgence of Authors' Self-Portraits." *Paris Review* 17 (Fall 1976): 117–129 [122]. Reprinted in *Self-Portrait: Book People Picture Themselves*. New York: Random House, 1976. P. 11.

"Fie on Bliss, and You Too, F. A. O. Schwarz." *Washington* (D.C.) *Post*, 19 December 1976, Potomac magazine, pp. 13, 44–45.

Preface to *William Styron: A Descriptive Bibliography* by James L. W. West III. Boston: G. K. Hall, 1977. P. vii.

[Statement about William Blackburn]. In *Duke Encounters*. Durham, N.C.: Duke University Office of Publications, 1977. Pp. 77–80.

"A Friend's Farewell to James Jones." *New York* 10 (6 June 1977): 40–41.

"'Race Is the Plague of Civilization': An Author's View." *U.S. News & World Report* 88 (28 January 1980): 65–66.

"Almost a Rhodes Scholar: A Personal Reminiscence." *South Atlantic Bulletin* 45 (May 1980): 1–7.

"In Praise of Vineyard Haven." *New York Times Magazine*, 15 June 1980, p. 30. Reprinted in *On the Vineyard*, edited by Peter Simon. New York: Anchor Press/Doubleday, 1980. Pp. 27–28.

E. BOOK AND RECORD REVIEWS

[Review of *An Almanac for Moderns*]. *The Archive* (Duke University) 60 (September 1946): 16–17.

"New Editions." *New York Review of Books* 1 (Special Issue [February] 1963): 43. [*Slave and Citizen: The Negro in the Americas* by Frank Tannenbaum.]

"Overcome." *New York Review of Books* 1 (26 September 1963): 18–19. [*American Negro Slave Revolts* by Herbert Aptheker.]

"An Elegy for F. Scott Fitzgerald." *New York Review of Books* 1 (28 November 1963): 1–3. [*The Letters of F. Scott Fitzgerald*, edited by Andrew Turnbull.]

"The Habit." *New York Review of Books* 1 (26 December 1963): 13–14. [*The Consumers Union Report on Smoking and the Public Interest* by Ruth and Edward Brecher, Arthur Herzog, Walter Goodman, and Gerald Walker.]

"A Southern Conscience." *New York Review of Books* 2 (2 April 1964): 3. [*A Southern Prophecy* by Lewis H. Blair.]

"Tootsie Rolls." *New York Review of Books* 2 (14 May 1964): 8–9. [*Candy* by Terry Southern and Mason Hoffenberg.]

"MacArthur." *New York Review of Books* 3 (8 October 1964): 3–5. [*Reminiscences* by Douglas MacArthur.]

"'John Fitzgerald Kennedy . . . As We Remember Him.'" *High Fidelity* 16 (January 1966): 38, 40. ["John Fitzgerald Kennedy . . . As We Remember Him," Columbia L2L 1017.]

"The Vice That Has No Name." *Harper's Magazine* 236 (February 1968): 97–100. [*Light on Dark Corners* . . . by B. G. Jefferis and J. L. Nichols.]

"The Shade of Thomas Wolfe." *Harper's Magazine* 236 (April 1968): 96, 98–104. [*Thomas Wolfe* by Andrew Turnbull.] Reprinted in *Thomas Wolfe: A Collection of Critical Essays*, edited by Louis D. Rubin, Jr. Englewood Cliffs, N.J.: Prentice-Hall, 1973. Pp. 97–107.

[Review of *The Joint* by James Blake]. *New York Times Book Review*, 25 April 1971, pp. 1, 10, 12. Reprinted as introduction to *The Joint* by James Blake. London: Secker & Warburg, 1972.

[Review of *The Court-Martial of Lt. Calley* by Richard Hammer and *Lieutenant Calley: His Own Story* by John Sack]. *New York Times Book Review*, 12 September 1971, pp. 1, 18, 20, 22, 24.

"The Red Badge of Literature." *Washington Monthly* 4 (March 1972): 32–34. [*365 Days* by Ronald J. Glasser.]

[Review of *The Arnheiter Affair* by Neil Sheehan]. *American Scholar* 41 (Summer 1972): 487–490.

[Review of *A Second Flowering: Works and Days of the Lost Generation* by Malcolm Cowley]. *New York Times Book Review*, 6 May 1973, pp. 8, 10, 12, 14.

"A Farewell to Arms." *New York Review of Books* 24 (23 June 1977): 3–4, 6. [*A Rumor of War* by Philip Caputo.]

"Hell Reconsidered." *New York Review of Books* 25 (29 June 1978): 10–12, 14. [*The Cunning of History* by Richard I. Rubenstein.]

F. POEMS

"The Terrible Case of Theodore Twaddle's Hiccups." *Scripts 'n Pranks* (Davidson College) 7 (December 1942): 11–12.

"Get All You Can: A Parody in Verse." *Scripts 'n Pranks* (Davidson College) 7 (May 1943): 6–7.

"October Sorrow (Chelsea, Vermont—Fall 1943)." *The Archive* (Duke University) 58 (September 1944): 18. [Published under the pseudonym Martin Kostler.]

G. LETTERS

"How Deep Is a Pin-Up?" *Esquire* 22 (December 1944): 10. [Signed by WS and J. A. Howell.]

"Letter to an Editor." *Paris Review* 1 (Spring 1953): 9–13.

"If You Write for Television . . . ." *New Republic* 140 (6 April 1959): 16.

"William Styron Writes PW about His New Novel." *Publishers Weekly* 177 (30 May 1960): 54–55. [SHF.]

"J. Edgar Hoover Is Wrong about Death Penalty." *New York Herald Tribune*, 11 June 1961, sec. 2, p. 1. [Signed by WS and James Baldwin.]

"V for Vamoose." *Esquire* 56 (August 1961): 12.

[Untitled letter]. In *Présences Contemporaines: Écrivains Américains d'Aujourd'hui* by Pierre Brodin. Paris: Nouvelles Éditions Debresse, 1964. Pp. 210–211.

[Untitled letter]. *New York Herald Tribune*, 25 April 1965, *New York* magazine, p. 20.

"Mr. Styron Replies." *Harper's Magazine* 230 (June 1965): 8.

[Untitled letter]. *Harper's Magazine* 232 (January 1966): 10, 12.

"Soviet Writers under Arrest." *New Republic* 154 (1 January 1966): 36, 38. [Public letter signed by WS and seventeen others.]

"An Appeal for Freedom: Fate of Soviet Writers." *London Times*, 31 January 1966, p. 11. [Public letter signed by WS and other writers.]

"An Open Letter." *Partisan Review* 33 (Spring 1966): 225–226. [Public letter signed by WS and several others.]

"An Open Letter." *Partisan Review* 35 (Spring 1968): 233. [Public letter signed by WS and several others.]

"Truth and Nat Turner: An Exchange: William Styron Replies." *The Nation* 206 (22 April 1968): 544–547. Reprinted in *The*

Nat Turner Rebellion: The Historical Event and the Modern Controversy, edited by Duff and Mitchell (see 2, A below). Pp. 196–202.

"Czechoslovakia." *New York Review of Books* 11 (2 January 1969): 42–43. [Signed by WS and five other writers.]

"Protest." *New York Review of Books* 12 (27 March 1969): 46. [Telegram signed by WS and several others.]

"'Nat Turner' Author Replies." *Boston Globe*, 10 May 1969, p. 6.

"Kuznetsov's Confession." *New York Times*, 14 September 1969, sec. 4, p. 13.

[Untitled letter]. In *This Is My Best in the Third Quarter of the Century*, edited by Whit Burnett. Garden City, N.Y: Doubleday, 1970. P. 361.

"Nat Turner and 'Dred.'" *New York Review of Books* 15 (19 November 1970): 52.

"Mr. Styron's Position." *Washington* (D.C.) *Post*, 8 February 1971, p. A19.

"A Letter from William Styron." *Barat Review* 6 (Spring/Summer 1971): 5.

[Untitled excerpt from letter]. In *Virginia Authors Past and Present*, edited by Welford Dunaway Taylor. Richmond: Virginia Association of Teachers of English, 1972. Pp. 108–109.

"Vidal Blue." *The Atlantic* 229 (May 1972): 27.

"Ford's Better Idea." *New York Review of Books* 19 (25 January 1973): 45–46. [Signed by WS and several others.]

"Red Leaves (Continued)." *New York Times Book Review*, 22 July 1973, p. 26.

[Untitled excerpt from letter]. In *Intellectual Skywriting: Literary Politics & "The New York Review of Books"* by Philip Nobile. New York: Charterhouse, 1974. Pp. 207–208.

"History versus Historical Fiction." *American Heritage* 25 (February 1974): 101.

"The End of the World, in 20 Words or Less." *Yale Daily News*, 17 April 1974, magazine, pp. 18–21. [20: facsimile of a letter.]

"Chira vs. Planning Board." *Vineyard Gazette* (Martha's Vineyard, Mass.), 12 September 1975, p. 12.

[Letter on editing of paperback SC]. *Time* 116 (22 September 1980): 4.

H. LIMITED SIGNED EDITIONS

Christchurch. Davidson, N.C.: Briarpatch Press, 1977.

Admiral Robert Penn Warren and the Snows of Winter. Winston-Salem, N.C.: Palaemon Press, 1978.

The Message of Auschwitz. Blacksburg, Va.: Press de la Warr, 1979.

Shadrach. Los Angeles: Sylvester & Orphanos, 1979.

II. Works about Styron

A. BOOKS

Aichinger, Peter. *The American Soldier in Fiction, 1880–1963: A History of Attitudes toward Warfare and the Military Establishment.* Ames: Iowa State University Press, 1975. Pp. 44, 46, 51, 56, 61, 67–68, 89–90, 103. [LM.]

Aldridge, John W. "The Society of Three Novels." In his *In Search of Heresy.* New York: McGraw-Hill, 1956. Pp. 126–148. [LDD.]

————. "William Styron and the Derivative Imagination." In his *Time to Murder and Create: The Contemporary Novel in Crisis.* New York: David McKay, 1966. Pp. 30–51. [SHF.] See also pp. 72, 91–93. [Some of this material reprinted from *Playboy* (see 2, B below).] Reprinted in his *The Devil in the Fire: Retrospective Essays on American Literature and Culture, 1951–1971.* New York: Harper's Magazine Press, 1972. Pp. 202–216.

Allen, Walter. *The Modern Novel in Britain and the United States.* New York: E. P. Dutton, 1964. Pp. 305–307. [LDD.]

Baker, John. "William Styron." In *Conversations with Writers, II,* edited by Matthew J. Bruccoli, C. E. Frazer Clark, Jr., Richard Layman, Margaret M. Duggan, Glenda G. Fedricci, and Cara L. White. Detroit: Gale, 1977. Vol. 3, pp. 257–282. [Interview.]

Baumbach, Jonathan. "Paradise Lost: *Lie Down in Darkness* by William Styron." In his *The Landscape of Nightmare: Studies in the Contemporary Novel.* New York: New York University Press, 1965. Pp. 123–137. [Reprinted from *South Atlantic Quarterly* (see 2, B below).]

Beja, Morris. *Epiphany in the Modern Novel*. Seattle: University of Washington Press, 1971. Pp. 42, 150, 212–213.

Bradbury, John M. *Renaissance in the South: A Critical History of the Literature, 1920–1960*. Chapel Hill: University of North Carolina Press, 1963. Pp. 122–123 and passim. [LDD and SHF.]

Brodin, Pierre. "William Styron." In his *Vingt-cinq Américains: Littérature & Littérateurs Américains des Années 1960*. Paris: Debresse, 1969. Pp. 223–226.

Bryant, Jerry H. *The Open Decision: The Contemporary American Novel and Its Intellectual Background*. New York: Free Press, 1970. Pp. 264–268. [SHF.]

Bryer, Jackson R., with the assistance of Mary Beth Hatem. *William Styron: A Reference Guide*. Boston: G. K. Hall, 1978. [Annotated checklist of works about WS.]

Butor, Michel. "Oedipus Americanus" preface to *La Proie des Flammes* [*Set This House on Fire*]. Translated by Maurice-Edgar Coindreau. Paris: Gallimard, 1962. Pp. vii–xx.

Butterworth, Keen. "William Styron." In *Dictionary of Literary Biography*. Vol. 2. *American Novelists since World War II*, edited by Jeffrey Helterman and Richard Layman. Detroit: Gale, 1978. Pp. 460–475.

Cerf, Bennett. *At Random: The Reminiscences of Bennett Cerf*. New York: Random House, 1977. Pp. 135, 136, 137, 238, 249, 254–256.

Chapsal, Madeleine. "William Styron." In her *Quinze Écrivains*. Paris: René Julliard, 1963. Pp. 173–181. [Interview reprinted from *L'Express* (see 2, B below).]

Clarke, John Henrik, ed. *William Styron's "Nat Turner": Ten Black Writers Respond*. Boston: Beacon Press, 1968.

Core, George, ed. *Southern Fiction Today: Renascence and Beyond*. Athens: University of Georgia Press, 1969.

Davis, Robert Gorham. "The American Individualist Tradition: Bellow and Styron." In *The Creative Present: Notes on Contemporary Fiction*, edited by Nona Balakian and Charles Simmons. Garden City, N.Y.: Doubleday, 1963. Pp. 111–141 [111–112, 130–141].

Detweiler, Robert. "William Styron and the Courage to Be." In his

Four Spiritual Crises in Mid-Century American Fiction. Gainesville: University of Florida Press, 1964. Pp. 6–13.

Duberman, Martin. "William Styron's *Nat Turner* and *Ten Black Writers Respond.*" In his *The Uncompleted Past.* New York: Random House, 1969. Pp. 203–222. [Reprinted reviews from *Village Voice* (see 2, D below) and *New York Times Book Review* (see 2, B below) plus "second thoughts" on both pieces.]

Duff, John B., and Peter M. Mitchell, eds. *The Nat Turner Rebellion: The Historical Event and the Modern Controversy.* New York: Harper & Row, 1971.

Edmiston, Susan, and Linda D. Cirino. *Literary New York: A History and Guide.* Boston: Houghton Mifflin, 1976. Pp. 97–98, 109.

An Exhibition: William Styron in Mid-Career. William R. Perkins Library, Duke University, 15 March–15 April 1976.

Finkelstein, Sidney. "Cold War, Religious Revival, and Family Alienation: William Styron, J. D. Salinger, and Edward Albee." In his *Existentialism and Alienation in American Literature.* New York: International Publishers, 1965. Pp. 211–242 [215–219, 223].

Fossum, Robert H. *William Styron: A Critical Essay.* Grand Rapids, Mich.: William B. Eerdmans, 1968.

Friedman, Melvin J. "William Styron." In *The Politics of Twentieth-Century Novelists,* edited by George A. Panichas. New York: Hawthorn Books, 1971. Pp. 335–350. Reprinted in his *William Styron* (see 2, A below).

————. *William Styron.* Popular Writers Series, no. 3. Bowling Green, Ohio: Bowling Green University Popular Press, 1974.

————, and A[ugust] J. Nigro, eds. *Configuration Critique de William Styron.* Paris: Minard, 1967.

————, and Irving Malin, eds. *William Styron's "The Confessions of Nat Turner": A Critical Handbook.* Belmont, Calif.: Wadsworth, 1970.

Fuller, Edmund. *Books with Men behind Them.* New York: Random House, 1962. Pp. 9–10. [SHF.]

Galloway, David D. "The Absurd Man as Tragic Hero" and "A William Styron Checklist." In his *The Absurd Hero in American Fiction.* Austin: University of Texas Press, 1966. Pp. 51–81 and

208–220. [Essay reprinted from *Texas Studies in Literature and Language* (see 2, B below).]

Gayle, Addison, Jr. *The Way of the New World: The Black Novel in America.* Garden City, N.Y.: Anchor Press/Doubleday, 1975. Pp. 234–237. [NT.]

Geismar, Maxwell. "William Styron: The End of Innocence." In his *American Moderns: From Rebellion to Conformity.* New York: Hill and Wang, 1958. Pp. 239–250. [LDD and LM.]

Genovese, Eugene D. "William Styron before the People's Court." In his *Red and Black: Marxian Explorations in Southern and Afro-American History.* New York: Pantheon, 1968. Pp. 200–217. [NT.]

Gindin, James. *Harvest of a Quiet Eye: The Novel of Compassion.* Bloomington: Indiana University Press, 1971. Pp. 349–350. [NT.]

Glicksberg, Charles I. *The Sexual Revolution in Modern American Literature.* The Hague: Martinus Nijhoff, 1971. Pp. 200–203. [SHF.]

Gossett, Louise Y. "The Cost of Freedom: William Styron." In her *Violence in Recent Southern Fiction.* Durham, N.C.: Duke University Press, 1965. Pp. 117–131.

Gray, Richard. *The Literature of Memory: Modern Writers of the American South.* Baltimore: Johns Hopkins University Press, 1977. Pp. 284–305. [Reprinted from *Dutch Quarterly Review of Anglo-American Letters* (see 2, B below).]

Hartt, Julian. *The Lost Image of Man.* Baton Rouge: Louisiana State University Press, 1963. Pp. 60–63. [LDD.]

Hassan, Ihab. "Encounter with Necessity: Three Novels by Styron, Swados, and Mailer." In his *Radical Innocence: Studies in the Contemporary American Novel.* Princeton, N.J.: Princeton University Press, 1961. Pp. 124–152. [LDD.] Reprinted in *On Contemporary Literature*, edited by Richard Kostelanetz. New York: Avon, 1964. Pp. 597–606. And reprinted in *William Styron's "The Confessions of Nat Turner": A Critical Handbook*, edited by Friedman and Malin (see 2, A above). Pp. 141–148.

———. *Contemporary American Literature 1945–1972: An Introduction.* New York: Frederick Ungar, 1973. Pp. 54–56.

Hays, Peter L. *The Limping Hero: Grotesques in Literature.* New

York: New York University Press, 1971. Pp. 88–95, 166–171.

Henderson, Harry B., III. *"The Fixer* and *The Confessions of Nat Turner:* The Individual Conscience in Crisis." In his *Versions of the Past: The Historical Imagination in American Fiction.* New York: Oxford University Press, 1974. Pp. 273–277.

Hoffman, Frederick J. "William Styron: The Metaphysical Hurt." In his *The Art of Southern Fiction: A Study of Some Modern Novelists.* Carbondale: Southern Illinois University Press, 1967. Pp. 144–161. Reprinted in *Configuration Critique de William Styron,* edited by Friedman and Nigro (see 2, A above). Pp. 33–56 (in French). Reprinted in *Frontiers of American Culture,* edited by Ray B. Browne, Richard H. Crowder, Virgil L. Lokke, and William T. Stafford. W. Lafayette, Ind.: Purdue University Studies, 1968. Pp. 69–87 (as "The Cure of 'Nothing': The Fiction of William Styron"). And reprinted in *William Styron's "The Confessions of Nat Turner": A Critical Handbook,* edited by Friedman and Malin (see 2, A above). Pp. 126–141.

Holman, C. Hugh. *The Immoderate Past: The Southern Writer and History.* 1976 Lamar Lectures at Wesleyan College. Athens: University of Georgia Press, 1977. Pp. 8, 10, 87–90. [NT.]

Hubbell, Jay B. *Who Are the Major American Writers?* Durham, N.C.: Duke University Press, 1972. P. 228.

Kaufmann, Walter. "Tragedy versus History: *The Confessions of Nat Turner.*" In his *Tragedy and Philosophy.* Garden City, N.Y.: Doubleday, 1968. Pp. 347–355.

Kazin, Alfred. "The Alone Generation." In his *Contemporaries.* Boston: Little, Brown, 1962. Pp. 214–216. [Reprinted from *Harper's Magazine* (see 2, B below).]

————. *Bright Book of Life: American Novelists and Storytellers from Hemingway to Mailer.* Boston: Little, Brown, 1971. Pp. 226–228, 290–291.

Kort, Wesley A. *"The Confessions of Nat Turner* and the Dynamic of Revolution." In his *Shriven Selves: Religious Problems in Recent American Fiction.* Philadelphia: Fortress Press, 1972. Pp. 116–140.

Kuehl, John. Appendix. In his *Write and Rewrite: A Study of the Creative Process.* New York: Meredith Press, 1967. Pp.

294–308. Also published under the title *Creative Writing & Rewriting* by Appleton-Century-Crofts, with same pagination. [Facsimile of holograph of chap. 1 of LM and the published version.]

Landor, Mikhail. "Centaur—Novels: Landor on Bellow, Updike, Styron and Trilling." In *Soviet Criticism of American Literature in the Sixties: An Anthology*, edited by Carl R. Proffer. Ann Arbor, Mich.: Ardis, 1972. Pp. 28–61 [27, 37–43, 55–59].

Leon, Philip W. *William Styron: An Annotated Bibliography of Criticism*. Westport, Conn.: Greenwood Press, 1978.

Ludwig, Jack. *Recent American Novelists*. University of Minnesota Pamphlets on American Writers, no. 22. Minneapolis: University of Minnesota Press, 1962. Pp. 31–34.

Lytle, Andrew. "The Hero with the Private Parts." In his *The Hero with the Private Parts*. Baton Rouge: Louisiana State University Press, 1966. Pp. 42–59. [50–55; reprinted from *Daedalus* (see 2, B below).]

McGinniss, Joe. *Heroes*. New York: Viking Press, 1976. Pp. 64–70.

Mackin, Cooper R. *William Styron*. Southern Writers Series, no. 7. Austin, Texas: Steck-Vaughn, 1969.

Mailer, Norman. *Advertisements for Myself*. New York: New American Library, 1960. Pp. 415–416.

Matthiessen, Peter, and George Plimpton. "William Styron." In *Writers at Work: The "Paris Review" Interviews*, edited by Malcolm Cowley. New York: Viking Press, 1959. Pp. 267–282. [Reprinted from *Paris Review* (see 2, B below).]

Meeker, Richard K. "The Youngest Generation of Southern Fiction Writers." In *Southern Writers: Appraisals in Our Time*, edited by R. C. Simonini, Jr. Charlottesville: University of Virginia Press, 1961. Pp. 162–191.

Mohrt, Michel. *Le Nouveau Roman Américain*. Paris: Gallimard, 1955. Pp. 171–174.

———. "Note du Traducteur." In *La Marche de Nuit* [*The Long March*]. Translated by Michel Mohrt. Paris: Gallimard, 1963. Pp. 7–9.

Morris, Robert K., and Irving Malin, eds. *The Achievement of*

William Styron. Athens: University of Georgia Press, 1975.

Morris, Willie. *North toward Home*. Boston: Houghton Mifflin, 1967. Pp. 396–400. [Reprinted from *Harper's Magazine* (see 2, B below).]

Morse, J. Mitchell. "Social Relevance, Literary Judgment, and the New Right." In his *The Irrelevant English Teacher*. Philadelphia: Temple University Press, 1972. Pp. 22–39. [Reprinted from *College English* (see 2, B below).]

Mudrick, Marvin. "Mailer and Styron" and "Postscript 1970." In his *On Culture and Literature*. New York: Horizon Press, 1970. Pp. 176–197, 198–199. [Reprinted from *Hudson Review* (see 2, B below).]

O'Connor, William Van. "John Updike and William Styron: The Burden of Talent." In *Contemporary American Novelists*, edited by Harry T. Moore. Carbondale: Southern Illinois University Press, 1964. Pp. 205–221.

Pearce, Richard. *William Styron*. University of Minnesota Pamphlets on American Writers, no. 98. Minneapolis: University of Minnesota Press, 1971. Reprinted in *American Writers: A Collection of Literary Biographies*, edited by Leonard Unger. New York: Charles Scribner's, 1974. Vol. 4, pp. 97–119.

Poirier, Richard. "A Literature of Law and Order." In his *The Performing Self: Compositions and Decompositions in the Language of Contemporary Life*. New York: Oxford University Press, 1971. Pp. 3–26. [5–7; reprinted from *Partisan Review* (see 2, B below).]

Rahv, Philip. Editor's introduction to *Eight Great American Short Novels*. New York: Berkley, 1963. Pp. 9–17. [16–17: LM.]

Ratner, Marc L. *William Styron*. Twayne's United States Authors Series, no. 196. New York: Twayne, 1972.

Robb, Kenneth A. "William Styron's Don Juan." In *Kierkegaard's Presence in Contemporary American Life: Essays from Various Sources*, edited by Lewis A. Lawson. Metuchen, N.J.: Scarecrow Press, 1970. Pp. 177–190. [Reprinted from *Critique* (see 2, B below).]

Rubin, Louis D., Jr. "William Styron: Notes on a Southern Writer in Our Time." In his *The Faraway Country: Writers of the Mod-*

ern South. Seattle: University of Washington Press, 1963. Pp. 185–230. Reprinted in *The Achievement of William Styron,* edited by Morris and Malin (see 2, A above). Pp. 51–87 (as "Notes on a Southern Writer in Our Time").

————. *The Curious Death of the Novel: Essays in American Literature.* Baton Rouge: Louisiana State University Press, 1967. Pp. 4, 9, 10, 20–22, 146–147, 277, 280, 286, 292.

————. "William Styron and Human Bondage: *The Confessions of Nat Turner.*" In *The Sounder Few: Essays from "The Hollins Critic,"* edited by R. H. W. Dillard, George Garrett, and John Rees Moore. Athens: University of Georgia Press, 1971. Pp. 305–317. [Reprinted from *Hollins Critic* (see 2, D below).]

————, Katherine Anne Porter, Flannery O'Connor, Caroline Gordon, and Madison Jones. *Recent Southern Fiction: A Panel Discussion.* Macon, Ga.: Wesleyan College, 1960. Pp. 8–10.

Sheed, Wilfrid. "William Styron: *The Confessions of Nat Turner.*" In his *The Morning After: Selected Essays and Reviews.* New York: Farrar, Straus and Giroux, 1971. Pp. 83–89. [Reprinted from *New York Times Book Review* (see 2, D below).]

Starke, C. J. *Black Portraiture in American Fiction.* New York: Basic Books, 1971. Pp. 120, 123–125.

Stevenson, David L. "William Styron and the Fiction of the Fifties." In *Recent American Fiction: Some Critical Views,* edited by Joseph L. Waldmeir. Boston: Houghton Mifflin, 1963. Pp. 265–274. [Reprinted from *Critique* (see 2, B below).]

Sullivan, Walter. *Death By Melancholy: Essays on Modern Southern Fiction.* Baton Rouge: Louisiana State University Press, 1972. Pp. 66, 67, 87, 88, 97–102, 115.

————. *A Requiem for the Renascence: The State of Fiction in the Modern South.* Mercer University Lamar Memorial Lectures, no. 18. Athens: University of Georgia Press, 1976. Pp. xxii–xxiii, 24, 70.

Taylor, Welford Dunaway, ed. *Virginia Authors Past and Present.* Richmond: Virginia Association of Teachers of English, 1972. Pp. 108–109.

Thelwell, Mike. "The White Nat Turner." In *Americans from Africa: Old Memories, New Moods,* vol. 2, edited by Peter I. Rose.

New York: Atherton Press, 1970. Pp. 103–115. [Reprinted from *Partisan Review* (see 2, B below).]

Urang, Gunnar. "The Voices of Tragedy in the Novels of William Styron." In *Adversity and Grace: Studies in Recent American Literature*, edited by Nathan A. Scott, Jr. Chicago: University of Chicago Press, 1968. Pp. 183–209.

Walcutt, Charles Child. "Idea Marching on One Leg." In his *Man's Changing Mask: Modes and Methods of Characterization in Fiction*. Minneapolis: University of Minnesota Press, 1966. Pp. 251–257. [LM.]

Watkins, Floyd C. *The Death of Art: Black and White in the Recent Southern Novel*. Mercer University Lamar Memorial Lectures, no. 13. Athens: University of Georgia Press, 1970. Pp. 8–9, 14, 38, 57, 67. [SHF.]

―――. "*The Confessions of Nat Turner:* History and Imagination." In his *In Time and Place: Some Origins of American Fiction*. Athens: University of Georgia Press, 1977. Pp. 51–70.

Weinberg, Helen. *The New Novel in America: The Kafkan Mode in Contemporary Fiction*. Ithaca, N.Y.: Cornell University Press, 1970. Pp. 124, 186, 191, 192–195, and passim.

West, James L. W., III. "Textual Note." In *Christchurch: An Address Delivered at Christchurch School on May 28, 1975* by William Styron. Davidson, N.C.: Briarpatch Press, 1977. P. 9.

―――. *William Styron: A Descriptive Bibliography*. Preface by William Styron. Boston: G. K. Hall, 1977.

―――. Afterword to *Admiral Robert Penn Warren and the Snows of Winter* by William Styron. Winston-Salem, N.C.: Palaemon Press, 1978.

B. PERIODICALS

"Accolade for Able Young Author." *Newport News* (Va.) *Times-Herald*, 24 July 1962, p. 6.

Akin, William E. "Toward an Impressionistic History: Pitfalls and Possibilities in William Styron's Meditation on History." *American Quarterly* 21 (Winter 1969): 805–812. [NT.]

Aldridge, John W. "Highbrow Authors and Middlebrow Books." *Playboy* 11 (April 1964): 119, 166–174 [172–174]. Reprinted in his *Time to Murder and Create* (see 2, A above). And reprinted in his *The Devil in the Fire* (see 2, A above).

Allis, Samuel. "The Literati and the Party of Styron's 'Choice.'" *Washington* (D.C.) *Post*, 13 June 1979, pp. E1, E3.

Anderson, Jervis. "Styron and His Black Critics." *Dissent* 16 (March–April 1969): 157–166.

Andrea. "Paris Report: All of a Sudden . . ." *Washington* (D.C.) *Star*, 15 April 1962, p. D3. [Styron conference in Paris.]

"Another Honor for a Native Son." *Newport News* (Va.) *Daily Press*, 7 February 1966, p. 4. [WS elected to National Institute of Arts and Letters.]

Aptheker, Herbert. "A Note on the History." *The Nation* 205 (16 October 1967): 375–376. Reprinted in *William Styron's "The Confessions of Nat Turner": A Critical Handbook*, edited by Friedman and Malin (see 2, A above). Pp. 89–92. And reprinted in *The Nat Turner Rebellion: The Historical Event and the Modern Controversy*, edited by Duff and Mitchell (see 2, A above). Pp. 191–195.

———. "Aptheker Defends Work against Styron Criticism." *New York Times*, 3 February 1968, p. 27.

———. "Truth and Nat Turner: An Exchange." *The Nation* 206 (22 April 1968): 543–545. Reprinted in *The Nat Turner Rebellion: The Historical Event and the Modern Controversy*, edited by Duff and Mitchell (see 2, A above). Pp. 195–202.

———. "Nat Turner." *New York Times Book Review*, 1 September 1968, p. 10. [Letter to the editor.]

Arms, Valarie Meliotes. "An Interview with William Styron." *Contemporary Literature* 20 (Winter 1979): 1–12.

Arnavon, Cyrille. "Les Romans de William Styron." *Europe* 41 (September 1963): 54–66.

Arnell, Dave. "Styron on 'Nat Turner': Novelist Says 'Love' May Be Path to Racial Peace." *Springfield* (Ohio) *Sun*, 22 November 1967, pp. 1, 4. [Account of lecture by WS.]

Askin, Denise. "The Half-Loaf of Learning: A Religious Theme in *The Confessions of Nat Turner*." *Christianity and Literature* 21 (Spring 1972): 8–11. Reprinted, slightly revised, in *Notes on Modern American Literature* 3 (Winter 1978): Item 6.

Askounis, Christina. "Rose (Styron) Is a Rose Is a Poet, and Comes

Home to Give Reading." *Baltimore News American*, 4 December 1968, sec. B, p. 1.

Atlas, James. "A Talk with William Styron." *New York Times Book Review*, 27 May 1979, pp. 1, 18.

Bailinson, Frank. "Styron Answers 'Turner' Critics: In Rare Response, He Says He Held to 'Central Truth.'" *New York Times*, 11 February 1968, p. 59. [Interview.]

Baker, Mary Jane, et al. "We Hitch Our Wagons." *Mademoiselle* 39 (August 1954): 266–269 [268: interview].

"Bantam's Choice." *Washington* (D.C.) *Star*, 10 August 1980, p. F2. [Editorial protesting Bantam's mass-marketing of SC.]

Barnes, Clive. "Stage: Playwriting Debut for Styron." *New York Times*, 17 December 1972, p. 67. [Review of Yale Repertory Theatre production of CS.]

Baro, Gene. "A Sampling of New Writers." *New York Herald Tribune Book Review*, 8 February 1953, p. 12. [Review of first issue of *Discovery* with mention of LM.]

Barr, Donald. "Lively and Unprecious." *New York Times Book Review*, 1 November 1959, p. 40. [Review of *Best Short Stories from "The Paris Review"* with mention of WS's introduction.]

Barzelay, Douglas, and Robert Sussman. "William Styron on *The Confessions of Nat Turner:* A Yale Lit Interview." *Yale Literary Magazine* 137 (Fall 1968): 24–35.

Baumbach, Jonathan. "Paradise Lost: The Novels of William Styron." *South Atlantic Quarterly* 63 (Spring 1964): 207–217. Reprinted in his *The Landscape of Nightmare* (see 2, A above).

Becker, John E., S.J. "Nat Turner and the Secular Humanist." *Review for Religious* 27 (May 1968): 411–419.

Behar, Jack. "History and Fiction." *Novel* 3 (Spring 1970): 260–265 [263–265: NT].

Bennett, Lerone, Jr. "The Case against Styron's Nat Turner." *Ebony* 23 (October 1968): 148–150, 154–157. Reprinted from Clarke's *William Styron's "Nat Turner"* (see 2, A above).

Benson, Alice R. "Techniques in the Twentieth Century Novel for Relating the Particular to the Universal: *Set This House on Fire.*" *Papers of the Michigan Academy of Science, Arts, and Letters* 47 (1962): 587–594.

Bergman, B. A. "Cover to Cover: Big Bash for Novel by Styron." *Philadelphia Bulletin*, 24 June 1979, sec. D, p. 10.

Bernstein, Jeremy, Harold Bloom, Robert Boyers, et al. "American Writers: Who's Up, Who's Down?" *Esquire* 88 (August 1977): 77–81 [80].

Bilotta, James D. "Critique of Styron's *Confessions of Nat Turner*." *Negro History Bulletin* 38 (December 1974–January 1975): 326–327.

"Biographical Sketches of Persons Selected for the Pulitzer Prizes for 1968." *New York Times*, 7 May 1968, p. 34.

Blatchford, Edward. "William Styron at Yale: Four Hours of Questions." *Yale Daily News*, 8 January 1965, p. 1.

Blau, Eleanor. "Styron's 'Sophie's Choice' Banned by South Africa." *New York Times*, 13 November 1979, p. C12.

"Books." *Duke University Alumni Register* 37 (October 1951): 251. [Biographical sketch.]

"Books: Advance-Guard Advance." *Newsweek* 41 (30 March 1953): 94, 97–98 [94: WS and *Paris Review* and *Discovery*].

Borders, William. "M'Carthy Gaining in Connecticut." *New York Times*, 10 March 1968, p. 46. [WS as delegate to Democratic Convention.]

Brandriff, Welles T. "The Role of Order and Disorder in *The Long March*." *English Journal* 56 (January 1967): 54–59.

Bready, James H. "About Books and Authors." *Baltimore Sunday Sun*, 24 March 1963, sec. A, p. 5. [WS at Johns Hopkins.]

Brickhouse, Bob. "Styron Studied the 'Human Terms' of Slavery." *Richmond* (Va.) *Times-Dispatch*, 15 April 1971, pp. A1, A2. [Interview.]

Brièrre, Annie. "William Styron." *Les Nouvelles Littéraires*, no. 1302, 14 August 1952, p. 4.

———. "William Styron à Paris." *France U.S.A.*, no. 158, March 1962, p. 2.

———. "La Proie des Critiques." *Les Nouvelles Littéraires* 40 (22 March 1962): 8. [Interview.]

Brooks, Rae. *Harper's Magazine* 219 (November 1959): 116–118. [Review of *Best Short Stories from "The Paris Review"* with mention of WS's introduction.]

Brown, Cecil M. *Negro Digest* 17 (August 1968): 91. [Review of Clarke's *William Styron's "Nat Turner."*]

Brunaur, Dalma H. "Black and White: The Archetypal Myth and Its Development." *Barat Review* 6 (Spring/Summer 1971): 12–19.

Brustein, Robert. "Styron's Choice." *Vogue* 169 (July 1979): 166, 202–203.

Bryant, Jerry H. "The Hopeful Stoicism of William Styron." *South Atlantic Quarterly* 62 (Autumn 1963): 539–550.

Buchwald, Art. "Capitol Punishment—A Last Resort: The Treaty of Martha's Vineyard." *Washington* (D.C.) *Post*, 7 August 1977, p. E1. [Syndicated humor column.]

Bulgheroni, Marisa. "William Styron: Il Romanziere, Il Tempo e la Storia." *Studi Americani* 16 (1970): 407–428.

Burger, Nash K. "Truth or Consequence: Books and Book Reviewing." *South Atlantic Quarterly* 68 (Spring 1969): 152–166 [155–160: NT].

Burkman, Katherine H., Anna Mary Wells, Stephen Tallackson, Geoffrey D. Clark, and Carole A. Parks. "Confessions Reviewed." *Saturday Review* 51 (13 July 1968): 21. [Letters to the editor.]

Bushnell, Nina. "The Quest for Nat Turner." *Newport News* (Va.) *Daily Press*, 27 April 1973, p. 13. [Interview.]

Calta, Louis. "Muriel Spark Calls for New Art Forms." *New York Times*, 27 May 1970, p. 40. [WS awarded Howells Medal for Fiction by National Academy of Arts and Letters.]

Cannon, Patricia R. "Nat Turner: God, Man, or Beast?" *Barat Review* 6 (Spring/Summer 1971): 25–28.

Canzoneri, Robert, and Page Stegner. "An Interview with William Styron." *Per/Se* 1 (Summer 1966): 37–44.

Carver, Wayne. "The Grand Inquisitor's Long March." *Denver Quarterly* 1 (Summer 1966): 37–64. [LM and Dostoevski's *The Legend of the Grand Inquisitor.*]

Casciato, Arthur D. "His Editor's Hand: Hiram Haydn's Changes in Styron's *Lie Down in Darkness*." *Studies in Bibliography* 33 (1980): 263–276.

————, and James L. W. West III. "William Styron and *The South-*

ampton Insurrection." *American Literature* 52 (January 1981): 564–577.

"Catch $95." *Newsweek* 63 (9 March 1964): 83–84 [84: influence of movies on WS's technique].

Chambers, Andrea. "From Slavery to Holocaust, Author Bill Styron Makes Best-Selling Choices." *People* 12 (23 July 1979): 67–70. [Interview.]

C[hapsal], M[adeleine]. "Entretien." *L'Express*, 8 March 1962, pp. 26–27. [Interview.] Reprinted in her *Quinze Écrivains* (see 2, A above).

Cheshire, Ardner R., Jr. "The Recollective Structure of *The Confessions of Nat Turner.*" *Southern Review* n.s. 12 (Winter 1976): 110–121.

Cheyer, A. H. "WLB Biography: William Styron." *Wilson Library Bulletin* 36 (April 1962): 691.

Chisolm, Elise T. "Rose Styron Is a Romantic Poet Who Listens to Voices of Children." *Baltimore Evening Sun*, 4 December 1968, p. B2. [Interview with Mrs. Styron.]

[Clark, Geoffrey]. "Reflections." *Ploughshares* 1 (December 1972): 82–84. [Interview.]

[Coates, John T.] "The Men among Us: Profile of a Best-Selling Author." *New Englander* 35 (November 1961): 18.

Cockshutt, Rod. "Books: An Evening with William and Bill." *Raleigh* (N.C.) *News and Observer*, 18 April 1971, p. 6IV. [WS and Willie Morris.]

Coles, Robert. "Arguments: The Turner Thesis." *Partisan Review* 35 (Summer 1968): 412–414.

Cooke, Michael. "Nat Turner: Another Response." *Yale Review* 58 (Winter 1969): 295–301. [Review of Clarke's *William Styron's "Nat Turner."*]

Core, George. "*The Confessions of Nat Turner* and the Burden of the Past." *Southern Literary Journal* 2 (Spring 1970): 117–134. Reprinted in *The Achievement of William Styron*, edited by Morris and Malin (see 2, A above). Pp. 150–167.

"Countries of the English-Speaking World: News from the United States." *Times Literary Supplement* (London), 5 August 1955, pp. II–III. [LDD.]

C[ousins], N[orman]. "Editor's Page: When Writers Meet." *Saturday Review* n.s. 4 (17 September 1977): 8–9, 57–59 [58: WS at Moscow conference of American and Soviet writers].

Cowley, Malcolm. "American Novels since the War." *New Republic* 129 (28 December 1953): 16–18. [LDD.]

Cross, Leslie. "The Reading Glass." *Milwaukee Journal*, 16 September 1951, editorial section, p. 5. [Biographical sketch.]

Cunliffe, Marcus. "Black Culture and White America." *Encounter* 34 (January 1970): 22–35 [29–31].

Curtis, Bruce. "Fiction, Myth, and History in William Styron's *Nat Turner.*" *University College Quarterly* 16 (January 1971): 27–32.

Davidson, Ted. "Countering Styron's Stereotypes." *Christian Century* 86 (15 January 1969): 89–90. [Review of Clarke's *William Styron's "Nat Turner."*]

Davis, John Roderick. "Kuznetsov's Dilemma." *New York Times*, 27 August 1969, p. 42. [Letter to the editor on WS's recommendation that Kuznetsov not defect.]

Davis, Robert Gorham. "In a Ravelled World Love Endures." *New York Times Book Review*, 26 December 1954, pp. 1, 13.

———. "Styron and the Students." *Critique* 3 (Summer 1960): 37–46. [SHF.]

De Biasio, Giordana. "*Lie Down in Darkness*: Libertà e Destino nella 'Domestic Tragedy' Styroniana." *Annali* (Feltre, Italy), 1974, pp. 281–295.

Dempsey, David. "Talk with William Styron." *New York Times Book Review*, 9 September 1951, p. 27.

Doar, Harriet. "Styron: 'Human Being in Conflict.'" *Charlotte* (N.C.) *Observer*, 24 March 1963, p. 4D. [Interview.]

———. "Southern Writing: He's for It." *Charlotte* (N.C.) *Observer*, 9 June 1963, p. 17A. [Interview with Hiram Haydn.]

———. "Interview with William Styron." *Red Clay Reader* 1 (1964): 26–30.

Dommergues, Pierre. "L'Ambiguïté de L'Innocence." *Langues Modernes* 59 (March–April 1965): 54–59.

———. "William Styron à Paris." *Le Monde*, 26 April 1974, pp. 19, 26. [Interview.]

Drake, Robert. "Signs of the Times or Signs for All Times?" *Christian Century* 85 (25 September 1968): 1204–1206. [NT and *The Fixer*.]

Duberman, Martin. "Historical Fictions." *New York Times Book Review*, 11 August 1968, pp. 1, 26–27. [Review of Clarke's *William Styron's "Nat Turner."*] Reprinted in his *The Uncompleted Past* (see 2, A above). And reprinted in *William Styron's "The Confessions of Nat Turner": A Critical Handbook*, edited by Friedman and Malin (see 2, A above). Pp. 112–116.

Duffer, Ken. "Styron Recovering from His Life as Nat Turner." *Winston-Salem* (N.C.) *Journal and Sentinel*, 2 April 1967, p. C4. [Interview.]

———. "A Revolt Revisited: Now Nat Turner as He Might Have Written It." *Winston-Salem* (N.C.) *Journal and Sentinel*, 17 December 1967, p. D6. [Review of Daniel Panger's *Ol' Prophet Nat*.]

Durden, Robert F. "William Styron and His Black Critics." *South Atlantic Quarterly* 68 (Spring 1969): 181–187. [Review of Clarke's *William Styron's "Nat Turner."*]

Eggenschwiler, David. "Tragedy and Melodrama in *The Confessions of Nat Turner*." *Twentieth Century Literature* 20 (January 1974): 19–33.

"Ex-Antiwar Figures Say Vietnam Abuses Rights." *New York Times*, 31 May 1979, p. A5. [WS as signer of petition protesting human rights violations in Vietnam.]

F., E. [Introduction to "Shadrach"]. *Esquire* 90 (21 November 1978): 82.

"Facts and Fiction: Some Virginia Scenes and Situations as Viewed by Novelist." *Norfolk Virginian-Pilot*, 9 September 1951, part 5, p. 5. [LDD.]

"Famous Peninsula Writer Interviewed When Latest Book Published in France." *Newport News* (Va.) *Daily Press*, 27 May 1962, p. 4D. [Excerpts from English translation of interview with Madeleine Chapsal (see 2, B above).]

Ferguson, Anna Lawrence. "Bits about Books: New Styron Novel." *Norfolk Virginian-Pilot and Portsmouth Star*, 1 May 1960, p. 6F. [SHF.]

Fielding, Andrew. "William Styron: An 'Unfamous' Great Writer Brings Out a New Novel, *Sophie's Choice*." *Horizon* 22 (June 1979): 60–67. [Interview and biographical sketch.]

Firestone, Bruce M. "A Rose Is a Rose Is a Columbine: *Citizen Kane* and William Styron's *Nat Turner*." *Literature/Film Quarterly* 5 (Spring 1977): 118–124.

Flanders, Jane. "William Styron's Southern Myth." *Louisiana Studies* 15 (Fall 1976): 263–278.

"For Bill Styron, It's Work, Tennis, Parties." *People* 4 (21 July 1975): 7.

Forkner, Ben, and Gilbert Schricke. "An Interview with William Styron." *Southern Review* n.s. 10 (Autumn 1974): 923–934.

Fosburgh, Lacey. "Styron and Miller Defend Yevtushenko against Charges in British Press of Hypocrisy." *New York Times*, 25 November 1968, p. 15.

Foster, Richard. "An Orgy of Commerce: William Styron's *Set This House on Fire*." *Critique* 3 (Summer 1960): 59–70.

Franklin, Jimmie L. "*Nat Turner* and Black History." *Indian Journal of American Studies* 1 (November 1971): 1–6.

Fremont-Smith, Eliot. "Nat Turner I: The Controversy." *New York Times*, 1 August 1968, p. 29. [Review of Clarke's *William Styron's "Nat Turner."*]

————. "Nat Turner II: What Myth Will Serve?" *New York Times*, 2 August 1968, p. 31. [Review of Clarke's *William Styron's "Nat Turner."*]

Friedman, Joseph J. "Non-Conformity and the Writer." *Venture* 2 (Winter 1957): 23–31 [27, 29: LDD].

Friedman, Melvin J. "William Styron: An Interim Appraisal." *English Journal* 50 (March 1961): 149–158, 192. Reprinted, revised, as preface to *Configuration Critique de William Styron*, edited by Friedman and Nigro (see 2, A above). Pp. 7–31. Reprinted in *William Styron's "The Confessions of Nat Turner": A Critical Handbook*, edited by Friedman and Malin (see 2, A above). Pp. 175–186. And reprinted in Friedman's *William Styron* (see 2, A above).

————. "The Cracked Vase." *Romance Notes* 7 (Spring 1966): 127–129. [SHF and *Le Rouge et Le Noir*.]

————. "William Styron and the *Nouveau Roman*." *Proceedings of the Comparative Literature Symposium* (Texas Tech University) 5 (1972): 121–137. Reprinted, abridged and in English, from *Configuration Critique de William Styron*, edited by Friedman and Nigro (see 2, A above). And reprinted in Friedman's *William Styron* (see 2, A above).

————. "Dislocations of Setting and Word: Notes on American Fiction since 1950." *Studies in American Fiction* 5 (Spring 1977): 79–98 [79–81, 89].

Fuentes, Carlos. "Unslavish Fidelity." *Times Literary Supplement* (London), 16 May 1968, p. 505. [Letter to the editor.]

————. "William Styron in Mexico." Translated by Margaret Peden. *Review* 17 (Spring 1976): 67–70.

Galloway, David D. "The Absurd Man as Tragic Hero: The Novels of William Styron." *Texas Studies in Literature and Language* 6 (Winter 1965): 512–534. Reprinted in his *The Absurd Hero in American Fiction* (see 2, A above).

Geismar, Maxwell. "The End of Something." *The Nation* 176 (14 March 1953): 230–231 [230: review of the first issue of *Discovery* with mention of LM].

————. "The Post-War Generation in Arts and Letters." *Saturday Review of Literature* 36 (14 March 1953): 11–12, 60.

Geltman, Max. "Men and Ideas: How Much Literary License?" *National Review* 20 (24 September 1968): 967–969. [NT.]

Genovese, Eugene D. "The Nat Turner Case." *New York Review of Books* 11 (12 September 1968): 34–37. [Review of Clarke's *William Styron's "Nat Turner."*] Reprinted in *The Nat Turner Rebellion: The Historical Event and the Modern Controversy*, edited by Duff and Mitchell (see 2, A above). Pp. 203–216.

————. "An Exchange on 'Nat Turner.'" *New York Review of Books* 11 (7 November 1968): 34–36. Reprinted in *The Nat Turner Rebellion: The Historical Event and the Modern Controversy*, edited by Duff and Mitchell (see 2, A above). Pp. 224–227.

Gentry, Curt. "A Bookman's Notebook: Stories That Disprove a Critical Fiction." *San Francisco Chronicle*, 8 December 1959, p. 41. [Review of *Best Short Stories from "The Paris Review"* with mention of WS's introduction.]

G[eoffrey], N[orman]. "Backstage with Esquire." *Esquire* 86 (September 1976): 38.

Gilman, Richard. "Nat Turner Revisited." *New Republic* 158 (27 April 1968): 23–26, 28, 32. Reprinted in *William Styron's "The Confessions of Nat Turner": A Critical Handbook*, edited by Friedman and Malin (see 2, A above). Pp. 104–111. And reprinted in *The Nat Turner Rebellion: The Historical Event and the Modern Controversy*, edited by Duff and Mitchell (see 2, A above). Pp. 228–237.

Gold, Sylviane. "A Night on the Vineyard: Mingling with the BPs, Eastern Division." *Boston Phoenix*, 15 July 1980, sec. 3, pp. 3, 15.

Goodwyn, Wrenda. "William Styron Remembers Past." *Newport News* (Va.) *Times-Herald*, 26 May 1973, p. 6S. [Interview.]

Gossman, Otis. "Bits about Books: Raising a Writer." *Norfolk Virginian-Pilot and Portsmouth Star*, 29 May 1960, p. 14A. [Interview with WS's father.]

Gray, Francine Du Plessix. "Confessions of William Styron." *Washington* (D.C.) *Post*, 20 May 1979, *Book World*, pp. E1, E6. See also *Detroit News*, 24 June 1979, pp. 2F, 3F. [Interview.]

Gray, Richard. "Victims and History and Agents of Revolution: An Approach to William Styron." *Dutch Quarterly Review of Anglo-American Letters* 5 (no. 1, 1975): 3–23. Reprinted in his *The Literature of Memory* (see 2, A above).

Gresset, Michel. "Sur William Styron." *Mercure de France* 350 (February 1964): 297–303.

———. "William Styron." *La Nouvelle Revue Française* 204 (December 1969): 898–907.

Griffin, Jack, Jerry Homsy, and Gene Stelzig. "A Conversation with William Styron." *The Handle* (University of Pennsylvania) 2 (Spring 1965): 16–29.

Gross, Seymour L., and Eileen Bender. "History, Politics and Literature: The Myth of Nat Turner." *American Quarterly* 23 (October 1971): 486–518. Reprinted in *The Achievement of William Styron*, edited by Morris and Malin (see 2, A above). Pp. 168–207.

Gunod, Roberta Zipper. "An Anomaly of 'and': A Linguistic Comparison of William Styron's *The Confessions of Nat Turner* with Claude Brown's *Manchild in the Promised Land* and Ralph Ellison's *Invisible Man.*" *Linguistics in Literature* 2 (Summer 1977): 19–42 [19–21, 24–26, 29–32, 37–42].

Halpern, Daniel. "Checking In with William Styron." *Esquire* 78 (August 1972): 142–143. [Interview.]

Hamilton, Charles V. "Nat Turner Reconsidered: The Fiction and the Reality." *Saturday Review* 51 (22 June 1968): 22–23. Reprinted in *William Styron's "Nat Turner": Ten Black Writers Respond*, edited by Clarke (see 2, A above). Pp. 73–78.

Hansen, Harry. "Beginning of a Novelist: Releasing Toy Balloons." *Chicago Sunday Tribune Magazine of Books*, 23 September 1951, p. 12. [Biographical sketch.]

Harding, Vincent. "An Exchange on 'Nat Turner.'" *New York Review of Books* 11 (7 November 1968): 31–33. Reprinted in *The Nat Turner Rebellion: The Historical Event and the Modern Controversy*, edited by Duff and Mitchell (see 2, A above). Pp. 217–224.

Harmetz, Aljean. "Pakula Will Film 'Sophie's Choice.'" *New York Times*, 29 May 1979, p. C10.

———. "'Sophie' Film Deal Was Dream." *New York Times*, 24 July 1979, p. C5.

Harris, Judith. "Styron Ignores End of the Novel." *Rome* (Italy) *Daily American*, 3 May 1967, p. 4. [Interview.]

Harrison, Katharine. "Critics Laud Styron Style; New Novel Comes off Press." *Newport News* (Va.) *Daily Press*, 9 September 1951, p. 14C. [Excerpts from reviews of LDD and biographical sketch.]

Hassan, Ihab. "The Avant-Garde: Which Way Is Forward?" *The Nation* 193 (18 November 1961): 396–399.

———. "The Character of Post-War Fiction in America." *English Journal* 51 (January 1962): 1–8 [2, 4, 7].

———. "The Novel of Outrage: A Minority Voice in Postwar American Fiction." *American Scholar* 34 (Spring 1965): 239–253 [243–244].

Havird, David. "Novelist Styron Pays Social Visit." *The Gamecock* (University of South Carolina, Columbia, S.C.), 28 January 1974, pp. 4, 7. [WS as guest in James Dickey's seminar.]

Hays, Peter L. "The Nature of Rebellion in *The Long March*." *Critique* 8 (Winter 1965–1966): 70–74.

H[azard], E[loise] P[erry]. "The Author." *Saturday Review of Literature* 34 (15 September 1951): 12. [Biographical sketch.]

———. "Eight Fiction Finds." *Saturday Review of Literature* 35 (16 February 1952): 16–18 [17].

Hiers, John T. "The Graveyard Epiphany in Modern Southern Fiction: Transcendence of Selfhood." *Southern Humanities Review* 9 (Fall 1975): 389–403 [400–401].

Hodges, Betty. "Betty Hodges' Book Nook." *Durham* (N.C.) *Herald*, 19 April 1959, p. 5D. [WS's comments on SHF.]

———. "Betty Hodges' Book Nook." *Durham* (N.C.) *Morning Herald*, 24 January 1960, p. 5D. [SHF.]

———. "Betty Hodges' Book Nook." *Durham* (N.C.) *Morning Herald*, 7 January 1968, p. 5D. [Review of Daniel Panger's *Ol' Prophet Nat*.]

———. "Betty Hodges' Book Nook." *Durham* (N.C.) *Morning Herald*, 3 March 1968, p. 5D. [NT.]

Holder, Alan. "Styron's Slave: *The Confessions of Nat Turner*." *South Atlantic Quarterly* 68 (Spring 1969): 167–180.

Holley, Fred S. "New Periodical: Styron's Story Dominates." *Norfolk Virginian-Pilot*, 8 February 1953, part 2, p. 10. [Review of first issue of *Discovery*, with mention of LM.]

Hooker, Pat. "Paris Review's Short Stories." *Roanoke* (Va.) *Times*, 25 October 1959, p. B12. [Review of *Best Short Stories from "The Paris Review"* with mention of WS's introduction.]

"The Housatonic." *Horizon* 2 (May 1960): 10–29 [28].

Howard, Jane. "Rose Styron." *Vogue* 151 (May 1968): 184–189, 274–275.

"Howe and Styron to Write Book Column for Harper's." *New York Times*, 26 October 1967, p. 40.

Hutchens, John K. "On the Books: On an Author." *New York Herald Tribune Book Review*, 9 September 1951, p. 2.

Johansson, Eric. "Lettres: Les Sortilèges de la Mauvaise Conscience." *Démocratie*, 27 June 1963, p. 10.

Juin, Hubert. "Rencontre avec William Styron." *Les Lettres Françaises*, 1–8 March 1962, p. 5. [Interview.]

Kakutani, Michiko. "Publishing: Shakespeare, a Feminist View."

New York Times, 1 August 1980, p. C21. [SC as mass-audience paperback.]

Kazin, Alfred. "The Alone Generation." *Harper's Magazine* 219 (October 1959): 127–131. Reprinted in his *Contemporaries* (see 2, A above).

Kelly, Frederic. "William Styron Tells the Story of the Nat Turner Rebellion." *New Haven* (Conn.) *Register*, 14 August 1966, Sunday pictorial section, pp. 7–9. [Interview.]

Kernan, Michael. "The Prophetic Outrage of William Styron." *Washington* (D.C.) *Post*, 18 May 1979, pp. C1, C4. See also *St. Petersburg* (Fla.) *Times*, 1 July 1979, p. 3G; *Cincinnati Enquirer*, 22 July 1979. [Interview.]

Kihss, Peter. "Pulitzer to Styron Novel; No Prize Given for Drama." *New York Times*, 7 May 1968, pp. 1, 34.

Kisor, Henry. "One for the Books—The Challenge of Auschwitz: Why Styron Wrote 'Sophie.'" *Chicago Sun-Times*, 3 June 1979, *Show* section, pp. 10–11. [Interview.]

Klemesrud, Judy. "Party Hails Publication of Jones's Last Novel." *New York Times*, 23 February 1978, p. C15.

Klotz, Marvin. "The Triumph Over Time: Narrative Form in William Faulkner and William Styron." *Mississippi Quarterly* 17 (Winter 1963–1964): 9–20.

Kostelanetz, Richard. "The Bad Criticism of This Age." *Minnesota Review* 4 (Spring 1964): 387–414 [391, 392, 393, 396, 408].

Krebs, Albin. "Notes on People." *New York Times*, 31 March 1972, p. 14. [WS appointed Honorary Consultant at Library of Congress.]

Kuznetsov, Feliks. "A Soviet Reply to 5 U.S. Writers." *New York Times*, 8 September 1979, p. 21.

Lask, Thomas. "Book Ends: William Styron's 'Choice.'" *New York Times Book Review*, 7 January 1979, p. 43. [Interview.]

Las Vergnas, Raymond. "Étoiles Anglo-Américaines: Nathanael West, William Styron, Robert Penn Warren, Carson McCullers, V. Sackville-West." *Les Annales*, August 1962, p. 33.

Lawson, John Howard. "William Styron: Darkness and Fire in the Modern Novel." *Mainstream* 13 (October 1960): 9–18. [SHF.]

Lawson, Lewis. "Cass Kinsolving: Kierkegaardian Man of Despair." *Wisconsin Studies in Contemporary Literature* 3 (Fall 1962): 54–66.

Le Clec'h, Guy. "Un 'Grand' de la Nouvelle Vague Américaine: William Styron." *Le Figaro Littéraire*, 24 February 1962, p. 3. [Interview.]

Leo, John. "Some Negroes Accuse Styron of Distorting Nat Turner's Life." *New York Times*, 1 February 1968, p. 34.

Leon, Philip W. "*The Lost Boy* and a Lost Girl." *Southern Literary Journal* 9 (Fall 1976): 61–69. [LDD and chap. 5 of *Look Homeward, Angel*.]

Leonard, Mary Anne. "NN Life Set Styron on Pulitzer Path." *Newport News* (Va.) *Times-Herald*, 28 April 1973, p. 20.

Lerman, Leo. "Something to Talk About: Bulletin." *Mademoiselle* 34 (January 1952): 112–113, 154 [112, 154: interview].

Lerner, Max. "The Generations." *New York Post*, 17 September 1951, p. 24. [LDD.]

Lewis, R. W. B. "American Letters: A Projection." *Yale Review* 51 (December 1961): 211–226.

———, and C. Vann Woodward. "Slavery in the First Person." *Yale Alumni Magazine* 31 (November 1967): 33–39. [Interview.] Reprinted in *William Styron's "The Confessions of Nat Turner": A Critical Handbook*, edited by Friedman and Malin (see 2, A above). Pp. 51–58.

Lichtenstein, G. "The Exiles." *New Statesman and Nation* 55 (6 September 1958): 320.

"'Lie Down in Darkness.'" *Newport News* (Va.) *Daily Press*, 23 November 1951, p. 4. [Editorial.]

Lobiondo, Joan. "William Styron: Learning from Past?" *Danbury* (Conn.) *News-Times*, 4 July 1976, pp. A1, A10. [Interview.]

"Local Author Important, W & M Professor Says." *Newport News* (Va.) *Daily Press*, 16 November 1951, p. 2.

Long, Robert Emmet. "The Vogue of Gatsby's Guest List." *Fitzgerald/Hemingway Annual* 1 (1969): 23–25 [23–24: LDD].

"Love Story." *Washington* (D.C.) *Post*, 29 January 1971, p. A18. [Editorial.]

Lowrey, Janet. "William Styron Reminisces." *Lynchburg* (Va.) *News*, 24 April 1977, pp. C9, C14. [Interview.]

———. "A 'Transplanted Southerner' Talks about Writing." *Sweet Briar News* (Sweet Briar College), 29 April 1977, p. 8.

Luedtke, Carol L. "*The Sound and the Fury* and *Lie Down in Darkness:* Some Comparisons." *Literatur in Wissenschaft und Unterricht* 4 (1971): 45–51.

Lukas, J. Anthony. "'Om,' Ginsberg's Hindu Chant, Fails to Charm a Judge in Chicago." *New York Times*, 13 December 1969, p. 19. [WS as witness at trial of "Chicago Seven."]

Lytle, Andrew. "Impressionism, the Ego, and the First Person." *Daedalus* 92 (Spring 1963): 281–296 [288–292]. Reprinted in his *The Hero with the Private Parts* (see 2, A above).

MacBeath, Innis. "Miller Defends Yevtushenko." *London Times*, 26 November 1968, p. 5.

McDonnell, Thomas P. "Novelist Shamefully Maligned by Critics." *The Pilot* (Boston), 2 November 1968, p. 4. [NT.]

McGehee, Overton. "Styron's Native State Still Has a Hold on Him." *Charlottesville* (Va.) *Daily Progress*, 25 May 1980, p. B1. [Interview.]

McGill, Ralph. "Astigmatic Critics—." *Atlanta Constitution*, 19 February 1968, p. 1. [NT.]

McGrory, Mary. "Reading and Writing: Hard-Boiled Marines Realize Claims of Literature, Defer Reservist Writer." *Washington* (D.C.) *Sunday Star*, 5 August 1951, p. C3.

McNamara, Eugene. "William Styron's *Long March*: Absurdity and Authority." *Western Humanities Review* 15 (Summer 1961): 267–272.

———. "The Post-Modern American Novel." *Queen's Quarterly* 69 (Summer 1962): 265–275.

Mailer, Norman. "Norman Mailer vs. Nine Writers." *Esquire* 60 (July 1963): 63–69, 105.

Malin, Irving. "Nat Turner." *Catholic World* 208 (October 1968): 43–44. [Review of Clarke's *William Styron's "Nat Turner."*]

Markos, Donald W. "Margaret Whitehead in *The Confessions of Nat Turner*." *Studies in the Novel* 4 (Spring 1972): 52–59.

"Martha's Troubled Vineyard." *Time* 102 (30 July 1973): 42–43. [WS in support of bill limiting commercialization of Martha's Vineyard.]

Marx, Leo. "The Highbrow and the Housewife." *New Republic* 133 (31 October 1955): 19–20 [20: LM].

Mason, Robert. "Teacher Guided, Publisher Fired Him: Encouragement and a Kick Made Bill Styron a Writer." *Norfolk Virginian-Pilot*, 9 September 1951, part 5, p. 5. [Biographical sketch and interview with WS's father.]

Match, Richard. "Duke Student Verse." *New York Herald Tribune Weekly Book Review*, 3 February 1946, p. 16. [Review of *One and Twenty: Duke Narrative and Verse* with mention of WS's "Autumn."]

Matthiessen, Peter, and George Plimpton. "William Styron." *Paris Review* 2 (Spring 1954): 42–57. Reprinted in *Writers at Work*, edited by Cowley (see 2, A above).

Mellard, James M. "Racism, Formula, and Popular Fiction." *Journal of Popular Culture* 5 (Summer 1971): 10–37 [34, 35: NT].

Mellen, Joan. "Polemics—William Styron: The Absence of a Social Definition." *Novel* 4 (Winter 1971): 158–170.

"'Men . . . with Genius for Platitude,' He Tells Tufts Graduates: Galbraith Assails LBJ Violence Panel Members." *Boston Herald Traveler*, 10 June 1968, p. 3. [WS gets honorary degree at Tufts.]

Menn, Thorpe. "Books of the Day." *Kansas City Star*, 4 July 1959, p. 16. [Review of *Best Short Stories from "The Paris Review"* with mention of WS's introduction.]

Meras, Phyllis. "The Author." *Saturday Review* 50 (7 October 1967): 30. [Interview.]

Meyer, June. "Spokesman for the Blacks." *The Nation* 205 (4 December 1967): 597–599 [597: NT].

Middleton, Harry. "Reading: An Evening with the Reticent William Styron." *Figaro* (New Orleans), 7 May 1979.

Mills, Hilary. "Publishing Notes: Styron's Latest Takes Off." *Washington* (D.C.) *Star*, 17 June 1979, *Sunday Calendar* section, p. B12.

Mitgang, Herbert. "50 Writers Demand Book-Award Boycott." *New York Times*, 9 August 1979, p. C15.

———. "Styron and Wolfe Lead Book-Award Winners." *New York Times*, 2 May 1980, p. C24.

Mohrt, Michel. "Michel Mohrt Présente la Première Révélation du Roman Américain Depuis la Guerre: J'ai Vécu Avec William Styron la Dolce Vita." *Arts*, no. 786 (7–13 September 1960): 3.

———. "Les Trois Obsessions de William Styron: Le Péché, Le Désespoir, Le Désir d'Évasion." *Arts*, no. 858 (28 February–8 March 1962): 3. [Interview.]

———. "William Styron: 'J'Écris l'Histoire d'un Illuminé qui Tuait par Devoir." *Nouveau Candide*, no. 70 (29 August 1962): 70. [Interview.]

Monaghan, Charles. "Portrait of a Man Reading." *Book World* (*Chicago Tribune*, *Washington* [D.C.] *Post*), 27 October 1968, p. 8. [Interview.]

Moore, L. Hugh. "Robert Penn Warren, William Styron, and the Use of Greek Myth." *Critique* 8 (Winter 1965–1966): 75–87.

Morris, Willie. "The Bear on Madison Avenue: A Provincial in New York, Part II." *Harper's Magazine* 235 (July 1967): 60–68 [67–68]. Reprinted in his *North toward Home* (see 2, A above).

Morse, J. Mitchell. "Social Relevance, Literary Judgment, and the New Right; or, The Inadvertent Confessions of William Styron." *College English* 30 (May 1969): 605–616. Reprinted in his *The Irrelevant English Teacher* (see 2, A above).

Morton, James Parks, Edith Wythosgrod, Rosemary Ruether, Michael D. Ryan, and Irving Greenberg. "Auschwitz Symposium: Reply to a Critic." *New York Times*, 25 July 1974, p. 40. [Letters to the editor in response to WS's "Auschwitz's Message."]

Moyano, Maria Clara. "Speaking Volumes: The Confessions of William Styron." *Book World* (*Chicago Tribune*, *Washington* (D.C.) *Post*), 1 October 1967, p. 6. [Interview.]

Mudrick, Marvin. "Mailer and Styron: Guests of the Establishment." *Hudson Review* 17 (Autumn 1964): 346–366. Reprinted in his *On Culture and Literature* (see 2, A above).

Mullen, Jean S. "Styron's Nat Turner: A Search for Humanity." *Barat Review* 6 (Spring/Summer 1971): 6–11.

Nakahara, Liz. "Personalities." *Washington* (D.C.) *Post*, 14 November 1979, p. B2. [SC banned in South Africa.]

Nelson, Norman K. "Personality of the Week: Bill Styron of Duke Called Second Wolfe." *Charlotte* (N.C.) *Observer*, 23 September 1951, p. 12D. See also *Asheville* (N.C.) *Citizen*, 23 September 1951. [Biographical sketch.]

Nenadál, Radoslav. "The Patterning of a Modern Hero in William Styron's *Set This House on Fire*." *Prague Studies in English* 15 (1973): 83–96.

Nichols, Lewis. "Background." *New York Times Book Review*, 5 June 1960, p. 8. [SHF.]

———. "In and Out of Books." *New York Times Book Review*, 15 April 1962, p. 8. [French enthusiasm for SHF.]

Nigro, August. "*The Long March:* The Expansive Hero in a Closed World." *Critique* 9, no. 3 (1967): 103–112.

Nolte, William H. "Styron's Meditation on Saviors." *Southwest Review* 58 (Autumn 1973): 338–348. [NT.]

"The Novelist as a Rebel Slave." *Life* 63 (13 October 1967): 51–52, 54.

Normand, J[ean]. "L'Homme Mystifié: Les Héros de Bellow, Albee, Styron, et Mailer." *Études Anglaises* 22 (October–December 1969): 370–385 [378–381].

Oates, Stephen B. "Children of Darkness." *American Heritage* 24 (October 1973): 42–47, 89–91 [91: NT].

O'Connell, Shaun. "Expense of Spirit: The Vision of William Styron." *Critique* 8 (Winter 1965–1966): 20–33.

———. "Styron's Nat Turner . . . ." *The Nation* 205 (16 October 1967): 373–374.

———. "William Styron: In the Refracted Light of Reminiscence." *Boston Sunday Globe*, 27 April 1975, magazine, pp. 30, 32–39. [Interview.]

Oliver, Joan. "Bill Styron." *The Archive* (Duke University) 65 (Fall 1951): 18–19. [Biographical sketch.]

O'Rourke, Elizabeth. *Best Sellers* 19 (1 November 1959): 259. [Review of *Best Stories from "The Paris Review"* with mention of WS's introduction.]

"Our Own 'Impulse toward Excellence.'" *Charlotte* (N.C.) *News*, 24 April 1963, p. 10A.

Ownbey, Ray. "Discussions with William Styron." *Mississippi Quarterly* 30 (Spring 1977): 283–295. [Interview.]

Parke, Mary Eugenia. "Facts and Fiction: Critics of Styron's Novel Agree Only on His Talent." *Norfolk Virginian-Pilot*, 7 October 1951, part 5, p. 5. [LDD.]

————. "Facts & Fiction: Styron Story Featured in Original Anthology." *Norfolk Virginian-Pilot*, 4 January 1953, part 5, p. 7. [LM.]

————. "Facts & Fiction: Promising Americans in France." *Norfolk Virginian-Pilot*, 12 April 1953, part 2, p. 13. [WS and *Paris Review*.]

"'Pathetic' Characters in Today's Literature." *Durham* (N.C.) *Morning Herald*, 14 September 1951, sec. 1, p. 4. [Editorial on LDD.]

Perosa, Sergio. "Incontri Americani." *Studi Americani* 17 (1971): 379–438 [389–395: interview].

Perry, J. Douglas, Jr. "Gothic as Vortex: The Form of Horror in Capote, Faulkner, and Styron." *Modern Fiction Studies* 19 (Summer 1973): 153–167. [SHF.]

Peyre, Henri. "Is Literature Dead? Or Dying?" *Michigan Quarterly Review* 12 (Fall 1973): 297–313 [301, 303].

Phillips, John. "Styron Unlocked." *Vogue* 150 (December 1967): 216–217, 267–271, 278. [Interview.]

Pickens, Donald K. "Uncle Tom Becomes Nat Turner: A Commentary on Two American Heroes." *Negro American Literature Forum* 3 (Summer 1969): 45–48.

Pinsker, Sanford. "Christ as Revolutionary / Revolutionary as Christ: The Hero in Bernard Malamud's *The Fixer* and William Styron's *The Confessions of Nat Turner*." *Barat Review* 6 (Spring/Summer 1971): 29–37 [35–37].

Plimpton, George. "William Styron: A Shared Ideal." *New York Times Book Review*, 8 October 1967, pp. 2, 3, 30, 32, 34. Reprinted in *William Styron's "The Confessions of Nat Turner": A Critical Handbook*, edited by Friedman and Malin (see 2, A above). Pp. 36–42.

Poirier, Richard. "A Literature of Law and Order." *Partisan Review* 36, no. 2 (1969): 189–204. Reprinted in his *The Performing Self* (see 2, A above).

Prasad, Thakur Guru. "*Lie Down in Darkness:* A Portrait of the Modern Phenomenon." *Indian Journal of English Studies* 10 (1969): 71–80.

"Professor and Writers." *Duke Alumni Register* 49 (April 1963): 10–11.

"A Pulitzer For Mr. Styron." *Newport News* (Va.) *Daily Press*, 8 May 1968, p. 4. [Editorial.]

Quinby, Brie. "Author William Styron's Winning Choice." *Little Rock Democrat*, 11 November 1979, *Family Weekly* magazine, p. 25. [Nationally syndicated interview.]

Ragan, Sam. "Southern Accent." *Raleigh* (N.C.) *News and Observer*, 16 September 1951, sec. 4, p. 5. [WS and the reception of LDD.]

―――. "Southern Accent." *Raleigh* (N.C.) *News and Observer*, 19 June 1960, sec. 3, p. 5. [SHF.]

[Rahv, Philip]. "The Editor Interviews William Styron." *Modern Occasions* 1 (Fall 1971): 501–510.

Ratner, Marc L. "The Rebel Purged: Styron's *The Long March*." *Arlington Quarterly* 2 (Autumn 1969): 27–42. Reprinted in his *William Styron* (see 2, A above).

―――. "Styron's Rebel." *American Quarterly* 21 (Fall 1969): 595–608. [NT.] Reprinted, expanded, in his *William Styron* (see 2, A above).

―――. "Rebellion of Wrath and Laughter: Styron's *Set This House on Fire*." *Southern Review* n.s. 7 (Autumn 1971): 1007–1020. Reprinted in his *William Styron* (see 2, A above).

Raymont, Henry. "P.E.N. Congress May Discuss Censorship of Soviet Writers." *New York Times*, 12 August 1969, p. 36. [WS quoted on plight of Soviet writers.]

―――. "Italian Poet Gets $10,000 Prize; Styron Is Cited for 'Nat Turner.'" *New York Times*, 14 March 1970, p. 28. [WS awarded Howells Medal for Fiction from National Academy of Arts and Letters.]

―――. "Book Unit Rejects 'Love Story.'" *New York Times*, 22 January 1971, p. 16. [WS, as juror for National Book Award for Fiction, comments on group's refusal to consider Segal's *Love Story*.]

Rewald, Alice. "Deux Entretiens: William Styron." *La Quinzaine Littéraire* (Paris), 15–31 October 1967, pp. 12–13. [Interview.]

Robb, Kenneth A. "William Styron's Don Juan." *Critique* 8 (Winter 1965–1966): 34–46. [SHF.] Reprinted in *Kierkegaard's Presence in Contemporary American Life: Essays from Various Sources*, edited by Lawson (see 2, A above).

Roberts, Steven V. "Over the 'Nat Turner' Screenplay Subsides [*sic*]." *New York Times*, 31 March 1969, p. 28. [On controversy about screen version.]

R[osebury], C[elia]. "Interview—Aptheker on Styron's Nat Turner: From Rebel Slave to Racist Monster." *People's World* (San Francisco), 4 November 1967, p. 7.

Rosen, Jackie. "Brief Encounter Spawns Novel: Styron Tops Best Sellers with Story of 'Sophie.'" *Newport News* (Va.) *Times-Herald*, 18 August 1979, *Leisure 79* section, p. L1. [Interview.]

Rosenthal, Jean. "William Styron." *Informations et Documents*, no. 158, 15 March 1962, p. 24.

Roth, Philip. "Writing American Fiction." *Commentary* 31 (March 1961): 223–233 [226, 232–233].

Rubin, Louis D., Jr. "The Difficulties of Being a Southern Writer Today." *Journal of Southern History* 29 (November 1963): 486–494.

————. "An Interview With . . . William Styron." *Hollins College Bulletin* 14 (November 1963): 8–11.

Sachs, Viola. "Contemporary American Fiction and Some Nineteenth Century Patterns." *Kwartalnik Neofilogizny* 13 (First Quarter 1966): 3–29 [6–7, 15–16, 27–28].

de Saint Phalle, Thérèse. "William Styron (Heritier Littéraire de Faulkner)." *Le Figaro Littéraire*, 1–7 July 1965, p. 16.

————. "William Styron: 'En U.R.S.S.—et en France—Je Suis Chez Moi.'" *Le Figaro Littéraire*, 28 October–3 November 1968, p. 26. [Interview.]

Salisbury, Harrison E. "Kuznetsov Backs Soviet on China." *New York Times*, 24 August 1969, p. 20. [Kuznetsov replies to WS's statement that he should not have defected.]

Salomon, Michel. "Interview avec William Styron: Intolérable Amerique." *Magazine Littéraire* 27 (March 1969): 24–25.

Saradhi, K. P. "The Agony of a Slave Negro: Theme and Technique in Styron's *Nat Turner*." *Osmania Journal of English Studies* 9, no. 1 (1972): 11–19. See also *Literary Half-Yearly* 16 (January 1975): 41–51.

Sauder, Ron. "Styron Recalls Days at Christchurch." *Richmond* (Va.) *Times-Dispatch*, 25 May 1975, pp. A1, A2. [Interview.]

Schaap, Dick. "Interview with William Styron." *Chicago Sun-*

Times, 8 October 1967, *Book Week* section, pp. 2, 11. See also *San Francisco Sunday Examiner and Chronicle*, 15 October 1967, *This World* section, pp. 39, 46.

Scheick, William J. "Discarded Watermelon Rinds: The Rainbow Aesthetic of Styron's *Lie Down in Darkness*." *Modern Fiction Studies* 24 (Summer 1978): 247–254.

Schickel, Richard. "The Old Criticism and the New Novel." *Wisconsin Studies in Contemporary Literature* 5 (Winter–Spring 1964): 26–36.

Schneider, Harold W. "Two Bibliographies: Saul Bellow, William Styron." *Critique* 3 (Summer 1960): 71–91.

Schwartz, Tony. "The Choosing of 'Sophie.'" *Newsweek* 93 (28 May 1979): 89, 91. [Interview.]

Sears, Robert B. "Author Chides Critics—Reviewers Go Astray by 'Thinking': Styron." *Roanoke* (Va.) *Times*, 3 March 1963, p. B2. [WS at Hollins College.]

Shapiro, Herbert. "*The Confessions of Nat Turner*: William Styron and His Critics." *Negro American Literature Forum* 9 (Winter 1975): 99–104.

Shepard, Richard F. "Stage and Literary Names Enlist for Candidates." *New York Times*, 14 August 1968, p. 40. [WS as cosponsor of fundraising party for McCarthy.]

Shepherd, Allen. "'Hopeless Paradox' and *The Confessions of Nat Turner*." *Recherches Anglaises et Américaines* 4 (1971): 87–91.

Simmonds, Anne. "A Successful Young Writer Hails from the Peninsula." *Newport News* (Va.) *Times-Herald*, 2 June 1960, p. 17.

Sink, D. Michael. "A Response to Critics: *The Confessions of Nat Turner*." *Clearing House* 48 (October 1973): 125–126.

Sitkoff, Harvard, and Michael Wreszin. "Whose Nat Turner: William Styron vs. the Black Intellectuals." *Midstream* 14 (November 1968): 10–20.

"Six Get Honorary Degrees from Duke." *Durham* (N.C.) *Sun*, 3 June 1968, sec. B, p. 1.

Slavitt, David R. "Poetry, Novels, and Critics: A Reply." *Yale Review* 51 (March 1962): 502–504.

Smith, Harrison. "Prose of Promise." *Saturday Review of Literature* 35 (16 February 1952): 15–16, 42–43 [15: LDD].

Smith, Harry. "Bestsellers Nobody Reads." *The Smith* 10 (November 1968): 182–184. [NT.]

Stair, Gobin. "Beacon Press on Styron." *Boston Globe*, 30 April 1969, p. 22. [Letter to the editor defending Clarke's *William Styron's "Nat Turner."*]

Stanford, Mike. "An Interview with William Styron." *The Archive* (Duke University) 89 (Spring 1977): 84–93.

Stevenson, David L. "Fiction's Unfamiliar Face." *The Nation* 187 (1 November 1958): 307–309. [LDD.]

———. "Styron and the Fiction of the Fifties." *Critique* 3 (Summer 1960): 47–58.

Stone, Peter H. "A Conversation with William Styron." *Look Magazine* n.s. 2 (August 1979): 33–36.

Strine, Mary S. "*The Confessions of Nat Turner:* Styron's 'Meditation on History' as Rhetorical Act." *Quarterly Journal of Speech* 64 (October 1978): 246–266.

Stuttaford, Genevieve. "PW Interviews: William Styron." *Publishers Weekly* 215 (21 May 1979): 10–11.

"Styron Addresses 1975 Graduates." *The Stingaree: Christchurch Student Alumni News* 55 (Summer 1975): 1.

"Styron Authors *Life* Story on Faulkner Rites." *Newport News* (Va.) *Daily Press*. 24 July 1962, pp. 1, 16.

"Styron Feels 'Establishment.'" *Waterbury* (Conn.) *Republican*, 7 May 1968, pp. 1, 2. [Interview.]

"Styron, Sweet Briar and Sophie." *Sweet Briar College Alumnae Magazine* 47 (Summer 1977): 10–13.

"Styron Uses River Theme for Graduates." *Richmond* (Va.) *Times-Dispatch*, 12 May 1980, p. B4.

"Styron Writes His First Play." *New York Times*, 12 December 1971, p. 62.

Sullivan, Jeremiah J. "Conflict in the Modern American Novel." *Ball State University Forum* 15 (Spring 1974): 28–36 [33–34: NT].

Sussman, Robert. "The Case against William Styron's *Nat Turner.*" *Yale Literary Magazine* 137 (Fall 1968): 20–23.

Suter, Anthony. "Transcendence and Failure: William Styron's *Lie Down in Darkness.*" *Caliban 12* (Toulouse) 11 (1975): 157–166.

Swanson, William J. "William Faulkner and William Styron: Notes on Religion." *Cimarron Review*, no. 7, March 1969, pp. 57–66. [*The Sound and the Fury* and LDD.]

——. "Religious Implications in *The Confessions of Nat Turner.*" *Cimarron Review*, no. 12, July 1970, pp. 57–66.

Tallmer, Jerry. "A Brave Face to Auschwitz." *New York Post*, 2 June 1979, p. 17. [Interview.]

Taylor, Robert. "The Contentions of William Styron." *Boston Sunday Globe*, 20 April 1969, mgazine, pp. 6–11, 13. See also *Washington* (D.C.) *Post*, 11 May 1969, p. 5B. [Interview.]

"Teacher Is Backed in Stand on Pledge." *New York Times*, 23 February 1970, p. 24. [WS as signer of statement supporting Roxbury, Conn., teacher who refused to say Pledge of Allegiance with her class.]

Thelwell, Michael. "Mr. William Styron and the Rev. Turner." *Massachusetts Review* 9 (Winter 1968): 7–29. Reprinted in *William Styron's "Nat Turner": Ten Black Writers Respond*, edited by Clarke (see 2, A above). Pp. 79–91. And reprinted in *The Nat Turner Rebellion: The Historical Event and the Modern Controversy*, edited by Duff and Mitchell (see 2, A above). Pp. 181–190.

——. "Arguments: The Turner Thesis." *Partisan Review* 35 (Summer 1968): 403–412. Reprinted in *Americans from Africa*, vol. 2, edited by Rose (see 2, A above).

——. "An Exchange on 'Nat Turner.'" *New York Review of Books* 11 (7 November 1968): 34.

Thomas, Emory M. "Ten Views of the Man Who Would Not Die." *Saturday Review* 51 (17 August 1968): 23–24. [Review of Clarke's *William Styron's "Nat Turner."*]

Thompson, F. H. "Hell Is Not Giving." *Prairie Schooner* 37 (Summer 1963): 183–185.

Thorp, Willard. "The Southern Mode." *South Atlantic Quarterly* 63 (Autumn 1964): 576–582 [578–579].

"Three Fights for Justice." *Time* 106 (29 December 1975): 32. [WS, Arthur Miller, and others urging reopening of case against Connecticut teenager convicted of manslaughter in 1973.]

Tischler, Nancy M. "Negro Literature and Classic Form." *Contem-*

porary Literature 10 (Summer 1969): 352–365. [NT and *Invisible Man.*]

———. *"The Confessions of Nat Turner*: A Symposium—Introduction." *Barat Review* 6 (Spring/Summer 1971): 3–4.

Tragle, Henry Irving. "Styron and His Sources." *Massachusetts Review* 11 (Winter 1970): 134–153.

———. "'Credibility Gap' Seen as Reason for Change in Movie Plan." *Richmond* (Va.) *Times-Dispatch*, 12 February 1970, p. A14. [On proposed film version of NT.]

Trocard, Catherine. "William Styron and the Historical Novel." *Neohelicon* 3, no. 1–2 (1975): 373–382.

Tyler, Betty. "Bill Styron Works on New Novel in Roxbury Isolation." *Bridgeport* (Conn.) *Sunday Post*, 18 May 1958, p. B3. See also *Richmond* (Va.) *Times-Dispatch*, 25 May 1958, pp. 1L, 4L. [Interview.]

Tyrmand, Leopold. "Yevtushenko's Career." *New York Times*, 8 December 1968, sec. 4, p. 13. [Letter to the editor in response to WS's defense of Yevtushenko.]

Urang, Gunnar. "The Broader Vision: William Styron's *Set This House on Fire.*" *Critique* 8 (Winter 1965–1966): 47–69.

"U.S. Authors Protest Suppression of Soviet Writers." *New York Times*, 12 August 1979, p. 5.

Uya, Okon E. "Race, Ideology and Scholarship in the United States: William Styron's *Nat Turner* and Its Critics." *American Studies International* 15 (Winter 1976): 63–81.

Vanderbilt, Kermit. "Writers of the Troubled Sixties." *The Nation* 217 (17 December 1973): 661–665 [661, 664].

Via, Dan O., Jr. "Law and Grace in Styron's *Set This House on Fire.*" *Journal of Religion* 51 (April 1971): 125–136.

Waldmeir, Joseph. "Quest without Faith." *The Nation* 193 (18 November 1961): 390–396.

Warren, Robert Penn. "William Styron." *Book-of-the-Month Club News*, October 1967, pp. 6–7, 14.

Wechsler, James A. "A Lonely Anger." *New York Post*, 17 October 1967, p. 49. [NT.]

Weiler, A. H. "Styron Charges 'Black Pressure' on Turner Film." *New York Times*, 28 January 1970, p. 48. [Interview.]

Wells, Anna Mary. "An Exchange on 'Nat Turner.'" *New York Review of Books* 11 (7 November 1968): 31.

West, James L. W., III. "A Bibliographer's Interview with William Styron." *Costerus* n.s. 4 (1975): 13–29.

————, ed. "William Styron's Afterword to *The Long March*." *Mississippi Quarterly* 28 (Spring 1975): 185–189.

————, and August J. Nigro. "William Blackburn and His Pupils: A Conversation." *Mississippi Quarterly* 31 (Fall 1978): 605–614.

White, John. "The Novelist as Historian: William Styron and American Negro Slavery." *Journal of American Studies* 4 (February 1971): 233–245.

White, Poppy Cannon. "Poppy's Notes: 'The African' vs. Nat Turner." *New York Amsterdam News*, 9 December 1967, p. 17. [NT and Harold Courlander's *The African*.]

Whitman, Alden. "William Styron Examines the Negro Upheaval." *New York Times*, 5 August 1967, p. 13. [Interview.]

————. "Styron Discloses Protest in Soviet: Criticized Jailing of Writers during Visit to Moscow." *New York Times*, 1 November 1968, p. 21. [Interview.]

Whitney, Blair. "Nat Turner's Mysticism." *Barat Review* 6 (Spring/Summer 1971): 21–24.

Wicker, Tom. "In the Nation: What Sense in Censorship?" *New York Times*, 3 April 1969, p. 42. [On censoring projected film version of NT as racist.]

Williams, Ernest P. "William Styron and His Ten Black Critics: A Belated Meditation." *Phylon* 37 (June 1976): 189–195.

Winfrey, Carey. "Ex-Postmaster's Indictment Stirs Roxbury." *New York Times*, 12 January 1978, p. 33.

Winner, Arthur. "Adjustment, Tragic Humanism and Italy." *Studi Americani* 7 (1961): 311–361 [316–321, 338–361: SHF].

W[ise], J[ames]. "Dubious Submission & Willing Fate." *Duke Alumni Register* 57 (November 1971): 4–8. [WS at Duke's literary festival.]

Woodruf, David. "Southampton County Most Likely Location for $4 Million Movie on Nat Turner Rebellion." *Franklin* (Va.) *Tidewater News*, 26 September 1969, p. 1.

"The World of Nat Turner." *Boston Sunday Globe*, 22 October 1967, p. 4A. [Editorial.]

"'Writing Can't Be Taught': Professor, Novelist Talk about Success." *Charlotte* (N.C.) *Observer*, 27 January 1952, p. 15C. [WS returns to Duke to speak to creative writing class.]

C. DOCTORAL DISSERTATIONS

Alexander, Roberta May. "The Fictional Portrayal of Popular Movements." University of California, San Diego, 1979. [Includes section on NT.]

Arms, Valarie Meliotes. "William Styron's Literary Career." Temple University, 1977.

Baumbach, Jonathan. "The Theme of Guilt and Redemption in the Post–Second World War Novel." Stanford University, 1961.

Bolton, Richard Russell. "Portrayal of the Garrison Military in American Fiction, 1946–1970." Washington State University, 1972. [Includes section on LM.]

Cheshire, Ardner R., Jr. "The Theme of Redemption in the Fiction of William Styron." Louisiana State University, 1973.

Coale, Samuel Chase, V. "The Role of the South in the Fiction of William Faulkner, Carson McCullers, Flannery O'Connor, and William Styron." Brown University, 1970.

Corodimas, Peter Nicholas. "Guilt and Redemption in the Novels of William Styron." Ohio State University, 1971.

Firestone, Bruce M. "A Study of William Styron's Fiction." University of North Carolina, Chapel Hill, 1975.

Galloway, David D. "The Absurd Hero in Contemporary Fiction: The Works of John Updike, William Styron, Saul Bellow, and J. D. Salinger." University of Buffalo, 1962.

Goodley, Nancy C. "All Flesh Is Grass: Despair and Affirmation in *Lie Down in Darkness*." American University, 1975.

Halpern, Jeanne Weinstein. "Form and Image in Contemporary American Biography." University of Michigan, 1977. [Includes section on NT.]

Hiers, John Turner. "Traditional Death Customs in Modern Southern Fiction." Emory University, 1974. [Includes section on LDD.]

Hoerchner, Susan Jane. "'I Have to Keep the Two Things Separate': Polarity in Women in the Contemporary American Novel." Emory University, 1973. [Includes section on LDD.]

Hux, Samuel H. "American Myth and Existential Vision: The Indigenous Existentialism of Mailer, Bellow, Styron, and Ellison." University of Connecticut, 1966.

Kime, Benna Kay. "A Critical Study of the Technique of William Styron." Tulane University, 1971.

Kochanek, Patricia Sharpe. "In Pursuit of Proteus: A Piagetian Approach to the Structure of the Grotesque in American Fiction of the Fifties." Pennsylvania State University, 1972. [Includes section on LDD and SHF.]

Lang, John Douglas. "William Styron: The Christian Imagination." Stanford University, 1975.

Leon, Philip W. "Idea and Technique in the Novels of William Styron." George Peabody College for Teachers, 1974.

Luttrell, William. "Tragic and Comic Modes in Twentieth-Century American Literature: William Styron and Joseph Heller." Bowling Green State University, 1969.

Mewshaw, Michael Francis. "Thematic and Stylistic Problems in the Work of William Styron." University of Virginia, 1970.

Mills, Eva Bamberger. "The Development of William Styron's Artistic Consciousness: A Study of the Relationship between Life and Work." University of Cincinnati, 1976.

Morgan, Henry Grady, Jr. "The World as Prison: A Study of the Novels of William Styron." University of Colorado, 1973.

Nelson, Doris L. "The Contemporary American Family Novel: A Study in Metaphor." University of Southern California, 1970. [Includes section on LDD.]

Nigro, August. "William Styron and the Adamic Tradition." University of Maryland, 1964.

O'Connell, Shaun V. "The Contexts of William Styron's *The Confessions of Nat Turner*." University of Massachusetts, 1970.

Ownbey, Ray Wilson. "To Choose Being: The Function of Order and Disorder in William Styron's Fiction." University of Utah, 1972.

Palm, Elaine Amanda. "The Integrative Vision: Ritual Action in the Novels of William Styron." University of Rhode Island, 1978.

Peterson, Sandra Marny. "The View from the Gallows: The Criminal Confession in American Literature." Northwestern University, 1972. [Includes section on NT.]

Scott, James B. "The Individual and Society: Norman Mailer versus William Styron." Syracuse University, 1964.

Sisney, Mary Frances. "Black Fiction: To Discriminate or Not to Discriminate. A Comparative and Rhetorical Study of *Native Son*, *Invisible Man*, *The Man Who Cried I Am*, *Intruder in the Dust*, and *The Confessions of Nat Turner*." University of Southern California, 1979.

Strine, Mary Susan. "The Novel as Rhetorical Act: An Interpretation of the Major Fiction of William Styron." University of Washington, 1972.

Swanson, William Joseph. "William Styron, Eloquent Protestant." University of Northern Colorado, 1972.

Wild, Fredric Max, Jr. "'A Plank in Reason': Time, Space and the Perception of the Self in the Modern Novel." Ohio State University, 1973. [Includes section on LDD.]

D. BOOK REVIEWS

Lie Down in Darkness

Aldridge, John W. "In a Place Where Love Is a Stranger." *New York Times Book Review*, 9 September 1951, p. 5.

Ault, Phil. "The Parents' Sins." *Los Angeles Mirror*, 21 September 1951, p. 30.

Bale, Joy. "Into the Dark of the Heart." *Louisville Courier-Journal*, 16 September 1951, sec. 3, p. 10.

Bedell, W. D. "William Styron: Bitter Story Hits Home." *Houston Post*, 9 September 1951, sec. 1, p. 22.

Bell, Blake Kennedy. "Gifted New Pen Is Indigo-Dipped: William Styron's First Novel Shows Talent." *Tulsa Daily World*, 23 September 1951, sec. 5, p. 9.

Blackman, Eugene J. *Boston Sunday Post*, 16 September 1951, p. 52.

Bloomfield, Paul. "New Novels." *Manchester* (England) *Guardian*, 21 March 1952, p. 4.

"Books New and Noticeable." *Cleveland Plain Dealer*, 16 September 1951, p. 33D.

Breen, Melwyn. "Southern Bloom in Dust." *Saturday Night* (Toronto) 67 (27 October 1951): 22.

Breit, Harvey. "Dissolution of a Family." *Atlantic Monthly* 188 (October 1951): 78–80.

Broaddus, Marian Howe. "Glancing Through the New Books with Marian Howe Broaddus." *El Paso Times*, 16 September 1951, p. 8.

Brown, Alexander C. *"Lie Down in Darkness:* A Review." *Newport News* (Va.) *Daily Press*, 9 September 1951, p. 4D.

Buffalo Courier-Express, 9 September 1951, p. 22D.

Bullock, Dick. "Southern Locale." *Charleston* (S.C.) *News and Courier*, 16 September 1951, sec. C, p. 1.

Burdick, Richard. "A Remarkable First Novel Treats Group of Fascinating People with Great Insight." *Sacramento Bee*, 14 June 1952, p. 27.

Byam, Milton S. *Library Journal* 76 (15 September 1951): 1423–1424.

C., H. B. "Family Which Destroys Itself." *Worcester* (Mass.) *Sunday Telegram*, 9 September 1951, sec. B, p. 11.

C[ady], E[rnest]. "Impressive First Novel Surmounts Handicap of Overworked Theme." *Columbus* (Ohio) *Dispatch*, 9 September 1951, p. F7.

Carter, Ruth S. "Depth and Power Found in 'Lie Down in Darkness.'" *Houston Chronicle*, 9 September 1951, p. E5.

Chang, Diana. "The Emotionally Mature Jew." *Congress Weekly* 19 (18 February 1952): 15–16.

Chapin, Ruth. "Twilight of the South." *Christian Science Monitor*, 4 October 1951, p. 11.

Cowley, Malcolm. "The Faulkner Pattern." *New Republic* 125 (8 October 1951): 19–20.

Crume, Paul. "Strong Novel of Virginia Tragedy." *Dallas Morning News*, 9 September 1951, part 6, p. 7.

"Dark Misery." *Newsweek* 38 (10 September 1951): 106–107.

Davis, Richard. "Debt Acknowledged." *Little Rock Gazette*, 11 November 1951, p. 6F.

Davis, Robert Gorham. "A Grasp of Moral Realities." *American Scholar* 21 (Winter 1951–1952): 114, 116.

"Depressed Areas." *Times Literary Supplement* (London), 28 March 1952, p. 217.

Derleth, August. "Idea Is Good but It Needs a Little Editing." *Chicago Sunday Tribune Magazine of Books*, 9 September 1951, p. 3.

Donnelly, Tom. "We Need a Few Hard Superlatives around Here." *Washington* (D.C.) *Daily News*, 7 September 1951, p. 37.

Downing, Francis. "The Young: A Lost Generation." *Commonweal* 54 (5 October 1951): 619–620.

Dwight, Ogden G. "Year's Third New Major Writer, Styron, Hailed for Brilliant Novel." *Des Moines* (Iowa) *Sunday Register*, 9 September 1951, p. 11W.

E[arl], L[eonard] F[rancis]. "Depressing Family Tale." *Winnipeg* (Manitoba) *Tribune*, 20 October 1951, p. 13.

Elwood, Irene. "Family Has Everything, Loses All." *Los Angeles Times*, 16 September 1951, sec. 4, p. 5.

Fane, Vernon. "The World of Books." *The Sphere* 209 (12 April 1952): 76.

Farber, James. "Parade of Books." *New York Journal American*, 29 September 1951, p. 8. See also *Baltimore News Post*, 29 September 1951; *Seattle Intelligencer*, 29 September 1951; *Milwaukee Sentinel*, 29 September 1951; *Albany* (N.Y.) *Times-Union*, 30 September.

Fowler, Robert. "Virginian Writes Lucid Prose." *Greensboro* (N.C.) *Daily News*, 9 September 1951, feature section, p. 3.

Gannett, Lewis. "Books and Things." *New York Herald Tribune*, 11 September 1951, p. 25.

Gardner, R. H. "A Promising First Novel and Another." *Baltimore Evening Sun*, 25 October 1951, p. 30.

Geismar, Maxwell. "Domestic Tragedy in Virginia." *Saturday Review of Literature* 34 (15 September 1951): 12–13.

Gould, John. "Frank Appraisals of Latest Books." *Wichita Falls* (Tex.) *Times*, 14 October 1951, p. 9D.

Gould, Ray. "Astonishing First Novel Is Brilliant." *Montgomery* (Ala.) *Advertiser*, 4 November 1951, p. 9D.

Govan, Christine Noble. "Story of Weak Family Is Plea for More Maturity in Adults." *Chattanooga Times*, 16 September 1951, p. 19.

G[reening], M[arjorie] M. "About Books . . . ." *Michigan City* (Ind.) *News-Dispatch*, 4 October 1951, p. 10.

Grove, Lee. "Memorable First Novel Demolishes a Family." *Washington* (D.C.) *Post*, 9 September 1951, p. 6B.

H., A. B. *Punch* 222 (30 April 1952): 550.

Heth, Edward Harris. "A Torrential New Talent." *Milwaukee Journal*, 16 September 1951, sec. 5, p. 5.

Hill, Bob. "Looking at Books." *Spokane* (Wash.) *Chronicle*, 13 September 1951, p. 32.

Horan, Kenneth. "Willa Cather's World: Two Problem Novels." *Dallas Times-Herald*, 16 September 1951, sec. 8, p. 3.

Hoyt, Elizabeth North. "Disintegration." *Cedar Rapids* (Iowa) *Gazette*, 7 October 1951, sec. 3, p. 8.

"Human Frailties." *London Times*, 22 March 1952, p. 8.

Hunt, Howard. "Evil Likewise Begins at Home in New Novel." *San Antonio Express*, 16 September 1951, p. 4D.

Janeway, Elizabeth. "Private Emotions Privately Felt." *New Leader* 35 (21 January 1952): 25.

Johnson, Pamela Hansford. "Father Was Eccentric." *John O'London's Weekly* 61 (9 May 1952): 464.

Johnson, Stanley. "Again the Decay of an Old Southern Family— This Time with Success." *Salt Lake Tribune*, 14 October 1951, magazine section, p. 4M.

Jones, Carter Brooke. "Work of Virginia's William Styron Hailed as Extraordinary First Novel." *Washington* (D.C.) *Sunday Star*, 9 September 1951, p. 3C.

Jones, Howard Mumford. "A Rich, Moving Novel Introduces a Young Writer of Great Talent." *New York Herald Tribune Book Review*, 9 September 1951, p. 3.

Kelley, James E. "Promising First Novel: Violence of Love and Hate." *Denver Post*, 9 September 1951, p. 6E.

Kimmel, L. F. "Eagle Eye on Books." *Wichita* (Kans.) *Eagle*, 19 September 1951, p. 6.

Kirby, John Pendy. *Virginia Quarterly Review* 28 (Winter 1952): 129–130.

Lambert, J. W. "New Novels: Every Man in His Humour." *London Sunday Times*, 30 March 1952, p. 3.

Laning, Clair. "Books and People . . . ." *Oakville* (Ontario) *Record-Star*, 11 October 1951.

L[aycock], E[dward] A. "An Exciting Discovery: William Styron Writes Magnificent First Novel about a Tragic Family." *Boston Sunday Globe*, 9 September 1951, p. 27A.

M., M. *Kingston* (Ontario) *Whig-Standard*, 22 December 1951, p. 4.

MacGregor, Martha. "Impressive First Novel by a Talented 26-Year-Old Writer." *New York Post*, 9 September 1951, p. 12M.

McHugh, Miriam. "Today's Books." *Trenton* (N.J.) *Trentonian*, 22 September 1951, p. 13.

MacLaren, Hale. "Looks at Books." *La Jolla* (Calif.) *Light*, 27 December 1951, p. 3B.

Mason, Robert. "Story of the Spirit Is Rich in Poetry and Insight: William Styron of Newport News, 26, Is Suddenly a Major Novelist." *Norfolk Virginian-Pilot*, 9 September 1951, part 5, p. 4.

Melton, Amos. "Fine Talent Is Misused In 1st Novel." *Fort Worth Star-Telegram*, 23 September 1951, sec. 2, p. 11.

Morgan-Powell, S. "Some New Novels: English and American Tales Provide a Striking Contrast." *Montreal Star*, 20 October 1951, p. 20.

Morrissy, W. B. "Disintegration of a Family." *Montreal Gazette*, 27 October 1951, p. 27.

Morton, Joseph J. *Brooklyn Eagle*, 16 September 1951, p. 27.

Mossman, Josef. "Horrid Limbo of Lost Souls." *Detroit News*, 23 September 1951, home and society section, p. 17.

Munn, L. S. "Mature Young Talent Seen in 'Lie Down in Darkness.'" *Springfield* (Mass.) *Sunday Republican*, 30 September 1951, p. 10B.

New Yorker 27 (29 September 1951): 118–119.

Nicholson, Henry. "Unhappiness Dissected." *Rochester* (N.Y.) *Democrat and Chronicle*, 30 September 1951, p. 10D.

North, Sterling. "Sterling North Reviews the New Books: An Important First Novel." *New York World Telegram*, 11 September 1951, p. 26. See also *Toledo Blade*, 30 September 1951.

O'Brien, Alfred, Jr. "*Lie Down in Darkness.*" *Commonweal* 55 (19 October 1951): 43–44.

O'Connor, Richard. "*Lie Down in Darkness.*" *Los Angeles Herald Express*, 22 September 1951, sec. A, p. 12.

O'Dell, Scott. "New Novelist Makes Auspicious Debut." *Los Angeles Daily News*, 15 September 1951, p. 8.

O'Leary, Theodore M. "Styron's Remarkable First Novel." *Kansas City* (Mo.) *Star*, 29 September 1951, p. 16.

P., A. F. "Wealth Does Not Bring Happiness." *Hamilton* (Ontario) *Spectator*, 27 October 1951, p. 16.

Pace, Norma W. "*Lie Down in Darkness:* A Puzzler." *Lexington* (Ky.) *Herald-Leader*, 23 September 1951, p. 23.

Pasley, Gertrude. "Unhappy People." *Newark* (N.J.) *Sunday News*, 16 September 1951, sec. 4, p. 88.

Prescott, Orville. "Books of the Times." *New York Times*, 10 September 1951, p. 19.

Price, Emerson. "Hails Young Author's First Novel." *Cleveland Press*, 11 September 1951, p. 18.

Ragan, Marjorie. "A New Southern Author Shows Literary Promise." *Raleigh* (N.C.) *News and Observer*, 16 September 1951, sec. 4, p. 5.

Retail Bookseller 54 (September 1951): 104.

Robinson, Frances. *Book-of-the-Month Club News*, September 1951, p. 14.

R[obinson], O[live] C. "*Lie Down in Darkness.*" *Lewiston* (Maine) *Sun*, 13 September 1951, p. 4.

Rockwell, Kenneth. "First Novel Introduces Major Literary Talent." *Dallas Times-Herald*, 9 September 1951, sec. 7, p. 3.

R[ogers], W. G. "First Novel 'Remarkable.'" *Omaha Sunday World Herald*, 16 September 1951, p. 28G. See also *Trenton* (N.J.) *Times*, 30 September 1951; *Manchester* (N.H.) *News*, 9 September 1951; *Scranton* (Pa.) *Tribune*, 14 October 1951; *San Mateo* (Calif.) *Times*, 11 September 1951; *Keene* (N.H.) *Sentinel*, 13 September 1951; *Woonsocket* (R.I.) *Call*, 27 September 1951; *Binghamton* (N.Y.) *Press*, 9 September 1951; *Phoenix Gazette*,

11 September 1951; *Aberdeen* (Wash.) *World*, 12 September 1951; *Bakersfield* (Calif.) *Californian*, 11 September 1951.

Rothermel, J. F. "Needed: A Good Editor. A Tragic Story involving Twisted People and Told with Powerful Writing." *Birmingham* (Ala.) *News*, 9 September 1951, sec. F, p. 6.

Rubin, Louis D., Jr. "Two Significant Southern Novels Point to Importance of Religious Faith in Society." *Richmond* (Va.) *News Leader*, 10 September 1951, p. 11.

————. "What to Do about Chaos." *Hopkins Review* 5 (Fall 1951): 65–68.

S., A. *Canadian Forum* 31 (January 1952): 239.

S., F. G. *South Bend* (Ind.) *Tribune*, 18 October 1951, sec. 1, p. 8.

Scott, Eleanor M. *Providence* (R.I.) *Sunday Journal*, 9 September 1951, sec. 6, p. 8.

Scott, J. D. "New Novels." *New Statesman and Nation* 43 (19 April 1952): 472–473.

Sessler, Betty. *Richmond* (Va.) *Times-Dispatch*, 16 September 1951, p. 8A.

Sherman, John K. "First Novel Stamps Young Writer as Great." *Minneapolis Sunday Tribune*, 30 September 1951, feature-news section, p. 6.

Smith, Harrison. "Young Writer Depicts Trials of Human Soul." *Buffalo Evening News*, 8 September 1951, magazine section, p. 7. See also *Charlotte* (N.C.) *Observer*, 9 September 1951, p. 14D; *Philadelphia Sunday Bulletin*, 9 September 1951, magazine section, p. 6; *Easton* (Pa.) *Express*, 8 September 1951; *Roanoke* (Va.) *Times*, 9 September 1951; *Youngstown* (Ohio) *Vindicator*, 9 September 1951; *Hartford Times*, 8 September 1951; *Brattleboro* (Vt.) *Reformer*, 5 September 1951; *San Diego Union*, 9 September 1951.

Snyder, Marjorie B. "Love, Hate, Passion All in His Book." *Boston Sunday Herald*, 9 September 1951, sec. 1, p. 6.

[Spectorsky, A. C.] "Worth Reading." *Charm* 75 (October 1951): 30.

Stix, Frederick, W. *Cincinnati Enquirer*, 9 September 1951, sec. 3, p. 13.

Sullivan, Julian T. "Decay and Death Fertilize Fine New Creative

Talent." *Indianapolis Star*, 16 September 1951, sec. 6, p. 14.

Swados, Harvey. "First Novel." *The Nation* 272 (24 November 1951): 453.

"Tensions and Adjustments." *The Scotsman* (Edinburgh), 3 April 1952, p. 9.

Thickens, Jean Wiley. "Book Review: 'Lie Down in Darkness' Not Pleasant but It's Interesting." *Appleton* (Wis.) *Post-Crescent*, 10 April 1952, p. 14.

Toney, Sara D. "The Mariners Bookstall." *Gloucester* (Mass.) *Daily Times*, 3 October 1951, p. 9.

Truax, Charles. "New Novel of Family's Tragedy Hailed." *Dayton Daily News*, 16 September 1951, sec. 2, p. 9.

Turner, E. S. "'Lie Down in Darkness' Reveals a New Talent." *Syracuse Herald*, 16 September 1951, features section, p. 37.

"The Unbeautiful and Damned." *Time* 58 (10 September 1951): 106, 108.

Wallace, Margaret. "Of a Nobel Laureate and Other Novelists." *Independent Woman* 30 (November 1951): 325.

Weeks, Mabel. "First Novel Shoots Straight to Heart." *Long Beach* (Calif.) *Press-Telegram*, 9 September 1951, *Southland* magazine, p. 13.

Winn, Elizabeth S. "The Bookshelf." *El Paso Herald-Post*, 20 October 1951, p. 4.

Wynne, Leslie B. "Remarkable First Novel." *Pasadena* (Calif.) *Star News*, 18 November 1951, sec. 1, p. 23.

Yaffe, James. *Yale Review* 41 (Winter 1952): viii.

Ziegner, Edward. "Here's a First, Not a Last, We Hope." *Indianapolis News*, 8 September 1951, p. 2.

Set This House on Fire

Adams, Phoebe. *Atlantic Monthly* 206 (July 1960): 97–98.

Aldinger, Beatrice I. *Charleston* (S.C.) *News & Courier*, 5 June 1960, sec. C, p. 13.

Alexander, Charles. "Comes Now Styron with His Second Novel of Moderns." *Albany* (Oreg.) *Democrat-Herald*, 30 July 1960, p. 10.

Barley, Rex. "Styron's Second Novel Falls Short of First." *Los Angeles Mirror News*, 20 June 1960, part 2, p. 2.

Baro, Gene. "Styron's New Novel: Search for the Meaning of Evil." *New York Herald Tribune Book Review*, 5 June 1960, pp. 1, 12.

Baudrillard, Jean. "'La Proie des Flammes.'" *Les Temps Modernes* 17 (June 1962): 1928–1937.

Betts, Doris. "Serious Violent Novel." *Houston Post*, 12 June 1960, Houston Now section, p. 36.

Bonnichon, André. "William Styron et le Second Oedipe." *Études* 315 (October 1962): 94–103.

Borklund, Elmer. "Fiction of Violence and Pain." *Commentary* 30 (November 1960): 452–454.

Boroff, David. "The Styron Novel." *New York Post*, 5 June 1960, magazine section, p. 11.

Bourg, Gene. "Italy Is Scene of American Drama." *New Orleans Times-Picayune*, 19 June 1960, sec. 2, p. 3.

Bourniquel, Camille. "De la Difficulté d'être . . . Américain." *Esprit* 30 (May 1962): 818–824 [820–824].

Bradley, Van Allen. "Bradley on Books: Second Styron Novel Close to a Masterpiece." *Chicago Daily News*, 4 June 1960, p. 13.

Breit, Harvey. "A Second Novel." *Partisan Review* 27 (Summer 1960): 561–563.

Bruni, Thomas G. *Lehigh Valley* (Pa.) *Labor Herald*, 29 June 1960, p. 5.

Bryden, Ronald. "Near Amalfi." *The Spectator*, no. 6921, 17 February 1961, pp. 232–233.

[Burton, Hal]. "A Novel of Rare Quality." *Newsday* (Garden City, N.Y.), 4 June 1960, p. 31.

Chaffee, Norman. "Examination of Good, Evil." *Tulsa Sunday World*, 10 July 1960, *Your World* magazine, p. 17.

Cheney, Frances Neel. "Rich, Sensitive Prose; Eye for Detail." *Nashville Banner*, 3 June 1960, p. 24.

Cleary, Pal. "New Fiction." *Books and Bookmen* 8 (March 1961): 27.

Covici, Pascal, Jr. "Powerful Vision for Our Time." *Dallas Morning News*, 5 June 1960, sec. 5, p. 6.

Creed, Howard. "Styron Doesn't Set Reviewer on Fire." *Birmingham* (Ala.) *News*, 21 August 1960, p. 8E.

Culligan, Glendy. "Styron Returns—Jury Still Hung." *Washington* (D.C.) *Post*, 5 June 1960, p. 6E.

Cunningham, Bill. "Styron Novel Is Intricate." *San Antonio Express and News*, 10 July 1960, p. 5G.

Curley, Thomas F. "The Quarrel with Time in American Fiction." *American Scholar* 29 (Autumn 1960): 552–560 [558–560].

Dahms, Joseph G. *America* 103 (18 June 1960): 380–381.

Daniels, N. A. "The Identity of Opposites." *People's World* (San Francisco), 9 July 1960, p. 6.

Dawkins, Cecil. "Our Man in Italy: A Study of Evil and Its Expiation." *Milwaukee Journal*, 5 June 1960, sec. 5, p. 4.

Didion, Joan. "Fiction Chronicle: Inadequate Mirrors." *National Review* 8 (2 July 1960): 430–431.

Dwight, Ogden G. "In 'Set This House on Fire' Styron Has Quite a Blaze." *Des Moines Sunday Register*, 3 July 1960, p. 11G.

"Empty Soul Blues." *Time* 74 (6 June 1960): 98.

Evans, Derro. "Fiction Gains New Stature with William Styron Novel." *Amarillo* (Tex.) *Sunday News-Globe*, 5 June 1960, p. 6C.

Fenton, Charles A. "William Styron and the Age of the Slob." *South Atlantic Quarterly* 59 (Autumn 1960): 469–476.

French, Marion Flood. "Maine Bookmarks." *Bangor Daily News*, 18–19 June 1960, p. 7.

Fuller, Edmund. "A Picture of Hell by a Writer of Maturing Vision." *Chicago Sunday Tribune Magazine of Books*, 5 June 1960, p. 3.

Gentry, Curt. "Styron's Superb Third Novel." *San Francisco Sunday Chronicle*, 5 June 1960, *This World* magazine, p. 22.

George, Daniel. "Recent Fiction: Bearer of the World's Despair." *London Daily Telegraph and Morning Post*, 17 February 1961, p. 19.

Gillon, Diana, and Meir Gillon. "Fiction of the Week: Extraordinary Vices." *London Sunday Times*, 19 February 1961, magazine section, p. 27.

Griffin, Lloyd W. *Library Journal* 85 (15 June 1960): 2458.

Gross, John. "Degenerates Abroad." *London Sunday Telegraph*, 19 February 1961, p. 7.

Hall, Barbara Hodge. "New Novel by Styron Is Gripping." *Anniston* (Ala.) *Star*, 10 July 1960, p. 6B.

Hayes, E. Nelson. "Novels by Styron and Fifield." *Providence* (R.I.) *Sunday Journal*, 5 June 1960, p. 20W.

Hicks, Granville. "After the Fury, a Time of Peace." *Saturday Review of Literature* 43 (4 June 1960): 13.

Highet, Gilbert. *Book-of-the-Month Club News*, May, 1960, p. 7.

Hill, Susan. *Time and Tide* 42 (24 February 1961): 285.

Hodges, Betty. "Betty Hodges' Book Nook." *Durham* (N.C.) *Morning Herald*, 3 July 1960, p. 5D.

Hoey, Reid A. "Styron's New Novel of Good and Evil," *Baltimore Sunday Sun*, 6 June 1960, sec. A, p. 5.

Hollander, John. *Yale Review* 50 (Fall 1960): 152–153.

Hummel, Joseph W. "'Set This House on Fire': Novel Stresses Finding Identity." *Columbia Missourian*, 12 June 1960, sec. B, p. 7.

Hunter, Anna C. "Styron Fulfills Promise with Explosive New Novel." *Savannah* (Ga.) *Morning News*, 5 June 1960, magazine section, p. 14.

Hutchens, John K. *New York Herald Tribune*, 3 June 1960, p. 11.

Hutchison, Ruth. "Reviewer's Corner: Styron's New Book May Raise Alarms." *Bethlehem* (Pa.) *Globe-Times*, 11 June 1960, sec. 3, p. 19.

Johnson, C. W. "Finding New Pieces in Old Tale." *Springfield* (Mo.) *Sunday News & Leader*, 5 June 1960, p. B5.

J[ones], C[arter] B[rooke]. "Mr. Styron's New Novel Is a Disappointment." *Washington* (D.C.) *Sunday Star*, 5 June 1960, p. 11C.

"Just Out: A Kind of Tenderness." *Newsweek* 55 (6 June 1960): 117–118.

Kaufman, Clarence. "Second Styron Novel Proof of Major Talent." *Lincoln* (Nebr.) *Sunday Journal and Star*, 5 June 1960, p. 12B.

Kenney, Herbert, Jr. "Moralizing Binge Spoils Styron Talent." *Indianapolis News*, 6 August 1960, p. 2.

Kirsch, Robert R. "Books and People: Styron's 'House' Nears Greatness." *Los Angeles Times*, 5 June 1960, sec. C, p. 7.

Kohler, Dayton. "Virginia Author: Styron Treats Moral Issues Dramatically." *Richmond* (Va.) *News Leader*, 8 June 1960, p. 13.

Kohn, Sherwood. "The Book Scene: Styron . . . an Heir of Camus?" *Louisville Times*, 15 June 1960, p. 11.

Krieger, Robert E. "Unending Nightmare of Good versus Evil." *Worcester* (Mass.) *Sunday Telegram*, 5 June 1960, sec. E, p. 9.

L., E. H. "New Book Plenty Hot: It Deserves to Burn." *Salt Lake City Tribune*, 14 August 1960, p. 15W.

L., T. C. "New Book Suffers from Overwriting." *Columbia* (S.C.) *Record*, 17 November 1960, p. 4D.

L[aycock], E[dward] A. "American Spoiled Boy: Styron's Third Novel Shocking, Powerful Picture of Degradation." *Boston Sunday Globe*, 5 June 1960, p. 7A.

Layton, Mike. "Critics' Predictions Fulfilled by Styron." *Olympia* (Wash.) *Sunday Olympian*, 12 June 1960, p. 22.

Lea, George. "New Novel Won't Set House on Fire." *Chicago Sun-Times*, 10 July 1960, sec. 3, p. 5.

LeMaire, Marcel. "Some Recent American Novels and Essays." *Revue des Langues Vivantes* 28 (January–February 1962): 70–78 [72–74].

"Life, Death of Sadistic Millionaire." *Miami Herald*, 12 June 1960, p. 14J.

Lindau, Betsy. *Asheville* (N.C.) *Citizen-Times*, 5 June 1960, p. 3D.

Littlewood, Sandra. "Bad, Good Are Mixed in Styron." *Sacramento Bee*, 5 June 1960, p. L30.

Lowman, Ann. "Too Much Retrospect Mars Styron's Second." *Columbus* (Ohio) *Sunday Dispatch*, 26 June 1960, *TAB* section, p. 12.

"Lucidity Could Do Wonders." *Charlotte* (N.C.) *News*, 4 June 1960, p. 7B.

McDermott, Stephanie. "Arty People Flounder in Own Morass." *St. Louis Globe Democrat*, 5 June 1960, p. 4F.

McManis, John. "Such Fascinating Villains." *Detroit News*, 5 June 1960, p. 3F.

Malcolm, Donald. "Books: False Alarms." *New Yorker* 36 (4 June 1960): 152–154.

Malin, Irving. "Styron Probes Ancient Truths in New Novel." *Fort Wayne News-Sentinel*, 4 June 1960, p. 4.

Mason, Robert. "Characters Clash in Heroic Conflict." *Norfolk Virginian-Pilot and Portsmouth Star*, 5 June 1960, p. 8F.

May, William. "A Disappointment." *Newark* (N.J.) *Sunday News*, 12 June 1960, sec. 2, p. W22.

Miller, Karl. "An American Revenger." *The Observer* (London), 19 February 1961, p. 29.

Miller, Nolan. *Antioch Review* 20 (Summer 1960): 256.

Mizener, Arthur. "Some People of Our Time." *New York Times Book Review*, 5 June 1960, pp. 5, 26.

Monaghan, Charles. "Styronic Manner." *Commonweal* 72 (22 July 1960): 380.

Mooney, Harry, Jr. "Styron Raises Issues, Faces Them Squarely, but Novel Is Seriously Marred by Author's Undisciplined Rhetoric." *Pittsburgh Press*, 5 June 1960, sec. 5, p. 14.

Moreland, John. "Critic on the Hearth . . . ." *Oakland* (Calif.) *Tribune*, 15 June 1960, p. D23.

Murray, James G. *The Critic* 19 (August–September 1960): 37.

Newberry, Mike. "Shock of Recognition." *Mainstream* 13 (September 1960): 61–63.

"New Fiction." *London Times*, 16 February 1961, p. 15.

New Mexico Quarterly 30 (Winter 1960–1961): 412.

"New Novels: On the Operatic Scale." *The Scotsman* (Edinburgh), 25 February 1961, *Week-End* magazine, p. 2.

Nichols, Luther. "Styron's Literary Shock Treatment." *San Francisco Examiner*, 29 May 1960, *Highlight* section, p. 6.

Norman, Sue. "Styron Survives Second Novel Test in Style." *San Angelo* (Tex.) *Standard Times*, 11 September 1960, sec. B, p. 8.

O'Brien, E. D. "A Literary Lounger." *Illustrated London News* 238 (11 March 1961): 412.

O'Leary, Theodore M. "All the Elements of Greatness." *Kansas City* (Mo.) *Star*, 4 June 1960, p. 18.

Peckham, Stanton. "Styron's Second Novel Fulfills Promise." *Denver Sunday Post*, 5 June 1960, *Roundup* section, p. 9.

Perkin, Robert L. "Important Fiction." *Rocky Mountain News* (Denver), 26 June 1960, p. 14A.

Pickrel, Paul. "Heroic Proportions." *Harper's Magazine* 221 (July 1960): 93.

Prescott, Orville. "Books of the Times." *New York Times*, 3 June 1960, p. 29.

Price, Emerson. "Magnificent Novel Portrays Man Trapped by His Own Folly." *Cleveland Press*, 7 June 1960, p. 28.

Price, R. G. G. "New Novels." *Punch* 240 (15 March 1961): 441–442.

"A Quick Look at the Rest of the Books." *London Evening Standard*, 28 February 1961, p. 17.

Ragan, Marjorie. "A Brilliant Fire of Tragedy." *Raleigh* (N.C.) *News and Observer*, 5 June 1960, sec. 3, p. 5.

Richman, Charles. "Books." *Brooklyn* (N.Y.) *Record*, 17 June 1960, p. 6.

Rogers, W. G. "Killing in Italy Theme of New Styron Novel." *Cleveland Plain Dealer*, 12 June 1960, p. 8H. See also *Santa Barbara* (Calif.) *News Press*, 5 June 1960; *Long Beach* (Calif.) *Independent Press Telegram*, 12 June 1960.

Rohm, Zeta. *Seattle Post-Intelligencer*, 11 June 1960, p. 13.

Rothberg, Abraham. "Styron's Appointment in Sambuco." *New Leader* 43 (4–11 July 1960): 24–27.

Rowe, Percy. "Monster and Madman: Meet the Terrible Twins." *Toronto Telegram*, 8 October 1960, p. 59.

Rubin, Louis D., Jr. *Baltimore Evening Sun*, 3 June 1960, p. 30.
———. "An Artist in Bonds." *Sewanee Review* 69 (Winter 1961): 174–179.

Scott, Paul. *New Statesman and Nation* 61 (17 February 1961): 270–271.

Sherman, John K. "Melodrama of Good and Evil Probes Human Undercurrents." *Minneapolis Tribune*, 12 June 1960, p. 6E.

Sinclair, Reid B. "From the Fiction Shelf: Prodigious Effort by Virginian." *Richmond* (Va.) *Times-Dispatch*, 26 June 1960, p. 10L.

Snyder, Mary Rennels. "Behind the Backs of Books & Authors." *Gary* (Ind.) *Post-Tribune*, 5 June 1960, p. D9.

Southern, Terry. *The Nation* 191 (19 November 1960): 382.

Stratton, James C. "Footnotes and Fancies: Moral Decay Exam Reveals and Revolts." *Stillwater* (Okla.) *News-Press*, 24 April 1960, p. 9.

Sullivan, Walter. "New Styron Disappoints." *Nashville Tennessean*, 19 June 1960, p. 10D.

Taylor, Robert W. "World of Books." *Diplomat* 11 (July 1960): 40.

Tyler, Betty. "Roxbury Author's Second: Provocative, Disturbing." *Bridgeport* (Conn.) *Sunday Post*, 29 May 1960, p. C4.

Tyndareus. "Recent Fiction." *John O'London's* 4 (23 February 1961): 218.

Virginia Quarterly Review 36 (Autumn 1960): civ, cvi.

W., J. "Books in Review." *Auburn* (N.Y.) *Citizen-Advertiser*, 4 June 1960, p. 4.

Wade, Gerald. "Conflict of Evil and Search for Peace Is Awesomely Told." *Beaumont* (Tex.) *Journal*, 17 June 1960, p. 20.

Watts, Harold H. "Assembly of Horrors." *St. Louis Post-Dispatch*, 19 June 1960, p. 4B.

"What Happened at Sambuco." *Times Literary Supplement* (London), 17 February 1961, p. 101.

Wyrick, Green D. "Book Review." *Emporia* (Kans.) *Gazette*, 25 February 1961, p. 4. See also *Larned* (Kans.) *Daily Tiller & Toiler*, 24 February 1961: *Wellington* (Kans.) *Monitor-Press*, 23 February 1961.

Yarus, W. P. "*Set This House on Fire:* Novelist Grows in Stature." *Charlotte* (N.C.) *Observer*, 12 June 1960, p. 7B.

The Long March

Ancrum, Calhoun. "This Week's Reading: Novella Reflects Genius of Styron." *Charleston* (S.C.) *News and Courier*, 7 April 1968, p. 12C.

Anders, Smiley. "Some of Early Power of Top Writer Shown." *Baton Rouge* (La.) *Advocate*, 5 May 1968, sec. F, p. 2.

Bryden, Ronald. "Time of War." *The Spectator*, no. 6980, 6 April 1962, p. 454.

Collamore, Elizabeth. "Waste and Death." *Hartford Courant*, 14 April 1968, magazine section, p. 15.

Davis, Paxton. "Styron, Jarrell in New Reprints." *Roanoke* (Va.) *Times*, 5 May 1968, p. E14.

"Early Styron." *Dallas Morning News*, 26 May 1968, p. 32 A.

"Eight Dead Boys." *Times Literary Supplement* (London), 6 April 1962, p. 229.

F., C. A. "Military Psychology." *New Orleans Times-Picayune*, 16 June 1968, sec. 3, p. 2.

"Fiction in Brief." *Punch* 242 (9 May 1962): 735.

Green, Peter. "Growing Up in Golders Green." *London Daily Telegraph and Morning Post*, 6 April 1962, p. 19.

Hughes, David. "Well Worth the Effort." *London Sunday Times*, 8 April 1962, p. 32.

"New Fiction." *London Times*, 5 April 1962, p. 13.

"New Fiction." *The Times Weekly Review* (London), 12 April 1962, p. 10.

Phipers, Todd. "Tedious Journey." *Rocky Mountain News* (Denver), 14 July 1968, *Startime* section, p. 19.

Scannell, Vernon. "New Novels." *The Listener* 67 (19 April 1962): 701.

Scott, Glenn. "Bookmarks: Battles." *Norfolk Virginian-Pilot*, 7 April 1968, p. C6.

Sudler, Barbara. "War Story 'The Long March' Reissued between Hard Covers." *Denver Sunday Post*, 5 May 1968, *Roundup* section, p. 13.

Zane, Maitland. "Down Yoknapatawpha Way." *Time and Tide* 43 (12 April 1962): 30.

The Confessions of Nat Turner

America 117 (25 November 1967): 666.

America 118 (24 February 1968): 269.

Ancrum, Calhoun. "Novel by Styron Gets Rave Notices." *Charleston* (S.C.) *News and Courier*, 31 December 1967, p. 2D.

Aptheker, Herbert. "Styron—Turner and Nat Turner: Myth and Truth." *Political Affairs* 46 (October 1967): 40–50.

Artopoeus, John B. "'A Meditation on History.'" *Newark* (N.J.) *Sunday News*, 8 October 1967, sec. 1, p. A6.

Barkham, John. "Sixty Whites Were Killed in 1831 Slave Riots." *Youngstown* (Ohio) *Vindicator*, 8 October 1967, p. 12B. See also *Woodland* (Calif.) *Democrat*, 18 October 1967; *Lewiston* (Idaho) *Tribune*, 15 October 1967; *Albany* (N.Y.) *Times-Union*, 8 October 1967; *Waukegan* (Ill.) *News Sun*, 8 October 1967; *Grand Rapids* (Mich.) *Press*, 8 October 1967.

Bauer, Malcolm. "Swords That Made 'Sore Slaughter.'" *Portland Sunday Oregonian*, 15 October 1967, p. F3.

Bell, Bernard W. "The Confessions of Styron." *American Dialog* 5 (Spring 1968): 3–7.

Benke, Dick. "Plight of Negro Slaves Mirrored by Nat Turner." *Pasadena* (Calif.) *Independent Star News*, 15 October 1967, p. B8.

Bernstein, Victor. "Black Power, 1831." *Hadassah Magazine* 49 (November 1967): 16, 37.

Bickham, Jack M. "Truth Hurts." *Oklahoma City Sunday Oklahoman*, 8 October 1967, sec. 1, p. 28.

Billings, Claude. "'Confessions' Bares Negro Slave Revolt." *Indianapolis Star*, 17 December 1967, sec. 8, p. 7.

Birdsell, Roger. "The Reading Lamp: Styron's Black Hamlet." *South Bend* (Ind.) *Tribune*, 15 October 1967, sec. 1, p. 16.

Birlchaui, John. "Nat Turner's Rampage Told." *Tucson* (Ariz.) *Daily Citizen*, 2 December 1967, *Olé* magazine, p. 7.

Black, Kay Pittman. "Agonies of Slavery Recounted in Novel about Nat Turner." *Memphis Press-Scimitar*, 22 September 1967, p. 6.

Blackwood's Magazine, 304 (August 1968): 191–192.

Bradley, Van Allen. "Styron Tells Slave's Saga." *Memphis Commercial Appeal*, 15 October 1967, sec. 5, p. 6. See also *Birmingham* (Ala.) *News*, 15 October 1967; *Chicago Daily News*, 7 October 1967; *Albany* (N.Y.) *Knickerbocker-News*, 14 October 1967.

Brendon, Piers. "From Jungle to Plateau." *Books and Bookmen* 13 (July 1968): 32.

Brown, Cecil M. *Negro Digest* 17 (February 1968): 51–52, 89–91.

Bryden, Ronald. "Slave Rising." *New Statesman* 75 (3 May 1968): 586–587.

Buckmaster, Henrietta. "Racism, 1831: The Fire Last Time." *Christian Science Monitor*, 12 October 1967, p. 5.

Bunke, Joan. "Styron Novel Is Powerful as Fiction and Sermon." *Des Moines* (Iowa) *Register*, 15 October 1967, p. 7T.

Butcher, Fanny. *Chicago Tribune*, 25 October 1967, sec. 1, p. 22.

C., S. J. "Styron's Search for One Man's Soul." *Baltimore News American*, 8 October 1967, p. 2G.

Callanan, Kathleen B. "Curl Up & Read." *Seventeen* 27 (January 1968): 116.

Casey, Kevin. "Fiction: Act of God." *Irish Times* (Dublin), 18 May 1968, p. 8.

Choice 5 (March 1968): 54.

Clemons, Joel. "Author Dramatizes Event Masterfully." *Charleston* (S.C.) *News and Courier*, 31 December 1967, p. 2D.

Cole, Verne. "Novel of Revolt." *Fresno* (Calif.) *Bee*, 12 November 1967, p. 17F.

Coles, Robert. "Blacklash." *Partisan Review* 35 (Winter 1968): 128–133.

Collier, Peter. "Saga of Rebellion." *The Progressive* 31 (December 1967): 41–42.

Collins, L. M. "Exam: Don't Flunk It!" *Nashville Tennessean*, 1 October 1967, p. 6B.

Cook, Bruce. "Fiction Verifies the Facts of a Tidewater Tale." *National Observer*, 9 October 1967, p. 22.

Cooke, Michael. "Nat Turner's Revolt." *Yale Review* 57 (Winter 1968): 273–278.

Core, George. "*Nat Turner* and the Final Reckoning of Things." *Southern Review* n.s. 4 (Summer 1968): 745–751.

Coyle, William. "A Major American Novel." *Springfield* (Ohio) *Sun*, 28 October 1967, sec. 1, p. 6.

Cunningham, Dick. "Styron Writes of Negro with Inside-Out View." *Minneapolis Tribune*, 8 October 1967, p. 6E.

Currie, Edward. "Author William Styron: Era's Clarion." *Rocky Mountain News* (Denver), 22 October 1967, *Startime* section, p. 19.

Davis, Paxton. "Mr. Styron and His Nat Turner." *Roanoke* (Va.) *Times*, 29 October 1967, p. D7.

Delany, Lloyd Tom. "A Psychologist Looks at *The Confessions of Nat Turner*." *Psychology Today* 1 (January 1968): 11–14.

Derleth, August. "Books of the Times: Wm Styron's Fourth Novel." *Capital Times* (Madison, Wis.), 19 October 1967, sec. 1, p. 27.

Dixon, Donald C. *Reading Guide* (University of Virginia Law School) 23 (December 1967): 1–3.

Driver, Tom F. "Black Consciousness through a White Scrim." *Motive* 28 (February 1968): 56–58.

Duberman, Martin. "Books." *Village Voice* 13 (14 December 1967): 8, 9, 16. Reprinted in his *The Uncompleted Past* (see 2, A above).

Duffer, Ken. "Nat Turner: Slave to a Terrible Vision." *Winston-Salem* (N.C.) *Journal and Sentinel*, 8 October 1967, p. D6.

"*Ebony* Book Shelf." *Ebony* 23 (December 1967): 20.

Emmanuel, Pierre. "L'Histoire d'une Solitude." *Preuves*, no. 217 (April 1969): 17–20.

Enright, D. J. "The Caliban Story." *The Listener* 79 (2 May 1968): 557–559.

Fadiman, Clifton. *Book-of-the-Month Club News*, October 1967, pp. 2–5.

Fanning, Garth. "Nat Turner's Revolt Haunts Us." *Sacramento Bee*, 24 December 1967, *Valley Leisure* section, p. L17.

Fauchereau, Serge. "Oncle Nat et Oncle Tom." *La Quinzaine Littéraire* 70 (15 April 1969): 5–6.

Favre, Gregory. "Can White Man Get inside Skin of Black Man Turner?" *Dayton Daily News*, 22 October 1967, *Dayton Leisure* magazine, p. 13.

Ferguson, Charles A. "Styron Revises Story of Slave Revolt of 1831." *New Orleans Times-Picayune*, 29 October 1967, p. 12.

Fournier, Norman. "Rise and Fall of a Slave." *Portland* (Maine) *Telegram*, 8 October 1967, p. 4D.

Franklin, John Hope. "A Meditation on History." *Chicago Sun-Times*, 8 October 1967, *Book Week* section, pp. 1, 11.

Fremont-Smith, Eliot. "Books of the Times: A Sword Is Sharpened." *New York Times*, 3 October 1967, p. 45.

———. "Books of the Times: 'The Confessions of Nat Turner'—II." *New York Times*, 4 October 1967, p. 45.

French, Philip. "Styron and Stowe." *Financial Times* (London), 9 May 1968, p. 10.

Friedman, Melvin J. "*The Confessions of Nat Turner*: The Convergence of 'Nonfiction Novel' and 'Meditation on History.'" *Journal of Popular Culture* 1 (Fall 1967): 166–175. Reprinted, abridged, in *University of Wisconsin at Milwaukee Magazine*, Spring 1968, pp. 3–7.

Fuller, Edmund. "Power and Eloquence in New Styron Novel." *Wall Street Journal*, 4 October 1967, p. 16.

Garrett, James. "Styron Attempts Probe on Negro Character." *Cleveland Press*, 13 October 1967, *In* magazine, p. 17.

Gewirtz, Jacob. "Black & White." *Jewish Chronicle* (London), no. 5176, 5 July 1968, p. 20.

Goodheart, Eugene. "When Slaves Revolt." *Midstream* 14 (January 1968): 69–72.

Goodwin, John. "Bestseller Exposes Roots of Race Problem." *Eternity* 19 (March 1968): 42–43.

Green, Florence. "Styron Returns South." *Houston Chronicle*, 1 October 1967, *Zest* magazine, p. 18.

Green, Martin. "The Need for a New Liberalism." *The Month* (London) n.s. 40 (September 1968): 141–147 [143–144].

Greene, A. C. "The Printed Page." *Dallas Times Herald*, 15 October 1967, sec. E, p. 13.

Greenleaf, Richard. "Styron's Anti-Negro Novel Is Libel on Nat Turner." *The Worker*, 8 October 1967, p. 5.

Greenwood, Walter B. "Nat Turner's Revolt a Tragic Comment on Slavery's Evils." *Buffalo Evening News*, 14 October 1967, p. 12B.

Gresset, Michel. "*Les Confessions de Nat Turner: L'Histoire Réelle et le Roman*—un Sociodrame *Américain*." *Preuves*, no. 217, April 1969, pp. 3–5.

Griffin, Lloyd W. *Library Journal* 92 (1 October 1967): 3448–3449.

Grimes, Roy. "Books and Things." *Victoria* (Tex.) *Advocate*, 15 October 1967, *Fun* section, p. 10.

Grosvenor, Peter. "Inside the Mind of a Rebel Slave." *London Daily Express*, 2 May 1968, p. 13.

H., S. "Novel of Slave Revolt Eloquent." *San Antonio Express*, 8 October 1967, p. 3H.

Hairston, Loyle. "William Styron's Dilemma: Nat Turner in the Rogues' Gallery—Some Thoughts on William Styron's Novel, *The Confessions of Nat Turner*." *Freedomways* 8 (Winter 1968): 7, 12.

Hall, Joan Joffe. "Jehovah's Rebel Slave." *Houston Post*, 22 October 1967, *Spotlight* section, p. 12.

Haltrecht, Montague. "A Moment of Truth in Virginia." *London Sunday Times*, 5 May 1968, p. 56.

Hamilton, Iain. "Recent Fiction." *London Daily Telegraph and Morning Post*, 2 May 1968, p. 22.

Harnack, Curtis. "The Quiddities of Detail." *Kenyon Review* 30 (Winter 1968): 125–132.

Harwi, Robert. "Styron Novel Presents Fiction at Highest Level." *Wichita* (Kans.) *Sunday Eagle and Beacon*, 3 December 1967, p. 10C.

Heise, Kenan. *Extension* 62 (December 1967): 54.

Herman, Dick. "Is Grim Message of Slavery Just Beginning to Be Felt?" *Lincoln* (Nebr.) *Sunday Journal and Star*, 15 October 1967, p. 15F.

Hicks, Granville. "Race Riot, 1831." *Saturday Review* 50 (7 October 1967): 29–31.

———. "Five for Year's End." *Saturday Review* 50 (30 December 1967): 19.

Hicks, Walter J. "The Futile Insurrection." *Baltimore Sunday Sun*, 15 October 1967, p. 5D.

Higby, Jim. "'Nat Turner' Chronicles Slave Revolt." *Buffalo Couier-Express*, 19 November 1967, p. 87.

Hodgart, Patricia. "New Fiction: Tragedy and Compassion in the Deep South." *Illustrated London News* 252 (18 May 1968): 34.

Hogan, William. "William Styron's American Tragedy." *San Francisco Chronicle*, 9 October 1967, p. 43.

———. "Further Thoughts on the Styron Novel." *San Francisco Chronicle*, 10 October 1967, p. 39.

Hoyt, Charles Alva. "Summation of Slavery." *Louisville Courier-Journal & Times*, 15 October 1967, p. E5.

Hoyt, Elizabeth N. "Story of Negro Uprising in 1831." *Cedar Rapids* (Iowa) *Gazette*, 8 October 1967, pp. 2C, 23C.

Hurt, Richard L. "Slavery's Quiet Resistance." *Boston Sunday Globe*, 8 October 1967, p. 43A.

"The Idea of Hope." *Time* 90 (13 October 1967): 110, 113.

"In the Book World." *Chicago's American*, 8 October 1967, sec. 3, p. 5.

Ingle, H. L. "Meditation on History." *Chattanooga Times*, 12 November 1967, p. 30.

Kauffmann, Stanley. "Styron's Unwritten Novel." *Hudson Review* 20 (Winter 1967–1968): 675–679.

Kazin, Alfred. "Instinct for Tragedy: A Message in Black and White." *Book World* (*Chicago Tribune, Washington* [D.C.] *Post*), 8 October 1967, pp. 1, 22.

Keown, Don. "The Book Pages: Two New and Different Novels by Veterans Styron and Uris." *San Rafael* (Calif.) *Independent-Journal*, 7 October 1967, p. M15.

Kincaid, Anne. *Library Journal* 92 (15 November 1967): 4274.

Kirkus 35 (1 August 1967): 905.

Kirsch, Robert. "The Virginia Slave Revolt." *Los Angeles Times*, 8 October 1967, *Calendar* section, p. 36.

Kohler, Roy. "Bloody Page in History: Controversial Slave Revolt Recalled." *Pittsburgh Press*, 8 October 1967, sec. 6, p. 6.

Krupat, Arnold. "The Shock of Nat Turner." *Catholic World* 206 (February 1968): 226–228.

LaHaye, Judson. *Best Sellers* 27 (1 November 1967): 308.

Lane, Jack C. "Three Days of 'Indiscriminate Massacre.'" *Orlando* (Fla.) *Sentinel*, 5 November 1967, *Florida* magazine, p. 16F.

Layton, Mike. "A Negro Slave Revolt and What It Tells Us." *Olympia* (Wash.) *Sunday Olympian*, 28 October 1967, p. 27.

Lehan, Richard. *Contemporary Literature* 9 (Autumn 1968): 540–542.

Lewis, Claude. "Slavery, Murder, and God." *Philadelphia Sunday Bulletin*, 15 October 1967, *Books and Art* section, p. 3.

Lewis, R. W. B. "A Yale Bookshelf—Topic: Fiction 1967." *Yale Alumni Magazine* 31 (November 1967): 9.

Lister, Richard. "Brought Terrifyingly Alive: How Nat Turner Led the Slaves in Revolt." *London Evening Standard*, 7 May 1968, p. 10.

Livingston, Jean. "Three Days That Shook a Small World." *Quincy* (Mass.) *Patriot-Ledger*, 1 November 1967, p. 44.

Long, James. *Oregon Journal* (Portland), 11 November 1967, p. 6J.

Lynch, Donna. "*Confessions of Nat Turner*: Doubts This Novel Worth the Praise It Has Received." *Baton Rouge* (La.) *Advocate*, 29 October 1967, sec. E, p. 2.

McCormick, Jay. "An American Tragedy: Lessons That the Gallows Failed to Teach." *Detroit News*, 8 October 1967, p. 3E.

McGroarty, Joseph G. "'Nat Turner': A Racial Tract for Our Times?" *The Tablet* (Brooklyn, N.Y.) 60 (16 November 1967): 13.

McMillan, Dougald. "Come In, Mr. Styron. Sit Down, Mr. Styron. No, Mr. Styron, 'Nat Turner' Is Not a Great Book. Rather, Mr. Styron, It Is Bad, Bad." *North Carolina Anvil* (Durham), 9 December 1967, p. 5.

McNeill, Robert. *Presbyterian Survey* 58 (February 1968): 26–27.

McPherson, James Lowell. "America's Slave Revolt." *Dissent* 15 (January–February 1968): 86–89.

Malin, Irving. "Nat's Confessions." *University of Denver Quarterly* 2 (Winter 1968): 92–96. Reprinted in *William Styron's "The*

Confessions of Nat Turner": A Critical Handbook, edited by Fried-man and Malin (see 2, A above). Pp. 84–88.

Mason, Robert. "A Brilliant 'Meditation on History': Nat Turner, From Birth to Rebellion." *Norfolk Virginian-Pilot and Portsmouth Star*, 8 October 1967, p. 6C.

Menn, Thorpe. "Books of the Day." *Kansas City* (Mo.) *Star*, 8 October 1967, p. 6E.

Miller, William Lee. "The Meditations of William Styron." *The Reporter* 37 (16 November 1967): 42, 44, 46, 49.

Molineux, Will. "Newport News–Born William Styron Covers Tragic 1831 Slave Revolt." *Newport News–Hampton* (Va.) *Daily Press*, 29 October 1967, *New Dominion* magazine, p. 10.

Moody, Minnie Hite. "Documentary Novel Is Pegged to 1831 Revolt." *Columbus* (Ohio) *Sunday Dispatch*, 22 October 1967, *TAB* section, p. 14.

Moynahan, Julian. "A Virginian Spartacus." *The Observer* (London), 5 May 1968, p. 27.

Moynihan, John. "Fiction: Who Gets Slain?" *London Sunday Telegraph*, 5 May 1968, p. 14.

Mulchrone, Vincent. "The First Hot Summer of Black Power." *London Daily Mail*, 3 May 1968, p. 10.

Murray, Albert. "A Troublesome Property." *New Leader* 10 (4 December 1967): 18–21. Reprinted in *The Nat Turner Rebellion: The Historical Event and the Modern Controversy*, edited by Duff and Mitchell (see 2, A above). Pp. 174–180.

Murrell, Helen. "Turner Confesses While Waiting Hangman's Noose." *Abilene* (Tex.) *Reporter-News*, 3 December 1967, p. 13C.

Myers, Arthur. "He Speaks for His Own." *Hartford Courant*, 12 November 1967, magazine section, p. 13.

"Nat Turner." *Marquette* (Mich.) *Mining Journal*, 18 January 1968, p. 12.

Newcomb, Horace. "William Styron and the Act of Memory: *The Confessions of Nat Turner*." *Chicago Review* 20, no. 1 (1968): 86–94.

Nolte, William H. "Fact Novel of Revolt in Hot Summer of 1831." *St. Louis Sunday Post-Dispatch*, 8 October 1967, p. 4D. See also *Columbia* (S.C.) *State & Record*, 22 October 1967.

Osborne, Lorraine. "Styron Pens Powerful Novel around Story of

Slave Revolt." *Bridgeport* (Conn.) *Sunday Post*, 22 October 1967, p. E4.

Ottaway, Robert. "Ottaway on Thursday." *London Daily Sketch*, 2 May 1968, p. 8.

Parker, Roy, Jr. "Styron's Nat Turner: Fact Transmuted into Art." *Raleigh* (N.C.) *News and Observer*, 29 October 1967, sec. 3, p. 3.

Patterson, Ann. "Rebellion of a Slave." *Arizona Republic* (Phoenix), 29 October 1967, p. N9.

Patteson, Richard. "A Glimmer of Compassion, Humility and Pride." *Charleston* (W. Va.) *Sunday Gazette-Mail*, 17 December 1967, p. 19m.

Penne, Leo. "Out from the Vicious Circle." *Seattle Post-Intelligencer*, 22 October 1967, *Northwest Today* section, p. 4.

Platt, Gerald M. "A Sociologist Looks at *The Confessions of Nat Turner*." *Psychology Today* 1 (January 1968): 14–15.

Powers, James. "Book Reviews." *Hollywood* (Calif.) *Reporter*, 29 September 1967, p. 6.

Playboy 14 (November 1967): 32.

Price, R. G. G. "New Fiction." *Punch* 254 (1 May 1968): 652.

Publishers Weekly 192 (31 July 1967): 53.

Q[uill], G[ynter]. "Revolt of Negro Slaves Echoes over the Years." *Waco* (Tex.) *Tribune-Herald*, 5 November 1967, p. 13D.

Rahv, Philip. "Through the Midst of Jerusalem." *New York Review of Books* 9 (26 October 1967): 6, 8, 10. Reprinted in *The Nat Turner Rebellion: The Historical Event and the Modern Controversy*, edited by Duff and Mitchell (see 2, A above). Pp. 238–244.

Raymond, Robert. "Fine Novel Describes Early U.S. Slave Revolt." *Staten Island* (N.Y.) *Advance*, 22 October 1967, p. B6.

Redding, Saunders, "A Fateful Lightning in the Southern Sky." *Providence* (R.I.) *Sunday Journal*, 29 October 1967, p. 18W.

Richter, David H. *Chicago Literary Review* 5 (October 1967): 1, 10–11.

Robertson, Don. " 'Nat Turner': One View—Styron Is a Brave Failure." *Cleveland Plain Dealer*, 15 October 1967, p. 8H.

Robinson, Charles K. "Book Review: *Confessions of Nat Turner*."

The Setonian (Seton Hall University, South Orange, N.J.) 42 (22 November 1967): 6.

Rothchild, Sylvia. "The Bookshelf." *Jewish Advocate* (Boston), 21 December 1967, sec. 2, p. 16.

Rubin, Louis D., Jr. "Books: Eloquent Story of a Slave Rebellion." *Washington* (D.C.) *Sunday Star*, 8 October 1967, p. 14G.

————. "William Styron and Human Bondage: *The Confessions of Nat Turner*." *Hollins Critic* 4 (December 1967): 1–12. Reprinted in *William Styron's "The Confessions of Nat Turner": A Critical Handbook*, edited by Friedman and Malin (see 2, A above). Pp. 72–84.

S., D. L. "The New Books." *Seattle Argus*, 27 October 1967, p. 8.

Sass, Samuel. "Book Review: The Tragic Story of a Suicidal Negro Revolt." *Berkshire Eagle* (Pittsfield, Mass.), 18 November 1967, p. 14.

Schlesinger, Arthur, Jr. *Vogue* 150 (1 October 1967): 143.

Schlueter, Paul. "Soul Torment." *Christian Century* 85 (21 February 1968): 234–235.

Schroth, Raymond A. "Nat Turner's Sword." *America* 117 (14 October 1967): 416.

Schwartz, Joseph. "Negro Revolt of 1831 Flares Again in a 'Big' Novel of Fall." *Milwaukee Journal*, 8 October 1967, sec. 5, p. 4.

Seymour-Smith, Martin. "The Reality of Nat Turner." *The Scotsman* (Edinburgh), 11 May 1968, *Week-End Scotsman* section, p. 5.

Shaw, Russell. *The Sign* 47 (January 1968): 63.

Sheed, Wilfrid. "The Slave Who Became a Man." *New York Times Book Review*, 8 October 1967, pp. 1–3, 30, 32, 34. Reprinted in *William Styron's "The Confessions of Nat Turner": A Critical Handbook*, edited by Friedman and Malin (see 2, A above). Pp. 59–63. And reprinted in Sheed's *The Morning After* (see 2, A above).

Sherman, John K. "Portrays Negro View: Novel Illuminates History." *Minneapolis Star*, 10 October 1967, p. 4E.

"Short Reviews." *London Sun*, 2 May 1968, p. 8.

Shrapnel, Norman. "A French Lesson." *Manchester* (England) *Guardian*, 3 May 1968, p. 7.

Sinclair, Andrew. "Most Deliberate Revolt." *New Society* 11 (2 May 1968): 647.

Smiley, Nixon. "Slave's History Retold: Novel Sheds Understanding." *Miami Herald*, 8 October 1967, p. 7F.

Smith, Miles A. "Slave Revolt of 1831 Is Recounted." *Indianapolis News*, 21 October 1967, p. 30. See also *St. Louis Globe Democrat*, 21 October 1967; *Neodesha* (Kans.) *Daily Sun*, 13 October 1967; *Sacramento Union*, 22 October 1967.

Sokolov, Raymond A. "Into the Mind of Nat Turner." *Newsweek* 70 (16 October 1967): 65–69. Reprinted in *William Styron's "The Confessions of Nat Turner": A Critical Handbook*, edited by Friedman and Malin (see 2, A above). Pp. 42–50.

Spearman, Walter. "'Confessions of Nat Turner' Is Important Book: A Vivid Account of Revolt and Slaughter." *Chapel Hill* (N.C.) *Weekly*, 15 October 1967, p. 4.

Stalder, Majorie Bright. "Books." *Hemet* (Calif.) *News*, 7 October 1967, sec. 2, p. 2.

Steiner, George. "Books: The Fire Last Time." *New Yorker* 43 (25 November 1967): 236, 238, 241–242, 244.

Sudler, Barbara. "Nat Turner Led Revolt to Bring Purpose to Slaves' Lives." *Denver Sunday Post*, 15 October 1967, *Roundup* section, p. 12.

Tanner, Tony. "The Negro's Revenge." *The Spectator*, no. 7297, 3 May 1968, pp. 596–597.

Thomas, Sidney. "Slave Broke His Chains." *Atlanta Journal and Constitution*, 12 November 1967, p. 10D.

Thompson, John. "Rise and Slay!" *Commentary* 44 (November 1967): 81–85.

Tucker, Martin. *Commonweal* 87 (22 December 1967): 388–389.

Turner, Darwin T. *Journal of Negro History* 53 (April 1968): 183–186.

Turney, Charles. "Virginian's Novel Seeks 'Meditation on History.'" *Richmond* (Va.) *Times-Dispatch*, 15 October 1967, p. 5F.

"Unslavish Fidelity: The Confessions of William Styron." *Times Literary Supplement* (London), 9 May 1968, p. 480.

Virginia Quarterly Review, 44 (Winter 1968): viii.

Vittum, Henry E. "A Review." *Plymouth* (N.H.) *Record*, 18 January 1968, p. A6. See also *Bristol* (N.H.) *Enterprise*, 28 March 1968.

Vizinczey, Stephen. "America: A Fearful Fiction in Biblical Prose." *London Times*, 4 May 1968, p. 20.

W., B. "The Negro Fury: A Vital Insight." *Long Beach* (Calif.) *Independent Press-Telegram*, 18 November 1967, p. 6A.

Wade, Gerald. "'The Only Effective U.S. Negro Revolt.'" *Omaha* (Nebr.) *Sunday World-Herald*, 29 October 1967, magazine section, p. 36.

Walsh, Anne C. "William Styron Writes 'Autobiography' of First Slave Uprising Leader." *Phoenix Gazette*, 18 October 1967, p. 17.

Weber, R. B. "Styron's Power Creates a Real Being." *Louisville Times*, 13 October 1967, p. 11A.

Weeks, Edward. *Atlantic Monthly* 220 (November 1967): 130, 132.

Wellejus, Ed. "The Bookshelf." *Erie* (Pa.) *Times-News*, 29 October 1967, p. 11F.

White, Poppy Cannon. "Poppy's Notes: 'Confessions of Nat Turner.'" *New York Amsterdam News*, 25 November 1967, p. 15.

Williams, Ernest E. "Novel on Slave Uprising Skillful." *Fort Wayne News-Sentinel*, 28 October 1967, p. 4A.

Winfrey, Lee. "Mr. Styron's Superb Novel: When a Negro Slave Rebelled." *Detroit Free Press*, 8 October 1967, p. 5B.

Wolff, Geoffrey. "Slavery Intersects Present." *Washington* (D.C.) *Post*, 24 October 1967, p. A16.

Woodward, C. Vann. "Confessions of a Rebel: 1831." *New Republic* 157 (7 October 1967): 25–28. Reprinted in *The Nat Turner Rebellion: The Historical Event and the Modern Controversy*, edited by Duff and Mitchell (see 2, A above). Pp. 168–173.

Wright, Giles E. "Life of Real Slave Treated in Top Novel." *Los Angeles Herald Examiner*, 8 October 1967, p. 4J.

Yardley, Jonathan. "Mr. Styron's Monumental 'Meditation on History.'" *Greensboro* (N.C.) *Daily News*, 8 October 1967, p. D3.

In the Clap Shack

Brockway, Jody. *Theatre Crafts* 6 (June 1973): 44.

Fussell, B. H. "On the Trail of the Lonesome Dramaturge." *Hudson Review* 26 (Winter 1973): 753–762 [745].

Leon, Philip W. "Styron Publishes First Play." *Nashville Tennessean*, 2 September 1973, p. 10E.

Malin, Irving. "Styron's Play." *Southern Literary Journal* 6 (Spring 1974): 151–157.

Publishers Weekly 203 (7 May 1973): 63.

Spearman, Walter. *Chapel Hill* (N.C.) *Weekly*, 8 July 1973, p. 4C.

Washington (D.C.) *Post*, 15 July 1973, *Book World* section, p. 15.

Sophie's Choice

Adachi, Ken. "Flawed but Moving View of Holocaust." *Toronto Star*, 23 June 1979, p. B7.

Aldridge, John W. "Styron's Heavy Freight: Sex, Guilt, and the Holocaust Too." *Harper's Magazine* 259 (September 1979): 95–98.

Allen, Bruce. "Losses and Bereavements." *Baltimore Sun*, 10 June 1979, p. D5.

Alter, Robert. "Styron's Stingo." *Saturday Review* 6 (7 July 1979): 42–43.

Amiel, Barbara. "Clothed in a Suit of Secondhand Pain." *Maclean's* 92 (11 June 1979): 46.

Bandler, Michael J. *American Way* (June 1979): 131.

Barkham, John. "*Sophie's Choice.*" *Newport News* (Va.) *Daily Press*, 10 June 1979, *Panorama* section, p. 11. See also *Federal Times*, 4 June 1979, p. 23.

Barton, Rick. *The Cresset* 43 (December 1979): 27–28.

Beatty, Jack. *New Republic* 180 (30 June 1979): 38–40.

Becker, Stephen. "A Dazzling, Stunning Masterwork of the Holocaust." *Chicago Sun-Times*, 3 June 1979, *Book Week* section, p. 10. See also *Sacramento Union*, 1 July 1979, p. C7; *Lincoln* (Nebr.) *Sunday Journal and Star*, 24 June 1979, p. 8H.

Bell, Pearl K. "Evil & William Styron." *Commentary* 68 (August 1979): 57–59.

Birnbaum, Beth. "Books: Life after a Death Camp." *Rutgers Daily Targum* (Rutgers University, New Brunswick, N.J.), 15 February 1980.

Booklist 75 (1 May 1979): 1348.

Boozer, William. "Styron Has Produced Another Masterpiece." *Nashville Banner*, 16 June 1979.

Bray, Ashlin. "Agony after the Death Camps." *Wilmington* (Del.) *News-Journal*, 17 June 1979, sec. F, p. 6.

Bunke, Joan. "Forget? Never!" *Des Moines* (Iowa) *Sunday Register*, 10 June 1979, p. 4C.

Bunting, Josiah, III. "A Novel in the Narrative Tradition: William Styron Reflects on Holocaust's Legacy of Evil, Guilt, Suffering." *Richmond* (Va.) *News Leader*, 13 June 1979, p. 15.

Burgess, Anthony. "Brooklyn Liebestod." *The Observer* (London), 9 September 1979, p. 36.

Carson, Herbert L. "Styron Risks Much—and Succeeds." *Grand Rapids* (Mich.) *Press*, 8 July 1979, p. 9G.

Carter, Albert Howard, III. "Choice of Love Springs from Squalid Memories." *St. Petersburg* (Fla.) *Times*, 1 July 1979, p. 3G.

Carter, Ron. "Styron Novel Probes Evil of Nazism." *Richmond* (Va.) *Times-Dispatch*, 8 July 1979, p. G5.

Caute, David. "The Longest Journey." *New Statesman* 98 (7 September 1979): 344–345.

Cernyak, Susan E. "Holocaust: Fiction and Documentation." *Cross Currents* 29 (Fall 1979): 349–353 [349–352].

Coale, Sam. "Styron Still Chases Evil and Guilt." *East-Side West-Side* (Providence, R.I.) 6 (14 June 1979): 2A.

Cole, Diane. "Styron's Choice." *National Jewish Monthly* 94 (November 1979): 46, 48–50, 52.

Cole, William. "Styron's Finest." *Cue* 48 (20 July 1979): 114.

Corbett, Bob. "Styron's Cluttered Tale of Guilt." *San Diego Evening Tribune*, 29 June 1979.

Crone, Moira. "Books." *City Paper* (Baltimore, Md.), 7 September 1979, p. 42.

Cunningham, John R. "Evil Plays Role in 'Choice.'" *Pittsburgh Press*, 15 July 1979, p. P6.

Davis, Paxton. "Styron's Fine New Novel Confronts the Holocaust." *Roanoke* (Va.) *Times & World-News*, 15 July 1979, p. F4.

Day, Frank. "'Sophie's Choice': Styron's Superb Portrait of the Novelist as a Young Man." *Charlotte* (N.C.) *Observer*, 3 June 1979, p. 8F.

DeMott, Benjamin. "Styron's Survivor: An Honest Witness." *Atlantic Monthly* 244 (July 1979): 77–79.

Dexter, Bruce. "Not Styron's Best: Dark Secrets." *San Diego Union*, 17 June 1979, *Books* section, pp. 1, 8.

Duhamel, P. Albert. "I've Been Reading: Few Interesting Moments to Ford Autobiography." *Boston Herald American*, 3 June 1979, p. D6.

Edlin, Joseph J. *St. Louis Jewish Light*, 15 August 1979, p. 7.

Elliott, Janice. "Shadow of Auschwitz." *London Sunday Telegraph*, 9 September 1979, p. 12.

Epstein, Leslie. "Novel and Novella." *The Nation* 229 (7 July 1979): 22–23.

Eyrich, Claire. "Into the Vortex of Sophie's Grief." *Fort Worth Star-Telegram*, 3 June 1979, p. 8f.

Feinstein, Elaine. "Fiction." *London Times*, 6 December 1979, p. 13.

Fiedler, Leslie A. "Styron's Choice: A Novel about Auschwitz." *Psychology Today* 13 (July 1979): 102, 104, 106, 108.

Firestone, Bea. "Reader's 'Choice' Becomes Best-Seller." *Kansas City* (Mo.) *Jewish Chronicle*, 29 June 1979, p. 15.

Fisher, Emma. *The Spectator*, no. 7892, 13 October 1979, p. 23.

Foreman, Robin Shea. "William Styron Addresses Prejudice and Its Guilt." *Winston-Salem* (N.C.) *Journal*, 1 July 1979, p. C4.

Frakes, James R. "Styron's Risky Use of Holocaust Misfires." *Cleveland Plain Dealer*, 10 June 1979, sec. 5, p. 22.

Francis, Michael J. "'Sophie's Choice' Called Marvelous Novel, Worthy of Its Extravagant Publicity." *South Bend* (Ind.) *Tribune*, 8 July 1979, *Michiana* section, p. 19.

Freedman, Richard. "An Artistic Triumph about the Persistence of Evil." *Newsday* (Garden City, N.Y.), 3 June 1979, *Ideas* section, p. 20.

Fremont-Smith, Eliot. "Making Book: Styron's Verdict." *Village Voice* 24 (4 June 1979): 89–90.

Friedman, Melvin J. *American Book Review* 2 (October 1979): 17.

Friedman, Robert. "Books in Brief." *New York Post*, 16 June 1979, p. 17.

Fuller, Edmund. "Moral Probing Flawed by Onanistic Dalliance." *Wall Street Journal*, 18 June 1979, p. 22.

Fussell, Paul. "An American Masterpiece." *Washington* (D.C.) *Post*, 20 May 1979, *Book World* section, pp. E1, E6.

Gardner, John. "A Novel of Evil." *New York Times Book Review*, 27 May 1979, pp. 1, 16–17.

Gerchick, Ruth. "In Print." *Scarsdale* (N.Y.) *Inquirer*, 7 June 1979, sec. 1, p. 6.

Getzfred, Mark. "Life's Choices Relived in Novel." *Grand Island* (Nebr.) *Daily Independent*, 21 July 1979, p. 2D.

Godwin, Gail. "A Search through the Darkness of the Holocaust." *Chicago Tribune*, 27 May 1979, *Book World* section, p. 1.

Goodman, Walter. "Artless Morality." *New Leader* 62 (21 May 1979): 10–11.

Gordon, Charles. "Books: Guilt, Big Guilt, in Best Novel of Year." *Ottawa Citizen*, 30 June 1979, p. 52.

Gray, Paul. "Riddle of a Violent Century." *Time* 113 (11 June 1979): 86, 88.

Grossman, Edward. *Hadassah Magazine* 61 (January 1980): 21.

Grumbach, Doris. "A Season Redolent of Worthy Fiction." *Chronicle of Higher Education* 28 (25 June 1979): R12, R13.

Gunn, Janet Varner. "Bonding." *Christian Century* 97 (2 April 1980): 383–384.

Hall, Cody. "'Sophie's Choice' Deep, Dark Descent." *Anniston* (Ala.) *Star*, 1 July 1979, p. 17C.

Hand, Judson. "Books: A Styron in Wolfe's Clothing." *New York Daily News*, 27 May 1979, *Leisure* section, p. 22.

Harris, Roger. "The Book Shelf: Styron Weaves a Grim Tale of the Holocaust." *Newark* (N.J.) *Star Ledger*, 27 May 1979, sec. 4, p. 14.

Hastings, Selina. "Recent Fiction." *London Daily Telegraph*, 6 September 1979, p. 15.

Hayes, E. Nelson. "'One of the Great Fictions of Our Time': Hatred, Evil and the Psychology of Survival." *Worcester* (Mass.) *Sunday Telegram*, 15 July 1979, p. 8E. See also *Boston Ledger*, 15–21 June 1979, pp. 24, 26.

Hearon, Shelby. "Lingering Guilt: Unanswered Questions of the Holocaust." *Dallas Morning News*, 24 June 1979, p. 5G.

Houston, Levin. "Styron's New Novel: An Award-Winner." *Freder-*

icksburg (Va.) *Free Lance-Star*, 16 June 1979, *Town & Country* magazine, p. 12.

Hutner, Geraldine. "Styron's Maelstrom." *Princeton* (N.J.) *Spectrum*, 1 August 1979, pp. 7–8.

Jacobs, Gerald. "Human Counterpoint." *Jewish Chronicle*, 28 September, 1979, p. 18.

Jaynes, Roger. "Souls of Auschwitz." *Milwaukee Journal*, 15 July 1979, part 5, p. 5.

Jeffress, Jim. "They Also Sin Who Merely Stand and Wait." *San Jose* (Calif.) *Mercury News*, 15 July 1979, p. 8B.

Jenkins, Ray. "The Book Shelf: Stunning Novel Examines Essence of Evil." *Montgomery Advertiser–Alabama Journal*, 3 June 1979, p. 16B.

Johnson, Alexandra. "Guilt as Slavemaster." *Christian Science Monitor*, 11 June 1979, p. B1.

Jones, Malcolm. "Styron's Sophie: A Sorrowful Tale." *Greensboro* (N.C.) *Daily News*, 8 July 1979, p. G5.

Jordan, Peter. "Styron's 'Sophie' Fulfills Ambitions." *Nashville Tennessean*, 17 June 1979, p. 10F.

Keller, Karl. "Linking the Southern and Jewish Literary Modes." *Los Angeles Times*, 27 May 1979, *Book Review* section, p. 16.

Kellough, Bill. *Tulsa World*, 8 July 1979, sec. F, p. 6.

Kelso, Dorothy H. "'Sophie's Choice': A Meditation on Evil." *Quincy* (Mass.) *Patriot Ledger*, 22 June 1979.

Kirkus 47 (1 April 1979): 410.

Kissel, Howard. *Women's Wear Daily*, 25 May 1979, sec. 1, p. 56.

Knight-Johnson, Bea. "Good versus Evil in Gothic Prose." *Pacific Sun* (Mill Valley, Calif.), 6–12 July 1979, pp. 19–20.

Koon, William. *Library Journal* 104 (1 June 1979): 1280–1281.

Krisher, Trudy. "Spellbinding, Courageous, Important, One of the Best Novels in Years . . . : Styron's Sophie's Choice." *Dayton Journal Herald*, 16 June 1979.

Lang, Joel. "Novel of Courage and Tragedy." *Hartford Courant*, 24 June 1979, p. 8G.

La Prada, Darrell. "Styron's Artful Ordeal." *Virginian-Pilot and The Ledger Star* (Norfolk, Va.), 24 June 1979, p. C6.

Larrieu, Kay. "'Sophie's Choice': Challenging, Inviting." *Manassas*

(Va.) *Journal Messenger*, 17 August 1979, *Weekend World* section, pp. 6, 9.

La Salle, Peter. "A Choice of Sorts." *America* 141 (28 July 1979): 38–39.

Lehmann-Haupt, Christopher. "Books of the Times." *New York Times*, 29 May 1979, p. C11. See also *Minneapolis Tribune*, 17 June 1979, p. 14G; *Santa Rosa* (Calif.) *Press Democrat*, 8 July 1979; *Toledo Blade*, 10 June 1979, sec. G, p. 10.

Leon, Philip W. "New Styron Novel a Winner." *Charleston* (S.C.) *Sunday*, 27 May 1979, p. 4E.

———. "A Vast Dehumanization." *Virginia Quarterly Review* 55 (Autumn 1979): 740–747.

Levine, Lawrence. "*Sophie's Choice:* Southern Fried Poland." *In These Times* (Chicago), 5 January–7 February 1980, pp. 15–16.

Levy, Paul. "American Giants." *Books and Bookmen* 25 (December 1979): 13–15 [14].

Liebrum, Martha. "In Mighty 'Southern Gothic,' Styron Weaves Several Themes." *Houston Post*, 10 June 1979, p. 8AA.

Malin, Irving. "At the Crossroads." *Present Tense* 7 (Winter 1980): 55–56.

Massie, Allan. "The Styron Style." *The Scotsman* (Edinburgh), 8 September 1979, *Weekend Scotsman* section, p. 3.

May, Derwent. "A Southerner and a Pole." *The Listener* 102 (6 September 1979): 318.

Maza, Michael. "Out of the Holocaust and into the Frying Pan." *Detroit News*, 24 June 1979, p. 2F.

Middleton, Harry. "Styron's 'Choice' Is to Confront Man's Evil Side." *Figaro* (New Orleans), 10 September 1979, p. 22.

Mills, Moylan C. "Styron Novel Acclaimed as 'Magnificent Work.'" *Philadelphia Bulletin*, 1 July 1979, sec. E, p. 4.

Milton, Edith. "Looking Backward: Six Novels." *Yale Review* 69 (Autumn 1979): 89–103 [90–94].

Morris, Robert K. "Styron Weaves a Writer's Holocaust." *St. Louis Globe-Democrat*, 2–3 June 1979, p. 4E.

Murray, James G. *The Critic* 38 (October 1979): 2, 8.

Navrozov, Lev. "*Moujik* 'n' Pulp Sandwich." *Chronicles of Culture* (Rockford College, Rockford, Ill.) 3 (November/December 1979): 7–12.

New Yorker 55 (18 June 1979): 109–110.

Northhouse, Donna. "Confrontation with Evil." *Lone Star Book Review* (Dallas, Tex.) 1 (July 1979): 4, 12.

Oates, Joyce Carol. "'A Blockbuster of a Story.'" *Mademoiselle* 85 (August 1979): 74, 76.

O'Leary, Theodore M. "Styron's Novel Shows the World Has Enough Guilt to Go Around." *Kansas City* (Mo.) *Star*, 22 July 1979, pp. 4E, 12E.

Olson, Clarence E. "The Faces of Evil." *St. Louis Post-Dispatch*, 17 June 1979, p. 4E.

Ott, William. "A Traumatic Decision." *Seattle Times*, 29 July 1979, magazine section, p. 14.

Palmer, Gail Branscome. "A Powerful New Novel Tells of Prejudice, Guilt." *Columbus* (Ohio) *Dispatch*, 1 July 1979, p. I6.

Peterson, Thane. "Guilt and Flaccid Intellectualism." *Twin Cities Reader* (Minneapolis), 24 August 1979, pp. 27–28.

Pintarich, Paul. "Haunting Truth, Insight Fire 'Sophie's Choice.'" *Portland Sunday Oregonian*, 17 June 1979, p. D4.

Prescott, Peter S. "Trials of a Survivor." *Newsweek* 93 (28 May 1979): 89.

Price, K[athleen] McCormick. "Styron Uses Multiple Themes in 'Sophie's Choice.'" *Denver Sunday Post*, 17 June 1979, *Roundup* section, p. 24. See also *San Diego Magazine* 31 (June 1979): 80, 82, 84.

Publishers Weekly 215 (16 April 1979): 70.

Ratliff, Judith. "'Sophie' Goes On and On . . . ." *Arizona Daily Star* (Tucson), 9 September 1979, p. 5I.

Reed, Kit. "'Sophie's Choice' Explores Love, Evil." *New Haven* (Conn.) *Register*, 8 July 1979, p. D5.

Reynolds, Stanley. "Brooklyn Secrets." *Manchester* (England) *Guardian*, 6 September 1979, p. 12.

Robertson, William K. "In Styron's Novel, Holocaust Horrors." *Miami Herald*, 3 June 1979, p. 7E.

Rose, Dan A. "William Styron's New Novel Dares the Holocaust Theme." *Providence* (R.I.) *Sunday Journal*, 10 June 1979, p. H18.

Rosen, Albert. "Styron's 'Sophie's Choice': A Great Novel Generally, for Jews." *Detroit Jewish News*, 7 September 1979, p. 12.

Rosen, Jackie. "Sophie's Story Best Seller for Styron." *Newport News* (Va.) *Times-Herald*, 18 August 1979, p. L2.

Rosenfeld, Alvin H. "The Holocaust According to William Styron." *Midstream* 25 (December 1979): 43–49.

Schopen, Bernard. "'Sophie's Choice' an Excursion into Evil." *Reno Evening Gazette-Nevada State Journal*, 15 July 1979, *Nevada Arts* section, p. 2B.

Sipper, Ralph B. "The Heart of Darkness." *San Francisco Chronicle*, 22 April 1979, *Spring Books* section, pp. 1, 12.

Spearman, Walter. "The Literary Lantern." *The Pilot* (Southern Pines, N.C.), 18 July 1979, sec. B, p. 4.

Starr, William W. "Assignment: Books." *The State* (Columbia, S.C.), 20 May 1979, p. 4E.

Stella, Charles. "The Holocaust: Who Can Ever Understand?" *Cleveland Press*, 7 June 1979, p. D20.

Stinnett, Caskie. "A Stark Tragedy of Tortured and Twisted People." *Boston Sunday Globe*, 3 June 1979, pp. A7, A9.

Styron, Nell Joslin. "'Sophie's Choice.'" *Raleigh* (N.C.) *News and Observer*, 9 September 1979, p. 6IV.

Swindell, Larry. "The Novel We'll Be Talking about All Summer Long." *Philadelphia Inquirer*, 10 June 1979, p. 16F.

Symons, Julian. "The Penalties of Survival." *Times Literary Supplement* (London), 30 November 1979, p. 77.

Talmey, Allene. "Books." *Vogue* 169 (June 1979): 34.

Tatum, Bil. "Styron's 'Sophie' Intense, Moving." *Springfield* (Mass.) *News and Leader*, 18 August 1979.

Taylor, Alex. "A Long Day's Journey into Manhood." *Vancouver* (B.C.) *Sun*, 17 August 1979, *Leisure & TV Week* section, p. 33L.

Taylor, Clement. *Best Sellers* 39 (September 1979): 201.

Thomas, Phil. "William Styron's First Work since '68 Is 'Sophie's Choice.'" *Monterey* (Calif.) *Sunday Peninsula Herald*, 19 August 1979, p. 6C. See also *San Antonio Star*, 29 July 1979: *Jacksonville* (Fla.) *Times-Union and Journal*, 15 July 1979, p. F8; *Asheville* (N.C.) *Citizen-Times*, 15 July 1979, p. 7L; *Torrance* (Calif.) *Daily Breeze*, 13 July 1979; *Memphis Press Scimitar*, 7 July 1979; *Buffalo Courier Express*, 16 July 1979.

Thomas, Sidney. "'Sophie's Choice' Is Searing, Unforgettable." *Atlanta Journal and Constitution*, 8 July 1979, p. 4E.

Thompson, Francis J. "Styron's Variation on Dostoevski." *Tampa Bay* (Fla.) *Tribune-Times*, 17 June 1979, p. 5C.

Towers, Robert. "Stingo's Story." *New York Review of Books* 26 (19 July 1979): 12, 14–16.

Toye, Randall. "William Styron Fails Miserably with New Novel." *Hamilton* (Ontario) *Spectator*, 28 July 1979, *Canadian* magazine, p. 33.

Wade, Rosalind. "Quarterly Fiction Review." *Contemporary Review* 236 (January 1980): 45–49 [45–46].

Wellejus, Ed. "Poland's Travail." *Erie* (Pa.) *Times*, 29 June 1979, p. 5A.

Wells, Lawrence. "William Styron's New Novel Is Masterpiece of Good and Evil." *The Clarion-Ledger and Jackson* (Miss.) *Daily News*, 12 August 1979, sec. G, p. 4.

Wesker, Arnold. "Art between Truth & Fiction: Thoughts on William Styron's Novel." *Encounter* 54 (January 1980): 48, 50, 52, 54–57.

Woessner, Robert. "Styron Asks Hard Questions." *Green Bay* (Wis.) *Press Gazette*, 24 June 1979, sec. A, p. 6.

Wolff, Geoffrey. "Appalling Choices—in Styron's Fiction." *Esquire* 91 (3–19 July 1979): 16, 19.

Yardley, Jonathan. "Breathtaking New Fiction from Styron." *Washington* (D.C.) *Star*, 13 May 1979, *Sunday Calendar* section, pp. B1, B10.

Zarroli, Jim. "Styron's Latest Novel a Tale of Intolerance and Its Ironic Effects." *Daily Collegian* (Pennsylvania State University, State College), 16 July 1979, p. 10.

Ziff, Larzer. "Books: Breaking Sacred Silences." *Commonweal* 106 (11 May 1979): 277–278.

Notes on Contributors

ROBERT K. MORRIS, professor of English at the City College of the City University of New York, is the author of *The Novels of Anthony Powell, The Consolations of Ambiguity: An Essay on the Novels of Anthony Burgess, Continuance and Change: The Contemporary British Novel Sequence*, and *Paradoxes of Order*, as well as a number of reviews and articles on contemporary British and American literature. He has also edited *Old Lines, New Forces: Essays on the Contemporary British Novel, 1960–1970*.

IRVING MALIN, professor of English at the City College of the City University of New York, is the author of *William Faulkner: An Interpretation, New American Gothic, Jews and Americans, Saul Bellow's Fiction, Isaac Bashevis Singer*, and *Nathanael West's Novels*. He has edited critical collections of essays on Bellow, Singer, Capote, and contemporary American Jewish literature, as well as a casebook (with Melvin J. Friedman) on *The Confessions of Nat Turner*. He contributes reviews regularly to numerous periodicals.

JACKSON R. BRYER, professor of English at the University of Maryland, is the author of *The Critical Reputation of F. Scott Fitzgerald*, editor of *Sixteen Modern American Authors: A Survey of Research and Criticism*, and coeditor of *Dear Scott/Dear Max: The Fitzgerald-Perkins Correspondence, F. Scott Fitzgerald in His Own Time: A Miscellany*, F. Scott Fitzgerald's *Basil and Josephine Stories*, and *William Styron: A Reference Guide*.

ARDNER R. CHESHIRE, JR. restores houses in Tucson and teaches American literature, the literature of science and human values, and technical writing at the University of Arizona. His articles have appeared in *The Wordsworth Circle, CLA Journal, The Technical Writing Teacher*, and other publications.

GEORGE CORE, formerly senior editor of the University of Georgia Press, is now editor of the *Sewanee Review*. He is also the editor of two books and the coeditor of two others. His articles and reviews have appeared in the *Southern Review*, the *Southern Literary Journal*, the *Michigan Quarterly Review*, and other periodicals.

JANE FLANDERS teaches American literature and women's studies at the University of Pittsburgh, with a special interest in writers of the American South. She has published, in addition to book reviews and pieces on the teaching of English as a profession, articles about Katherine Anne Porter's "Old Mortality," *Pale Horse, Pale Rider*, and her early nonfiction.

JAN B. GORDON, professor of English at the University of Singapore, has lectured for the State Department as far afield as Dacca, Rangoon, and Port-au-Prince. His essays on Victorian and modern literature have appeared in the *Southern Review*, *Criticism*, the *Journal of Arts and Aesthetics Criticism*, *Kenyon Review*, *Victorian Studies*, *Commonweal*, *ELH*, and *Modern Fiction Studies*. He has also coedited a collection of essays on the fin de siècle entitled *Decadence and the Eighteen Nineties*.

PHILIP W. LEON is associate professor of English at the Citadel and the author of *William Styron: An Annotated Bibliography of Criticism*. His articles and reviews have appeared in the *Southern Literary Journal*, the *Virginia Quarterly Review*, and the *Mississippi Quarterly*, as well as other periodicals.

JOHN O. LYONS, professor of English at the University of Wisconsin at Madison, is the author of *The College Novel in America*, *The Invention of the Self: The Hinge of Consciousness in the Eighteenth Century*, and a number of articles on contemporary literature. He has also been a Fulbright lecturer in Iraq, Iran, and Turkey.

RICHARD PEARCE is professor of English at Wheaton College in Massachusetts. He has written the University of Minnesota pamphlet *William Styron* (republished in Scribner's *American Authors*) and *Stages of the Clown: Perspectives on Modern Fiction from Dos-*

toyevsky to Beckett, as well as edited *Critical Essays on Thomas Pynchon*.

ROBERT PHILLIPS, writer, editor, anthologist, is the author or editor of *Inner Weather* (poems), *The Land of Lost Content* (short stories), *Aspects of Alice* (a critical anthology), *The Confessional Poets* (criticism), *Moonstruck* (an anthology of poetry about the moon), *Denton Welch* (criticism), *William Goyen* (criticism), *Delmore Schwartz' Last and Lost Poems*, and *Running On Empty* (poems). His essays and reviews have appeared in the *New York Times Book Review*, the *Saturday Review*, *Commonweal*, *Centennial Review*, and elsewhere, and his poetry in most of the major literary periodicals.

LOUIS D. RUBIN, JR., University Distinguished Professor of English at the University of North Carolina, is one of the most important contemporary critics of American literature. Among his many books are *The Faraway Country*, *The Writer in the South*, *The Teller in the Tale*, and most recently *Wary Fugitives*. He is coeditor of the *Southern Literary Journal* and the editor of *Thomas Wolfe*, *The Comic Tradition in American Literature*, and other books.

MARY S. STRINE, associate professor of communication at the University of Utah, is the author of reviews and articles on modern critical theory, the rhetoric of literary forms, and the relationship between American literature and culture. She is the book review editor for *Literature in Performance* and is a member of the editorial board for *Liberal and Fine Arts Review*.

Metropolitan Desegregation

Metropolitan Desegregation

Edited by
Robert L. Green
University of the District of Columbia
Washington, D.C.

With the assistance of
Frances S. Thomas
Michigan State University
East Lansing, Michigan

LIBRARY

PLENUM PRESS • NEW YORK AND LONDON

Library of Congress Cataloging in Publication Data

Main entry under title:

Metropolitan desegregation.

Includes bibliographies and index.
1. School integration—Delaware—New Castle County—Addresses, essays, lectures. I.
Green, Robert Lee. II. Thomas, Frances S.
LC214.22.D3M48   1985   370.19′342   85-12032
ISBN 0-306-41964-5

Research for Chapters 2,5,7 and 8 was supported by a grant from the Rockefeller Foundation,
Division of Social Sciences. Special thanks are due Dr. Bruce Williams, Assistant Director for
the Social Sciences Division, for his encouragement and support.

Some of the material in Chapter 9 was abstracted from "Third-Generation School Desegregation Issues: An Agenda for the Future," by R. Griffore, in *Procedures and Pilot Research to
Develop an Agenda for Desegregation Studies* (1981), which was funded entirely by the U.S.
Department of Education. The Department of Education disclaims any official endorsement
of the materials, and no product endorsement should be inferred.

Parts of Chapter 8 are adapted from material that appeared in *The Urban Review,* Volume 13,
Number 2, Summer 1981, and Volume 16, Number 2, 1984.

©1985 Plenum Press, New York
A Division of Plenum Publishing Corporation
233 Spring Street, New York, N.Y. 10013

Printed in the United States of America

This book is dedicated to the memory of our colleague, Rick D. Rapaport, whose joyous, creative, productive life (1954–1985) was dedicated to the pursuit of justice, peace, and human dignity, and to a better future for the victims of oppression and discrimination all over the world—fellow human beings who need from each of us the kind of commitment, caring, and love exemplified in Rick's short life. Rick's work lives on in the lives of the many children of many colors who are showing us the way to make America work, and their parents, teachers, and school administrators who dare to believe in the American ideal for which desegregation stands. To them this book is also dedicated.

Contributors

Joe T. Darden Dean, Urban Affairs Programs, Michigan State University, East Lansing, Michigan

Robert L. Green President, University of the District of Columbia, Washington, District of Columbia

Robert J. Griffore Department of Family and Child Ecology, Michigan State University, East Lansing, Michigan

Margaret A. Parsons Greater Flint Health Maintenance Organization, Flint, Michigan

Diana Pearce Center for National Policy Review, Catholic University School of Law, Washington, District of Columbia

Julie Schmidt Department of Educational Studies, University of Delaware, Newark, Delaware

John H. Schweitzer Urban Affairs Programs, Michigan State University, East Lansing, Michigan

Cassandra A. Simmons Urban Affairs Programs, Affirmative Action Graduate Financial Assistance Program, Michigan State University, East Lansing, Michigan

Frances S. Thomas Urban Affairs Programs, Michigan State University, East Lansing, Michigan

Meyer Weinberg Horace Mann Bond Center for Equal Education, University of Massachusetts, Amherst, Massachusetts

Preface

Most of the findings in this book are based on the work of a team of researchers from Urban Affairs Programs at Michigan State University. From 1976 to 1981, the team observed the progress of school desegregation in metropolitan Wilmington, Delaware, which encompasses New Castle County. The project was made possible by a grant from the Rockefeller Foundation, Division of Social Sciences.

Metropolitan desegregation is a strategy deserving of national attention because this country's black population has become increasingly concentrated within central cities. Desegregation solutions must be found that encompass America's white suburbs as well as its urban areas.

In a 1977 statement, the U.S. Commission on Civil Rights called metropolitan school desegregation "the last frontier to be crossed in the long judicial effort to make equal educational opportunity . . . a living reality." Moreover, the National Task Force on Desegregation Strategies concluded in 1979,

> The simple demographic fact is that many large city school districts cannot desegregate by themselves. For children in such districts, the best hope for attending a desegregated school lies in the implementation of metropolitan desegregation strategies—i.e., desegregation plans which do not stop at the city line, but rather encompass at least some of the surrounding suburban areas. (p. 1)

The Michigan State University research team began its investigation in New Castle County, Delaware, after a three-judge federal district court ruled that area schools were illegally segregated between districts.[1] The court determined that governmental action affecting the entire region had contributed to the racial separation of the primarily black urban core from its ring of nearly all-white suburbs. The court consolidated Wilmington and its surrounding suburban school districts, and then ordered countywide busing to desegregate the schools throughout the metropolitan area.

In its 5-year study, the research team assessed the attitudes and academic achievement levels of selected students as well as the attitudes of selected teachers and parents in New Castle County. In four of the nine chapters of this book, members of the MSU team present the data from this case study and discuss the conclusions that were drawn. Other writers from other institutions analyze pre-

[1]*Evans v. Buchanan,* 416 F. Supp. 328 (1976).

vious research on school desegregation in order to provide a context for the Wilmington/New Castle County study.

In the first chapter, the legal and educational history of school segregation and desegregation is set forth. The position advocated is that of the United States Commission on Civil Rights, which stated in 1979 that "no more important challenge faces the Nation than the elimination of all discrimination from our public schools" (p. viii).

In the second chapter, the history of school desegregation in New Castle County is reviewed. Emphasis is placed on the political context within which desegregation occurred and the political waves that flowed in its wake. The analysis is based on media coverage of the desegregation process and on interviews with many of the participants.

In Chapter 3, educational components in desegregation remedies are described. Increasingly, the judicial system has come to recognize the need to alter the policies of desegregating districts in order to help undereducated minority children catch up, and to counteract the deleterious effects of past segregated schooling. The author analyzes the legal justification, the educational need, and the effectiveness of the various components.

In Chapter 4, research findings are presented on the relationship between residential and educational segregation and the effects of school desegregation on this relationship. The author of this chapter has undertaken ground-breaking research on the effects of neighborhood racial composition on racial attitudes and on attitudes about school desegregation.

Attitudes about race and education, as expressed by students and parents from New Castle County neighborhoods of varying racial compositions, are analyzed in Chapter 5. The data show that neighborhood racial composition accounts for differences in attitudes not accounted for by race *per se*.

Chapter 6 presents a summary of selected research on relationships between school desegregation and academic achievement. The author notes that results vary depending on the methodology of the research and the sincerity of the desegregation effort. The conclusion is presented that successful desegregation can improve academic achievement for black and other minority students without inflicting educational damage on white students.

The achievement data from the New Castle County study are analyzed in Chapter 7. The findings indicate that for both black and white pupils there was a definite increase in achievement after desegregation. Achievement gains were generally greater for black pupils; for pupils at the elementary level, both black and white; and for all pupils in the area of mathematics.

In Chapter 8, the author examines the attitudes of New Castle County students and parents about race, schools, and education, before and after school desegregation. She observes that the most positive attitudes about race were evidenced at the earliest grades, suggesting that younger children are more likely than their older siblings to learn positive racial attitudes through school deseg-

regation. Differences in attitudes and attitudinal changes related to variables such as race, sex, and socioeconomic status are also noted.

In the final chapter, recent trends in desegregation research are traced, focusing on the family's role in children's educational achievement in desegregated schools. The author also discusses new directions for research on education and desegregation, and suggests an ecological perspective as a framework for conceptualizing school desegregation and organizing future research.

It is our hope that the information provided in this book will enlarge public understanding of desegregation in general, and metropolitan desegregation in particular. Students of America's progress toward the goal of equal educational opportunities for all children may find the data from the study of metropolitan desegregation in Wilmington/New Castle County, Delaware, to be of particular interest. The authors share the conviction that integrated education is necessary to prepare children—of all races—for full participation in our multiracial world.

This study of metropolitan desegregation could not have been completed without the assistance of numerous colleagues. Thanks are due Rick D. Rapaport for excellent researching services; Dr. Joe T. Darden for coordinating tasks; and Barbara Gaffield, Roberta Grange, Shirley Hoksbergen, and Marie McNutt for typing the manuscript. Special appreciation is due Dr. Frances Thomas for her services in critiquing and editing the various chapters. On behalf of the authors, I want to express our gratitude for the assistance of these persons.

ROBERT L. GREEN

Contents

CHAPTER 6

IMPROVING EDUCATION IN DESEGREGATED SCHOOLS 143

Meyer Weinberg

CHAPTER 7

SCHOOL AND INDIVIDUAL ACHIEVEMENT FOLLOWING
DESEGREGATION IN NEW CASTLE COUNTY, DELAWARE 161

John H. Schweitzer

CHAPTER 8

PARENTS' AND STUDENTS' ATTITUDE CHANGES RELATED TO SCHOOL
DESEGREGATION IN NEW CASTLE COUNTY, DELAWARE 185

Margaret A. Parsons

1

Desegregation

ROBERT L. GREEN

In September 1978, buses rolled throughout metropolitan Wilmington, Delaware. In so doing, they rolled past the major legal boundary blocking efforts to desegregate the nation's schools: city limits. The buses carried children from virtually all-black neighborhoods in the central city to formerly all-white classrooms in the suburbs. They also brought suburban white children to schools in the black community. The exchange of students marked the first time that a court had compelled school children to cross former school district boundaries for the purpose of desegregation.

THE NEED TO DESEGREGATE AMERICAN EDUCATION

The advisability of metropolitan school desegregation is not predicated on any value inherent in placing young people on school buses. Some might prefer that racial integration occur more "organically," through the mingling of minority and majority group members on jobs and in neighborhoods, and in the schools only after neighborhoods have been desegregated. Unfortunately, this is unrealistic. More than two centuries of slavery and nearly another of legal and quasi-legal segregation have left a residue of irrational fear and suspicion that makes substantial residential integration unlikely in the near future. Furthermore, the vestiges of inferior segregated schooling, along with present-day discrimination, make successful black competition in the job market difficult. The employment situation for blacks is improving only slowly and incrementally, and then only in response to considerable legal and political pressure.

ROBERT L. GREEN ● President, University of the District of Columbia, Washington, District of Columbia 20008.

Education, therefore, must lead in efforts to integrate blacks into the main-stream of American society. Because schools play an important role in trans-mitting a society's culture and values (Bullivant, 1982), they should be teaching, by lesson and experience, the benefits of racial harmony. Nazi Germany dem-onstrates the potential negative power of education in this regard. School children began receiving indoctrination at the age of 6, and many joined the fanatic Hitler Youth organization at age 10. "We were too young to doubt the validity of what we heard," a former Hitler Youth leader (Hecht, 1982) wrote. Near the end of World War II, when defeat seemed obvious to most adults, Hitler Youth boys of 16 were still willing to join the militia. "Many of the . . . men 60 and older who had also been drafted quickly surrendered or disappeared in the general chaos," he wrote. "But not the Hitler Youth. To many of us, defeat was worse than death. It was a form of state-induced madness." If children can be taught destructive lessons like Nazi fanaticism, imagine the constructive force that could be unleashed if society committed itself with comparable rigor to develop its positive potential.

Desegregation in education must precede progress in employment and hous-ing for yet another reason: segregated schooling tends to be inferior schooling, which leaves minority group members at a disadvantage when competing in the job market. Employment statistics for black Americans tell a bleak tale (U.S. Department of Labor, 1983). In December 1982, this country's unemployment rate was 10.3%; for blacks, the rate was nearly twice as high, with 20.2% jobless. Even more discouraging, nearly half of all black teenagers who wanted and were looking for jobs could not find them. Much of this inequity results from overt and covert racial discrimination. In addition, two structural changes underway in the national economy have compounded the problem. First, count-less industrial plants that once provided black employment in Northern urban areas have closed up shop and exported their jobs to the suburbs, the South, or overseas. Second, other plants that once employed blacks have closed altogether, victims of changing technologies and international competition. American blacks, who have yet to overcome two and a half centuries of slavery, are bearing a disproportionate share of the suffering wrought by these changes.

Meanwhile, the nation's public schools (particularly urban public schools) are failing to provide many American children (particularly minority children) with the basic school skills (Levine & Havighurst, 1977). It has become ac-ceptable to blame the children, their parents, or their neighborhoods for the schools' failures. It seems clear, however, that with about 25 million American adults functionally illiterate (Lubow, Howard, Begley, LaBrecque, & Morris, 1978), unable to manage necessary transactions requiring minimal ability to read and write, the schools themselves must account for the problem. This seems especially clear given the racial and ethnic composition of the nation's functional illiterates: 44% of all blacks and 56% of those with Spanish surnames read at

the lowest ability level, compared with 16% of the white population (Kozol, 1980).

The United States education system prepares many minority group Americans only for menial labor, the military, or unemployment. Consequently, minority group Americans in disproportionate numbers do menial work, staff the military, or do nothing economically productive at all. According to U.S. government statistics for 1983 (U.S. Dept. of Labor, 1983), blacks, who constitute 11.7% of the American population, provide 39.1% of the housekeepers, 41.1% of the garbage collectors, and 48.5% of the cleaners and servants. They provide only 6.9% of the engineers, 3.6% of the lawyers, and 2.4% of the airplane pilots. Meanwhile, America's military is becoming increasingly black, rising steadily from 11.4% in 1971 to 21.6% in 1980. As robots and computers increasingly take on society's menial labor, vast numbers of minorities will likely be relegated to the armed forces or the welfare lines. Our only alternative is to improve public education. Apart from obvious moral considerations, a concern for national defense, economic productivity, and social harmony should encourage Americans to look favorably on ways to prepare all children to participate productively in our society.

Researchers of social conditions often uncover relationships that can be interpreted in subjective ways. Biased analysis can yield inappropriate conclusions. For example, when public schools in Chicago are listed in order from those serving the most affluent to those serving the least affluent neighborhoods, the list roughly approximates a ranking of schools from the highest to the lowest in academic achievement. That same list parallels one indicating the racial composition of the schools, with one end showing a high concentration of whites and the other end showing a high concentration of blacks (Green, 1981b, p. 15). Some might interpret this to mean that blacks are inherently less intelligent and deserve to be at the low end of the economic range. The fact is, however, that some schools with very high concentrations of black students do very well to promote high academic achievement among all children, regardless of race. Therefore, something other than demography must be afflicting those schools with low levels of achievement. That something is pervasive racial discrimination (Green, 1977, 1981a).

SEGREGATION

Although white Americans often find it difficult to comprehend the extent of racial discrimination in this country, the facts show that American society has routinely and systematically limited the opportunities of its minority population. This discrimination has been particularly apparent in the public schools.

To understand school segregation, and consequently the need for deseg-

regation, one must keep in mind this nation's history. The vast majority of black Americans are on this continent because their ancestors were kidnapped in Africa and brought here by force. With violence and terror, a white power structure kept "law and order" on the plantations for more than 200 years, while enslaved blacks produced much of this country's early wealth. Very few learned to read. The law forbade it, and the white legal system enforced no statute in the slave code more rigidly than that against educating black slaves. The first such law appeared in South Carolina in 1740 (Washington, 1900). By 1829, the Georgia legislature had expanded the prohibition to include "free persons of color." Whites who broke that law could be fined up to $500 and imprisoned indefinitely. A black person guilty of the same "crime" faced a fine or a vicious whipping.

This law enforcement may seem peculiar today, but people in power have long known the political wisdom of restricting education: uneducated people are more easily controlled. Thus, even with the cessation of slavery and the adoption of the Constitutional amendments that were supposed to confer on blacks the rights of American citizenship, true liberation did not follow. After Reconstruction, the South settled into a dark era of structural segregation which disorganized, undereducated blacks were in no position to resist. Southern segregation was enforced, under sanction of law, with a violence and terror only slightly less than that used during slavery. Meanwhile, wave after wave of blacks streamed out of the South to jobs in the growing industrial centers of the North. In response, Northern whites developed a somewhat more subtle form of segregation nearly as effective as that employed in the South.

There would be little purpose in distinguishing between the Northern and Southern versions of urban segregation were not the distinction emphasized by the courts in school desegregation law. As Robert L. Carter, president of the National Committee against Discrimination in Housing, told a U.S. Senate committee in 1970, Northern-style *de facto* segregation and Southern-style *de jure* segregation are very much the same—"except the South has been more open and candid in its approach to the question" (U.S. Senate, 1971, p. 2645). Segregation harms the children of both races, whether separation results from official action or from officially sanctioned private choices. However, the judicial system has lent great weight to the differences between the two, so I will address each.

Educational segregation in the South was a straightforward affair. Jim Crow laws established, with neither pretense nor apology, separate schools for black children. Although in 1896 the Supreme Court, in *Plessy v. Ferguson,*[1] told black Americans that their separate facilities were supposed to be equal to those of white, experience told them otherwise. As Wilkinson (1979) wrote, "In time, equal became a ghost word, a balm for the nation's conscience, a token of the law's hollow symmetry and logic, but quite irrelevant insofar as the Negro was

[1] 163 U.S. 537 (1896).

concerned" (p. 19). The irrelevance and hypocrisy of "separate but equal" showed clearly 3 years after the doctrine was announced. In 1899, the Supreme Court allowed the Richmond County Board of Education to meet a financial emergency by closing its separate black schools. "The colored school children of the county would not be advanced in the matter of their education by a decree compelling the defendant Board to cease giving support to a high school for white children," the Court reasoned.[2]

Even when schools for black children were provided, facilities were substantially inferior to those offered white children. For example, South Carolina in 1915 spent nearly 10 times as much to educate each white child as it spent for each black child (Bell, 1973, p. 452). In 1931, six Southern states (Alabama, Arkansas, Florida, Georgia, and the Carolinas) spent more than 3 times as much. This should surprise no one, because the parents and grandparents of white children traditionally have served on the school boards that make the allocation decisions, whereas black parents and grandparents, until recently, have stood by powerless. The Supreme Court only recognized the obvious when in 1954 it ruled in the landmark *Brown* decision that "separate educational facilities are inherently unequal."[3]

In the North, segregation in education began long before the Civil War. By the 1830s, whether by statute or by custom, black children attended separate schools in nearly every community in the North (Litwack, 1973). Early Northern school segregation resembled that in the South. In the 19th century, for example, a committee of the Ohio Legislature rejected a petition to grant blacks a share of education money because the benefits of education—"morality, virtue, and wisdom"—were important only for whites (p. 441). In the 1870s, after the courts required Ohio officials to educate blacks, the state legislature passed a law allowing school boards to consolidate districts in order to economically provide separate schools for black students (p. 443).

Northern education segregation in the 19th century involved relatively few blacks, because so few lived in the North at that time. Migration out of the rural South increased near the end of the century due to sagging agricultural production, and intensified as Northern industrialists recruited blacks as strike breakers. As this migration continued in the early decades of this century, the segregationist strategy of Northern whites expanded to include efforts aimed at keeping blacks and whites not only in separate schools, but in separate residential neighborhoods as well. Some local authorities enacted ordinances requiring segregated residential neighborhoods, but these were ruled unconstitutional by the Supreme Court in 1917.[4] As the century progressed, however, segregationists developed more artful machinations that achieved the same effect.

---

[2] *Cumming v. Richmond Board of Education,* 175 U.S. 528 (1899), 544.

[3] *Brown v. Board of Education,* 347 U.S. 483 (1953), 495.

[4] *Buchanan v. Warley,* 245 U.S. 60 (1917).

White men in virtually every institution of American society worked to channel this black migration into the country's urban ghettos. The federal government contributed greatly to this process. In 1938, for example, the Federal Housing Administration's underwriting manual for loan agents (U.S. FHA, 1938) counted "inharmonious racial groups" among its list of "adverse influences" that could jeopardize property values (para. 935). The FHA warned particularly that, in suburban areas, loan agents should make certain that insured properties were encumbered by "effective restrictive covenants" to prohibit "the occupancy of properties except by the race for which they are intended" (para. 979). Furthermore, appraisers were told to undervalue properties in racially mixed neighborhoods. This encouraged white families to relocate in suburbs with skyrocketing land values rather than in central cities where values were on the decline.

George Romney, Secretary of Housing and Urban Development in the early 1970s, testified before a Senate committee (U.S. Senate, 1971) that "an unwritten but well-understood agreement between financial interests and FHA," called for lenders to "redline" many central city neighborhoods. Romney said these predominantly minority enclaves were thereby doomed to "an unfavorable economic future" (p. 2755). Loans in areas with unfavorable futures were discouraged. Thus in 1972, a U.S. Senate subcommittee concluded that the FHA and the Veterans' Administration (VA) had financed more than $120 billion of new housing, of which "less than 2% has been available to non-white families, and much of that on a strictly segregated basis" (U.S. Senate, 1972, p. 249).

Public housing policies have exacerbated the segregative effect of federal loan programs. Subsidized projects have provided poor people less than one-tenth the number of units that have been provided upper-income families with federal financing (National Advisory Commission, 1968, p. 474). Yet the site selection for these poverty projects reinforces the view that the federal government consciously set out to ghettoize urban blacks. If we compare a map of public housing built in the city of Chicago with a map indicating neighborhoods with the highest concentrations of black residents, we discover that the two maps coincide (Green, 1981b, pp. 650, 680). In metropolitan Indianapolis, all 10 low-income housing projects built between 1966 and 1970 were sited within the city limits; none was built in the suburbs (Taylor, 1979). All 10 Indianapolis projects opened 50% to 75% black, and became 98% black soon thereafter. In 1962, 80% of all subsidized public housing was either all white or all black (Grier & Grier, 1968, p. 128).

The government has operated what amounts to a two-tier housing policy: it has subsidized single family dwellings in the suburbs, primarily for the white middle class, and central city projects, primarily for poor blacks. As the U.S. Senate Select Committee on Equal Educational Opportunity reported in 1972, "The federal government's involvement in residential segregation was not a matter of inadvertence or neglect. It was conscious, stated policy" (p. 249).

Policies and practices of the United States real estate industry have rein-

forced the federal government's efforts to segregate American cities. The most prestigious national organization of homesellers, the National Association of Real Estate Boards (NAREB, now known as the National Association of Realtors),[5] operated according to an overt segregationist policy long after 1948, when restrictive covenants were finally deemed unconstitutional (U.S. Commission on Civil Rights, 1973). The organization adopted an open housing policy only in 1968, with the passage of the 1968 Civil Rights Act, legislation that the realtors had strongly opposed.

Despite extensive legislation intended to reduce residential segregation, the racial isolation of black Americans decreased little in the 1960s and 1970s (Orfield, 1977, p. 45). In fact, racial isolation in metropolitan areas may actually have increased (deLeeuw, Schnare, & Struyk, 1977, p. 152). This has resulted in part from the lack of a comprehensive desegregation policy, and in part from a failure to enforce the laws that do exist. After 4 years of the community block grant program, the Department of Housing and Urban Development never cited civil rights violations as the basis for disapproving an application. Rather, the Department allowed known violations to continue (U.S. Commission on Civil rights, 1979b, p. 6). Furthermore, research in the late 1970s (Orfield, 1979) indicated that widespread discrimination and steering—the use of subtle influence to direct home buyers to racially homogeneous neighborhoods—still infected the housing market. In addition, public officials have developed a host of methods to manipulate zoning and other statutes to further segregation (Dimond, 1981, p. 74). Despite public perceptions to the contrary (Orfield, 1977), the nation has made little progress toward housing desegregation.

Housing segregation does not derive from the inability of black families to afford integrated housing. As demographers Karl and Alma Taeuber (1965) have pointed out, "The net effect of economic factors in explaining residential segregation is slight" (p. 94). If Detroit residents in 1970 had been distributed between the central city and the suburbs strictly according to income, 67% of the area's blacks would have lived in the suburbs (Orfield, 1977, p. 46). As it was, the urban-suburban boundary line was much more a racial than an economic demarcation, with the city 43.7% black, and some suburbs more than 99% white. Dearborn, a middle-class suburb, was less than 1% black in the early 1970s. It is further significant to note that Detroit's blacks have been more segregated than the city's other ethnic groups (Taeuber, 1975, p. 839).

In short, Northern residential segregation derives from the willful acts of public officials and others operating under official sanction. These actions continue to the present day, as do the psychological and economic reverberations of actions taken in the past. As Orfield (1977) noted, "The principal restraints on the mobility of [black families] appear to be the momentum of past expec-

---

[5] Members of NAREB claim sole use of the term "realtor." It has been estimated (Denton, 1967, p. 54) that brokers on NAREB's boards handled 90% of all real estate transactions.

tations, continuing pervasive segregationist practices in the real estate industry, and the mounting inflation-fueled intitial costs of purchasing a home" (p. 47). Given all this, one must wonder at those who would attribute residential segregation to "unknown and perhaps unknowable factors."[6]

In recent years, school board officials facing desegregation lawsuits have been inclined to acknowledge state and local responsibility for segregated housing patterns, while maintaining their own innocence of complicity in creating segregated schools. In 1967, however, the U.S. Commission on Civil Rights found that "the policies and practices of school systems also have an impact. These policies are seldom neutral in effect. They either reduce or reinforce racial concentrations in the schools" (p. 39).

Extensive litigation has shown repeatedly that school policies and practices have tended to reinforce rather than reduce the school effects of residential segregation. One commentator (Smedley, 1973) has summarized the various school-related practices that courts have deemed unconstitutionally segregative:

> Revision of attendance zone boundaries as population shifts with racial implications occurred; failure to revise boundaries to alleviate overcrowding of schools with student bodies of predominantly one race and to prevent underusage of schools with student bodies of predominantly the other race; location of new school buildings and use of portable classrooms in a manner resulting in a minimization of integration of student bodies; fixing the size of new buildings so that they have a capacity to serve only the uniracial area surrounding them; assignment of teachers and administrators in a way which indicated that certain schools were intended primarily for white students and certain other schools were intended primarily for black students; establishing bus transportation routes which tended to take black students to predominantly black schools rather than to predominantly white schools nearer to their homes; voluntary student transfers in situations which enabled white students to avoid attending predominantly black schools; use of optional attendance zones for racially changing residential areas, thus allowing students to choose not to attend a school in which they would be in a racial minority; failure to adopt recommended school reorganization plans which would have resulted in greater desegregation of student bodies; and allocation of school operating and maintenance funds in a way which perpetuated the inferior quality of predominantly black schools and thereby discouraged white students from attending them. (pp. 424–425)

School boards in both the North and South have used such policies with great effect. By 1974, despite two decades of desegregation litigation, two thirds of all black students in the country attended majority black schools (U.S. Commission on Civil Rights, 1977). Two black students in five attended intensely segregated schools, in which more than 90% of their fellow students were black. In the nation's 26 largest standard metropolitan statistical areas, fully three quarters of all black public school children attended intensely segregated schools. The figures vary somewhat between regions. In the South, where desegregation litigation began first and has been pursued longest, 23% of the black children

---

[6] *Milliken v. Bradley*, 418 U.S. 717 (1974), 756 (Stewart, J., concurring).

attended intensely segregated schools in 1974. In the Midwest, the figure was almost two out of three, or 62% (Center for National Policy Review, 1977).

Segregation is no accident. It is the foreseeable result of conscious policy decisions by whites in power. Its extremely negative effects on black children particularly, but upon white children as well, make it offensive and dangerous policy. The inferior education many black children obtain in segregated schools leaves them unprepared to compete in the job market with better-schooled whites. In addition, both black and white children, taught in separate schools, develop erroneous perceptions about themselves and one another. As the district court in one desegregation case stated, segregated schools "damage the minds of all children who attend them—the Negro, the white, the poor and the affluent— and block the attainment of broader goals of democratic education, whether the segregation occurs by law or by fact."[7]

Former National Education Association President Donald Morrison recognized this in 1972, when in response to President Nixon's anti-busing rhetoric, he stated that

> school segregation is as wrong educationally as it is constitutionally. It provides a poor learning environment. It instills feelings of inferiority in black children and robs them of the confidence they need to learn. It limits their ambitions and aspirations. It gives them a wholly unrealistic concept of the world into which they will emerge upon leaving school. And it has an adverse effect on the attitudes and expectations of teachers. (Morrison, 1972, p. 538)

J. Kenneth Morland (1972) found that children in segregated schools develop positive attitudes about their own race, and at the same time develop negative notions about members of the other race. However, black children are likely to take this a step further by internalizing the negative implications of segregated schooling. As Nancy St. John (1975) concluded from her review of desegregation research, "To separate [black children] from others of similar age and qualifications solely because of their race generates a feeling of inferiority as to their status in the community that may affect their hearts and minds in a way unlikely ever to be undone" (p. 46).

Segregation's harms are not confined to black children. A statement by social scientists filed during the 1954 *Brown* litigation argued that, in the long run, white children also suffer. As summarized by Schofield (1981), the statement contended that

> white children living under government-enforced segregation may develop unrealistic self-appraisals and experience moral conflict as they discover the gap between adult emphasis on values such as justice and brotherhood and a social system which fosters prejudice and discrimination. (p. 227)

Although segregation injures both black and white children by fostering unhealthy attitudes, blacks suffer a far greater debilitation: an unequal education

---

[7] *Hobson v. Hansen*, 269 F. Supp. 401 (1967), 406.

that does not prepare them to participate fully in American life. This inequality can be readily observed. For example, according to Green and Cohen (1979), black and white children tested as equals when they entered the Kalamazoo, Michigan, public schools. Under segregated schooling, an achievement gap, with whites outscoring blacks, opened during the first few years and widened as the children progressed through school. After desegregation, however, that gap began to close. A survey of national data in the mid-1960s (Coleman *et al.*, 1966) showed a similar tendency for the disparity between black and white achievement levels to increase as students moved through school. In the 6th grade, whites outperformed blacks in verbal achievement by the equivalent of 1.5 years; by the 12th grade, the gap had doubled to 3 years.

The Kerner Commission (National Advisory Commission, 1968) blamed centuries of white racism, including that endemic to the country's educational system, for the conditions of distrust and despair that led to the violent disturbances of the late 1960s. Since then, the lives of some blacks have improved. In certain basic ways, however, most blacks are still oppressed. Millions of black Americans have seen little significant change; they have only grown older and more frustrated.

I favor educational desegregation because I believe all children deserve a better, more just future than they are likely to get with segregated schooling. We are all in this world together, and together we face countless global perils. Contending with the threat of nuclear annihilation would provide plentiful challenge even to a world undivided by issues of race. But divided we are, and it is a potentially explosive division. We must address the problem directly, and educational desegregation is one critical place to start. If we do not learn to live together, we will certainly die together. If children do not learn new ways to cooperate and coexist, who will?

DESEGREGATION

School desegregation is a political, social, and educational issue. It is also a deeply personal issue. As Nathaniel Jones, then General Counsel for the NAACP, reminded a desegregation conference sponsored by Michigan State University in 1976:

> When school desegregation reaches the point of litigation, it is because the political process has been unresponsive. Parents who are really concerned about their children's education have found it necessary to look to the legal process to seek vindication. The plaintiffs on whose behalf these suits are brought are not phantoms. They are real-live people concerned about their children. (p. iv)

Even before the Civil War, black parents began legal efforts to enable their children to gain access to white schools. In 1950, a Massachusetts court upheld

the legality of school segregation, denying that it violated the state's constitutional guarantee of equality for black citizens.[8] Numerous legal actions after the Civil War also usually resulted in adverse decisions. According to Bell (1973), these decisions were often based on the premise that race was a reasonable basis for classification, and so state laws requiring segregation were simple regulations, and not abridgement of rights protected by the 13th and 14th Amendments.

The courts in these early cases based their decisions on the availability of separate schools for blacks. This doctrine of "separate but equal" was later enshrined by the Supreme Court in *Plessey v. Ferguson* in 1896.

> The object of the [Fourteenth] Amendment was undoubtedly to enforce the absolute equality of the two races before the law, but in the nature of things it could not have been intended to abolish distinctions based upon color, or to enforce social, as distinguished from political equality, or comingling of the two races upon terms unsatisfactory to either.[9]

The Supreme Court only 3 years later made a mockery of *Plessey's* call for equality, sustaining a ruling by the Georgia Supreme Court that allowed a school board to close its black high school for purely economic reasons.[10] Thus, for more than half a century preceding the *Brown* decision in 1954, the courts rebuffed black parents not only in their efforts to attain integration, but also in their efforts to assure equality of their children's separate educational opportunities.

The Supreme Court finally began to erode the "separate but equal" doctrine in 1950. In *Sweatt v. Painter,*[11] a black student had been barred from the University of Texas Law School and consigned to a separate all-black facility. The Supreme Court noted that the white school offered, among other things, a larger faculty, more course variety, and a better library. Due to the inequality of the two institutions, the Court ordered the plaintiff's admission to the white law school. The Supreme Court, however, explicitly refused in *Sweatt* to rule on the constitutionality of the *Plessey* "separate but equal" doctrine. This awaited the decision in 1954 of *Brown v. Board of Education.*[12]

Five cases had been consolidated into *Brown,* and the Supreme Court exercised jurisdiction to decide whether separate educational facilities for black and white children violated the rights of blacks to equal protection of the law under the Fourteenth Amendment.

> Here, unlike *Sweatt v. Painter,* there are findings below that the Negro and white schools involved have been equalized, or are being equalized, with respect to build-

---

[8] *Roberts v. City of Boston,* 59 Mass. 198 (1850), cited in *Brown v. Board of Education,* 347 U.S. 483 (1954), 491.

[9] 163 U.S. 537 (1896), 544.

[10] *Cumming v. Richmond County Board of Education,* 175 U.S. 528 (1890).

[11] 339 U.S. 629 (1950).

[12] 347 U.S. 483 (1954).

ings, curricula, qualifications and salaries of teachers, and other "tangible" factors.
Our decision, therefore, cannot turn on merely a comparison of these tangible factors . . . We must look instead to the effect of segregation itself on public education.[13]

In assessing that effect, the Court found "separate" to be incompatible with
"equal," and repudiated the premises of the *Plessey* doctrine:

> Whatever may have been the extent of psychological knowledge at the time of *Plessey
> v. Ferguson,* this finding [that segregation deprives black children of benefits they
> would receive in integrated schools] is amply supported by modern authority. Any
> language in *Plessey v. Ferguson* contrary to this finding is rejected.
>
> We conclude that in the field of public education the doctrine of "separate but
> equal" has no place. Separate educational facilties are inherently unequal. Therefore,
> we hold that the plaintiffs . . . are, by reason of the segregation complained of,
> deprived of the equal protection of the laws guaranteed by the Fourteenth Amend-
> ment.[14]

The Supreme Court remanded the *Brown* cases to their respective district
courts for remedies. The cases reappeared before the Justices in *Brown II*[15] a
year later, at which time the Court refused to grant plaintiffs' request for immediate integration. The Justices' gradualist approach required only that the
defendants make a "prompt and reasonable start toward full compliance" with
the *Brown I* ruling. "Once such a start has been made," the Court continued,
"the courts may find that additional time is necessary."[16] Finally, the Court again
remanded the cases,[17] calling on the district courts to bring about nondiscriminatory school admission with "all deliberate speed."[18]

The "prompt and reasonable start" and " all deliberate speed" qualifiers may
have seemed at the time to offer fair allowance for administrative difficulties
school districts were likely to encounter in the desegregation process. However,
the provisions turned out to provide loopholes for the obstructionists. As Robert
Carter (1973) wrote:

> The formula adopted by the Court—requiring a "good faith" start in the transformation
> from a dual to a unitary school system, with compliance being accomplished with
> "all deliberate speed"—was a grave mistake. . . . Until *Brown II,* constitutional rights
> had been defined as personal and present. In the exercise of that ephemeral quality
> called judicial statesmanship, the Warren Court sacrificed individual and immediate
> vindication of the newly discovered right to desegregated education in favor of a mass
> solution.
>
> The Court undoubtedly failed to realize the depth and nature of the problem.
> It . . . apparently believed that its show of compassion and understanding of the

---

[13] *Id.* at 492.

[14] *Id.* at 494–495.

[15] *Brown v. Board of Education (Brown II),* U.S. 294 (1955).

[16] *Id.* at 300.

[17] Except the Delaware case, in which the lower court had ordered the admission of black children
to the previously all-white schools.

[18] *Brown II,* 349 U.S. 294 (1955), 301.

problem facing the white South would help develop a willingness to comply. Instead
the "all deliberate speed" formula allowed the hope that resistance to the constitutional
imperative would succeed. (pp. 456–457)

It was only after a decade of delay that the Court finally determined in 1964
that "the time for mere 'deliberate speed' has run out."[19] In the interim, very
little progress had been made, with less than 2% of Southern black children
attending school with white students in the 1963–64 school year (Carter, 1973,
p. 460).

White Southern officials had developed numerous methods of resisting segregation. Among the most prevalent was the so-called "freedom-of-choice" system, under which children of either race were supposedly entitled to attend either
the formerly black or the formerly white schools. Predictably, most white children
continued to attend white schools, and few black children were willing to risk
the physical danger and psychological pressure of crossing the color line. The
constitutionality of a freedom-of-choice plan in New Kent County, Virginia,
was addressed by the Supreme Court in 1968. The Court ruled that

a plan that at this late date fails to provide meaningful assurance of prompt and
effective disestablishment of a dual system is . . . intolerable. . . . The burden of a
school board today is to come forward with a plan that promises realistically to work,
and promises realistically to work *now*.[20]

The Court noted that in the 3 years of freedom-of-choice, no white child
had chosen to attend the "black" school; and that although 115 black children
had enrolled in the "white" school in 1967, 85% of the black children still
attended the "black" school. "In other words," the Court ruled, "the school
system remains a dual system." The Court ordered the district to "convert permanently to a system without a 'white' and a 'Negro' school, but just schools."[21]

Having announced unequivocally in 1968 its intent to disestablish dual
school systems, the Supreme Court finally set out in 1971 to clarify the methods
school officials legitimately could employ to effectuate that end. Although *Swann
v. Charlotte-Mecklenburg Board of Education*[22] dealt in particular with the question of busing, three other issues were also addressed. First, the Court ruled
permissible the use of racial quotas as a "starting point in the process of shaping
a remedy."[23] Second, the Court found that, although the existence of one-race
schools does not necessarily indicate the existence of illegal segregation, "in a
system with a history of segregation, the need . . . to assure a school authority's
compliance with its constitutional duty warrants a presumption against schools

[19] *Griffen v. County School Board of Prince Edward County*, 377 U.S. 218 (1964), 234.
[20] *Green v. County School Board of New Kent County*, 391 U.S. 430 (1968), 438–39 (emphasis in
original).
[21] *Id.* at 441–442.
[22] 402 U.S. 1 (1971).
[23] *Id.* at 25.

that are substantially disproportionate in their racial composition."[24] Third, the Court approved the manipulation of attendance area boundary lines, and the clustering of noncontiguous attendance zones, for the purpose of achieving a more proportional racial mix within individual schools. As Chief Justice Burger wrote on behalf of the Court:

> Absent a constitutional violation, there would be no basis for judicially ordering assignment of students on a racial basis. All things being equal, with no history of discrimination, it might well be desirable to assign pupils to schools nearest their homes. But all things are not equal in a system that has been deliberately constructed and maintained to enforce racial segregation. The remedy for such segregation may be administratively awkward, inconvenient, and even bizarre in some situations and may impose burdens on some; but all awkwardness and inconvenience cannot be avoided in the interim period when adjustments are being made to eliminate the dual school systems.[25]

The Court then turned to the issue of student transportation. First, it noted that bus transportation had long been "an integral part of the public education system," and that 18 million (39%) of the nation's school children had been transported to school by bus the previous year—few of those for desegregation. Because, in the Court's view, segregation in Charlotte-Mecklenburg could be eliminated only by assigning children to relatively distant schools, and because busing was an acceptable means of transportation, the Court concluded that "the remedial techniques used by the District Court's order were within the Court's power to provide equitable relief."[26]

In the 1960s, the Supreme Court had focused almost exclusively on segregation in the rural South. *Swann*, in 1971, was the first urban case. Two years later, the Court turned its attention to the North.[27] In the 1973 case, *Keyes v. School Dist. No. 1*,[28] black plaintiffs in Denver originally had sought to desegregate the schools in only one small section of the city, known as Park Hill. The Supreme Court affirmed the lower courts' findings of segregation in the Park Hill area, thus providing Northern blacks a blueprint for proving segregation in districts with no history of overt segregatory policy:

> The District Court found that by the construction of a new, relatively small elementary school . . . in the middle of the Negro community west of Park Hill, by the gerry-mandering of student attendance zones, by the use of so-called "optional" zones, and by the excessive use of mobile classroom units, among other things, the respondent School Board had engaged over almost a decade after 1960 in an unconstitutional policy of deliberate racial segregation with respect to Park Hill schools.[29]

---

[24] *Id.* at 26.

[25] *Id.* at 28.

[26] *Id.* at 30.

[27] The Supreme Court had previously refused to hear cases in Kansas City, Cincinnati, and Gary, Indiana (Wilkinson, 1979, p. 341).

[28] *Keyes v. School Dist. No. 1*, 413 U.S. 189 (1973).

[29] *Id.* at 192.

The Court went further, however, and held that the entire district should undergo desegregation.

> Where plaintiffs prove that the school authorities have carried out a systematic program of segregation affecting a substantial portion of the students, schools, teachers, and facilities within the school system, it is only common sense to conclude that there exists a predicate for a finding of the existence of a dual school system.[30]

Thus, in *Keyes,* the Supreme Court determined that a Northern district without a history of Jim Crow laws could be called to account for its more subtle form of segregation; and that plaintiffs need not prove segregative intent for each and every school, only establish a pattern of segregative intent in a "significant portion" of the district.

The *Keyes* decision hinged on the distinction between *de jure* and *de facto* segregation. The majority held that "the differentiating factor . . . is purpose or intent to segregate."[31] Justice Powell, however, saw that this distinction has little meaning, and based his support for desegregation in Denver on broader grounds. In a concurring opinion, he called upon his colleagues to

> abandon a distinction which has long since outlived its time. . . . I would hold simply that where segregated public schools exist within a school district to a substantial degree, there is a *prima facie* case that the duly constituted public authorities are sufficiently responsible to warrant imposing on them a nationally applicable burden to demonstrate they nevertheless are operating a genuinely integrated school system.[32]

Powell added in a footnote that the court's *de jure-de facto* distinction reflected an inaccurate view of history. "If one goes back far enough," he wrote, "it is possible that all racial segregation, wherever occurring and whether or not confined to the schools, has at some time been supported or maintained by government action."[33]

However, the Court's majority maintained the *de jure-de facto* distinction, and black plaintiffs have been required to expend financial and legal resources to prove official complicity in each and every case. The Court's ruling in 1973 foreshadowed the 1975 decision in which it refused to order urban-suburban student reassignment to remedy urban-suburban school segregation in Detroit.

METROPOLITAN DESEGREGATION

In 1970, George Romney, then Secretary of Housing and Urban Development, recognized the racial nature of the boundary lines separating the cities from the suburbs:

[30] *Id.* at 201.
[31] *Id.* at 208; emphasis in original.
[32] *Id.* at 219–224.
[33] *Id.* at 228.

Metropolitan areas today consist of miles of slums, miles of grey areas, and miles of
sprawling suburbs. . . . These are the miles which separate the black and the poor
from good schools, and from new promising job opportunities. And with this physical
separation has come a decreasing ability of people of different backgrounds to communicate with each other about the problems which clearly affect everyone. (U.S.
Senate, 1972, p. 246)

In 1977, the Commission on Civil Rights called metropolitan school desegregation "the last major frontier to be crossed in the long judicial effort to
make equal educational opportunity . . . a living reality" (p. 75). The increasing
concentration of this country's black population within its central cities requires
desegregation solutions that encompass its equally concentrated white suburbs
as well.

Nationwide, about one in five public school students is a member of a racial
or ethnic minority (Center for National Policy Review, 1977). In the 20 to 30
largest school districts, where about one-half of these children live, minorities
comprise about 60% of school enrollments. On average, the enrollment of the
10 largest districts is 70% minority. In Chicago, 93% of the city's black children
attend schools with minority enrollments over 90%; in Los Angeles, 79% of the
black children attend such schools; in Philadelphia and Houston, 78%. Meanwhile, white children are equally isolated in the suburbs. In Baltimore, for
example, minority children constitute 70% of the school population; the surrounding suburbs are 92% white. Prior to metropolitan desegregation in Wilmington, that city's schools were 85% minority, while its adjacent suburbs were
94% white (Bell, 1978, p. 10). The National Task Force on Desegregation
Strategies (Rashman, 1979) concluded that

the simple demographic fact is that many large city school districts cannot desegregate
by themselves. For children in such districts, the best hope for attending a desegregated
school lies in the implementation of metropolitan school desegregation strategies—
i.e., desegregation plans which do not stop at the city line, but rather encompass at
least some of the surrounding suburban areas. (p. 1)

Critics argue that the nation's courts have no business ordering metropolitan
desegregation. They contend: (1) that it is not the fault of suburban whites that
disproportionate numbers of blacks live in the central cities; (2) that cross-district
busing wastes time and money; and (3) that multidistrict remedies jeopardize
parents' ability to exercise local control over the schools.

This thinking ignores crucial facts. The truth regarding the concentrations
of blacks in central cities is, as stated by the Commission on Civil Rights (1977),
that

the concentration of blacks is not to any significant degree the result of individual
choice or even income differences among the races. Rather, such segregation has
come about because of discriminatory practices of important institutions in our society,
practices which government has tolerated, fostered, and in some instances mandated.
Despite changes in national policy, many of these practices persist to the present day.
(pp. 14–15)

I have already discussed some of the forces responsible for residential segregation. These were brought to bear with a vengeance to keep blacks out of the suburbs: the FHA and the VA refused loan guarantees to "inharmonious elements"; real estate boards considered it a matter of business ethics to maintain racially pure neighborhoods; public housing for the poor was located exclusively within central cities; and financial institutions utilized redlining to maintain segregation. Furthermore, when blacks did make it out of the central cities, they usually found themselves in black suburbs as segregated as the neighborhoods they had left (Darden, 1977).

In recent years, skyrocketing construction costs and prohibitive interest rates helped maintain the rigidity of this segregation. Blacks who did not buy or build integrated suburban housing in the 1950s and 1960s could scarcely afford to do so in 1980. Thus the effects of past discrimination linger. Meanwhile, many whites left the central cities. This may have been motivated partially by a racist response to the black influx, but considerable financial incentive existed as well. During the 1950s and 1960s, 80% of the new jobs created in large metropolitan areas were located in the suburbs (U.S. Senate, 1972, p. 247).

Thus, numerous social trends have converged to leave the nation's central cities disproportionately poor, disproportionately minority, and disproportionately powerless to do anything about it. These conditions are magnified in the public schools. As long ago as 1967, the Commission on Civil Rights realized that

> the trend toward racial and economic isolation between city and suburbs also has been reinforced by the manner in which schools are financed. Education, like many other governmental functions, is financed in large part from property taxes levied by local jurisdictions. Under this system of financing, the adequacy of educational services is heavily dependent upon the adequacy of each community's tax base. With the increasing loss of their more affluent white population, central cities also have suffered a pronounced erosion of their fiscal capacity. At the same time the need for city services has increased, particularly in the older and larger cities. The combination of rising costs and the declining tax base has weakened the cities' capacity to support education at levels comparable to those in the suburbs. As the gap between educational services in the cities and the suburbs has widened, more affluent white families have been afforded further inducement to leave the cities, again intensifying racial and economic isolation and further widening the gap. (p. 25)

The Commission noted that cities were spending a third more per capita for welfare and twice as much per capita for public safety as their suburban counterparts, whereas suburbs were able to spend $1\frac{1}{2}$ times as much per capita for education (p. 26).

The Kerner Commission (National Advisory Commission, 1968) found that in the 1960s Detroit's suburban school districts were spending $500 more on each student than was Detroit proper. The Detroit district would have had to spend an additional $13 million to hire 16,650 teachers in order to bring its student–teacher ratio into line with that of its suburbs. Rectifying disparities in school facilities would have cost many millions more.

Within this context, the suburbs and their residents share responsibility, if only indirectly, for conditions in the central cities. As the Kerner Commission concluded,

> What white Americans have never fully understood—but what the Negro can never forget—is that white society is deeply implicated in the ghetto. White institutions created it, white institutions maintain it, and white society condones it. (p. 2)

Others who oppose metropolitan school desegregation argue that interdistrict busing wastes time and money. The fact is, metropolitan remedies are likely to require little if any more busing than district-only plans. The racial nature of city boundary lines accounts for this apparent anomaly. Densely populated black areas just inside city limits are often geographically close to dense concentrations of white families just past the city lines. Often, busing both ways across the line would desegregate more easily and more effectively than would busing all the way across the city district. In Richmond, Virginia, for example, where the Supreme Court rejected an interdistrict remedy, the U.S. Commission on Civil Rights (1977) found that

> most central city schools located close to the district line were predominantly black in enrollment, while most suburban schools close to the district line were virtually all white. If assignment of children across district lines had been mandated, desegregation would not have posed major, logistical problems. Indeed, in some cases, the need for busing to accomplish inter-district desegregation may be far less than what would be required to desegregate within the district. (p. 55)

The third criticism of metropolitan desegregation involves the fear that large consolidated districts jeopardize local community control over the schools. Although this fear is understandable, experience has shown that there need be no conflict between the existence of a large district, consolidated for the purpose of student reassignment, and the creation of smaller subunits allowing effective parental participation in school decision-making. Many large districts have recognized the need for decentralized administration, even in the absence of school desegregation. The New York City School District, for example, established community subdistricts, whose locally elected boards had broad authority to hire school personnel and make decisions about subdistricts' budgets and curricula (U.S. Commission on Civil Rights, 1977, p. 50). As the Commission noted,

> There is nothing inherent in the concept of metropolitan school desegregtion to prevent devising structures which will maximize parental participation in school affairs. Nor does a metropolitan remedy jeopardize the prerogative of the States or local governments to experiment at the local level or to tailor educational programs to local needs. (p. 50)

Other potential administrative difficulties associated with metropolitan desegregation can be overcome with similar ease. School district reorganization has been common for several decades, and 48 states have established procedures for consolidation, annexation, or merger (Taylor, 1977, p. 118). Furthermore,

numerous districts in the South and the Southwest already organize within county rather than city boundaries. Metropolitan desegregation provides a workable approach to the pressing problems of urban-suburban school segregation.

The majority of the Supreme Court, however, thought otherwise when it first squarely addressed the proposition in 1974. In the Detroit case, *Milliken v. Bradley*,[34] the Court reversed a lower court order that had called for busing across the city boundary between Detroit and 53 of its surrounding suburban districts. Thurgood Marshall in dissent called the decision a "giant step backward" from earlier desegregation efforts.[35] However, although giving little solace to the children in Detroit's still-segregated schools, one positive result did emerge from the *Milliken* ruling. In his concurring opinion, Justice Stewart[36] laid out the conditions under which an interdistrict remedy could be justified. In so doing, he provided the blueprint that the New Castle County litigants would later successfully follow.

All parties to the Detroit litigation agreed that state and local officials had operated the district's schools in violation of the Constitution. The district court concluded that "governmental actions and inactions at all levels, federal, state, and local, have combined with those of private organizations . . . to maintain racial segregation throughout the Detroit metropolitan area."[37]

Moreover, the lower court found that the Detroit Board of Education had magnified the effects of discriminatory housing by creating and maintaining optional attendance zones with the "natural, probable, foreseeable and actual effect" of furthering segregation (p. 587).[38] The court also found that the school district had drawn attendance zones "along north-south lines despite [its] awareness that drawing boundary lines in an east-west direction would result in significantly greater desegregation."[39] Also, the court ruled that in its transportation program, designed to relieve overcrowding, the school board had bused black children to predominantly black schools beyond or away from closer white schools with available space, and that school construction policies tended to exacerbate segregation.[40]

Insofar as state-sanctioned segregation was concerned, the Detroit case was clearcut in the mode of *Keyes*. However, the demographic fact that Detroit's schools in 1973 were 70% black, whereas its surrounding suburbs were 81% white, led the district court to conclude that a Detroit-only student reassignment plan would not work. It held that a Detroit-only plan "would not accomplish

[34] 418 U.S. 717 (1974).
[35] *Id.* at 781 (Marshall, J., dissenting).
[36] *Id.* at 753 (Stewart, J., concurring).
[37] *Bradley v. Milliken,* 338 F. Supp. 582 (1971), 587.
[38] *Id.* at 587.
[39] *Id.* at 2588.
[40] *Id.*

desegregation . . . within the corporate geographic limits of the Detroit school system for a solution to the problem."[41]

The district court based its reasoning on sound legal principles. First, education is a state function, as also is the enforcement of the Constitution's equal protection requirement. Because it had ultimate authority for the delegation of its educational responsibility, the State of Michigan had been implicated in the segregation of Detroit's schools. Thus, the court concluded that "school district lines are simply matters of political convenience and may not be used to deny Constitutional rights."[42] A metropolitan plan was the best method to "achieve the greatest degree of actual desegregation to the end that, upon implementation, no school, grade or classroom [would be] substantially disproportionate to the overall pupil racial composition."[43]

The appeals court agreed that "the State has committed *de jure* acts of segregation and that the State controls the instrumentalities whose action is necessary to remedy the harmful effects of the State acts."[44]

The Supreme Court rejected this line of reasoning, relying in particular on its belief that "the notion that school district lines may be casually ignored or treated as a mere administrative convenience is contrary to the history of public education in our country. No single tradition in public education is more deeply rooted than local control over the operation of schools."[45] The Court was repelled by the notion that "the metropolitan remedy would require, in effect, consolidation of 54 independent school districts historically administered as separate units into a vast new super school district."[46] The Court also noted "logistical and other serious problems attending large-scale transportation of students," as well as "an array of other problems in financing and operating this new school system."[47] The inclusion of these concerns in the opinion is hard to explain, given the Court's later admission that "of course, no state law is above the Constitution. School district lines are not . . . sacrosanct."[48]

The Court finally turned "to address, for the first time, the validity of a remedy mandating a cross-district or interdistrict consolidation to remedy the condition of segregation found to exist in only one district."[49] This phrasing telegraphed the result, ignoring as it did the proven fact of state-sanctioned violations.

---

[41] 418 U.S. 717 (1974), 732–733, quoting Pet. App. 51a–57a.
[42] *Id*. at 589.
[43] 345 F. Supp. 914 (1972), 918.
[44] 484 F. 2d 215 (1973), 249.
[45] 418 U.S. 717 (1974), 741.
[46] *Id*. at 743.
[47] *Id*.
[48] *Id*. at 744.
[49] *Id*.

The record before us, voluminous as it is, contains evidence of *de jure* segregated conditions only in the Detroit schools; indeed, that was the theory on which the litigation was initially based. . . . With no showing of significant violation by the 53 outlying school districts and no evidence of any interdistrict violation or effect, the court went beyond the original theory of the case . . . and mandated a metropolitan area remedy. To approve the remedy ordered by the Court would impose on the outlying districts, not shown to have committed any constitutional violation, a wholly impermissible remedy based on a standard not hinted at in *Brown I* and *II* or any holding of this Court.[50]

Chief Justice Burger, who authorized the majority opinion, then turned to consider the appropriate remedy. He stressed that

all remedies are [designed] to restore the victims of discriminatory conduct to the position they would have occupied in the absence of such conduct. Disparate treatment of white and Negro children occurred within the Detroit school system and not elsewhere, and on the record the remedy must be limited to that system.[51]

The Court thereupon remanded the case to the lower courts to formulate a decree limited to Detroit only. Burger made only passing reference to potential factual circumstances that might call for an interdistrict remedy. Justice Stewart, however, devoted much of his concurring opinion to such a discussion:

Were it to be shown, for example, that state officials had contributed to the separation of the races by drawing or redrawing school district lines . . . by transfer of school units between districts . . . or by purposeful, racially discriminatory use of state housing or zoning laws, then a decree calling for transfer of pupils across district lines or for restructuring of district lines might well be appropriate.[52]

Stewart overlooked the state violations and violations by state-delegated authorities that had been proved in the Detroit case.

Since the mere fact of different racial composition in contiguous districts does not iself imply or constitute a violation of the Equal Protection Clause in the absence of a showing that such disparity was imposed, fostered, or encouraged by the State or its political sub-divisions, it follows that no inter-district violation was shown in this case.[53]

Stewart then compounded his oversight in a footnote, the meaning of which is nearly incomprehensible:

The record here does not support the claim made by the respondents that white and Negro students within Detroit who otherwise would have attended school together were separated by acts of the State or its sub-divisions. However, segregative acts within the city alone cannot be presumed to have produced . . . an increase in the number of Negro students in *the city as a whole*. It is this essential fact of a predom-

---

[50] *Id.* at 745.

[51] 418 U.S. 717 (1974), 746.

[52] 418 U.S. 717 (1974), 755 (Stewart, J., concurring).

[53] 418 U.S. 717 (1974), 756 (Stewart, J., concurring).

inantly Negro school population in Detroit—caused by unknown and perhaps unknowable factors such as in-migration, birth rates, economic changes, or cumulative
acts of private racial fears—that accounts for the "growing core of Negro schools,"
a "core" that has grown to include virtually the entire city.[54]

As Pettigrew (1974) has said, many aspects of human societies may derive
from "unknown and perhaps unknowable" causes. However,

the tight, unremitting containment of urban blacks over the past half century within
the bowels of American cities is not one of them. In fact, most social scientists who
specialize in American race relations would agree, I believe, that housing segregation
is one of the better understood processes in our realm of study. (p. 62)

Much has been written criticizing the Court's decision. The criticisms have
ranged from the analytical to the emotional. Justice Marshall's dissent combined
the best of both:

The rights at issue in this case are too fundamental to be abridged on grounds as
superficial as those relied on by the majority today. We deal here with the right of
all our children, whatever their race, to an equal start in life and to an equal opportunity
to reach their full potential as citizens. . . . Our nation, I fear, will be ill-served by
the Court's refusal to remedy separate and unequal education, for unless our children
begin to learn together, there is little hope that our people will ever learn to live
together.[55]

Marshall stressed that the majority's "most serious analytical flaw" was its
failure to consider the district court's "explicit finding that a Detroit-only decree . . . 'would not accomplish desegregation.' "[56] Before addressing the problem of remedy, however, Marshall attacked the majority view that the district
court, having failed to find an interdistrict violation, had focused excessively on
the issue of metropolitan-wide racial balance.

Contrary to the suggestions in the Court's opinion, the basis for affording a desegregation remedy in this case was not some perceived racial imbalance either between
schools within a single school district or between independent school districts. What
we confront here is "a systematic program of segregation affecting a substantial portion
of the students, school . . . and facilities within the school district" [Keyes, 413 U.S.
189, 201]. The Constitutional violation here was . . . the purposeful, intentional,
massive, *de jure* segregation of the Detroit city schools.[57]

Marshall then reviewed the role of the State of Michigan in the segregation
of Detroit's schools:

The actions of the State itself directly contributed to Detroit's segregation. Under the
Fourteenth Amendment, the State is ultimately responsible for the actions of its local
agencies. And, finally, given the structure of Michigan's educational system, Detroit's

---

[54] *Id.* (emphasis in original).

[55] 418 U.S. 717 (1974), 783 (Marshall, J., dissenting). Douglas, Brennan and White joined in the
dissent.

[56] *Id.*

[57] *Id.* at 785.

segregation cannot be viewed as the problem of an independent and separate entity. Michigan operates a single state-wide system of education, a substantial part of which was shown to be segregated in this case.[58]

Marshall then came to the matter of remedy:

> We held in *Swann* . . . that when *de jure* segregation is shown, school authorities must make "every effort to achieve the greatest possible degree of actual desegregation." [402 U.S., at 26]. This is the operative standard. . . . If these words have any meaning at all, surely it is that school authorities must, to the extent possible, take all practicable steps to assure that Negro and white children in fact go to school together. This is, in the final analysis, what desegregation of the schools is all about. The flaw of a Detroit-only decree is not that it does not reach some ideal of racial balance or mixing. It simply does not promise to achieve desegregation at all.[60]

Marshall then pointed out that the tri-county Detroit metropolitan area functions as a "single cohesive unit," and is regarded as such by its residents.

> About 40 percent of the residents of the two suburban counties included in the desegregation plan work in Wayne County, in which Detroit is situated. Many residents of the city work in the suburbs. The three counties participate in a wide variety of cooperative governmental ventures on a metropolitan-wide basis, including a metropolitan transit system, park authority, water and sewer system, and council of governments. The Federal Government has classified the tri-county area as a Standard Metropolitan Statistical Area, indicating that it is an area of "economic and social integration."[60]

Thus, given state responsibility for the segregation existing in the Detroit area, the inability to remedy that segregation with a Detroit-only plan, and the existing interdependence of the city and its suburbs, Marshall concluded that circumstances justified a metropolitan, interdistrict remedy. He rejected the majority's contention that such a plan would violate the *Swann* dictum limiting the remedy to the scope of the violation.

> In school segregation cases, as in other equitable causes, a remedy which effectively cures the violation is what is required. . . . No more is necessary, but we can tolerate no less. To read this principle as barring a district court from imposing the only effective remedy for past segregation and remit the order to a potentially ineffective alternative is, in my view, to turn a simple commonsense rule into a cruel and meaningless paradox.[61]

Marshall's reasoning and pleading were for naught. As already mentioned, the case was remanded for the formulation of a decree limited to Detroit proper. Some good, however, did derive from the Detroit litigation. Justice Stewart had outlined the proofs that would be necessary to justify a metropolitan remedy. The NAACP lawyers and plaintiffs in the Wilmington case, *Evans v. Buchanan*,

[58] *Id.* at 797–798.
[59] *Id.* at 802–803.
[60] *Id.* at 804.
[61] *Id.* at 406–407.

had been watching the Detroit developments with great interest, and they ultimately tailored their efforts to elicit a metropolitan remedy.

Since *Evans,* the Supreme Court has reaffirmed its reluctant approval of metropolitan school desegregation remedies, most notably in the Indianapolis case.[62] In that case, the Court ordered busing across still-existing school district lines to effect the first truly *interdistrict* desegregation plan. (In *Evans,* as in the Louisville, Kentucky, case, several districts were merged to form a single district, which was then desegregated.) The Court determined in the Indianapolis case that the plaintiffs had met the *Milliken* requirement that discriminatory practices in one district must have contributed to the segregation in another in order to justify a metropolitan remedy. Two such violations were proved. First, Indianapolis in 1969 had reorganized most civil government on a countywide basis, while specifically excluding the schools. This confined 95% of the county's black population to a segregated education in the inner city. Second, public housing authorities had sited all low-income subsidized housing in segregated black neighborhoods, reinforcing the already severe residential segregation. Based on these examples of discrimination by the suburban districts and the State of Illinois, the Court ordered suburban participation in Indianapolis's desegregation plan.

Two possible future avenues for streamlining efforts toward racial integration are now under consideration by leading desegregation strategists. William Taylor (1979), former staff director for the U.S. Commission on Civil Rights, and now Executive Director of the Center for National Policy Review, supports an approach attacking housing segregation and school segregation in single, combined lawsuits. As Taylor sees it, the Federal Justice Department would most effectively spearhead such an effort, which would also call for cooperation between the Department of Education and the Department of Housing and Urban Development.

Another possibility, dealing exclusively with school desegregation, would have plaintiffs sue state governments for segregation found to exist anywhere in each state. This approach would ease for defendants the financial burden of expensive litigation, and would also focus legal responsibility where it belongs: with the states. Each state board of education would then take on the task of desegregating each individual school district under its jurisdiction.

The administrative and legislative branches of the federal government can also provide initiative and direction in the desegregation process. Potential benefits can be seen in a brief look at the early and mid–1960s, when both the White House and Congress were aiding, rather than obstructing, the struggle for racial justice (Hirt, 1981; Leubsdorf, 1977). The 1964 Civil Rights Act, along with subsequent enforcement efforts, provides the best example to date of effective legislative-administrative cooperation in school desegregation. The 1964 Act called on the Attorney General to initiate desegregation lawsuits, and on the

---

[62] *U.S. v. Board of School Commissioners,* 573 F 2d 400, Aff'd, 439 U.S. 824 (1978).

Commissioner of Education to provide technical assistance to desegregating school districts. It also forbade discrimination in programs receiving federal aid, thus allowing federal agencies to withhold funding from segregated districts. In 1965, when Congress began allocating significant amounts of money to local school districts, the Department of Health, Education and Welfare worked to ensure that districts receiving aid made strides toward ending unconstitutional segregation.

As Orfield (1979) has noted, a combined legislative-administrative approach can have effects beyond the individual districts involved.

> Beginning in 1956, the Civil Rights groups fought consistently for a law requiring nondiscrimination in all programs receiving federal funds. . . . When it was written into law as Title VI of the 1964 Civil Rights Act, it soon became the key to desegregation of the South. After the Johnson Administration made a credible threat to cut off federal aid, desegregation of the schools of the rural South was nearly finished within four years. . . . In only a very small fraction of cases were actual cutoffs necessary and those were usually short term. (p. 26)

Orfield contends that legislative and administrative support can also increase the effectiveness of judicial action:

> When the pronouncement of a new Supreme Court requirement is followed rapidly by executive branch action adopting the new standards and vigorously enforcing them, those who discriminate must risk the combined force of administrative and judicial action. Use of such cooperative strategies had a major impact on Southern school desegregation during the Johnson Administration. Many districts concluded that change was inevitable and decided to comply rather than to first lose their federal funds and then be hit by Justice Department action anyway. (p. 24)

OPPOSITION TO SCHOOL DESEGREGATION

In 1983, the Supreme Court reaffirmed its tenuous commitment to desegregating America's schools by refusing to reopen the Nashville case.[63] The Reagan Administration, as part of its wide-ranging effort to undermine federal enforcement of civil rights laws, had supported the attempt to overturn the busing plan already underway in that city.[64] In Congress, meanwhile, conservative senators and representatives were trying to achieve through legislation what their counterparts had failed to accomplish through litigation. The Helms-Johnston Amendment would impose limits on court-ordered busing and would prohibit the Justice Department from pursuing suits that might require school districts to bus students past the schools nearest their homes.[65]

---

[63] *Metropolitan County Board of Education of Nashville and Davidson County, Tennessee v. Kelly Cert, denied,* 103 S. Ct. 834 (1983).

[64] For an in-depth discussion of the Reagan Administration's performance on Civil Rights enforcement, see Leadership Conference, 1982.

[65] For an in-depth discussion, see Citizens Commission on Civil Rights, 1982.

Constitutional, legal, educational, psychological, and social considerations aside, these maneuvers misread American public opinion. Opposition to desegregation generally, or to busing in particular, is not as broad or as deep as conservative politicians would like to believe. It is true that a 1981 CBS/*New York Times* poll showed that, in abstract terms, three quarters of all Americans opposed busing. However, in communities that had actually undergone or were considering desegregation by busing, 70% of the people had accepted the idea and were not actively opposed (Citizens Commission, 1982, p. 91). Even more telling is a 1981 Harris survey of families who had personally participated in busing for desegregation. Of white families, 48% rated their experience as very satisfactory, whereas 37% rated their experience as partly satisfactory—an overall positive rating of 85%. Black families were even more likely to develop positive attitudes about busing, with 96% rating it either very or partly satisfactory (Citizens Commission, 1982, p. 92).

Conservative politicians repeatedly have hoped to generate political advantage by appealing to the electorate's lowest common denominator on the busing issue. For example, President Ford, running for election in the summer of 1976, announced his "busing attack" despite a poll released the previous day indicating that the American public did not perceive busing to be a major issue (Green, 1976). President Reagan's midterm shift in emphasis from the faltering economy to a new attack on busing (along with efforts to push through tuition tax credits and school prayer) represents a similar political maneuver.

However, neither Ford nor Reagan offered feasible alternatives that effectively would desegregate the country's schools. Actually, busing is not now, nor has it ever been, the primary issue. As the U.S. Commission on Civil Rights (1967) stated:

> We do not hesitate to bus our children long distances in rural areas, or, in cities, to private schools or to schools offering special advantages. Thus, the issue is not whether . . . busing [is] bad, *per se,* but whether the interests of our children will be served or impaired by particular proposals or solutions. (p. 196)

The busing issue has been blown out of proportion. Whereas more than half of all school children ride buses to school, only about 3.5% do so for reasons of desegregation (Rist, 1978, p. 40). Many desegregation plans require only a marginal increase in a district's busing; and, in many districts with histories of busing *for* segregation, desegregation actually results in a reduction of busing. For example, 90% of the 300 Southern desegregation plans approved by the Department of Health, Education, and Welfare in 1969 actually showed decreases in total busing in their respective districts (U.S. Commission on Civil Rights, 1977, p. 71).

James E. Allen (1969), former U.S. Commissioner of Education, has said that the purpose of school busing is to "get a child safely to a better education," and that it is therefore a reasonable justification for busing. The real issue, of

course, is not busing, but desegregation. U.S. Appeals Court Judge George Edwards (1976) realized this in the mid–1970s.

> The morning after Labor Day in 1971 my wife and I drove down to Detroit from our cottage through the rural thumb country of Michigan. We passed . . . and stopped for . . . dozens of yellow school buses picking up hundreds of farm children . . . all white. It reminded us that busing gave us a fine system of consolidated schools all over rural America with well-nigh unanimous approval. That was also the morning when the school desegregation order for Pontiac, Michigan, went into effect. On the car radio we heard that the fleet of buses had been bombed and set afire. Proofs in a federal court criminal trial later showed that this was the work of the Ku Klux Klan. The Ku Klux Klan doesn't hate buses. Its whole history shows that it simply hates blacks.

The bombing of school buses is only the most extreme method of opposing and resisting desegregation. As Leubsdorf (1977) has pointed out,

> in many cases, unfortunately, the outsiders interfering with desegregation are themselves state officials. . . . Courts have thus confronted attempts to keep schools open and segregated through the use of police and proclamations, through transfer and control of schools away from law-abiding administrators and through injunctive and criminal proceedings. . . . Desegregated schools have also been deprived of funds or accreditation, or closed entirely, often in connection with schemes to subsidize segregated private schools. Sometimes . . . officials limit themselves to blocking the funding needed for desegregation expenses, or attempt to forbid desegregative busing, or carve up the school district. (p. 63)

However, despite these efforts, the courts have held steadfast to their contention, first announced in *Brown II* that "the vitality of these constitutional principles cannot be allowed to yield simply because of disagreement with them."[66] Even in the face of violent opposition, desegregation must proceed: "Law and order are not here to be preserved by depriving the Negro children of their constitutional rights."[67] This principle has been restated continuously, as by the district court in the Boston case: "No amount of public or parental opposition will excuse avoidance by school officials of constitutional rights."[68]

Much anti-busing sentiment has been cloaked in the rhetoric of support for the so-called neighborhood school. As already discussed, the Supreme Court overturned Detroit's multidistrict plan largely because the plan violated this supposed tradition. In fact, however, the notion of neighborhood schools has grown to mythic proportions only since it has become a tool with which to fight school desegregation.

In the not-too-distant past, public schools were not necessarily neighborhood schools. In the early decades of this century, American schools were likely to

[66] *Brown v. Board of Education (Brown II)*, 349 U.S. 294 (1955), 300.
[67] *Cooper v. Aaron*, 358 U.S. 1 (1958), 16.
[68] *Morgan v. Hennigan*, 379 F. Supp. 410 (1974), 482.

serve large regions embracing no particular homogeneous neighborhoods. In most communities, rural and urban youngsters attended the same schools. The United States Commission on Civil Rights (1967) has further noted that in recent years many urban district attendance areas have not conformed to any consistently meaningful definition of "neighborhood."

> Traditional neighborhoods—self-contained, cohesive communities—do not, in fact, appear to be the basis for neighborhood attendance policy. Instead, the common rationale for neighborhood attendance rests more on convenience. . . . Attendance areas are commonly defined, not by boundaries of communities, but by reference to population density, the size of schools in geographic boundaries such as highways and railroads. (pp. 40–41)

Thus, the neighborhood school is not a deeply rooted tradition, but a co-incidental by-product of "convenience." Attendance areas have shrunk "not because of decisions that it is necessary today for children to attend schools closer to their homes than in the past, but rather as a result of increasing population density" (p. 41). The coincidental nature of neighborhood school attendance areas is clearly shown in Oakland, California, where some elementary school attendance areas are sometimes as much as 10 times larger than others. Nor does consideration of optimal school size determine attendance zone boundaries. In 1965, for example, Chicago elementary schools ranged in enrollment from 93 to 2,539 students.

The underlying weakness of many districts' commitment to neighborhood schools is evidenced in the frequency with which that supposed commitment is violated by allowing students to cross zone lines to escape schools in which they would be in the racial minority. As was found in the Boston case, "Evidence established that the neighborhood school policy of Boston was so selective as hardly to have amounted to a policy at all and that several practices of [the school board] . . . were antithetical to a neighborhood school system."[69]

In 1968, the Supreme Court laid down the law: "The burden of a school board today is to come forward with a plan that promises realistically to work, and promises realistically to work *now*."[70] In 1971, the Supreme Court finally declared that student reassignment based on race was "one tool absolutely essential to fulfillment of [the] constitutional obligation to eliminate existing dual school systems."[71] All students need quality education, and all should receive that education in circumstances where they learn to interact in our multiracial world.

The schools serve as agents of the state. Benefits of public education should be distributed equally to all, whether urban, suburban, or rural. Parents should

---

[69] *Id.* at 412.

[70] *Green v. County School Board of New Castle County,* 391 U.S. 430 (1968), 439 (emphasis in original).

[71] *North Carolina State Board of Education v. Swann,* 402 U.S. 43 (1971), 46.

not be able to buy into "better" public schools for their children by buying homes in "better" neighborhoods.

John H. Lawrence (1971), superintendent of schools in Shaker Heights, Ohio, has said that busing offers "the most practical and most economical way to provide quality education for pupils in our elementary schools. In reality we have only broadened the geographic base of the child's neighborhood at an earlier age than is usually done" (p. 40).

The president of an organization purporting to support neighborhood schools admitted that his group's real concern was neither busing nor the proximity of children's homes to their school buildings. Rather, he acknowledged that his support for anti-busing legislation arose from "a perception of what has happened to the quality of education" following desegregation (Citizens Commission, 1982, pp. 79–80). If spreading educational resources equally across a school district results in a diminution of the quality of education for white children, it would argue *for* rather than against desegregation. Such a result would provide proof positive of pre-desegregation educational disparities. However, a bipartisan group of former federal officials monitoring federal anti-discrimination enforcement has argued convincingly that the perception of reduced educational quality following desegregation is erroneous. After close analysis, the Citizens Commission on Civil Rights (1982) concluded that "social science data has shown that this 'perception' is a product of ignorance, and that it tends to change radically as people acquire actual experience with busing" (p. 80).

Another erroneous perception manipulated by busing critics to bolster their argument is that school desegregation has caused the exodus of white families from the central cities to the suburbs. This debate raged with particular force in the mid-1970s, when Professor James Coleman initiated "an unprecedented campaign by a sociologist to influence public policy" (Pettigrew & Green, 1976, p. 4). Coleman's so-called "white flight" thesis was marred by serious methodological and conceptual problems.

Evidence shows that although extensive school desegregation in non-metropolitan areas may hasten white flight in its first year, it has little cumulative effect when measured over the course of several years. Moreover, the lack of significant white flight in medium-sized cities or in larger countywide school systems indicates that flight occurs only when whites believe there is somewhere to which they can escape. This argues not for the abandonment of judicial enforcement of the Constitution, but for the expansion of desegregation remedies to encompass the suburbs as well as the central cities. As the National Task Force on Desegregation Strategies (Rashman, 1979) reported:

> If suburban, as well as city, schools are desegregated, no incentive will exist for white parents to flee city school districts in order to live in districts where schools are predominantly white. In fact, metropolitan school desegregation can actually contribute to maintaining integrated neighborhoods by exempting such neighborhoods from the desegregation plan. (pp. 7–8)

The media must bear some burden of responsibility for both the extent of the opposition that exists, and for the general public's impression that such opposition is more extensive than it actually is. The Kerner Commission (National Advisory Commission, 1968) noted that

> important segments of the media failed to report adequately on the causes and con-
> sequences of civil disorders and on the underlying problems of race relations. They
> have not communicated to the majority of their audience—which is white—a sense
> of the degradation, misery, and hopelessness of life in the ghetto. (p. 20)

William Grant (1976), education writer for the *Detroit Free Press,* has pointed out that this deficiency in media coverage applies particularly in the treatment of school desegregation litigation.

> In most cities, it appears that a court-ordered busing plan suddenly bursts forth from
> the clouds. The media seldom pay much attention to the court proceedings designed
> to discover whether or not a school system is guilty of segregating its schools. . . . It
> is not until after a finding of a constitutional violation and the discussion of a remedy
> that most people, including the media, become interested. And then the talk focuses
> almost exclusively on busing. (p. 82)

The media's tendency to accentuate conflict compounds the likelihood that coverage will generate more heat than light. Edwin Diamond (1975), reporting on media treatment of the Boston desegregation story, quoted a wire service editor who said:

> In the first four weeks, we were writing one lead every hour, and we got to the point
> where we'd lead with fights involving five or six people with no injuries. The problem
> was that some of the stuff wasn't worth reporting. Everybody—New York, the sub-
> scribers—was keyed up about "the Boston situation," and so you've got to come up
> with a story, even though there wasn't a story there. (p. 10)

Conflict generates more exciting news copy than does cooperation. But experience has shown that cooperation can achieve successful school desegregation. White opposition can be overcome by careful planning and strong leadership. As Willie and Greenblatt (1981) concluded in their study of 10 school systems under court order:

> The officials themselves need not be in favor of the court order to prevent violent
> resistance. Their public pronouncements may be neutral if they take a strong position
> asserting that the law will be enforced. . . . When public officals speak out against
> court orders to desegregate the public schools, they stimulate resistance . . . which
> may get out of hand. . . . Judicial appeals . . . sometimes are taken as a sign that
> resistance by any means will be tolerated. (p. 324)

Pettigrew's (1974) research indicates that resistance arises when community leaders signal that resistance may be effective. Conversely, when leaders rally behind a desegregation program, resistance tends to be minimal (Willie & Greenblatt, 1981, pp. 15–16). Lansing, Michigan, provides a fine example of the

latter situation. In the early 1970s, the city's school board initiated a voluntary desegregation program for the upper elementary grades. With the strong support of the district's superintendent and cooperating community leadership, the plan proceeded without racial incident. This is impressive, in that only 50 miles separate Lansing from Pontiac, where extensive violence accompanied that city's desegregation program.

An especially insidious manifestation of white opposition is expressed when black children are "resegregated" within the walls of supposedly desegregated schools. In such schools, black children are shunted into special classes that effectively separate them from mainstream educational experiences. Resegregation and other indignities often associated with desegregation have convinced many black leaders to oppose school integration. Although this emotional response is understandable, it is reactive. It results not from the failure of school desegregation efforts to benefit children, but from the frequent failure of school boards to implement effectively their desegregation mandates. The major objection by blacks to school desegregation relates to the disproportionate burden on the black community of most desegregation remedies. Examples of this burden include one-way busing, closures of schools in black neighborhoods, harsh discipline of black pupils, and the dismissal or demotion of black faculty and administrators after desegregation. These undesirable practices require great vigilance to ensure fair, effective desegregation programs, but they do not justify abandoning desegregation efforts.

THE FUTURE OF SCHOOL DESEGREGATION

There has been progress. Throughout the country, increasing numbers of blacks are graduating from high school (Green *et al.*, 1981). However, much remains to be done. Despite the gains, proportionately more blacks than whites still drop out (or are pushed out) of the nation's public schools. Segregation has actually increased in some areas (Orfield, 1982). In 1975, 23 million Americans over the age of 15 were illiterate (Rowan & Mazie, 1977). In that group could be found about half of the country's unemployed 16- to 21-year-olds, about half the nation's welfare recipients, and a great percentage of the inmates in the nation's prisons. A year of study at a state university in the Midwest costs about $4,000. A year in a state prison—much less productive for both the participant and for society—costs the taxpayer $2\frac{1}{2}$ times as much. Humanistic considerations aside, we cannot afford to let our education system deteriorate further.

The Kerner Commission (National Advisory Commission, 1968) recommended desegregation as a "priority education strategy," but that priority has not been actualized. Blacks have seen old promises unfulfilled as national leaders have backed away from the obligation to enforce the Constitution. In the early

1980s, the assistant attorney general in charge of civil rights enforcement refused "to compel children who don't choose to have an integrated education to have one" (Leadership Conference on Civil Rights, 1982, p. 7). The attorney general, the nation's chief law enforcement agent, called on the courts to limit their own enforcement efforts. He insisted that they should heed "the groundswell of conservatism evidenced by the 1980 elections," warning against "serious attacks on the independence and legitimacy of the courts" (p. 33).

Seven years after the Kerner Commission issued its report, sociologist James Coleman in 1975 called on blacks to limit their legal efforts to bring about school desegregation (Kerner, Kelly, & Moore, 1975). Coleman's contention—that school desegregation, especially busing, had failed—was as erroneous then as are the echoes we hear today. Nathaniel Jones, then chief counsel for the NAACP, noted the inconsistency of Coleman's exhortations in 1975:

> Less than a decade ago, white people were telling black people to get out of the streets, stop public protesting, and go use our constitutional safeguards through the courts. Now that we have followed that advice successfully in American cities, Coleman tells us to stop using the courts for they are an inappropriate source for remedies. Can black people seriously be expected to listen to him? (Pettigrew & Green, 1976, p. 11)

We could not listen to Coleman in the 1970s, and we cannot in the 1980s listen to his political heirs. Desegregation has not "failed." The dismal fact is that it has barely been tried. In the few instances where school officials have worked sincerely to provide quality education for all students, most students of all races have prospered. In the other, unfortunately, more prevalent cases, reasons other than desegregation explain whatever failure has occurred. School desegregation has not failed. Many boards of education have failed. Many teachers, counselors, and school administrators have failed. State and national officials too numerous to count have failed. And the nation's teacher education institutions have failed. The responsibility must be put where it belongs. Separate and unequal schooling has been around for a long time, and it will require a strong and persistent effort to eradicate it.

This may be difficult to comprehend among whites, who for nearly 30 years have read headlines about the fight for school desegregation. Conditioned by television to expect 30- or 60-minute resolutions of complex human dramas, our national mind seems impatient with the slow pace of social change. Blacks also believe that progress proceeds too slowly, and so the confrontation continues. Civil rights advocates since the beginning have been told that their timing has been bad and their tactics inflammatory. But for those who need, the time must always be now; and for those who hold advantage, the time is never right. Jackie Robinson, Rosa Parks, Martin Luther King, Jr., sit-ins, freedom rides, and the *Brown* decision—all were controversial. And all have been vehicles of much needed change.

We must each, in the milieu in which we live and work, treatment of all people. Equal quality education is one pai treatment. I am reminded of the story of an old man who wa Someone asked him why plant a tree unlikely to bear fruit in the old man responded, "I did not find the world desolate when as my fathers planted for me before I was born, so I plant for come after me." To allow a child to enter adult life without ad ,..... training is to plant a tree in rocky and infertile soil, to deprive it of water and sun, to consign it to a gnarled and stunted growth.

The problem we address in school desegregation is not unique to the schools, nor does it hinge entirely on the differences between black and white. The problem pervades every institution in society at each and every level, and it involves virtually all relationships between those with power and those without. Schools are not the only front on which we must wage the battle for racial justice. Poor and minority people need better housing, better nutrition, better health care, and better jobs. Hunger, illness, and oppressive home environment are barriers to effective education, and we must address these deficiencies before our efforts in the schools can achieve complete success.

Minority members and the poor have much in common. The separation of the races has protected and reinforced the concentration of power in the existing elite, itself but a small portion of white society. Segregation drives a wedge of fear and hostility between poor blacks and poor whites, two groups that share oppression as much as they compete for society's crumbs. This competition drives the wedge deeper by the day.

Poor whites and disadvantaged minorities must learn that their interests converge with those of most black Americans. Desegregation limited within city boundaries often accentuates the conflict between the poor of both races, while exempting upper-class whites in the suburbs. This argues for urban/suburban desegregation, as well as for integration according to socioeconomic status. Rich and poor, black and white—we must all learn to live together.

The need to incorporate and celebrate social diversity in the schools does not end with race or class. Children of all kinds—female and male, minority ethnicity or minority lifestyle—must achieve their legitimate places in this country's classrooms. The education of American youth must include in its curricula, both explicit and implicit, respect for this diversity.

Our country's future lies in its children. Only by seeing that all of our children are educated effectively in an atmosphere of love and respect can we hope to solve the complex problems we face. The country that put a man on the moon ought to be able to put its children in schools that work, and ultimately to put educated adults to work at meaningful jobs. Children are our best investment. They are not a high-risk investment. When we invest time, energy, love, and attention in young people, they will return all that with interest.

REFERENCES

Allen, J. (1969). Integration is better education. *Integrated Education, 7,* (5), 30–31.

Bell, D. (1973). *Race, racism and American law.* Boston: Little, Brown.

Bell, D. (1978). The mirage of metropolitan school remedies. *Legal analysis, 2,* 1–12.

Bullivant, B. (1982). Power and control in the multi-ethnic school: Toward a conceptual model. *Ethnic and Racial Studies, 5,* 53–70.

Carter, R. (1980). The Warren Court and desegregation (pp. 381–384). In D. Bell (Ed.), *Race, racism and American law.* Boston: Little, Brown.

Center for National Policy Review. (1977). *Trends in black school desegregation, 1970–74.* Washington, DC: National Institute of Education.

Citizens Commission on Civil Rights. (1982). *"There is no liberty . . ."—A report on Congressional efforts to curb the federal courts and undermine the Brown decision.* Washington, DC: Author.

Coleman, J. S., Campbell, E. Q., Hobson, C. J., McPartland, J., Mood, A. M., Weinfeld, F. D., & York, R. L. (1966). *Equality of educational opportunity.* Washington, DC: U.S. Department of Health, Education, and Welfare, U.S. Government Printing Office.

Coleman, J. S., Kelly, S. D., & Moore, J. A. (1975, April). *Recent trends in school integration.* Paper presented at the annual meeting of the American Educational Research Association, Washington, DC.

Darden, J. T. (1977). Blacks in the suburbs: Their number is rising but patterns of segregation persist. *Vital Statistics, 27,* 1–4.

deLeeuw, F., Schnare, A. B., & Struyk, R. J. (1976). Housing. In W. Gorham and N. Glazer (Eds.), *The urban predicament* (pp. 119–178). Washington, DC: Urban Institute.

Denton, J. (1967). *Apartheid American style.* Berkeley: Diablo Press.

Diamond, E. (1975). Boston: The agony of responsibility. *Columbia Journalism Review, 13,* 9–15.

Diamond, P. (1981). Toward ending segregation in the 1980s. *The Urban Review, 13,* 73–83.

Edwards, G. (1976, June). *Issues and options.* Address, U.S. Court of Appeals for the Sixth Circuit, Chicago, IL.

Grant, W. (1976). The media and school desegregation. In Michigan State University, College of Urban Development (Ed.), *School desegregation: Making it work* (pp. 71–89). East Lansing: Michigan State University, College of Urban Development.

Green, R. L. (1976). A social scientist's view of school desegregation: National politics, attitude change and school achievement. In Michigan State University, College of Urban Development (Ed.), *School Desegregation: Making it work* (pp. 9–31). East Lansing: Michigan State University, College of Urban Development.

Green, R. L. (1977). *The urban challenge—poverty and race.* Chicago: Follett.

Green, R. L. (1981a). *Consultants' research report, student desegregation plan for the Chicago Public Schools. P. 1: Educational components.* East Lansing: Michigan State University.

Green, R. L. (1981b). *Student desegregation plan for the Chicago public schools: Recommendations on educational components.* East Lansing: Michigan State University.

Green, R. L., & Cohen, W. (1979). *An evaluation of the results of the school desegregation order in Oliver v. Kalamazoo Board of Education.* East Lansing: Michigan State University.

Green, R. L., Darden, J. T., Griffore, R. J., Parsons, M. A., Schmidt, J., & Schweitzer, J. H. (1982). *Metropolitan school desegregation in New Castle County, Delaware: Final report to the Rockefeller Foundation.* East Lansing, MI: Michigan State University, Urban Affairs Programs.

Green, R. L., Darden, J. T., Hirt, J., Simmons, C. A., Tenbrunsel, T., Thomas, F., Thomas, J., & Thomas, R. (1981). *Discrimination and the welfare of urban minorities.* Springfield, IL: Charles C. Thomas.

Grier, E., & Grier, G. (1968). Equality and beyond: Housing segregation in the Great Society. In

B. Friedan & R. Morris (Eds.), *Urban Planning and Social Policy* (pp. 122–147). New York: Basic Books.

Hecht, A. (1982, November 28). The Hitler Youth: Dictator's fanatics. *Detroit Free Press*, p. 1.

Hirt, J. (1981). Current federal policies on school desegregation: Constitutional justice or benign neglect? *The Urban Review*, 13, 57–63.

Jones, N. (1976). Educational desegregation: Problems and prospects. In Michigan State University, College of Urban Development (Ed.), *School desegregation: Making it work* (pp. xi–xx). East Lansing: Michigan State University, College of Urban Development.

Kozol, J. (1980). How we can win: A plan to reach and teach twenty-five million illiterate adults. *Wilson Library Bulletin*, 54, 640–644.

Lawrence, J. H. (1971). Desegregation in Shaker Heights. *Integrated Education, IX*, 40–41.

Leadership Conference on Civil Rights. (1982). *Without justice: A report on the conduct of the Justice Department on civil rights in 1981–82*. Washington, DC: Author.

Leubsdorf, J. (1977). Completing the desegregation remedy. *Boston University Law Review, 57*, 39–95.

Levine, D., & Havighurst, R. (1977). *The future of big-city schools*. Berkeley: McCutcham.

Litwack, L. (1973). North of slavery. In D. Bell (Ed), *Race, racism and American law* (pp. 440–442). Boston: Little, Brown.

Lubow, A., Howard, L. Begley, S., LaBrecque, R., Morris, H. (1978, November 6). The blight of illiteracy. *Newsweek*, pp. 106–112.

Morland, J. (1972). *Racial attitudes in school children: From kindergarten through high school*. Washington, DC: U.S. Department of Health, Education, and Welfare, Office of Education, National Center for Educational Research and Development.

National Advisory Commission on Civil Disorders. (1968). *Report of the National Advisory Commission on Civil Disorders*. New York: New York Times Company.

Orfield, G. (1977). If wishes were houses then busing could stop: Demographic trends and desegregation policy. In National Institute of Education (Ed.), *School desegregation in metropolitan areas: Choices and prospects* (pp. 43–57). Washington, DC: U.S. Department of Health, Education, and Welfare.

Orfield, G. (1979). Federal agencies and urban segregation: Steps toward coordinated action. In Ford Foundation (Ed.), *Racial segregation: Two policy views*. New York: Ford Foundation.

Orfield, G. (1982). *Desegregation of black and Hispanic students from 1968 to 1980*. Washington, DC: Joint Center for Political Studies.

Pettigrew, T. (1974). A sociological view of the post-Milliken era. In U.S. Commission on Civil Rights, (Ed.), *Milliken v. Bradley: The implications for metropolitan desegregation* (pp. 53–67). Washington, DC: U.S. Commission on Civil Rights.

Pettigrew, T., & Green, R. (1976). School desegregation in large cities: A critique of the Coleman "white flight" thesis. *Harvard Educational Review, 46*, 1–53.

Rashman, M. (1979). *Metropolitan school desegregation: A report and recommendations of the National Task Force on Desegregation Strategies*. Denver: Education Commission of the States.

Rist, R. (1978). Sorting out the issues. *Civil Rights Digest, 10*, 40–43.

Rowan, C., & Maxie, D. (1977, January). Johnny's parents can't read either. *Reader's Digest, 110*, 153–156.

St. John, N. (1975). *School desegregation: Outcomes for children*. New York: Wiley.

Schofield, J. (1981) Uncharted territory: Speculations on some positive effects of desegregation on white students. *The Urban Review, 13*, 227–242.

Smedley, T. A. (1973). Developments in the law of school desegregation. *Vanderbilt Law Review, 26*, 405–452.

Taeuber, K. (1975). Demographic perspectives on housing and school segregation. *Wayne Law Review, 21*, 833–850.

Taeuber, K., & Taeuber, A. (1965). *Negroes in cities*. Chicago: Aldine.

Taylor, W. (1977). Metropolitan remedies for public school discrimination: the neglected option. In National Institute of Education (Ed.), *School desegregation in metropolitan areas: Choices and prospects* (pp. 115–121). Washington, DC: U.S. Department of Health, Education, and Welfare.

Taylor, W. (1979). Mounting a concerted federal attack on urban segregation: A preliminary exploration. In Ford Foundation (Ed.), *Racial segregation: Two policy views* (pp. 45–47). New York: Ford Foundation.

United States Commission on Civil Rights. (1967). *Racial isolation in the public schools.* Washington, DC: U.S. Government Printing Office.

United States Commission on Civil Rights. (1973). *Understanding fair housing: A report of the Commission, 1973.* Washington, DC: United States Government Printing Office.

United States Commission on Civil Rights. (1977). *Statement on metropolitan school desegregation.* Washington, DC: Author.

United States Commission on Civil Rights. (1979a). *Desegregation of the nation's public schools: A status report.* Washington, DC: U.S. Government Printing Office.

United States Commission on Civil Rights. (1979b). *The federal fair housing effort.* Washington, DC: U.S. Government Printing Office.

United States Department of Labor, Bureau of Labor Statistics. (1983). *Employment and Earnings, 30.*

United States Federal Housing Administration. (1938). *Underwriting manual.* Washington, DC: U.S. Government Printing Office.

United States Senate. (1971) *Hearings before the Select Committee on Equal Educational Opportunity.* U.S. Senate, August 25–27 and September 1, 1970, 91st Congress, 2d session.

United States Senate. (1972). *Report of the Select Committee on Equal Educational Opportunity.* Washington, DC: U.S. Government Printing Office.

Washington, B. (1900). The education of the Negro. In N. M. Butler (Ed.), *Education in the United States* (Vol. 1) (pp. 893–936). Albany, NY: Lyon.

The wayward busing issue. (May, 1972). *Phi Delta Kappan, 53,* 537–538.

Wilkinson, J. (1979). *From Brown to Bakke.* New York: Oxford Univ. Press.

Willie, C. & Greenblatt, S. (1981). *Community politics and educational change—ten school systems under court order.* New York: Longman.

2

School Desegregation in New Castle County, Delaware

HISTORICAL BACKGROUND

JULIE SCHMIDT

A lawsuit filed in 1971 in the U.S. District Court of Delaware renewed litigation for school desegregation in Delaware's northern New Castle County. Five black parents residing in the city of Wilmington petitioned the federal court to grant the Constitutional rights of their children (and those similarly situated) to an equal educational opportunity. At that time, the plaintiffs sought a remedy that would portion sections of the city district with the contiguous suburban school districts. Following several years of judicial hearings, the U.S. District Court ruled in favor of the plaintiffs' petition, but fashioned a remedy that grouped the bulk of the county into a single school district, thus ordering the nation's first metropolitan school desegregation remedy.[1]

This chapter reviews the causes of the initiation of the 1971 lawsuit and the political/legal events that shaped the resolution of the conflict. An overview is presented of the various desegregation issues, some of which began prior to the litigation. Community responses to this issue and its ramifications are also reviewed.

HISTORICAL BACKGROUND

Prior to 1896, educational opportunities for Delaware's black children had been neglected, except for the efforts of black leaders themselves (Hoffecker,

[1] *Evans v. Buchanan*, 379 F. Supp. 1218 (1974).

JULIE SCHMIDT ● Department of Educational Studies, University of Delaware, Newark, Delaware 19713.

1973; Maddan, 1969).[2] Later, when the state provided public education for all its children, it did so on a racially discriminatory basis (Hoffecker, 1974, pp. 138–140). The state's policy of "separate but equal" education was soon sanctioned under the 1896 *Plessy v. Ferguson* decision.[3]

The state of Delaware followed the spirit of the *Plessy* doctrine for decades. The state provided racially separate educational opportunities that failed, by most accounts, to fulfill the promise of equal educational opportunities for black and white children. Separate but unequal was more readily available in the Delaware public school system (Hoffecker, 1973, pp. 138–143).

Brown litigation in Delaware underscored the state's inability to deliver on the guarantee of equality implicit in the *Plessy* doctrine. *Brown* litigation, pursued in the state courts by black plaintiffs, demonstrated the persistence of unequal educational opportunities for black children.[4] These litigants enjoyed limited success within the confines of the prevailing law sanctioning "separate but equal." However, their early desegregation efforts were not without longer-range consequences.

In their immediate victory, these initial plaintiffs won relief from the unconstitutional denial of their rights and were granted admission to the nearby all-white schools, which the state court found "superior" to the all-black schools.[5] On a more long-term basis, this lawsuit served as a platform from which litigants launched an appeal to the Supreme Court for the dissolution of the *Plessy* doctrine itself.

In 1954, the state was drawn into the national arena, along with four other states whose racially segregatory practices were brought before the Supreme Court for review. Plaintiffs in the famous *Brown v. Topeka Board of Education* were successful in their challenge of the prevailing doctrine established in 1896.[6] The standard of "separate but equal" in the field of public education was struck down by the High Court. In its place, the justices decreed that the principle of equal educational opportunity required an end to state-mandated segregation.

Like other states in the nation operating a dual school system based on race, the state of Delaware was ordered to dismantle its segregated system gradually and to replace it with a unitary system of public education.[7] The state's task of eliminating its dual school system dovetailed, to some extent, with its educational objective of consolidating several smaller districts into larger organizational units. For the most part, state school officials dismantled the colored districts by con-

---

[2] Public education in Delaware began in 1829 with the passage of the Free School Act. In 1866, the Delaware Association for the Moral Improvement and Education of Colored People maintained schools in all three counties in Delaware. In 1881, the state appropriated funds for the black schools.

[3] Delaware, Constitution, Art. 10, sec. 1; *Plessy v. Ferguson,* 163 U.S. 156 (1896).

[4] *Gebhart v. Belton,* 91 A. 2d. 137 (Del. 1952).

[5] Ibid.

[6] *Brown v. Board of Education of Topeka et al.,* 349 U.S. 486 (1954).

[7] *Brown v. Board of Education of Topeka et al.,* 347 U.S. 294 (1955).

solidating them with the former all-white districts into unitary ones (Mowrey, 1974).

In the city of Wilmington, this typical method of desegregation was not feasible, because attendance zones had been used to segregate the students by race. Thus, the redrawing of these boundaries served as the primary method of mixing the races. Following the procedure of optional attendance zones, school officials in the city boasted of their early success in achieving complete desegregation by 1957.[8]

However, the city school officials had not attained a racial mixture that established racially unidentifiable schools. In the transition to a unitary system, city school officials never compelled their students to attend schools located in the newly drawn attendance zones. Some city students elected to stay in their former schools.[9] Hence, a pattern of racial separation within the city schools continued.

Several factors contributed to the racial separation existing between city and suburban public school students. Starting in the 1930s, and continuing for the next 30 years, the population of New Castle County increased dramatically.[10] Most of the growth occurred in the suburbs. The rapid increase in population brought pressure on the State Board of Education to construct additional schools and reorganize districts into larger, more efficient units. Official responses to the burgeoning growth in population were often accompanied by racially discriminatory housing and real estate practices that exacerbated the racial disparity between city and suburban school populations.[11]

With additional impetus from the 1964 Civil Rights Act, the state board pursued its task of desegregation and set aside its other pressing goal of reorganization. In 1966 the State Board of Education phased out the remaining colored school district in southern Delaware and announced the completion of

[8] *Evans v. Buchanan*, 379 F. Supp. 1218, 1228-30 (Del. 1975).

[9] Ibid. All five of Wilmington's all-black schools prior to 1954 had remained over 90% black for 20 years. With the exception of two suburban districts (De La Warr and Appoquinimink), all suburban districts' 1973 pupil enrollments showed a white population of 89.5% or higher.

[10] U.S. Department of Commerce, Bureau of Census (Delaware 1940–1970).

General Population

Year	Wilmington		New Castle County*	
	White	Nonwhite	White	Nonwhite
1940	98,175	14,327	159,018	20,446
1950	93,031	17,325	193,052	25,827
1960	70,721	25,106	271,168	36,278
1970	44,901	35,080	290,345	48,894

* Excludes Wilmington

[11] *Evans v. Buchanan*, 393 F. Supp. 428, 432–437 (Del. 1975).

the desegregation effort. State school officials then felt free to pursue reorganization of school districts without a view to additional desegregation.[12]

During these years, some Wilmington school activists considered the state's upcoming reorganization effort as a vehicle for addressing the increasing racial disparity between the city and suburban school populations in New Castle County. These citizens pressured state school officials to carve up the city district and merge those sections with parts of the suburban districts to alleviate, in part, what these residents considered *de facto* racial segregation. State school officials refused to consider the issue because they felt the public schools were by then desegregated.[13] The state's eventual reorganization effort in 1968 not only further entrenched the city's segregated school system, but prevented city efforts to alter the situation. State law confined the school district boundaries to the city's boundaries; therefore, no mergers with suburban districts were possible.[14] The state's prohibition of any modification of those boundaries effectively locked the city children into a racially segregatory school system. With so few white students remaining in the city schools, Wilmington school officials were reluctant to disperse them in order to improve the racial mixture in the schools.[15]

It was after the passage of the 1968 Reorganization Act that city activists pursued a judicial course of action to end the racial segregation in their schools. City activists sought a court decree to enable them to merge portions of their district with the outlying suburban districts for purposes of improving educational opportunities (Schmidt, 1979, pp. 167–178). These actions culminated in 1971 in the reopening of an earlier desegregation lawsuit (*Evans v. Buchanan,* originally filed in 1956) to compel state officials to carry out the mandate of the *Brown* ruling. The five black parents who reopened the lawsuit were joined one year clater by the Wilmington Board of Education as party plaintiffs (Schmidt, 1979, pp. 178–183).[16]

Three timely Supreme Court cases were to affect the legal outcome of this 1971 desegregation litigation. In 1968, the Supreme Court clarified its expectations for desegregation remedies ordered in its 1955 *Brown II* decision. The earlier stipulation that permitted gradual desegregation of dual school systems was withdrawn by the Supreme Court in its 1968 *Green* decision.[17] To the Court, 20 years of transition to a dual school system was long enough. The Court now placed responsible school authorities in the position of assuming an "affirmative duty" to desegregate immediately, and to the greatest extent feasible.[18]

In 1972, the Supreme Court ruled (*Swann v. Charlotte-Mecklenburg*) that

---

[12] Wilmington (Del.) *Morning News,* 10 February 1965; Del., State Superintendent, Annual Report (1964–65); Interview with Assistant State Superintendent, 12 June 1978.

[13] Interview with State Superintendent, 30 November 1977.

[14] Educational Advancement Act, 14 Delaware Code 292, secs. 1026, 1004, 1025 (1968).

[15] Interview with former school superintendent, 8 March 1978.

[16] Minutes of the meeting of the Wilmington Board of Education, 19 June 1972.

[17] *Green et al. v. County School Board of New Kent County et al.,* 391 U.S. 432 (1968).

[18] Ibid.

in areas with a history of a dual school system, plaintiffs need not prove fresh intent to segregate in order to obtain relief from past segregatory practices.[19] The Court specified certain measures and tools available to school authorities to reach the goal of the maximum degree of desegregation feasible. Among these provisions was busing of students for purposes of desegregation. The Court noted that transportation had long been used by school districts in their educational systems, and it was considered to be an acceptable tool for desegregation purposes.[20]

The Court also addressed the issue of racial balance or racial quotas in the newly desegregated schools. Use of such indicators was limited, according to the Court. It was not seeking to impose any particular racial balance; instead, school officials were permitted to look at the racial balance in schools for guidance in measuring the extent to which schools had been desegregated.[21]

A third Supreme Court ruling affecting the outcome of the Delaware litigation concerned the interdistrict nature of the remedy. In the *Milliken v. Bradley* decision of 1975, the Court determined that interdistrict remedies were permissible only in cases where the courts had obtained evidence of a Constitutional violation whose very scope and nature required interdistrict relief.[22]

At one time or another in the *Evans* litigation, these cases influenced the course of the remedy. The 1968 *Green* decision opened the way for the plaintiffs to seek additional relief from the state for past segregatory practices. *Green* compelled state officials to eliminate all vestiges of racial segregation immediately. Within *Green,* the obvious segregation in the city school district became reclassified as *de jure* segregation.

The *Swann* decision mandated that the Wilmington school district desegregate its school system by some effective measure, and that busing not be rejected out of hand as an available measure. City school officials believed that any plan they devised to disperse their declining white student population would only aggravate the racial disparity by causing the white parents to withdraw their students from the city's public schools.[23] *Swann* propelled city school officials to pursue another course of action and opened the doors for a remedy using busing for desegregation. *The Milliken* decision also had a bearing on the Delaware case, for it paved the way for a court-ordered interdistrict remedy, the first of its kind in the nation.

---

[19] *Swann et al. v. Charlotte-Mecklenburg Board of Education et al.,* 402 U.S. 1 (1971).

[20] Ibid.

[21] Ibid.

[22] *Milliken, Governor of Michigan et al. v. Bradley et al.,* 418 U.S. 711 (1974).

[23] Letter from J. Stanley Pottinger to Dr. Gene Geisert, Wilmington Public Schools, 17 June 1971, p. 2. Pottinger wrote: "A review of fall 1970 student enrollments and assignment data by your district to this office (Office of Civil Rights) indicates that your system has one or more schools that may be subject to further desegregation steps under the *Swann* decision in order to ensure your district's continued compliance with Title VI of the Civil Rights Act of 1964." Interview with former school superintendent, 8 March 1978.

EVANS V. BUCHANAN—LIABILITY AND REMEDY

During the liability phase of the trial, in the early 1970s, the plaintiffs proved the existence of the vestiges of past discriminatory practices by the state, including unconstitutional government practices in real estate, low-income housing policies, and transportation for nonpublic students. All of these past discriminatory practices contributed to the racial disparity between the city district and the outlying suburban districts.[24] One of the most damaging pieces of evidence presented in court had been the state's 1968 Reorganization Act, which effectively locked in the city district and compelled children living there to attend racially segregated schools.[25] Because of this and other actions, the district court determined that the Constitutional violations against the plaintiffs were interdistrict in scope and therefore required correctional measures that were interdistrict.[26]

The district court ordered relief for the plaintiffs in two ways. First, state authorities were required to submit a desegregation plan that in some way reorganized the city and suburban districts into a unitary system. (All but one suburban district had become part of the remedy when contiguous districts persuaded the court that the exclusion of the noncontiguous districts would create a haven for white flight. The court accepted this argument, and included the noncontiguous districts because they too had participated in the state's prior practices of racial segregation.)[27]

Secondly, the Court ensured the plaintiffs' Constitutional rights by fashioning a default remedy based on current state reorganization principles. According to the state's 1968 Reorganization Act, only whole districts could be merged during consolidation. Extrapolation of this principle led the district court to consolidate the entire county (thus merging whole districts) into a single unitary system.[28] The court's remedy, announced in 1976, would take effect only if responsible state authorities failed to meet their Constitutional duty to submit an acceptable alternative plan.

PUBLIC BODIES AND DESEGREGATION PLANS

Wilmington school officials, under compulsion from *Swann* to complete the desegregation of their schools, joined the *Evans* litigation in 1972 as party plaintiffs. The decision, made initially by the city's white superintendent and a

---

[24] *Evans v. Buchanan*, 379 F. Supp. 1223–1224 (Del., 1974); *Evans v. Buchanan*, 393 F. Supp. 428–437 (Del., 1975).

[25] Ibid.

[26] *Evans v. Buchanan*, 416 F. Supp. 328 (Del., 1976).

[27] Ibid.

[28] Ibid.

mostly black board of education, continued under the leadership of the newly hired black superintendent. The members of the board were divided, however, over their support for the lawsuit. The majority supporting entry did so for several reasons. These members were committed to the concept of integration and were convinced that their current school system offered only a "separate and unequal" educational opportunity for children. By merging the city district with the outlying suburban districts, the board hoped to provide city students with an education on a par with that provided for suburban students. Board members opposed to intervention believed that merging with the white suburbs would be harmful for the majority-black city children; these members viewed the suburbs as a racially hostile environment (Schmidt, 1979).

A further consideration for those black board members who opposed the plan was that they had recently acquired power in the city school system for the first time in its history. From that position of power, they felt that their commitment to the "special educational needs" of the city children could best be met. These members also held the view that national desegregation efforts had demonstrated that blacks did not receive their fair share of administrative posts following desegregation. In addition, they believed the desegregation would increase both the drop-out rate and the suspension rate for blacks. To their minds, discipline would not be free from racial prejudice (Schmidt, 1979). Thus it was a divided city board and a divided community that embarked on this legal excursion in 1972.

The board's official entry into the lawsuit proved critical. Board members believed that their presence in the litigation would give them more control over the final remedy imposed by the court, and to some extent this proved accurate. In case of protracted litigation, legal standing before the court was secured by the board's position as party plaintiffs. Additionally, the board had considerable financial resources at its disposal (compared to the five black plaintiffs) and was able to finance the high-powered litigation. The board retained the services of nationally prominent desegregation attorneys who eventually won the suit, including reimbursement of legal fees. Thus, state money paid for the legal fees of both the defendants and the plaintiffs (Schmidt, 1979).

Suburban districts did not become active participants in the litigation until the close of the liability phase, when the court pointed toward an interdistrict remedy. In 1975, the suburban districts filed motions as party defendants to the suit.[29] As mentioned earlier, the contiguous districts were successful in including the noncontiguous districts in the area to be desegregated. As party defendants, the suburban boards either filed their own appeals or joined with the state to

[29] The suburban districts included: Alfred I. duPont, Alexis I. duPont, Appoquinimink, Claymont, Conrad, De La Warr, Marshallton-McKean, Mt. Pleasant, Newark, New Castle-Gunning Bedford and Stanton. Appoquinimink, in the southernmost portion of the county, had already achieved a fairly integrated school system and was not included in the subsequent "desegregation area" of New Castle County.

seek a reversal of the district court's findings. Considerable effort and many years were devoted by the suburban boards to an unsuccessful campaign against the desegregation decree.

The defendant suburban boards and the state took the position that they had done no wrong to be remedied by the court. Many state officials thought that a single district remedy was undesirable and that a multidistrict solution satisfied state traditions.[30]

In 1976, the court ordered a desegregation remedy from state officials. It also created a five-member Interim Board of Education to develop the court's default remedy for the plaintiffs. The task of the interim board quickly became politically impossible. The same individuals, meeting by day to plan for a desegregation remedy that most of them opposed, met by night as strategists to pursue their litigant interest in reversing the decree.[31] (City board members did not experience this dual role.) Certain interim board members, who believed that the case could require remedial action on their part, signaled acceptance of the court's findings with respect to the liability and remedy in the litigation.

These desegregation planners were given 1 year to prepare for the implementation of a unitary system. The court also allowed for a 2-year transition to full desegregation. By way of guidance, the court permitted a racial ratio in the range of 10% to 35% for each grade, class, and school in the new district.[32] Subsequent county plans that sent children across district lines irked state officials and failed to reorganize districts as required by the court's decree. Maintaining existing district lines was unacceptable, both under the court order and by state tradition. Part of the state's commitment to a multidistrict plan stemmed from the desire to preserve local control in the form of smaller districts. Sending children across district lines compromised the enfranchisement of the parents of these children. Interim board members, representing their constituents, drifted further from their assigned task of devising a default single-district remedy to be adopted in case of default by the state board. The state began to devise its own multidistrict plans and pupil assignments apart from the wavering interim board.[33]

The greatest achievement of the interim board was its organization of task forces. Several members of both suburban and city communities became more aware of the imminent desegregation of their schools and wished to play an active role. For some individuals, this meant an active role against desegregation; for others, it meant either a neutral role or a supportive role.

[30] Interview with Interim Board member, 3 October 1977.

[31] Interviews with Interim Board members: 16 March 1978; 30 March 1978; 10 April 1978; 23 January 1978; 18 April 1978; 3 October 1977; 18 January 1978.

[32] *Evans v. Buchanan*, 416 F. Supp. 328 (Del., 1976). Under the court's order, secondary grades were to be desegregated during the first year. So-called "rising seniors" were exempted from participating in the desegregation remedy.

[33] Wilmington (Delaware) *News Journal,* 3 March 1977.

Task force members included superintendents, school staff, and community activists. Since all districts had been operating as discrete entities, this year gave these various actors the opportunity to meet and exchange ideas with others in the county. Information on courses, students, and finances was gathered by these task forces for the use of the interim board members. Information was also gathered by the Superintendent's Council.

Despite this, the interim board was unable to pursue a steady course. One contingent of members drafted plans and rationales that created temporary districts and assigned students to grade centers—measures that could easily be undone upon a legal reversal.[34] Other factions on the interim board developed countywide plans that the majority board disregarded.[35] The remaining board members attempted to find a compromise between the two opposing camps by proposing a three-district remedy as a middle ground for those who favored six districts and those who favored one district.[36] No consensus was reached by interim board members, however.

Following a ruling from the Third Circuit Court of Appeals,[37] which upheld the findings of the lower court but discarded the racial ratio guidelines, the state board disbanded the interim board in July of 1977.[38] Meanwhile, the state board had failed to win legislative support for its own three-district plan. After the Circuit Court outlined the requirements of the remedy, state officials in charge of the legal strategy altered their course. Rather than follow the ruling of the majority of judges in the Circuit decision, the state officials adopted a course that seemed to reflect the dissenting opinion expressed in the Circuit Court decision. The key words that guided recalcitrant state officials were in the dissenter's remark that the remedy should place the victims of the violation in the position they would have been in "but for" the violation against them.[39]

Here the state board followed the advice of high ranking state officials, including state legislators, who proceeded to characterize the desegregation case (which they had earlier called a racial balance suit) now as a suit to ensure that black students in the city would attend suburban schools.[40] (The De La Warr district, which housed the county's second largest black population, had been considered a black district by desegregation planners prior to this point; it was now lumped in with the white districts under this strategy.)

[34] Memo to Interim Board of Education from J. Reardon, 9 September 1976.

[35] Interviews with Interim Board members: 16 March 1978; 30 March 1978; 10 April 1978; 23 January 1978; 18 April 1978; 3 October 1977; 18 January 1978.

[36] Ibid., Minutes from Interim Board meeting, 16 March 1977.

[37] *Evans v. Buchanan*, 555 F. sd. 373 (3rd Cir., 1977).

[38] Wilmington (Delaware) *News Journal*, 8 June 1977.

[39] Report to the State Board of Education, June, 1977, pp. 3, 6–23; Wilmington (Delaware) *News Journal* 25 June 1977.

[40] Appellant's Reply Brief in U.S. Court of Appeals for the Third Circuit, "Report of the State Board of Education Required by the Opinion and Order of the Circuit Court of Appeals in This Case." (Summer, 1977), pp. 17–18.

The state, discarding its three-district plan, now readied its new desegregation proposal for the court. This "but for" plan, also called *reverse volunteerism,* reflected the state's new strategy of seeking a stay of desegregation in the hope that a review of the case by the Supreme Court would reverse the lower decree to the state's advantage, defendant's favor. The "but for" plan attempted to calculate the number of black city children who would have attended suburban schools except for the Constitutional violations committed against them. On arriving at various figures supposedly corresponding to each violation, the state board submitted the plan to the district court for its review in the summer of 1977.[41]

Three weeks of evidentiary hearings followed. Testimony and evidence submitted to the court showed that the plan was flawed on procedural, substantive, and equitable grounds. The district court objected to the voluntary nature of the plan, which reassigned certain black students to suburban schools although leaving them the freedom to remain in their current school. The plan's failure to promise to desegregate the county schools to the greatest extent feasible, coupled with its imposition of the burden of desegregation only on the victims of the violation, constituted the chief reasons for the district court's rejection of it. The district court was compelled to grant the defendants their stay of desegregation, but only on a limited basis.[42]

When a timely Supreme Court denial of review confirmed the lower court's position,[43] the district court then reactivated the earlier board to plan only for the desegregation of a single countywide unitary district in conformity with the 1976 court's default provision. As with the earlier ruling, the district court again invited state officials to come forth at any time with an alternative plan of their own.[44]

Several factors accounted for the success of the planning board's development of a single district remedy. After the Supreme Court denied review of the case in the early part of the fall, planning board members finally accepted the inevitability of desegregation and were more committed to serious remedies. Also, the court played a more active role than it had previously done, requiring the planning board to submit biweekly reports of its progress to the court.

The size of the planning board was set at five members, and this enhanced consensus. Board members were instructed not to pursue multidistrict plans. Although the planning board members continued to exhibit factional disputes, with many decisions made on a 3–2 split vote, nevertheless the board did achieve its overall task of devising a default desegregation plan.

[41] Wilmington (Delaware) *Morning News,* 27 May 1977; *Morning News,* 16 June 1977; *Morning News,* 27 June 1977; *Morning News,* 19 June 1977; *News Journal,* 25 June 1977; *News Journal* 6 July 1977.

[42] *Evans v. Buchanan,* 435 F. Supp. 832 (Del., 1977).

[43] Wilmington (Delaware *News Journal,* 5 August 1977.

[44] *Evans v. Buchanan,* 435 F. Supp. 832 (Del., 1977).

PUPIL ASSIGNMENTS

One of the most controversial issues confronting board members and community activists was that of pupil reassignment in desegregation. The original district court findings and orders called for reassignment of both students and staff in order to eliminate the racial identifiability of the county school system. Some of the early desegregation plans (at one point totaling over 19 separate proposals) split the reassignment of students over a 2-year period, reassigning the upper grades the first year of desegregation. When the 1976 court handed down its decision, it exempted "rising seniors" from reassignment, allowing them to complete their final high school year in their home district.[45] However, the 1977 stay of desegregation cancelled that extension and all grades were ordered to desegregate immediately.

Another pupil assignment plan that developed in the early stages reflected suburban community interests. County school officials considered a pupil assignment plan that established grade centers in the city (and De La Warr) schools offering grades 5–9.[46] The grade center approach was a compromise for the suburban districts in that it demonstrated a commitment to two-way busing on the part of city and suburban populations.

One prevailing misconception among community, school, and public officials during the litigation was the belief that the High Court was requiring a racial balance. To that end, board members designed pupil assignments that would mix the school populations in the same racial proportion as the county's overall population. That racial ratio was 80:20 white to black.[47] In 1977, desegregation planners sought such a mirror image in the school population. By locating grade centers in the city and transporting suburban children to them for 2 of their 12 years of education, the planners could achieve that desired racial balance. The middle years were selected for the grade centers because the majority of desegregation planners believed that these years would be more acceptable to the suburban parents, most of whom viewed the early and later years of the educational experience in their home district as most valuable.[48]

Wilmington and De La Warr desegregation planners opposed these measures. Both districts objected to the loss of their school systems, especially their high schools. The conversion of their schools into grade centers was viewed as a punitive measure against them for bringing the litigation initially. District

---

[45] *Evans v. Buchanan,* 416 F. Supp. 328 (Del., 1976).

[46] Wilmington (Delaware) *News Journal,* 5 January 1977; *News Journal,* 6 January 1977; *News Journal,* 11 January 1977. Minutes from the Interim Board meetings, 13 January 1977; 10 January 1977.

[47] Ibid., Interview with Interim Board member, 3 October 1977.

[48] Ibid., Interviews with Planning Board members: 22 August 1978; 19 July 1978; 24 February 1978; 23 January 1978.

planners also felt that it would harm the black students to see that their high schools were considered inferior to the suburban schools.[49]

In an effort to gain some measure of equity in this aspect of desegregation planning, the city representative on the planning board, together with certain city school administrators, secretly designed an alternative pupil assignment plan to submit to the district court. In this plan, *Plan W*, the city representative claimed that the capacity in the city school system allowed for a greater number of years for suburban children to attend city schools.[50] The city representative also challenged the dominant 10–2 plan by arguing that a more equitable arrangement would be achieved if the number of years were increased that members of both races (but not necessarily each member of both races) would be transported to either city or suburban schools. In this scheme of 6–6, blacks and whites would be bused an average of 6 years of their educational experience.[51]

Suburban board members were divided on this issue. The majority of them were committed to the principle that a stable and equitable arrangement in pupil assignments could only be achieved by treating all suburban students alike and by treating all city students alike. The plan which bused both races for an *average* of 6 years meant, in practice, that some students would be bused for 12 years of their education and other students, of the same race, would be bused for none of those years.[52] One member of the board objected to the treatment of the city schools as grade centers only, and noted that black parents considered the early and later years of education to be just as critical as did the white parents.[53]

When the majority (10–2) and minority (6–6) pupil assignment plans were finally submitted to the district court in the fall of 1977, the court, comparing both plans, decided that equity necessitated the lessening of the burden of busing on the victims of discrimination. The court then sequestered its own pupil assignment committee to flesh out various 9–3 pupil assignment proposals.[54]

Among its other tasks, the committee recommended that several schools be closed. Thus, two of the most controversial issues in this litigation, pupil assignments and school closings, were sheltered from intense public pressure. The district court also ordered its pupil assignment committee to retain a 1–12 grade structure in the city. The pupil assignment committee worked under a court gag order, put in place to help insulate the committee from political pressures. The

[49] Ibid.

[50] Interview with Planning Board member, 23 January 1978.

[51] Ibid., Participant Observer at 1977 District Court hearings.

[52] Interview with Planning Board member, 3 August 1978.

[53] Interview with Planning Board member, 22 August 1978; Wilmington (Delaware) *Morning News*, 23 January 1977; *Morning News*, January 28, 1977.

[54] *Evans v. Buchanan*, 477 F. Supp. 982 (Del., 1978).

pupil assignment committee developed various pupil assignment configurations and continued informally to seek an 80:20 racial ratio in all county schools.[55]

On learning that a 9–3 pupil assignment plan was feasible, the court ordered the planning board to select one of those schemes.[56] Not all board members were pleased with the final 9–3 plan. A few members sought exemptions for certain seniors who were to be transferred their final year. The majority on the board, however, prohibited any special treatment in hopes of bringing fairness to the entire community.[57]

The already-approved four attendance zones for the countywide district were modified by the planning board in conformity with the new pupil assignments so that no students were bused to schools outside their attendance area. Public dissemination of the pupil assignment plan lessened the uncertainty over school assignments for parents in the community. It enabled some individuals to begin making plans to familiarize the community with its new schools. Board members were satisfied with the adjustable attendance zones in the countywide district, enabling them to maintain fairly similar racial ratios among the four attendance areas.

With pupil assignments available to the public, the planning board members turned their attention to other concerns. Decisions on discipline policies, school closings, and teacher contracts awaited board action. These issues were not resolved without great dissatisfaction on the part of both the community and the staff. For the first 3 years of desegregation, officials of the single district had to cope with one or more of these trying conflicts.

With encouragement from business, religious, social, political, and community groups, the county board began its first year of desegregation peacefully in 1978. The board operated a countywide desegregated district for 3 years. State opposition to the single district remained steady until the state board finally won legislative and judicial support for a multidistrict arrangement beginning in the fourth year of desegregation.

FIRST THREE YEARS OF DESEGREGATION

One of the most difficult reorganization issues to confront desegregation planners stemmed from the disparate economies found among the 11 component

---

[55] Interviews with Pupil Assignment Committee members: 25 February 1980; 15 November 1978. The Pupil Assignment Committee members all agreed that three-year grade centers enhanced educational program offerings. Members made no attempt to divide Wilmington in order to redistribute its wealth among the suburban areas.

[56] *Evans v. Buchanan*, 477 F. Supp. 982 (Del., 1978).

[57] Wilmington (Delaware) *Morning News*, 14 April 1978.

county districts. The districts varied in their relative wealth and relative degree of teacher union strength, and consequently in financial support for public education. Reorganization tossed these distinct communities into one pool and proved to be the catalyst for the adjustment of tax rates to enable leveling-up of teachers' salaries. Desegregation planners perceived that it was impossible to expect staff to work in comparable positions in the same buildings at different salary levels. Teachers, too, grasped the district's untenable position and demanded that all salaries be leveled-up to the highest pay scale, that of the Wilmington school teachers.[58]

Attitudes in the community were divided on this issue. Wilmington teachers, who already enjoyed the highest pay scale and recalled the absence of suburban support for their 1975 teachers' strike, lacked the incentive to join the drive for higher salaries. Others in the community believed that the suburban teachers seized the moment and greedily sought a windfall of higher incomes. A third faction in the community felt that equity was best rendered in uniformity of pay scales and subscribed to the principle of equal pay for equal work.[59]

Teachers in the county began the first year of desegregation in 1978 without a contract and without settlement of several outstanding issues, including pay scales. Nevertheless, teachers were committed to a peaceful transition to desegregated education and temporarily were willing to overlook the absence of a negotiated contract. By mid-October, however, the suburban-based union members had reached the limit of their patience with the district administration. Mounting frustration over the delay in signing a contract between the suburban-based teachers' union and the central administration pressed the union toward a severe job action. In the latter part of October, the membership voted overwhelmingly for a strike.[60]

The teachers' strike lasted 6 weeks. Division and mistrust continued. Before the strike was over, several different parties (the board, the governor, teachers, parents, union officials, arbitrators, and even the district court judge) were involved in an examination of the district's financial resources. With public pressure leaning in the teachers' favor, the county board agreed to level-up salaries over a 3-year period. Wilmington teachers did not escape suburban resentment for their failure to support the teachers' strike.[61]

The aftermath of the strike gradually faded as a new problem arose in the form of the state's four-district reorganization scheme. The community's sense

---

[58] Wilmington (Delaware) *Morning News*, 6 May 1977; *Morning News*, 18 November 1977; *Morning News*, 14–19 1977.

[59] Ibid., Participant Observer at various community meetings.

[60] In October, unresolved contract issues included: job security, grievance procedures, class size, discipline codes, leveling-up of salaries. See Wilmington (Delaware) *Morning News*, 5, 8, 11, 13 October 1978; Newark (Delaware) *Weekly Post*, 11 October 1978.

[61] Three years earlier, the NCCEA failed to support the WFT strike in Wilmington. Wilmington (Delaware) *Morning News*, 5, 6 October 1978.

of relief at the cessation of the strike quickly disappeared when the state announced its intention of dismantling the single district. The thought of further disruption in the public schools united the county in strong opposition to the state's proposal. Long-time multidistrict advocates lent their support to the rejection of the multidistrict plan and urged the state to wait for a more propitious moment to advance its reorganization plan. The state prudently withdrew its four-district plan in the face of almost universal public disapproval.[62]

Two years later, in 1980, under more favorable circumstances, including a direct invitation from the Third Circuit Court of Appeals, the state board, with the endorsement of the state legislature, secured judicial approval for transition to a multidistrict form of school organization. Some members of the county board of education protested the division of the single district and the consequent loss of flexibility in adjusting attendance zones for purposes of racial balance. Other members voiced their concern that a change to four districts would generate a likelihood of increased turmoil and instability—primarily in the form of white flight. Black representatives to the board objected to the plan because they felt that it fragmented the highly desirable and effective convergence of minority interests achieved under the management of a central administration and board for the entire county.[63]

The interests supporting a multidistrict plan prevailed in court, but not without certain conditions. These attached conditions indicated a change in the district court's position toward a monitoring agency. (The 1976 court did not see a need for such an agency.) The attached conditions also demonstrated the difficulties encountered by the county district over the preceding 3 years.[64]

ANCILLARY RELIEF AND FINANCIAL TURMOIL

Pupil assignments and teachers' contracts were only two of the complex and politically unpopular questions faced by the county's desegregation planners. Those two concerns tended to divide the county board from the community, but the issues of tax rates and ancillary relief strained the relationship between the county board and the state.

Even more than pupil assignments, the issue of ancillary relief highlighted the differing assumptions among school officials about the nature of desegregation. Ancillary relief had been sanctioned by the Supreme Court in its 1975

---

[62] Wilmington (Delaware) *Morning News,* 9 February 1979.

[63] *Evans v. Buchanan,* 512 F. Supp. 839 (1981); "Public Comment on the proposed Reorganization of the New Castle County School District," (Dover, Delaware: Department of Public Instruction, November 20, 1980); "Regulations for the Reorganization of New Castle County School District," (Dover, Delaware: Department of Public Instruction, November 20, 1980); Wilmington (Delaware) *News Journal,* 15 November 1980.

[64] Ibid.

Milliken II decision.[65] Desegregation, explained the High Court, entailed more than the physical reassignment of pupils to new schools. Remedial aid to the victims of segregation addressed the educational deficiencies engendered by the inequality of opportunity.

Based on this rationale for correcting some of the inequities connected to racial segregation, the 1976 district court ordered a spectrum of ancillary relief measures. Included were in-service training for staff; reading and communications programs; human relations training; and a host of racially nonidentifiable practices pertaining to such matters as instructional materials, discipline policies, guidance counseling, and school closings, openings, and expansions.[66]

The state opposed the provision of ancillary relief services, partly because the state was targeted to finance them. Also, the state viewed desegregation solely in terms of pupil assignments. County school officials, on the other hand, had testified to the merits of ancillary relief and greatly desired its inclusion in any desegregation remedy.[67]

Funding for ancillary relief was based on a formula that placed a diminishing share of the burden on the state and an increasing absorption of the costs by the county district. Money from the Emergency School Aid Act (ESAA), used to help finance ancillary relief programs, also decreased from an initial $6.7 million to $2.9 million in the third year. (The district had been strapped for money ever since the state legislature readjusted the tax rate downward.) Thus, the district felt the financial pinch of this added cost.[68]

While it was available, ESAA money benefited both black and white students in the county schools. Administrators of the grant money were thankful for the large initial amounts since the district court had never specified how much should be spent on ancillary relief. ESAA administrators believed that, if left to itself, the state's provision of ancillary relief would have been minuscule by comparison.[69]

The district's financial crisis was due to factors other than ancillary relief services. When the state had failed to submit a suitable desegregation remedy to the court, the judge authorized the implementation of a default single-district alternative. The district court set a range of permissible tax rates for the county district to provide for the current level of funding for education and for desegregation-related expenses incurred by the county board of education.[70]

---

[65] *Milliken, Governor of Michigan et al. v. Bradley et al.*, 433 U.S. 267 (1975).

[66] *Evans v. Buchanan*, 416 F. Supp. 328 (Del., 1976).

[67] Ibid., *Evans v. Buchanan*, 447 F. Supp. 982 (1982).

[68] Interview with ESAA Administrator, 15 September 1981.

[69] Ibid.

[70] *Evans v. Buchanan*, 447 F. Supp. 982 (1978); "State Board Resolution Establishing Maximum Tax Rate for the Single Judicially Reorganized School District in New Castle County Pursuant to Senate Bill 457, April 17, 1978; Wilmington (Delaware) *Morning News*, 24 February 1978; *Morning News*, 28 April 1978.

In the winter of 1978, after the district court suggested a tax range, outraged state officials sought a lower rate through a legal appeal to the Third Circuit Court. The Third Circuit Court upheld the state's lower tax rate, to the dismay of county school officials, who were now asked to operate their school system with less money than available prior to desegregation.[71] Some of the state's motivation stemmed from a desire to lessen the burden of taxation on certain county districts that saw their tax rate nearly double under the court's calculations.

The Third Circuit Court's ruling in favor of the state came as a mixed blessing to its petitioners. The Court agreed that the state was empowered to set the tax rate for the county district; however, the county district was not free to spend its revenues without certain attached conditions. First and foremost, the district's finances had to meet desegregation-related costs; only after satisfying those superceding obligations was the district free to spend its resources on other educational objectives.[72]

The state's success in reducing the tax rate for the single district began a vicious cycle of economic cutbacks and layoffs entailing constant movement of personnel among the district's schools. In its second year of desegregation the county board pursued its only available course of action for increasing its revenues. It held a tax referendum for the county's endorsement. The community, however, frustrated and bitter about the desegregation issue, the management of the district, and the worsening general economic climate, expressed their opposition in a rousing defeat of the tax increase by a 10–1 margin.[73]

Mismanagement and cutbacks took their toll on the single district. The county board closed schools to save money and continued to lay off personnel. The ensuing disruptions from these actions generated more instability in the district. Parents threatened to withdraw their children from the schools; staff members were demoralized by the constant shifts in personnel.[74]

The lack of support for the single district convinced county residents that the state would only lend its assistance under a multidistrict arrangement. When, by the third year of desegregation, the state did devise an acceptable four-district plan, the public was ready to support the transition.

---

[71] *Evans v. Buchanan*, 455 F. Supp. 715 (Del., 1978); "Petition for Writ of Mandamus," filed by State Department of Justice, State of Delaware, Floyd Abrams, Special Counsel for the State, to the U.S. Third Circuit Court of Appeals, 1978.

[72] *Evans v. Buchanan*, 468 F. Supp. 944 (Del., 1979).

[73] Wilmington (Delaware) *Morning News*, 25 September 1980; *Morning News*, 23 October 1980.

[74] Wilmington (Delaware) *Morning News*, 24 April 1980; Newark (Delaware) *Weekly Post*, 30 April 1980; *News Journal*, 27 April 1980; *Morning News*, 15 May 1980; *Weekly Post*, 14 May 1980; *News Journal*, 15 June 1980; *Morning News*, 18 July 1980; *Morning News*, 14 July 1980; *Morning News*, 5 March 1980; Participant Observer at Parents' Review Committee Meeting, 18 March 1980.

STATE LEGISLATURE

Through the years, the state legislature had adopted a resistant and obstructive position toward racial desegregation of the county's public schools. In the mid-1960s, the legislature refused to desegregate the city schools fully and later maneuvered to overturn the court's decree. Strategies of opposition included trying to impeach the district court judges hearing the case, delaying the funding of transportation for desegregation, and capitalizing on the anti-busing sentiment in the county.

State legislators objected strongly to the court's intrusion into the local arena. The specter of "forced busing" descended on lawmakers, who quickly pursued voluntary means of desegregation, including voluntary transfer plans and magnet schools. Early in the litigation, lawmakers latched onto the notion that any action on their part to desegregate the schools would jeopardize their success in the appeals process.[75]

The state's 2-year voluntary transfer plan (majority to minority exchanges) in 1975–1976 failed to alter the racial identifiability of the county schools to any substantial degree. Most of the transfers were one-way, with black students seeking to leave majority-black schools and enter mostly white schools in the suburbs (Bresnahan & Showell, 1977).[76]

Magnet schools, which were favored by several county and state desegregation planners, also failed to desegregate the county schools. Part of the reason was that the necessary endorsement for winning federal money for magnet schools was not forthcoming from the predominantly black districts in the county.[77]

When these measures were abandoned, the state then offered its "reverse volunteerism" plan in the summer of 1977. Again, the state included a "voluntary" component in the plan, but with a twist. Black city students were reassigned to suburban schools but could elect to remain in their city schools. Not until all appeals were exhausted did the state legislature grant the state board the power to redivide the county district.[78]

The court accepted the state's "good faith" in preparing a four-district plan. However, because of certain other desegregation-related concerns, the court advised the state to establish a monitoring agency to report regularly to the court. The court also wanted the state to finance a study of the administration of discipline in the county schools, with an eye to racial prejudice.

[75] Interview with State Legislator, 24 July 1978.

[76] House Bill 1198, signed by Governor Tribbitt on June 25, 1976; Wilmington (Delaware) *Morning News*, 12 August 1977; *Morning News*, 8 June 1977.

[77] Participant Observer at Magnet School Meeting, 4 August 1977.

[78] *Evans v. Buchanan*, 435 F. Supp. 832 (1977); Wilmington (Delaware) *News Journal*, 29 May 1977; *Morning News*, 19 June 1977; *News Journal*, 17 May 1980; *News Journal*, 17 May 1980; *Morning News*, 20 June 1980.

STUDENT CODE OF CONDUCT

In July of 1978, the county desegregation planners began to draft a student code of conduct. Although certain districts, such as Wilmington, did not permit the use of corporal punishment, other districts did. Disagreement among the staff and public was strong. In the end, the board included a corporal punishment provision in the code because it appeared that public sentiment favored it.[79]

The most troublesome problems with the code of conduct revolved around various interpretations by school administrators. In the first year of desegregation, the code and punishments were handled by classroom teachers. With the resulting racially disproportionate number of suspensions, however, pressure mounted to revise the reporting system.[80]

The primary infractions during the first year of desegregation were fights on buses and on school property. The discrepancy between black and white suspensions continued in the next year. The county board member representing the city district pursued his request for an independent study of the entire suspension procedure in the county schools. This board member also voiced his concern over the disproportionate number of black students placed in special education classes. Eventually, the matter was brought before the district court in hearings on the state's four-district plan. The plaintiffs argued that an independent study of suspension, expulsion, and dropout rates in the district was necessary. These racially disproportionate rates signaled to some the fact that the district had not completed its transition to a unitary school system.[81]

The state offered to finance such a study, to please the court. The court, convinced of the state's "good faith," permitted the reorganization of the single district into four districts, with the stipulation that a monitoring agency be established along with the independent investigation of discipline.

COMMUNITY REACTION

The community's response to the desegregation litigation was largely antagonistic. Agreement in the city of Wilmington over the desirability of the lawsuit was not to be found among the black community. The suburban communities were overwhelmingly opposed to the consequences of the litigation,

[79] Wilmington (Delaware) *Morning News,* 17 July 1978; *Morning News,* 21 July 1978; Interviews with county board members: 22 August 1978; 3 August 1978.

[80] Wilmington (Delaware) *News Journal,* 6 May 1979; Newark (Delaware) *Weekly Post,* 14 February 1979; *News Journal,* 31 March 1979.

[81] Wilmington (Delaware) *News Journal,* 6 May 1979; Minutes of the New Castle County Board of Education meetings: 25 January 1980; 24 July 1980; 28 August 1980; Memo to Dr. Carroll Biggs from Dr. Richard Linnett, 17 January 1980.

which meant disruption of established ways and busing of students away from their neighborhood schools.

The minimal support for desegregation came largely from religious sectors and certain groups in the city of Wilmington. The U. S. Department of Justice placed a community relations specialist in the county to help smooth the way for a peaceful transition to desegregation.[82] In addition to religious leaders, a small group of citizens, including university professionals, school administrators, members of civic associations like the League of Women Voters, and school activists began early in the mid-1970s to prepare the community and the students for the upcoming change in their school environments.

Most of the early preparations involved either workshops or conferences about desegregation and the major issues connected with the transition. In these early meetings, ways were explored to educate the public about the nature of the lawsuit and to ensure fair treatment of students in the desegregated setting. Although these small groups attempted to win larger support from such public bodies as the interim board of education, they were handicapped by individuals who remained unconvinced of the inevitability of desegregation and objected to plans to prepare the community for it.[83]

The most extensive response to desegregation came from citizens opposed to the lawsuit. Opposition to desegregation took two forms: withdrawal to non-public schools and organization into the county's Positive Action Committee— the spearhead of anti-busing sentiment. From 1975 to 1978, over 1,500 children were enrolled in Christian schools in the county. In April of 1978, two new nonpublic schools opened their doors in New Castle County. By 1979, eight new schools had opened in the county. Most of these schools were offering grades 1–8, which coincided with the majority of busing years for suburban students. However, public school administrators did not view these schools and their enrollments as constituting substantial white flight from the district.[84]

In the first year of desegregation, the county school population totalled 55,000 students—an enrollment decline of approximately 9%. In the second year, there was an 8% decline, but in the third year, the decline was only 5.6%.[85] Prior to the fourth year of desegregation, population projections estimated a decline in District I's enrollment, an unpredictable pattern in District II, a stable pattern in District III, and an increase in District IV.

District officials did not consider these figures as proof of white flight. By the third year of desegregation, the enrollments in the nonpublic schools had begun to decline after a 5- to 6-year increase. Parochial schools were not showing

---

[82] Interview with Community Relations Service Officer, 5 February 1979.

[83] Interview with Alliance members: 22 September 1978; 30 May 1978; Interview with DCSD members, 9 November 1978; 12 December 1978; 20 December 1977; 25 August 1978.

[84] Interview with Head Start official, 21 May 1980; Interview with top school official, 29 April 1981; Wilmington (Delaware) *Morning News,* 28 February 1978; *Morning News,* 5 April 1978; *Morning News,* 25 April 1978.

[85] Interview with top school official, 29 April 1981.

large increases in their enrollments, and private schools showed a decrease by the third year of desegregation. Also, nearby out-of-state schools were not showing large increases in their enrollment either. Thus, the 5.6% decline in the third year was attributed to the lower birth rate and not to white flight. However, it was clear that the enrollments in the county's Christian schools had come entirely from the county population, whereas other nonpublic schools in the county drew in part from out-of-state and downstate pupils.[86]

Parents and others who felt that they could not work with or express their opposition to desegregation through school boards or school organizations took part in community demonstrations against desegregation. In the spring of 1977, pupil protests among junior and senior high school students marked early resistance to desegregation. These student protests were repeated nearly one year later with more secondary school students.[87] In 1978, over 370 pupils picketed outside their school buildings. The momentum carried through the week until over 3,000 students had joined in some sort of protest activity. Protesting students tended to receive the support of their parents.[88]

Some parents formed an organization called Concerned Parents for Childrens' Rights. Although they planned for future demonstrations against "forced busing," at no time did any group advocate violent opposition to desegregation. Eventually even this group of parents joined in more formal school liaisons for parental input into school affairs.[89] In the spring of 1978, another group of anti-busing parents formed a loose coalition against desegregation, but within weeks the coalition collapsed from lack of support.[90]

The core of the anti-busing public joined the county's Positive Action Committee. This organization, whose membership reached a peak of over 10,000 in 1975, served as the focus for anti-busing sentiment and resistance strategies. The Committee at no point encouraged violent opposition to desegregation. The PAC proved to be an effective wielder of influence in the state legislature in securing legal assistance for the state lawmakers in this litigation.[91]

The Committee also distributed pamphlets updating the national anti-busing movement. PAC's height of influence was reached in 1978 when its president

---

[86] Interview with top school official, 19 April 1981.

[87] Wilmington (Delaware) News Journal, 26 March 1977. Students protested at the Brandywine Junior High School in Marshallton-McKean School District.

[88] Wilmington (Delaware) Morning News, 21 March 1978. Junior high (and eventually senior high) students protested in the Stanton School District. Morning News, 22 March 1978; Morning News, 23 March 1978. For a full week prior to spring break, nearly 3,000 students participated in nonviolent protests against "forced busing."

[89] Wilmington (Delaware) Morning News, 13 April 1978; Morning News, 8 April 1978.

[90] Wilmington (Delaware) Morning News, 3 April 1978; Morning News, 25 April 1978. This final spurt of anti-busing activity manifested itself in Claymont.

[91] For a profile of PAC's leader, James Venema, see Philadelphia Bulletin, 20 July 1975. For an extensive review of PAC's activities see Jeffrey A. Raffel's The Politics of School Desegregation, (Philadelphia: Temple University Press, 1980), pp. 154–173 in passim.

made his bid for the Republican nomination to the U.S. Senate. However, the candidate failed to win widespread party support. When desegregation began peacefully in the county, citizens slowly resigned themselves to the inevitability of desegregation. The membership in the Positive Action Committee dropped dramatically. Nevertheless, the committee continued to be unwilling to cooperate with the growing sentiment that sought a neutral ground between anti-busing and pro-busing positions.[92]

An organization that became known as the Citizens' Alliance for Public Education grew out of cooperative efforts among black and white city and suburban school activists and organizations. This group attracted pro-busing members of the community, because it advocated a position of lawful acceptance of desegregation. It also attracted members of several diverse religious, community, business, social, and school organization. Police, clergy, parent–teacher organizations, and others joined under this one umbrella organization to advocate a peaceful transition to desegregation. The group overcame racial strains that had developed between the city-based Parent Teachers Organization and the community-based PTA. The Citizens' Alliance was very active in educating the public and in supporting the local school officials empowered to supervise the operation of the county schools. As the four-district plan emerged and citizen interest in desegregation dwindled, the Alliance finally disbanded.[93]

Over time these activists channeled their energies into the newly established CACs (Citizen Advisory Councils) set up in the county and then in each of the four discrete districts in the county. Here parents and teachers expressed their concerns on a wide range of issues that now constituted their school agenda. These issues included disciplinary measures, affirmative action policies, staff reductions, racial balance, ability grouping, declining pupil enrollments, curriculum, financing, minority parent participation, and attitudes toward desegregation and school closings.[94]

In some districts, black leaders were able to continue their established contacts with school district administrators through the Wilmington Community Leaders. This group, organized in the first years of desegregation, served as a focus for black interests and influence in school affairs. Not all of the four new districts continued this informal communication.[95]

Although discipline issues continued to remain highly controversial, school

---

[92] Wilmington (Delaware) *Morning News,* 13 July 1978. At no time did PAC actively join the Citizens' Alliance.

[93] Interviews with Citizens' Alliance for Public Education members: 30 May 1978; 22 September 1978.

[94] Highlights of Minutes of New Castle County School District's citizens Advisory Councils (1978–1981) for Areas I, II, III, IV.

[95] Interview with federal officer, 25 August 1981; Interview with school administrator, summer, 1981; Minutes from the Wilmington Community Leaders meetings; 9 January 1978 through 28 November 1980.

officials noted that the racial climate in the schools had improved over the years. These officials concluded that the stable feeder patterns had probably contributed to the familiarity students had with each other by the time they reached junior high. Students were also more aware of school rules by the secondary years.[96]

SUMMARY

What began in the 1950s as an effort to achieve equal educational opportunities for blacks culminated in a final lawsuit litigated in the mid-1970s. This third phase of the *Evans* litigation ushered in a dramatic change in the public school system for New Castle County. A district court, finding that interdistrict violations required interdistrict relief, ordered state officials to submit an acceptable desegregation/reorganization scheme that promised to provide for immediate fulfillment of the plaintiffs' constitutional rights. However, strong opposition to the judicial branch and to racial integration fostered protracted litigation coupled with a general void of political leadership in the community.

This void was eventually filled by the county's school board members, community activists, teachers, parents, and others. Under a cloak of law-abidingness, a large segment of the community was drawn into the public arena in order to influence a range of concerns, including white flight, ability grouping, pupil assignments, affirmative action, teachers' contracts, school closings, racial balance, and local control.

The court's provision of a unitary district in the form of a single countywide system failed to secure the support of state officials. After 3 years of operation, the state then developed a responsible desegregation remedy that divided the county into four districts, retaining the previous pupil assignment plan. New school boards were now invested with the responsibility of restoring public support of the schools as well as ensuring quality education and fair treatment of the diverse populations in their school districts.

REFERENCES

Bresnahan, R. B. & Showell, H. I. (1977, February). *Report on voluntary student transfer program.* Dover, DE: Department of Public Instruction.

Hoffecker, C. (Ed.). (1973). *Readings in Delaware history.* Newark, DE: Univ. of Delaware Press.

Madden, K. C. (1969). *History of education in Delaware.* Dover, DE: Department of Public Instruction.

Mowrey, R. C. (1974). *Delaware school district organization and boundaries.* Dover, DE: Department of Public Instruction.

Schmidt J. A. (1979). *School desegregation in Wilmington, Delaware: A case study in non-decision-making.* Unpublished master's thesis, University of Delaware, Newark, DE.

---

[96] Interviews with top school officials: 28 April 1981; 29 April 1981.

3

Educational Components

CASSANDRA A. SIMMONS

In 1978, on the first day of school desegregation in New Castle County, students confronted a challenge more profound than merely riding a school bus or adjusting to a strange, new school building. Most white students had to face for the first time the reality of living in a multiracial world. Few students of either race were prepared for the clash of cultures that would inevitably occur. Racial minority children, most of them poor and undereducated, had to confront the affluence and relatively advanced academic status of their new suburban classmates. White children, most of them middle-class, had to confront the impoverished environment surrounding inner-city schools. In addition, all students had to contend with the racial stereotypes fostered by our race-conscious society.

Educators in New Castle County's desegregated schools were venturing on a complex mission. It is true that dedication and skill are required to teach a homogeneous class composed of children of similar family background and comparable academic achievement. In a heterogeneous classroom, however, with students of different race, socioeconomic status, and educational experience, even more is demanded. Teachers must teach not only one type of student, but all types of students. Teachers must dedicate themselves not only to the white and the well-to-do, but to the black and brown and the poor as well.

Teachers and administrators are often little better prepared than their students to cope with desegregation. Many carry with them long histories of personal prejudice, and few have had constructive interracial experiences. School systems themselves, used to dealing with racially and culturally homogeneous student populations, often carry structural vestiges of their segregated pasts. Furthermore, many minority students enter desegregation with accumulated educational and psychological deficits from years of inferior, segregated schooling. Many ma-

CASSANDRA A. SIMMONS ● Urban Affairs Programs, Affirmative Action Graduate Financial Assistance Program, Michigan State University, East Lansing, Michigan 48824.

jority students, on the other hand, enter with dangerous and erroneous perceptions of innate superiority. Merely reassigning pupils is not enough if the goal is to equalize education for all children.

The judicial system in recent years has come to share this view, and judges now often include in their desegregation decrees requirements that schools modify discriminatory policies and practices. As the Supreme Court ruled in 1977, "Pupil assignment alone does not automatically remedy the impact of previous unlawful educational isolation; the consequences linger and can be dealt with only by independent measures."[1] With that statement, the Court sanctioned the use of "educational components" in the Detroit desegregation case. The Court approved a district court decree ordering the Detroit Public Schools and the State of Michigan to share the cost of four specific procedures: remedial reading classes for the victims of prior segregation; in-service training sessions to sensitize school personnel to the needs of multiracial schools; cessation of the misuse of standardized tests; and modification of discriminatory counseling and career guidance programs.

Less than 2 years later, the district court in the New Castle County case included a 6-point battery of educational components in its decree. By that time, the necessity of including these components was generally accepted. In the words of the district court: "That ancillary relief is necessary and essential to accomplish the transition to unitary racially non-discriminatory schooling and to overcome the vestige effects of *de jure* segregation in Northern New Castle County is amply supported and indeed undisputed on the record."[2] Along with three of the four *Milliken II* components—in-service training, unbiased counseling, and remedial reading—the court in *Evans v. Buchanan* also required a nondiscriminatory curriculum, a human relations program, and a racially evenhanded discipline policy. In other cases, judges have required districts to address problems in faculty discrimination, tracking, parental involvement, and extracurricular activities.

Educational components are judicial answers to educational and social questions. That they only recently have been considered integral to desegregation planning indicates a weakness in the judicial system. Judges may lack the special competence required to address desegregation issues that are fundamentally educational in nature. However, the courts have come to recognize the need for these components, and judges have called on specialists to design remedies aimed at rectifying the effects of past constitutional violations.

Among the specialists assisting desegregating school districts have been a number of desegregation teams from Michigan State University. These consultants, under the direction of Dr. Robert L. Green, former Dean of Urban Affairs Programs at Michigan State University and presently President of the University of the District of Columbia, have provided expert testimony in nearly

---

[1] *Milliken v. Bradley (Milliken II)*, 433 U.S. 267 (1977), 287–288.
[2] *Evans v. Buchanan*, 447 F. Supp. 982 (1978), 1014.

20 desegregation cases. In fact, Dr. Green introduced the term *educational components* during testimony as the NAACP's primary educational expert witness in the Detroit litigation.[3] Team members have consulted in numerous school districts, including Columbus, Indianapolis, Dallas, and Los Angeles, to analyze the need for ancillary relief, and to design educational components for inclusion in court orders. The team also developed educational components for a consent decree in the Chicago case (Green, 1981a, b), perhaps the most comprehensive battery of educational components yet designed.

THE LAW

The educational components ordered in *Milliken II, Evans,* and the Chicago consent decree represent the culmination of decades of school desegregation litigation. They evince a judicial reach into the classroom that would have seemed inconceivable when the Supreme Court decided the first *Brown* case in 1954.[4] However, since the Court did evaluate *Brown* in terms of the educational deprivation suffered by the plaintiff black children, this provided the seed that grew into educational components.

Desegregation litigation usually progresses in two phases. First, plaintiffs must prove the existence of Constitutional violations. Second, the presiding court must devise a strategy to remedy those violations. Educational components arise in the remedial phase, which itself has evolved into a two-pronged attack on segregation. The first prong involves the elimination of the most basic violation, the separate education of white and black children in white and black schools. Student reassignment accomplishes physical desegregation among school buildings. (Resegregation within nominally desegregated schools has arisen, however, and some educational components seek to prevent or dismantle this violation of judicial intent.) The second prong of the remedy process strives to rectify the unequal results of past segregated schooling, and some educational components address these inequalities.

The Supreme Court in *Brown I* did not specifically delineate the scope of remedies appropriate in desegregation cases. However, the Court's emphasis on the negative educational effects of segregated education framed the remedial approach that developed in the following decades. The Court, considering public education "in the light of its full development and its present place in American life," determined that education is "a principal instrument in awakening the child to cultural values, in preparing him for later special training, and in helping him adjust normally to his environment." The Court concluded: "In these days it is doubtful that any child may reasonably be expected to succeed in life if he is denied the opportunity of an education."[5]

---

[3] *Bradley v. Milliken,* 402 F. Suppl. 1096 (1975).
[4] *Brown v. Board of Education,* 347 U.S. 483 (1954).
[5] *Id.* at 492–493.

The Court found that segregation in education "generates [in black children] a feeling of inferiority as to their status in the community that may affect their hearts and minds in a way unlikely ever to be undone."[6] Then, citing "modern authority" in psychology, the Court agreed with a lower court that segregation "has a detrimental effect on the colored children," tending to "deprive them of some of the benefits they would receive in a racial[ly] integrated school system."[7] Based on this reasoning, the Court concluded that "in the field of public education the doctrine of 'separate but equal' has no place. Separate educational facilities are inherently unequal. Therefore, we hold that the plaintiffs . . . are, by reason of the segregation complained of, deprived of the equal protection of the laws."[8]

Two key elements of the Court's rationale in *Brown I* foreshadowed the development of educational components. First, as mentioned, the primary justification for finding segregation unconstitutional lay in that system's negative educational treatment of black children, along with the psychological and emotional ramifications of that treatment. Second, the Court relied on the lessons of social science to buttress its finding.

The Court remanded the *Brown I* cases to the lower courts, acknowledging that judges would face "considerable complexity" in formulating remedial decrees.[9] The Court offered no guidelines, however, to indicate how the damage identified by the Justices might be undone.

In 1955, when the cases reappeared on the Supreme Court's docket in *Brown II*, the tribunal provided only vague assistance:

> Full implementation of these constitutional principles may require solution of varied local school problems. School authorities have the primary responsibility for elucidating, assessing, and solving these problems; courts will have to consider whether the action of the school authorities constitutes good faith implementation of the governing constitutional principles.[10]

The Court then once more remanded the cases for further litigation, noting that the lower courts, due to their proximity to local conditions, were best qualified to perform the task. The Court stressed that, in addressing the "varied local school problems," the lower courts should be "guided by equitable principles." The law of equity, the Court explained, is "characterized by a practical flexibility in shaping its remedies and by a facility for adjusting and reconciling public and private needs." The Court noted that admission of black children to schools on a nondiscriminatory basis may require "elimination of a variety of obstacles."[11]

[6] *Id.* at 494.
[7] *Id.*
[8] *Id.* at 495.
[9] *Id.*
[10] *Brown v. Board of Education of Topeka (Brown II),* 349 U.S. 294 (1955), 299.
[11] *Id.* at 300.

The "practical flexibility" of equity law has been well tested by school desegregation. Even the plaintiffs have underestimated the problems inherent in abruptly mixing educationally disadvantaged black children with white children who have received the benefits of the best public schools. Further, few persons anticipated the resourcefulness of many state and local officials in their efforts to delay, resist, and subvert the desegregation process.

For nearly a decade following *Brown II,* desegregation plaintiffs made little progress in their efforts to persuade courts to order effective desegregation remedies. School boards made full and creative use of the "all deliberate speed" dictum[12] to resist or delay desegregation (Carter, 1973, p. 458). Finally, in the mid-1960s, the Supreme Court lost patience and declared that "the time for mere 'deliberate speed' has run out."[13] In subsequent litigation, the courts at last began to stress the necessity for *effective* desegregation remedies. Although the Supreme Court focused primarily on pupil reassignment to eliminate districtwide segregation, the language used to justify judicial involvement would later be referred to in support of educational components.

In 1968, the Supreme Court required a formerly *de jure* segregated system to go beyond an ineffective "freedom-of-choice" student assignment plan in order to eliminate segregation "root and branch."[14] The Court ruled that "the obligation . . . is to assess the effectiveness of a proposed plan in achieving desegregation. . . . It is incumbent upon the school board to establish that its proposed plan promises meaningful and immediate progress toward disestablishing state-imposed segregation."[15] The term *disestablish* has been taken to require that school boards go beyond racially neutral practices and enact policies that root out the effects of past segregation.

In 1971, the Supreme Court was even more explicit. In affirming the use of school buses for desegregation, it ruled that school boards must not only dismantle segregation, but must also "eliminate from the public schools all vestiges of state-imposed segregation."[16] The Court went on to explain:

> Once a right and a violation have been shown, the scope of a district court's equitable powers to remedy past wrongs is broad. . . . The task is to correct . . . the condition that offends the constitution. . . . As with any equity case, the nature of the violation determines the scope of the remedy.[17]

Milliken II, in 1977, marked the first time a party in a desegregation suit argued for a comprehensive battery of educational components.[18] Although fed-

---

[12] *Id.*

[13] *Griffin v. School Board of Prince Edward County,* 377 U.S. 218 (1964), 234.

[14] *Green v. County School Board of New Castle County,* 391 U.S. 430 (1968), 438.

[15] *Id.* at 439.

[16] *Swann v. Charlotte-Mecklenberg Board of Education,* 402 U.S. 1 (1971), 15.

[17] *Id.* at 15–16.

[18] *Milliken v. Bradley,* 433 U.S. 267 (1977).

eral district courts had been ordering individual components for nearly 10 years prior to that, it was in *Milliken II* that the educational need and legal justification clearly converged to establish educational components in the mainstream of desegregation law.

In *Milliken I,* in 1974, the Supreme Court had rejected an interdistrict reassignment plan lower courts had ordered for the Detroit metropolitan area.[19] The lower courts had determined that that remedy was necessary for two reasons. First, plaintiffs had proved state government complicity in the segregation between the city and its suburbs. Second, the Detroit public schools had too few white students to create meaningful desegregation. The Supreme Court, however, remanded the case for a remedy limited to Detroit proper.

On remand, the district court in 1975 found it "impossible to avoid having a substantial number of all-black or nearly all-black schools in a school district that is over 70% black."[20] The judge then rejected the plaintiff's proposal, which, despite substantial busing, left most Detroit schools between 75% and 90% black. "An appropriate desegregation plan," the court reasoned, "must carefully balance the costs of desegregation techniques against the possible results to be achieved. Where the benefits to be gained are negligible, those techniques should be adopted sparingly."[21]

The court preferred a plan offered by the Detroit Board of Education, a plan that called for considerably less busing but included several educational components. After submitting the proposal to experts for budgetary and educational analysis, the courts ruled that

> the majority of the educational components included in the Detroit Board plan are essential for a school district undergoing desegregation. While it is true that the delivery of quality desegregated educational services is the obligation of the school board, nevertheless this court deems it essential to mandate educational components where they are needed to remedy effects of past segregation, to assure a successful desegregative effort and to minimize the possibility of resegregation.[22]

When the district court finally issued its ruling on educational components in the spring of 1976, it ordered "comprehensive programs" in four areas: reading and communication skills; in-service training; counseling and career guidance; and testing.[23] The State of Michigan (which, as a co-defendant in the desegregation suit, had been charged with funding half the cost of these components) appealed to the circuit court. As that court framed the argument,

> the Michigan State defendants . . . [contend] that there is no violation which justifies these remedies and that the District Judge exceeded his lawful authority. . . . The

---

[19] *Milliken v. Bradley,* 418 U.S. 717 (1974).

[20] *Bradley v. Milliken,* 402 F. Supp. 1096 (1975), 1102.

[21] *Id.*

[22] *Id.* at 1118.

[23] *See Bradley v. Milliken,* 540 F. 2d 229 (1976), 240.

Detroit Board of Education, on the other hand, contends that all the Educational Components are within the scope of the equity powers of the court to remedy racial segregation in the Detroit schools because they help eliminate vestiges of discrimination and because they are a necessary part of the long-range desegregation plan.[24]

The circuit court agreed with the Detroit Board, and affirmed the judgment of the district court. Once again, the State Board appealed, and once again *Milliken v. Bradley* was before the Supreme Court, which agreed to hear the case to settle two questions:

Namely, whether a District Court can, as part of a desegregation decree, order compensatory or remedial eduational programs for school children who have been subjected to past acts of *de jure* segregation, and whether . . . a federal court can require state officials found responsible for constitutional violations to bear part of the costs of those programs.[25]

The Court noted that although it had never specifically ruled on remedial educational programs, the "general principles" governing its resolution of the issue had been "well settled by the prior decisions of this court."[26] The Court did not accept the State Board's argument that, since the constitutional violation found by the district court was racial segregation, the lower court had exceeded its power by ordering a remedy going beyond pupil reassignment. "This contention misconstrues the principle petitioners seek to invoke," the Court ruled, "and we reject their argument."[27]

The Court ruled that federal courts exceed their "appropriate limits" only if they seek to eliminate "a condition that does not violate the Constitution, or does not flow from such a violation."[28] Educational components in *Milliken II* constituted no such excess.

The "condition" offending the Constitution is Detroit's *de jure* segregated school system, which was so pervasively and consistently segregated that the District Court found that the need for educational components flowed directly from constitutional violations by both state and local officials. These specific educational remedies, although normally left to the discretion of the elected school board and professional educators, were deemed necessary to restore the victims of discriminatory conduct to the position they would have enjoyed in terms of education had these four components been provided in a non-discriminatory manner in a school system free from pervasive *de jure* racial segregation. . . . Discriminatory student assignment policies can themselves manifest and breed other inequalities built into a dual system founded on racial discrimination. Federal courts need not, and cannot, close their eyes to inequalities, shown by the record, which flow from a longstanding segregated system.[29]

---

[24] *Id.* at 241.
[25] *Milliken v. Bradley*, 433 U.S. 267 (1977), 269.
[26] *Id.* at 279.
[27] *Id.* at 281.
[28] *Id.* at 282.
[29] *Id.* at 282–283.

The Court thus determined that "the decree before us was aptly tailored to remedy the consequences of the constitutional violation,"[30] and ordered the State and Detroit School Boards to share the cost of implementing that decree.

THE COMPONENTS

Educational components can be defined as court-ordered interventions in the internal policies and practices of desegregating schools or school districts. These interventions are designed to overcome the vestiges of past segregation or to prevent or dismantle resegregation, and thereby to insure greater equity of education for all children. The following discussion separates components for the purpose of analysis. However, in the actual experience of children in school, textbooks and testing, for example, blend with factors such as counseling and discipline policy to create the school's overall climate. Potential positive effects of one component can be undermined by the failure to address other problems. Similarly, a remedy in one area can contribute to the effectiveness of remedies in other areas.

The attitudes and expectations of administrators and teachers are pivotal factors in the success or failure of school desegregation. Constructive effort addressing these intangible elements of the school environment underlies successful implementation of the programmatic educational components. A discussion of specific programmatic components first will provide context for the later discussion of in-service training to modify the attitudes and behaviors of school personnel.

Overcoming the Vestiges of Segregated Schooling

"Separate facilities are inherently unequal."[31] The import of that statement may sometimes be lost through frequent repetition. The words, however, are true, and their implication is clear. Separate facilities provided for minority children have most often been inferior facilities.

One way to gauge the degree of inferiority is to compare the per student financial support afforded black and white children in segregated school districts. In Washington, D.C., in the mid-1960s, for example, the median annual per pupil expenditure for white children ($392) exceeded that of black children ($292) by more than one third.[32] In 1964, school districts throughout the South spent on the average more than one third more money on white students ($165) than on black students ($115) (Bell, 1973, p. 452). These expenditure differentials,

---

[30] *Id.* at 287.
[31] *Brown v. Board of Education of Topeka,* 347 U.S. 483 (1954), 495.
[32] *Hobson v. Hansen,* 269 F. Supp. 401 (1967), 406.

by no means rare, are not abstractions. They manifest themselves all too concretely in the education of black pupils. One critical aspect is that because of expenditure differentials, administrators and teachers in minority schools have often had inferior credentials (Havighurst, 1977; National Advisory Commission, 1968).

An analysis of national survey data by the U. S. Commission on Civil Rights (1977) found "noticeable differences in the quality of school facilities available to Negro and white students in the Nation's metropolitan areas" (p. 92). The Commission noted that whites more often attended schools with more extensive libraries, and were also more likely to attend schools with science laboratories. The Commission found similar disparities in the school curricula offered students of different races, with

> whites more often . . . in schools which had advanced courses in particular subjects, such as science and language. They also were more likely to be in schools with fewer pupils per teacher. In most cities . . . it was found that schools with nearly all-Negro enrollments were overcrowded more often than nearly all-white schools. (p. 92)

As a consequence of these inequalities, many black children entering desegregating schools need special assistance to catch up academically. The courts have recognized this necessity since 1966, when a South Carolina district court directed a school district to include remedial education courses in its desegregation program. "Because the weaknesses of a dual school system may already have affected many children, the court would be remiss in its duty if any desegregation plan were approved which did not provide for remedial education courses. They shall be included in the plan."[33]

In 1967, a federal appeals court in the South expressed a similar view: "The defendants shall provide remedial education programs which permit students attending or who have previously attended segregated schools to overcome past inadequacies in their education."[34] Two years later, that same court determined that remedial programs "are an integral part of a program for compensatory education to be provided Negro students who have long been disadvantaged by the inequities and discrimination inherent in the dual school system."[35]

Other courts have reached similar conclusions, and the Supreme Court specifically affirmed remedial education programs in *Milliken II*. As the district court has phrased it, "We find that a comprehensive reading instruction program, together with appropriate remedial reading classes, are essential to a successful desegregative effort. Intensified reading instruction is basic to an educational system's obligation to every child in the school community."[36]

Remedial education programs address only one vestige of segregation—the

---

[33] *Miller v. School District 2, Clarendon County, South Carolina*, 256 F. Supp. 370 (1966), 377.

[34] *U.S. v. Jefferson County Board of Education*, 380 F. 2d 385 (1967) 394.

[35] *Plaquemines Parish School Baord v. United States*, 415 F. 2d 817 (1969), 831.

[36] *Bradley v. Milliken*, 402 F. Supp. 1096 (1975), 1118–1119.

disparity in academic achievement between black and white children. Other vestiges also require attention, including the curricular differentials between schools, and the racism that pervades formerly segregated systems.

After desegregation, school districts may make an effort to equalize facilities and curricula among schools. However, districts often allow great inequalities to persist in the teaching, testing, and treatment of minority and majority students. As Green (1981b) pointed out in the recommendations on educational components for the Chicago consent decree, "These inequalities are not necessarily attributable to official action or inaction—and may, in fact, be contrary to the stated policies of the school system—but they do exist in most of the nation's major urban areas" (p. 11). School districts should consciously strive for the greatest possible reduction of system-wide disparities. Course offerings and course content in the basic subjects should reflect parity among the system's schools, with students "able to transfer from one school to another and find a level of curricular offerings relatively equal. All students should have access to college preparatory courses as well as vocational training and specialized courses" (p. 23).

School districts should also eliminate programs and materials imbued with explicit or implicit racial or cultural bias. Reading primers in which Dick, Jane, Mom, Dad, and all their friends are white and middle-class do not reflect the experiences common to children who are black and poor. History texts that neglect the contributions by blacks to the development of this nation deprive all children, black and white, of a well-rounded appreciation of the racial and ethnic diversity that characterizes this country. These concerns were addressed directly by the court in the New Castle County case: "Curricular offerings and programs must preserve respect for the racial and ethnic backgrounds of all students. To that end, instructional materials, texts, and other curriculum aids should be free of racial bias."[37]

Lichter and Johnson (1969) found that multiethnic materials can make a difference. White second graders who used a multiethnic reader showed more positive racial attitudes than comparable white second graders who used traditional materials. In Williamsburg County, South Carolina, it was found that revised teaching methods, combined with staff desegregation and the addition of courses that included black culture, were associated with dramatically improved achievement among poor, black pupils (U.S. Commission on Civil Rights, 1977). Both black and white children achieved similar gains in Hillsboro County, Florida, after that district underwent curriculum revision, staff desegregation, and special training for school personnel (U.S. Commission on Civil Rights, 1976b).

It is not enough, however, to add black history units to traditional social

---

[37] *Evans V. Buchanan*, 447 F. Supp. 982 (1978), 1016.

studies classes. As Solomon and Young (1968) pointed out, "Afro-American history by itself does not rectify all the white-supremacist distortions of our history." Black history, when added to "standard" history, can give children information about black America, but it also conveys a secondary message. In the words of Green (1979):

> Black and other minority children can still perceive themselves as afterthoughts, while white children can still develop superior attitudes about their cultures. Thus, we see that special minority culture classes . . . may . . . provide a dangerous and damaging perspective. The entire curriculum must be reworked in a way that gives respect to all children from all backgrounds and gives proper perspective to all racial and ethnic groups. (p. 6)

In 1976, the National Council for the Social Studies established a set of curriculum guidelines for multiethnic education. These guidelines helped delineate the task faced by educators in eliminating the vestiges of racial bias from the school curriculum. Paraphrasing the Council's guidelines:

1. Ethnic pluralism should permeate the total school environment.
2. School policies and procedures should foster positive multiethnic interactions and understanding among students, teachers, and support staff.
3. The school staff should reflect the ethnic pluralism within American society.
4. Schools should have systematic, comprehensive, mandatory, and continuing staff development programs.
5. The multiethnic curriculum should provide each student with continuous opportunities to develop a better sense of worth.
6. The multiethnic curriculum should help students develop decision-making abilities, social participation skills, and a sense of political efficacy as the necessary bases for effective citizenship in an ethnically pluralistic nation.
7. The multiethnic curriculum should help students develop the skills necessary for effective interpersonal and interethnic group interactions.
8. The multiethnic curriculum should be comprehensive in scope and sequence, should provide holistic views of ethnic groups, and should be an integral part of the total school curriculum.
9. Interdisciplinary and multidisciplinary approaches should be used in designing and implementing the multiethnic curriculum.
10. Schools should conduct ongoing, systematic evaluations of the goals and instructional methods used in teaching about ethnicity.

Implementing these guidelines requires a concerted effort, but the mental, emotional, and economic well-being of our country's children is at stake.

Overcoming Resegregation in Desegregating Schools

In August 1977, District Court Judge Noel Fox ordered the Board of Education in Kalamazoo, Michigan, to report on the progress achieved in 4 years of school desegregation.[38] The remedy Judge Fox had ordered in 1974 relied primarily on student reassignment. Judge Fox appointed Robert Green, then Dean of the College of Urban Development at Michigan State University, and Wilbur J. Cohen, then Dean Emeritus of the School of Education at The University of Michigan, to undertake the evaluation. The resulting report (Green & Cohen, 1979) concluded that "although the district has made substantial progress in meeting the court order regarding the racial distribution among schools, certain academic programs in 1978–1979 were as segregated by race as the school buildings were prior to the Judge's desegregation order" (p. 292).

Resegregation can be defined as the separation of children by race or ethnicity within the walls of a nominally desegregated school. To determine the extent of resegregation in Kalamazoo, the researchers undertook an exhaustive analysis of the racial composition of each classroom in the district. This "course enrollment analysis" revealed that 10 out of 11 junior high courses evaluated were nonrepresentative in black enrollment in 1978–1979, and that the number of nonrepresentative courses had risen in recent years. The extent of course segregation was found to have increased in the high schools. Furthermore, blacks were found disproportionately in lower-level courses, out of the college preparatory sequence. A course enrollment analysis in the Chicago public schools (Green, 1981a) yielded similar results.

Eyler, Cook, Tompkins, Trent, and Ward (1981) have described three sources of resegregation. The three interrelate and reinforce one another, but can usefully be separated for the purpose of discussion. The first, oldest, and least defensible of these is racism. Racism can manifest itself in numerous ways. It may be overt and calculated, as was the so-called intact busing discovered in Benton Harbor, Michigan, where black youngsters were being bused from black neighborhoods to white schools, isolated in black classrooms for the day, and then returned to the black neighborhoods in the afternoon. Or racism may be subtle and/or inadvertent such as the "institutional racism" described by Hughes, Gordon, and Hillman (1980):

> Institutional racism, by definition, is composed of those factors and organizational practices, procedures, and rules, not necessarily conscious, that keep certain groups of people in an inferior status not because they are of the specific group but because of the effects of the accepted practices. For example, a regulation requiring that members of the girls' drill team wear their hair at shoulder length will automatically keep many black girls from participating, although the rule is not overtly racist.

---

[38] Court order, Judge Noel Fox, August 15, 1977. In *Michele Olliver v. Kalamazoo Board of Education. See* 368 F. Supp. 143 (1973).

> Similarly, high laboratory fees, while seemingly necessary, will keep economically
> deprived students from participating in certain academic courses. (p. 146)

Racism may also contribute to resegregation through excessively harsh discipline of minority children, which can lead to disproportionately high suspension and expulsion rates; and through discriminatory treatment of minority children participating in extracurricular activities. These issues will be addressed later.

A second source of resegregation is the fragmented nature of public education policy. Separate governmental agencies, implementing programs authorized by diverse legislation, may undermine one another's efforts. As Eyler *et al.* (1981) noted,

> While courts and some agencies may be making policies which mandate or facilitate
> integration, other agencies may develop programs which seem at cross-purposes with
> integration. Just as government supports both tobacco crops and warnings on cigarette
> packages, public policy about education is made in a variety of decision-making
> arenas . . . which may conflict. For example, categorical aid programs which require
> or allow disadvantaged students to be removed from the classroom for compensatory
> services will have a resegregation effect. (p. 212)

The third source of resegregation results from "the traditional response of schools to student diversity" (p. 211). This is the most important and most difficult to counteract of resegregative influences, for it pervades most day-to-day school policy-making decisions, and is often cloaked in the rhetoric of eduational necessity.

> Students are sorted and categorized and programs matched to their apparent needs.
> Behavioral standards are adopted to reduce diversity and students who do not conform
> are excluded. To the extent that race and ethnicity are associated with criteria used
> to sort or exclude students, these processes will result in racial imbalance in classes
> and racial disproportionality in exclusion. Resegregation results. (p. 211)

This sorting is most evident in curricular tracking and the clustering of students into homogeneous learning groups. Both tracking and ability grouping characterize some children as "slow learners." It is neither coincidence nor evidence of genetic inferiority that these lower groups are usually populated disproportionately by minority children from previously segregated schools. On the contrary, that concentration is evidence of the lingering effects of segregated schools' inferior education. Grouping and tracking perpetuate those effects. Biased testing programs and discriminatory counseling practices often exacerbate the problem.

The district court in *Milliken II* recognized the necessity of mandating thorough desegregation, stating that "an effective and feasible remedy must prevent resegregation at all costs. To ignore the possibility of resegregation would risk further injury to Detroit school children, both black and white."[39] School

---

[39] *Bradley v. Milliken (Milliken II)*, 402 F. Supp. 1096 (1975).

policies must be modified if desegregation is to succeed. As Leubsdorf (1977) noted in his groundbreaking tract on ancillary relief in desegregation cases, "To rearrange the system but leave the poison circulating within it is to ensure that discrimination will continue in new forms" (p. 46).

Testing and Tracking.   Standardized testing and curriculum tracking deal the most devastating blows in the resegregation of minority students. Judged inferior by overreliance on the results of inappropriate tests, disproportionate numbers of minority children are separated into so-called special education or compensatory education curriculum tracks. Once so placed, these children do not receive the academic training necessary to overcome whatever educational deficiencies they may actually have. Low expectations, teacher indifference, and administrative apathy finish the job. These educational attitudes and procedures defeat the purpose of desegregation by separating black and white children within schools. They also inflict an even greater harm by branding many minority children with undeserved labels that can limit their options throughout their lives.

It is taken as an article of faith by many, educators and lay people alike, that testing and tracking as we know them today are essential components of the educational process. However, as Kirp (1973) pointed out in his analysis of the constitutional policy implications of student classifications, "only during the past 60 years have schools devoted considerable effort to classifying and sorting students. The proto-typical common school . . . was designed to provide a common educational experience for all comers" (p. 714).

Kirp noted that the public schools responded to European immigration at the turn of the century by offering "opportunity classes" to help newcomers overcome their language barriers and prepare for regular school. This innovation marked the beginning of differentiated curricula. At first, the aim was for children ultimately to join the mainstream. As industrialization swept the land, however, even greater differentiation was promoted. It can be argued that this arose to sort children for the convenience of their future employers, not for their own benefit. Intelligence tests grew to meet the need of student classification, and lent an aura of scientific respectability to this elitist and educationally suspect practice.

These tests, despite their many supporters, have proved unreliable. Still, educators cling to them with almost mystical devotion. As Robert Green (1974) wrote:

> Test scores are sometimes used like tea leaves. Gypsies read great truths from tea leaves; often educators read great truths from test scores. Neither reading is necessarily valid but many people believe them. Superstition has grown up around the science of aptitude and intelligence testing, so much so that the use of these tests is frequently not scientific at all. (p. 68)

Three examples indicate the failure of these tests to measure accurately what they are supposed to measure. First, a 1965 study of black high school students showed no correlation between students' verbal scores on the School

and College Ability Tests and their grade point achievement levels (Green & Farquahr, 1965). Second, scores on the Scholastic Aptitude Test (SAT) have been shown to predict less than 12% of the variance of the grades of first-year college students (Ford & Campos, 1977). Finally Green (1975) tells a story that brings these impersonal statistics into focus in an individual life:

> When Robert Williams was 15 years old, he earned an IQ test score of 82. Given this low result, Williams' high school counselor suggested he take up bricklaying as a career. But Williams ignored the advice and went on to earn a B.A. . . . , an M.A. . . . , and a Ph.D. . . . Today, Williams is a well-known psychologist and crusader against the misuse of IQ tests. (p. 1)

As ineffective as most tests prove to be generally, they are even less accurate in assessing the potential of poor and minority children. Test bias—unfairness of the test itself—results when a test does not measure the same dimensions for all who take it. A 1975 study of the authors of some of the nation's most widely used standardized tests (Green & Griffore, 1976) showed that 95% were white males with degrees from prestigious universities. It should come as no surprise, therefore, to find that test items presuppose exposure to middle-class experience and that test examples rarely correspond to the lives of poor and minority children. Partly as a result of the training and experience of their authors, tests usually presume language usage common to the white middle class. Consequently, minority children often score relatively poorly due to the cultural bias of the test, rather than to any lack of intelligence (e.g., Hunt, 1972). Furthermore, majority children have often had the opportunity to develop a certain "test-wiseness," the ability to pick up and use subtle clues to speed their progress through the test. This skill substitutes for a portion of the generalized "intelligence" the test purports to measure.

More could be said regarding the bias inherent in most standardized tests, but the irresponsible use of these tests is an even greater cause for concern. The primary such use is for the placement of students in differentiated curriculum tracks. A 1974 National Education Association study revealed that 70% of the schools in large and medium sized districts practiced some form of ability grouping. Findley and Bryan (1971) reported that about 82% of the districts they studied used standardized tests as a criterion, sometimes the only criterion, for student placement.

The misuse of standardized tests is often compounded by inconsistent and biased student evaluations by school personnel. Simmons (1979) found that teachers and counselors in a desegregating midwestern school system reported that the primary information sources used to place minority students in language arts programs were "teacher perceptions and student motivation." The teachers later attributed the disproportionate enrollment of minority children in lower status reading classes to (1) lack of parental support; (2) economic and environmental factors; (3) less ability and low language skills; and (4) a limited range of experiences (p. 129). The misuse of standardized tests, combined with the

belief that negative environmental factors limit the potential achievement of black children, can create a self-reinforcing cycle.

That cycle entraps many thousands of black youngsters. In one midwestern high school, black children were 3 times more likely than whites to be in remedial reading classes (Green & Cohen, 1979, p. 132). Blacks were consistently over-represented in basic math and general education courses, whereas never over-represented in advanced or college preparatory classes. In Chicago, blacks were 3 times more likely than whites to land in classes for the "educable mentally handicapped" (Green, 1981a, p. 68). A study of Florida (State of Florida, 1979) yielded similar results. A study by the Stanford Research Institute showed that teachers identified black children 3.5 times more often than white children as being mentally retarded ("Teachers Say," 1976). Oakes' research and literature review (1982) reinforced the conclusion that track levels tend to correlate with socioeconomic status and race, with poor and minority students in the lower tracks.

When low-track minority children are reevaluated with nonbiased instruments, it has often been shown that their low placement was inappropriate. In Riverside, California, for example, 91% of the black students assigned to programs for educable mentally handicapped were later found to have been incorrectly evaluated (Mercer, 1973). A group of children once assigned to the lowest two tracks in the Washington, D.C. school system were later reassessed and two thirds were found to have been misclassified.[40]

Moreover, tracking systems tend to be inflexible. The chance misplacement of a child in a slow elementary school track can foreclose options at each subsequent phase of his or her educational career. A desegregating school district in the early 1970s exemplified the ridiculous extremes to which this can be taken (Green, 1976). As first graders, children were tested and assigned to 12 different ability groups. The researchers found that the tracks were so rigid that most stayed in their original track until they graduated or dropped out of school. As Green and Cohen (1979) concluded with regard to tracking in Kalamazoo:

> While the District has stated that students freely make their own choices of classes in which they enroll, in reality, little free choice is involved. Once a student is placed in a reading class, or in a lower-track math class, this limits other "free choices," not only at the time the decision is made, but for all subsequent school years. (p. 154)

There is no proof to support the contention that a narrow range of student ability within a classroom provides meaningful educational benefits. On the contrary, significant evidence indicates the opposite, that tracking and other forms of ability grouping actually lead to reduced achievement for lower-track children, with little if any benefit to their high-track classmates. Furthermore, since tracking so often results in racial segregation, it can cause emotional and psychological as well as educational harm.

[40] *Smuck v. Hobson*, 408 F. 2d 175 (1969), 187.

Bryson and Bentley (1980) conducted an in-depth review of the research on tracking and ability grouping in their analysis of the legal implications of school sorting methods. They concluded that tracking causes all but above average students to "lose ground instead of gaining" (p. 15). The authors focused extensively on a representative study (Goldberg, Passow, & Justman, 1966), which, as summarized by Bryson and Bentley, found that:

1. Simply narrowing the ability range, without specifically designed variations in program for the several ability levels, does not result in consistently greater academic achievement for any group of pupils.
2. In the lower ability levels, narrowing the ability range caused teachers to set lower expectation standards for students. Teachers generally tended to underestimate the capabilities of pupils in lower-track courses.
3. Most teachers found more success in teaching a given subject to several ability levels simultaneously than in teaching all subjects to narrow-range classes.

The Goldberg *et al.* (1966) study concluded that "ability grouping is inherently neither good nor bad. It is neutral. Its value depends upon the way in which it is used" (p. 168).

Findley and Bryan (1971) found data to be similarly inconclusive:

> Ability grouping . . . shows no consistent positive value for helping students . . . to learn better. Taking all studies into account, the balance of findings is chiefly of no strong effect, either favorable or unfavorable. Among the studies showing significant effects the slight preponderance of evidence showing the practice favorable for the learning of high ability students is more than offset by evidence of unfavorable effects on the learning of average and low ability groups, particularly the latter. (p.54)

The Goldberg study's conclusion (that ability grouping is "neutral") is applicable only with respect to cognitive outcomes. It is far from true in the noncognitive realm of emotions and psyche. Although grouping may render no marked academic advantage or disadvantage, it does convey a strong and lasting message to all involved. The U.S. Commission on Civil Rights (1967) found that black students in nominally desegregated schools, when "accorded separate treatment, with others of their race, in a way that is obvious to them as they travel through their classes, felt inferior and stigmatized" (pp. 86–87). As Kirp (1973) concluded:

> The harm caused by between-school segregation appeared to the Commission far less substantial than the harm caused from within-school segregation: while between-school segregation resulted from the relatively impersonal criterion of neighborhood residence, within-school segregation was clearly caused by personal and pejorative judgments of ability. (p.762)

Stigma is defined as "a stain or reproach on one's reputation." The labels that usually accompany low-track status, such as "mentally retarded" or "emo-

tionally impaired," affect the child's self-image, and also the attitudes of teachers and classmates. Again quoting Kirp:

> These adverse school classifications reduce both the individual's sense of self-worth and his value in the eyes of others. . . . The school's inclination to cope with a particular learning or social problem by isolating those who share that problem reinforces the child's sense of stigma. (pp. 733–734)

And the stigma, once attached, tends to cling. The effects

> do not cease at the time the child leaves school, for schools significantly are society's most active labelers. The schools label more persons as mentally retarded [and] share their labels with more other organizations . . . than any other formal organization in the community. (Kirp, p. 736)

The effects of the stigma associated with low-track placement are usually compounded by an educational experience substantially different from that received in higher tracks. Some analysts (Bowles & Gintes, 1976) have contended that tracking serves to help reproduce society's power distribution in coming generations by differentiating knowledge acquired by children of varying social, economic, and racial backgrounds. Oakes' (1982) research on the curricular content of various track levels supported this contention:

> High-track classes were presented with instructional topics traditionally associated with preparation for higher education. Teachers of high-track classes tended to list as a part of course content activities and skills that required higher levels of cognition . . . [and] to be concerned that their students learn behaviors that would enable them to function autonomously and think critically. Students in low-track classes, on the other hand, rarely encountered these types of learnings. . . . Activities and skills listed by teachers usually required only low-level cognitive processes. The non-subject-related behaviors included as course content were those that encouraged student conformity to rules and expectations. (pp. 111–112)

Taken together, testing and tracking conspire to maintain, within the walls of supposedly desegregated schools, the dual educational system that characterized segregation. As a result of inferior educational preparation, minority children enter desegregation with academic achievement levels lagging behind those of their new white schoolmates. Culturally biased standardized testing, combined with teacher evaluations tainted by discriminatory low expectations, consistently place disproportionate numbers of minority children in the lowest academic tracks. There, these children receive a diluted curriculum that, rather than help them catch up, in fact causes them to fall further behind.

In the landmark case addressing testing and tracking,[41] a black parent sued (among others) the superintendent of the Washington, D.C. public schools. The superintendent, Carl Hansen, had written *The Four-Track Curriculum for Today's High Schools* (Hansen, 1964), a book that explained and defended the

---

[41] *Hobson v. Hansen*, 269 F. Supp. 401 (1967).

tracking system. The district court judge drew extensively from Hansen's book in framing a 118-page opinion that focused primarily on the racial impetus and racially identifiable effects of that system. Washington, D.C. schools initiated the tracking system in 1956, 2 years after being ordered in one of the *Brown* cases to desegregate. In his testimony, Hansen conceded that

> to describe the origin of the four-track system without reference to desegrega-
> tion . . . would be to by-pass one of the most significant causes of its being. Deseg-
> regation was a precipitant of the four-track development in the District's high schools.[42]

The court ruled that, despite evidence supporting the school district's claim that tracking was not racially motivated, "there is no escaping the fact that the track system was specifically a response to problems created by the sudden commingling of numerous educationally retarded Negro students with the better educated white students."[43] Moreover, the court could not ignore that

> of all the possible forms of ability grouping . . . [the District chose] the one that—
> with the exception of completely segregated schools—involves the greatest amount
> of physical separation by grouping students in wholly distinct, homogeneous curric-
> ulum levels. It cannot ignore that the immediate and known effect of this separation
> would be to insulate the more academically developed white student from his less
> fortunate black schoolmate, thus minimizing the impact of integration.[44]

The court noted that Hansen's system divided children into four student types. "He assumes," the court continued, "that each of these types of students has a maximum level of academic capability and, most importantly, that the level of ability can be accurately ascertained."[45] However, the court found, "the evidence that the defendants are in no position to make such judgments about the learning capacity of the majority of District school children is persuasive."[46] The court then deliberated extensively on standardized testing. In an analysis that touched on many issues addressed earlier in this chapter, the court concluded that

> the aptitude tests used to assign children to the various tracks are standardized primarily
> on white middle class children. Since these tests do not relate to the Negro and
> disadvantaged child, track assignment relegates Negro and disadvantaged children to
> the lower tracks from which, because of the reduced curriculum and the absence of
> adequate remedial and compensatory education, as well as continued inappropriate
> testing, the chance of escape is remote.[47]

The court noted the existence of racially identifiable results of the D.C. tracking system, particularly that "as they proceeded through the Washington

[42] *Id*. at 442.
[43] *Id*.
[44] *Id*. at 443.
[45] *Id*. at 444.
[46] *Id*. at 447.
[47] *Id*. at 407.

school system, the reading scores primarily of the Negro and poor children, but not the white and middle class, fall increasingly behind the national norm."[48]

Finally, the court determined that the "infirmities" in the Washington, D.C. tracking system, "deprived the poor and a majority of the Negro students in the District of Columbia of their Constitutional right to equal educational opportunities."[49] To remedy this unconstitutional denial of equal opportunity, the court declared that "the track system simply must be abolished. In practice, if not in concept, it discriminates against the disadvantaged child, particularly the Negro."[50]

The appeals court limited the effect of *Hobson v. Hansen* to the specific tracking system in effect in Washington, D.C. at the time of the ruling. Under the name *Smuck v. Hobson*, the appeals court permitted "full scope for such ability groupings" as existed at the time of the appeal in 1969.[51] As Kirp (1973) has said, school administrators under the *Smuck* ruling "retained . . . the full panoply of student differentiation, while simply changing labels" (p. 753).

However, litigation in the years since has clarified that school personnel must consider the effects on desegregation of any testing or tracking procedure. In 1970, a federal appeals court prohibited a district court remedy that would have allowed the assignment of children to schools according to their performance on achievement tests. The court ruled that "testing cannot be employed . . . until unitary school systems have been established."[52] In 1971, a Louisiana district court prohibited grouping children into class levels based on standardized tests, ruling that

> the educational policy used . . . to assign black students on the basis of presently used testing violates their Fourteenth Amendment rights to be treated equally with white students. Homogeneous grouping is educationally detrimental to students assigned to the lower sections, and blacks comprise a disproportionate number of the students in the lower sections.[53]

Also in 1971, an unemployment case ruled unconstitutional the use of tests that result in disproportionate failure rates by black applicants.[54] In 1972, a federal appeals court ruled that, although the Constitution does not require absolute racial balance in classes for the mentally retarded, it does require that the tests used to place children in those classes be racially nonbiased.[55] The same year, school officials in San Francisco contended that IQ tests were acceptable despite their racial bias because they offered "the best means of classification

---

[48] *Id.* at 406.
[49] *Id.* at 511.
[50] *Id.* at 515.
[51] 408 F. 2d 175 (1969), 189.
[52] *Singleton v. Jackson Municipal Separate School District*, 419 F. 2d 1211 (1970), 1219.
[53] *Moses v. Washington Parish School Board*, 330 F. Supp. 1340 (1971), 1345.
[54] *Griggs v. Duke Power Company*, 401 U.S. 424 (1971).
[55] *Copeland v. School Board of City of Portsmouth, Virginia*, 464 F. 2d 932 (1972).

currently available."[56] The district court disallowed continued use of tests, holding that the need to treat "truly mentally retarded children" in a special manner

> does not, however, justify depriving black children of their right to equal protection of the laws. Indeed, the absence of any rational means of identifying children in need of such treatment can hardly render acceptable an otherwise concededly irrational means, such as the I.Q. test as it is presently administered to black students.[57]

In 1975, a circuit court in Texas ruled that ability grouping is not unconstitutional *per se*.[58] However, in that same year a Mississippi appeals court forbade the use of ability groups that result in racially segregated classrooms, at least until previously segregated districts had been integrated long enough to prevent the assignment of children to lower groups based on educational disparities resulting from prior segregation.[59] Also in 1975, a district court judge in Boston prohibited the use of an arbitrary test score cutoff for admission to Boston's advanced "examination schools," if that standard prevented desegregation.[60] The judge also mandated that "special needs" students should be assigned to schools according to regular assignment procedures.

By the Supreme Court's 1977 ruling in *Milliken II*, both testing and tracking had been under judicial attack for nearly a decade. The issue of tracking did not arise in the Detroit litigation; however, the district court did direct the school district to implement a nonbiased testing program:

> The Detroit Board and State Board of Education are constitutionally mandated to eliminate all vestiges of discrimination, including discrimination through improper testing. Thus, the Detroit Board and the State Board of Education must devise a program that will ensure that testing design, content and procedures are adaptable to a desegregated school system.[61]

The Supreme Court, noting that lower courts had previously "altered" or even suspended testing programs employed by school systems undergoing desegregation, concluded that the district court's remedy "was aptly tailored to remedy the consequences of the Constitutional violation."[62]

The desegregation research team from Michigan State University's Urban Affairs Programs has been requested to formulate educational component recommendations for several desegregating school districts (Green, 1978, 1980, 1981a, 1981b). Recommendations have been based on the proven unconstitutionality and educational inappropriateness of biased testing and tracking procedures. The recommendations for Chicago's consent decree (Green, 1981b),

[56] *Larry P. v. Wilson Riles*, 343 F. Supp. 1306 (1972), 1313.
[57] *Id.*
[58] *Morales v. Shannon*, 516 F. 2d 411 (1975).
[59] *McNeal v. Tate County School District*, 408 F. 2d 1017 (1975).
[60] *Morgan v. Kerrigan*, 401 F. Supp. 216 (1975).
[61] *Bradley v. Milliken*, 402 F. Supp. 1096 (1975), 1142.
[62] *Milliken v. Bradley*, 433 U.S. 267 (1977), 286–287.

for example, called on the district to "discontinue the use of standard individual tests of intelligence as the sole or primary source of information in the special education screening and evaluation of black and Hispanic children" (p. 46).

Alterations in testing and tracking procedures require school personnel to adjust their thinking about student potential, and to adjust their instructional philosophies to accommodate a wider range of student achievement levels in each classroom. Such adjustments are never easy. However, it is even more difficult for the victims of unfair practices to construct productive lives after having been stigmatized by the educational system.

Discipline. Quality education requires a sane, orderly school environment. Children sometimes misbehave, so schools must develop procedures to deal with that misbehavior. Setting the standards of acceptable behavior in a desegregating school requires the recognition of possible cultural bias. White administrators and teachers confronting minority students for the first time must ensure that disciplinary procedures are appropriate and fairly administered.

The U. S. Department of Health, Education, and Welfare (1975) found that schools expel minority students at almost twice the rate for white students. Some observers (Larkin, 1979; Miller, 1975) have argued that racial inequality in school suspensions is related to desegregation. Studies of desegregating school districts bear this out. For example, the number of suspensions in Louisville doubled the first year of desegregation (Project Student Concerns, 1977). Significant increases were also noted in Columbus, Ohio (Columbus, 1980) and Milwaukee (Southern Regional Council, 1979). In Hillsboro County (Tampa), Florida, the overall suspension rate nearly doubled in the first year of desegregation (U.S. Commission on Civil Rights, 1976c). Minority students, comprising only 20% of the district's enrollment, accounted for about half the suspensions. In Prince George's County, Maryland, a district with a 25% black student body, about 46% of the students suspended in the mid-1970s were black (U.S. Commission on Civil Rights, 1976a, p. 328). In 1982, the Board of Education in Ann Arbor, Michigan, launched an investigation to determine why black students in that district were four times as likely to be suspended as their white schoolmates (Child, 1982). Other research (Arnez, 1976; Kaeser, 1979; Yudof, 1975) showed similar findings across the country. Furthermore, blacks were found to be not only more likely to be suspended, but also likely to be suspended more frequently (Children's Defense Fund, 1974) and for longer durations (Hall, 1978).

Schools within the same district have often exhibited substantial variations in their rates of student suspension. The fact that "many schools and districts with high minority enrollments do not suspend minority students at a higher rate" (Eyler *et al.,* 1981, p. 304) argues against blaming these disparities on qualities inherent in minority children. Rather,

> these differences in suspension rates seem to reflect the ways in which particular principals and teachers apply rules. Some educators do not use suspension at all; others use it infrequently; others use it frequently for a wide range of offenses. It is

in school districts that use it frequently that the disproportion of minorities is also high. (p. 304)

In 1974, a Texas court found that "racism . . . is the chief cause of the disproportionate number of blacks being suspended and given corporal punishment" after desegregation in Dallas.[63] The court went on to order "an affirmative program" to effectuate "a change of attitude of both the School Board and [school district] officials." That program, ruled the court, must train teachers, counselors, and students "to deal with institutional racism."[64]

In 1975, the Supreme Court determined that public education bequeathed a property right, and that the Constitution guaranteed due process procedures before administrators could deprive students of that right. "Having chosen to extend the right to an education," the court rules, "Ohio may not withdraw that right on grounds of misconduct absent fundamentally fair procedures to determine whether the misconduct has occurred."[65]

Discipline issues also arose in the Detroit case, in which the district court expressed its concern both for the prevention of school disruption, and for the protection of student rights. The court placed a high priority on the institution of a uniform code of conduct. As the court explained its reasoning:

> Children living, learning and playing together convert a building into a human institution with . . . an identifiable environment. It is this environment that the Detroit Board is constitutionally bound to protect in order to assure that every student can enjoy the right to a happy, healthy and rewarding school experience. . . . Both students and teachers must feel secure in their person and in their ability to perform their respective functions. . . . The court will not, of course, attempt to substitute its judgment for the discretion of school administrative personnel in dealing with student violations of the Code. The court will ensure, however, that all Detroit students are afforded minimal rights of due process.[66]

Although the district court did not include the discipline component in its ultimate *Milliken II* order,[67] the district court in the New Castle County case did require the newly created metropolitan district to "develop a code of rights and responsibilities regarding such issues as student conduct and suspension and expulsion, and to ensure administration of the code in an unbiased manner."[68]

The recommendations prepared for the Chicago consent decree (Green, 1981b) by Michigan State University consultants included a comprehensive discipline component that calls on the district to "approach discipline problems from a holistic perspective, with strategies for preventing unacceptable conduct,

---

[63] *Hawkins v. Coleman*, 376 F. Supp. 1330 (1974), 1337.
[64] *Id.* at 1338.
[65] *Goss v. Lopez*, 419 U.S. 565 (1975), 567.
[66] *Bradley v. Milliken*, 402 F. Supp. 1096 (1975), 1142.
[67] *See Bradley v. Milliken*, 540 F. 2d 420 (1976).
[68] *Evans v. Buchanan*, 447 F. Supp. 892 (1978), 1016–1017.

managing such conduct when it occurs, and following up with remedial activities subsequent to such conduct" (p. 69).

Other components of a desegregation plan can help prevent unacceptable conduct by integrating minority students into the mainstream of school life. Students who feel they are a part of an institution are less likely to disrupt it than those who do not. Furthermore, research indicates that children favor discipline when it is administered fairly and consistently, and when it allows them to feel safe and to work effectively (Children's Defense Fund, 1974).

It is important that discipline policies not only be fair, but also that they be clearly understood and be perceived to be fair. In light of this, MSU's desegregation team (Green, 1981b, pp. 69–70) recommended that the Chicago schools implement the following recommendations:

- Develop in concert with administrators, teachers, students, and citizens a uniform code of student conduct.
- Codify the penalties that would be applicable system-wide, yet retain administrative flexibility in application.
- Enforce in a uniform and equitable manner the new code.
- Furnish the uniform code to every principal, faculty member, and student, so that they may become familiar with its contents.
- Make maximum use of alternative methods (e.g., in-school suspension centers, time-out rooms, peer counseling, and work-study alternatives) for dealing with student suspensions in cases of non-dangerous, non-violent offenses which do not have a seriously disruptive effect on the educational process.

As with most other components, the modification of disciplinary procedures requires educators to rethink their responses to classroom phenomena. Change is never easy, and less so when required in the often tense circumstances accompanying disciplinary actions. As with most other components, prethinking by means of preservice and in-service training can ease the transition.

Extracurricular Activities

An effective school learning climate must be complemented with an effective school social climate. This is especially true in desegregated secondary schools, where reassignment of students and desegregation have disrupted the traditional sources of school spirit. . . . In order to establish bonds of loyalty between new students . . . and old students . . . it is important that the secondary school . . . strengthen the extracurricular program, especially athletics, music, art, drama, and dance. (Green, 1981a p. 165)

Extracurricular activities, when promoted and administered with integration in mind, are more likely than classrooms to offer the conditions of cooperative equal status interaction that Allport (1954) considered favorable to positive interracial contact. As Crain (1981) summed it up, "Classroom activities are normally structured so as to maximize competition among students for limited rewards. Equal status contact is virtually precluded . . . as are cooperative relations" (p. 125). Extracurricular activities, however, offer a place to impress on children a sense of common interest and common humanity.

Schofield (1981) suggested that "unless schools take steps to prevent it, a great many extracurricular activities become typed as black or white" (p. 132), and thus carry resegregation into the sports teams, music and drama groups, and other clubs. Scherer and Slawski (1981), however, indicated that where black and white children share a common task, interracial contact increases significantly. As Schofield (1981) concluded:

> Although the impact of cooperation on non-academic tasks has not been as closely studied [as has classroom cooperation], it too seems conducive to positive relations. Further, it is clear that resegregation of widely valued extracurricular activities like athletics can lead to tensions and resentment. Thus, strategies which are effective in encouraging cooperative contact in such activities seem likely to lead to more positive intergroup relations. (p. 135)

Hughes *et al.* (1980) noted that, in addition to overt racism, socioeconomic factors may contribute to extracurricular segregation. For example, requirements that members of cheerleading squads possess skills learned at paid clinics, or that members of certain teams purchase equipment or finance travel, restrict participation to relatively well-to-do-students. School history, the authors observed, may also be an inadvertently discriminatory factor. For example, a previously white school with a chapter of Future Farmers of America and a Chess Club may not have groups such as a Soul Music Club or a Black Heritage Club.

In 1967, a federal appeals court alluded to the constitutional necessity of ending discrimination in extracurricular activities, remarking that "the necessity of overcoming the effects of the dual school system in this circuit requires integration of faculties, facilities, and activities as well as students."[69] The following year, a district court in Alabama applied that ruling to athletics, finding that "it is without serious question that athletic programs in the various high schools . . . are an integral part of the public school system."[70]

In 1971, a Texas appeals court was even more specific:

> Defendants shall not permit . . . activities run in connection with the elementary and secondary educational program . . . which, whether by intent, inaction, or inadvertence, [result] in segregation or other discrimination against students on the ground of race, color, or national origin. These extracurricular activities include, but are not limited to, student government organizations, athletic teams for inter-scholastic competition, clubs, hobby groups, student newspaper staffs, annual staffs, band, band majorettes, and cheerleaders.[71]

Thus by 1975, clear precedent was already in place when the district court in *Milliken II* addressed the need for desegregation in extracurricular activities. After stressing that such activities are "essential supportive programs in a system

[69] *U.S. v. Jefferson County Board of Education,* 380 F. 2d 385 (1967), 389.
[70] *Lee v. Macon County Board of Education,* 283 F. Supp. 194 (1968), 197.
[71] *U.S. v. State of Texas,* 447 F. 2d 441 (1971), 445.

undergoing desegregation,"[72] the court called for the Detroit Board to develop a specific plan to address desegregation of extracurriculars. That component ultimately was omitted from the district court's order.

More recent batteries of educational components, however, have included requirements addressing desegregation of nonacademic programs. For example, in the consent decree in San Francisco, the parties agreed that "it is important to ensure that the extracurricular activities of [the district] are available to all students on a basis which is consistent with the obligation to avoid segregation and provide equal educational opportunity." The decree went on to require the State of California to submit a program "for monitoring extracurricular activities to find out the extent to which students from the various groups do or do not participate in various activities and to develop methods for informing them formally about their opportunities to participate."[73]

Desegregation must be a goal for all aspects of school life. Efforts to integrate activities such as athletic teams and school-based clubs are key elements of a desegregation plan.

Parental and Community Involvement. The transition to desegregated schools progresses much more smoothly when students, parents, and the general public support the process (Willie & Greenblatt, 1981). Opposition, on the other hand, can undermine desegregation efforts. The U.S. Commission on Civil Rights (Wilkinson, 1979) found opposition to have occurred in the early years of desegregation in Boston: "A virtual total lack of support . . . by public and private leaders . . . reinforced the opposition view that desegregation would never come to pass" (p. 209).

District Judge Garrity addressed Boston's anti-busing sentiment by creating new mechanisms to involve parents and other interested community members in the educational system.[74] Dentler (1977) reported that after desegregation, parental involvement in Boston "increased tremendously." It seems that the passions aroused in the busing controversy were channeled into improving the quality of education in that system. As Green, Canup, and Hebert (1978) stated:

> The primary change was a dramatic rise in parental involvement. Desegregation pinched awake many a parent who had been complacent about schools up to that point. Parents were found visiting and working in offices, classes, and libraries in great numbers. And when people began to take notice, they discovered that their past apathy had been allowing the schools to coast along inefficiently and without accountability. . . . Perhaps most significantly, the inability of the school to deal with a variety of student types was exposed. As the schools became better, student trouble subsided. (p. 9)

---

[72] *Bradley v. Milliken*, 402 F. Supp. 1096 (1975), 1143.

[73] *San Francisco NAACP v. San Francisco Unified School District*, N.D. Cal., Civil NO. C–78–1445 WHO. Consent Decree, p. 18.

[74] *Morgan v. Kerrigan*, 401 F. Supp. 216 (1975).

Desegregation presents an opportunity to increase parental and community participation in the schools. This participation can lead to better education for school children. Researchers have identified numerous potential benefits from more widespread participation in school decision-making. Gittle (1971) found that participating students generally achieved a heightened sense of mastery over their environments, and that participating minority students acquired attitudes strongly related to subsequent academic success. The research of Altshuler (1970) indicated that participation can reduce community fragmentation and impersonality, and can also increase cooperation among people who usually are competitive. According to McNeely (1973), opportunities for involvement in school-related activities can increase civic participation among racially homogeneous, low socioeconomic status sectors in the community. Wilcox (1970) found that increased community involvement in educational decision-making can lead to sharp declines in suspension, decreased vandalism, and more positive attitudes about the schools among students and teachers.

Researchers have also found specific gains associated with community participation in the desegregation process. Interracial interaction among students has increased, either in connection with students' own involvement (Weinberg, 1977) or with that of their parents (Struzziery, 1977). Other researchers (Raffel, 1980; Willie & Greenblatt, 1981) have noted that community participation is related to a reduction in community race- or class-based tensions surrounding desegregation. Doulson, reported by Bryant, Chesler, and Crowfoot (1979) ascertained that student participation in the planning and implementation of desegregation is related positively to reading and math scores. According to Bryant et al., improved test scores were significantly associated with students' feelings that they had exercised a meaningful influence over their educational environment.

The federal courts began including community participation components in their desegregation remedies as early as 1971.[75] Although the Supreme Court did not include the participation component in its *Milliken II* ruling, the district court in the Detroit case did outline the parameters for such a program. An "effective community relations program," according to the district court, would

> develop a partnership between the community and the schools and . . . cooperate with traditional groups such as parent–teacher organizations and local school advisory boards. There should be a cooperative flow of information from the school to the community and from the community to the school. Open and free discussion and participation in the desegregation process should be encouraged.[76]

The district court also called on the school district to incorporate community involvement in its extracurricular programs. These programs, the court said, "can acquaint students with the many fine institutions in the Detroit area, which

---

[75] *U.S. v. State of Texas,* 342 F. Supp. 24 (1971); *aff'd.* 466 F. 2d 518 (5 Cir. 1972).
[76] *Bradley v. Milliken,* 402 F. Supp. 1096 (1975), 1143.

have indicated their interest in aiding the court in providing quality education to Detroit school children." These institutions include the local art institute and the city's public library, as well as two colleges in the Detroit area.[77]

Achieving quality education is difficult even under the most harmonious circumstances. Desegregation can be unsettling to whatever harmony exists in a district. For that reason, civic leaders must work to create the broadest possible base of community support for the schools during desegregation. Community involvement components are, therefore, important additions to desegregation planning.

In-service Training

> Social acceptance and better education do not automatically occur by causing a school to be composed of students from different races or ethnic backgrounds. . . . Unless there is conscious, sensitive planning, the recently desegregated school is frequently characterized by student (and faculty) hostility, resentment, and an inadequate administrative response system. It is a school in which neither staff nor students accept one another, and ultimately resegregation is a likely possibility. (Hughes, *et al.*, 1980, p. 141)

Among the most important factors in determining the success or failure of a desegregation plan are the attitudes and expectations of school personnel (Bosma, 1977; Chesler, Guskin, & Erenberg, 1969; Raffel, 1980). Studies of school climate (Brookover, Beady, Flood, Schweitzer, & Wisenbaker, 1979; Lezotte, Hathaway, Miller, Passalacqua, & Brookover, 1980) indicate that teachers and administrators, more than any other factors, can determine a school's level of student achievement. Teachers can also do much to foster a favorable atmosphere for positive interracial contact (Cohen, 1980; Smith, Downs, & Lachman, 1973).

Few educators would deny the importance of unbiased teachers, counselors, and administrators in achieving successful desegregation. However, researchers (Banks, 1972; Bowles & Gintes, 1973; Gottlieb, 1964; Simmons, 1979) have found that teachers and counselors do in fact have different feelings toward majority and minority children. Frequently, these attitudes reflect stereotypes based on both race and social status (Green & Cohen, 1979; Simmons, 1979; Washington, 1979; Yee, 1969).

The effects of these differing expectations have already been shown in the context of tracking, discipline, and extracurricular activities. Such specific effects must be addressed at a structural level by components designed to root out their institutional sources. However, unless the individual biases of school personnel are also addressed, the institution will likely develop conditions reflecting those biases.

In a handbook for desegregation planners, Hughes, Gordon, and Hillman (1980) highlighted problems common in desegregated districts. These included

[77] *Id.* at 1144.

low academic expectations for minority students, biased teaching materials, tracking unrelated to true ability, biased counseling, failure to relate to minority children as individuals, biased discipline, and dishonesty. The authors concluded that "these problems can be expected, and there is a need to provide in-service training to deal with them" (p. 136).

As Green (1981b) stated in the recommendations for the Chicago Consent Decree:

> There are numerous critical issues in the implementation of the systemwide student desegregation plan, as roles will be redefined and educational goals reestablished. This will necessitate the development or strengthening of pedagogical and administrative skills. . . . Accordingly, the district must assume the obligation to help its staff members through the transition period, providing training designed to develop new skills and attitudes that will enable staff members to cope with their dynamic situation. (p. 75)

The courts began to recognize this obligation in the late 1960s. A Louisiana federal district court in 1969 ruled that "in-service teacher training programs shall be offered so that teachers may remedy any inadequacies in their preparation, and so that they may be better prepared to deal with the problems arising from school desegregation."[78] By 1975, a circuit court counted in-service training programs among the "actions necessary to plan for successful student and faculty desegregation."[79]

Thus, the district judge in the Detroit case drew on considerable consistent precedent when he held that:

> a comprehensive in-service training program is essential to a system undergoing desegregation. A conversion to a unitary system cannot be successful absent an in-service training program for all teachers and staff. All participants in the desegregation process must be prepared to deal with new experiences that inevitably arise.[80]

The court called for training programs in teacher expectations, human relations, minority culture, testing, and discipline.

The *Milliken II* district court addressed with particular specificity the importance of teacher attitudes and expectations:

> It is known that teachers' attitudes toward students are affected by desegregation. These attitudes play a critical part in the atmosphere of a school and affect the pulse of the school system. Teachers, both white and black, often have unhealthy expectations of the ability and worth of students of the opposite race. Moreover, it is known that teachers' expectations vary with socio-economic variations among students. These expectations must, through training, be reoriented to ensure that academic achievement of black students in the desegregation process is not impeded.[81]

---

[78] *Smith v. St. Tamany Parish School Board*, 302 F. Supp. 106 (1969), 110.

[79] *U.S. v. State of Missouri*, 523 F 2d 885 (1975), 887.

[80] *Bradley v. Milliken*, 402 F. Supp. 1096 (1975), 1139.

[81] *Id.*

The U.S. Supreme Court approved the district court's order in *Milliken II,* finding that "the decree . . . was aptly tailored to remedy the consequences of the constitutional violation."[82] By 1978, the district court in the New Castle County case ruled that "in-service training is essential," and ordered the consolidated school board to "formulate and implement a comprehensive in-service training program for teachers, administrators, and other staff."[83]

Perhaps the most comprehensive in-service training program yet implemented was undertaken in Memphis, beginning in 1982 (Green, 1983). Under the terms of a consent decree, 22 nearly all-black schools were targeted for intensive efforts to upgrade their academic climates. Based on the belief that virtually all children can learn if effectively taught, the Memphis Effective Schools Project was organized to improve five factors that researchers have found to be critical in distinguishing effective from ineffective schools.

1. Strong and effective administrative leadership in instruction and management.
2. Greater emphasis on, and time devoted to, basic reading and mathematics.
3. A safe and orderly school environment that allows teachers and pupils to focus their energies on academic achievement.
4. A climate of expectations that virtually all children can learn under appropriate conditions.
5. The use of assessment instruments to provide continuous feedback on the effects of instruction. (Green, 1983, p. 2)

Most evaluations of in-service training programs measure only participants' reactions, rather than the actual impact of training on classroom behavior (Carney, 1979; Roye, 1970). However, staff training in communication skills, individualized instruction methods, teaching effectiveness, leadership effectiveness, and the use of bilingual materials, have been shown to contribute to more successful desegregation (King, 1980; King & Galindo, 1980; Williams, 1980). Rokenson and Preston (1976) studied Houston teachers who had undergone intensive in-service workshops designed to promote, among other things, positive interracial attitudes. The researchers found that workshop participants tended to be less prejudiced, and to have more favorable attitudes toward integration, than teachers who had not participated.

Teacher attitudes influence many elements of a school's climate. The potential benefits of in-service training can be greatly enhanced when programs are skillfully designed and implemented. There must be close cooperation between the outside experts hired to design the program and the local school personnel who will put the program's lessons into practice. In particular, teachers must participate as early as possible in the planning stages to assure that the program addresses their needs (Green, Parsons, & Thomas, 1981).

Green (1978) recommended a comprehensive set of goals for an effective

---

[82] *Milliken v. Bradley,* 433 U.S. 275 (1977), 287.
[83] *Evans v. Buchanan,* 447 F. Supp 982 (1978), 1015.

in-service training program in the Indianapolis desegregation case. He urged the creation of a program designed

- To promote interracial cooperation and understanding among students, teachers, administrators, and all support staff in order to prevent minor concerns and irritations from developing into major conflict situations.
- To assist support staff in their understanding of the uniqueness of all students, and to develop skills which will enable them to deal effectively with conflict situations specifically related to racial desegregation.
- To help professional staff develop skills which prevent social and academic resegregation from occurring.
- To assist the total staff in understanding the impact of school desegregation on all students.
- To assist teachers in understanding their role in establishing different standards, expectations of failure, and differential performance of students from racially and economically diverse backgrounds, and to work against this phenomenon.
- To increase the level of sensitivity to minorities.
- To develop an awareness of personal and institutional racism, and to eradicate its effects within the desegregation area.
- To develop the capacity to understand and accept racial and cultural diversity (Green, 1978, p. 24).

The accomplishment of these essential goals will require more than an afternoon's seminar. For this reason, educators must address in-service training not as an isolated event, but as an ongoing process. This process of developing positive attitudes should begin in the nation's teacher training institutions, and should continue in a conscious ongoing manner throughout the careers of all educators. As Robert W. Cole (1982), editor of *Phi Delta Kappan,* wrote:

The rationales for an effective system of inservice training in *every* school district are simple. Knowledge changes. Best practice changes. Both are altered by time, research, technology, and any number of other factors. An educator's education does not end on graduation day; it is only beginning. To stagnate is to be a less effective educator, and the education profession is too vital to allow room for people whose minds stopped growing the day they entered their first classroom. (p. 370, emphasis in original).

CONCLUSION

School desegregation is both a social ideal and a judicial response to the historical fact of unconstitutional school segregation. Busing may be necessary to achieve desegregation, and metropolitan busing may be necessary if residential patterns dictate. All boundaries obstructing desegregation must be addressed— by local or state policies where possible, by court order if necessary. Educational components address the most nebulous, but perhaps the most pernicious of these boundaries: those of personal prejudice and institutional bias, and those involving the academic and emotional effects of past segregation.

Some argue that educational components go too far, that they subvert local

control of the schools and substitute the vagaries of the adversarial judicial process for the more reasoned analysis of educational professionals. A review of the history of educational component litigation indicates, however, that these judicial interventions consistently have arisen from educational need. Professionals knowledgeable in the problems facing desegregating schools have designed components to meet the requirements of particular local conditions. Some court orders have established programs that actually increase community access to school decision-making.

The purpose of educational components is to help all children achieve high academic standards. If minority children have been permitted to lag behind in inferior segregated schools, the discrepancy must be addressed as part of the desegregation process. Segregation was imposed to enforce a caste system, with blacks and other minorities at the low end of the social spectrum. When problems develop after children from various points along that spectrum are placed in the same classroom, we must remember that these problems grow not from desegregation, but from segregation and inferior schooling. As Weinberg (1975) has said, desegregation does not create problems; it uncovers them.

In uncovering these problems, desegregation can benefit poor- and/or low-achieving white children as much as it benefits minority children. As the superintendent of the Wilmington schools remarked (Minter, 1976), desegregation can "provide educators and communities with opportunities for making substantive changes in educational programs being offered to children. It can provide an opportunity to develop a new curriculum that will meet the needs, talents, and abilities of all children" (p. 40).

In her landmark study of desegregation outcomes, St. John (1975) found that some desegregation plans seemed to work, whereas others did not:

> School desegregation is a many-sided phenomenon. . . . Whether the potential benefit outweighs the potential harm depends not only on the circumstances of individual pupils involved but above all on how well schools adapt to meet the challenge of a biracial population. For too long, courts, schoolmen, and social scientists have been obsessed with questions of quantity rather than quality, with mathematical ratios, quotas, and balance, rather than with the educational process itself. The real task—to translate desegregation into integration—still remains. (pp. xi–xii)

In the years since St. John's writing, educational components have done much to direct the focus of desegregation back to the educational process, and to begin the task of translating school desegregation into true school integration.

REFERENCES

Allport, G. (1954). *The nature of prejudice*. New York: Addison-Wesley.
Altshuler, A. A. (1970). *Community control*. Indianapolis: Pegasus.

Arnez, N. L. (1976). Desegregation of public schools: A discriminatory process. *Journal of Afro-American Issues, 4*, 274–282.

Banks, J. (1972). Racial prejudice and the black self-concept. In J. Banks & J. Grambs (Eds.), *Black self-concept* (pp. 5–35). New York: McGraw Hill.

Bell, D. (1973). *Race, racism, and American law*. Boston: Little, Brown.

Bosma, B. (1977). The role of teachers in school desegregation. *Integrated Education, 15*, 106–111.

Bowles, S., & Gintes, H. (1973). *I.Q. in the U.S. class structure*. New York: Warner Modular.

Bowles, S., & Gintes, H. (1976). *Schooling in capitalist America*. New York: Basic Books.

Brookover, W., Beady, C., Flood, P., Schweitzer, J., & Wisenbaker, J. (1979). *School social systems and student achievement: Schools can make a difference*. New York: Praeger.

Bryant, B. I., Chesler, M. A., & Crowfoot, J. E. (1979). Student perception in school desegregation: Programs and problems. *Integrated Education, 17*, 43–47.

Bryson, J. E., & Bentley, C. P. (1980). *Ability grouping of public school students: Legal aspects of classification and tracking methods*. Charlottesville, VA: Michie.

Carney, M. (Ed.), (1979). *In-service training in desegregated school districts: Eastern region case studies*. Washington DC: U.S. Department of Health, Education and Welfare, National Institute of Education.

Carter, R. (1973). The Warren Court and desegregation. In D. Bell (Ed.), *Race, racism and American law* (pp. 381–384). Boston: Little, Brown.

Chesler, M., Guskin, J., & Erenberg, P. (1969). *Planning educational change: Vol. 2. Human resources in school desegregation*. Washington, DC: U.S. Government Printing Office.

Child, C., (1982, December 2). Suspension policies face bias inquiry. *Ann Arbor (Michigan) News*, p. 1,2.

Children's Defense Fund. (1974). *Children out of school in America*. Washington, DC: Children's Defense Fund, Washington Research Projects.

Cohen, E. (1980). Design and redesign of the desegregated school: Problems of status, power, and conflict. In W. Stephen & J. Feagin (Eds.), *School desegregation: Past, present, and future* (pp. 251–280). New York: Flenum Press.

Cole, R. W. (1982). "In-service" is not a verb. *Phi Delta Kappan, 63*, 370.

Columbus Public Schools. (1980, March 25). *Report on the status of desegregation to the Federal District Court, Penick v. Columbus Board of Education*, Columbus, OH.

Crain, R. G. (1981). Making desegregation work: Extracurricular activities. *The Urban Review, 13*, 125–127.

Dentler, R. A. (1977). Educational implications of desegregation in Boston. In D. U. Levine & R. J. Havighurst (Eds.), *The future of big-city schools* (pp. 177–191). Berkeley: McCutchen.

Eyler, J., Cook, V., Tompkins, R., Trent, W., & Ward, L. (1981). Resegregation: Segregation within desegregated schools. In Vanderbilt University, Institute for Public Policy Studies, Center for Educational and Human Development Policy (Ed.), *Assessment of current knowledge about the effectiveness of school desegregation strategies* (pp. 126–162). Nashville: Vanderbilt University.

Findley, W., & Bryan, M. (1971). *Ability grouping: 1970: Status, impact and alternatives*. Athens, GA: Center for Educational Improvement.

Ford, S. F., & Campos, S. (1977). *Summary of validity data from the admissions testing program validity study service*. New York: College Entrance Examination Board.

Gittel, M. (1971). *Demonstration for social change*. New York: Queens College, Institute for community studies.

Goldberg, M. L., Passow, H., & Justman, J. (1966). *The effects of ability grouping*. New York: Teachers College Press.

Gottlieb, D., (1964). Teaching and students: The views of Negro and white teachers. *Sociology and Education, 27*, 145–153.

Green, R. L. (1974). The awesome danger of intelligence tests. *Ebony, 29*, 68–72.

Green, R. L. (1975). *IQ equals poor clue*. Unpublished manuscript, Michigan State University.

Green, R. L. (1976, February). *School desegregation: What can the staff expect?* Paper presented before the staff of the Wilmington Public Schools, Wilmington, DE.

Green, R. L. (1978, July). *Metropolitan desegregation: Educational considerations*. Deposition for Buckley v. Board of School Commissioners of the City of Indianapolis. East Lansing, MI.

Green, R. L. (1979, February). *Living in a multicultural world*. Paper presented at Rearing Children of Good Will Conference, Greater Detroit Round Table, Detroit, MI.

Green, R. L. (1980). *Educational Components for Tasby v. Estes*. East Lansing, MI: Michigan State University, College of Urban Development.

Green, R. L. (1981a). *Consultants' research report, student desegregation plan for the Chicago Public Schools. Pt. 1: Educational components*. East Lansing, MI: Michigan State University, College of Urban Development.

Green, R. L. (1981b). *Student desegregation plan for the Chicago public schools: Recommendations on educational components*. East Lansing, MI: Michigan State University, College of Urban Development.

Green, R. L. (1983). *Consultants' interim report, February, 1983: Memphis Effective Schools Project*. East Lansing, MI: Michigan State University, Urban Affairs Programs.

Green, R. L., & Cohen, W. (1979). *An evaluation of the results of the school desegregation order in Michelle Oliver v. Kalamazoo Board of Eduation*. East Lansing, MI: Michigan State University.

Green, R. L., & Farquhar, W. W. (1965). Negro academic motivation and scholastic achievement. *Journal of Educational Psychology, 56*, 241–243.

Green, R. L., & Griffore R. J. (1976, March). *School desegregation, testing, and the urgent need for equity in education*. Paper presented at the Association for Supervision and Curriculum Development Conference, Miami, FL.

Green, R. L., Canup, T., & Herbert, H. (1978). *Can children gain from desegregation?* Paper prepared for the Kentucky Commission on Human Rights. East Lansing, MI: Michigan State University, College of Urban Development.

Green, R. L., Parsons, M., & Thomas, F. (1981). Desegregation: The unfinished agenda. *Educational Leadership, 38*, 282–285.

Hall, L. (1978). Race and suspension: A second generation desegregation problem. In C. D. Moody, J. Williams, & C. B. Vergon (Eds.), *Student rights and discipline* (pp. 47–54). Ann Arbor, MI: University of Michigan, School of Education.

Hansen, C. F. (1964). *Four-track curriculum for today's high schools*. Englewood Cliffs, NJ: Prentice-Hall.

Havighurst, R. (1977). *Education in metropolitan areas*. Boston: Allyn & Bacon.

Hughes, L. W., Gordon, W. M., & Hillman, L. W. (1980). *Desegregating America's schools*. New York: Longman.

Hunt, B. C. (1972). Black dialect and third and fourth graders' performance on the Gray Oral Reading Test. *Reading Research Quarterly, 25*, 430–437.

Kaeser, S. C. (1979). Suspensions in school discipline. *Education and Urban Society, 11*, 465–486.

King, A. (1980). *Executive summary of final report on analyses of self development programs and other strategies to improve education in desegregated schools, 1978–1979*. Austin, TX: Southwest Educational Development Lab.

King, A., & Galindo, L. (1980). *Identification of effective staff development/in-service education strategies to integrate desegregated schools*. Paper presented at the American Educational Research Association Annual Meeting, Boston, MA.

Kirp, D. L. (1973). Schools as sorters: The constitutional implications of student classification. *University of Pennsylvania Law Review, 121*(4), 705–797.

Larkin, J. (1979). School desegregation and student suspension: A look at one school system. *Education and Urban Society, 11*, 485–495.

Leubsdorf, J. (1977). Completing the desegregation remedy. *Boston University Law Review, 57,* 39–95.

Lezotte, L., Hathaway, D., Miller, S., Passalacqua, J., & Brookover, W. (1980). *School learning climate and student achievement.* East Lansing, MI: Michigan State University, College of Urban Development and College of Education.

Lichter, J. H., & Johnson, D. W. (1969). Changes in attitudes toward Negroes of white elementary. school students after use of multiethnic readers. *Journal of Educational Psychology, 60*(2), 148–152.

McNeely, R. L. (1973). *In public education, is community participation the answer?* Waltham, MA: Brandeis University, Heller School.

Mercer, J. (1973). *Labeling the mentally retarded.* Berkeley: University of Calif. Press.

Miller, J. D. (1975). Student suspension in Boston: Derailing desegregation. *Inequality in Education, 20,* 16–18.

Minter, T. K. (1976). How does a district mobilize for desegregation? In Michigan State University, College of Urban Development (Ed.), *School desegregation: Making it work* (pp. 39–58). East Lansing, MI: Michigan State University, College of Urban Development.

National Advisory Commission on Civil Disorders. (1968). *Report of the National Advisory Commission on Civil Disorders.* New York: New York Times Company.

National Council for the Social Studies. (1976). *Curriculum guidelines for multiethnic education.* Arlington, VA: Author.

National Education Association. (1974). *Survey of programs and practices of public school students.* Washington, DC: Author.

Oakes, J. (1982). The reproduction of inequity: The content of secondary school tracking. *The Urban Review, 14*(2), 107–120.

Project Student Concerns. (1977). *Interim report.* Louisville, KY: Jefferson County Education Consortium.

Raffel, J. A. (1980). *The politics of school desegregation.* Philadelphia: Temple Univ. Press.

Rokenson, J., & Preston, J. D. (1976). Equal status contact and modification of racial prejudice: A reexamination of the contact hypothesis. *Social Forces, 54,* 911–924.

Roye, W. (1970). *An evaluation of an in-service training program which focuses on assisting educators of School District 65 to develop some common understanding about crucial integration issues.* New York: Columbia University.

St. John, N. (1975). *School desegregation: Outcomes for children.* New York: Wiley.

Scherer, J., & Slawski, E. (1981). Desegregation: Advantages to whites. *Urban Review, 13,* 217–225.

Schofield, J. W. (1981). Desegregation school practices and student race relations. In Vanderbilt University, Institute for Public Policy Studies, Center for Education and Human Development Policy (Ed.), *Assessment of current knowledge about the effectiveness of school desegregation strategies* (pp. 58–103). Nashville, TN: Vanderbilt University.

Simmons, C. A. (1979). *Racial bias of teachers and counselors in the assignment of incoming seventh graders to ability groups within a desegregated school district.* Unpublished doctoral dissertation, Michigan State University, East Lansing, MI.

Smith, A., Downs, A., & Lachman, M. (1973). *Achieving effective desegregation.* Lexington, MA: D.C. Heath.

Solomon, B., & Young, B. (1968). Racism in U.S. history: Unweaving the threads. *Changing Education, 2*(4), 7–13.

Southern Regional Council. (1979). A conflict of cultures. *Southern Exposure, 7*(2), 126–298.

State of Florida, Department of Education. (1979, April). *Statistical Report,* Series 79–21, pp. 28–29.

Struzziery, J. (1977). School climate and racial attitudes. *Integrated Education, 15*(6), 100–102.

Teachers say poor blacks most often handicapped. (1976). *Phi Delta Kappan, 57,* 561.

United States Commission on Civil Rights. (1967). *Racial isolation in the schools.* Washington, DC: U.S. Government Printing Office.

United States Commission on Civil Rights. (1976a). *A long day's journey into light: School deseg-regation in Prince George's County*. Washington, DC: U.S. Government Printing Office.

United States Commission on Civil Rights. (1976b). Hearing, Tampa, Florida, March 29–31.

United States Commission on Civil Rights (1977). *Williamsburg County, SC: Case study of deseg-regation*. Washington, DC: U.S. Government Printing Office.

United States Department of Health, Education, and Welfare. (1975, September). *Fact sheet: Student discipline*. Washington, DC: Author.

Washington, V. (1979). The role of teacher behavior in school desegregation. *Educational Horizons, 57*, 145–151.

Weinberg, M. (1975). The relationship between school desegregation and academic achievement: A review of the research. *Law and Contemporary Problems, 39*, 241–270.

Weinberg, M. (1977). *Minority students: A research appraisal*. Washington, DC: National Institute of Education.

Wilcox, P. (1970). Integration or separatism in education: K–12. *Integrated Education: Race and Schools, 8*(1).

Wilkinson, J. H. (1979). *From Brown to Bakke: The Supreme Court and school integration, 1954–1978*. New York: Oxford Univ. Press.

Williams D. (1980). *Validation of effective staff development/in-service education strategies*. Paper presented at the American Educational Research Association Annual Meeting, Boston, MA.

Willie, C. V., & Greenblatt, S. L. (1981). *Community politics and educational change: Ten school systems under court order*. New York: Longman.

Yee, A. H. (1969). Source and direction of causal influence in teacher-pupil relations. *Journal of Educational Psychology, 59*, 275–282.

Yudof, M. G. (1975). Suspension and expulsion of black students from the public schools: Academic capital punishment and the Constitution. *Law and Contemporary Problems, 39*, 374–411.

4

Beyond Busing

NEW EVIDENCE ON THE IMPACT OF METROPOLITAN SCHOOL
DESEGREGATION ON HOUSING SEGREGATION

DIANA PEARCE

Wilmington is one of the first large Northern cities to desegregate its schools on a metropolitan basis. But is not the first city[1] to have metropolitan school desegregation. Particularly in the South, where school systems are often organized on a countywide basis, many urban communities have had areawide school desegregation since the early seventies. The experiences of these cities, in the South as well as elsewhere, can be a guide and prospectus as to Wilmington's future. In this chapter, I will focus on the impact of metropolitan school desegregation on housing patterns. The question I will address is whether the elimination of segregation in the schools of an urban community results in less segregated housing.

The relationship between school desegregation and housing desegregation is of great policy importance. Most Americans support integrated education, and most Americans would probably agree that desegregation of housing is the preferable way to achieve integrated schools. Yet over the past decades, levels of residential segregation have remained quite high (Sorenson, Taeuber, & Hollingsworth, 1975; Taeuber & Taeuber, 1965; Van Valey, Roof, & Wilcox, 1977). Except in those places where the schools have been desegregated, these high levels of residential segregation have been reflected in correspondingly high

---

[1] Unless otherwise stated, "city" should be taken to mean metropolitan area; other designations, such as urban area and urban community, should also be understood to be interchangeable with the more exact albeit cumbersome term, "entire metropolitan area."

DIANA PEARCE ● Center for National Policy Review, Catholic University School of Law, Washington, District of Columbia 20064.

levels of school segregation. As a result, the school segregation that was once mandated by dual school system laws in the South is now found in all parts of the country, buttressed now by housing segregation.

The level of segregation in housing is usually seen as determining school segregation levels; if housing is very segregated, so will be the schools. But urban processes are seldom so simple or unidirectional. In this chapter, I will put forth evidence that demonstrates the impact that schools have on housing, such that segregated schools reinforce housing segregation, and desegregated schools produce desegregation in residential patterns. In addition, I will outline some of the dynamics involved in these processes.

The question of the impact of schools on housing is really two questions: (1) Do segregated schools reinforce segregated housing patterns? (2) Do desegregated schools reinforce desegregation in housing? The first question has been most directly addressed by the Supreme Court, when it took note of the reciprocal effects that segregated schools had on housing, and in turn on the schools:

> The location of schools may thus influence the patterns of residential development of a metropolitan area and have important impact on the composition of inner-city neighborhoods. . . . School board decisions may well promote segregated residential patterns, which, when combined with "neighborhood zoning," further lock the school system into the mold of separation of the races. (*Swann v. Charlotte-Mecklenburg,* 402 U.S. 1, 1971, at 20–21)

Although observations to the same effect have been made by others, there has not been a systematic attempt to document this phenomenon using social science methods.

The second question, however, which asks whether school desegregation has caused housing to become desegregated, has been addressed by a number of social scientists as well as by other observers and the courts, doing so under the rubric of white flight. Beginning with the report by Coleman and his associates (1975), it has been argued that when central city schools are desegregated, involving large amounts of reassignment and transportation of pupils (often under federal court order), substantial losses of white students occur. Although some authors have debated the magnitude of these effects, there is a general consensus that such a loss occurs in the first year after implementation of the plan, or its major portions (Farley, Richards, & Wurdock, 1980; Rossell, 1978).

Such white flight studies, however, address only one part of the question posed above, for they narrow the question in several important ways. First, virtually every study has examined groups of cities or school districts that include few or no metropolitan school districts. That is, they look at cities in which the desegregating district is the central city, surrounded by predominantly or all-white suburban areas; minority students are concentrated overwhelmingly in the central city. Because the option of private/parochial schools has been limited in most cities to high- and middle-income families, available white enclaves have become very important as destinations of the white flight. Where metropolitan

districts have been included, the factor of "metropolitanness" has been found to lower the level of loss of white students (Farley *et al.*, 1980). In short, whether there is white flight depends on whether there is some place to which one can flee.

A second way in which the debate on white flight narrows the question of the relationship between school and housing desegregation is that the focus is on too short a time frame. Those studies that have examined a relatively long period of time, such as 5 years, have come to somewhat different conclusions from those that focus on the first few years before and after desegregation. Although the loss of white students usually occurs most severely in the first year after the implementation of desegregation, some school systems have found that after 4 or 5 years not only are enrollment patterns back to normal, but in some cases the losses are less than they were before desegregation (Bosco & Robin, 1976; Rossell, 1978). Changes in the way housing is marketed, and even more so, changes in housing patterns, take time to become apparent. Dramatic changes in the level of segregation in school systems can happen very quickly, whereas segregation levels in housing change much more slowly. Thus, using too short a time span may well result in misleading conclusions.

A third way in which the white flight debate has narrowed the question of school desegregation's impact on housing is by examining only the negative effects (mainly white flight) that undermine residential integration and not the positive effects, direct and indirect, that reinforce integration in housing patterns. When combined with samples limited to central city-type districts and an insufficient time frame, findings of negative impacts may be both partial and misleading.

RESEARCH DESIGN

This study seeks to overcome the limitations of previous research by examining long-term, structural changes; by including metropolitan as well as central city districts in the sample; and by considering evidence of positive as well as negative impacts of school racial policies on neighborhood integration. By examining a set of cities, some with segregated and some with desegregated schools, I will approach simultaneously the two questions—whether segregated schools promote segregated housing, and whether desegregated schools promote desegregated housing. Likewise, the principal hypothesis being tested in this paper is a twin one: that segregated schools reinforce housing segregation, and that metropolitan school desegregation results in lowered levels of housing segregation.

Why metropolitan school desegregation? First, it removes white enclaves, at least in terms of the schools. One reason many whites seek out all-white residential areas is that they prefer all-white schools, either because they believe

them to have a larger share of resources or for racial reasons. When schools are desegregated on a metropolitan basis, however, all schools become roughly equal in terms of racial composition.[2] No matter where one lives, one's children will attend an integrated school.

Metropolitan desegregation not only unhooks school racial composition from neighborhood composition; it also neutralizes and may even reverse the incentives in the housing market. Before desegregation, white parents in a neighborhood experiencing an influx of minorities often faced the dilemma that if they accepted the integration of the school and neighborhood, their children might well be the last white students in the school. With metropolitan school desegregation, increasing numbers of minority families in a neighborhood will not affect the school racial composition; under some plans, such integrated neighborhoods become the only ones that have a neighborhood school (and are exempt from busing).

Obviously the definition of metropolitan is crucial to any study that examines the impact of metropolitan school desegregation. A narrow definition of metropolitan school desegregation would limit the pool of possible cases to those cities that have had a court-ordered merger of city and suburban districts pursuant to a desegregation plan. There are only two such cases: New Castle County (Wilmington, Delaware) and Jefferson County (Louisville, Kentucky). But there are many more school districts organized on an areawide basis. Some of these are county districts, a common pattern in the South. These districts contain both the central city and most or all of the suburban ring. Others are unusually large city districts that encompass what would ordinarily be called suburban areas. Still others have evolved from mid-century consolidations of once rural single-school districts that have subsequently become urban/suburban areas. Because the crucial factor in our hypothesis is not a district's legal history, but rather the degree to which the school district does or does not contain white enclaves that can be used as white flight destinations, we have chosen to define as *metropolitan* those school districts that encompass all or most of that urban community's housing market.

The design of the study is quite simple: we have compared the experiences of several pairs of urban communities, with each pair chosen to be as alike as possible, except that one has had metropolitan school desegregation and the other

---

[2] Of course, some desegregation plans have exempted some schools, leaving them predominantly one race, whereas other plans have wide variation between schools in the percent minority/black. For exactness, each sentence should begin with a phrase, "to the extent that desegregation means racial balance in all of the metropolitan community's schools . . ." Because that is cumbersome, we will refer to communities as if we dealt with two clear-cut ideal types, "segregated" and "desegregated," rather than the real but imperfect situations that characterize most cities. Nevertheless, whereas some schools may be segregated in the "communities with desegregated schools," and some schools integrated in the "communities with segregated schools," the relative difference in levels of segregation is quite high.

has had partial or no desegregation of its schools. To obtain the pairs, I began with a list of cities (including the suburban ring) that (1) have had a metropolitan school desegregation plan (i.e., one that covers most of the city's housing market) for at least 5 years, (2) have a minimum of 10% minority enrollment in the schools, and (3) had a population of at least 100,000 in 1970. Cities were then chosen from this list where there was a control city as similar as possible in terms of size, percent minority, ethnic mix, and region, but had either not desegregated or else had only desegregated schools in a portion of the housing market.[3] The pairs were selected so as to maximize variation in such areas as size; the ethnic mix of the minority population; region; and length and type of desegregation. The final study sample consists of seven pairs of cities, a number large enough to reveal consistent patterns, yet small enough to permit detailed analysis of specific cities. As a group, the cities represent a wide range, for example, some pairs are quite large, some quite small, some have significant Hispanic minorities, some virtually none. But since these cities are not randomly sampled they do not represent some larger universe of cities. The pairs chosen and the basic facts are shown in Table 1.

The city of *Charlotte-Mecklenburg County[4] was the first large school system to desegregate its schools using busing; its countywide desegregation plan was implemented under court order in 1970. *Charlotte is paired with Richmond, another Southern city similar in size and racial makeup. In Richmond, an effort to expand its citywide desegregation plan to a metropolitan one was prevented when the Supreme Court failed to approve it. For the second pair, the *Tampa-St. Petersburg standard metropolitan statistical area (SMSA) is considered one urban area, although each county surrounding the cities (Hillsborough and Pinellas, respectively) has its own school system with its own history. Nonetheless, all of Florida's school districts were desegregated under court order more or less simultaneously in 1970–1971. This contrasts sharply with the spotty and partial desegregation experienced in its pair city of Atlanta and its suburban cities and counties. The third pair, *Greenville (South Carolina) and Augusta (Georgia), both have countywide school systems: but several of Augusta's suburban areas are in another county, thus providing predominantly white enclaves.

In the Northeast, there are no districts that are truly metropolitan. *Springfield (Massachusetts), however, includes substantial portions of its housing

---

[3] Note that the cities chosen for matching may actually have some school desegregation which is partial and/or covering the central city only. This is especially true in the South, where almost every school district has experienced some desegregation. When referring to such communities as Richmond, then, as a "community with segregated schools," we are highlighting the fact that, in contrast to its counterpart, Charlotte, a substantial portion of Richmond schools are segregated, and not that every school or school district within the metropolitan area is segregated.

[4] Cities with asterisks before their names are those with metropolitan (as defined here) school desegregation.

Table 1.   Housing Segregation in Seven

		Population[a]			School enrollment[b]			
City pairs	Total[c]	% Increase 1960–1970	% Black 1970	Total[c]	% Black	% Hispanic	% Minority	Date
*Charlotte, NC	409	29.2	23.1	97	28.4	.4	30.1	1970
1. Richmond, VA	518	18.9	25.1	116	31.4	.7	32.4	1970
*Tampa-St. Petersburg	1,013	31.1	10.8	188	17.2	5.6	25.2	1971
2. Atlanta	1,390	36.7	22.3	321	26.7	1.0	27.8	1973
*Greenville, NC	300	15.2	17.1	67	18.9	.3	19.3	1970
3. Augusta	253	27.8	17.0	59	33.9	.6	35.2	1972
*Springfield, MA	164	−6.1	12.6	30	24.0	7.7	32.4	1974
4. Bridgeport, CT	157	−0.1	17.3	24	34.0	21.2	55.7	1969
*Racine	170	20.5	6.2	41	9.2	4.7	14.4	1974
5. Saginaw, MI	220	15.2	12.2	55	16.7	5.1	22.1	1972
*Wichita	277	8.6	9.7	57	16.4	2.4	19.8	1971
6. Tulsa	322	26.7	10.6	71	15.4	.8	20.1	1971
*Riverside	140	66.1	5.2	26	9.3	14.2	24.6	1966
7. San Bernardino	104	13.4	14.0	34	15.6	20.9	37.3	1970

[a] Data from U.S. Bureau of the Census, 1970 Census of Population and Housing. The Population statistics for the city pairs 1, 2, 3, and 5 are for the SMSA (the Standard Metropolitan Statistical Area). In the remaining three pairs, statistics are for the city only.

[b] Data from U.S. Bureau of the Census, 1970 Census of Population and Housing. School enrollment data on pairs, 1, 2, 3, and 5 (the SMSA pairs) come from the 1970 census. School enrollment for the other pairs (4, 6, and 7) are taken from U.S. Department of Health, Education and Welfare/Office for Civil Rights, *Directory of Public Elementary and Secondary Schools in Selected Districts/Fall 1972.*

[c] Population in thousands.

[d] Data from R. Farley, *"Final Report,"* NIE Grant #G 79-015. Data used is from school racial enrollment statistics

Sets of Paired U.S. Cities (1960–1970)

	School Segregation		Housing Segregation[f]		
Plan type/area covered	School segregation indices		Segregation indices (by census tract)		% Change 1960– 1970
	I[d]	II[e]	1960	1970	
Court-ordered/county-wide	13.1	12.5	75.6	72.3	−4.4
Court-ordered/city only	29.1	—	74.9	76.6	+2.8
Tampa					
Court-ordered/county-wide	15.9	19.6	83.6	84.5	+1.1
St. Petersburg					
	25.3	26.8			
Court-ordered/city only	75.3 (1974)	74.2	77.1	81.7	+6.0
Court-ordered/county-wide	12.3	—	38.1	42.7	+12.1
Court-ordered/one county	—	—	72.2	58.6	−18.8
Court-ordered/citywide	19.4 (1974)	17.0	9	77.4	—
Board-ordered/partial city	47.1	44.6	66.3	73.1	+7.5
Board-ordered/city-suburban		19.1	9	76.2	—
Voluntary/partial city		80.0	81.6	83.7	+2.6
HEW-ordered/citywide plan	16.5 (1972)	17.0	88.5	87.0	−1.7
Court-ordered/partial city plan	73.9 (1972)	71.5	88.6	85.5	−3.5
Board-ordered/citywide plan	23.7	23.6	75.8	57.0	−24.8
Board-ordered/partial city plan	46.3	39.1	71.4	73.0	+2.2

collected by the Office of Civil Rights (OCR), U.S. Department of Health, Education & Welfare. Date is 1971 unless otherwise indicated, and is the black-white index of dissimilarity.

[e] Data from C. H. Rossell, "*Assessing the Unintended Impacts of Public Policy: School Desegregation and Resegregation*" 1978, the National Institute of Education Appendix 1. Date is 1971 unless otherwise indicated.

[f] Data from U.S. Census, as calculated and published in T. Van Valey, W. D. Roof, and J. E. Wilcox, "Trends in Residential Segregation: 1960–1970," *American Journal of Sociology* 82 (January, 1977): p. 26–84. Figures are calculated for the whole SMSA, except for Riverside and San Bernardino, which are the same SMSA; the figures for these two cities are for each city only.

* Starred cities have metropolitan-wide school desegregation.

market, whereas its control city, Bridgeport (Connecticut), is surrounded by white suburban areas that are excluded from the predominantly minority Bridgeport school district. In the Midwest, *Racine (Wisconsin), which voluntarily desegregated its schools in 1974, was a district consolidated from the city and many small, mostly rural districts. Saginaw (Michigan), on the other hand, is a similar Midwestern city that has had virtually no school desegregation. *Wichita (Kansas) is a city that contains most of its suburban areas within the boundaries of the city and the school district; its mate, Tulsa (Oklahoma), has only a partial desegregation plan, which does not even include all of the city, nor any of the suburbs, within the school district's boundaries. Finally, *Riverside and San Bernardino, although included in the same SMSA by the Census Bureau, have in fact had very different experiences with school desegregation. *Riverside, which includes a major portion of its housing market within the school district, has had a board-ordered plan since 1966, whereas San Bernardino did not begin any significant amount of desegregation until the late seventies.[5]

In this paper, the index of dissimilarity is used to measure both housing and school segregation.[6] This measure ranges from 0 to 100. Zero indicates that there is no segregation, that is, that each unit (such as a census tract or a school) has the same proportion of minority and majority as the city (or school district) as a whole. As one approaches a score of 100, one is approaching perfect segregation, at which point the two groups are completely segregated from each other. The index can also be interpreted as the percent of population of either race that would have to move, if there were to be complete desegregation (Taeuber & Taeuber, 1965).

The last three columns of Table 1 trace the trends in levels of segregation over the 1960–1970 decade for the city pairs. With the exception of *Riverside, which desegregated its schools in 1965, this decade is predesegregation for all the study cities. With the exception of *Riverside and the Augusta-*Greenville pair, this set of indices shows no strong trends toward either increased or de-

---

[5] The South is somewhat overrepresented because more of its school systems have been desegregated, and at an earlier point, than is true of other regions of the country; also, more of its school districts are countywide, resulting in more situations in which school desegregation is *ipso facto* metropolitan in coverage. Further details of the sampling process are available from the author (Pearce, *The Selection of Matched City Pairs in an Impact Study of School Desegregation on Housing,* January 29, 1979).

[6] The index was used extensively by the Taeubers (1965) to measure residential segregation in American cities. The formula for the index is: I.D. $= [(\Sigma|x_i - y_i|)/2] \times 100$ where $x_i =$ the proportion of the x population (e.g., blacks) found in unit i; $y_i =$ the proportion of the y population (e.g., whites) found in unit i. Although other measures are stronger in certain ways, this index was chosen because (1) it is widely used to measure segregation, thus permitting easy comparisons of findings; (2) it is, for a social science measure, intuitively straightforward, and (3) although theoretically there are differences between indexes, empirically various indexes are very highly correlated (Taeubers, 1965, App. I).

creased residential segregation during the seventies.[7] Aside from those three, these cities exemplify the trend, documented by other researchers, of small decreases in residential segregation during the decade of the sixties (Van Valey et al., 1977).

More important, in comparison to their respective counterparts, the cities that desegregated their schools in the seventies did not enter the decade with substantially lower levels of residential segregation, nor with rapidly decreasing levels of segregation. Thus, not only in terms of the criterion variables (size, ethnic mix, and so forth), but also in terms of levels and dynamics of residential segregation, each city was closely matched with its counterpart before one of the pair experienced metropolitan desegregation. (Because *Riverside's school desegregation occurred in the previous decade, it is necessary to compare the 1960 figures in the case of the *Riverside–San Bernardino pair.)

The data analyzed and reported here are varied, in terms of source, type, and quality, ranging from official censuses (such as that of Richmond) to anecdotes in newsletters of open housing groups. The data include:

- interviews with school officials
- school district enrollment data
- OCR data on school racial composition
- interviews with housing officials
- planning organization documents, reports, and records
- interviews with open housing advocates and civil rights lawyers
- censuses (U.S. and local)
- simulated homeseekers' visits to real estate agents
- newspaper reports and articles[8]
- housing advertisements
- academic reports

Most of the information was obtained during visits by the researcher to each of the cities of the study. In each city that had metropolitan desegregation, an attempt was made to obtain information about housing opportunities and housing patterns previous to desegregation as well as information on trends after 1970. The intent was not just to compile quantitative data, however, but rather to obtain information on all relevant aspects of community life that might provide insight into how, and under what circumstances, school desegregation enhances residential integration.

---

[7] From the figures, it appears that Greenville had moved from an old Southern pattern of less residential segregation to a more Northern style residential pattern and hence higher level of segregation. See below for further discussion of Augusta.

[8] Most of these were obtained from the extensive clippings files at the Center for Equal Education (University of Massachusetts at Amherst).

FINDINGS

The impact of school segregation/desegregation on housing patterns was also measured with the index of dissimilarity. Instead of using the SMSA, however, as the definition of the urban area, the more geographically limited Urbanized Area was used. The SMSA includes all of each county that has either a portion of the central city and/or suburban areas in it; the Urbanized Area, by contrast, excludes rural portions of the various counties, including within it the city and its suburban ring. This distinction is especially important in the South, where the inclusion of small essentially rural discrete all-black and all-white settlements in the same census tract may be interpreted as increased suburban residential integration.

Demographic data on census tract racial composition were obtained, for the latest possible date, from three types of sources: censuses (local or special U.S. census), school enrollment data, and estimates by planning officials. Because these overlapped in several cities, it was possible to estimate what the magnitude and direction of bias was for the noncensus-based estimates.

The federal government did a special census in Richmond in 1978 as a dry run for the 1980 census. Since it included separate figures, by race, on school-age children, it was possible to calculate an index for school-age children alone, as well as the population as a whole. The two indices were 70.4 for all ages, and 75.0 for school-age children, a difference of 4.6 points. In other cities, school enrollment data (for elementary schools only) were used if there was no desegregation plan in effect (e.g., Bridgeport). Where school enrollments reflected reassignment of some students out of their residential area, either (1) kindergarten enrollment data were used, if kindergarten was excluded from the plan, or (2) estimates of the number of nonresident students by school and by race together with school racial totals were used to calculate the residential enrollment of each school. (It was assumed that nonresident minority students came from residentially segregated areas, a conservative rule that would lead to overestimating levels of residential segregation in cities with desegregated schools.)[9] In five of the cities where both school and census-type information was available,

---

[9] Although this is a reasonbly accurate assumption about minority students in *Wichita as well as in most other cities that use busing to achieve desegregation, it is less likely to hold with white students. This is because a large proportion of the white pupils are bused voluntarily to magnet schools; some of these students come from integrated rather than all-white areas. Thus, the assumption that all bused students live in ghettoes probably overestimates the level of segregation, but by a small amount. Black students' school assignments in *Wichita are determined by their address (i.e., their location in ghetto areas), and the overwhelming majority are bused to school. White students either volunteer or are chosen on the basis of a birthdate lottery.

For *Riverside, the 1978 student busing data, together with school enrollment data, were used to estimate neighborhood racial composition. These data were especially compiled for this study by the *Riverside school system and are not ordinarily kept from year to year.

the school-based figures were consistently slightly higher, averaging 2.6 points higher, which is close to the Richmond census-based differential between total population and school-age population. The two California cities, *Riverside and San Bernardino, however, had estimates based on school population that averaged 11 points lower, rather than higher, than those based on total counts. Unlike other urban areas included in our study, a substantial portion of new housing developments and subdivisions in southern California are adult-only and/or retirement communities, so that the total population in these two cities may very well be more segregated than are families with school-age children.[10]

A third source of data on residential trends is that of planning department estimates. Because census tract and elementary school attendance areas differ in number of units and areas covered, school enrollment data are used at two points in time (pre- and postdesegregation, generally 1970 and 1976–1978, respectively).

In order of preference, demographic data from censuses, school enrollment, and planning official estimates were used to calculate segregation indices for the city pairs; these are presented in Table 2. A per-year average change in the level of the index was computed, (see column 5); and by extrapolation, 1980 levels of segregation were estimated for each of the study cities (column 7). These figures show that, in each case, the city that has experienced metropolitan school desegregation (the starred city in each pair) has a much larger reduction in residential segregation than its counterpart. There is, of course, variation in this pattern, with the desegregation effect much larger in some cities than others.

One important difference among cities with metropolitan school desegregation is the length of time since implementation of desegregation. The city with the longest experience is that of *Riverside, whose schools were desegregated in 1965. As was stated above, the effect of that desegregation on housing patterns was already apparent by 1970. Though *Riverside's index of dissimilarity had been 4 points above that of San Bernardino in 1960, by a decade later (and 5 years into desegregation), it was almost 12 points below. It was estimated that by 1980 it would have dropped another 17 points or more (see Table 2). This suggests that the effect of desegregation is not a temporary phenomenon, but rather one that continuously reduces segregation, even well into the second decade.

The two cities that have had the shortest experience with desegregation, *Racine and *Springfield, completed their desegregation in 1974–1975. Whereas *Racine has shown, relative to its counterpart and absolutely, a greater amount

---

[10] For 1970, calculation of the indexes of dissimilarity for *Tampa and *St. Petersburg lends support to this interpretation. (In both cases, the countywide school systems were desegregated in 1971.) In 1970, *Tampa-Hillsborough's school index was higher than the residential index (85.0 vs. 82.8), whereas *St. Petersburg-Pinellas, which has had a large influx of mostly white retirees, is the opposite, with its school index lower than its residential index (71.1 vs. 93.4).

Table 2. Segregation Level[a] Estimates Based on School[e] and Demographic Data for Seven Sets of Paired U.S. Cities, 1970–1980

	City	(1) 1970 index[b]	(2) Post-1970 index	(3) Year of data	(4) Source	(5) Rate of change/year	(6) 1980 estimate	(7) Percentage change, 1970–1980
1.	*Charlotte	84.1	67.7	1976	Public school enrollment by race, by census tract	−2.73	56.8	−32.7%
	Richmond	83.5	70.4	1978	U.S. Special Census	−1.64	67.1	−19.6%
	*Tampa-St. Petersburg	87.7	77.1	1977/1976	Planning Department Estimate of Population (Tampa)/U.S. Special Census (St. Petersburg)	−1.63	71.4	−18.6%
2.	Atlanta	83.8	77.7	1978	Atlanta Regional Commission	−.76	76.2	−9.1%
	*Greenville	59.9	50.3	1976	U.S. Special Census	−1.60	43.9	−26.7%
3.	Augusta	68.7	—	—	—	—	—	—
4.	*Springfield	71.9[c]	69.6	1978	Kindergarten enrollment	−.58	68.4	−4.9%
	Bridgeport[d]	71.1[c]	71.2	1976	School enrollment data, HEW (OCR)	+.02	71.3	+.3%

5.	*Racine	72.8[c]	62.5	1978	School enrollment and busing data, Racine school system	−1.29	59.9	−17.7%
	Saginaw	85.8[c]	78.8	1978	School enrollment, Saginaw metropolitan area, HEW (OCR)	−.88	77.0	−10.2%
6.	*Wichita	86.3	77.3	1978	Household enumeration (census)	−1.12	75.1	−13.0%
	Tulsa	89.8	85.5	1978	Planning Department and school estimates combined (see text)	−.54	84.4	−6.0%
7.	*Riverside	58.8	44.7	1978	1978 Special Census	−1.76	41.2	−30.0%
	San Bernardino	70.5	62.8	1975	San Bernardino Census of Ethnic Population	−1.54	55.1	−21.8%

[a] The measure used is the index of dissimilarity (see text).

[b] Unless otherwise indicated, data in this column are calculated from 1970 census data, and are for the urbanized area (see text).

[c] Estimates in these cities are based on the same schools used for the post-1970 estimate; the data are from 1972 in the case of Bridgeport, 1974 in the case of Springfield, and 1970 in the other cities.

[d] For districts surrounding Bridgeport, when data was not available on a school by school basis, it was assumed that all minority children were equally distributed among that district's schools; thus this estimate is conservatively low.

[e] All school data is for elementary schools only.

* Starred cities have metropolitan-wide school desegregation.

of housing desegregation in the seventies, *Springfield has not. The major differences between *Racine and *Springfield are their respective regions and school district organizations. Whereas *Racine's school system covers half of a county and encompasses all of its suburban areas as well as some rural ones, *Springfield covers only that city.

Although it is not as metropolitan as *Racine, *Springfield is more metropolitan than its counterpart, Bridgeport, and has reduced housing segregation more. In fact, Bridgeport is the only city in the study in which segregation appears to be actually increasing. This suggests that the older cities of the Northeast, with their declining industries and built-up housing stock, as well as population loss, may be less responsive to the effects of school desegregation than are cities in other regions. In short, the lesser effect of school desegregation on housing in *Springfield is probably the result of a combination of the three factors of regional location, school district organization, and relatively recent school desegregation.

Two of the cities without metropolitan school desegregation have nevertheless had substantial reduction in levels of housing segregation; these are San Bernardino and Richmond. In the case of San Bernardino, although the reduction is substantial, it is still considerably less than that experienced by its counterpart city, *Riverside. What this implies is that the California cities may be experiencing more rapid desegregation of housing than is true of other areas, so that school desegregation in this situation is an accelerating factor. This is consistent with other aspects of housing. In many ways, these cities have characteristics that are the direct opposite of those in the Northeast, for they are expanding geographically, population-wise, and economically.

In the case of Richmond, one is confronted with a very different set of circumstances, from California on the one hand, and the Northeast on the other. In particular, there are two attributes of Richmond that distinguish it from the other cities in this study. First, Richmond has experienced a considerable amount of gentrification, with the historical renovation of several central city areas, such as the Fan District and Church Hill. But the influx of whites that is generally associated with such gentrification is probably not contributing much quantitatively to Richmond's reduction of housing segregation. Calculation of separate indexes for the city alone and the suburbs alone reveals that the city is much more segregated, with a score of 73.0 compared to the suburban index of 56.7 (indexes of dissimilarity computed from the 1978 Census). Richmond is also distinctive in its experience with school desegregation. Although Richmond has not had metropolitan desegregation, the city and the suburban county systems have been desegregated in varying degrees. The city school system reduced its segregation from an index of 91.9 in 1968 to 31.9 in 1976, whereas Chesterfield County's 1976 index was 44.7 and Henrico County's was 58.0. It may be that if the systems are large enough (the three school districts of Richmond, Henrico County, and Chesterfield County include virtually the entire metropolitan area),

and if there is a sizable proportion of minority students in the suburban as well as the city populations (both counties are over 10% minority), then the desegregation of these systems may diminish housing segregation, differing only in degree from the impact of metropolitan-wide desegregation on each.

HISPANICS AND HOUSING SEGREGATION

In three of the city pairs, Hispanics constitute a substantial minority group. The data, however, are more limited than that available on the black population. In Table 3, the levels of housing segregation have been calculated using school enrollment data in the manner described above.

Clearly the dynamics of Hispanic segregation are different from those for blacks. Hispanics in both of the Northeast cities are more segregated than are blacks in those cities; moreover, that segregation shows no sign of decreasing. Although Hispanics in the two Midwestern cities are not as segregated as blacks, there was no apparent decrease in the seventies, and perhaps even an increase in levels of segregation in both cities. Of the six cities, then, only in *Riverside is there any decrease in the estimated level of segregation among Hispanics.

The trends in the first four cities suggest that Hispanics are going through a period of ghettoization that replicates the experience of blacks. Perhaps because Hispanics have generally low income levels, they are often unable, in cities that do not have expanding economies, to take advantage of the increased open

Table 3.   Residential Segregation Indexes for the Hispanic Population[a] in Three Sets of Paired U.S. Cities, 1963–1978

City	First index	Date	Second index	Date	Change (points per year)	Source of data[a]
*Springfield	81.4	1974	82.5	1978	+.3	School enrollment (kindergarten)
Bridgeport	77.5	1972	81.8	1976	+1.1	School enrollment
*Racine	53.4	1972	54.0	1978	+.1	School enrollment/ busing figures
Saginaw	51.9	1970	58.7	1978	+.8	School enrollment
*Riverside	61.6	1963	27.2	1978	−2.3	School enrollment/ busing figures
San Bernardino	52.9	1970	56.1	1978	+.4	School enrollment

[a] Data are for elementary schools only; see text for description of how figures are calculated in desegregated districts.
* Starred cities have metropolitan-wide school desegregation.

housing opportunities that apparently result from school desegregation. Only in *Riverside, in the economic growth climate of California, does the factor of school desegregation have an impact on Hispanic housing segregation levels. Alternatively, there may be much more hostility to Hispanics in the Northeast and Midwest, whereas in the West, the degree of Hispanicization of Anglo culture raises the question of which group is assimilating the other.

Finally, many Hispanics have lived in the California cities longer, even generations longer, than their Anglo neighbors. This is in sharp contrast to the Midwest and Northeast, where the recent large and rapid influx of Hispanics has led to the development of *barrios*. In addition, bilingual programs developed for many of these students can actually increase rather than decrease their segregation in schools. The effect of school desegregation programs on Hispanic housing patterns thus may be blocked until Hispanic students are included in the desegregation program in ways comparable to other minority students.

In sum, the patterns of residential segregation for Hispanics in these six cities suggest that the Hispanic experience is much more varied than that of blacks. We have suggested four factors that may contribute to that variation: the strength or weakness of the urban economies where they have migrated, cultural hostility, time since migration, and the relationship between bilingual programs and segregation. Further research utilizing the 1980 census as well as other data may suggest additional factors. Clearly, research on the relationship between school desegregation and Hispanic housing segregation requires knowledge of factors unique to the Hispanic housing segregation—factors such as migration patterns (including return and remigration), bilingualism, bilingual programs and their relation to within-school segregation, and differences between different Hispanic groups (Puerto Rican, Mexican-American, Cuban).

This detailed examination of several study cities as well as the experiences of Hispanics suggests that the general conclusion—that cities with metropolitan-wide school desegregation have experienced greater reductions in housing segregation than similar cities without school desegregation on a metropolitan basis—should be augmented under the following conditions:

1. The effect of metropolitan school desegregation on housing is not concentrated in the first few years, but rather continues to be manifest, at least into the second decade, in steadily decreasing levels of housing segregation.
2. The amount of impact of metropolitan school desegregation is related to how metropolitan the school desegregation actually is, i.e., the more metropolitan the larger the impact on housing patterns.
3. A growing housing market probably enhances the effects of metropolitan school desegregation, whereas metropolises that are not experiencing growth will be less responsive to the impact of metropolitan school desegregation. In terms of size and region, smaller cities and/or the cities

of the South and West ought to exhibit, other things being equal, stronger impacts of metropolitan school desegregation than those which are larger and/or are located in the Northeast and Midwest.

4. Whether the housing segregation of Hispanics is less in cities with metropolitan school desegregation depends, as described above, on factors significant for blacks and also on factors unique to the Hispanic experience, such as bilingual programs and migration patterns.

DISCUSSION: THE DYNAMICS OF RACIAL INTEGRATION

School and housing desegregation can only be mutually supportive if the increased housing integration that is associated with metropolitan school desegregation includes substantial numbers of families with school-age children. The data available permitted us to examine that aspect of racial change in only one city pair, that of *Charlotte and Richmond. The data reveal a trend toward the city and the suburbs of Richmond becoming demographically quite differentiated, particularly in contrast to *Charlotte. In Richmond the suburbs are increasingly the domain of white families with school-age children, whereas the city's demography is dominated by black families with children and white families without children of school age. The contrast between Richmond and *Charlotte is shown by the figures in Table 4.

In Richmond over four times as many white children live in the average suburban tract, as compared to the average city census tract, whereas the ratio for *Charlotte is only 2.7. The opposite is true for black children. In Richmond the average city census tract has almost four times as many black children as

Table 4.   Comparison of Richmond (1978) and *Charlotte (1976) Distribution of School-Age Children, by Race[a]

	Mean number school-age children per census tract			
	White		Black	
	Richmond	*Charlotte	Richmond	*Charlotte
Total	399	699	183	357
City	141	516	310	376
Suburbs	600	1,397	84	286
City:suburbs ratio	4.2	2.7	.27	.77

[a] Data from Richmond, 1978 Special Census; Charlotte, School Enrollment by Census Tract (1976).
* Starred cities have metropolitan-wide school desegregation.

the average suburban tract, but in *Charlotte, the average number of black children in suburban tracts is much closer to the city tract averages. The sharp distinction found in Richmond between the city as a place primarily for adults and black families, and the suburbs as a place for white families, with children, is much less sharply drawn in *Charlotte. Whether the blurring of the city–suburb distinction helped facilitate school desegregation or is only one result of it cannot be answered with this data. What is clear is that both the city and the suburban areas of *Charlotte continue to attract both black and white families, thus providing a sound basis for further residential desegregation.

A second aspect, explored in this study, of the dynamics of racial integration addresses the question of whether the apparent increase in residential integration found in cities with metropolitan-type school desegregation is in fact only temporary, a transitional phase between segregated white and segregated minority neighborhoods. In the past, segregated ghetto areas have been maintained, in spite of increased numbers of minorities, by expanding these areas on a block-by-block basis. Thus, at any one point in time, one could find neighborhoods that appeared to be racially integrated but were in fact undergoing rapid racial change and soon would be resegregated. How rapidly this occurred was directly related to the number of neighborhoods or blocks involved. At one extreme, if all of the excess housing demands that could not be met within the ghetto were concentrated on one block at a time, then change in each of the successive blocks would be quite rapid, and segregation would be maintained at a high level. At the other extreme, if all excess demands were satisfied more or less randomly throughout the metropolitan housing market, then there would be very little resegregation and a rising level of integration.

Which of these two extremes best fits the residential patterns of the study cities? Is the increase in integration in the cities that have had metropolitan desegregation real and lasting or only a transitory stage snapshot? To answer these questions, Table 5 was constructed using the same sources of demographic data used in Table 2.

The hypothesis being tested here is that metropolitan school desegregation, by breaking down barriers throughout the area's housing market, results in increases in black percentages that are similar across different neighborhoods. The contrasting pattern, expected in metropolitan areas without areawide school desegregation, is the resegregation scenario described above, in which relatively few areas experience very large increases in proportion black, whereas most areas have little or no increase in percent black.

Because in a given census tract, what is rapid racial change is relative to what is going on in the city as a whole, I have begun by calculating what the mean increase in percent black is for the city as a whole (for those cities which had comparable census-based data for two points in time). The standard deviation for the increase in percent black, given in column 3 of Table 5, gives a measure of the spread or variation between tracts. The smaller the standard deviation is,

Table 5. Change in Magnitude and Distribution of Percentage Black Following School Desegregation in Seven U.S. Cities[a] 1970 and Post-1970

| | Percentage black | | | | Change in percentage black | | Census tracts with increases in percentage black that are more than twice the citywide mean | | |
| | (1) 1970 | | (2) Post-1970 | | (3) Citywide | | (4) | (5) | (6) |
City (N)[b]	M	SD	M	SD	M	SD	Number of such tracts	Mean increase in percentage black	Percentage of total population in these tracts
*Greenville (18)	35.6	30.5	39.1	31.3	+3.4	9.0	5	14.3	29.9
*Tampa-St. Petersburg (155)	15.1	30.0	20.1	30.7	+5.0	11.5	27	25.7	14.7
Atlanta (242)	25.8	38.1	32.9	38.3	+7.1	16.4	43	36.8	14.5
*Wichita (88)	9.0	23.6	10.5	24.7	+1.5	4.8	18	7.3	19.4
Tulsa (105)	9.2	25.7	10.8	27.4	+1.6	7.0	13	15.1	12.0
*Riverside (52)	5.5	9.4	5.5	7.9	-.1	6.1	36	2.2[c]	72.7
San Bernardino (36)	9.0	15.1	13.3	31.2	+4.3	16.0	2	52.9	5.5

[a] Cities which had comparable census-based data for two points in time.
[b] Number in parentheses is total number of census tracts.
[c] Because Riverside's mean is negative, this figure is the average of all census tracts with a positive increase in percentage black.
* Starred cities have metropolitan-wide school desegregation.

the more the average census tract's experience resembled that of the city as a whole; put another way, the smaller the standard deviation, the larger the number of neighborhoods that experienced an increase in the percent black similar to the citywide increase.

In the second half of the table, I examine in detail those tracts that experienced, relative to their city, very large increases in percent black, using twice the citywide mean as the threshold. In column 5, the average increase in percent black in these rapidly changing blocks is given; by referring back to column 3, one can see how much faster these tracts are changing compared to the city as a whole. Finally, in the last column, the percent of the total population found in these rapidly increasing tracts is given, in order to test the notion that these tracts are a handful of areas near the expanding edge of ghetto areas.

Although the number of cities looked at here is small, the results suggest that, relative to their counterpart cities, those with metropolitan school desegregation have less variation across the city in percent black (as shown by the standard deviation in column 3), and that relatively large increases in percent black are not concentrated in a very small number of neighborhoods. Likewise, the figures in Table 5 suggest that at least some of the apparent residential integration in cities such as San Bernardino or Tulsa is unstable. Of course, this analysis is only suggestive; analysis that would confirm these results, however, would have to examine a much larger number of cities, and/or examine several cities' experience on a neighborhood-by-neighborhood basis. Although these findings are both limited in their applicability and highly tentative, they do hint at the possibility that school desegregation not only reduces housing segregation, but also profoundly affects the dynamics of racial change in American neighborhoods.

CONCLUSION: TOWARD A THEORY OF METROPOLITAN DESEGREGATION

This examination of seven pairs of cities has revealed a remarkably consistent pattern. Compared to similar cities that have had no or only partial desegregation, cities that have had metropolitan-wide school desegregation have experienced substantially greater reductions in housing segregation.

Areawide school desegregation also affects indirectly, by the way it alters housing market practices, the neighborhood choices made by white and minority families. I have reported these findings elsewhere (Pearce, 1981), but briefly the data show that (1) where schools are racially identifiable, they are more often used in advertising and advice to steer homeseekers along racial lines, and (2) housing agents in areas with metropolitan desegregation plans are less parochial and more positive about a broader range of neighborhoods than agents in cities with partial or no school desegregation. For example, I found that schools

mentioned in real estate advertisements were virtually always white schools; not a single advertisement named a predominantly minority school.

But why does this association hold? Is it just coincidence, or does metropolitan school desegregation, directly or indirectly, cause housing patterns to also become integrated? An exploratory study such as this cannot definitely answer a question of causation, but the data do provide some important insights into the dynamics of school/housing segregation/desegregation. They suggest that the impact of broad school desegregation on housing choices is apparent at three levels, that of the individual, the neighborhood, and the metropolis.

At the individual level, desegregated schools provide, under the best of circumstances, positive interracial encounters. Parents, as well as teachers and students, work together rather than in competition. Most of the interaction, of course, involves young students who bring to the experience fewer preconceptions than do older persons; this enhances the positive effects.

Also at the individual level, fears of both majority and minority parents are reduced. After school desegregation, black families considering moving into white neighborhoods know that their children are not the first black or minority children encountered by their prospective neighbors. Indeed, because of busing, black parents or their children may already have friends or acquaintances living in white neighborhoods.

The above sociopsychological effects, however, are true of schools that are integrated by central city or partial desegregation, and even to some extent of schools temporarily integrated while a neighborhood goes through racial transition. What is distinctive about metropolitan desegregation is that the individual-level experiences are supported by the neighborhood and metropolitan impacts, rather than undercut as is the case with partial desegregation.

At the neighborhood level, as stated above, a metropolitan desegregation plan by definition removes white enclaves as far as the schools are concerned. If minority families move into one's neighborhood, one can flee residential integration, but not school integration. Most plans go one step further than this, by exempting integrated neighborhoods from busing. The power of this incentive for neighborhoods should not be underestimated, for it counteracts negative market tendencies and reinforces positive individual inclinations. Without metropolitan desegregation, the white family that remains in a neighborhood that is becoming racially mixed is likely to find itself the victim of real estate speculations and, very quickly, in the minority, as the market concentrates minority housing demands on that one area. With metropolitan desegregation, a very different incentive is operating for white families. By accepting and even encouraging housing integration, the white families in such neighborhoods may become the only ones in the metropolitan area whose children are not bused. In short, that neighborhood is likely to maintain or reacquire its neighborhood school.

For blacks, these incentives support the strong preferences of the over-

whelming majority of black families for racially mixed housing. As has been demonstrated elsewhere, many black families have the financial potential to live outside the ghetto, but have encountered noneconomic barriers to doing so. Or, if they have overcome these obstacles, they have found out very quickly that the racially mixed neighborhood to which they have moved is in fact racially transitional. In the context of metropolitan school desegregation, however, a move out of the ghetto may exempt minority children from busing and may also, by contributing to racial balance in their new neighborhood, eventually exempt the white children living there. These factors may help to make the black families welcome. Thus, when racially integrated neighborhoods are exempt from busing, such policy becomes a stabilizing factor.

In some instances, neighborhoods have become advocates of public policies that support and encourage stable housing integration. Two examples of this were found in *Charlotte (North Carolina). In the first instance, the Community Relations Commission worked with housing officials and real estate brokers to persuade predominantly white neighborhoods to accept scattered site public housing. The local communities were receptive to the idea because, under the assumption that a majority of the occupants would be minority families, it would reduce the amount of busing necessary for integration, and could lead to exemption for all children in the neighborhood. In the second instance, white residents of a neighborhood threatened with a familiar pattern of rapid racial transition did not flee. Instead, they stayed and fought the efforts of some realtors to engage in blockbusting and other tactics. If the area were allowed to resegregate, the white families who moved out and the black families who moved in would find that their children would be bused to school.

At the metropolitan level, the impact of school desegregation is manifested in several ways. For instance, school desegregation on a metropolitan scale sometimes results in a substantial increase in resources from outside the school system, a rejuvenation of the system, and a more equal distribution of resources between schools in the system. In *Racine, federal monies were obtained under the ESAA Act; this amounted to $800,000 the first year and almost a million dollars the second year. These resources enabled Racine not only to develop many new and innovative programs, but also to build a planetarium for the schools (and the community). In *Springfield, state aid was used to build a magnet school that includes not only excellent educational facilities, but also resources that are available to the community (e.g., library, swimming pool, day care center, and Hispanic Community Center).

The increased resources and overhaul of the system often result in new programs, including magnet schools. The latter may draw their students from throughout the community and are usually located in schools that were previously predominantly minority. Such programs and schools have two effects on housing choices. First, such schools decrease the importance of where one lives, because participation in the magnet schools is not contingent on residential location.

Second, by putting new programs and new schools in areas of minority concentration, the schools within a system become more equal in their attractiveness. In both instances, by making schools throughout the system more equal in their appeal, where one lives becomes less crucial, and differentials in resources between neighborhoods are reduced.

Finally, at the metropolitan level, school desegregation puts a major institution behind the principle of equal opportunity. And, unlike a metropolis with only some of its school districts desegregated, there are not competing implicitly prosegregation educational institutions. The legitimacy and authority thus lent to being pro integration are not of course limited to educational issues. This is not to say that school officials automatically become ardent and articulate civil rights activists. Rather, it simply makes integration orthodox. For example, if racially integrated school groups are seen in public places (museums, historic landmarks, etc.), then racially integrated groups in a restaurant are no longer perceived as unusual, or as a threat to the status quo. With racially mixed schools a fact of life for almost a decade, even in cities in the South, the initiating of fair housing laws or enforcement actions is not only perceived as nonthreatening, it is not even news.

In sum, the meaning of acting in prointegration ways is very different between areas where there is metropolitan school desegregation and areas where there is not. In the latter case, if one prefers racial integration, one must live in neighborhoods that are going through rapid transition and sometimes manipulation by the unscrupulous, send one's children to schools that are often overcrowded, and move frequently (to stay ahead of resegregation). In short, whether one is white or black, one must pay high costs for the short-lived benefit of racial integration. In contrast, in the context of metropolitan school desegregation, acting in prointegration ways is rational. It would be irrational to choose a segregated neighborhood, from which one's children must be bused, particularly if one values a neighborhood school over an integrated neighborhood with a walk-in school. Hence, metropolitan school desegregation has converted the choice of racially integrated housing from one that is irrational and costly to one that is rational and beneficial.

Whether at the individual, neighborhood, or metropolitan level, it should be noted that most of the observed effects of metropolitan school desegregation have occurred without major emphasis on this issue by either school or housing officials. Although the integrated neighborhood exemption was a part of most of the plans implemented in the study cities, it was not strongly emphasized or publicized frequently. Although busing was not well liked, it was treated as inevitable in most cases. With the exceptions noted above, few housing officials took advantage of the argument that such policies as scattered-site public housing or increased enforcement of fair housing laws, by integrating neighborhoods, would reduce busing. If observable housing pattern changes associated with metropolitan school desegregation can occur without officials making the con-

nection explicit, then even a few well-targeted efforts by schools and/or housing officials may well have very large impacts in terms of increasing and stabilizing racial integration in neighborhoods.

In the long run, metropolitan school desegregation may alter the character of urban neighborhoods in fundamental ways that go far beyond questions of racial and ethnic composition. Although these data cover too short a time period to document these changes, it is worthwhile to reflect briefly on these possibilities. If black families seeking racially integrated living no longer have to move frequently to stay ahead of the expanding edge of the ghetto, and if white families do not flee neighborhoods as they become integrated, then logically both groups would move less often. Aside from the personal benefits, this suggests that such neighborhoods would resemble less the way station typical of the urban neighborhood of the mid-20th century, and more the stable community of a more distant past. But unlike the villages of other times and places, these communities would not be differentiated along ethnic or linguistic lines. Each would be a microcosm of the larger community. For that reason, and because many individual residents would be involved in citywide programs (such as magnet schools, but also vocationally and recreationally), the increased neighborhood loyalty would not be parochial in nature. Rather, it would be balanced by a commitment to the community as a whole, and both commitments would recognize the values of a multicultural society.

How soon, if at all, cities like Wilmington will resemble the above scenario is at best a guess. But preliminary analyses of the 1980 census, as well as the findings presented here, clearly indicate that cities with metropolitan-wide school desegregation are experiencing more and more rapid housing integration than those with only partial or no desegregation of their public schools. This is leading to a fundamental divergence in the character of urban life among American cities. The difference is one of overcoming racial barriers to equal opportunities and getting on with other issues versus continuing to wrestle with racial inequality of opportunity. It may well be that by the turn of the century the contrast in growing up that used to distinguish city children from country children will be replaced by the very different experience of growing up in the cities which have, as opposed to those which have not, had desegregation of their schools and housing. America may indeed be moving toward two societies, not the two envisioned by the Kerner Commission, but rather two that are set apart by whether or not they have begun the process of breaking down the barriers to equal opportunity.

REFERENCES

Bosco, J. J., & Stanley R. S. (1976). White flight from busing? *Urban Education, 11,* 263–273.
Coleman, J. S. (1975, October). Racial segregation in the schools: New research with new policy implications. *Phi Delta Kappa,* 75–79.

Farley, R., Richards, T. & Wurdock, C. (1980). School desegregation and white flight: An investigation of competing models and their discrepant findings. *Sociology of Education 53*, 123–139.

Pearce, D. M. (1981). Deciphering the dynamics of segregation: The role of schools in the housing choice process. *The Urban Review, 13,* 85–101.

Rossell, C. H. (1978). School desegregation and community social change. *Law and Contemporary Problems, 42.*

Sorenson, A., Taeuber, K., & Hollingsworth, L. (1974). Indexes of racial residential segregation for 109 cities in the United States, 1940 to 1970. *Institute for Research on Poverty Discussion Papers*. Madison: University of Wisconsin, 7–9.

Swann v. Charlotte-Mecklenburg. 402 U.S. 1 (1971).

Taeuber, K. E., & Taeuber, A. (1965). *Negroes in Cities*. New York: Atheneum.

Van Valey, T. L., Roof, W. C. & Wilcox, J. E. Trends in residential segregation: 1960–1970. *American Journal of Sociology, 82.*

5

Neighborhood Racial Composition and School Desegregation in New Castle County, Delaware

JOE T. DARDEN

The racial composition of American schools has been strongly influenced by neighborhood racial composition. In order to gain a better understanding of school desegregation, it is useful to examine racial and demographic patterns in communities undergoing desegregation. In this chapter, an assessment is made of demographic characteristics and enrollment trends related to desegregation in New Castle County, Delaware, following a court-ordered metropolitan desegregation plan instituted in 1978. The relations between neighborhood racial composition and attitudes and between neighborhood racial composition and achievement are also investigated.

The city of Wilmington, located in New Castle County, was the only Standard Metropolitan Statistical Area (SMSA) in Delaware in 1970. The central city of Wilmington is an area of population decline. For example, from 1960 to 1970, the population of Wilmington declined by 16% from 96,000 to 80,000. This decline was caused by a loss of 26,000 whites and a gain of only 10,000 nonwhites, mostly blacks. The white population loss resulted from a net out-migration of 26,000 persons, equivalent to 37% of the total white population of Wilmington in 1960. The natural increase of the white population of Wilmington was minimal, amounting to only 500 for the 1960–1970 decade. The growth of Wilmington central city's population of blacks was due in almost equal part to natural increase (5,500) and net immigration (5,000). As a result of these changes, the black population increased from 26% to 44% of Wilmington's total popu-

JOE T. DARDEN ● Dean, Urban Affairs Programs, Michigan State University, East Lansing, Michigan 48824.

lation. In 1970, blacks in Wilmington's central city were 61.4% residentially segregated.

In the suburban areas, that is, outside the central city of Wilmington, blacks increased by 21%. Few blacks were moving to the suburbs, however. The increase was due mainly to excess births over deaths, rather than to migration. Only 1,598 blacks moved to the suburbs from 1960 to 1970 (U.S. Department of Commerce, 1971). By contrast, the white population in the suburbs, which increased by 26%, grew more through net migration (52,000) than through natural increase (39,000).

In 1970, blacks comprised 12.7% of Wilmington's SMSA, that is, New Castle County, for a total of 48,869 blacks, compared to 335,246 whites. Blacks, however, were disproportionately living in the central city in 1970: 35,072 in contrast to 13,797 in the suburbs. Suburban blacks were slightly more segregated (63%) than those in the central city (61.4%).

From 1970 to 1980, the total population of New Castle County increased from 385,856 to 399,002 or by 3.4%. Most of this increase was due to a 23.2% change in the black population from 48,869 in 1970 to 60,242 by 1980. The white population changed from 335,246 to 331,552 or by −1.1% over the decade (U.S. Department of Commerce, 1981).

Unlike New Castle County, the total population of Wilmington continued to decline from 80,386 in 1970 to 70,197 in 1980 (−12.7%). The decline was due primarily to the continuing outmigration of whites, a loss not balanced by the small increase (2.2%) in the black population. Thus, by 1980, Wilmington had become a majority black city with 35,858 blacks and 31,663 whites.

Although Wilmington's central city black population increased only minimally over the 1970–1980 decade, the growth of Wilmington's suburban black population was substantial. The black population in the suburbs increased from 13,797 in 1970 to 24,384 in 1980 or by 76.7% (U.S. Department of Commerce, 1981). In 1980, blacks comprised 18.1% of New Castle County's population, up from 12.7% in 1970. Of all blacks in New Castle County, 40.4% lived in the suburbs in 1980 compared to only 28.2% in 1970.

THE RELATION BETWEEN DISCRIMINATORY HOUSING PRACTICES AND SCHOOL ENROLLMENT PATTERNS

Prior to school desegregation in 1978, 74,916 students were attending school in New Castle County. Of that number 56,480 or 75.4% were white, and 16,716 or 22.3% were black. Eighty-two percent of the blacks attended school in the Wilmington school district, whereas only 10% of the whites attended school in Wilmington. This disparity in school attendance patterns on the basis of race did not occur by chance. New Castle County has had a history of racial segregation.

Before the 1978 District Court desegregation decision, New Castle County schools were highly segregated. The extent of segregation is clearly revealed by indexes of segregation (dissimilarity) (Table 1). Data on enrollment by race were made available in 1958. At that time, the elementary schools in New Castle County were 71.7% segregated. By 1959, segregation had increased to 76.4%. Racial data for 1960 were unavailable. During the decade of the sixties, segregation reached its peak in the elementary schools of New Castle County. In 1965, black children in the elementary schools were 83.9% segregated, the highest level of segregation since the 1954 *Brown v. Board of Education* school desegregation decision (Table 1 and Figure 1). The elementary schools were 81.7% segregated in 1971, when five black parents from Wilmington filed suit for supplementary relief from the segregated school system in the Wilmington school district. This suit reopened the *Evans v. Buchanan* suit that was initiated in 1956 to assure admission to public schools in Delaware on a racially nondiscriminatory basis. The elementary schools were 78.8% segregated in 1974, when a three-judge panel ruled that a unitary school system had not been established in Wilmington and required the defendant State Board of Education to submit alternate desegregation plans. In 1976, the District Court established a five-member Interim Board of Education to oversee the reorganization of the newly created New Castle County school district and to provide for pupil assignment for an interdistrict desegregation remedy. By 1976, the elementary schools were 73.7% segregated. The index of segregation stood at 70.3% in 1977 when the Federal District Court judge, retaining jurisdiction in the *Evans* suit, granted the defendant's motion for a second stay of the order to desegregate the New Castle County Schools. Thus, from 1958 to 1977, the elementary schools of New Castle County remained at an average level of segregation of 78.0%. It was not until

Table 1.   Racial Segregation in the Elementary Schools[a]

Year	Segregation index	Year	Segregation index
1958	71.7	1970	80.3
1959	76.4	1971	81.7
1961	69.5	1972	80.4
1962	69.7	1973	82.0
1963	78.6	1974	78.8
1964	81.7	1975	79.1
1965	83.9	1976	73.7
1966	79.1	1977	70.3
1967	80.9	1978	14.7
1968	83.3	1979	17.5
1969	81.6		

[a] Data from State of Delaware, Department of Public Instruction. *Racial and Ethnic Pupil Enrollment*, September 30, 1958–1979.

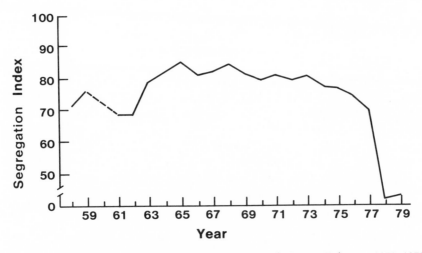

Figure 1.   Trends in elementary school segregation in New Castle County, Delaware, 1958–1979.

implementation of the *Evans v. Buchanan* desegregation order that segregation
in the elementary schools dropped from 70.3% in 1977 to 14.7% in 1978.

In 1958, the junior high schools of New Castle County were 65.2% segregated (Table 2 and Figure 2). By 1959, segregation increased to 67.7%. As
in the elementary schools, junior high school segregation reached its peak during
the decade of the sixties, rising to 81.8% in 1969. In 1971, the junior high
schools were 67.4% segregated. By 1974, segregation had declined to 45.6%.
However, during 1975 and 1976, segregation again rose—this time to 57.7%,
the highest level since 1971. This increase was followed by a steep decline to

Table 2.   Racial Segregation in the Junior High Schools[a]

Year	Segregation index	Year	Segregation index
1958	65.2	1970	62.7
1959	67.7	1971	67.4
1961	71.0	1972	56.8
1962	71.0	1973	51.8
1963	74.0	1974	45.6
1964	72.5	1975	52.6
1965	77.5	1976	57.7
1966	75.1	1977	27.5
1967	79.4	1978	7.1
1968	80.2	1979	5.9
1969	81.8		

[a] Data from State of Delaware, Department of Public Instruction. *Racial and Ethnic
Pupil Enrollment,* September 30, 1958–1979.

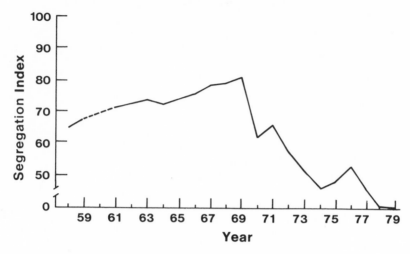

Figure 2.   Trends in junior high school segregation in New Castle County, Delaware, 1958–1979.

27.5% in 1977. Thus, from 1958 to 1977, the average level of segregation in the junior high schools was 65.1%.

In 1969, when the middle school concept was introduced into New Castle County, the schools were 68.3% segregated (Table 3 and Figure 3). By 1971, the middle schools had become 77.1% segregated, and by 1974, the figure had increased to 80.8%. On the eve of court-ordered desegregation in 1977, the index was 51.2%. Between 1969 and 1977 the average level of segregation was 73.8%.

In 1958, the high schools of New Castle County were 58.8% segregated (Table 4 and Figure 4). In 1959, segregation increased to 63.4%. By 1971, segregation had increased to 78.4% and peaked in 1973 at 82%. During 1974, however, segregation dropped from 82% to 70.5%. By 1976, the high schools were 74.3% segregated. On the eve of the court-ordered desegregation, the high schools in New Castle County were 58.8% segregated (Table 4). Thus, from

Table 3.   Racial Segregation in the Middle Schools[a]

Year	Segregation index	Year	Segregation index
1969	68.3	1974	80.8
1970	74.8	1975	81.8
1971	77.1	1976	78.1
1972	82.2	1977	51.2
1973	70.2	1978	7.1

[a] Data from State of Delaware, Department of Public Instruction. *Racial and Ethnic Pupil Enrollment*, September 30, 1969–1978.

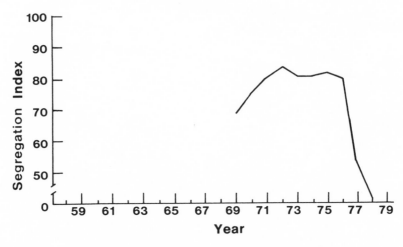

Figure 3.   Trends in middle school segregation in New Castle County, Delaware, 1969–1979.

1958 to 1977, the average level of segregation in the high schools stood at 67.9%.

These data indicate that through the years New Castle County's entire school system had been racially segregated. Only after the 1978 court order was there a substantial reduction in segregation. Segregation in the elementary schools was reduced from 78.0% to 16.1%, and in the junior high schools from 65.1% to 6.5%. In the middle schools, segregation was reduced from 73.8% to 7.1%, and in the high schools from 67.9% to 6.3% (Table 5).

Table 4.   Racial Segregation in the High Schools[a]

Year	Segregation index	Year	Segregation index
1958	58.8	1970	76.6
1959	63.4	1971	78.4
1961	56.5	1972	78.9
1962	58.3	1973	82.0
1963	64.5	1974	70.5
1964	62.0	1975	79.0
1965	53.0	1976	74.3
1966	62.7	1977	58.8
1967	69.0	1978	5.7
1968	70.2	1979	6.9
1969	74.3		

[a] Data from State of Delaware, Department of Public Instruction. *Racial and Ethnic Pupil Enrollment*, September 30, 1958–1979.

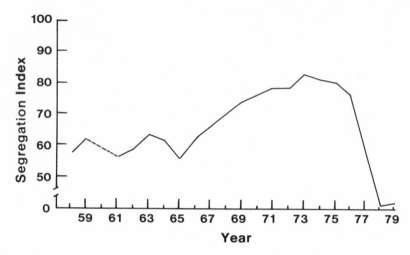

Figure 4. Trends in high school segregation in New Castle County, Delaware, 1958–1979.

In the *Evans v. Buchanan* decision, the state was faulted for its sanction and encouragement of the dramatic Wilmington population shifts, all of which ultimately bore on school attendance patterns. Discriminatory housing practices also contributed to this violation. Prior to the 1968 Federal Fair Housing Act, racial discrimination was actively encouraged in housing rentals and sales in Wilmington's suburbs. The real estate industry encouraged these practices, and the State authorized them. Among its findings, the District Court noted the use of racially restrictive covenants. Although racially restrictive covenants had been ruled unenforceable by the U. S. Supreme Court in 1948, they were recorded on real estate deeds in Wilmington's suburbs until 1973.

During this same period, however, the National Association of Real Estate Boards' Code of Ethics equated racial discrimination with good realtor practices.

Table 5. Mean Levels of Racial Segregation[a]

Schools	Before desegregation mean index	After desegregation mean index
Elementary schools	78.0	16.1
Junior high schools	65.1	6.5
Middle schools	73.8	7.1
High schools	67.9	6.3

[a] Data from State of Delaware, Department of Public Instruction. *Racial and Ethnic Pupil Enrollment,* September 30, 1958–1979.

It was not until 1970 that these provisions were finally removed from the Code of Ethics. The District Court found that in 1965 the Greater Wilmington Board of Realtors had established, in conjunction with these practices, a multilist that enabled sellers to indicate whether they would sell their houses to minorities. "Open" listings indicated a willingness to sell to minorities. According to the State Human Relations Commission, only 7% of suburban listings were open, compared with 51% in Wilmington. A housing practice that also contributed to racial segregation in Wilmington's schools came from the Wilmington Housing Authority. Only minimal efforts were made to locate low-income housing outside the corporate city limits, even though the Authority was fully empowered to do so. The few efforts to locate housing in the suburbs met with great resistance from white suburban residents. The net effect of these policies was to concentrate the poor, most of whom were black or members of other racial minorities, in the city of Wilmington (*Evans v. Buchanan,* 1976).

The State of Delaware had recently passed a law that provided public transportation for children from nonpublic schools to travel across district lines to other nonpublic schools. The majority of students profiting from this state aid were white pupils. Thus, the State of Delaware had also contributed to the racial segregation of the Wilmington public schools.

The Court ordered the defendants to draw up two types of desegregation plans: one confined to Wilmington, and one that included Wilmington and its suburbs. On January 9, 1978, the District Court handed down its desegregation remedy. It was a compromise of the basic concerns expressed by both plaintiffs and defendants.

Judge Murray Schwartz settled the remedial issues before the bar. He chose the pupil assignment concept, outlined the nature of ancillary relief, established the governance structure of the desegregated district, and defined the proper role of the Federal Court in assuring the removal of the dual school system.

The Court chose a compromise (9–3) pupil assignment plan. Blacks were to be transported to the suburban schools for 9 years, and whites were to be transported to Wilmington schools for 3 years.

However, the District Court adhered to the Congressional Act relating to the assignment of pupils for school desegregation. The 1974 U. S. Equal Education Opportunities and Transportation of Students Act listed several criteria courts must consider in pursuing desegregation remedies. Congress intended that courts should provide for the use of neighborhood schools to the greatest extent possible; should permit majority to minority transfers; should gerrymander attendance zones and alter grade structures; should construct new schools; and should use magnet schools. These methods were insufficient for effective desegregation in Wilmington. Given the constraints of the interdistrict remedy, the District Court inescapably employed busing of pupils for desegregation. No pupil transportation plan had been shown to violate the conditions on busing expressed by the Supreme Court in *Swann v. Mecklenburg Board of Education* (1971).

THE RELATION BETWEEN NEIGHBORHOOD RACIAL COMPOSITION AND PARENT AND STUDENT ATTITUDES AFTER SCHOOL DESEGREGATION

This section presents a reevaluation of the racial attitudes of a sample of parents and students in Metropolitan Wilmington after 3 years of school desegregation. The specific objective was to determine the differences in attitudes of parents and students living in neighborhoods with different levels of racial composition.

The findings can best be interpreted in the context of the growing number of studies of degree of citizen satisfaction with urban services such as schools, parks, police protection, and garbage collection (Aberback & Walker, 1970; Fowler, 1974; Rich, 1979; U. S. Department of Housing and Urban Development, 1978). The findings of past research suggest that differences in neighborhood racial composition often influence the quantity and/or quality of encounters, both direct and indirect, with municipal services. In other words, in all-black neighborhoods, garbage is collected less frequently; police come less quickly or act less concerned about adequate enforcement; parks are fewer or less cared for; and teachers and school administrators are less qualified or less concerned (Schuman & Gruenberg, 1981, p. 168). These interpretations all assume that the racial composition of the neighborhood leads to differential treatment, which in turn leads to differences in satisfaction between blacks and whites (Durand, 1973; Jacobs, 1972; Maimon, 1970; Rossi, Berk & Edison, 1970; U.S. Advisory Commission on Civil Disorders, 1968). Residents in all-black or mostly black neighborhoods receive objectively worse services than residents in white neighborhoods. The objective reality is related to the residents' perceptions that are transformed into levels of dissatisfaction (Schuman & Gruenberg, 1981, p. 160). Schuman and Gruenberg concluded, therefore, that racial differences in attitudes toward schools are not due to race *per se,* but to the racial composition of neighborhoods. Persons, black and white, living in predominantly black neighborhoods were most dissatisfied with schools and other services. Thus, it appears that neighborhood racial composition is of critical importance in explaining variations of racial attitudes.

Although the present study is generally similar to past studies of urban service distributions, it differs in several respects. First, attitudes toward three services—namely, garbage collection, police protection, and parks and playgrounds—are not assessed. Second, attitudes toward schools, the one service chosen, are assessed in greater depth. Third, differences are assessed among neighborhoods throughout the metropolitan area instead of in the central city only. Fourth, this study is based on a sample composed of the same respondents over time rather than being an age-cohort analysis of population surveys (e.g., Durand, 1976).

Data were obtained in the spring of 1978, prior to desegregation, through

questionnaires administered to 2,333 families in five former school districts within New Castle County, Delaware (Metropolitan Wilmington). Separate questionnaires were filled out by parents and students. The districts included Wilmington, De La Warr, Mt. Pleasant, Newark, and Marshallton-McKean. As a result of the Supreme Court decision in *Evans v. Buchanan* (1976), these five districts were consolidated with six additional districts within metropolitan Wilmington in 1978 and became the single school district of New Castle County. Although no data were obtained from six of the former districts, the sample is believed to be generally representative of households in New Castle County.

In the spring of 1979, 1980, and 1981, follow-up questionnaires were sent to the same 2,333 families, resulting in 298 questionnaires as the final data base. The sample distribution by racial composition of neighborhood is presented in Table 6. Of the respondents, approximately 28% lived in all-white neighborhoods and 57% lived in mostly white neighborhoods. Six percent lived in mostly black neighborhoods. Families living in half-black/half-white neighborhoods represented about 4% of the families. Due to the extremely small percentage of respondents (three) from all-black neighborhoods, the group was excluded from the analysis. Thus, the total sample size consisted of 291 respondents over the 4-year study period.

This particular inquiry concerns the extent to which the observed racial differences in attitudes are related to neighborhood differences. Therefore, respondents were asked to describe racial composition of their neighborhoods in answer to the following question: Is the racial composition of your neighborhood (1) all-white, (2) mostly white, (3) about half-white and half-black, (4) mostly black, or (5) all-black? Based on the factor analysis, the attitudinal items were grouped into six unidimensional subscales for the parents and six for the students. Reliability coefficients were computed for each of the six parent scales and each of the six student scales. Coefficient alpha was the reliability measure used.

Table 6.   Sample Distribution by Racial Composition of Neighborhood

	1978		1979		1980		1981	
	Number	%	Number	%	Number	%	Number	%
All-white	83	27.9	69	23.2	71	23.8	69	23.2
Mostly white	171	57.4	179	60.1	183	61.4	181	60.7
Half-black/ half-white	13	4.4	17	5.7	15	5.0	19	6.4
Mostly black	19	6.4	19	6.4	18	6.0	22	7.4
All-black	8	2.7	6	2.0	6	2.0	5	1.7
Unknown	4	1.3	8	2.7	5	1.7	2	0.7
Totals	298	100.0	298	100.0	298	100.0	298	100.0

Reliability estimates for the student scales ranged from .96 to .44, and estimates for the parent scales ranged from .85 to .55. Analysis of variance was used to test for overall differences among neighborhoods. *Post hoc* comparisons were then performed using the Tukey procedure with alpha set at .05.

Parent Attitudes Three Years after School Desegregation

After 3 years of metropolitan school desegregation, there were observable changes in parental attitudes, based on the sample studied, but significant differences by neighborhood racial composition persisted. Parents in all-white neighborhoods maintained the least positive racial attitudes over the 3-year period. The racial attitudes of these parents dropped from a score of 3.27 in 1978 to 3.14 in 1981 (Table 7). The greatest change occurred after the first year of desegregation. During the second and third years, the racial attitudes seemed to stabilize, changing only slightly. The racial attitudes of parents in mostly white neighborhoods followed a similar pattern, declining from a score of 3.56 to 3.45 after 3 years. The racial attitudes of parents in half-black/half-white neighborhoods became slightly more positive after the first year of desegregation, but changed in a less positive direction during the second and third years. On the other hand, the racial attitudes of parents in mostly black neighborhoods consistently became more positive following each year of desegregation (Table 7). Therefore, after 3 years of court-ordered desegregation, there was no overall reduction in racial attitude differences by neighborhood racial composition. Unlike racial attitudes, however, parental attitudes toward school desegregation became more positive after 3 years of school desegregation in all-white and mostly white neighborhoods and less positive in half-black/half-white and mostly black neighborhoods. Parents in half-black/half-white neighborhoods, however, maintained the most positive attitudes toward school desegregation, whereas parents in all-white neighborhoods had the least positive attitudes (Table 7).

Parental attitudes toward perceived school quality became less positive in all-white, mostly white and half-black/half-white neighborhoods. Parents' perceived school quality in mostly black neighborhoods was essentially the same after 3 years of desegregation. In the third year, parents' perceptions of school quality, like their racial attitudes, tended to be less positive in all categories of neighborhoods (Table 7).

Parents' evaluation and expectations of their child's performance became less positive in all-white, mostly white and half-black/half-white neighborhoods. In mostly black neighborhoods, parents' evaluation and expectations of their child's performance became slightly more positive. Despite these changes, however, significant differences between neighborhoods still existed after 3 years of desegregation. Prior to desegregation, parents in half-black/half-white neighborhoods had the least positive evaluation and expectations of their child's per-

Table 7. Parents' Mean Scale Scores by Racial Composition of Neighborhood

Scale	1978	1979	1980	1981	F Groups	F Repeated measures	F Groups × repeated measures
Racial attitudes					12.57*	1.35	1.64
All-white	3.27	3.13	3.15	3.14			
Mostly white	3.56	3.48	3.47	3.45			
Half-black/half-white	3.99	4.01	3.85	3.71			
Mostly black	3.74	3.79	3.88	3.92			
Attitudes toward school					13.24*	5.34*	1.76
desegregation							
All-white	2.21	2.41	2.54	2.44			
Mostly white	2.32	2.67	2.72	2.59			
Half-black/half-white	3.27	3.45	3.25	3.15			
Mostly black	3.24	3.18	3.53	3.06			
Perceived school quality					2.75*	15.00*	1.86
All-white	3.93	3.56	3.44	3.48			
Mostly white	3.99	3.39	3.49	3.49			
Half-black/half-white	3.98	3.47	3.63	3.81			
Mostly black	4.03	3.64	3.96	4.03			
Evaluation and expectations					6.49*	1.13	0.44
of child's performance							
All-white	4.22	4.20	4.20	4.17			
Mostly white	4.13	4.33	4.33	4.28			
Half-black/half-white	3.93	3.88	3.80	3.74			
Mostly black	4.10	4.15	4.09	4.13			
Importance of education					.33	3.06*	0.65
All-white	4.74	4.63	4.62	4.61			
Mostly white	4.71	4.63	4.67	4.67			
Half-black/half-white	4.82	4.70	4.67	4.67			
Mostly black	4.65	4.60	4.65	4.67			
Social status					15.36*	2.13	1.02
All-white	3.41	3.43	3.37	3.41			
Mostly white	3.43	3.45	3.46	3.47			
Half-black/half-white	2.83	2.98	2.96	2.90			
Mostly black	2.97	3.06	3.08	2.94			

Note: Scale scores from 1.00 (least positive) to 5.00 (most positive).
* Significant at the $p < .05$ level.

formance, followed by parents in mostly black, all-white, and mostly white neighborhoods, in that order. This ordering of expectations by neighborhoods did not change after 3 years of desegregation.

In summary, based on the sample studied, after 3 years of court-ordered desegregation in New Castle County there was little observable reduction in the difference in parental attitudes by neighborhood racial composition. The greatest difference found in the samples existed in racial attitudes held by parents in

Table 8.   Range of Parent Attitudes by Neighborhood Racial Composition Three Years after Court-Ordered Metropolitan School Desegregation

Attitudes	Most positive		Least positive		Difference
Racial attitudes	Mostly black	3.92	All-white	3.14	.78
Attitudes toward school desegregation	Half-black/ half-white	3.15	All-white	2.44	.71
Perceived school quality	Mostly black	4.03	All-white	3.48	.55
Evaluation and expectations of child's performance	Mostly white	4.28	Half-black/ half-white	3.74	.54
Importance of education	Half-black/ half-white	4.67	All-white	4.61	.06
Social status	Mostly white	3.47	Half-black/ half-white	2.90	.57

Note: Scale scores range from 1.00 (least positive) to 5.00 (most positive).

mostly black compared with all-white neighborhoods. The second highest difference gap was found in the attitudes toward school desegregation held by parents in half-black/half-white neighborhoods compared with parents in all-white neighborhoods (Table 8). The smallest difference gap was found in parents' attitudes toward the importance of education.

Student Attitudes Three Years after School Desegregation

Similar to their parents, students in all-white neighborhoods had the least positive racial attitudes before desegregation and 3 years afterwards. After the first year of desegregation, the racial attitudes of students in all-white, mostly white, and half-black/half-white neighborhoods became less positive. These attitudes stabilized the following 2 years, remaining at a level less positive than before desegregation. On the other hand, students in mostly black neighborhoods had more positive racial attitudes after the first year of desegregation and maintained more positive attitudes after 3 years of desegregation. The general finding was that school desegregation did not appear to be related to a reduction in the gap in student racial attitudes by neighborhood racial composition. After 3 years of desegregation, racial attitudes became less positive in all neighborhoods (Table 9).

Educational self-concept on the part of students in all neighborhoods also became less positive after 3 years of desegregation. The greatest change occurred in mostly black neighborhoods where students' educational self-concept was most positive prior to desegregation. After 3 years of desegregation, students in all-white neighborhoods had the most positive educational self-concept. The

Table 9.   Students' Mean Scale Scores by Racial Composition of Neighborhoods

Scale	1978	1979	1980	1981	F Groups	F Repeated measures	F Groups × repeated measures
Racial attitudes					13.84*	3.60*	1.33
All-white	3.58	3.36	3.25	3.29			
Mostly white	3.82	3.63	3.59	3.50			
Half-black/half-white	4.23	4.11	4.11	3.99			
Mostly black	4.18	4.42	4.24	4.30			
Educational self-concept					2.97*	35.03*	2.91
All-white	4.16	4.18	4.20	3.92			
Mostly white	4.31	4.34	4.31	3.91			
Half-black/half-white	4.06	4.05	3.82	3.72			
Mostly black	4.37	4.46	4.06	3.80			
Importance of education					3.44*	2.44	1.33
All-white	4.59	4.53	4.47	4.43			
Mostly white	4.60	4.55	4.52	4.44			
Half-black/half-white	4.72	4.72	4.65	4.61			
Mostly black	4.61	4.82	4.70	4.77			
School academic climate					0.73	4.74*	0.97
All-white	4.21	4.17	4.11	4.20			
Mostly white	4.28	4.13	4.16	4.14			
Half-black/half-white	4.35	4.15	3.98	3.91			
Mostly black	4.17	4.07	3.97	4.05			
Sense of control					0.64	0.63	3.08
All-white	4.28	4.46	4.37	4.38			
Mostly white	4.44	4.45	4.40	4.35			
Half-black/half-white	4.49	4.22	4.32	4.05			
Mostly black	4.07	4.22	4.52	4.60			
Future aspirations					6.17*	1.79	0.96
All-white	4.07	4.19	4.11	4.13			
Mostly white	4.03	4.11	4.13	4.04			
Half-black/half-white	3.35	3.55	3.33	3.55			
Mostly black	3.84	3.85	3.65	3.80			

Note: Scale scores from 1.00 (least positive) to 5.00 (most positive).
* Significant at the $p < .05$ level.

least positive educational self-concept was found by students living in half-black/half-white neighborhoods (Table 9).

The perception of the importance of education declined each year following desegregation in all-white, mostly white, and half-black/half-white neighborhoods. Only in mostly black neighborhoods was there an increase. Thus, significant differences in perception of the importance of education still existed by neighborhood racial composition 3 years after desegregation. The importance of education score, like that of racial attitudes, increased along a continuum from all-white to mostly black neighborhoods (Table 9).

After 3 years of desegregation, students' perception of school academic climate became less positive in mostly white, half-black/half-white, and mostly black neighborhoods. Perception of academic climate by students living in all-white neighborhoods became less positive after the first year of desegregation, but returned to its original level after 3 years. Thus, students in all-white neighborhoods had the most positive perceptions of academic climate, and students in half-black/half-white neighborhoods had the least positive (Table 9). The differences were not significant, however.

School desegregation was related to an increase in students' sense of control in mostly black and all-white neighborhoods. On the other hand, students' sense of control actually decreased in mostly white and half-black/half-white neighborhoods. Thus, following 3 years of desegregation, students in mostly black neighborhoods had the most positive attitudes toward sense of control, whereas the least positives attitudes were found in half-black/half-white neighborhoods (Table 9). The differences were not significant by neighborhood, however.

Students' future aspirations increased slightly in all-white and half-black/half-white neighborhoods. Desegregation had no observable relation to aspirations of students in mostly white neighborhoods and there was only a slight decline in the aspirations of students in mostly black neighborhoods after a 3-year period. Thus, school desegregation notwithstanding, students in all-white neighborhoods maintained the highest future aspirations, whereas students in half-black/half-white neighborhoods had the lowest aspirations (Table 9).

In summary, after 3 years of court-ordered metropolitan school desegregation, there was no significant change in the difference gap in student attitudes by neighborhood racial composition. As was the case with the parents, the greatest difference gap in students' racial attitudes was found between students living in mostly black neighborhoods and those in all-white neighborhoods (Table 10). The

Table 10. Range of Student Attitudes by Neighborhood Racial Composition Three Years after Court-Ordered Metropolitan School Desegregation

Attitudes	Most positive		Least positive		Difference
Racial attitudes	Mostly black	4.30	All-white	3.29	1.01
Educational self-concept	All-white	3.92	Half-black/ half-white	3.72	.20
Importance of education	Mostly black	4.77	All-white	4.43	.34
School academic climate	All-white	4.20	Half-black/ half-white	3.91	.29
Sense of control	Mostly black	4.60	Half-black/ half-white	4.05	.55
Future aspirations	All-white	4.13	Half-black/ half-white	3.55	.58

Note: Scale scores range from 1.00 (least positive) to 5.00 (most positive).

least difference in student educational self-concept existed between all-white and half-black/half-white neighborhoods. It is apparent, therefore, that attitudes tended to vary spatially by neighborhood racial composition in the sample studied. Thus, school desegregation without neighborhood desegregation seems to have little relationship in attitude changes on the part of parents and students involved in the school desegregation process.

THE RELATION BETWEEN NEIGHBORHOOD RACIAL COMPOSITION AND STUDENT ACHIEVEMENT

Few empirical studies of the relation between desegregation and achievement have been done since 1975. Instead, recent research on academic achievement has concentrated on reevaluating the large number of studies completed during the early and mid-1970s. These reevaluations, with few exceptions, have reaffirmed the earlier findings on the relation between school desegregation and achievement. This reaffirmation concludes that (1) white student achievement has either improved or remained constant following desegregation, and (2) minority student achievement has generally improved following desegregation (College of Urban Development, 1976; Grant, Paige, & Sinett, 1979; Hawley, 1979; Hawley, 1981; Lemke, 1979; St. John, 1975; Stephen, 1978; Weinberg, 1977). For some minority students, however, academic achievement has remained constant or the gap between them and the majority students has increased. School desegregation, then, is not consistently followed by improvement for all minority students. Because school desegregation is followed by significant improvement in achievement for some minority students, it appears that certain characteristics beyond mere school desegregation may be involved. There is reason to believe that among those characteristics is the racial composition of the students' neighborhoods.

Past research suggests that differences in the neighborhood racial composition often influence (1) the nature of treatment by teachers and administrators (Schuman & Gruenberg, 1981) and (2) racial attitudes (Darden & Parsons, 1981). There is also reason to believe that neighborhood racial composition is related to achievement.

This section assesses the achievement of students in metropolitan Wilmington after 3 years of school desegregation. The specific objective is to determine the differences in achievement of students living in neighborhoods with different levels of racial composition.

Prior to the formation of the New Castle County School District, the 11 separate school districts had different testing programs. Therefore, no common achievement data were available prior to 1978. The California Achievement Test (CAT) was administered to all students in the new district in the fall of 1978, and also in the spring of 1979, 1980, and 1981. Achievement scores were

obtained for the 298 students who were participants in this study. The reading, mathematics, and total battery scores were reported in terms of national percentiles. Although the obtained sample of 298 students was not totally random, since data were obtained from students in only five former districts, the sample demographically includes the variety of households in New Castle County.

Because services, especially schools, are spatially distributed over neighborhoods, an investigation was made of the extent to which achievement differences are related to neighborhood differences. The first point of inquiry concerned perceived racial residential segregation, a phenomenon that has been proven, using objective indicators, to be extremely high in metropolitan areas (Citizens Commission on Civil Rights, 1983; Darden, 1977). On a questionnaire, respondents were asked to define the racial composition of their own neighborhoods. Each respondent was asked: Is your neighborhood (1) all-white, (2) mostly white, (3) about half-white and half-black, (4) mostly black, or (5) all-black?

Most of the respondents resided in mostly white neighborhoods and the least number of respondents resided in all-black neighborhoods. In fact, due to the extremely small number of respondents from all-black neighborhoods, this group was excluded from the analysis. Thus, the total sample size consisted of 291 respondents.

It was hypothesized that prior to desegregation the level of student achievement would decline from the all-white to mostly black neighborhoods. It was also hypothesized that following 3 years of school desegregation, (1) a decline would still exist but (2) the achievement gap between neighborhoods would narrow. In the investigation, analysis of variance was used to test for overall differences in achievement among neighborhoods.

Student Achievement before Metropolitan Desegregation

Significant differences existed in the achievement level of students by neighborhood racial composition in the fall of 1978, prior to desegregation. As expected, a decline occurred by racial composition of neighborhoods, ranging from the 75.4 percentile for students in all-white neighborhoods to the 28.6 percentile for students in mostly black neighborhoods, that is, a 46.8-point difference (Table 11).

Student Achievement Three Years after Metropolitan School Desegregation

After 3 years of court-ordered metropolitan school desegregation, the achievement level of students from all neighborhoods increased. Students from some neighborhoods experienced greater gains in achievement than others. The greatest gains occurred among students in half-black/half-white neighborhoods and in mostly black neighborhoods where the increase in achievement was 13.9

Table 11.   Achievement Gains Following Metropolitan School
Desegregation by Neighborhood Racial Composition

Neighborhood racial composition	Achievement score (total battery)		Achievement gains (total battery)
	(1978)	(1981)	
All-white	75.4	80.9	+5.5
Mostly white	73.4	81.0	+7.6
Half-black/half-white	31.6	45.5	+13.9
Mostly black	28.6	41.8	+13.2

and 13.2 points respectively (Table 11). The least gains occurred among students in all-white neighborhoods, where the increase was 5.5 points.

At the end of 3 years, the highest achieving neighborhoods were mostly white. All-white neighborhoods were second, followed by half-black/half-white and mostly black neighborhoods. The total battery scores ranged from the 41.8 percentile in mostly black neighborhoods to the 81.0 percentile in the mostly white neighborhoods, a difference of 39.2 points (Table 12). In short, following 3 years of desegregation, significant differences by neighborhood racial composition continued to exist. In reading, for example, students in mostly black neighborhoods scored at the 37th percentile, whereas students in mostly white neighborhoods scored at the 80.1 percentile. In math, students in half-black/half-white neighborhoods scored at the 45.1 percentile, where students in all-white neighborhoods scored at the 78.7 percentile (Table 12). As expected, however, the gap in achievement narrowed as students in mostly black and half-black/half-white neighborhoods made relatively greater gains in achievement than students from mostly white and all-white neighborhoods. Thus, the achievement gap narrowed from 46.8 points in 1978 (prior to desegregation) to 39.2 points in 1981.

Table 12.   Achievement Scores by Racial Composition of Neighborhood, Spring, 1981

Subtests	Neighborhood racial composition				Significance
	All-white	Mostly white	Half-black/half-white	Mostly black	
Reading	79.8	80.1	46.2	37.0	.000
Mathematics	78.7	78.0	45.1	47.0	.000
Total Battery	80.9	81.0	45.5	41.8	.000

Note: Achievement scores reported are national percentiles.

CONCLUSION

Neighborhood racial composition has historically had a strong influence on school racial composition. The schools of New Castle County were racially segregated until the District Court desegregation order in 1978.

Although school segregation was reduced, differences in racial attitudes by neighborhood racial composition did not change significantly. The data indicate that attitudes varied spatially by neighborhood racial composition. School desegregation without neighborhood racial integration appears to have little relationship to changes in the attitudes of parents and students.

Finally, academic achievement, like attitudes, tends to vary spatially by neighborhood racial composition. The data gathered in this study show that students from half-black/half-white neighborhoods experienced the greatest gains in achievement. In general, based on data gathered in this study, school desegregation in New Castle County, Delaware, has been associated with a reduction in the academic achievement gap between neighborhoods.

REFERENCES

Aberback, J. D., & Walker, J. L. (1970). The attitudes of white and blacks towards city services: Implications for policy making. In J. P. Crecine (Ed.), *Financing and metropolis* (pp. 519–537). Beverly Hills: Sage Publications.

Brown v. Board of Education, 347, U.S. 483 (1964).

Citizens Commission on Civil Rights (1983). *A decent home: A report on the continuing failure of the federal government to provide equal housing opportunity.* Washington, DC: Catholic University.

College of Urban Development (1976). *School desegregation: Making it work.* East Lansing, MI: Michigan State University.

Darden, J. T. (1977). Blacks in the suburbs: Their number is rising but patterns of segregation persist. *Vital Issues, 27,* 1–4.

Darden, J. T., & Parsons, M. A. (1981). The effect of neighborhood racial composition on black and white attitudes. *Urban Review, 13,* 103–109.

Durand, R. (1973). Neighborhood racial transition and the structuring of service evaluation. *Journal of Political Science, 1,* 1927–1935.

Durand, R. (1976). Some dynamics of urban service evaluations among blacks and whites. *Social Science Quarterly, 56,* 698–706.

Educational Advancement Act (1968) Title 14, Delaware, Ch. 292, sec. 1004, 1026.

Evans v. Buchanan, 416 F. Supp. 328 (D. Del., 1976).

Fowler, F. (1974). *Citizens' attitudes towards local government, services, and taxes.* Cambridge: Ballinger.

Grant, F., Paige, D., & Sinnett, M. (1979). Segregation/integration and black/white math achievement. *School Science and Mathematics, 79,* 111–114.

Hawley, W. D. (1979, February). Getting the facts straight about the effects of school integration. *Educational Leadership,* 314–321.

Hawley, W. D. (Ed.). (1981). *Increasing the effectiveness of school desegregation: Lessons from the research.* Washington, DC: National Institute of Education.

Jacobs, H. (1972). Contact with government agencies: A preliminary analysis of the distribution of government services. *Midwest Journal of Political Science, 16,* 143–146.

Lemke, E. A. (1979). The effects of busing on the achievement of white and black students. *Educational Studies,* 401–406.

Maimon, Z. (1970). The inner city impact. *Urban Affairs Quarterly, 6,* 233–247.

Rich, R. (1979). Neglected issues in the study of urban service distribution: A research agenda. *Urban Studies, 16,* 143–156.

Rossi, P. H., Berk, R. A., & Edison, B. K. (1970). *The roots of urban discontent.* New York: Wiley.

St. John, N. (1975). *School desegregation: Outcomes for children.* New York: Wiley.

Schuman, H., & Gruenberg, B. (1981). Dissatisfaction with city services: Is race an important factor? In J. T. Darden (Ed.), *The Ghetto: Readings with interpretations* (pp. 159–173). Port Washington, NY: Kennikat Press.

Stephan, W. G. (1978). School desegregation: An evaluation of predictions made in *Brown vs. Board of Education. Psychological Bulletin, 85,* 217–238.

Swann *et al.* v. Charlotte-Mecklenburg Board of Education *et al.,* 402, U.S. 1 (1971).

U.S. Advisory Commission on Civil Disorders (1968). *Report of the National Advisory Commission on Civil Disorders.* New York: Bantam Books.

U.S. Department of Commerce, Bureau of the Census (1971). *1970 census of population and housing: General demographic trends for metropolitan areas, 1960–1970, Final Report, PHC, Wilmington, Delaware.* Washington, DC: Government Printing Office.

U.S. Department of Commerce (1981). *1980 Census of population and housing.* Delaware PHC 80–v–9, Advance Reports. Washington, DC: Government Printing Office.

U.S. Department of Housing and Urban Development (1978). Office of Policy Development and Research. *A survey of citizens' views and concerns about urban life.* Final report. Washington, DC: Author.

Weinberg, M. (1977). *Minority students: A research appraisal.* Washington, DC: U.S. Government Printing Office.

6

Improving Education in Desegregated Schools

MEYER WEINBERG

During the mid-1960s, at the height of the civil rights movement, organized minority parents began demanding that their schools publish reading and mathematics test scores. Their purpose was to call attention to the almost certain achievement discrepancy between white and minority schools. By desegregating the schools, they hoped, achievement differences would be bridged or at least minimized. There thus existed a perceived link between desegregation and achievement. Public opinion polls during the 1970s found repeatedly that a belief that minority academic achievement would rise with desegregation was the principal reason for black support of desegregation. This view prevailed during struggles to initiate desegregation as well as to maintain it.

What lay behind this conviction? For one thing, it was expected that a desegregated school would receive more material support than would a minority-segregated one. In the South, particularly, glaring inequities between black and white schools had been typical before the *Brown* decision and continued long afterward. Stories abound of hitherto black schools being desegregated and suddenly receiving a new coat of paint, new textbooks, and visits by carpenters, plumbers, and electricians. Additional teachers were often assigned to the school. All in all, expenditures per pupil undoubtedly rose. It costs more to operate a desegregated school system than one in which a select few are educated and the rest are left to sink or swim.

For another thing, black parents believed that school authorities could no longer discriminate on a school-by-school basis because "their" children would now also be attending formerly all-black schools. Some have called this the

MEYER WEINBERG ● Horace Mann Bond Center for Equal Education, University of Massachusetts, Amherst, Massachusetts 01003.

143

hostage theory since it stresses the wish of white authorities to avoid harming their own children rather than a desire for equal treatment of all. The theory worked in practice, at least in some cases. In others, however, white school board members remained in office while sending their children to private schools. They then proceeded to reduce tax rates that financed the once-more black schools. The hostage theory was thus invalidated, and sharp disparities were restored in black and white educational opportunities.

An additional reason black parents believed in the desegregation–achievement tie was the conviction that being treated equally would release in black children a wave of learning. Still another factor at work was the belief by black parents that staff in the desegregated school would be committed to the task of raising all students' achievement. They also expected that school authorities would put aside the antagonism that had often characterized the period between filing of the lawsuit and issuance of the desegregation order. In too many instances, these hoped-for positive developments did not occur. Teacher complaints about black students' unreadiness to learn and their alleged predilection toward indiscipline often left little time for substantive instruction. Some school authorities failed to reorganize the newly desegregated school for more productive learning and settled for a mere change in racial ratios. In many cases, however, both teachers and administrators used their new opportunity to educational advantage.

Some educators offered an additional reason to hope for increased achievement. They asserted that black students from comparatively poor families would benefit by attending school with white middle-class classmates. Presumably, a sort of osmosis of academic motivation and accomplishment would occur whereby blacks would absorb the superior academic ways of whites. None of this was very precise, nor did it explain why poorer white students attending white schools failed to absorb the superior ways of their more affluent white classmates. The theory contained elements of racism insofar as it implied that blacks needed whites as spurs to achievement.

Before the mid-1960s, there were few actual cases of desegregation in the United States. Federal courts ordered desegregation during 1955–1965, but the process was speeded, at least in the South, by passage of the 1964 Civil Rights Act. A series of significant decisions by the U. S. Supreme Court during 1968–1973 spurred greatly the extension of desegregation.

When researchers examined these desegregated schools, what did they find? Many of the earliest studies of desegregation and achievement involved only single classrooms rather than schools. Only during the 1970s did evidence of desegregated school systems begin to come to light. Even then, the evidence was in some respects unsatisfactory because certain scientific precautions had not always been observed. In any practical process embracing entire school systems, this was inevitable. At times, findings of declines or advances in achievement were declared without having ascertained what the beginning levels

of achievement had been. Children of different races and classes were studied without distinguishing between the two. Students in segregated and desegregated classrooms were studied without sufficient assurance that the groups were directly comparable with respect to race, class, previous education, or even subject matter taught.

Nevertheless, the achievement effects of desegregation were measured more successfully than was the case in many social science studies of comparable topics. Inquiries antagonistic to desegregation frequently attacked desegregation studies for their alleged departure from some imagined perfect research methodology. Occasionally, desegregation studies may have tried too hastily to incorporate current research techniques being used in sociology, psychology, and anthropology. Compared with the general run of social science inquiry, however, desegregation studies of achievement have been on a par with other customary inquiries.

In general, desegregation has meant an improvement in academic achievement for black students, although a gap between black and white frequently endures. That deficiency, however, is a product not of desegregation but of the conditions that preceded it. Judging from ample legal and historical evidence, shortchanging minority children was an integral part of the system of segregation. Desegregation campaigns that are mounted without attention to educational improvement are incomplete, for they are fated to perpetuate the same planned deprivation that infused the system of segregation.

By and large, black parents' expectations that desegregation would improve their children's learning have proved to be justified. Two major works, by St. John (1975) and Weinberg (1977), examined a large body of research on the subject. Krol (1978) scrutinized all the studies examined by both predecessors and concluded that desegregation had "slightly positive" effects on achievement. Krol's study is by far the most comprehensive and rigorous evaluation of desegregation studies on achievement. In addition, the work by Crain and Mahard (1978) is consistent with Krol's findings. On the other hand, the Bradleys (1977) are more skeptical of existing studies and are unready to pronounce desegregation beneficial. At the same time, they regard as "tenuous" the contention of Armor (1972) that busing is ineffective.

Two overall observations must be added to the finding that desegregation benefits academic achievement. One, the benefit, although greater than any other actual practice tried on a large scale, is still not great enough. Desegregated schools, for whatever reasons, have yet to attain a parity of learning by white and black children. Two, the benefit does not automatically follow desegregation but seems to result only from a deliberate process of educational planning, consciously and conscientiously applied.

Thus, if we are to maximize learning in desegregated schools, we must search out the obstacles that may be frustrating effective education. "It is never wise or productive, either for the educational system or the teacher," wrote Stern

and Keislar (1977), "to insist that a program be implemented by someone who is basically antagonistic to it" (p. 75). How does this apply to desegregation programs in American schools? Frequently, the assumption is made that following a court order in a desegregation case, the course of events is more or less a technical one of joining resources and personnel. In fact, however, this is an oversimplification. Many of the value conflicts around desegregation do not disappear with the court order. They persist. In some cases, they are resolved creatively. We must examine both kinds of resolutions.

ATTITUDES OF SCHOOL OFFICIALS

Rodgers and Bullock (1976) reported on their study of 170 black and white school officials in 31 Georgia school districts. A majority (62%) expressed opposition to desegregation, with 32% saying they favored it. There was a clear racial separation of views; 9 out of 10 black officials favored desegregation. With reference to this latter finding, Rodgers and Bullock observed that "less universal support might have been expected since in some of the districts black administrators and teachers were demoted and dismissed as a consequence of the elimination of all-black schools" (p. 33).

When asked whether desegregation had harmful or beneficial effects on achievement in the schools, over half (59%) of the white officials thought there were harmful effects. Sixty-three percent of the blacks thought the impact had been positive. Responding to a question on the impact of desegregation on race relations, 40% of white and 79% of black officials thought the impact had been positive.

Rodgers and Bullock (1976) believed that their Georgia sample was typical of the Deep South. If so, there is reason for concern. They wrote: "We infer from the persisting white opposition to desegregation that Georgia officials will unilaterally do little to correct second generation desegregation problems" (p. 34). (These include racially discriminatory placements in special education, biased disciplinary measures, ability grouping, and others.)

Research by Stewart (1977), completed in 1977, supports Rodgers' and Bullock's (1976) pessimism. Taking Southern school districts as a whole, Stewart found that racially discriminatory placements in special education and the disproportionate replacement of black teachers increased during 1968–1974. On the other hand, over a shorter period, 1971–1974, racially discriminatory retentions of pupils and punishments for disciplinary infractions fell. In all four areas of investigation, however, the percentage of school districts found to be discriminating was 70% or higher; in most cases it was 80% or 90%.

Stewart also studied whether the legal agency utilized—HEW, Department of Justice, or a private lawyer—made any difference in solving second-generation desegregation problems. He found that the Department of Justice was compar-

atively ineffectual in moderating second-generation problems. (It should be remembered that these were mostly the years of the presidencies of Richard Nixon and Gerald Ford, neither of whom was devoted to strict enforcement of civil rights laws.) Stewart (1977) concluded that "blacks will continue to be the victims of discrimination in the desegregated school system of the South for the foreseeable future" (p. 56).

Maldonado and Byrne (1978), in an examination of the attitudes of non-Chicano educators in Utah toward Chicano students, reported that in Utah no Chicanos were on the state board of education, no local superintendent was a Chicano, only 4 of the state's 637 principals were Chicano, and only 2 Chicanos were members of the 40 local school boards in the state. Chicanos, who made up only 2% of certified employees in the state's schools, worked as noncertified employees in nearly one third of the districts.

Maldonado and Byrne (1978) contacted a random sample of 100 educators in the state of Utah. They established a typology of four perceptions of Chicano students: oppressed, copers, pathological, and noble poor. The perception of Chicanos as oppressed was based on a revolutionary strategy; as copers, on pluralistic strategies such as bilingual-bicultural programs; as pathological, on compensatory education strategies involving elimination of Spanish and other cultural elements; and as the noble poor, on separatist strategies involving separate schools for Chicanos, with Spanish as the medium of instruction. In this schema, respondents seemed to appraise the noble poor and copers positively, and pathologicals and oppressed negatively. Respondents were asked to rank each type from 1 to 4 with 1 as the highest. The pathological perspective was by far the most frequently indicated (Table 1).

At the same time, Anglo educators in Utah acknowledged that Chicano parents and leaders rejected the pathological perspective. By an analysis of subsamples, Maldonado and Byrne (1978) found that whereas the educators as a whole favored a pluralistic perspective, this was least true in rural or suburban-rural areas. "It is highly possible," wrote Maldonado and Byrne, "that for many educators the conception of the child failing because his home and culture fail

Table 1.   Ranking by 100 Utah Educators of Four Perceptions
of Chicano Students, 1978

Rank	Oppressed	Copers	Pathological	Noble poor
1	7	32	57	4
2	10	53	28	9
3	49	12	13	26
4	34	2	3	61

Note. From The Social Ecology of Chicanos in Utah (p. 100) by L.A. Maldonado and D.R. Byrne, 1978, Iowa City: Iowa Urban Community Research Center. Copyright 1978 by The Iowa Community Research Center. Adapted by permission.

remains an operational truth. Several years of observation of school people in Utah would seem to support this assertion" (p. 38).

The preceding research suggests that much that does or does not occur in the classroom depends on factors that extend beyond the immediate milieu of the classroom. (Teacher training institutions completely ignore the implications of this fact when they define field experience solely in terms of activity within a classroom.)

Let us now examine a series of studies involving teachers and students in desegregated schools.

TEACHERS AND STUDENTS IN DESEGREGATED SCHOOLS

Birdin (1978) questioned 1,250 black and white teachers in 12 Illinois school districts with reference to their feelings about race. He found that blacks were more apprehensive on school-related matters whereas whites were more so on intimate personal relationships such as dating or marrying over racial lines.

Other researchers studied teacher interaction with Mexican-American students. Sayavedra's (1976) research focused on five high schools in Laredo, Texas, and environs. Twenty teachers, 10 Anglo and 10 Chicano, were involved in 20 physical science classes in each of which there were at least 6 Anglo or 6 Chicano students. The researcher personally observed every classroom. Overall, both groups of teachers paid more attention to students for whom they held high academic expectations and tended to avoid interaction with students at the low end of the expectation scale. Chicano teacher-interaction with students was less related to ethnic membership; that is, Chicano teachers interacted productively with both Anglo and Chicano students. Chicano teachers also interacted more encouragingly with Chicano students than did the Anglo teachers. Sayavedra (1976) commented that "Mexican-American teachers may possibly be trying to encourage Mexican-American pupils to participate and to contribute to the class" (p. 103).

Because most public school teachers were Anglo, and because they tended less than their Chicano peers to interact productively with Chicano students, Sayavedra (1976) concluded, "The academic level of teacher–pupil interaction experienced by Mexican-American pupils is inferior to that experienced by Anglo-American pupils even when the teacher and pupils are predominantly Mexican-American" (p. 103). Part of the reason for this finding is the tendency noted above of both groups of teachers to avoid interaction with students for whom they have low expectations.

Laosa (1979) reported on his study of kindergarten and second-grade Anglo- and Mexican-American children in 14 classrooms in five Los Angeles area schools, all of which had some form of bilingual interaction. He classified each

of the Chicano children as English-dominant or non-English-dominant. Laosa then arranged 153 threesomes, each containing one Anglo, English-dominant; one Mexican-American, English-dominant; and another Mexican-American, non-English-dominant. Members of each threesome were closely matched by sex, occupational status of the head of their household, and reading and mathematics achievement scores. All teachers were Anglos, but each teacher had a Mexican-American aide.

In kindergarten classes, Laosa found, Chicano children experienced fewer "cognitively stimulating interactions" (1979, p. 60) than did Anglo children. Yet, as compared with second graders, Chicano kindergarteners "received fewer disapprovals" and more non-evaluative academic, or academically related, information from teachers than the Anglo children. Teachers' disapproving behavior toward children was more readily explained by students' language dominance than by ethnic group. Without respect to sex, non-English-dominant Chicano students experienced an increase in teacher disapprovals, from kindergarten to second grade. On the other hand, for English-dominant students, disapprovals diminished in the same period. Also as significant was the finding that between kindergarten and second grade, non-English-dominant Chicano students increased their attempts to gain the teacher's attention.

The combination of greater disapproval and less instruction, Laosa (1979) declared, can be deadly:

> This pernicious process could easily explain, at least partially, the allegations of low self-esteem and lack of motivation in Mexican American pupils and the observed academic failure for many members of this ethnic group. (p. 62)

Laosa also addressed the role of bilingual education in this situation:

> The findings indicate that bilingual, bicultural education—as it was implemented in the classrooms observed in this study—is not assurance of educational quality and equality of opportunity for ethnic minority and limited-English-speaking students. (p. 62)

In fact, very little bilingual instruction went on in these classrooms because none of the teachers was bilingual; only the aides were.

Carter, in research completed in 1976, more or less supported the Laosa study, at least in one important respect (Carter, 1976). She examined 100 Anglo and Chicano third- and fourth-grade teachers in four schools located in a Texas metropolitan center and in a South Texas town. The teachers listened to tape recordings of children speaking highly accented English, as well as virtually unaccented English, and were asked to express an opinion of the child's ability to learn, based wholly on the recording. Anglo teachers were more negative than Chicano teachers, but both groups of teachers were negative toward speakers of highly accented English. Teachers' attitudes toward children with accents were unaffected by whether the teacher had studied Spanish (Carter, 1976).

The Sayavedra, Laosa, and Carter studies lend support to earlier findings that stressed the fundamental inequality of learning conditions for Mexican-American children (Weinberg, 1977).

Daniels studied professional staff views at the Ribault Senior High School and its 11 feeder schools in Jacksonville, Florida (Daniels, 1974). The school had been desegregated by court order in 1971. Seventy staff members were interviewed 3 years after this date. During 1971–1972, the school had been closed three times because of student violence. By 1974, however, teachers in the Ribault elementary feeders agreed that student interaction was more positive than in 1971. Teacher reports stressed more cohesive and congenial relationships, at the sixth-grade level, among black and white boys than among girls.

Faculty relations improved greatly (Daniels, 1974):

> Several teachers on one faculty reported that prior to this study it was understood that black and white teachers did not communicate during school hours. If they wanted to make plans involving activities for students, they had to do it over the telephone in the afternoons or sneak and do it on school time. If a white teacher was seen communicating with a black teacher, then the white teacher was treated in the same negative manner by the principal, as the black teacher. (p. 37)

In 1972, in another school, teachers sat separately by race during staff meetings on desegregation.

By 1974, white student acceptance of black teachers had improved markedly. In general, teachers were said to be more empathic with students, but the situation varied from one feeder school to another. In one, School L, student hostility was said to have increased over 1971. In School F, on the other hand, relations had greatly improved. Teachers attributed much of the overall improvement in Ribault to in-service programs. Unfortunately, Daniels did not describe these programs.

Espinosa investigated what might be called the role of paternalism in teacher–minority student relationships as demonstrated in San Francisco high schools (Espinosa, 1975). He sought to understand the continued failure of poorly performing minority students in high school. What were the dynamics of student–teacher relations? Espinosa analyzed the experiences of 770 students in eight high schools; he used three suburban schools and one school of technology as controls. One thing soon became clear. Minority students who were performing poorly nevertheless believed they were putting out much effort; actually, they were not. What led them to believe otherwise? Espinosa writes that "their differences in effort and achievement are perpetuated by teacher behavior and academic standards" (p. 41).

What led Chicano and black students to overrate their academic effort, and how did teachers encourage such misperceptions? Of all ethnic groups, these students spent the least time on homework. They achieved at distinctly lower rates than did Anglo and Asian students, for example. They also indulged in widespread cutting of classes and were frequently absent all day without excuses.

At the same time, teachers were warm and informal with them, praising them frequently. Students interpreted such personal warmth as friendliness and as a positive evaluation of their academic efforts.

The teachers, for their part, saw the matter differently. They expected little of the lower-achieving Chicano and black students and graded them by low academic standards. Thus, observed Espinosa (1975), "students who are low in verbal and math skills as they enter high school can get better grades without improving their skills" (p. 93). Teachers substitute personal warmth for challenging academic standards. Espinosa is severe in his conclusion:

> These schools may be viewed as supporting an elaborate custodial system which cools-out students. Supportive teacher control mechanisms, such as warmth, tend to be a successful way of not only deceiving students about their personal performance but keeping students in school. (p. 93)

Along with other institutions, the school thus joins in the devaluation of minority achievement in a process of its own creation.

Gerald Adams studied the role of race and physical attractiveness in teacher–student relations in 25 preschools in four states (Adams, 1978). Adams presented 240 teachers with photographs of children of a high or low degree of attractiveness. Teachers were then asked to judge the intelligence and academic achievement of each child pictured. One hundred twenty-eight of the teachers were white and 112 were black. In general the findings were as follows (Adams, 1978):

> Preschool teachers judged white children as more intelligent than black children, physically attractive children more intelligent than less attractive youth, with white teachers predicting higher intelligence levels than black preschool teachers. . . . Academic achievement was expected by preschool teachers to be higher for white children than for black children; white teachers also judged higher achievement for physically attractive in comparison to unattractive children. (p. 33)

Thus, whiteness and attractiveness were the most highly valued characteristics. The highest academic achievement was predicted for physically attractive white males, the lowest for the least attractive black females.

Black and white teachers did not have significantly different views. This led Adams to state, "If the concept 'black is beautiful' is becoming more evident, the black preschool teachers revealed few signs of it" (Adams, 1978). The mere presence of black teachers as presumed models for the black children was of little, if any, help. "It seems reasonable to suggest," Adams concludes, "that all the 'modeling' effects in the world will have little or no positive effect upon the child's self-attitude, racial awareness, or personality development unless the teacher also holds strong and positive expectations for the child's potential" (pp. 38–39).

Marwit and colleagues also examined the influence of attractiveness and race on 137 teachers and 60 student-teachers in St. Louis (Marwit, Marwit, & Walker, 1978). The teachers were found to be influenced by a child's attrac-

tiveness but not by the child's race. Student-teachers were found to be more negatively influenced by black children's behavior after their practice teaching than before.

Gene Piché and others analyzed the role of black dialect in teacher–student interaction (Piché, Rubin, Turner, & Michlin, 1977). Fifty white teachers and 50 white preservice teachers read two compositions that were identical in content and vocabulary except for the presence in one of certain black dialect expressions. The researchers posed two problems: (1) Could the readers infer the racial identity of the writers? and (2) Is the teacher influenced by that knowledge in making qualitative judgments of the composition?

Teachers were able to identify the racially "white" or standard English versions but not the race of the writer of the nonstandard version. At the same time, teachers recognized the nonstandard version from the black dialect content. Further, these "black" compositions tended to be rated poorer in quality. "A general ethnocentric bias exists which affects teachers' judgments of the quality of students' written composition," wrote the researchers, "but . . . it bears no close relation to specific linguistic features of such writing" (Piché, Reuben, Turner, & Michlin, 1977, pp. 107–118).

The distinction is somewhat difficult to follow. Piché and his colleagues acknowledged that teachers' expectancies may affect children's achievement or at least the teacher's evaluation of achievement. They questioned, however, whether black dialectal expressions lead directly to teacher discrimination. The researchers seemed to be saying that the use of Black English does not invariably result in alienating teachers, causing them to be prejudicial to the Black English writers. Instead, they attributed the teacher prejudice to "a general ethnocentric bias." This may be a distinction without a difference.

A somewhat related study by Pietras and Lamb (1978), conducted during 1973–1974, dealt with 30 teachers of black children attending four all-black schools and one heavily white school. The investigators found that in-service work with these teachers on curricular and other problems seemed to be more beneficial than undergraduate and/or graduate level course work.

Joyce Riley examined the role of black teachers in the political socialization of black elementary students (Riley, 1975). By political socialization, Riley meant citizenship training. Fifty black teachers of K–6 black students in Cleveland, Philadelphia, Newburgh, and Poughkeepsie were interviewed. Riley pointed out a fact that is rarely highlighted: although in 1975 black teachers comprised only one twelfth of all public school teachers, they were teaching about three quarters of all black elementary students in the country. (This was because of the continuing segregation of many black children, especially in large city school systems.)

Although "a large majority" of these black teachers valued Afro-American history highly, fewer than half dealt with it "frequently" in the curriculum. Indeed, noted Riley, "the teachers . . . tended to stay away from issues of con-

troversy in the classroom" (p. 127). Most, as she noted, taught in predominantly black schools with black teachers and a black principal. "A large proportion of teachers who 'frequently' included issues of controversy in the classroom curriculum," observed Riley, "taught in . . . minority black [schools]" (Riley, 1975, p. 131). The socially quiescent approach of Riley's sample extended to the philosophy of education as well. Thus, she reported:

> Fifty-six percent . . . of all teachers sampled accepted the "victim" hypothesis. That is, they believed that learning problems of black youngsters are rooted in the home environment rather than the school system. (p. 120)

Judging from Riley's findings in schools in four cities, the Afro-American teacher of black children in mainly black schools was socializing the children to play roles not greatly different from those taught them in other American schools.

Washington (1978) probed the relation of teacher racial attitudes to effective instruction. Studying 10 second-grade classrooms in Indianapolis, she found that white and black teachers expressed prodesegregation sentiments, with those of the blacks being stronger. After four visits to each of the 10 classrooms, Washington found that, on the whole, black and white teachers were disproportionately negative in characterizing black children, whites more so than blacks. Teacher attitudes toward desegregation, however, seemed to make a difference. Black teachers most favorable to desegregation tended to perceive black children most positively. Conversely, white teachers least favorable to desegregation were slightly unfavorable to black children.

But Washington was not conducting a simple attitude study or a public opinion poll. She went beyond that and sought to determine the classroom consequences of teacher attitudes. Unexpectedly, she found that attitudes and practices were not always congruent with each other. Black teachers who strongly favored desegregation, for example, were found "more favorable in their instructional strategies toward white children than were white teachers" (Washington, 1978, p. 167). One white teacher, called Mrs. Q., illustrated another contradiction (Washington, 1978):

> While Mrs. Q. showed unfavorable attitudes toward ethnicity, and unfavorable perceptions of black children, her behavior toward black children in her classroom was positive/slightly favorable. (p. 142)

How did Washington account for this kind of finding? "Teachers," declared Washington, "appear to recognize that they have negative attitudes, yet when social pressure for a positive posture is asserted, this may lead to behavior which overcompensates for negative attitudes" (1978, p. 175). Such an interpretation is in line with recent thinking in the field of human relations. There is less emphasis on creating "right attitudes" and more on creating opportunities for changed behavior. Over time, it is hoped, repeated "right behavior" will transform less favorable attitudes into more wholesome ones. The relationship be-

tween attitudes and actions is far more complex than suggested by the shuttling from one to the other.

Most crucial, perhaps, is the need to explore the nature of Washington's "social pressure for a positive posture." What are the social forces that create new norms and values that affect the reconstruction of individual attitudes and behavior? How may these be encompassed in in-service programs for teachers in schools undergoing desegregation? More than 15 years ago Francis Keppel, then U.S. Commissioner of Education, exclaimed, "Thank God for the civil rights movement!" (Keppel, 1964). He meant that the movement was helping revolutionize education by placing new demands and approaches before the country. This is one form of "social pressure for a positive posture" by teachers.

Dolores Mathis studied 20 third- and fourth-grade classrooms in five Southeast schools—four suburban, one rural—to examine differences in teacher interactions with students of different races. She found that

> nearly half of all the black students in the classrooms under study were perceived by their teachers as severe disciplinary problems. . . . On the majority of the measures of verbal interaction between teacher and student there were gross disparities in favor of the white student. . . . Black teachers showed less partiality than white teachers to both ethnic student groups. . . . Black students fared better with black teachers. . . . White students received an overwhelming amount of positive teacher time, as well as interaction. (Mathis, 1975, pp. 70–71)

Peter Peretti analyzed the effects of teacher attitudes on the emergence of discipline problems in three desegregated Evanston, Illinois, schools (Peretti, 1976). His central finding was that the "teachers with a positive attitude toward busing for integration did have fewer discipline problems and required fewer discipline measures in their classrooms as compared to teachers with a negative attitude" (p. 136). Further, interracial interaction among students grew friendlier in classrooms where teachers had favorable attitudes toward the desegregation program. Just how teachers communicated their sentiments about desegregation to their students was not analyzed in detail, but Peretti observed that "students tend to know what the teacher thinks about their social climate" (1976, p. 139).

In a study in England, Kevin Majoribanks (1979) found that "modest" changes in student achievement were associated with changes in teacher perceptions of student behavior, at any given level of student intelligence and social environment. Majoribanks also reported that "at each level of teacher perceptions, increases in intelligence and social environment scores are related to sizable increments in academic achievement." He concluded that "if the children came from a deprived social environment or had a low level of intelligence and were perceived by teachers as having unfavorable school-related behavior, then they suffered a compounded deprivation in relation to achievement" (Majoribanks, 1979, p. 217). On the other hand, he reported, they overcame, in part, the disabilities of their environment and low IQ test scores if teachers perceived them favorably.

We now shift our perspective to other vantage points from which to view equity problems in the operation of desegregated schools. Whenever possible, we will examine schoolwide rather than individual teacher–student relationships.

EQUITY PROBLEMS IN DESEGREGATED SCHOOLS

George James Hagerty II studied a desegregated school in what he called "Midwest City," during 1976–1977 (Hagerty, 1978). Much of the work is a day-by-day account of events during the author's year there. Although it is true that after desegregation the incidence of violence in the school increased greatly, nevertheless, as Hagerty reported, "learning was proceeding." This held true, he observed, despite the school's "tension-filled atmosphere."

Prior to desegregation, initiated in 1974, the school had been virtually all-white, attended mainly by lower-class students, few of whom went on to college. At that time, the level of academic achievement was comparatively low and, according to Hagerty, "no true reading program had been established." The desegregation court order directed that remedial tutoring be instituted; curriculum reform also began. In 1976, when Hagerty arrived at the school, 9 out of 10 entering freshmen read below grade level; one tenth read only at second-grade level. The benevolence that resulted in curriculum reform and reading instruction did not infuse all aspects of the school; suspensions of blacks outnumbered those of whites by a ratio of 2.5 to 1.0 (Hagerty, 1978).

Hagerty studied the school during its third year of desegregation. Aside from instructional improvements, he reported "the initiation of a general community acceptance of desegregation" (1978, p. 71). Inside the school, Hagerty explained, black and white students who had known each other before desegregation (there could not have been many of these) communicated extensively, except during disturbances. White and black students who were new to each other communicated mainly within the formal confines of classroom routine. Throughout the first two years of desegregation, black and white students never sat at the same lunchroom tables, but during 1976–1977 they began to share tables for the first time.

Referring to desegregation, Hagerty asserted that "the value of this social change is its tendency to reawaken and refresh declining institutions" such as the school under study (Hagerty, 1978, p. 98). But the "reawakening" occurred only under an extraordinary court order that included, for a time, the imposition of a court-ordered receivership. A detailed history of the school's desegregation would undoubtedly uncover numerous other sources of change. These include the role of organized parents, the growing unacceptability of violence in school affairs, the deliberate use of differences over school desegregation for political advantage, and more.

Jean Ann Linney investigated school desegregation in Danville, Illinois, a

town of about 40,000 people (Linney, 1978). The desegregation plan provided for busing blacks to formerly white schools, but whites were not to be bused in return. In the fall of 1974, the plan was implemented. Linney collected data on 343 students for the two years preceding desegregation and for two years after.

Unlike Hagerty's school, apparently the Danville schools did not institute changes in curriculum and instructional practices. Achievement gaps between white and black children persisted through the two years of desegregation. Linney also found that bused black children were relatively isolated and friendless in the desegregated school, in contrast with the situation in their previous school. On the other hand, Linney found that black children attending a neighborhood desegregated school did gain in academic achievement and social acceptability. Apparently, this was not due to socioeconomic similarity with their white class-mates. Linney wrote that in Danville "there is no identifiable pattern of assign-ment based on socioeconomic level as is often common" (1978, p. 64). Neither Hagerty nor Linney studied systematically the role of teachers in effective change.

As for the existence of discriminatory treatment of students, Linney wrote: "There is some suggestion that after the desegregation black children are being placed in EMH (educable mentally handicapped) classes at a rate different from that prior to desegregation" (p. 143). But she also observed: "The appropriate data are not available to determine the extent to which special education place-ments for black students have increased following the desegregation, or if in fact they have definitely increased at all" (1978, p. 143).

Vera Wilson studied extracurricular activities in five Baltimore high schools during 1977 (Wilson, 1978). The schools ranged from 30% to 70% black. Wilson found racially disproportionate enrollment patterns in each of the schools; in most instances, blacks were disproportionately less enrolled in honors groups, whereas whites were disproportionately more enrolled in honors and service groups. In music and fine arts groups, black membership was disproportionately high. Whites, on the other hand, participated less in school cultural events but more in community and church groups.

Wilson (1978) reported that "in one majority white high school, an increase of 50% black membership in a cocurricular club or activity resulted in an exodus of white members" (p. 152). Although she did not indicate that this was always true, nevertheless Wilson wrote that the racial pattern of extracurricular activities attested to the existence of parallel social systems in the schools. "To augment separate or parallel social systems," Wilson concluded, "breeds racism."

Surprisingly few desegregation studies have examined actual classroom behavior. Researchers have preferred to administer questionnaires or other in-struments at two time points and record any difference. The difference has been assumed to be attributable to desegregation, provided certain statistical precau-tions have been taken. Terrence Scout, however, chose to test the theory, pro-pounded principally by Elizabeth Cohen (1975), that majority-white acceptance

of minority classmates will develop more readily if the two groups cooperate on common tasks (Scout, 1976). Competition within the work groups is expected to recede as all cooperate. The theory is important because it points to a feature of school organization that might need to be changed to facilitate integration, a step beyond desegregation.

Scout studied 372 Mexican-American ninth-graders in the Riverside-San Bernardino, California, area. They attended two schools: one experimental, in which cooperative, interethnic work teams were used; and one control, in which traditional organization prevailed. The former group had 161 students, the latter, 211.

The results were mixed. On the positive side, Mexican-American males in the cooperative work teams grew more positive in their perceptions of Anglo males. But the opposite was true for Mexican-American females; they grew less positive over time. Indeed, female Mexican-Americans in the comparison group grew even more negative than those in the experimental group. When male and female Mexican-Americans were grouped together within the experimental sample, it was found that there was "a decrease in their mean number of associates who are Anglo, while the comparison group reports an increase" (Scout, 1976, p. 2). White students in the experimental group did not show an increase in positive perceptions of Mexican-American students. Scout concluded that the Cohen theory is simply "not practical on a large scale at this time" (p. 95).

The question is: Did Scout in fact demonstrate this? It is doubtful that he did. For one thing, the Cohen (1975) theory, called the theory of "interracial interaction disability," depends on minority children being taught some knowledge which they then teach to white children. Presumably, the latter thus have a chance to view minority children in a new, socially valued role. It is not known to what degree Scout implemented such a procedure. Further, Scott himself notes some methodological weaknesses in his own study. For example, subjects were not randomly chosen nor were subjects in the two groups matched. The Anglos had a higher socioeconomic status than did the Mexican-Americans; and the Anglos in the comparison group had a higher socioeconomic status than did the Anglos in the experimental group. Mexican-Americans in both groups had a comparable status. Scout also reports that pretests were given "after the students had already been exposed to the treatment for about 2 months" (Scout, 1976, p. 71). Thus, the absence of the hoped-for experimental effect may be a consequence of failing to administer a pretest before the experimental treatment, that is, cooperative work groups and the like, began.

There is another problem with Scout's research design. He did not study the possible effects of teachers on interethnic student attitudes. Yet we know from earlier material relating to the Riverside schools that teacher attitudes underwent a long period of change, ranging from fear and rejection of minority children to more considerate and cooperative relations (Linsenmeier & Wortman,

1978; Weinberg, 1977). Teacher preference for Anglo children could easily help separate them from Mexican-American children and engender a mutual coolness between the groups.

Hillman and Davenport (1978) studied teacher–student interracial interaction in Detroit during 1976. Fifteen hundred teachers from 80 schools, K–12, attended a weekend workshop in human relations. Observers then sat in the classrooms of 306 of these teachers to analyze possible discrimination against black students. The researchers found a mixed rather than clear picture. White teachers of black students seemed to take special pains to get the lesson across to them. Hillman and Davenport were cautious in their conclusion. They raised the possibility that white teachers were straining to make the patterns appear to be equal. It is also possible that the patterns were in fact equal. Another possibility the authors did not mention is that the subjects of the study were not at all typical since they were drawn from a group of teachers who had volunteered to attend an in-service workshop. Among classroom teachers, such behavior is comparatively rare. In a real sense, the teachers in the sample were a self-selected group and thus oriented against discrimination in the classroom.

CONCLUSION

Desegregation research often proceeds, as does much of educational research, as though classrooms and schools were self-regulating mechanisms, subject principally to considerations of efficiency and technical proficiency. Thus, when desegregation is ordered, it is assumed that the school and its personnel will try their utmost to make a success of it. As we have seen, however, the empirical realities are frequently quite different. School board members and administrative officials may tend to resist the implementation of desegregation. The Rodgers and Bullock, and Stewart studies underscore the possibility of the growth of, rather than the diminution of, racial discrimination under desegregation. Federal regulatory agencies may fail their duty of enforcing court orders and statutes, to the detriment of desegregation; in this way, school resistance is encouraged.

Studies by Sayavedra, Laosa, and Carter underscore the continuing failure of many American schools to accord equal education to Hispanic children. The studies were made in Texas and California, where most Chicanos live. Espinosa's analysis of classroom paternalism, seldom recognized as such, adds to the documentation of the school as an agent of deprivation for minority youth.

Adams, Marwit et al., and Pietras and Lamb explored the educational destructiveness of white standards of physical attractiveness and spoken dialect. A striking finding by Adams concerned discrimination against black children by black teachers. Riley observed a similar phenomenon, reporting that black teachers were socializing black students to a subordinate social status. Washington

made the point that black teachers favorable to desegregation perceived black children most favorably.

Hagerty's study made evident that a desegregated school under virtual siege could manage to operate and even improve its educational offering. A federal court provided support. Dedicated school leadership was especially critical in whatever success was achieved. Linney recorded the academic and social gains of black children attending a desegregated neighborhood school and, contrariwise, the penalties of black children attending, via buses, a more distant desegregated school. The precise reasons for both outcomes are obscure.

Researchers have also examined extracurricular activities for their contribution to desegregation. Distinct racial patterns emerged in the studies reviewed here, but not uniformly. It is surprising that so few studies have been made of this area of student activity.

Perhaps the most significant aspect of this chapter is that nearly every action discussed is under the control of the school or school system in which it occurred. Neither fate nor history determined the action taken. The course of desegregation (or any major educational change, for that matter), depends greatly on the educational leadership that is brought to bear. Continuing patterns of discrimination are subject to administrative changes, should the school authorities wish to make them.

REFERENCES

Adams, G. R. (1978). Racial membership and physical attractiveness effects on preschool teachers' expectations. *Child Study Journal, 8,* 29–41.

Armor, D. J. (1972). The evidence on busing. *The Public Interest, 28,* 90–126.

Birdin, V. E. (1978). *A study of selected apprehensions of teachers working in schools predominantly of the opposite race.* Unpublished doctoral dissertation, Virginia Polytechnic and State University, Blacksburg, VA.

Bradley, L., & Bradley, G. (1977). The academic achievement of black students in desegregated schools. *Review of Educational Research, 47,* 399–449.

Carter, R. B. (1976). *A study of attitudes: Mexican-American and Anglo-American elementary teachers' judgment of Mexican-American bilingual children's speech.* Unpublished doctoral dissertation, University of Houston, Houston, TX.

Cohen, E. G. (1975). The effects of desegregation on race relations. *Law and Contemporary Problems, 39:*271–299.

Crain, R. L., & Mahard, R. E. (1978). Desegregation and black achievement: A review of the research. *Law and Contemporary Problems, 42,* 17–56.

Daniels, L. H. (1974). *Changes in opinions of professional staff in schools experiencing rapid integration.* Unpublished doctoral dissertation, University of Florida, Gainesville, FL.

Espinosa, R. W. (1975). *The impact of evaluation processes upon student effort in ethnic groups which vary in academic preparation.* Unpublished doctoral dissertation, Stanford University, Stanford, CA.

Hagerty, G. J., II. (1978). *Desegregation in a midwest city: A qualitative study of an urban, comprehensive high school and its interaction with community agencies.* Unpublished doctoral dissertation, Harvard University, Cambridge, MA.

Hillman, S. B., & Davenport, C. G. (1978). Teacher–student interactions in desegregated schools. *Journal of Educational Psychology, 70*, 545–553.

Keppel, F. (1964). Thank God for the civil rights movement. *Integrated Education, 2*, 9–12.

Krol, R. (1978). *A meta analysis of comparative research on the effects of desegregation on academic achievement.* Doctoral dissertation, Western Michigan University (University Microfilms No. 79–07962).

Laosa, L. M. (1979). Inequality in the classroom: Observational research on teacher-student interactions. *Aztlan, 8*, 51–67.

Linney, J. A. (1978). *A multivariate, multilevel analysis of a midwestern city's court ordered desegregation.* Unpublished doctoral dissertation, University of Illinois.

Linsenmeier, J. A. W., & Wortman, P. M. (1978). The Riverside school study of desegregation: A re-examination. *Research Review of Equal Education, 2*, 1–40.

Majoribanks, K. (1979). Intelligence, social environment, and academic achievement: A regression surface analysis. *Journal of Experimental Education, 47*, 346–351.

Maldonado, L. A., & Byrne, D. R. (1978). *The social ecology of Chicanos in Utah.* Iowa City: Iowa Urban Community Research Center.

Marwit, K. L., Marwit, S., & Walker, E. (1978). Effects of student race and physical attractiveness on teachers' judgments of transgressions. *Journal of Educational Psychology, 70*, (6), 911–915.

Mathis, D. W. (1975). *Difference in teacher interaction with Afro-American and Anglo-American students in the same classroom.* Unpublished doctoral dissertation, University of Michigan, Ann Arbor, MI.

Peretti, P. O. (1976). Effects of teachers' attitudes on discipline problems in schools recently desegregated. *Education, 97*, 136–140.

Piché, G. L., Ruben, D., Turner, L. J., & Michlin, M. L. (1977). Teachers' subjective evaluations of standard and black non-standard English compositions: A study of written language and attitudes. *Research in the Teaching of English, 44*, 60–72.

Pietras, T., & Lamb, R. (1978). Attitudes of selected elementary teachers toward non-standard black dialects. *Journal of Educational Research, 71*,292–297.

Riley, J. B. (1975). *Political socialization in the elementary school: The role of the Afro-American teacher.* Unpublished doctoral dissertation, University of Illinois.

Rodgers, H. R., Jr., & Bullock, C. S. III. (1976). The impact of school desegregation. *Integrateducation, 14*, 33–34.

St. John, N. H. (1975). *School desegregation: Outcomes for children.* New York: Wiley.

Sayavedra, L. (1976). *Teacher differential expectations and interactions with Mexican-American and Anglo-American secondary physical science students.* Unpublished doctoral dissertation, University of Texas.

Scout, T. M. (1976). *School desegregation to integration through changes in social structure.* Unpublished doctoral dissertation, University of California, Riverside, CA.

Stern, C., & Keislar, E. (1977). Teacher attitudes and attitude change: A research review. *Journal of Research and Development in Education, 10*, 63–76.

Stewart, J. E. (1977). *Second generation discrimination: Unequal educational opportunity in desegregated Southern schools.* Unpublished doctoral dissertation, University of Houston, Houston, TX.

Washington, V. (1978). *Desegregation attitudes, perceptions, and classroom behavior of black and white teachers of second grade: Group profiles and interrelationships in integrated settings.* Unpublished doctoral dissertation, Indiana University.

Weinberg, M. (1977). *Minority students: A research appraisal.* Washington, DC: U.S. Government Printing Office.

Wilson, V. I. (1978). *The relationship between racial composition of desegregated high schools and membership in co-curricular programs in Baltimore City.* Unpublished doctoral dissertation, Temple University, Philadelphia, PA.

7

School and Individual Achievement Following Desegregation in New Castle County, Delaware

JOHN H. SCHWEITZER

This study describes the academic achievement of the pupils of New Castle County, Delaware, during the first 3 years of school desegregation. Every school desegregation case has its own specific characteristics that limit the generalizability of the findings to other desegregation settings. In New Castle County there were many unique factors which, taken together, make this desegregation case different from all others. In that sense, this report represents a case study of a unique situation. It is felt, however, that this in-depth examination of academic achievement coincident with desegregation has generated findings that contribute to our understanding of educational outcomes associated with the desegregation process.

A major difference between this desegregation study and most others is that this one examines the impact of a metropolitan desegregation plan that created a single desegregated district from 11 previously separate and racially identifiable districts. The New Castle County School District was formed from the separate school districts of Alexis I. DuPont, Alfred I. DuPont, Claymont, Conrad, De La Warr, Marshallton-McKean, Mount Pleasant, New Castle-Gunning Bedford, Newark, Stanton, and Wilmington.

The first year of metropolitan-wide desegregation was relatively peaceful. At the opening of school in September 1978, there were occasional scattered demonstrations by parents and students, but for the most part school desegregation was grudgingly accepted. In October, however, teachers in the district

JOHN H. SCHWEITZER ● Urban Affairs Programs, Michigan State University, East Lansing, Michigan 48824.

walked out on strike, primarily over the issue of teachers' salaries. The 6-week strike may not only have affected pupil achievement, but it may also have influenced the racial climate of the schools in subtle ways. Attitudes in the community were sharply divided on the issue of teachers' salaries. Prior to desegregation, the Wilmington teachers, who were predominantly black, had the highest pay scale; they did not strongly support the strike. The predominantly white teachers of the suburban districts were the prime movers in the demand that all salaries be "leveled-up" to the highest pay scale. This difference in support for the strike along racial lines probably exacerbated racial tension in the schools.

Coincident with the first year of school desegregation was the adoption of a new competency-based curriculum. The new curriculum included the introduction of performance objectives and the use of a modified form of the mastery model of instruction. The fact that these changes in instruction and curriculum took place at the same time as the implementation of school desegregation makes it difficult to isolate the impact of desegregation on achievement.

Another factor that adds to the uniqueness of this study is its longitudinal research design. Whereas most desegregation studies report findings based on 1 or perhaps 2 years of desegregation, this study presents data spanning a 3-year period. Achievement data were collected at the beginning of school desegregation and at the end of each of the first 3 school years in the newly constituted desegregated district.

Other unique factors of this study relate to the school levels studied and the units of analysis. Data were collected from schools and students at the elementary, junior high, and senior high school levels. Separate analyses of the relationship of desegregation and achievement were conducted using the district, the school, and the individual pupil as units of analysis.

At each level of analysis, a number of questions were asked relating to desegregation and achievement. At the district level there were four major questions: What changes, if any, occurred in achievement during the first, second, and third years of desegregation? Were the changes in achievement comparable from year to year? Were the changes in achievement comparable at the elementary, junior high, and senior high levels? Were changes in mathematics achievement comparable to those in reading?

Two major questions were asked at the school level: What, if any, aspects of school racial climate were related to overall achievement level in the desegregated schools? In what ways, if any, do aspects of racial climate related to achievement differ between the junior high and senior high level?

At the individual level, the main question asked was: To what extent are the gains in achievement made by black pupils similar to the gains in achievement made by white pupils? In addition, five separate individual factors were examined, including gender, grade level, parents' initial attitude toward school desegregation, parents' perceived socioeconomic status (SES), and the racial com-

position of the school attended prior to desegregation. For each factor the questions asked were: How is this factor related to changes in achievement? In what ways, if any, does this factor interact with race to influence achievement?

METHOD

Prior to the formation of the New Castle County School District in 1978, the 11 original districts did not have a uniform testing program. Different standardized achievement tests were used in the various districts, and the tests were administered at different grade levels and at different points during the school year. Therefore, no common achievement data were available for the years before 1978.

The research directors of the separate districts realized that it was necessary to implement a common testing program for the new district. Although the legal maneuvering associated with the court order was still underway and the final outcome was uncertain, the research directors began meeting during the 1977–1978 school year to make plans for the possible formation of a single unified district. It was decided that districtwide achievement would be measured by the California Achievement Test (CAT).

The first administration of the CAT was in October 1978 at the beginning of the implementation of school desegregation. The test was given to all students in grades 1 through 12 in the new district. Grade 1 students took Level 11 of the CAT, grade 2 students took Level 12, and so on through grade 7. Students in grades 8 and 9 took Level 18; and grades 10, 11, and 12 were given Level 19. Form C of the CAT was used for all grade levels. The same tests were again administered in April 1979, in April 1980, and in May 1981. In each case, Form C was used, and the level of the test given to each grade was the same as in the first test administration.

The scores from these test administrations compose most of the data presented in this chapter. The October 1978 scores are used as baseline data. Although the students had been attending desegregated schools for about 1 month at the time of this test, it was felt that this short period would not invalidate the use of this test as a pretest. The three spring test administrations were used as posttests so that achievement levels could be examined after the first, second, and third years of school desegregation.

The test results, broken down by school and by grade within school, were published by the New Castle County School District (1979; 1980; 1981). For each grade level in each school, these yearly reports present the grade equivalent and national percentile means of those tested for the reading, language, and mathematics subtests as well as the total battery means.

The analyses presented in this chapter are based on the national percentile scores on the reading and mathematics subtests of the CAT. A disadvantage in

the use of percentile scores is that they provide only an ordinal level of measurement. It was felt, however, that this drawback was outweighed by the fact that percentile scores are directly comparable at each grade level. The only other available scores were grade equivalents, which have many limitations (Mehrens & Lehmann, 1973).

For the total district analysis, the results were based on the 90 schools that were open over the 3-year period of the study. The mean school achievement level in reading and mathematics was computed by averaging the mean national percentiles at each grade level within each school. A repeated-measures analysis of variance was computed on school means in reading and mathematics over the four testing periods.

It should be noted that the school means and the districtwide means at each testing period were not based on the same population of pupils. Among the reasons for this were pupil absences during the testing; dropping out; moving into, out of, or within the district; and graduation. The total number of pupils tested was 50,825 in 1978, 49,380 in 1979, 44,721 in 1980, and 43,278 in 1981. This indicates that there was a drop of almost 15% from the number of students tested in fall 1978 to the number of students tested in spring 1981. Most of this drop was because parents withdrew their children from the public schools in New Castle County.

The analysis of the relation of school characteristics to overall school achievement level was also based on the published results of the achievement test program. School means were obtained as described for each of the junior high and senior high schools in the district. These means were correlated with various measures of school climate to identify factors related to high achieving desegregated schools.

The analysis of achievement scores at the individual level was based on a different procedure. Two years prior to the implementation of school desegregation, meetings were held with each of the 11 superintendents to ask permission to conduct a study of the impact of desegregation. After extensive negotiations and meetings with school personnel, boards of education, and parent groups, five districts agreed to cooperate with the study. Each cooperating district—De La Warr, Marshallton-McKean, Mt. Pleasant, Newark, and Wilmington—provided a list of the names and addresses of the students enrolled during the 1977–1978 school year. From these lists, a random sample of families was selected. In spring 1978 each family received a cover letter briefly describing the study, a consent form, and student and parent questionnaires. A total of 2,333 families returned the consent forms and the student and parent questionnaires.

In the spring of each of the 3 years following desegregation, the participating families were contacted by mail and asked to fill out questionnaires. A total of 298 pairs of students and parents returned usable questionnaires in each year of the study. Because these families were voluntarily participating, the New Castle County School District agreed to provide individual achievement data for each

of the four test administrations. The exclusion of those students who had missed part or all of any of the achievement tests, and those whose racial/ethnic group was neither black nor white, left a sample of 218 pupils. Repeated-measures analyses of variance were computed on the achievement scores of these students to examine changes over time. Analyses were also made of the interaction of race and achievement with the factors of gender, SES, grade level, parents' attitude toward school desegregation, and racial composition of school attended prior to desegregation.

DISTRICTWIDE ACHIEVEMENT

In this section the results of the achievement testing for the total district at each of the four testing periods are presented. Because the data are based on the total population of the schools in the district and because all students in each school were tested, there is no real population to which the district results could be generalized. However, inferential statistical tests of significance were used to assist in the interpretation of the results and to allow a generalization of these findings to similar school districts.

The means of the 90 schools on the reading and mathematics subtests and on the CAT total score at each of the four test periods are presented in Table 1. The schools of New Castle County averaged slightly above national norms at the beginning of desegregation in 1978. During the 3 years of this study there was a gain of 12 percentile points in reading, 15 points in mathematics and a total gain of 14 points. Most of the gain (10 points) was made during the first

Table 1.   Mean School Achievement Scores (1978–1981)

		1978	1979	1980	1981
Elementary	Reading	51.0	63.1	63.1	65.8
schools	Mathematics	51.0	65.3	65.6	69.8
(N = 59)	Total battery	51.0	63.6	64.7	68.2
Junior high	Reading	56.1	61.8	61.5	63.8
schools	Mathematics	53.3	61.6	62.3	64.8
(N = 19)	Total battery	54.1	60.9	61.4	64.5
Senior high	Reading	57.1	60.8	61.8	62.7
schools	Mathematics	54.7	60.7	60.9	60.9
(N = 12)	Total battery	55.6	61.1	61.6	62.1
All schools	Reading	53.0	62.3	62.5	64.8
(N = 90)	Mathematics	52.0	63.7	64.1	67.4
	Total battery	52.2	62.7	63.6	66.6

year of desegregation. There was a 1-point gain in total achievement scores in the second year and a 3-point increase in the third year.

A repeated-measures analysis of variance was conducted on the school reading and mathematics achievement means. Results of this analysis are presented in Table 2. The gains made across years showed a high degree of significance. The significant interaction of year and grade level is graphically presented in Figure 1. This figure indicates that prior to desegregation the senior high schools had the highest level of achievement, the junior high schools scored slightly lower, and the elementary schools scored lowest. At the end of the first year, the elementary and senior high schools reversed positions. During the second year the changes in achievement were small at all levels, but in the third year the elementary schools again had the greatest gains. This finding is consistent with previous research that found that desegregation is most effective at the elementary school level in increasing achievement (Crain & Mahard, 1982).

The significant subtest effect shown in Table 2 means that overall the schools in the district scored higher in mathematics than in reading. The interaction of subtest and level is explained by these findings: the elementary schools averaged higher in mathematics acorss the 4 years; there was no real difference at the junior high level; and the senior high schools did better in reading.

The significant interaction of subtest and year is pictured in Figure 2. At the beginning of desegregation in 1978, the overall district reading scores averaged one point higher than the mathematics scores. At the end of the first year these figures were reversed, and by the end of the third year the math scores were $2\frac{1}{2}$ points higher than the reading scores.

The analysis of the districtwide changes in achievement coincident with the first 3 years of school desegregation in New Castle County leads to three major conclusions. First, there were major gains made in achievement, with the greatest gains coming during the first year, slight gains in the second year, and moderate gains in the third year; second, greater gains were made on the mathematics subtest than on the reading subtest; and third, the greatest gains were made in the elementary schools.

Table 2. Repeated Measures ANOVA of Verbal and Math Scores (1978–1981)

Source	df	F	Significance level
Level	2	.30	.742
Year	3	170.41	.000
Level by year	6	7.42	.000
Subtest	1	8.97	.004
Level by subtest	2	5.86	.004
Subtest by year	3	18.75	.000
Level by subtest by year	6	1.25	.285

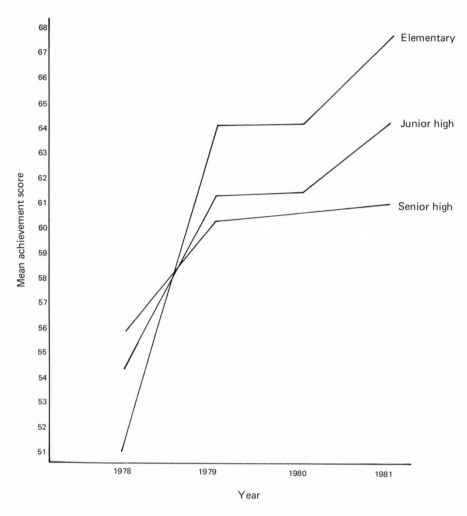

Figure 1.   Achievement score gains made by elementary, junior high and senior high schools, New Castle County, Delaware, 1978–1981.

INDIVIDUAL CHARACTERISTICS AND ACHIEVEMENT

Over the 3 years of this study, major gains in achievement took place in the New Castle County schools coincident with school desegregation. The purpose of this section is to examine whether the gains were consistent across different groups of children, or whether achievement gains varied with student characteristics. The analyses are based on the 218 students for whom test scores

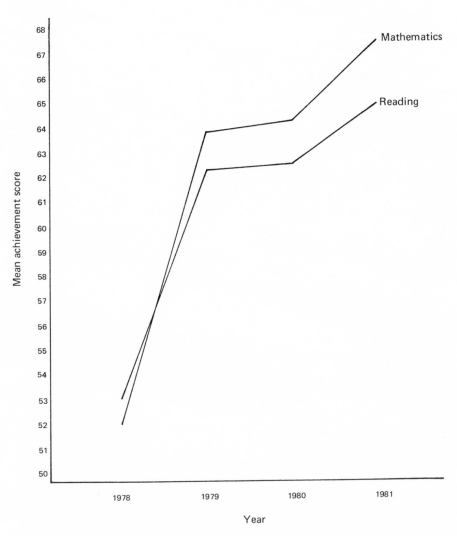

Figure 2.   Achievement gains on reading and mathematics subtests, New Castle County, Delaware, 1978–1981.

were available for all four testing periods and for whom we had complete de-mographic data.

This sample of 218 students should not be considered a random sample of the population of students in the New Castle County School District during the first 3 years of desegregation. As was noted earlier in the chapter, this sample consisted of students from only 5 of the 11 original districts. They were in grades

2 through 10 at the beginning of desegregation, and they and their parents had voluntarily participated over the 3 years of the study. The sample contained a higher proportion of whites and a lower proportion of blacks than were in the overall district. As might be expected with a sample like this, the mean test scores were consistently higher than the districtwide averages for each of the four test periods. However, the patterns of achievement gains made by the sample were similar to the districtwide pattern. In this sample, as well as in the whole district, most of the achievement gains came during the first year, greater gains were made by the elementary pupils, and greater gains were made in mathematics. In light of these similarities, the sample data can, with caution, be generalized to the entire district.

Repeated-measures analyses of variance were used to examine changes in achievement over time. The dependent variables were the national percentile reading and math scores on the CAT in 1978, 1979, 1980, and 1981. The student characteristics used as independent variables in the analyses of variance included race, gender, grade level immediately prior to implementation of desegregation, parents' SES, parents' initial attitude toward school desegregation, and racial composition of the school attended prior to desegregation. Because of the limited size of the sample, all these factors could not be included in a single analysis of variance. However, since student race was seen as the variable of greatest interest in this study of school desegregation, it was included with each of the other factors in an analysis of variance. In this way, the possible interaction of student race with the other variables could be examined. In each of the analyses of variance, the repeated-measures factors were years and subtests, that is, reading and mathematics.

Results of the analysis of variance of race and grade with the repeated-measures factors of years and subtest are presented in Table 3. The highly significant main effects of race and years indicate that there were differences in the achievement scores of blacks and whites, and that the test scores of the total sample increased substantially from 1978 at the beginning of desegregation to 1981 at the completion of 3 full years of desegregated education. This latter finding is consistent with the results, reported earlier in the chapter, based on the means of all the schools in the district.

Three significant interactions are reported in Table 3. The race-by-years interaction indicates that the changes in achievement were not the same for black and white pupils. Table 4 shows that the black students gained an average of 10 percentile points in achievement during the first year of desegregation, whereas the white students gained an average of 5 points during the same period. Both groups then showed only minor changes in achievement during the next 2 years. The finding of the apparently greater gains made by black pupils during the first year is tempered by the fact that a given percentile difference typically represents fewer raw score units near the median than at the extreme. Since the black students' mean was closer to the national median than the white students' mean,

Table 3. Repeated Measures ANOVA of Race, Grade, Subtest, and Year (1978–1981)

Source	df	F	Significance level
Race	1	58.73	.000
Grade	2	2.15	.119
Race by grade	1	.04	.845
Subtest	1	2.22	.137
Race by subtest	1	1.18	.278
Grade by subtest	2	.24	.788
Race by grade by subtest	1	.00	.945
Year	3	27.22	.000
Race by year	3	3.07	.027
Grade by year	6	2.19	.043
Race by grade by year	3	.34	.797
Subtest by year	3	4.63	.003
Race by subtest by year	3	.15	.931
Grade by subtest by year	6	.85	.531
Race by grade by subtest by year	3	1.36	.254

it could be argued that the greater gain in percentile points made by blacks did not reflect an actual closing of the achievement score gap. However, conversion of the percentile ranks to standard scores by assuming a normal distribution indicates that the gains made by the blacks in this sample were at least 1 1/2 times the gains made by the whites in the first year.

Table 4. Achievement Scores at Four Testing Periods (1978–1981)

	1978	1979	1980	1981
		Race		
Black (N = 27)	40.1	50.4	48.4	50.3
White (N = 191)	74.2	79.4	78.1	78.4
		Grade		
2–5 (N = 105)	71.7	79.1	78.2	79.4
6–8 (N = 92)	68.3	74.2	72.5	72.2
9–10 (N = 21)	68.5	71.9	74.8	72.6
		Subtest		
Reading	71.8	75.6	75.0	75.5
Mathematics	68.1	75.9	73.8	74.5
Total	70.0	75.8	74.4	75.0

There was also a significant interaction between grade and year. As can be seen in Table 4, this interaction comes from the fact that the students who were in grades two to five before desegregation gained almost 8 points during the course of the study whereas those in the upper grades gained an average of 4 points.

The means on the reading and mathematics subtests of the CAT by year are also presented in Table 4. The significant interaction between these two factors is caused by the larger gains on the mathematics subtest during the first year of desegregation. This is consistent with the results from the total district. In the next 2 years the reading scores of the sample stayed fairly constant while mathematics scores dropped and then rose slightly.

The second repeated-measures analysis of variance, using the factors of gender and race, is presented in Table 5.

The significant four-way interaction of race-by-sex-by-subtest-by-years may be understood by examining the means of the black and white males and the black and white females as presented in Table 6. White male and white female students had very similar patterns of mean scores. Both groups made gains during the first year of desegregation, both gained more in math than in reading, and both had fairly steady scores over the second and third years. The patterns of the black male and black female students were different from each other, and both were different from those of the white pupils. The black males made a very

Table 5. Repeated Measures ANOVA of Race, Sex, Subtest, and Year (1978–1981)

Source	df	F	Significance level
Race	1	59.02	.000
Sex	1	.73	.394
Race by sex	1	3.69	.056
Subtest	1	2.27	.133
Race by subtest	1	1.21	.273
Sex by subtest	1	2.51	.114
Race by sex by subtest	1	1.58	.210
Year	3	26.87	.000
Race by year	3	3.04	.029
Sex by year	3	.87	.454
Race by subtest by year	3	.12	.949
Subtest by year	3	4.73	.003
Race by subtest by year	3	.15	.929
Sex by subtest by year	3	1.97	.117
Race by sex by subtest by year	3	4.87	.002

Table 6.   Means on CAT Subtests (1978–1981)

Race and gender	Subtest	1978	1979	1980	1981
Black Males (N = 11)	Reading	32.5	36.2	39.1	41.5
	Math	34.6	53.5	44.5	43.3
Black Females (N = 16)	Reading	47.1	57.7	53.2	54.1
	Math	42.2	50.8	52.2	57.2
White Males (N = 99)	Reading	77.7	80.8	79.9	80.3
	Math	74.7	82.0	79.3	79.3
White Females (N = 92)	Reading	73.9	77.4	77.4	77.5
	Math	69.0	75.5	74.7	75.6

large gain in mathematics the first year and then dropped the next year, whereas their reading scores consistently rose over the 3 years. For black females the pattern was reversed. They made their largest gains in reading in the first year and then dropped slightly the next year, but their math scores rose consistently over the 3-year period. It is not known why the black males and black females had different patterns of achievement on the reading and mathematics subtests over the years, whereas the white males and females had patterns similar to each other.

In this sample, the black females generally outscored the black males, and the white males consistently outscored the white females. Table 6 indicates that the overall gains on combined test scores were the same for males and females. Black males made overall gains equal to those of black females, and the gains of white males and females were also equal to each other but less than the overall black gains.

The repeated-measures analysis of variance for the factors of race, SES, subtest, and years is presented in Table 7. The significant main effect of SES indicates that SES level is related to overall achievement. Students from higher- and middle-SES families scored higher than students from lower-SES families. SES did not interact significantly with any of the other factors. This means that the achievement gains made during the 3 years did not differ significantly for the different SES groups. Desegregated education did not appear to be related to differential outcomes for higher-, middle-, and lower-SES students of either race.

Table 7. Repeated Measures ANOVA of Race, SES, Subtest, and Year (1978–1981)

Source	df	F	Significance level
Race	1	60.30	.000
SES	2	4.29	.015
Race by SES	2	2.89	.058
Subtest	1	2.71	.101
Race by subtest	1	.70	.403
SES by subtest	2	.19	.827
Race by SES by subtest	2	.43	.648
Year	3	27.14	.000
Race by year	3	3.26	.021
SES by year	6	.84	.541
Race by SES by year	6	1.07	.379
Subtest by year	3	4.92	.002
Race by subtest by year	3	.22	.881
SES by subtest by year	6	1.02	.414
Race by SES by subtest by year	6	1.36	.228

The results of the repeated-measures analysis of variance of student race by racial composition of school attended before desegregation are presented in Table 8 and the means are given in Table 9. The significant main effect of school indicates that students attending predominantly white schools before desegregation scored higher overall compared with students attending predominantly black schools.

A significant interaction of race-by-school-by-years was found. Table 9 indicates that black students gained approximately 10 points on total score, with no difference between blacks who had attended black schools and those who had attended predominantly white schools. For white students, however, there was a big difference. Those who had been attending predominantly white schools gained an average of 4 points, but whites who had been attending predominantly black schools gained an average of 28 points after desegregation. Despite the small sample size, this finding suggests that future desegregation research should examine what happens to white pupils from mainly black schools when their schools are desegregated.

There are other significant interactions shown in Table 8. The significant interaction between race, school, and subtest is due to the fact that blacks in our sample who had attended black schools scored higher on the math subtest than on the reading subtest (Table 9). Although there was little difference between the overall reading scores and math scores of whites from white schools, both

Table 8. Repeated Measures ANOVA of Race, prior School
Composition, Subtest, and Year (1978–1981)

	df	F	Significance level
Race	1	62.31	.000
School	1	7.57	.006
Race by school	1	1.46	.228
Subtest	1	2.52	.114
Race by subtest	1	1.27	.260
School by subtest	1	2.15	.144
Race by school by subtest	1	5.78	.022
Year	3	28.88	.000
Race by year	3	3.09	.027
School by year	3	3.06	.028
Race by school by year	3	5.12	.002
Subtest by year	3	5.08	.002
Race by subtest by year	3	.14	.934
School by subtest by year	3	3.77	.011
Race by school by subtest by year	3	1.55	.199

Table 9. Mean Achievement Scores of Students by Racial Composition of School
Attended prior to Desegregation (1978–1981)

Prior school	Student race		1978	1979	1980	1981
Black	Black	Reading	29.8	35.3	36.4	39.4
	(N = 16)	Math	33.8	47.2	42.1	44.8
		Total	31.8	41.2	39.3	42.1
Black	White	Reading	54.5	78.8	79.8	85.8
	(N = 6)	Math	54.0	75.8	74.5	78.2
		Total	54.2	77.3	77.2	82.0
White	Black	Reading	57.6	68.7	63.5	62.9
	(N = 11)	Math	46.9	58.7	59.3	61.4
		Total	52.2	63.7	61.4	62.2
White	White	Reading	76.6	79.4	78.9	79.1
	(N = 185)	Math	72.6	79.4	77.7	77.7
		Total	74.6	79.4	78.3	78.4

blacks from white schools and whites from black schools were generally better at reading than at math.

Greater overall gains after desegregation were made by students originally from predominantly black schools. When the gains are considered by subtest, it is seen that students from black schools gained 10 points in both reading and math, whereas students from white schools gained 5 points in math and 2 points in reading.

Another individual factor that was postulated as having a possible relationship with achievement gains after school desegregation was parents' initial attitude toward desegregation in New Castle County. Based on preimplementation responses to questions about the desirability of school desegregation in New Castle County, parents were identified as being in favor of, neutral toward, or opposed to school desegregation.

The factor of attitude toward desegregation was included with race, subtest, and year in a repeated-measures analysis of variance. Results of this analysis, presented in Table 10, indicate that there was no overall difference in student achievement across the three levels of parental attitude. In addition, attitude did not interact significantly with any of the other factors. This means that although there were wide differences in the attitudes of parents of both races toward the

Table 10. Repeated Measures ANOVA of Race, Attitude toward School Desegregation, Subtest, and Year (1978–1981)

Source	df	F	Significance level
Race	1	64.96	.000
Attitude	1	1.92	.149
Race by attitude	1	.06	.944
Subtest	1	2.71	.101
Race by subtest	1	.86	.354
Attitude by subtest	2	2.11	.123
Race by attitude by subtest	2	.97	.381
Year	3	27.33	.000
Race by year	3	2.83	.030
Attitude by year	6	.76	.603
Race by attitude by year	6	.47	.829
Subtest by year	3	5.08	.002
Race by subtest by year	3	.15	.929
Attitude by subtest by year	6	1.65	.130
Race by attitude by subtest by year	6	.87	.515

desirability of school desegregation, these attitudes had no discernible relation to the achievement of children in a desegregated setting.

These analyses of individual characteristics and achievement have shown that the variables of race, grade level, racial composition of prior school, and, to a lesser extent, gender, were the most important intervening variables related to achievement scores in the desegregated schools of New Castle County. Black students made greater gains overall than white students, especially during the first year of desegregation. The total gains made by black male and female pupils were similar, but they had different patterns on the subtests over the years. White males and females gained relatively equally and had similar patterns on the subtests.

Greater overall gains were made in reading and mathematics by students who had attended predominantly black schools prior to desegregation. Black students from predominantly white schools gained as much as black students from segregated schools, but even greater gains seem to have been made by white students who had been attending predominantly black schools.

The greatest gains following implementation of the desegregation plan were made by students at the elementary level. Moderate gains were made by junior high pupils, and the smallest gains were made by pupils enrolled in senior high school at the beginning of desegregation. This finding was the same for both black and white pupils.

The SES level of parents and their initial attitude toward school desegregation in New Castle County did not appear to be important variables related to the achievement score gains of their children in the desegregated schools.

SCHOOL CHARACTERISTICS AND ACHIEVEMENT

Numerous studies have pointed out the need to consider school-level effects in the analysis of achievement data. Brookover, Schweitzer, Schneider, Beady, Flood, and Wisenbaker (1978), and Brookover, Beady, Flood, Schweitzer and Wisenbaker (1979) found that school achievement is highly related to school social climate. In reviews of the literature on effective schools (Mackenzie, 1983; Rowan, Bossert, & Dwyer, 1983), researchers have concluded that there are school characteristics that consistently distinguish between higher and lower achieving schools. Although it is generally agreed that there are school-level variables related to achievement, few studies of desegregation and achievement have included the school as a unit of analysis. Hawley (1980) observed that most researchers have studied the outcomes of school desegregation without identifying the school-level variables that might account for the differing outcomes. One variable that has been studied, however, is school racial climate. Several studies (Crain & Mahard, 1982; Forehand, Ragosta, & Rock, 1976)

have found that positive racial climate in the classroom is related to higher achievement of black pupils.

In this section of the chapter, school-level variables that are related to overall school achievement following desegregation are examined. The Department of Human Relations of the New Castle County School District collected data that were thought to be indicative of the overall school climate of the secondary schools during the first years of desegregation. The Human Relations Department was particularly concerned with maintaining a harmonious racial climate in the schools. To assist in this goal, a *climate indicator* was developed, using data from several sources, for each junior and senior high school in the district. The indicator gave the relative ranking of each school on a series of variables that could be indicative of the overall racial climate in the school. The 19 junior high schools and the 12 senior high schools were ranked separately. The climate indicators were used to identify potential trouble areas in each school where the school's energies might be focused and additional assistance provided in order to improve the climate. To explore whether school racial climate was related to school learning, the variables measured by the climate indicator were correlated with mean school achievement.

The variables that were thought to measure school racial climate included both objective and subjective indexes. The objective indexes, obtained from school records, were suspension and dropout rates, average attendance, rate of minority participation in student activities, and rate of disruptive incidents (including incidents of a racial nature). The subjective indexes were measured through surveys of the school personnel in each building. These variables were racial tension as perceived by the school community; teachers' interest in and use of multicultural materials and programs; and perceived need for tension-reducing activities, such as stress management workshops, crisis prevention programs, interpersonal relations programs, and community involvement programs.

In addition to overall suspension and dropout rates for each school, the disparity of these rates was examined for majority and minority students within each school. The disparity of suspension rates was determined by comparing, in each school, the percent of minority students with the percent of majority students suspended during the school year. A large disparity, indicating a potential source of trouble, could be due to overt or subtle racial policies on the part of the disciplinary personnel within the school. A disparity could also be due to a high level of racial tension in the school, causing minority students to be disproportionately involved in fights and other incidents leading to their suspension from school. In any case, a large disparity in suspension rates could be indicative of a school climate inimical to overall school achievement. During the first year of desegregation, there was great variation in the disparity of minority/majority suspensions in the 31 secondary schools. In one junior high

school, the rate of minority student suspension was only 60% of the rate of majority student suspensions, whereas in another junior high school minority students were suspended at a rate 13 times the majority rate.

The disparity of dropout rates between minority and majority students was also considered an indicator of the overall school climate that might impact on achievement. This variable was determined for each school in the same way as suspension-rate disparity. Average daily attendance rates broken down by race in each school were not available. Therefore, the rate of overall attendance, rather than disparity in attendance rates, was used as a measure of school climate.

Participation in extracurricular activities has been found to be an important factor related to school achievement, expectation, and future aspirations (Hanks & Eckland, 1976; Rehberg & Schafer, 1968; Schafer & Armer, 1968; Spady, 1970, 1971). In addition, participation in extracurricular programs has been shown to be related to students' interracial behavior and attitudes (Patchen, Davidson, Hofmann, & Brown, 1977). Therefore, a measure of participation in student activities was included as an indicator of school climate. A disparity of participation rates between majority and minority students was seen as a possible indicator of a school racial climate not conducive to overall achievement. Disparity of participation rates was measured in the same way as disparity of suspension rates.

Other indicators of the overall school climate obtained from the school records were the rate of incident reports during the year and the rate of crisis team responses. Incident reports were made for acts of student misbehavior, such as disruption of the orderly educational process, defiance of school personnel's authority, or vandalism. A team of human relations specialists made crisis team responses to incidents of a racial nature, such as fighting between pupils of different racial groups.

Another source of school climate data was a survey of the teachers and administrators in each of the secondary schools. From this survey the following indicators of climate were developed for each school: racial tension as perceived by the teachers and administrators; extent of use of multicultural materials by the teachers; degree of teacher interest in stress management workshops; degree of teacher interest in multicultural awareness workshops; and perceived need for programs in multicultural awareness, crisis prevention, interpersonal relations, and community involvement.

Overall school achievement was computed by averaging the mean total scale percentile scores on the CAT for each grade. Achievement scores broken down by racial group were not available, so the analysis was limited to examining the relationship of school racial climate to overall school achievement. The overall school achievement scores are based primarily on the achievement of white students who made up approximately 74% of the student body in each school.

Correlations between achievement and school climate indexes were computed separately for the 12 senior and 19 junior high schools that comprised the population of senior and junior high schools in the district. In interpreting these correlations, it is useful to know that a correlation of .49 would be statistically significant if the senior high schools were a sample from an infinite population and a correlation of .39 would be significant if the junior high schools were a sample from the same size population.

For the junior high schools in New Castle County, as shown in Table 11, five of the eight objective measures of school climate were strongly related to school achievement. As expected, attendance rate was highly correlated with achievement. Schools with higher overall performance on the achievement tests tended to have higher average attendance, and lower achieving schools had a poorer attendance rate.

The overall student dropout rate and the disparity of the minority dropout rate were both related to achievement in the expected way. Higher achieving schools had a lower dropout rate and a smaller difference in the dropout rates of minority and nonminority students. Lower achieving schools had a greater

Table 11.   Correlations of School Climate Indexes with
Overall School Achievement for the Junior High Schools
(1978–1981)

Indexes	Correlation
Objective	
Student suspensions	− .03
Disparity of minority suspensions	.59
Student dropouts	− .49
Disparity of minority dropouts	− .45
Attendance rate	.69
Incident reports	− .02
Crisis team responses	− .39
Minority participation in student activities	− .59
Subjective	
Racial tension	− .33
Use of multicultural materials	.45
Interest in multicultural awareness workshops	− .03
Need for multicultural awareness programs	− .04
Interest in stress management workshops	− .05
Need for crisis prevention programs	− .03
Need for interpersonal relations programs	.22
Need for community involvement programs	− .10

overall dropout rate, and minority students in these schools were more likely to drop out than nonminority students.

Student suspensions in the junior high schools were not related to achievement in the expected way. Overall student suspension rate showed no correlation with achievement, and the disparity of minority student suspension rate was positively related to student achievement. This means that higher achieving schools were more likely to suspend minority students than nonminority students, but there was little racial discrepancy in suspension rates in the lower achieving schools.

The level of minority participation in student activities showed a high negative correlation with achievement in the junior high schools. Minority students were less likely to participate in student activities in the higher achieving schools, whereas lower achieving schools had a higher rate of minority participation in student activites. The racial composition of the neighborhood in which the school was located was postulated as a possible intervening variable that could help to explain the negative correlation. The percent of minority students attending each school prior to desegregation was used as a proxy for neighborhood racial composition. Controlling for neighborhood composition reduced the correlation between minority participation and achievement to − .42. Another explanation for this unexpected relationship is the possibility that in the higher achieving schools, minority students had to spend more time on school work and therefore had less time for extacurricular activities.

The rate of crisis team responses was moderately related to school achievement. Higher achieving schools tended to have fewer incidents of a racial nature requiring a response by the human crisis team. There was no relationship between the rate of incident reports and school achievement, indicating that incidents of student misbehavior were equally high at high and low achieving schools.

Only three of the eight subjective indexes of school climate were related to school achievement at the junior high level. Perceived racial tension was moderately negatively correlated with achievement. Lower achieving schools were perceived to have higher levels of racial tension than were higher achieving schools. Higher achieving junior high schools were more likely to make use of multicultural materials and were slightly more likely to be perceived as needing interpersonal relations programs.

At the high school level there was a somewhat different pattern of relationships between school climate indexes and school achievement level, as shown in Table 12. Attendance rate and overall participation in student activities were positively related to school achievement. Objective indexes showing negative correlations with achievement were suspensions, dropouts, incident reports, and, to a lesser extent, crisis team responses. Lower achieving high schools generally had more suspensions, dropouts, incident reports, and crisis team responses.

Minority participation in student activities was negatively correlated with

Table 12. Correlations of School Climate Indexes with
Overall School Achievement for the Senior High
Schools (1978–1981)

Indexes	Correlation
Objective	
Student suspensions	− .48
Disparity of minority suspensions	.32
Student dropouts	− .42
Disparity of minority dropouts	.62
Attendance rate	.59
Incident reports	− .44
Crisis team responses	− .20
Participation in student activities	.37
Minority participation in student activities	− .40
Subjective	
Racial tension	− .37
Use of multicultural materials	− .08
Interest in multicultural awareness workshops	− .06
Need for multicultural awareness programs	− .23
Interest in stress management workshops	.29
Need for crisis prevention programs	− .28
Need for interpersonal relations programs	− .13
Need for community involvement programs	− .18

achievement, as was the case in the junior high schools, although the strength of the relationship was not as high. Controlling for the neighborhood composition reduced the correlation to − .30, but did not completely eliminate it. At the senior high school level, as at the junior high level, there was a tendency for less minority participation in student activities in higher achieving schools.

The disparities in minority student suspensions and dropouts were related to school achievement at the high school level. At high achieving schools, minorities had a higher dropout rate than nonminority students. There was less difference in the dropout rates of the two groups at lower achieving schools. The discrepancy in suspension rates was also related to achievement in the same way, although the correlation was not as high. These results show that discrepancies of minority dropout and suspension rates were related to overall achievement, but the data were not available to examine their relationship to minority pupil achievement.

Among the subjective indexes of school climate at the senior high level, only racial tension as perceived by the school personnel was related to school achievement. This relationship, equal in magnitude and direction to the junior

high correlation, indicated that there was more perceived racial tension at the lower achieving schools. The other subjective indexes were not related to school achievement.

In order to identify the best subset of variables related to overall school achievement, multiple-regression analyses were computed for the two groups of schools. Results of these analyses are shown in Table 13. In the junior high schools, the rate of participation in extracurricular activities by minority students and the perceived racial tension in the school were the two variables significantly related to school achievement in the regression equation. The other variables did not significantly increase the percent of variance in school achievement accounted for.

At the senior high school level, three variables accounted for 62% of the variance in achievement. These variables were the disparity of minority dropouts, the overall dropout rate, and the perceived racial tension. Racial tension was a significant variable in the multiple regression equation at both the junior high and senior high levels.

In interpreting these relationships between school climate measures and school achievement, no causation has been demonstrated. In the case of the relationship, found in junior and senior high schools, between racial tension and achievement, it is likely that neither factor was directly caused by the other. Instead, the observed correlation probably resulted from the interplay between these two factors and many other variables. More research in desegregated schools using school as the unit of analysis is needed to identify more clearly the direction of causation.

In spite of the absence of demonstrated causation, certain conclusions can be drawn. At the junior and senior high school levels, higher achieving schools were characterized by higher attendance rates, lower overall dropout rates, lower levels of perceived racial tension, a greater tendency to suspend minority stu-

Table 13. Multiple Regression of School Climate Indices with School Achievement (1978–1981)

Climate index	Simple R	Multiple R	R^2	R^2 Change	Significance
		Junior High			
Minority participation in student activities	.67	.67	.45	—	.009
Racial tension	− .33	.79	.62	.17	.007
		Senior High			
Disparity of minority dropouts	.62	.62	.38	—	.044
Dropout rate	− .42	.70	.49	.11	.041
Racial tension	− .37	.79	.62	.13	.027

dents, and less participation by minority pupils in student activities. Minority students were less likely to drop out of high achieving junior high schools, but more likely to drop out of the high achieving senior high schools. The high achieving senior high schools were characterized by less overall student mis-behavior, and the high achieving junior highs had fewer racial incidents and greater use of multicultural materials.

DISCUSSION

Significant gains in reading and mathematics were made by students of the New Castle County School District during the first 3 years of school desegre-gation. The gains were widespread and consistent throughout the district, but the greatest gains were made by elementary school pupils, on the mathematics subtest, and during the first year of desegregation. These findings were the same for the analysis based on all schools in the district using school mean as the unit of analysis, and for the analysis based on the sample of cooperating students using individual achievement scores as the unit of analysis. An additional finding based on the latter analysis was that greater gains were made by black students.

These gains cannot be attributed solely to the implementation of school desegregation; other factors must also be considered. One possible explanation for the gains was the teachers' strike that closed the schools for 6 weeks during the school year. According to this hypothesis, after the schools reopened the teachers eliminated many of the frills from their teaching and concentrated their instruction in the basics to make up for lost time. This had the effect of raising test scores on the spring test. There was not enough evidence to test the validity of this theory.

Another factor that coincided with the first year of school desegregation was the introduction of the new competency-based curriculum. It could be argued that this factor was at least partially responsible for the test score increase, but again the evidence was not sufficient for testing this theory. Still another expla-nation for the gains was that the fall test scores were low because they were administered before the students had time to adjust to their newly desegregated schools. Evidence against this argument is the fact that the entire district averaged above national norms at the first test period.

In the second and third years of school desegregation there was an overall gain of 4 points, with most of it coming in the third year. Achievement scores continued to rise in spite of the fact that overall enrollment and percent white were declining. The racial composition of the district changed from 74% white in 1978–1979 to 70% white in 1980–1981.

At the junior and senior high schools, a number of variables were char-acteristic of higher achieving schools. These included high attendance rates, lower overall dropout rates, greater suspension rates for minority pupils, lower

levels of minority participation in student activities, and lower levels of racial tension. The school level achievement scores were determined primarily by the 65% to 90% majority white pupils, so no conclusion should be drawn that these variables were related to minority pupil achievement.

The generalizability of the findings of this study is limited by the unique aspects of the school desegregation situation in New Castle County. The 6-week teacher strike and the implementation of the new curriculum were two factors in particular that influenced achievement test scores in unknown ways. However, certain conclusions can be drawn. There was a distinct increase in districtwide achievement over the 3 years, especially for elementary pupils, for black pupils, and in mathematics. This study demonstrates that metropolitan desegregation can provide the opportunity for attaining significant gains in achievement.

REFERENCES

Brookover, W. B., Schweitzer, J. H., Schneider, J. M., Beady, C. H., Flood, P. K., & Wisenbaker, J. M. (1978). Elementary school social climate and school achievement. *American Educational Research Journal, 15,* 301–318.

Brookover, W. B., Beady, C., Flood, P., Schweitzer, J., & Wisenbaker, J. (1979). *School social systems and student achievement: Schools can make a difference.* South Hadley, MA: Bergin.

Crain, R. L., & Mahard, R. E. (1982). *Desegregation plans that raise black achievement: A review of the research.* Santa Monica, CA: Rand Corporation.

Forehand, G. A., Ragosta, M., & Rock, D. A. (1976). *Conditions and processes of effective school desegregation.* Princeton, NJ: Educational Testing Service.

Hanks, M. P., & Eckland, B. K. (1976). Athletics and social participation in the educational attainment process. *Sociology of Education, 49,* 217–294.

Hawley, W. D. (1980). *Increasing the effectiveness of desegregated schools: Lessons from research.* Durham, NC: Center for Educational Policy, Duke University.

Mackenzie, D. E. (1983). Research for school improvement: An appraisal of some recent trends. *Educational Researcher, 12,* 5–17.

Mehrens, W. A., & Lehmann, I. J. (1973). *Measurement and evaluation in education and psychology.* New York: Holt, Rinehart, & Winston.

New Castle County School District. (1979, July). *Results of the California Achievement Tests, school year 1978–79.* Wilmington, DE.

New Castle County School District (1980, July). *Results of the California Achievement Tests, school year 1979–80.* Wilmington, DE.

New Castle County School District (1981, August). *Results of the California Achievement Tests, school year 1980–81.* Wilmington, DE.

Patchen, M., Davidson, J. D., Hofmann, G., & Brown, W. R. (1977). Determinants of students' interracial behavior and opinion change. *Sociology of Education, 50,* 55–75.

Rehberg, R. A., & Schafer, W. E. (1968). Participation in interscholastic athletics and college expectations. *American Journal of Sociology, 73,* 732–740.

Rowan, B., Bossert, S. T., & Dwyer, D. C. (1983). Research on effective schools: A cautionary note. *Educational Researcher, 12,* 24–31.

Schafer, W. E., & Armer, M. (1968). Athletes are not inferior students. *Transaction 6,* 21–26.

Spady, W. G. (1970). Lament for the letterman: Effects of peer status and extracurricular activities on goals and achievement. *American Journal of Sociology, 75,* 680–702.

Spady, W. G. (1971). Status, achievement, and motivation in the American high school. *School Review,* 379–403.

8

Parents' and Students' Attitude Changes Related to School Desegregation in New Castle County, Delaware

MARGARET A. PARSONS

Although many researchers have investigated the relation between school desegregation and academic achievement for minority and majority students, few have explored the relation between school desegregation and attitudinal variables. This latter category of outcomes is of critical importance for intrinsic reasons and for effects relative to academic achievement. Among questions that need to be examined are the following:

What attitudes do parents have regarding school desegregation prior to implementation? What attitudes do students have regarding school desegregation prior to implementation? In what ways, if any, do these attitudes change following implementation of desegregation? When do the changes, if any, occur (i.e., immediately following implementation, or after one or more years)?

In what ways, if any, do the changes differ for different groups of students (e.g., white, black, male, female)? In what ways, if any, do the changes differ for different groups of parents (e.g., low-income, middle-income, white, black)? Is there an observable relationship between the attitudes of parents and those of their children regarding school desegregation?

Examination is also needed of a second category of attitudinal variables in relation to school desegregation outcomes. This category includes such factors as attitudes about the importance of education, the quality of the school and its academic climate, students' self-concept regarding educational ability, students' academic goals and future aspirations, and parents' perceptions of their child's

MARGARET A. PARSONS ● Greater Flint Health Maintenance Organization, Flint, Michigan 48504.

academic performance, as well as their expectations and goals for the child. Information is needed not only on overall effects, but also on differential effects.

Questions that need to be examined include the following: What relationship, if any, exists between school desegregation and the educational self-concept of students? In what ways, if any, are the relationships different for majority students when compared with minority students? What relationship, if any, exists between school desegregation and academic climate or overall quality?

If changes in school climate are observed, in what ways, if any, do these changes have differential effects for different groups of students (e.g., white, black, elementary, secondary)? If one change associated with school desegregation appears to be an increase in students' future goals and aspirations, to what extent is this the case for different groups of students (e.g., black, white, male, female)?

More information is needed regarding changes related to desegregation implementation, and additional factors must also be examined as they interact with the implementation process. These factors include the community atmosphere regarding desegregation; the attitudes and behaviors of school district administrators, teachers, and other school staff members; and the role of the media. A better understanding of these additional factors can help to insure the successful implementation and administration of a school desegregation plan.

School and community characteristics should also be taken into account in examining attitudinal outcome and data. Relevant questions would include: What is the attitude (i.e., hostile, favorable, or neutral) of the community, or significant segments of the community, toward desegregation? What is the nature of the desegregation plan (e.g., voluntary, court-ordered, or consent decree)? What is the attitude of school district administrators and staff members? What school and/or community resources are available to support the implementation of the desegregation plan? What is the attitude of the media toward the desegregation plan?

Another set of characteristics to be taken into account in interpreting the findings of desegregation outcomes research are those of the families—parents and students—involved in the schools. Although these characteristics are generally not changeable, they should be taken into account in designing and implementing a school desegregation plan. Factors in this category would include the student's race, age, gender, and grade level at the time of initial implementation. Also included would be the parents' socioeconomic status and place of residence. All of these characteristics may interact with the overall desegregation plan and may be related to attitudinal outcomes.

Research on attitudinal outcomes is based on the assumption that school desegregation provides the opportunity for attitudinal change by increasing the opportunity for contact among students of different racial groups. For example, the amount of interaction among students of different racial groups has been

found to be the best predictor of interracial attitudes and behaviors, with more positive relationships existing among students who worked with members of another race (Slavin & Madden, 1979). Similarly, in a survey of Milwaukee schools, it was found that those students who already interacted as friends with members of other racial groups were more positive toward the idea of school desegregation, and, in fact, indicated a preference for attending an integrated school (*The Milwaukee Journal,* 1976).

Other studies have found positive changes in understanding others during the first 2 years of desegregation (Beers & Readon, 1974) and significant decreases in ethnic prejudice among black, white, and Mexican-American students following desegregation (Sheehan, 1980). In the Sheehan study, it was found that there were decreases in prejudice toward both the students' own ethnic group and toward other ethnic groups.

One question of concern in examining the assumption that increased contact will result in more positive racial attitudes is the nature of that contact. Much of the work in this area is based on Allport's (1954) theory of equal status contact conditions. Recent work has suggested that Allport's conditions for equal status contact may be necessary but not sufficient for improving interracial attitudes and relationships (Mercer, Iadicola, & Moore, 1980). For example, Cohen (1975, 1980) contends that race alone is a status condition in this society, and that additional strategies are needed to increase equal status interactions in the classroom. Many of the small group cooperative learning strategies that have been developed for classroom use (Johnson & Johnson, 1979) focus on the need to maximize equal status interactions in order to improve racial attitudes.

Closely related to attitudes toward members of other racial groups are attitudes toward school desegregation itself. Several studies have examined the attitudes of both students and parents toward school desegregation. Students have expressed positive attitudes toward desegregation as a means of addressing the problem of perceived racism in the school setting, reducing stereotypes about persons of other races, and learning to get along better with others in a multiracial environment (Fort Wayne Urban League, 1977; Regens & Bullock, 1979; Rosenthal, 1979). Students who have already experienced interracial contact are also more favorable toward school desegregation (*The Milwaukee Journal,* 1976).

Parental attitudes toward school desegregation appear to be related to the duration of desegregation, with opposition subsiding after the initial implementation year (Hawley, 1979; Serow & Solomon, 1979). Several factors have been found to be important in reducing parental opposition and improving the success of implementation. One important factor is the involvement of parents and other members of the community in the planning process prior to desegregation and in activities of the schools themselves during the initial stages of desegregation. Parents of students involved in magnet school programs have been found to be more supportive of busing for desegregation purposes than parents whose children

were not involved in such programs (Loveridge, 1978). Although parents' racial attitudes and their attitudes toward school desegregation appear to have some influence on their children's attitudes (Bullock & Stewart, 1977), this influence was found by St. John (1975) to decrease as students become older.

The influence of media coverage on parental attitudes has been examined by Allen & Sears (1979), who found that negative press reports of desegregation planning were followed by unfavorable reactions by white parents toward desegregation. The researchers' suggestion was that supportive media coverage and positive actions on the part of school officials could be instrumental in improving parental attitudes toward desegregation and in reducing uncertainty and fear surrounding desegregation implementation. For minority parents, desegregation is more likely to be seen as a means of improving educational outcomes for their children (Beck & Sobol, 1978; St. John, 1975), but concerns are often expressed about the disproportionate burden of transportation that frequently results for minority students under a desegregation plan (Alexander, 1979; Altevogt & Nusbaumer, 1978).

Student and parent characteristics that have been found to be important in outcomes related to racial attitudes include race (Schofield, 1981), parents' educational level (Alston & Crouch, 1978), and the child's grade level at the time of desegregation implementation. Of these variables, grade level and race have been examined most extensively. Results suggest that attitudes are positively related to grade level, so that more positive outcomes are found when desegregation begins in the early elementary grades (Erbe, 1977; Regens & Bullock, 1979).

Research in the area of educational attitudes indicates that school desegregation can be accompanied by an improvement in student self-esteem and sense of control within the academic setting. Beers and Readon (1974), for example, found an increase in self-esteem and interest in school among grade school students in a desegregated school system, whereas Sheehan (1980) reported increased self-esteem among black students and increased sense of control among black and Mexican-American students following school desegregation.

A major difficulty with most research on the outcomes of school desegregation is the lack of long-term involvement. Studies are either cross-sectional, comparing students in a desegregated school setting with similar students in a segregated setting, or they focus only on changes during the first year of desegregation. There is also a need to look more closely at not only the overall attitudinal outcomes but also the relation between these outcomes and student, parent, and community characteristics (Schofield, 1981).

The study described here focused on racial and educational outcomes for parents and students in a large metropolitan school district following the implementation of a court-ordered desegregation plan. Attitudes were measured before the implementation of the plan and for 3 consecutive years following implementation, in order to examine the continuing effects of a desegregation plan.

BACKGROUND

Following prolonged litigation, the school districts in New Castle County, Delaware, were ordered to implement a metropolitan school desegregation plan. These districts included the inner-city Wilmington school district and the 10 surrounding suburban districts. Because the court had found the city and the suburban districts to be involved in the segregation measures, all districts were ordered to be involved in the desegregation remedy. This order included the dissolution of the individual school district boundaries and administrations and the formation of one countywide school district, with one central administrative structure. In September 1978, this reorganization was finalized and students were reassigned to schools within the new district to achieve proportional racial representation in all of the schools within the county.

Although community opposition to desegregation had been generally prolonged and bitter in the suburban districts, and desegregation had been resisted by the Delaware state government, actual implementation was relatively successful and without major incident. The first year of desegregation proceeded generally peacefully, with the exception of scattered demonstrations by parents and students in the spring preceding implementation and in the fall of the first year. The year was also marked by a 6-week strike by teachers in the new district over such issues as salary, workload, and reassignments due to the new desegregation plan. Significant district administration issues during the first year were the new tax rate for the single district, the pupil assignment plan, adoption of a uniform disciplinary code, and decisions about school closings.

School desegregation continued through the second year without major difficulties, although parents and other community members expressed concern about discipline issues in the junior and senior high schools. Financial difficulties occurred as the district experienced a continued decline in enrollment, coupled with a reduced tax rate. School closings were considered in response to the financial constraints but aroused considerable public opposition.

In a progress evaluation commissioned by the Delaware State Board of Education, it was noted that desegregation had been initiated without major racial disturbances. Teachers and administrators in the new district were commended for fostering positive educational goals, adapting to new students, and making efforts to provide an equal educational opportunity for all students in the county. Recommendations were made for improving communication throughout the single-district administrative structure, raising teaching staff morale, and increasing participation of minority parents in school activities.

During the third year of desegregation, the district continued to experience financial difficulties due to a continuing decline in enrollment, a low tax rate, and decreasing financial support from the state. The possibility of staff layoffs and concern for affirmative action in hiring and promotion were major personnel issues. Black parents and other members of the black community expressed

concern about disproportionate numbers of suspensions, following desegregation, for black students in some areas of the district, whereas Hispanic parents worried about the possible loss of bilingual programs that emphasized cultural identity and heritage.

In an outside commissioned evaluation of the second and third years of school desegregation, questions were raised regarding the loss of funding for teaching staff in special programs, the disproportionate suspension rates for minority students, the loss of morale among district principals, and the use of achievement test scores. Recommendations were made regarding a revision of the disciplinary code, implementation of alternative disciplinary programs, achievement testing for students in all grades, and the need for more long-term planning regarding personnel procedures.

During the fourth year of desegregation, following additional litigation, the single countywide district was divided into four autonomous school districts, each with its own superintendent and elected board of education. These new districts roughly paralleled the attendance areas in the single district. The State Board of Education was charged with the overall responsibility for assuring desegregation in pupil assignments under the new four-district division.

METHOD

In 1979, prior to desegregation implementation, negotiations to obtain permission for data collection were conducted by the research team with the superintendent in each of the 11 districts. Due to both the uncertainty regarding the final desegregation plan to be implemented and strong community opposition to desegregation, only the superintendent from Wilmington initially agreed to participate. After extensive discussions, four additional suburban district superintendents gave permission for data collection in their districts. Thus, a total of 5 of the 11 districts in New Castle County participated in the study.

Although these districts constituted only a portion of the final single-county district, they represented a range of racial and socioeconomic characteristics. With the inclusion of the Wilmington and De La Warr districts, the final sample covered more than 75% of the minority students and 40% of the majority students within the county schools. The Wilmington school district, located in eastern New Castle County, was ranked lowest of the 11 districts in socioeconomic status. This district also had the largest proportion of minority residents: 44% in 1976, prior to desegregation. The suburban De La Warr district, adjacent to Wilmington, was made up largely of blue-collar working-class families and ranked 10th in the county in socioeconomic status. The De La Warr population was 34% minority. The Marshallton-McKean district ranked 6th in the county in socioeconomic status and contained only a 5% minority population. The Mt. Pleasant district was 5th in socioeconomic status, with a 3% minority population. The Newark district, which included the residential areas surrounding the Uni-

versity of Delaware, was 4th in the county in socioeconomic status and also had only a small minority population.

Questionnaire Development

All attitude data were collected through questionnaires sent to parents and students. These questionnaires contained items requesting extensive demographic data, as well as items designed to measure several dimensions of racial and educational attitudes. Items were developed through an extensive process that included the use of items from previously published or developed scales, and, where necessary, the use of new items to measure certain dimensions not covered by previously developed scales. The student questionnaire was piloted on a group of elementary students to check for appropriate reading level. After initial questionnaire development, meetings were held with each district superintendent to allow for their review of the questionnaires. Public meetings for questionnaire review were also held in each of the participating districts, and some revisions were made before final permission for use of the questionnaires was given.

After the initial round of data collection, factor analyses were run separately for the parent and student questionnaire items. Based on the factor-analysis results, five measures were developed for parents' attitudes and six for students' attitudes. A measure of family social status was also developed. All measures were in the form of 5-point Likert scales, ranging from 1.00 (least positive) to 5.00 (most positive). These measures were as follows:

I. *Racial attitudes*
    A. *Parents' racial attitudes.* Measures attitudes about relations and interactions between blacks and whites. Higher scores indicate more positive attitudes toward race relations.
    B. *Parents' attitudes toward school desegregation.* Measures attitudes about the desirability of school desegregation in general and for New Castle County in particular. Higher scores indicate a more positive attitude toward school desegregation.
    C. *Students' racial attitudes.* Measures attitudes about relations between blacks and whites and interactions between black students and white students. Items are similar to those used in parents' racial attitudes scale. Higher scores indicate more positive attitudes toward race relations.
II. *Educational attitudes*
    A. *Parents' perceived school quality.* Measures parents' attitudes regarding the quality of their child's school. Higher scores indicate more positive perceptions.
    B. *Parents' evaluation and expectation of child's performance.* Measures parents' evaluation of their child's academic performance and abilities. Higher scores indicate more positive evaluations.
    C. *Parents' perception of importance of education.* Measures parents'

attitudes about the importance of educational attainment for their child. Higher scores indicate greater emphasis on the importance of education.

D. *Students' educational self-concept.* Measures students' self-evaluation of academic ability and perceptions of parents' and teachers' evaluations of students' academic ability. Higher scores indicate more positive evaluations.

E. *Students' future aspirations.* Measures students' academic goals and their perceptions of the goals held for them by parents and teachers. Higher scores indicate more ambitious academic goals.

F. *School academic climate.* Measures school climate in terms of perceived peer and teacher expectations for academic achievement within the school. Higher scores indicate perceptions of greater emphasis on academic attainment in the school.

G. *Students' importance of education.* Measures students' attitudes about the importance of educational attainment and perceptions of parents' values regarding educational attainment. Higher scores indicate greater emphasis on the importance of education.

H. *Students' sense of control.* Measures students' attitudes about their ability to control their academic achievement and goals. Higher scores indicate a greater sense of personal control.

III. *Social status.* Measures family social status based on parents' perceptions of relative education, income, and prestige. Higher scores indicate higher social status.

Sample and Data Collection

Development of a sampling design was limited by two major constraints prior to the onset of the study. The first of these constraints was the need to obtain data in the spring of 1978, before implementation of the desegregation plan, as a baseline to examine attitude changes following implementation. The second constraint was the uncertainty of pupil assignments and of the specific nature of the final desegregation plan. Thus, when setting up the original sampling design, the researchers were unable to select a sample stratified on whether the students would be bused to school for desegregation during the following year. It was also impossible to take into account school assignments following desegregation. Given these constraints, a decision was made to sample randomly from all families with students enrolled in the five districts participating in the study, with no stratification on variables related to school assignment following desegregation.

Lists of names and addresses for enrolled students and their families were provided by the five districts participating in the study. A decision was made to mail questionnaires to students' homes rather than to administer questionnaires to students in their classrooms. There were several reasons for this decision. First of these was the desire to eliminate the possible effects on the students of

teacher bias. Second was the need to administer the questionnaire only to students whose parents had given consent. This specified condition would have created difficulties for the classroom teachers, as not all students in a classroom would be filling out the questionnaires. Finally, data were needed for both students and their parents, and it was easier to have matching student–parent pairs when the questionnaires were sent directly to the homes. Each family received a packet containing a cover letter explaining the purposes of the study, an informed consent form, and student and parent questionnaires.

The initial round of data collection occurred during the spring of 1978. Questionnaire packets were mailed to 16,500 families in New Castle County. Telephone followup was also conducted for those families who did not respond to the original mailing. A total of 2,333 usable pairs of parent and student questionnaires were obtained for this first round, for a response rate of 14%. For each of the 3 years following desegregation implementation (1979, 1980, and 1981), questionnaires were again sent in the spring to those families who had previously responded. New families were not added to the mailing list after the first round, and graduating seniors were deleted. The attrition rate also reflected those families who moved from the district or sent their children to private schools after the first year. In the spring of 1979, the first year following desegregation, a total of 1,027 usable questionnaire pairs were received. In 1980, 492 questionnaire pairs were returned by those who had responded in both of the 2 previous years. In 1981, a final sample of 298 student/parent questionnaire pairs was obtained. This final sample included only New Castle County students and parents for whom complete questionnaire data were available for all 4 years of the study.

The final sample contained 14% black families, 82% white families, and 4% for whom race was either "other, or unknown." Compared to the population distribution in the school district, black families were slightly underrepresented, and white families were slightly overrepresented. The student sample was relatively evenly divided between males and females, but the parent sample was almost three-quarters female. The final student sample distribution by grade showed a fairly even distribution from grades 5 through 12. Because no new students were added to the sample after 1978, no first-, second-, or third-grade students, and only 3 fourth-grade students were included in the final sample. Residents of the former De La Warr and Wilmington school districts were underrepresented in the final sample, whereas residents of the suburban districts of Marshallton-McKean, Mt. Pleasant, and Newark were somewhat overrepresented. The mean age of the parents was 43 years.

Data Analysis

Because data were available for the same subjects at four points in time, repeated-measures analyses of variance were used. These analyses examined (1) overall changes in the dependent attitude measures across time (2) overall group

differences based on the several intervening variables, and (3) group-by-repeated-measures interactions for each pair of attitude measures and intervening variables. These interaction measures indicated whether differential changes in attitudes occurred over time for any given intervening variable. The intervening variables examined were race, child's grade level immediately prior to desegregation implementation, gender, former school district (prior to desegregation and district reorganization), parents' perceived social status, and parents' initial attitude toward school desegregation.

RESULTS

Overall, attitudes among parents and students in the group of 298 respondents changed somewhat during the first year of desegregation implementation and then stabilized at these levels during the second year. Additional slight attitudinal changes were evident during the third year of desegregation. Specifically, racial attitudes of both parents and students became slightly less positive immediately following desegregation implementation and then remained unchanged for the next two years. For parents, the most notable changes were in attitudes toward school desegregation and in perceived school quality. Attitudes toward desegregation became substantially more positive immediately following desegregation implementation, improved slightly again during the second year, and then became slightly less positive during the third year. Parents' perceptions of school quality declined substantially during the first year of desegregation and then improved very slightly during the next 2 years.

Students' perceptions of their school academic climate also became slightly less positive during the first year of desegregation and then remained the same during the next 2 years. Both students' educational self-concept and their view of the importance of education showed a slightly different pattern, remaining unchanged for the first 2 years of desegregation and then declining slightly during the third year.

Additional results are presented separately for racial attitudes and for educational attitudes. Under each set of attitudinal variables, the overall changes across time are presented for parents and for students. Following this, the effects of each of the intervening variables on the separate attitudinal variables are discussed. Overall changes are presented and data on individual attitudinal variables and the accompanying intervening variables are presented in tables for each section.

Racial Attitudes

Changes in parents' racial attitudes over time were relatively slight, but there were significant effects for several of the intervening variables examined (Tables 1 and 2). Parents' racial attitudes became slightly less positive immediately following desegregation implementation and then showed no further change

Table 1.   Parents' Racial Attitudes and Attitudes toward Desegregation and Students' Racial Attitudes

	Year				F
Scale	1978	1979	1980	1981	Repeated measures
Parents					
Racial attitudes	3.54	3.46	3.46	3.43	4.37*
Attitudes toward desegregation	2.43	2.70	2.77	2.63	20.93*
Students					
Racial attitudes	3.83	3.67	3.61	3.56	15.52*

Note. Data reported are mean scale scores, ranging from 1.00 (least positive) to 5.00 (most positive).
* $p < .05$.

during the succeeding years of desegregation. For each year in which attitudes were measured, black parents had more positive racial attitudes than did white parents. Racial attitudes were also less positive among parents from the suburban districts of Mt. Pleasant, Newark, and Marshallton-McKean than they were among parents from either De La Warr or Wilmington. Parents from the middle

Table 2.   Parents' Racial Attitudes

					F		
	Year						Groups ×
Group	1978	1979	1980	1981	Groups	Repeated measures	repeated measures
Race					30.82*	1.46	0.35
Black	3.93	3.90	3.90	3.89			
White	3.45	3.38	3.35	3.33			
Student's grade level					1.46	2.58	0.77
Elementary	3.58	3.48	3.53	3.51			
Junior high	3.53	3.45	3.42	3.38			
Senior high	3.34	3.36	3.30	3.25			
Social status					5.71*	1.04	1.02
Low	3.60	3.67	3.74	3.55			
Middle	3.42	3.37	3.31	3.31			
High	3.67	3.54	3.60	3.56			
Former district					12.42*	1.09	0.72
Wilmington	4.04	4.04	4.02	3.98			
De La Warr	3.97	4.20	3.85	3.95			
Mt. Pleasant	3.44	3.44	3.42	3.34			
Newark	3.57	3.44	3.44	3.42			
Marshallton-McKean	3.22	3.13	3.13	3.18			

Note. Data reported are mean scale scores, ranging from 1.00 (least positive) to 5.00 (most positive).
* $p < .05$.

social status group reported the least positive racial attitudes. And finally, mothers and fathers did not differ in their reported racial attitudes. There was a positive relationship between parents' racial attitudes and their initial attitudes toward school desegregation; that is, parents with the most positive racial attitudes also had the most positive initial attitude toward school desegregation and parents with the least positive racial attitudes had the least positive initial attitude toward school desegregation.

The most noticeable change in parents' attitudes during the course of the study was with respect to school desegregation itself (Table 3). These attitudes were significantly more positive following implementation of the desegregation order than they had been in the year preceding implementation. Further, attitudes toward desegregation continued at this improved level during the next 2 years of desegregation. This pattern of increased positive attitudes toward desegregation generally held when the different intervening variables were taken into account. Parents did differ initially in the value of their attitudes toward desegregation, and this gap did not close during the time of the study. For example, black parents' attitudes toward school desegregation were consistently more

Table 3. Parents' Attitudes toward School Desegregation

| | | Year | | | | F | |
Group	1978	1979	1980	1981	Groups	Repeated measures	Groups × repeated measures
Race					38.58*	6.53*	2.07
Black	3.17	3.18	3.39	3.19			
White	2.27	2.60	2.64	2.51			
Student's grade level					2.36	11.58*	0.62
Elementary	2.43	2.73	2.87	2.69			
Junior high	2.48	2.73	2.73	2.62			
Senior high	2.16	2.44	2.45	2.33			
Social status					3.46*	3.85*	1.15
Low	3.07	3.32	3.10	3.18			
Middle	2.40	2.62	2.72	2.52			
High	2.41	2.75	2.81	2.72			
Former district					9.27*	3.81*	1.15
Wilmington	3.33	3.24	3.39	3.29			
De La Warr	3.25	3.35	3.45	3.40			
Mt. Pleasant	2.43	2.76	2.70	2.63			
Newark	2.28	2.55	2.64	2.50			
Marshallton-McKean	2.22	2.61	2.77	2.62			

Note. Data reported are mean scale scores, ranging from 1.00 (least positive) to 5.00 (most positive).
* $p < .05$.

Table 4.   Students' Racial Attitudes

	Year				F		Groups × repeated measures
Group	1978	1979	1980	1981	Groups	Repeated measures	
Race					51.36*	2.25	4.60*
Black	4.23	4.36	4.28	4.28			
White	3.74	3.53	3.46	3.41			
Student's grade level					5.04*	11.40*	0.61
Elementary	3.93	3.84	3.74	3.69			
Junior high	3.76	3.54	3.50	3.46			
Senior high	3.70	3.37	3.44	3.35			
Social status					1.23	4.42*	1.28
Low	3.90	3.74	3.53	3.94			
Middle	3.79	3.60	3.58	3.46			
High	3.87	3.74	3.66	3.65			
Former district					10.63*	4.34*	1.34
Wilmington	4.20	4.31	4.26	4.36			
De La Warr	4.30	4.35	4.10	3.87			
Mt. Pleasant	3.70	3.46	3.41	3.31			
Newark	3.86	3.67	3.62	3.54			
Marshallton-McKean	3.62	3.46	3.35	3.35			

Note. Data reported are mean scale scores, ranging from 1.00 (least positive) to 5.00 (most positive).
* $p < .05$.

positive than those of white parents. For black parents, there was also a slight deviation from the pattern of change, with more positive attitudes occurring during the second year after implementation rather than during the first year. Parents from Wilmington and De La Warr also had more positive attitudes than did parents from the other suburban districts (Mt. Pleasant, Newark, and Mar-shallton-McKean). Social status was a significant intervening variable, with parents from the low social status group having more positive attitudes toward school desegregation than parents from either the middle or high social status groups. And, as in the case of parents' racial attitudes, there were no differences between mothers and fathers in attitudes toward school desegregation.

As with parents, students became slightly less positive in their racial attitudes in the year immediately following desegregation implementation and then showed no significant further change during the next 2 years (Table 4). Race, initial grade level, former district, and parents' initial attitudes toward desegregation were all significant intervening variables relative to students' racial attitudes. For each year measured, black students had more positive racial attitudes than did white students, as was the case with their parents. Also similar to their

parents, students from Wilmington and De La Warr had the most positive racial attitudes each year, whereas students from the suburban districts of Mt. Pleasant and Marshallton-McKean had the least positive attitudes. For each year, racial attitudes were most positive for elementary students, less positive for junior high students, and least positive for senior high students. This is in contrast to parents' racial attitudes, which were not affected by their child's grade level. Although parents' attitudes were affected to some extent by their social status, students' attitudes were not. Male and female students did not differ significantly in their reported racial attitudes. For students, there was a significant positive relationship between their parents' initial attitude toward school desegregation and their own racial attitudes.

Educational Attitudes

The most significant change in parents' educational attitudes was in their perceptions of school quality (Tables 5 and 6). Perceived school quality dropped noticeably in the year immediately following desegregation implementation and did not recover during the next 2 years. Although there was some effect for intervening variables, in general this pattern held even when the intervening variables were taken into account. The two intervening variables that were significant were race and former school district. Black parents and white parents had approximately the same perceptions of school quality prior to desegregation and reported the same drop in perceived school quality immediately following

Table 5.   Parents' and Students' Educational Attitudes

	Year				F
Scale	1978	1979	1980	1981	Repeated measures
Parents					
Perceived school quality	3.98	3.46	3.53	3.56	45.88*
Evaluation and expectations of child's performance	4.25	4.25	4.24	4.20	1.46
Importance of education	4.71	4.65	4.65	4.65	4.62*
Students					
Educational self-concept	4.27	4.30	4.24	3.90	76.31*
Future aspirations	3.96	4.06	4.03	4.00	2.21
School academic climate	4.25	4.13	4.12	4.13	5.11*
Importance of education	4.61	4.58	4.54	4.49	8.59*
Sense of control	4.37	4.42	4.39	4.36	0.69

Note. Data reported are mean scale scores, ranging from 1.00 (least positive) to 5.00 (most positive).
* $p < .05$.

Table 6.   Parents' Perceived School Quality

	Year				F		
Group	1978	1979	1980	1981	Groups	Repeated measures	Groups × repeated measures
Race					6.30*	19.89*	7.31*
Black	3.97	3.50	3.82	3.98			
White	4.00	3.46	3.47	3.47			
Student's grade level					0.97	27.73*	0.62
Elementary	4.06	3.47	3.57	3.57			
Junior high	3.90	3.41	3.50	3.51			
Senior high	3.93	3.45	3.32	3.58			
Social status					0.38	8.61*	2.93*
Low	3.67	3.67	3.38	3.58			
Middle	4.07	3.38	3.53	3.48			
High	3.92	3.53	3.56	3.65			
Former district					2.48*	4.63*	2.97*
Wilmington	4.03	3.58	3.83	4.02			
De La Warr	3.62	3.69	3.75	3.75			
Mt. Pleasant	3.92	3.53	3.55	3.62			
Newark	4.12	3.41	3.45	3.48			
Marshallton-McKean	3.68	3.44	3.50	3.39			

Note. Data reported are mean scale scores, ranging from 1.00 (least positive) to 5.00 (most positive).
* $p < .05$.

desegregation. For black parents, however, perceptions of school quality improved during the succeeding years of desegregation and in the third year reached the level held prior to desegregation. For white parents, however, the initial decline was not followed by subsequent improvement during the duration of the study. In regard to the quality of education in a former district, parents from the former De La Warr district initially had the least positive perceptions of their school's quality, but these perceptions became slightly more positive immediately following desegregation implementation.

Overall, there were no significant changes in parents' evaluations and expectations regarding their child's academic performance following desegregation (Table 7). Several of the intervening variables did have an observable effect on these attitudes, however. For example, white parents consistently had higher expectations for their child's academic performance than did black parents. Parents from suburban Newark, which included the University of Delaware area, had the highest expectations for their children, whereas parents from Wilmington and De La Warr had the lowest expectations. Social status was also related to parents' expectations for their child's performance, with parents in the high social status group having the highest expectations for their children. Expecta-

Table 7. Parents' Evaluation and Expectations of Students' Performance

	Year				F		
							Groups ×
						Repeated	repeated
Group	1978	1979	1980	1981	Groups	measures	measures
Race					13.19*	2.00	0.55
Black	4.08	3.96	3.97	3.92			
White	4.27	4.29	4.28	4.25			
Student's grade level					5.58*	0.49	2.14*
Elementary	4.35	4.32	4.38	4.35			
Junior high	4.19	4.18	4.12	4.06			
Senior high	4.11	4.21	4.20	4.20			
Social status					20.68*	6.36*	3.05*
Low	4.03	4.00	3.78	3.53			
Middle	4.08	4.13	4.09	4.07			
High	4.45	4.40	4.43	4.40			
Former district					5.49*	2.45	1.29
Wilmington	4.08	3.92	3.90	3.90			
De La Warr	4.17	4.08	3.67	3.83			
Mt. Pleasant	4.24	4.24	4.22	4.18			
Newark	4.35	4.38	4.36	4.30			
Marshallton-McKean	4.09	4.15	4.17	4.16			

Note. Data reported are mean scale scores, ranging from 1.00 (least positive) to 5.00 (most positive).
* $p < .05$.

tions of parents from both the high and the middle social status group remained about the same over time, whereas expectations of parents from the low social status group declined. Grade level also had an effect, with parents of elementary school children having higher expectations for their children than parents of either junior or senior high school students. Mothers and fathers did not differ in their expectations regarding their child's academic performance.

For parents, attitudes about the importance of education declined very slightly immediately following desegregation and then remained unchanged during the next 2 years (Table 8). These attitudes were not significantly affected by race, social status, former school district, or gender. Parents' attitudes were affected by their child's initial grade level, however. Parents of elementary students placed the most importance on education, followed by parents of junior high students. Parents of senior high students expressed the least emphasis on the importance of education. Even for this breakdown by level of schooling, however, scores were relatively high for all parents.

Observable changes in students' educational self-concept did not occur immediately following desegregation implementation (Table 9). During the third

year of desegregation, however, there was a slight drop in this measure for all students in the sample. This pattern of unchanged self-concept until the third year's decline was not significantly affected by any of the intervening variables measured, although some of these variables did account for differences initially and following desegregation. For black students and for students from the low social status group, the decrease in educational self-concept began during the second, rather than the third, year of desegregation. Educational self-concept was more positive among students in the elementary grades than among either junior or senior high school students. Students from the high social status group also had a more positive educational self-concept than students from the low or middle social status groups. Educational self-concept did not vary significantly according to race, gender, or the students' former school district.

With respect to the parents' evaluations of their child's academic performance, no significant change occurred following desegregation. Although race, grade level, former district, and social status all affected parents' evaluations of their child's academic performance, grade level and social status were the only significant factors affecting the students' own educational self-concept.

Table 8.   Parents' Perception of Importance of Education

| | Year | | | | F | | |
Group	1978	1979	1980	1981	Groups	Repeated measures	Groups × repeated measures
Race					0.00	3.06*	0.89
Black	4.72	4.66	4.69	4.61			
White	4.72	4.66	4.65	4.66			
Student's grade level					14.82*	3.81*	1.39
Elementary	4.79	4.71	4.72	4.74			
Junior high	4.71	4.60	4.67	4.63			
Senior high	4.51	4.49	4.39	4.35			
Social status					0.74	2.74*	0.76
Low	4.88	4.73	4.67	4.67			
Middle	4.71	4.60	4.65	4.63			
High	4.70	4.66	4.68	4.67			
Former district					0.58	1.18	0.71
Wilmington	4.68	4.62	4.72	4.61			
De La Warr	4.88	4.91	4.71	4.82			
Mt. Pleasant	4.67	4.66	4.62	4.65			
Newark	4.72	4.62	4.65	4.66			
Marshallton-McKean	4.78	4.64	4.68	4.65			

Note. Data reported are mean scale scores, ranging from 1.00 (least positive) to 5.00 (most positive).
* $p < .05$.

Table 9.   Students' Educational Self-Concept

	Year				F		
Group	1978	1979	1980	1981	Groups	Repeated measures	Groups × repeated measures
Race					1.64	41.78*	2.83*
Black	4.24	4.29	4.04	3.82			
White	4.28	4.30	4.28	3.91			
Student's grade level					5.00*	37.85*	1.26
Elementary	4.37	4.40	4.35	3.97			
Junior high	4.22	4.22	4.15	3.83			
Senior high	4.14	4.23	4.23	3.98			
Social status					8.51*	27.85*	1.04
Low	4.24	4.29	3.98	3.71			
Middle	4.21	4.17	4.16	3.81			
High	4.37	4.44	4.36	4.02			
Former district					2.33	26.26*	2.95*
Wilmington	4.32	4.32	3.93	3.78			
De La Warr	4.13	4.37	4.13	3.83			
Mt. Pleasant	4.22	4.14	4.10	3.81			
Newark	4.34	4.37	4.35	3.96			
Marshallton-McKean	4.14	4.29	4.31	3.91			

Note. Data reported are mean scale scores, ranging from 1.00 (least positive) to 5.00 (most positive).
* $p < .05$.

Overall, the future aspirations of the students in the sample did not change significantly following desegregation (Table 10). For each year, white students had higher future aspirations than black students. Students from Wilmington had the lowest future aspirations, and students from Newark, the highest. Students' future aspirations increased with increasing social status. There was no gender or grade level effect on aspirations.

Findings on students' future aspirations were consistent with those on parents' evaluations and expectations for their child's academic performance. Students' future aspirations and parents' expectations remained essentially unchanged following desegregation. Both factors were positively related to social status and showed consistent patterns in regard to race and former school district.

Students' perceptions of their school's academic climate became slightly less positive immediately following desegregation implementation (Table 11). These perceptions then remained essentially unchanged during the succeeding years of the study. In comparison, parents' perceptions of school quality dropped more than those of the students during the first year of desegregation, and then

Table 10.   Students' Future Aspirations

| | Year | | | | F | | |
Group	1978	1979	1980	1981	Groups	Repeated measures	Groups × repeated measures
Race					16.42*	2.09	1.29
Black	3.59	3.74	3.54	3.67			
White	4.02	4.12	4.11	4.06			
Student's grade level					2.53	2.48	3.06*
Elementary	3.99	4.12	4.16	4.13			
Junior high	3.94	4.01	3.88	3.84			
Senior high	3.96	4.12	4.19	4.27			
Social status					18.63*	1.22	0.61
Low	3.70	3.88	3.61	3.67			
Middle	3.76	3.82	3.83	3.83			
High	4.23	4.37	4.30	4.26			
Former district					7.99*	0.79	1.31
Wilmington	3.36	3.59	3.28	3.45			
De La Warr	3.93	3.87	3.87	4.00			
Mt. Pleasant	3.91	4.18	4.06	4.05			
Newark	4.14	4.17	4.19	4.11			
Marshallton-McKean	3.92	3.97	4.05	4.03			

Note. Data reported are mean scale scores, ranging from 1.00 (least positive) to 5.00 (most positive).
* $p < .05$.

remained unchanged at that lower level in succeeding years. School academic climate was perceived to be somewhat more positive by white students than by black students. Students from Newark generally reported the most positive school academic climate, and students from De La Warr reported the least positive climate. School academic climate was perceived most positively by elementary students, less positively by junior high students, and least positively by senior high students. Social status and gender did not affect students' perceptions of their school's academic climate.

Students' perception of the importance of education decreased consistently but very slightly in each of the years following desegregation implementation (Table 12). The only intervening variable that did not measurably affect students' attitudes regarding the importance of education was social status. For each year, the black students in the sample considered education to be more important than did the white students. Elementary students considered education to be most important, followed by junior high students, and then senior high students, in a pattern similar to parents' attitudes about the importance of education. Education

Table 11. Students' Perception of School Academic Climate

| | | Year | | | | F | |
Group	1978	1979	1980	1981	Groups	Repeated measures	Groups × repeated measures
Race					4.02*	5.46*	0.86
Black	4.23	3.96	4.00	3.99			
White	4.26	4.15	4.13	4.15			
Student's grade level					11.79*	2.77*	1.99
Elementary	4.41	4.32	4.20	4.19			
Junior high	4.17	4.97	4.06	4.10			
Senior high	4.04	3.99	3.99	3.99			
Social status					0.88	2.43	1.22
Low	4.28	4.27	4.00	4.05			
Middle	4.27	4.08	4.12	4.12			
High	4.25	4.23	4.17	4.19			
Former district					2.81*	2.29	0.46
Wilmington	4.17	3.93	4.02	3.93			
De La Warr	4.00	4.00	3.68	3.92			
Mt. Pleasant	4.18	4.07	4.10	4.10			
Newark	4.29	4.22	4.17	4.21			
Marshallton-McKean	4.31	4.09	4.12	4.13			

Note. Data reported are mean scale scores, ranging from 1.00 (least positive) to 5.00 (most positive).
* $p < .05$.

Table 12. Students' Perception of Importance of Education

| | | Year | | | | F | |
Group	1978	1979	1980	1981	Groups	Repeated measures	Groups × repeated measures
Race					10.46*	1.73	3.15*
Black	4.65	4.76	4.70	4.70			
White	4.60	4.55	4.51	4.45			
Student's grade level					28.80*	10.65*	4.22*
Elementary	4.67	4.72	4.66	4.67			
Junior high	4.62	4.49	4.49	4.39			
Senior high	4.34	4.32	4.19	4.05			
Social status					0.85	4.03*	0.64
Low	4.70	4.69	4.78	4.53			
Middle	4.62	4.57	4.52	4.49			
High	4.59	4.57	4.54	4.46			
Former district					3.26*	1.33	1.52
Wilmington	4.61	4.70	4.64	4.73			
De La Warr	4.74	4.86	4.86	4.77			
Mt. Pleasant	4.50	4.49	4.41	4.39			
Newark	4.64	4.56	4.57	4.47			
Marshallton-McKean	4.65	4.62	4.49	4.45			

Note. Data reported are mean scale scores, ranging from 1.00 (least positive) to 5.00 (most positive).
* $p < .05$.

was considered most important by students from De La Warr and least important by students from the Mt. Pleasant district. Female students considered education to be more important than did male students; this was the only significant effect for gender found in the study.

Students' sense of control relative to their academic achievement and future goals did not change overall following desegregation implementation (Table 13). Nor was a sense of control significantly related to former school district, gender, or grade level immediately prior to desegregation. Social status and race were, however, related to differences in a sense of control. Prior to desegregation and in the year following implementation, a sense of control was perceived as higher by white students than by black students. In the second and third years of desegregation, however, black students reported a greater sense of control than did white students. Prior to desegregation, a sense of control was perceived as highest by students from the low social status group. Following desegregation, however, a sense of control was perceived as highest in each succeeding year by students from the high social status group.

Table 13. Students' Sense of Control

| | | | | | | F | |
| | | Year | | | | Repeated | Groups × repeated |
Group	1978	1979	1980	1981	Groups	measures	measures
Race					0.34	1.36	3.31*
Black	4.22	4.28	4.49	4.41			
White	4.40	4.44	4.37	4.35			
Student's grade level					2.11	1.18	1.83
Elementary	4.37	4.47	4.48	4.49			
Junior high	4.40	4.36	4.34	4.27			
Senior high	4.32	4.48	4.24	4.26			
Social status					3.62*	0.38	1.12
Low	4.54	4.42	4.38	4.30			
Middle	4.30	4.30	4.37	4.35			
High	4.45	4.56	4.45	4.43			
Former district					2.28	0.17	0.84
Wilmington	4.21	4.25	4.39	4.35			
De La Warr	4.60	4.53	4.33	4.60			
Mt. Pleasant	4.27	4.41	4.20	4.17			
Newark	4.46	4.46	4.47	4.43			
Marshallton-McKean	4.33	4.42	4.40	4.37			

Note. Data reported are mean scale scores, ranging from 1.00 (least positive) to 5.00 (most positive).
* $p < .05$.

DISCUSSION

Following 3 years of metropolitan school desegregation in New Castle County, Delaware, the overall changes in attitudes among both parents and students participating in the study were slight. Moreover, the observable attitude changes occurred mainly during the year immediately following desegregation implementation. Attitudes did not change significantly in either a positive or negative direction during the succeeding years of desegregation. This finding is significant in light of the prolonged opposition to desegregation in New Castle County prior to implementation, the massive administrative reorganization, and the substantial amount of both student and staff reassignment.

The most noticeable overall attitude changes were those that occurred among parents during the first year of desegregation: a decline in perceived school quality and an improvement in attitudes toward school desegregation itself. The decline in perceived school quality should be considered in light of conditions during the first year of desegregation. Chief of these conditions was a prolonged teachers' strike during the fall of the year. Teachers expressed dissatisfaction over a range of issues, including salary scales, classroom and building reassignment procedures, and additional job expectations resulting from the desegregation order. New curricular and testing programs were also instituted district-wide to replace the programs used previously by the 11 separate former school districts. Thus, it is important to consider any attitude changes in light of all the events occurring in the New Castle County School District at this time, some of which were not directly related to the school desegregation order.

In the introduction to this chapter, several questions were posed regarding the relationship of school desegregation and racial and educational attitudes for parents and students. One question was whether school desegregation was accompanied by significant changes in attitudes on the part of parents and/or students. Overall, the answer for the sample studied in New Castle County was that racial attitudes did not improve. In fact, during the first year, racial attitudes became slightly less positive for both students and parents, and the decreased level remained constant as desegregation continued. One factor to be considered in examining this outcome is the fact that opposition and litigation continued in the community and the school district during the 3 years of the study. This opposition centered around the issue of district organization, with the county finally being redistricted to form four school districts rather than one. The ongoing turmoil made more difficult the attempts by teachers, staff, administrators, students, parents, and the community to move forward with the business of education under desegregation.

Another area of inquiry was whether changes in attitudes were the same for all students and parents, and, if not, what the differences might be. Although the overall patterns of change did not differ greatly according to the intervening

variables examined, there were initial differences for these variables which, in most instances, held across time. Thus, in general, desegregation in New Castle County was not associated with differential effects for blacks and whites; for men and women; for families with elementary, junior high, or senior high students; for families with differing social status; or for families from the five different former school districts. Differences that were apparent prior to desegregation remained during the 3 years of the study. For example, desegregation was not related to differential changes that would have narrowed the gap in racial attitudes between black parents and white parents, or between black students and white students.

The data indicate that there were positive changes in attitudes toward desegregation itself. This finding is subject to a variety of interpretations. One explanation, particularly in light of the strong and continued opposition to desegregation up to and even following implementation of the court order, is that expectations of what desegregation would be like were worse than the actual implementation. Once desegregation was actually implemented, with little violence and no major conflict, parents may have realized that desegregation was not going to be as negative as they had feared.

The educational attitudes of students appeared to change only slightly. The one consistent finding was a decrease in educational self-concept during the third year of desegregation. Because grade level differences were found consistently for educational self-concept, it may be that this overall pattern is a developmental phenomenon, unrelated to desegregation. Students did not perceive a decline, or an improvement, in their school's academic climate, even though their parents perceived a decline in school quality. These attitudinal findings should be viewed with the fact in mind that actual achievement for students improved throughout the school district following desegregation.

Changes associated with desegregation were not the same for all of the parents and students in the study. Race appeared to be an important intervening variable, both initially and over time. Child's grade level at the time of desegregation implementation also appeared to be related to racial and educational attitudes. The results reported here agree with other research findings of more positive racial attitudes among minority members (e.g., Beck & Sobol, 1978) and more positive racial attitudes and adjustment to school desegregation among elementary school students (Erbe, 1977).

Although only 5 of the 11 former school districts in New Castle County were sampled, comparisons of demographic characteristics indicate that the study sample was reasonably representative of the county population as a whole. Although some aspects of the desegregation process in New Castle County were unique, the findings presented here may prove useful to other schools and communities involved in the implementation and maintenance of a school desegregation plan.

REFERENCES

Alexander, D. (1979, April). *An investigation into the absence of black parental involvement in desegregated schools.* Paper presented at the annual meeting of the American Educational Research Association, San Francisco. (ERIC Document Reproduction Service No. ED 173 480)

Allen, H. M., Jr., & Sears, O. (1979). *White opposition to busing in Los Angeles: Is self-interest rejuvenated?* Paper presented at the annual meeting of the American Psychological Association, Toronto, Canada. (ERIC Document Reproduction Service No. ED 166 353)

Allport, G. W. (1954). *The nature of prejudice.* Cambridge, MA: Addison-Wesley.

Alston, J. P., & Crouch, B. (1978). White acceptance of three degrees of school desegregation. *Phylon, 39,* 216–224.

Altevogt, B., & Nusbaumer, M. (1978). Black parents and desegregation in Fort Wayne. *Integrated Education, 16,* 31–34.

Beck, W. W., & Sobol, M. G. (1978). *Perception versus reality in educational attitudes.* Paper presented at the annual meeting of the Southwest Educational Research Association, Austin, Texas. (ERIC Document Reproduction Service No. ED 155 268)

Beers, J. S., & Readon, F. J. (1974). Racial balancing in Harrisburg, achievement and attitudinal changes. *Integrated Education, 12,* 35–38.

Bullock, C. S., & Stewart, J. (1977). Perceived parental and student racial attitudes. *Integrated Education, 15,* 120–122.

Cohen, E. (1975). The effects of desegregation on race relations. *Law and Contemporary Problems, 39,* 271–299.

Cohen, E. (1980). Design and redesign of the desegregated school: Problems of status, power, and conflict. In W. Stephan & J. Feagin (Eds.), *School desegregation: Past, present, and future* (pp. 251–280). New York: Plenum Press.

Erbe, B. M. (1977). Student attitudes and behavior in a desegregated school system. *Integrated Education, 15,*123–125.

Fort Wayne Urban League. (1977). What high school students think of desegregation. *Integrated Education, 15,* 131–133.

Hawley, W. D. (1979). Getting the facts straight about the effects of school desegregation. *Educational Leadership, 36,* 314–321.

Johnson, D., & Johnson, R. (1979). Cooperation, competition and individualization. In H. Walber (Ed.), *Educational environments and effects* (pp. 101–119). Berkeley, CA: McCutchen.

Loveridge, R. L. (1978). *Parent perceptions of magnet schools as a method of desegregation.* Paper presented at the annual meeting of the American Educational Research Association, Toronto, Canada. (ERIC Document Reproduction Service No. ED 170 384)

Mercer, J. R., Iadicola, P., & Moore, H. (1980). Building effective multiethnic schools: evolving models and paradigms. In W. Stephan & J. Feagin (Eds.), *School desegregation: Past, present and future* (pp. 281–308). New York: Plenum Press.

Milwaukee Journal. (1976). Students view desegregation in Milwaukee. *Integrated Education, 14,* 43–51.

Regens, J. L., & Bullock, C. S. III. (1979) Congruity of racial attitudes among black and white students. *Social Science Quarterly, 60,* 511–522.

Rosenthal, S. J. (1979). Racism and desegregation at Old Dominion University. *Integrated Education, 17,* 40–42.

St. John, N. H. (1975). *School desegregation: Outcomes for children.* New York: Wiley.

Schofield, J. W. (1981). Desegregation school practices and student race relations outcomes. In W. Hawley (Ed.), *Assessment of current knowledge of school desegregation strategies: Vol. 5, A review of the empirical research on desegregation: Community response, race relations, academic achievement and resegregation* (pp. 88–171). Nashville, TN: Vanderbilt University, Center for Education and Human Development Policy, Institute for Public Policy Studies.

Serow, R. C., & Solomon, D. (1979). *The proximity hypothesis of parental support for desegregation*. Washington, DC: National Institute of Education (ERIC Document Reproduction Service No. 171 824).

Sheehan, D. C. (1980). A study of attitude change in desegregated intermediate schools. *Sociology of Education, 53,* 51–59.

Slavin, R. E., & Madden, N. A. (1979). School practices that improve race relations. *American Educational Research Journal, 16,* 169–180.

9

School Desegregation
SOME ECOLOGICAL AND RESEARCH ISSUES

ROBERT J. GRIFFORE

School desegregation is a phenomenon that must be understood in relation to the context in which it occurs. It is an ecological event involving virtually every American institution and social process. It is rooted in such basic social realities as racial and social class segregation; it involves major American institutions including the school and the family; and remedies proposed and implemented have rested on the Constitution and a growing body of case law.

Yet the treatment of school desegregation as an ecological phenomenon has been cursory at best. The ways in which school desegregation has modified and complicated linkages among elements of the human ecosystem remain largely ignored. The roots of this problem may be illuminated by an analysis of the sociology of knowledge relative to school desegregation. Such an analysis may offer a useful perspective from which to understand some of the dynamics that have tended to restrict and limit the extant dominant view of school desegregation. This approach investigates the rationale for and uses made of knowledge, as well as the relative importance and power of those who would benefit from the knowledge.

This chapter includes material abstracted from R. Griffore, "Third Generation School Desegregation Issues: An Agenda for the Future." In *Procedures and Pilot Research to Develop an Agenda for Desegregation Studies*, which was funded entirely by the U.S. Department of Education. The Department of Education disclaims any official endorsement of the materials, and no product endorsement should be inferred.

ROBERT J. GRIFFORE ● Department of Family and Child Ecology, Michigan State University, East Lansing, Michigan 48824.

Historiography in school desegregation usually involves legal and political dimensions very heavily; thus, school desegregation history is not an ecological history. It does not, for example, systematically involve the educative process in a balanced fashion. In particular, educative contexts outside the school, such as the family, have been virtually ignored.

In school desegregation history, it has been more or less common practice to divide the early development of school desegregation into two periods. One deals with first-generation issues, particularly the elimination of dual school systems and *de jure* and *de facto* segregation. The other deals with second-generation issues, such as the resegregation of desegregated schools and the various means by which segregated schools are maintained.

In recent years, considerable attention has been devoted to educational programs and achievement outcomes in desegregated schools. Educational components of school desegregation have thus represented a pivotal movement away from first- and second-generation issues. In the realm of educational issues, and achievement in particular, an ecological perspective is of great relevance. One group of factors that may be expected to be related to achievement outcomes consists of specific processes and methods of school desegregation. Here an ecological approach would consider, for example, the interrelationships of public opinion, the family, and particular modes of desegregation.

A second and relatively well-documented approach to explaining achievement outcomes relies on school factors, particularly school academic climate. Another group of possible explanatory factors involves student background variables, such as race and social class. However, such status variables may actually serve as poor proxies for other more relevant variables, such as family educational processes, actual parental behavior, the influence of siblings, and parental goals for education.

Many of these important family variables have been ignored, often due to the unchallenged parochialism of researchers. To the extent that research and intervention efforts are targeted toward schools, resources also tend to be targeted toward the schools and remain available for educational researchers. At the same time, resources for research and intervention with families may be diminished. The explicit recognition of the school or the family as the dominant influence on educational achievement, in general as well as in the context of school desegregation, involves the control of substantial resources and power. Thus, advocates of the dominance of either the family or the school in this equation typically portray the other's role as relatively minor.

Equally counterproductive to a balanced ecological approach are the tendencies of educational researchers to employ convenient rather than appropriate research techniques and to adhere to biased values in planning their research. If educational research were less encumbered by these restrictions, it might produce information useful to a range of interests and constituencies. This chapter will

suggest ways in which a balanced ecological approach to research might produce knowledge with diverse uses and applications.

AN ECOLOGICAL PERSPECTIVE

School desegregation has provided a classic example of the large-scale implementation of social engineering without the knowledge of predictable consequences. Fundamentally, desegregation seeks to eliminate dual school systems and provide educational equity for all students. However, its actual range of outcomes is complicated by the complexity of the ways in which school desegregation interacts with the ecological contexts in which it occurs. Whereas the Constitution and case law together provide the rationale for desegregation wherever it occurs, the ecological variables that mediate its outcomes variously involve local social class characteristics, the extent of racial segregation in the schools, the mechanisms by which segregated schools have been achieved and maintained, the teaching and administrative characteristics of the school system, public sentiment surrounding desegregation, local housing patterns, unique family variables, and other diverse factors.

The range of outcomes and consequences of desegregation and desegregation's relation to diverse mediating variables indeed may have augmented the tendency to see this phenomenon in reductionist terms. Moreover, reductionist terms are typically more productive of policy-relevant conclusions. Ultimately, the complex reality of desegregation will be recognized, and its recognition may be facilitated through an understanding of the underlying dynamics of the reductionism that obscures the complexity.

The conduct of research and the pursuit of knowledge may be understood on several levels. At a personal level, a variety of motives might be identified; in a discipline or defined area of study, certain ideological, political, existential, social, and cultural influences might guide and stimulate work in particular directions.

The sociology of scientific knowledge has directed attention toward the influences of "the invisible college." This is a network of colleagues who, although perhaps widely dispersed geographically, maintain an effective communication network. Through this network, they share recent advances in their domain of scholarly activity and perhaps foster their particular motives and ideological positions as well.

The sociology of scientific knowledge also describes ways in which researchers working within the boundaries of a discipline address themselves to interests beyond these boundaries. Thus, the focus is on the relationship between the pursuit of knowledge and the interests of diverse constituencies.

In the case of school desegregation, the research issues, the various con-

stituencies, and the many changes that have occurred over the years are linked together in interesting ways. We will first examine some of these historical trends relating research directions and the interests of various constituencies.

FIRST- AND SECOND-GENERATION ISSUES

As typically framed, the history of school desegregation is essentially a legal history, heavily influenced by group conflict (Orfield, 1978). It has become both useful and conventional to distinguish between first-generation issues and second-generation issues in school desegregation. First-generation issues were related to achieving that for which *Brown v. Topeka* provided the legal basis. Although the Supreme Court ruled that no state shall "deny to any person within its jurisdiction the equal protection of the laws," it was left to the states to find ways to ensure that equal protection became a reality in the realm of education. Thus, following *Brown,* attention was devoted primarily to the elimination of segregated school systems, in compliance with the law. In the South, *de jure* segregation, the result of official segregation policies and practices, was the target. In the North, the focus was on *de facto* segregation, said not to result from official policy. In both cases, however, the major goal was to eliminate dual school systems, in order that white and minority students could attend school together. The techniques by which this might be accomplished and the extent of the progress toward this goal constituted the fundamental first-generation issues in the realm of school desegregation.

The attainment of substantial progress toward the goal of eliminating dual school systems eventually became problematic. Although segregated schooling may have been reduced to some extent, there remained many of the motives and political foundations that had consistently led to segregated schools. Therefore, to the extent segregated schooling was reduced, efforts were made to develop new and creative means of maintaining segregation between white and minority pupils in school districts, and in buildings within districts. These techniques produced a set of second-generation issues in school desegregation. Although the range of these techniques is rather extensive, the following three examples will serve to illustrate the concept of second-generation issues:

1. placement of minority students in special education classes and low ability groups in disproportionate numbers
2. use of excessively harsh and discriminatory discipline measures with minority students
3. use of discriminatory practices against minority teachers and staff

These techniques have proved effective in resegregating students into predominantly minority schools and/or classrooms.

Evidence of the disproportionate placement of minority students in special education classes has been cited by Mercer (1971). A principal mechanism for such placement has been the IQ test score, although questions have been raised concerning whether the IQ score is an inherently culturally biased indicator (Meyers, Sundstrom, & Yoshida, 1975).

In addition to special education placement, ability grouping has also been used to resegregate students in desegregated schools (Samuda, 1975). Indeed, this practice has been responsible for resegregation in several states (Mills & Bryan, 1976).

Resegregation may also be accomplished by removing black students from school. There is evidence that minority students have been kept out of school more often by harsh disciplinary measures than have white students (U.S. Department of Health, Education, and Welfare, 1975). Some school districts have been charged with discriminatory disciplinary practices under Title VI of the 1964 Civil Rights Act and the Emergency School Aid Act of 1973 (Bullock, 1978).

Discriminatory practices against minority faculty and staff have provided another means of resisting the goals of full integration and have maintained an open door for resegregative practices. The courts have recognized the importance of faculty and staff desegregation, and they have dealt with appropriate assignment patterns in several districts, including Boston, Tampa, and Louisville (U.S. Commission on Civil Rights, 1976a).

DESEGREGATION AND PUPIL ACHIEVEMENT

Beyond these second-generation issues, perhaps no other question has arisen with such frequency or interest as the impact of school desegregation on pupil achievement. Attorneys and judges have been interested in this question primarily because such information is needed to assess the outcomes of diverse desegregation plans. Generally, the available evidence has been advocacy-based and inconclusive. Yet the testimony of expert witnesses has been accepted readily, in spite of its probably inherent biases. Indeed, expert witnesses for the opposing parties to a legal suit might claim that desegregation alternatively improves pupil achievement or jeopardizes it, citing two very different and mutually exclusive complements of research studies in support of these positions. Judges and attorneys have heard expert witnesses present completely opposite testimony, often involving statistical arguments and technical language. Thus, researchers' efforts have often been used for the purpose of advocacy.

Consequently, there has remained a crucial and unanswered question: Why is desegregation followed by significantly enhanced achievement in some schools and districts, whereas in other schools and districts there is little or no change, or the white–minority achievement gap may actually increase? To date, research

has not accounted for differences in the impact of desegregation on achievement across districts or across buildings within districts. Thus, a basic problem has not been solved, and the effect of desegregation on white and minority achievement still cannot be predicted with accuracy (Weinberg, 1977).

EXPLAINING EDUCATIONAL OUTCOMES

To answer the question of where to search for explanations of achievement outcome differences across desegregated schools, it is useful to take a historical perspective. Educational researchers have long attempted to understand why in some schools pupils achieve at high levels, whereas in others they do not. We may now pose the question more specifically for desegregated schools, with the expectation that some of the findings of research on the general question also apply to the specific case of desegregated schools.

One place to begin the search for insight into this matter would be school input and composition variables. The research most clearly associated with these variables is that of Coleman *et al.* (1966), which is best known for its conclusion that the influence of the school on educational outcomes is relatively small, compared to home background factors. This line of inquiry also produced Jencks' (1972) general conclusion that schools contribute very little to levels of intellectual inequality across groups.

A popular hypothesis in line with this research is that because socioeconomic and home characteristics are of critical importance, minority students could achieve better if they attended school with white middle-class students. It appears, however, that this notion may not be based in fact (St. John, 1975). Moreover, the feasibility of maintaining predetermined specific student body racial and socioeconomic compositions may be questioned.

In addition, there may be problems inherent in the evidence supporting socioeconomic background and composition factors, beginning with the Coleman *et al.* (1966) *Equality of educational opportunity* (EEOP) report that initially advocated the importance of these factors. For example, Bowles and Levin (1968) argued that Coleman's regression analysis may have overestimated the effect of background variables on pupil achievement, relative to school factors. Another problem may lie in the possibility of misinterpreting the EEOP findings. These findings do not mean that school has no effect on pupil achievement, but rather that school factors do not necessarily explain large proportions of pupil achievement variance (Armor, 1972).

Another problem inherent in these broad background factors is that they do not contribute significantly to an ecological analysis. These variables are an imprecise representation of certain aspects of the ecosystem surrounding educational outcomes. Race and social class should not be substituted as proxy variables for a range of family process variables that may be operationally defined

with a greater degree of precision. These family processes include, for example, parental behavior and sibling behavior, relative to directly encouraging or perhaps discouraging children's achievement. Also included are complicated facets of the interface between the family and the school.

THE FAMILY, ACHIEVEMENT, AND DESEGREGATION

To understand the depth and scope of the role of the family in the educative process, one might begin with a review of some of the outcomes of early education programs involving parents. Based on such a review, Bronfenbrenner (1974) observed that intellectual gains coincident with programs involving parents were longer lasting than either completely home-based programs or completely school-based programs. Because parents and children remain together after the school-based processes have ceased, certain aspects of the treatment may be sustained, thereby having a continued influence. Bronfenbrenner (1974) concluded that the family is the most effective system in which to foster child development, and that relative to the child's intellectual development, totally school-based interventions are not as likely to produce sustained effects as are cooperative home–school efforts.

Bronfenbrenner's conclusion is consistent with the findings of Goodson and Hess (1975). After reviewing 29 preschool programs, which involved parents in varying degrees, they concluded that in general the programs were effective for school readiness, and that these programs were likely to provide children with a relatively lasting achievement advantage. Moreover, programs that focused more heavily on parents were more likely to produce the greatest educational benefits for children, and particularly efficacious were one-to-one parent–teacher modes of operation.

Whereas these program outcomes are, in themselves, important, Goodson and Hess (1975) observed that parents' sense of personal control also improved, and that parents' resulting behavior changes tended to benefit other children in the home. Thus, it would appear that programs to assist parents in teaching their children may be expected not only to produce significant and lasting educational benefits, but also to have a positive effect on parents' general educative behavior.

Other studies have produced findings consistent with these conclusions. For example, White and Watts (1973) studied mother–child interaction and found that mothers who were most successful in an educative capacity regularly stimulate their children and challenge and encourage them intellectually. In a study at the Appalachian Educational Laboratory, Gotts (1978) also reported consistent findings.

Whereas the home–school relationship at the preschool level demonstrates the effectiveness of the family vis-à-vis educational outcomes, other research conducted on school-aged populations corroborates the finding. For example,

Project Follow Through programs specifically designed to build contextual factors into the educational process have been very successful (House, Glass, McLean, & Walker, 1977).

Some research has sought to document the existence of the influence of the family on achievement, and other studies have described some family process variables and parent–child interaction variables that might explain this effect (Bloom, 1964). In one of these investigations, Wolf (1964) described 13 separate process variables while studying the mothers of 11-year-old children. These 13 variables collectively formed three environmental press factors that together explained approximately one half of these children's IQ score variance. In another study, six family environmental variables were found to account for between 30% and 60% of the variance on subscales of the Metropolitan Achievement Test (Dave, 1963). Thus, it appears that both intelligence and achievement variance are explained by family environment variables.

Marjoribanks (1972) conducted a study in southern Ontario that indicated that approximately half the variance in the tested children's verbal performance could be explained by sociopsychological factors in the family environment. Moreover, Walberg and Marjoribanks (1973) found that different family stimulation patterns were related to specific abilities.

In conjunction with these studies, there have been numerous attempts to describe different models of family variables as they related to children's intellectual performance. Walberg and Marjoribanks (1976) have reviewed 12 such models. A principal distinguishing shortcoming of many of these models is their focus on fixed or background variables, such as socioeconomic status, rather than alterable, and operationally definable process variables. To the extent models of family influence incorporate such variables as family size, socioeconomic status, and ethnicity, they include factors presumably fixed and unalterable by educational intervention.

Substantial space has been devoted here to the effects of family environment on achievement. This is necessary due to the typically perfunctory way educational researchers have treated the role of the family. If one seeks to identify the complement of variables that explain pupil achievement, either in general, or specifically in desegregated schools, the role of the family must be seriously considered.

SCHOOL LEARNING CLIMATE AND ACHIEVEMENT

Recently, educational researchers have focused on the relationship between school learning climate and pupil achievement. Identifying the learning climate factors that make schools effective for all pupils has become a preoccupation among educational researchers for a good reason—namely, that these factors

can powerfully influence the achievement of pupils at all levels. Indeed, there is a very persuasive body of research linking achievement outcomes with school learning climate (Brookover & Schneider, 1975; Brookover, Gigliotti, Henderson, & Schneider, 1973; Brookover, Beady, Flood, Schweitzer, & Wisenbaker, 1979). These studies indicate that a large proportion of achievement variance may be explained by school climate indicators.

At the classroom level, Anderson (1970) found that climate variables measured by the Learning Environment Inventory exercised a powerful force on achievement. At the building level, climate variables can also exercise a powerful influence. In one study, six climate variables accounted for a significant proportion of math achievement variance, and when these climate variables were controlled, socioeconomic status became insignificant in explaining achievement (McDill, Meyers, & Rigsby, 1967).

Brookover and Lezotte (1977) conducted a study of six improving schools, and two declining schools, relative to pupil achievement, over a 3-year period. A favorable academic climate was found to explain the achievement increases in the improving schools. Specifically, in the improving schools there was significantly greater attention given to basic reading and mathematics objectives than was the case in declining schools. Also, in the improving schools, more teachers tended to believe that all pupils could master the basic objectives. In addition, the principals in improving schools were more likely to assume more responsibility for teaching basic skills than were those in declining schools. Indeed, in the improving schools, the principal played the role of instructional leader rather than allowing the teachers to carry this responsibility alone. This is consistent with the overall greater acceptance of a model of accountability in the improving schools.

Other studies have noted similar characteristics of learning climate. Madden, Lawson, and Sweet (1976) studied 21 pairs of elementary schools differing on the basis of pupils' standardized achievement scores but matched on other school characteristics. Within pairs, higher achievement was accounted for substantially by such factors as higher teacher satisfaction, better administrative support services, less grouping for instructional purposes, more adult volunteers, greater access to materials outside the classroom, higher teacher expectations, more intensive student monitoring, and greater support from building principals.

An important aspect of the overall school learning climate is the observable student prestige order that exists in the school. This status structure may vary across schools such that some schools place all students in differentiated status levels, whereas in other schools all students occupy relatively equal status levels.

It is quite possible that schools may expect less from lower-status students, and it is reasonable to hypothesize that these low expectations apply particularly to lower-status minority students. Cohen (1980) has proposed that differentiated statuses that are associated with racial and ethnic characteristics are associated

with differential expectations. Thus, low-status minority students may be expected to achieve at levels lower than other students who have both racial and school status-structure advantages.

The probable influence of status structures on pupil achievement provides a basis for suspecting that by changing classroom status structures in multiracial classrooms, measurable improvement may be produced in the achievement of low-status students.

School learning climate may also heavily involve specific measurable teacher variables shown to be associated with pupil achievement. Teacher indirectness is one such variable (Herman, 1967). Teacher acceptance of students' ideas is also positively related to pupil achievement (Perkins, 1965). Teacher praise (Wright & Nuthall, 1970), teacher questioning of behavior (Wallen, 1966) and teacher use of reinforcement (Hewett, Taylor, & Artuso, 1969) are also positively related to achievement.

Although school learning climate is a potent force on pupil achievement, there has been little research on its impact in desegregated schools. However, St. John (1975) observed that levels of expectations, school norms, and the overall organization of instruction may explain some achievement gains coincident with desegregation.

DESEGREGATION PROCESS VARIABLES

Another domain of factors in which explanations of achievement variance may be found includes specific processes and methods of school desegregation. This brings into play, in an ecological framework, the influence of public opinion. Although little systematic empirical work has been done to document the impact of public opinion on desegregation, experience indicates that it can be a potent force. A concerned populace, aroused by the specter of deleterious educational outcomes, is capable of manifesting sufficient influence to demonstrate that social policy ultimately must be responsive to public opinion.

School desegregation does not independently affect school achievement; rather, it interacts with other contemporaneous factors. Therefore, its outcomes are unpredictable unless they are understood in the context of these other factors. Moreover, the influence of these other factors can lead to the realization of desirable educational outcomes.

The interaction of judicial decisions and public opinion may introduce educational issues into the implementation of school desegregation. Pupil transportation in a desegregation plan is only one of many factors that influence a wide range of educational outcomes. Public opinion may call for such ancillary programs as curriculum revision, instructional development, in-service training, and specific modes of community involvement. For example, the Hillsborough County, Florida, School District implemented a staff desegregation program

(U.S. Commission on Civil Rights, 1976b), incorporating both a program for training teachers in human relations and an effort to increase the number of minorities on staff (National Institute of Education, 1977).

In the Williamsburg, South Carolina, district, desegregation involved the use of individualized instruction, black culture curriculum, staff desegregation, and human relations training (U.S Commission on Civil Rights, 1977).

In several cases, specific classroom learning techniques have been employed coincident with desegregation. For example, in Baltimore, Slavin (1977) introduced the use of biracial cooperative learning teams, a technique that can lead to achievement increases for both black and white students.

An example of extensive community involvement in the implementation of a desegregation plan is provided by Charlotte-Mecklenburg, North Carolina. Mini-school boards and other community involvement techniques together elicited the participation of 10,000 community volunteers for the schools (National Institute of Education, 1977).

These particular features of specific desegregation plans may be considered in the context of the proposition that if one applies the same treatment to diverse situations, the differences across these situations may be expected to increase in some fashion. Uniformity applied to diversity augments that diversity. Bereiter (1969) observed this phenomenon in recognizing that the highest degree of equity cannot be attained by presenting all pupils with uniform instruction. Offering the same level of instruction to children with dissimilar levels of prior achievement will produce even greater achievement variance. Perhaps in an analogous fashion, uniform school-desegregation plans may be expected to produce a wide range of outcomes across dissimilar school systems. Therefore, specificity and ecological considerations should guide desegregation in each case.

ECOLOGICAL RAMIFICATIONS

An ecological framework that relates desegregation outcomes to such factors as public opinion implies a multidirectional pattern of influence. Desegregation affects and is affected by social organizations and institutions that compose the public. Among these organizations is the family. Although the effects of desegregation on family life are important, they are little understood. Some studies, such as that of Green, Darden, Griffore, Parsons, Schmidt, and Schweitzer (1982), have measured various parental attitudes, which may be proxies for actual indicators of the impact of desegregation on family interaction patterns and for ecological variables affecting the family. Other studies have focused on white flight to the suburbs, a phenomenon which may be an inferred indicator of family dynamics (Coleman, Kelly, & Moore, 1975; Rossell, 1978). The impact of demographic variables on reactions to school desegregation has also been investigated. For example, in Berkeley, California, Jensen (1970) studied

racial differences in attitude as related to differences in length of residence, educational attainment, and homeownership status.

Yet there has been a relative dearth of research on the effects of desegregation on family interaction patterns. It is true that parents' attitudes correspond to some degree to the impact of desegregation on their children (Beck & Sobol, 1978; Serow & Solomon, 1979), but larger-scale family impacts have generally failed to attract educational researchers' attention. One exception is a study conducted in New Castle County, Delaware, in the framework of a countywide metropolitan desegregation plan (Griffore, 1982). A sample of parents whose children were involved in the desegregation plan were surveyed to determine the extent to which desegregation caused conflicts in the family.

One of the focal areas was conflict between parents' work schedules and childrens' schedules involving busing to and from school. In general, parents reported that family conflict increased slightly coincident with school desegregation. Parents also were asked whether, as a direct consequence of desegregation, they found the need to pay for special child care services. Approximately 7% of the respondents indicated they did, and the average expenditure was $52.50 per month. Approximately 6% also indicated that they needed to assume other expenses directly attributable to desegregation, and these other expenses averaged approximately $30. In addition, 15% of the respondents reported difficulty in their work that they attributed directly to desegregation.

Additional research on the impact of desegregation on the family is clearly indicated, particularly if it illuminates the relationships that may develop between the school, parents, siblings, and pupils within specific modes of school desegregation. Unfortunately, the zeitgeist among educational researchers suggests that such family-relevant issues will continue to be ignored. The research that now has currency is that which suggests that the schools are the most important locus of influence on students' educational achievement, and that the family's influence is too minimal to justify any additional attention. This research seeks to demonstrate that school-related variables are very powerful determinants of pupil achievement; that many schools are doing a poor job; that schools could benefit greatly from programs designed to improve their learning climate characteristics; and that this effort merits all available resources.

Holding the schools accountable for educational improvements serves another purpose—namely, relieving the family of this responsibility. To the extent low pupil achievement can be linked to institutional weaknesses in the school, it is not associated with racial and/or cultural characteristics of the family. In desegregated districts where minority children consistently score lower than white pupils on achievement tests, blaming the minority family is obviously a problematic approach, and it is not surprising that the schools have usually been expected to assume the burden of accountability. Nevertheless, ignoring the impact of the family on achievement in desegregated schools diminishes the

likelihood that the role of the family will be considered by educational researchers. An important area of concern will thus continue to be overlooked.

FUTURE DIRECTIONS FOR DESEGREGATION RESEARCH

The increased role of the judiciary in educational policy-making has decreased the role of educational research. Desegregation research has contributed to this situation by building a large and inconsistent body of literature. Why have educational researchers been attracted to school desegregation? Perhaps it is because they have been attracted to large quasi-experimental situations, more than to the nature of the experiment *per se*. But if researchers believe that a good way to understand education is through experimentation, they might also welcome the opportunity to exercise more control over the nature of the treatment. They might also be interested in a much more comprehensive network of educationally relevant variables from which hypotheses could be derived and tested systematically. There is no compelling reason why the only large-scale, quasi-experimental educational research concerning issues of discrimination should be conducted by the courts. Although school desegregation as an experiment has a legitimate rationale, the failure to experiment more broadly with the schools is unfulfilling and ultimately wasteful. What researchers have learned from their experience with desegregation as an ecological experiment may be applied extensively.

Bronfenbrenner (1976) has described an ecological framework for educational research that defines relevant variables in a nested arrangement of environmental systems and that involves experimentation to transform the relationships among these systems. School desegregation is an example of an experimental treatment involving these environmental systems.

One environmental system is the *microsystem,* the place in which learners engage in specified activities and roles at specified times. The *mesosystem* is formed by the interrelations of the several settings that contain the learner at some point in time. These settings include the school, the family, and the peer group. The notion of the *exosystem* is predicated on the fact that the mesosystem is extended to the domain of concrete social structures and major institutions of society, including mass media, government agencies, transportation, and the many service professions. The concrete representatives of the major institutions of society are conceptualized in their abstract and global sense in the *macrosystem*. The macrosystem also conceptually represents the underlying ideology and the basic meanings of society.

Ecologically framed educational experiments have certain characteristics (Bronfenbrenner, 1976, 1979). An ecological approach involves the investigation of reciprocal relationships between learners and all aspects of the environmental

systems in the educational process. Learning outcomes are affected by all levels of environmental systems, and ecologically framed research recognizes this complex system of relationships.

With respect to generalizability, the requirements of ecological research are reminiscent of Brunswik's (1956) notion of probabilistic functionalism. That is, ecological research should involve as many different types of settings as possible so that generalizability of findings will be enhanced. Moreover, ecological educational research should involve the "innovative restructuring of prevailing ecological systems in ways that depart from existing institutional ideologies and structures by redefining goals, roles, and activities and providing interconnections between systems previously isolated from each other" (Bronfenbrenner, 1976, p. 14).

In this ecological approach to research, there lies the possibility of gaining a more thorough understanding of educational institutions by transforming them profoundly. Thus far, one of the few such transforming experiments whose results can be seen on a large scale is school desegregation. There is as yet little evidence concerning the results of other ecological experiments in similar magnitude.

Educational research would do well to conform to the basic requirements for ecological research by utilizing experiments that effect transformations on the ecosystem. Understanding educational institutions and the educative process ultimately depends on understanding the ecology of education. In recent years, the courts have assumed increasing power and authority in desegregation experiments, but neither the courts nor researchers have taken the leadership in challenging the contemporary status of the ecology of education by conducting even more profound experiments.

DESEGREGATION RESEARCH: CLIENTS AND CONSTITUENCIES

Whereas the courts have been a major constituency of desegregation research, the opportunity to conduct research that might have important policy implications has also in effect made researchers their own clients. Such an opportunity sets the stage for the emergence of researchers' own biases, prejudices, values, and preconceived notions.

To suggest that desegregation research and educational research are frequently value-laden is to understate the case. Indeed, this is inevitable, and arguments to the contrary are quite likely self-serving. Broguslaw (1967) described the process by which current professional and academic goals may be shaped by values acquired very early in life. The cloak of ethical neutrality is often a technique utilized by researchers who either cannot or will not recognize the framework of values that guide their work.

A classic example may be found in research concerning white flight as a consequence of desegregation. Coleman et al. (1975) embarked on a campaign

designed to demonstrate that desegregation produces white flight to the suburbs from central city school districts. Critics charged that Coleman had gone beyond his data in drawing conclusions, and that the research revealed a biased perspective (Pettigrew & Green, 1976). It is likely that both parties in this debate were guided by a substratum of firmly held values. In a debate where contradictory conclusions may be drawn from the same data, that value system wins the day which has the greatest political currency.

If desegregation research is to transcend the status of advocacy based on biased viewpoints, researchers must not only understand their own values; they must be willing to consider the values of others. That is, researchers should

1. understand their own values,
2. publicly state their values,
3. understand how they acquired these values,
4. have the courage to support these values,
5. be willing to accept objectively established truth even if it is inconsistent with their values, and
6. be willing to consider modifying their values.

There is no place in desegregation research for rigidity that is rooted in personal values that are impervious to factual data. Indeed, to the extent that political realities and the rigidity of individual values impact on desegregation research (and educational research, in general), the fundamental integrity of the research is in jeopardy.

NEW CLIENTS FOR DESEGREGATION RESEARCH

In 1980, the author participated in convening, at Michigan State University, three school desegregation research symposia sponsored by the U.S. Department of Education. Participants in one symposium were school administrators and school board members from geographically diverse areas. The purpose of this symposium was to identify essential research questions that the participants believed should form the desegregation research agenda in the near future. Altogether, 55 questions arose, some of which may be categorized and paraphrased as follows (Griffore, 1981):

1. In what ways, if any, is desegregation related to changed educational outcomes?
2. In what ways, if any, is desegregation related to racial relations?
3. What is the attitude of the public toward desegregation?
4. How can public attitudes about desegregation be changed?
5. What are the political ramifications and dimensions of desegregation?

6. In what ways can various segments of the community play significant roles in desegregation?
7. How should desegregation be accomplished for the best overall results?

These summary questions do not adequately reflect the insights and experiences that school administrators and board members brought to the symposium. Nevertheless, the questions suggest the range of concerns of the participants, many of whom had had a long involvement with desegregation.

A second symposium was held for attorneys and judges who had been involved in desegregation. Again, several researchable questions were generated. These questions might be categorized and stated as follows (Griffore, 1981):

1. What types of desegregation plans are most likely to be successful?
2. What are the outcomes of desegregation, both long-term and short-term?
3. What is the community's reaction to desegregation likely to be?
4. What are some of the characteristics of good teaching, and in particular, what type of instruction is likely to be most successful with minority students?

Again, these general questions do not adequately express the high level of insight that informed these attorneys' and judges' thinking about desegregation research.

Desegregation researchers, in addition to addressing both their own personal needs and the informational needs of educational administrators and the courts, should consider addressing the needs of other professionals who become involved in school desegregation. The third of the symposia convened at Michigan State University serves as an illustration. The purpose of this symposium was to explore ways in which desegregation could more effectively respond to the needs of media professionals. Participants in this symposium included newspaper reporters and television reporters, all of whom had been involved in covering desegregation in diverse geographic regions of the country. In the course of the discussion, the following provocative questions were generated (Griffore, 1981):

1. What is the public interested in learning about desegregation?
2. What dimensions of desegregation could be better covered by the media?
3. In what ways could the media work with school and community officials to effect a beneficial impact on the desegregation effort?
4. How does the presence of the media impact on desegregation?
5. What are the principal sources of information about desegregation for students, parents, and teachers?
6. How does the influence of the media compare to that of personal communication?
7. What types of information can be counterproductive to school desegregation?

8. In what ways could communication be facilitated between education officials and media personnel?

In addition, media personnel raised numerous questions concerning typical or predictable outcomes of desegregation for pupils, families, and communities. These participants demonstrated a truly ecological perspective in their views on the ramifications of desegregation, a perspective that representatives of other professions might well emulate.

SUMMARY

Setting an agenda for desegregation research in the future should involve broadening and expanding extant boundaries. Issues of importance to diverse constituencies should be considered important. Researchers' biases and subjective orientation, although inevitably influencing the research process, should not be permitted to restrict the scope of investigation. The most comprehensive perspective possible should be taken on the processes and products of school desegregation in the framework of the ecology of education. In retrospect, we can say that out of the phenomenon of desegregation, an extremely wide-ranging and powerful quasi-experiment, we have learned a number of fundamental facts about the relationship of education to the social and institutional exosystem.

REFERENCES

Anderson, G. J. (1970). Effects of classroom social climate on individual learning. *American Educational Research Journal, 7,* 135–152.

Armor, D. J. (1972). School and family effects on black and white achievement: A reexamination of USOE data. In F. Mosteller & D. P. Moynihan (Eds.), *On equality of educational opportunity* (pp. 168–229). New York: Vintage.

Beck, W. W., & Sobol, M. G. (1978, January 27). *Perception versus reality in educational attitudes toward school desegregation.* Paper presented at the Annual Meeting of the Southwest Educational Research Association, Austin, TX.

Bereiter, C. (1969). The future of individual differences. *Harvard Educational Review, 39,* 310–318.

Bloom, B. S. (1964). *Stability and change in human characteristics.* New York: Wiley.

Bowles, S., & Levin, H. J. (1968). The determinants of scholastic achievement: An appraisal of some recent evidence. *Journal of Human Resources, 3,* 3–24.

Broguslaw, R. (1967). Ethics and the social scientist. In I. L. Horowitz (Ed.), *The rise and fall of project Camelot* (pp. 107–127). Cambridge, MA: MIT Press.

Bronfenbrenner, U. (1974). *A report on longitudinal evaluation of preschool programs. Vol. 2.* Ithaca, NY: Cornell University Press.

Bronfenbrenner, U. (1976). The experimental ecology of education. *Educational Researcher, 5,* 5–15.

Bronfenbrenner, U. (1979). *The ecology of human development.* Cambridge, MA: Harvard University Press.

Brookover, W. B., Beady, C., Flood, P., Schweitzer, J., & Wisenbaker, J. (1979). *School social systems and student achievement: Schools can make a difference.* New York: Praeger.

Brookover, W. B., Gigliotti, R., Henderson, R., & Schneider, J. (1973). *Elementary school environment and school achievement.* East Lansing, MI: College of Urban Development, Michigan State University.

Brookover, W. B., & Lezotte, L. W. (1977). *Changes in school characteristics coincident with changes in student achievement.* East Lansing, MI: College of Urban Development, Michigan State University.

Brookover, W. B., & Schneider, J. (1975). Academic environments and elementary school achievement. *Journal of Research and Development in Education, 9,* 83–91.

Brunswik, E. (1956). The conceptual framework of psychology. *International Encyclopedia of Unified Science. Vol. 1, Pt. 2.* Chicago: University of Chicago Press.

Bullock, C. S. (1978). Federal law and school discrimination in the North. *Journal of Negro Education, 47,* 113–131.

Cohen, E. G. (1980). Design and redesign of the desegregated school: Problems of status, power and conflict. In W. G. Stephan & J. R. Feagin (Eds.), *School desegregation: Past, present and future* (pp. 251–280). New York: Plenum Press.

Coleman, J., Campbell, E. Q., Hobson, C. J., McPartland, J., Mood, A. M., Weinfelt, F. D., & York, R. C. (1966). *Equality of educational opportunity.* Washington, DC: U. S. Government Printing Office.

Coleman, J. S., Kelly, S. D., & Moore, J. A. (1975). *Trends in school desegregation, 1968–1973.* Unpublished paper, The Urban Institute, Washington, DC.

Dave, R. (1963). *The identification and measurement of environmental process variables that are related to educational achievement.* Unpublished doctoral dissertation, University of Chicago, Chicago, IL.

Goodson, B. D., & Hess, R. D. (1975). *Parents as teachers of young children: An evaluative review of some contemporary concepts and programs.* Washington, DC: Bureau of Educational Personnel Development.

Gotts, E. (1978). *Final report: Appalachian Educational Laboratory.*

Green, R. L., Darden, J., Griffore, R., Parsons, M., Schmidt, J., & Schweitzer, J. (1982). *Metropolitan school desegregation in New Castle County, Delaware. Final report to the Rockefeller Foundation.* East Lansing, MI: Urban Affairs Programs, Michigan State University.

Griffore, R. J. (1981). Third-generation school desegregation issues: An agenda for the future. In *Procedures and pilot research to develop an agenda for desegregation studies* (pp. 149–227). *A final report to the U. S. Department of Education.* East Lansing, MI: Michigan State University.

Griffore, R. J. (1982). Effects of school desegregation in New Castle County, Delaware, on family life: A preliminary study. In R. L. Greene *et al. Metropolitan school desegregation in New Castle County, Delaware. A final report to the Rockefeller Foundation* (pp. 473–485). East Lansing, MI: Urban Affairs Programs, Michigan State University.

Herman, W. (1967). An analysis of the activities and verbal behavior of selected fifth grade social studies classes. *Classroom Interaction Newsletter, 2,* 27–29.

Hewett, F., Taylor, F., & Artuso, A. (1969). The Santa Monica Project: Evaluation of an engineered classroom design with emotionally disturbed children. *Exceptional Children, 35,* 523–529.

House, E. R., Glass, G. V., McLean, L. D., & Walker, D. F. (1977). *No simple answer: Critique of the "follow through" evaluation.* Urbana: University of Illinois.

Jencks, C. (1972). *Inequality.* New York: Harper & Row.

Jensen, A. R. (1970). *Parent and teacher attitudes toward integration and busing.* Berkeley, CA: California Teachers Assocation. (ERIC Document Reproduction Service No. ED 041 092).

Madden, J. V., Lawson, D. R., & Sweet, D. (1976). *School effectiveness study: State of California.* Paper presented at the annual meeting of the American Educational Research Association, San Francisco.

Majoribanks, K. (1972). Ethnic and environmental influences on mental abilities. *American Journal of Sociology, 78*, 323–337.

McDill, E. L., Meyers, E. O., & Rigsby, L. C. (1967). Institutional effects on the academic behavior of high school students. *Sociology of Education, 40*, 181–189.

Mercer, J. R. (1971). Institutionalized Anglocentrism: Labeling mental retardates in the public schools. In P. Orleans & W. Rusell, Jr. (Eds.), *Urban affairs annual review: Vol. 5. Race change, and urban society* (pp. 311–338). Los Angeles: Sage.

Meyers, C. E., Sundstrom, P. E., & Yoshida, R. K. (1974). The school psychologist and assessment in special education. *School Psychology Monographs, 2*, 3–57.

Mills, R., & Bryan, M., (1976). *Testing–grouping: The new segregation in southern schools.* Atlanta: Southern Regional Council.

National Institute of Education. (1977). *School desegregation in metropolitan areas.* Washington, DC: Department of Health, Education, and Welfare.

Orfield, G. (1978). *Must we bus?* Washington, DC: The Brookings Institution.

Perkins, H. (1965). Classroom behavior and underachievement. *American Educational Research Journal, 2*, 1–12.

Pettigrew, T. F., & Green, R. L. (1976). School desegregation in large cities: A critique of the Coleman "white flight" thesis. *Harvard Educational Review, 46*, 1–53.

Rossell, C. H. (1978). *Assessing the unintended impacts of public policy: School desegregation and resegregation.* Boston: Boston University.

St. John, N. H. (1975). *School desegregation: Outcomes for children.* New York: Wiley.

Samuda, R. J. (1975). *Psychological testing of American minorities.* New York: Harper & Row.

Serow, R. C., & Solomon, D. (1979). *The proximity hypothesis of parents' support for desegregation.* Washington, DC (ERIC Document Reproduction Service No. ED 171 824).

Slavin, R. E. (1977). How student learning teams can integrate the desegregated classroom. *Integrated Education, 15*, 56–58.

U. S. Commission on Civil Rights. (1976). *Fulfilling the letter and spirit of the law.* Washington, DC: U. S. Government Printing Office.

U. S. Commission on Civil Rights. (1976b, March). *Transcript of Tampa, Florida, hearings.* 29–31.

U. S. Commission on Civil Rights. (1977, June). *Williamsburg County, South Carolina, case study of desegregation.*

U. S. Department of Health, Education, and Welfare. (1975). *Factsheet, student discipline.*

Walberg, H., & Marjoribanks, K. (1973). Differential mental abilities and home environment: A canonical analysis. *Developmental Psychology, 9*, 363–368.

Walberg, H., & Marjoribanks, K. (1976). Family environment and cognitive development: Twelve analytic models. *Review of Educational Research, 46*, 527–551.

Wallen, N. (1966). *Relationships between teacher characteristics and student behavior. Part 3.* Salt Lake City: University of Utah Press.

Weinberg, M. (1977). *Minority students: A research appraisal.* Washington, DC: National Institute of Education.

White, B. L., & Watts, J. C. (1973). *Experience and environment. Vol. 1* Englewood Cliffs, NJ: Prentice-Hall.

Wolf, R. M. (1964). *The identification and measurement of environmental process variables related to intelligence.* Unpublished doctoral dissertation, University of Chicago, Chicago, IL.

Wright, C., & Nuthall, G. (1970). Relationships between teacher behaviors and pupil achievement in three experimental elementary science lessons. *American Educational Research Journal, 7*, 477–491.

Index

THE ACHIEVEMENT OF WILLIAM STYRON

The Allegheny Courthouse is connected to the county jail by a stone arch bridge over Ross Street. It is named the Bridge of Sighs because the design is based on the sixteenth-century Bridge of Sighs in Venice, Italy.

The uniquely Romanesque-designed Allegheny County Courthouse includes a courtyard allowing natural light and fresh air to reach most of the rooms in the building from the courtyard and street. The building, designed by Henry Hobson Richardson, was placed on the National Register of Historic Places in 1973.

From high on the edge of Mt. Washington, the bronze sculpture *Point of View,* by James A. West, overlooks Pittsburgh's Golden Triangle. The sculpture portrays the October 1770 face-to-face meeting between George Washington and Seneca leader Guyasuta. The meeting took place while Washington was exploring land along the Ohio River.

Built in 1764, Fort Pitt Block House, at Point State Park, is the only surviving structure from Fort Pitt, an important British fortification during the French and Indian War. Today it is owned and operated by the Fort Pitt Society of the Daughters of the American Revolution of Allegheny County.

The original fountain at 36-acre Point State Park was installed in 1974 and reconstructed in 2013. The fountain's spray reaches a height of 150 feet before falling into a 200-foot-wide circular basin. It uses 500,000 gallons of recirculated water and is operated during the spring, summer, and fall seasons.

The tip of Pittsburgh's Golden Triangle was once a busy industrial zone and later a slum. It was authorized to become a state park in 1945 and is now Point State Park. Owned and managed by the Pennsylvania Bureau of State Parks, it receives around three million visitors annually.

The Smithfield Street Bridge spanning the Monongahela River is the second oldest street bridge in the United States and listed as a National Historic Landmark. The bridge, which opened for traffic in 1883 and was widened in 1889 and 1911, uses lenticular trusses to carry enormous weight.

Fort Pitt Museum, at Point State Park, is operated by the Senator John Heinz History Center. Through interactive displays, artifacts, and life-size figures, the 12,000-square-foot museum demonstrates the important role western Pennsylvania played during the French and Indian War, the American Revolution, and the birth of Pittsburgh.

One of the life-size, life-like displays at the Fort Pitt Museum is of Tamaqua, also known as King Beaver (?-1771), a Lenni-Lenape Native American who was a respected peace advocate and diplomat between the British, French, and Iroquois during the French and Indian War era.

The economic, shipping, and especially the historic military strategic location of present day Pittsburgh is interpreted at the Fort Pitt Museum through displays and actual artifacts.

A 2006 study revealed there are 446 bridges in the city of Pittsburgh, three more bridges than in Venice, Italy. This officially makes Pittsburgh the city with the most bridges in the world. Here we can see several bridges crossing the Allegheny River.

The glass walls of PPG Place reflect images of surrounding buildings and resemble a painting in the Modernist style.

At Gateway Plaza, honey locust trees offer shade and a sense of nature among the high-rise buildings. The TreeVitalize Pittsburgh program has planted over 20,000 trees since 2008 to improve the quality of life, the environment, and business in the Pittsburgh area.

The 44-foot rose granite obelisk sits at the center of PPG Place, providing a refreshing refuge for the city's Central Business District employees and a must-have photo-op for visitors. At night, changing colored lights and jetted fountains offer a spectacular show.

Every winter the fountain area at PPG Plaza is converted into an ice skating rink that is 2,000-square-feet larger than New York City's Rockefeller Center. A 60-foot-tall holiday tree graces the rink's center.

The Spirits of Giving From Around the World exhibit, held seasonally at PPG Place Wintergarden, displays life-size "Santas" and original paintings of Christmas customs and folklore from around the world. Here a Ukrainian head of house brings in shafts of wheat to place in a corner of the house.

(Middle) Every year during the winter holiday season, a gingerbread house competition and model train display is held in the PPG Place Wintergarden.

(Bottom left) In winter when the fountain at Point State Park needs to be turned off, it is replaced with a giant holiday tree as part of the annual Pittsburgh Light Up the Night celebration.

(Below) The Market Square 33-foot-high modern holiday tree, adorned with red and white spheres, glimmers with 150,000 LED lights twinkling and frolicking to synchronized holiday music.

PNC Firstside Park in Pittsgh's Central Business District is a privately owned park. It is open to the public and especially appreciated by the banking center's 1,500 employees who find the 1½ acres of green space a natural retreat from their offices.

The beautiful classic brick façade on Saint Mary of Mercy Roman Catholic Church, located on Stanwix Street, contrasts with the modern shimmering glass towers of PPG.

A Pittsburgh landmark, the Union Trust building on Grant Street was built in 1917 combining fifteenth-century French Gothic and late North French architecture. Its original purpose was to serve as a 240-store shopping arcade. Today it houses offices and is listed on the National Register of Historic Places.

Located at Heinz Hall Plaza along Liberty Avenue at Sixth Street, the 1981 Angela Conner sculpture, Quartet, and water fountain find inspiration in the natural elements of wind, water, and light.

At night the water fountain at Heinz Hall Plaza displays a composition of constantly changing colored lights.

21

Heinz Hall for the Performing Arts was built in 1927 as a movie theatre named Loew's Penn Theatre. Renovated and reopened as Heinz Hall in 1971, it is now the cornerstone of the Cultural District. The 2,676-seat hall presents 200 variety performances yearly and is home to the Pittsburgh Symphony Orchestra.

Built in 1903, the Gayety Theater in Pittsburgh's Cultural District was originally a vaudeville house. It was renamed The Fulton in the 1930s when it became a full-time movie theater. In 1995 it was renovated and has been called the Byham Theater ever since.

Located in Pittsburgh's Cultural District, the Westin Convention Center consistently receives impeccable reviews. Opened in 1986, it has accommodated notables such as South African leader Nelson Mandela, presidential candidate Bill Clinton, President George W. Bush, and Vice President Dick Cheney.

Water gracefully falls from a series of vertical granite columns at the Mellon Green Fountain, highlighting the center of the park.

(Opposite page) Springtime ornamental flowering cherry trees and daffodils beautify Mellon Green in Pittsburgh's Central Business District. Surrounded by many prominent downtown office buildings, the green has been a popular lunchtime destination for downtown workers since it opened in 1985.

The top of the Park Building is adorned by colossal male architectural figure sculptures known as telamones that give the appearance of supporting the building. Telamone comes from an ancient Greek mythological word meaning "bearer" or "support." The building was built in 1896 on Fifth Avenue.

The iconic Fulton Building, built in 1906 in the Cultural District, served as an office building and a World War II VA hospital. From 2000 through 2001 it underwent significant renovations and is now the Renaissance Hotel. It was added to the National Register of Historic Places in 2002.

The skyscrapers in the Cultural District reflect the light from one another and create an abstract pattern.

The Keenan Building, with its red dome, has been a Pittsburgh landmark since it was constructed in 1907. Now dwarfed, it was once the tallest building in the city. The building was built by Col. Thomas J. Keenan, the principle owner of the forerunner newspaper to the Pittsburgh Press.

The trout sculpture outside the McCormick & Schmick's Seafood Restaurant building captures attention and is a downtown Pittsburgh landmark.

Holiday-decorated street lamps bring cheer and a holiday spirit to Pittsburgh's Central Business District.

A summer musical concert series is held yearly at US Steel Plaza on Grant Street. During the holiday season, the privately owned park, open to the public, also hosts a larger-than-life nativity scene known as the Pittsburgh Creche, which is sponsored by the ecumenical Christian Leaders Fellowship.

(Top left) Gardens and green space are found in all sizes and in numerous locations in downtown Pittsburgh. The Western Pennsylvania Conservancy maintains many of the garden plantings as seen here at Gateway Center.

(Top right) Part of a three-figure sculpture by James Simon, the Liberty Avenue Musicians in the Penn/Liberty Historic District of downtown Pittsburgh honors the musical heritage of the city. The cast concrete, clay figures tower 15 feet above the sidewalk. The sculpture was erected in 2003.

People in Pittsburgh always look up, in more ways than one. The top of Gulf Towers displays a pyramid of colored lights that change according to weather conditions, showing temperature, precipitation, humidity, and wind speed. If a Pittsburgh pro team has a winning game, the towers display black and gold lights.

33

Construction of the cathedral-like thirteenth- and fourteenth-century English Gothic style First Presbyterian Church on Sixth Avenue was contracted in 1905 on land donated by the heirs of William Penn.

Original stone and quartered oak beautify the interior of the First Presbyterian Church. Two 30-foot-high solid oak doors, each weighing two tons, are at the front of the sanctuary.

The Frick Building, built in 1902 on Grant Street, dominated the Pittsburgh skyline for fourteen years. When constructed, the building was considered rather innovative by having a basement power-generating plant and washrooms on all floors. Today it is listed on the National Register of Historic Places.

The ornamental bronze Kaufmann's clock was added to Pittsburgh's oldest department store's facade in 1913. The clock has since become a famous city landmark and meeting place.

Completed in 2003, the David L. Lawrence Convention Center, along the Allegheny River, was one of the world's most environmentally friendly buildings at the time it opened. Pittsburgh's steel bridges inspired the building's design.

The unique Tenth Street Water Feature flows beneath the David L. Lawrence Convention Center. This meandering pedestrian walkway descends 17 feet and is surrounded by a flowing stream with waterfalls, pools, and lights. It was built with private financial support with assistance from state and federal sources.

37

Five 85-foot-tall flag poles fly the American, Pennsylvania, Pittsburgh, Boy Scouts of America, and one of the historic predecessors of Old Glory flags at Flag Plaza-Scout Center on Bedford Avenue. Vivian W. Lehman donated the plaza to the BSA, Laurel Highlands Council, in memory of her husband Chester.

Next to Flag Plaza-Scout Center is an exact replica of the Liberty Bell that was cast in London's Whitechapel Foundry. The Boy Scouts use the bell during the Historic Flag Ceremony.

Robert Morris University's Pittsburgh campus in the downtown area is just twenty minutes away from its main campus in Moon Township. The university offers 60 undergraduate degree programs and 20 graduate degree programs. It has an enrollment of around 5,200 undergraduate and graduate students from 42 states and 32 nations.

The 720,000-square-foot Consol Energy Center was completed in 2010 and replaces the Civic Arena, also known as Mellon Arena. The center serves as home to NHL's Pittsburgh Penguins and the Arena Football League's Pittsburgh Power. Celebrities who have performed at the arena include Paul McCartney and Lady Gaga.

(Above) Located near the Strip District, the Senator John Heinz History Center, an Affiliate of the Smithsonian Institution, is the largest history museum in Pennsylvania. In addition to telling the story of Pittsburgh and Western Pennsylvania's contributions to the world, the six-floor museum houses the Western Pennsylvania Sports Museum.

From the 1920s until fast food chain restaurants took over in the 1960s, the Heinz Luncheonette catered to the lunchtime trade with healthy fast food at an economical price in a clean environment. Although gone from the American landscape, one has been recreated in the Senator John Heinz History Center.

(Top middle) In discovering 250 years of Pittsburgh history at the Senator John Heinz History Center, visitors learn the important contributions made by immigrants to the culture and economic growth of the region. Exhibits display the various ethnic clothing and cultures that enriched the city, such as the Slovak exhibit seen here.

(Top right) Abolition and civil rights struggles in Western Pennsylvania are interpreted at the Senator John Heinz History Center. In addition, the vital contributions that African Americans made to the nation and the city are honored in the museum's From Slavery to Freedom section.

One section of the Senator John Heinz History Center is designated as the Discovery Place. Through hands-on interactive exhibits and games, children can learn about 250 years of Pittsburgh history and culture from the Native Americans to the present high-tech economy.

Once home to mills and factories, Pittsburgh's Strip District became a produce wholesale center in the early twentieth century. Today the area has transformed into a historic district of unique shops, ethnic food providers, art studios, restaurants, and nightspots. "Strip" refers to the narrow section of land along the Allegheny River.

Unique, trendy, and cutting-edge costume jewelry is displayed on the open-air sidewalk by one of the Strip District's retailers.

The original Primanti Bros. restaurant in the Strip District has been a Pittsburgh tradition, with its unique sandwiches, since its founding in 1933 when it started catering to hungry truckers. Over the years it has received so much media attention that some employees are now celebrities themselves.

(Bottom left) The famous Primanti Bros. sandwich consists of the customer's choice of grilled meat, coleslaw, tomato slices, provolone, and French fries between two slices of Italian bread. If customers want the coleslaw and fries on the side, they will have to do it themselves, but very few actually do.

(Below) Beginning as a four-page weekly in 1786, The Gazette was the first newspaper west of the Allegheny Mountains. Today the Pittsburgh Post-Gazette is the largest daily newspaper serving metropolitan Pittsburgh and has won six Pulitzer prizes since 1938.

The Strip District's Pennsylvania Railroad Fruit Auction and Sales Building was constructed in 1926 as a wholesale center for produce shipped into Pittsburgh. It is now a market of multiple retailers called the Pittsburgh Public Market. The steeples of St. Stanislaus Catholic Church loom behind the building.

The rotunda of the former Pennsylvania Railroad Union Station at Liberty Avenue was constructed in 1903 of grayish-brown terra cotta. A central dome skylight lit the interior during the day. The station was converted to apartments in 1988, however the rotunda is listed on the National Register of Historic Places.

At night new LED lighting inside the fountain at Point State Park and around the fountain plaza celebrates Pittsburgh's modern image as a national model of urban revitalization through the arts. Point State Park hosts more than 3 million visitors a year.

Visitors are encouraged to pause to admire the graceful curves and inlaid cobblestones in the reflecting pool under the portal bridge at the entrance to the Great Lawn and the fountain at the newly reconstructed Point State Park.

Opened in 1926, the Ninth Street, or Rachel Carson, Bridge is one of three parallel bridges spanning the Allegheny River, collectively called The Three Sisters. On Earth Day 2006 the bridge was renamed the Rachel Carson Bridge in memory of the local world-renowned naturalist and environmentalist.

On May 27, 1907, Rachel Carson was born in this modest clapboard house overlooking the Allegheny River in Springdale. She went on to become a noted writer, naturalist, and ecologist. In 1962 she warned the world about the long-term negative effects of misusing pesticides in her groundbreaking book, Silent Spring.

Several posthumous recognitions have been given to Rachel Carson, but the one she might have personally appreciated is a 35-mile-long hiking trail dedicated in her honor. She hiked several of these areas in her youth. Shown here is the Rainbow Bridge along the trail in Harrison Hills Park.

The 277-foot-long riverboat Gateway Majestic sails on the Allegheny River near the 9th Street, or Rachel Carson, Bridge. The Majestic was built in 1987 in Florida and sailed through the Gulf of Mexico, then up the Mississippi and Ohio Rivers to arrive at Pittsburgh.

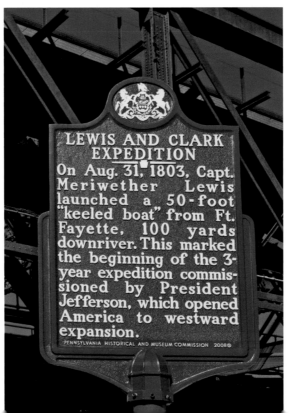

LEWIS AND CLARK
EXPEDITION
On Aug. 31, 1803, Capt.
Meriwether Lewis
launched a 50-foot
"keeled boat" from Ft.
Fayette, 100 yards
downriver. This marked
the beginning of the 3-
year expedition commis-
sioned by President
Jefferson, which opened
America to westward
expansion.
PENNSYLVANIA HISTORICAL AND MUSEUM COMMISSION 2008Ⓡ

In July 2013, the Sixteenth Street Bridge was renamed the David McCullough Bridge in honor of the native historian, author, and commentator. The 1,900-foot-long through-arch bridge was constructed in 1922 and spans the Allegheny River. It is now listed on the National Register of Historic Places.

Most people learn that the Lewis and Clark Expedition started from St. Louis, Missouri, in 1804. However the first leg of the 8,000-mile journey began on August 31, 1803, when Meriwether Lewis and his eleven volunteers set sail from Pittsburgh to meet Clark and his recruits assembling at Louisville, Kentucky.

49

Most, but not all, of Pittsburgh's downtown bridges were either constructed or later painted in the color Aztec Gold to match the city's official colors of black and gold.

Pittsburgh's bridges are not just for vehicle traffic, but are also very pedestrian friendly, as seen here at the Sixth Street, or Roberto Clemente, Bridge spanning the Allegheny. The bridge was renamed in 1998 in memory of the legendary Pittsburgh Pirate.

Beginning in 2009, "love locks" have been appearing on several Pittsburgh bridges. Inspired by a Serbian tale from World War I, the couple inscribes their names or initials on a padlock attached to the bridge railing and then tosses the key into the river to symbolize their unbreakable love.

Located on Pittsburgh's North Side, the National Aviary is said to be "America's only independent indoor nonprofit zoo dedicated exclusively to birds." It houses 500 birds representing more than 150 worldwide species, some rare. Visitors get up-close interaction with free-flying birds through large walk-through exhibits.

The Water Steps at Roberto Clemente Memorial Park along North Shore Drive, near Heinz Field, is not only an imaginative display of water landscaping, but also a place to wade and cool off on a hot summer's day. The park was named in honor of Pittsburgh Pirates great Roberto Clemente.

Playing his entire career in Pittsburgh between 1955 and 1972, Roberto Clemente's life and career ended tragically in an airplane crash as he was helping to deliver aid to Nicaragua earthquake victims. A bronze statue by Susan Walker honoring Clemente's 3,000th hit was erected in 1994 at PNC Park.

Willie Stargell, affectionately known as "Pops," is honored in another Susan Walker bronze sculpture erected in 2001 at PNC Park. Stargell played left field for the Pittsburgh Pirates from 1962 to 1982. During the Pirates' 1972 World Series victory, Stargell hit three home runs.

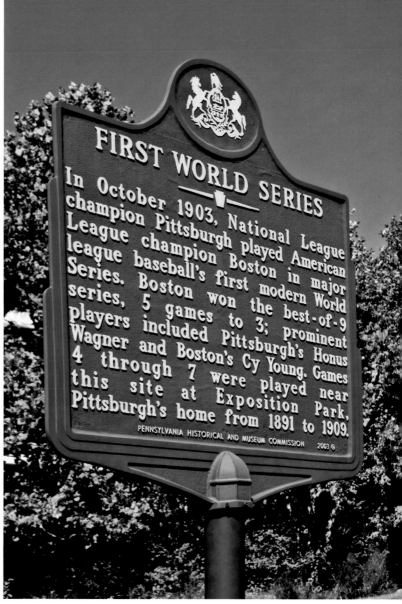

FIRST WORLD SERIES

In October 1903, National League champion Pittsburgh played American League champion Boston in major league baseball's first modern World Series. Boston won the best-of-9 series, 5 games to 3; prominent players included Pittsburgh's Honus Wagner and Boston's Cy Young. Games 4 through 7 were played near this site at Exposition Park, Pittsburgh's home from 1891 to 1909.

PENNSYLVANIA HISTORICAL AND MUSEUM COMMISSION 2003 ©

Near today's PNC Park, baseball's first modern Major League World Series was played, and it soon became a national obsession. While post-season games played from 1884 to 1903 were called "world series," they were considered to be exhibition games.

The Alcoa Building was built in 1998 along the North Shore Riverfront Park. The curving glass facade refers to Pittsburgh's rivers and the city's role in the glass industry. The Alcoa Corporate Center fills an entire block between the Rachel Carson and Andy Warhol Bridges.

The distinctive Alcoa Corporate Center building and the Seventh Street, or Andy Warhol, Bridge reflect in the Allegheny River at night.

For four weeks in the late summer of 2013, the Andy Warhol Bridge was covered with 580 knitted and crocheted panels in a community arts project called *Knit the Bridge*. It was possibly the largest "yarn bombing" in the world and was covered by the BBC, NPR, and the Huffington Post.

Opened in 1926, the Seventh Street Bridge was renamed the Andy Warhol Bridge in 2005 in honor of the late artist and Pittsburgh native. It is the only bridge in the United States named for a visual artist.

The Gateway Duchess, built in 1965, is 125 feet long and has a capacity of 310 passengers. Before coming to Pittsburgh in 1975, the riverboat was operated in Cleveland and Philadelphia. She is seen here sailing the Allegheny River near the 7th Street, or Andy Warhol, Bridge.

Pittsburgh Variations *by sculptor George Sugarman, on the North Shore, was installed in 1984. The abstract painted aluminum shapes reference the growth of Pittsburgh and represent the industry, business, finance, forests, and natural resources of Pennsylvania.*

Installed in 1984, Mythic Source *and* Piazza Lavoro *by sculptor Ned Smyth, at Allegheny Landing, honors Pittsburgh's contributions to American labor. The palm trees are used to remind viewers of nature and counterbalance the achievements of civilization.*

The Forks *by Isaac Witkin, a cast aluminum sculpture installed in 1984 at Allegheny Landing, represents the meeting of Pittsburgh's three rivers, Monongahela, Allegheny, and Ohio, and their impact on the city's economic development.*

Commissioned in 1984 by the construction company Mellon-Stuart, the bronze sculpture The Builders, by George Danhires, pays tribute to the builders of Pittsburgh's two renaissances. Located on the North Shore, the sculpture is based on photographs of two of the company's actual employees.

The Vietnam Veterans Memorial, on the North Shore at Riverfront Park, was erected in 1987 to honor Vietnam War veterans. Several artists took part in the final creation. The bronze figures symbolize soldiers reuniting with their families. The inverted lotus blossom is a Buddhist symbol for peace.

VIETNAM VETERANS
MONUMENT

A Ligonier blue rock marks the spot of the August 1763 Battle of Bushy Run fought between British forces moving west to Fort Pitt and a combined force of several Native American tribes. The Pennsylvania Historical and Museum Commission and the Bushy Run Battlefield Heritage Society administer the 213-acre battlefield.

The museum at the Westmoreland County Bushy Run Battlefield tells the story of the battle and life on the western Pennsylvania frontier in the eighteenth century. It includes the garments worn by the conflicting side.

In the eighteenth century, Pennsylvania's Allegheny Mountains and Ohio River Valley were the nation's frontiers with pioneers moving westward to establish homesteads and farms in the wilderness. The Bushy Run Battlefield contains a reconstructed log cabin typical of those built by frontier settlers.

(Opposite page) Three-foot-long fiberglass bass, created by Chris and Elizabeth Siefert, soar and turn in the wind next to the Children's Museum of Pittsburgh. Named in 2011 by Parents magazine as one of the nation's top ten children's museums, it seeks to inspire joy, creativity, and curiosity through interactive exhibits.

(Top left) The Fred Rogers Memorial Statue, located along North Shore Riverfront Park, was dedicated in 2009 in honor of the public television children's show personality and western Pennsylvania native. The 11-foot bronze statue is framed in an opening of the former Manchester Bridge pier named Tribute to Children.

(Top right) Susan Walker sculpted the bronze Law Enforcement Officers Memorial located along Riverfront Park near Heinz Field in 1996. Paid for by a non-profit organization, the memorial honors all law enforcement personnel, living and dead, and especially those who made the "supreme sacrifice."

The North Shore Riverfront Park and Trail, along the Ohio and Allegheny Rivers, is attractive to walkers and bicyclists for its stunning views of Pittsburgh's skyline. Native bird and butterfly species are also attracted to the native plants that have been re-established along the nearly mile-long park.

The Carnegie Science Center, on the banks of the Ohio River, offers hands-on exhibits that inspire and entertain, connecting science and technology with everyday life. The cone-shaped sculpture on top, titled E-Motion, displays a rainbow of different colors at night that change to reflect weather forecasts.

The Rivers Casino, along the Ohio River, opened in 2009 and is one of Pittsburgh's newest attractions. The casino has 3,000 slot machines, table games, four restaurants, a nightclub, and a 1,000-seat outdoor amphitheater. It reportedly produces several million dollars annually in county, city, and school taxes.

A popular outdoor exhibit at the Carnegie Science Center is the USS Requin, a Cold War-era submarine now permanently moored along the Ohio River. Daily tours are available, weather conditions permitting. During its service the submarine took on lengthy defense and scientific missions, some still classified today.

Flight 93 National Memorial in Somerset County is the nation's memorial to the forty passengers and crew who gave their lives on September 11, 2001, by overtaking a terrorist-hijacked airliner directed to the Nation's Capital. Wall of Names, positioned on the flight path, lists the names of the heroes.

Thirteen years in the making, the Southwestern Pennsylvania World War II Memorial was dedicated in December 2013, honoring those who fought in the war and those who labored on the home front. Constructed of granite panels, steel spires, and glass, the memorial interprets the war through photographs, diary entries, and quotations.

REUNION

"I flew…from Paris to Portugal to refuel; to Azores to refuel, and again to Newfoundland to refuel, and down to Delaware…I had to report…for final disembark, but I got some leave so I could meet my wife…She said she'd drive from where she was staying with her parents in Ohio…and be [in Pittsburgh] when I arrived. I got off the bus and walked in to the hotel and asked if Mrs. McConahey was registered 'Yes, she is.' Went up to her room…I knocked on the door, my knees very weak. Door opened and there she was. A long separation was over."

William M. McConahey, in Battalion Surgeon

William M. McConahey was born in Pittsburgh in 1919. As a Captain in the Army Medical Corps, he was with the 4th Division on D-Day and continued to serve in the European theater until after V-J Day. After the War he joined the medical faculty at the Mayo Clinic.

D-DAY LANDING

The D-Day assault of France on June 6, 1944 was the largest land-from-sea attack in military history. In his launch order, American General Dwight D. Eisenhower stated that the objective was to "bring about the destruction of the German war machine, the elimination of Nazi tyranny over the oppressed peoples of Europe…Your task will not be an easy one. Your enemy is well trained, well equipped and battle-hardened. He will fight savagely…"

Three days after D-Day, an eyewitness account appeared in the Pittsburgh Post-Gazette:

"We hit the beach at 7: a.m. We had just been riding in nice until the sailors let the ramp down. Then we got it…I fell on the boat floor when a bullet hit my arm. When we crawled into the water, mines blew up some of the fellows. When we got to the rocks, lots of us were gone. A couple of Navy fellows joined us…We separated and a fellow with me and I managed to dig a little hole. The shell fire blew the two sailors to bits."

THE END OF THE WAR

Hitler's suicide freed Germany from his fanatical determination to continue the war and led to its May 7, 1945 surrender to the Allies. In July, Japan was given an ultimatum to surrender unconditionally. When it refused, atomic bombs were dropped on Hiroshima and Nagasaki, killing 75,000 just on the days the bombs fell. The strikes led to Japan's declaration of surrender on August 15, 1945.

German and Japanese leaders were tried before international tribunals for their wartime conduct. Those found guilty were executed or sentenced to prison. American-led programs helped rebuild infrastructure and restore economies across Europe and Asia – including those of its principal foes. Russia's role in defeating Germany markedly altered postwar events by gaining domination of the Eastern and Central European countries its forces occupied at war's end. Soon, even Germany was partitioned by an "Iron Curtain" that divided the entire continent. And Russia was now a superpower engaged in a "Cold War" with the United States.

In 1961, President John F. Kennedy affirmed the principles for which he and so many others had bravely fought. He declared that America would again "pay any price, bear any burden, meet any hardship, support any friend and oppose any foe to assure the survival of liberty."

The focal point of Ohiopyle State Park is 20-foot-high Ohiopyle Falls on the Youghiogheny River. The Youghiogheny (yawki-gay-nee) flows fourteen miles through the park and is the best and most popular section of whitewater east of the Mississippi River. Under special regulations paddlers are allowed to run the falls.

Seen here passing through the borough of Ohiopyle, the Great Allegheny Passage, a former railroad corridor, is now a 150-mile trail for non-motorized recreation. Beginning at Pittsburgh's Point State Park, it continues to Cumberland, Maryland, where it joins the C&O Canal Towpath for another 185 continuous miles to Washington, DC.

Under the command of British Colonel George Washington, Fort Necessity was quickly and crudely built in Fayette County in 1754 during the French and Indian War. The battle that took place on July 3, 1754, was a victory for the French and Indians, with Washington surrendering.

Period-costumed historical interpreters demonstrate the lives and skills of the soldiers under the command of George Washington stationed at Fort Necessity. The site is now Fort Necessity National Battlefield and managed by the National Park Service.

(Opposite page) The General Edward Braddock Monument, located near the Monongahela River in Fayette County, honors the British commander-in-chief of the Thirteen Colonies during the French and Indian War. Mortally wounded in battle on July 9, 1755, his body was originally buried in the middle of the road to conceal his grave.

At the Pittsburgh Zoo a masai giraffe, Giraffa camelopardalis tippelskirchi, the tallest land mammal on Earth, uses its 18- to 20-inch-long tongue to grab some extra vegetation to help satisfy its diet of up to 75 pounds of food per day.

In addition to its educational and conservation programs, the Pittsburgh Zoo cares for and displays over 400 species, including twenty-two threatened or endangered species. Here a large endangered male western lowland gorilla, Gorilla gorilla gorilla, enjoys a snack of grass and clover in his open-air enclosure

(Opposite page) Built from 1913 to 1930, these Romanesque Revival and Beaux-Arts style buildings, in the Troy Hill neighborhood, once comprised the Heinz food-processing complex. They have now been converted to upscale apartments and added to the list of Pittsburgh History and Landmarks Foundation Historic Landmarks.

PPG Aquarium, a major component of the Pittsburgh Zoo, was renovated in 2000. This state-of-the-art aquarium displays and educates everything aquatic, from native Pennsylvania fish and aquatic amphibians, such as the increasing rare hellbender, to penguins and sharks.

Watching the beautiful moon jellyfish, Aurelia aurita, at PPG Aquarium can become a mesmerizing experience as they swim in their graceful, rhythmically pulsating movements.

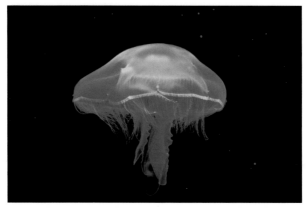

Built in 1912, the Allegheny Observatory is part of the Department of Physics and Astronomy at the University of Pittsburgh. Today its main research involves detection of extrasolar planets. It is listed on the National Register of Historical Places.

The Phipps Conservatory and Botanical Gardens in Schenley Park offers visitors nineteen indoor and outdoor gardens of natural wonder and beauty. The gardens were founded and given as a gift to the city in 1893 by Henry Phipps, a nineteenth-century millionaire and philanthropist.

A division of the Senator John Heinz History Center, Meadowcroft Rockshelter in Washington County is the archaeological site of the oldest human habitation in North America. Artifacts from the site show continual human habitation going back over 19,000 years to Paleo-Indian times. The site is a National Historic Landmark.

In addition to the archaeological site, Meadowcroft contains the Miller Museum on the family's former homestead. The museum has a vast and varied collection and displays of nineteenth-century rural life, including Delvin G. Miller's extraordinary eight-decade career in harness racing.

Passing through Pittsburgh and southwestern Pennsylvania, the Lincoln Highway stretches 3,389 miles from Times Square in New York City to Lincoln Park in San Francisco. Dedicated on October 31, 1913, it is affectionately called "The Main Street Across America" and was the first transcontinental automobile highway across the United States.

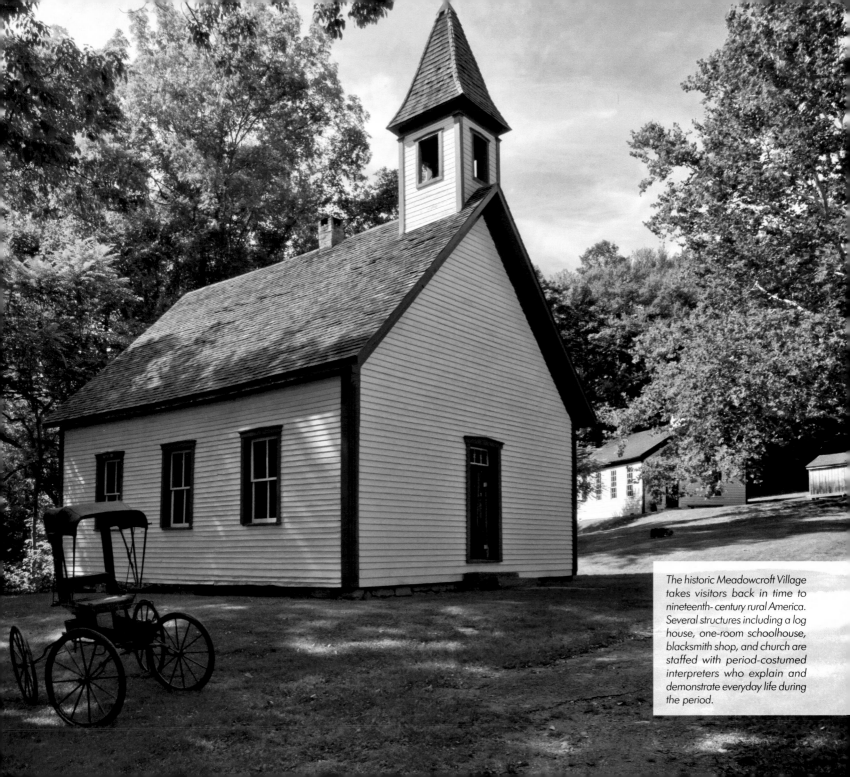

The historic Meadowcroft Village takes visitors back in time to nineteenth- century rural America. Several structures including a log house, one-room schoolhouse, blacksmith shop, and church are staffed with period-costumed interpreters who explain and demonstrate everyday life during the period.

The Soldiers' and Sailors' Memorial in the Oakland area was originally built as a memorial to Civil War veterans, but today it is a museum to honor all American war veterans.

Built in 1918, the Mary Schenley Memorial Fountain, at the entrance to Schenley Park, near the University of Pittsburgh, is also known as A Song to Nature. The two figures on top represent a reclining Pan, the Greek God of Shepherds, and a female singer above him playing the lyre.

(Opposite page) The 535-foot-high late Gothic Revival-style Cathedral of Learning at the University of Pittsburgh is the tallest educational building in the Western Hemisphere and towers above the surrounding Pittsburgh landscape.

The 42-story Cathedral of Learning contains the massive four-story gothic Commons Room used as a lobby, general study area, and for special events.

The Indian Nationality Room is an architectural tribute to India's preeminent seventh- to twelfth-century A.D. Nalanda University. This period is often referred to as the Indian Renaissance, a time of political and artistic unity and the peak of India's development of music, painting, literature, drama, and architecture.

The University of Pittsburgh's Cathedral of Learning contains twenty-nine Nationality Rooms, used as classrooms, honoring the ethnic groups that helped build Pittsburgh. The Austrian Room is decorated in the seventeenth- and eighteenth-century Baroque style. The crystal chandelier is patterned after the one in the formal dining hall of Vienna's Hofburg.

Dinosaurs in Their Time is one of the most popular exhibits at the Carnegie Museum of Natural History. Renovated and expanded in 2007, the exhibition scientifically and accurately illustrates the diversity of life during the Mesozoic Era, including the plants and animals that shared the environment at the time.

Eighty-four-foot long Dippy greets visitors to the Carnegie Museums of Art and Natural History. The landmark public sculpture was created in 1999 by the museums in recognition of the 100th anniversary of an expedition financed by Andrew Carnegie, which discovered the Diplodocus carnegii dinosaur fossils in Wyoming.

The Carnegie Museum of Natural History's Polar World, in the Wyckoff Hall of Arctic Life, is one of the largest exhibitions on Canadian Inuit culture in the United States. Its many exhibits also contain life-size and life-like dioramas such as this traditional sea mammal hunting scene.

In addition to special events and exhibits, the Carnegie Museum of Art has a permanent collection of over 35,000 objects including paintings, sculptures, drawings, photographs, film, video, digital imagery, architectural casts, decorative arts, and design.

The George A. Roberts Engineering Hall at Carnegie Mellon University is a hub for interdisciplinary research activities. Its various labs have significantly contributed to the success of major research.

Dedicated in 1938, the non-denominational Heinz Memorial Chapel at the University of Pittsburgh was a gift of John Heinz, founder of the H.J. Heinz Company, to honor his mother. Approximately 1,500 events, including religious services, tours, and concerts, are held annually in the chapel.

The neo-Gothic Heinz Memorial Chapel, designed by Charles Klauder, uses stone vaults, high ceilings with repeated arches, and twenty-three windows created by Charles Connick at his Boston studio. Constructed of Indiana limestone, the chapel's interior reaches a height of 100 feet at the nave.

Old Economy Village, operated by the Pennsylvania Historical & Museum Commission, is located about seventeen miles from downtown Pittsburgh in Beaver County. This state historical site and National Historic Landmark preserves and interprets the unique story and history of the Harmony Society, a highly successful nineteenth-century religious communal society.

Developed by the Civilian Conservation Corps (CCC) during the Great Depression, 3,075-acre North Park is a favorite place for jogging, biking, and strolling. In addition, it has an 18-hole golf course, 75-acre lake, ice-skating rink, swimming pool, nature center, and tennis courts.

The South Fork Fishing and Hunting Clubhouse in Saint Michael was the exclusive retreat for Pittsburgh's rich, who used it for parties, sailing, and fishing on the lake. Through negligence the lake's dam broke on May 31, 1889, causing $17 million in property damage and the loss of 2,209 lives.

The National Park Service restored the Unger House at the Johnstown Flood National Memorial in 1989, 100 years after the great flood. It was from this house that Elias Unger, president of the South Fork Club, noticed the water cresting the dam and desperately tried in vain to repair it.

The 635-foot high, forty-story PPG Place is often called "the crown jewel of the Pittsburgh skyline." The office tower's shimmering glass reflects the sky, rivers, hills, and buildings of Pittsburgh. The spires recall the city's historic neo-Gothic buildings while connecting with the newer modern geometric architectural style.

In the evening as the sun sets, the PPG Place tower receives the final sunlight in Pittsburgh and often reflects the color of a spectacular sunset farther west along the Ohio River.

On June 5, 2010, Pittsburgh residents and visitors broke the official Guinness World Record for the largest raft of canoes and kayaks. The event known as Paddle at the Point, off Point State Park, was part of Pittsburgh World Environment Day, when 1,619 canoeists and kayakers took part.

The Gateway Clipper Fleet moors at Station Square on the South Shore. Fully equipped and staffed, six riverboats tour Pittsburgh's three rivers year-round, offering sightseeing, dinner/dance, and entertainment cruises. Weddings, corporate meetings, and high school proms are held on the riverboats.

The days of highly polluted rivers in Pittsburgh now belong only in the history books. The rivers have made an epic comeback and are now sought after for recreation such as boating and fishing, as seen here on the Monongahela River near the Fort Pitt Bridge.

Heinz Field on the North Shore is reflected in the Ohio River. Opened in August 2001, the 65,500-seat, 1.49 million-square-foot stadium serves as home to the Pittsburgh Steelers and University of Pittsburgh Panthers American football teams. It replaces the former Three Rivers Stadium that served from 1970 to 2000.

Barge traffic is a common sight on Pittsburgh's rivers. According to the US Army Corps of Engineers, Pittsburgh is the busiest river port in the United States and the eleventh busiest port of any kind. The United States Coast Guard regulates shipping on the rivers.

The present Fort Pitt Bridge, spanning the Monongahela River near the confluence of the three rivers, was opened in 1959. It is a double-decked steel bowstring arch bridge with a total length of 1,207 feet and serves Interstate 376. The bridge has been featured in several Hollywood films.

(Above) Twenty-four artists of Pittsburgh's Industrial Arts Co-op created The Workers sculpture, dedicated in 2012 on the South Shore. It is a testament to the union of people, capital, rivers, and land that set Pittsburgh in motion.

(Top right) The original South Side Market House was built in 1893 but burned in 1914, then rebuilt in 1915. It was used to hold livestock and a fresh produce market. Today it serves as a senior citizen recreation center and was added to the National Register of Historic Places in 1976.

Pittsburgh is a city of hills. The hillside community of South Side Slopes is connected with narrow winding streets and a network of stairways. In addition to the reward of affordability and ample green spaces, residents are also guaranteed spectacular views of the city.

A familiar landmark on Pittsburgh's South Side is the gold onion-shaped domes of St. John the Baptist Ukrainian Catholic Church, whose history goes back to 1891. Christianity came to present-day Kyiv, Ukraine, in 988 A.D. and soon spread throughout Eastern Europe, including Russia many years later.

The South Side Flats, along the Monongahela River, has one of the largest Victorian main streets in the United States, with fifteen blocks of Carson Street named a National Historic District. To maintain the Victorian architecture, strict rules dictate the appearance of the building's exteriors.

101

The place to be on a summer afternoon is the fountain at Point State Park. Whether to jog, bike, fish, cool off by the fountain, or just to enjoy the beauty and take photographs, it is one of Pittsburgh's major attractions for both residents and tourists.

Once a bustling 40-acre freight and passenger complex for the Pittsburgh and Lake Erie Railroad, Station Square fell into despair with the decline of rail traffic in the 1970s. In the mid-1970s the area was revitalized into a magnificent indoor and outdoor shopping and entertainment complex.

The Fountain at Bessemer Court sits at the epicenter of Station Square. Every night, three times every hour, between mid-April and the Friday before Thanksgiving, hundreds of changing multi-colored water jets dance as high as 40 feet in the air, performing ten different water shows choreographed to music.

103

Pittsburgh's historical steel-making industry is remembered with a blast furnace blower erected at Station Square.

In addition to the Gateway Clipper Fleet, other charter companies sail Pittsburgh's rivers. The 110-passenger Fantasy, owned and operated by Pittsburgh Water Limo, is a two-level yacht complete with two bars and a dance floor.

Mid-nineteenth- and late-twentieth-century architectural styles are seen mixing in the Central Business District along the shore of the Monongahela River.

The Monongahela Incline, near the Smithfield Street Bridge, was built in 1870 to transport workers from Pittsburgh's downtown to their Mt. Washington homes 369 feet above. It is the oldest continuously operating funicular in the United States and, along with the Duquesne Incline, is one of two surviving funiculars in Pittsburgh.

MONONGAHELA
1870
INCLINE

The lights of Mt. Washington and the tracks of the Duquesne Incline reflect in the Ohio River at night.

USA Weekender's "2003 Annual Travel Report" ranked the breathtaking view of Pittsburgh's Golden Triangle, and the three rivers from Mount Washington, the second most beautiful place in America. From 800 feet below, the Duquesne Incline takes passengers up the steep slope.

As part of Station Square, Bessemer Court is an open area between the shops and restaurants that faces the Monongahela River and the Pittsburgh skyline. The court, dedicated to the city's steel heritage, is an area of enjoyment and relaxation for visitors.

An evening panoramic of Pittsburgh's downtown and the Monongahela River between the Fort Pitt Bridge and the Smithfield Street Bridge is viewed from Station Square's observation deck.

The last rays of the day's sunlight illuminate Pittsburgh's Gateway Clipper Fleet, moored for the night near Station Square and the railroad tracks that parallel the Monongahela River near Station Square.

Visitors to Station Square can take a set of stairs or ride an elevator to the top of a two-story observation deck to take in an outstanding view of the boats on the Monongahela River and of Pittsburgh's downtown skyline.

The Grand Concourse of the former Pittsburgh and Lake Erie Railroad Station has become a legendary dining destination since 1978. Dining guests are treated not only to an epicurean cuisine, but also a trip back in time to when railroad travel was elegant and stations were ornate works of art.

The Landmarks Building at Station Square, on the South Shore, was built in 1900 to house the Pittsburgh and Lake Erie Terminal Railroad Station. The building was remodeled in 1984 and now houses two restaurants. In 1974 it was added to the National Register of Historic Places.

Few scenes are more perfect and more inspiring than the view of Pittsburgh at night. American Pulitzer Prize-winning author Willa Sibert Cather said, "Pittsburgh was even more vital, more creative, more hungry for culture than New York. Pittsburgh was the birthplace of my writing." The same holds as true for many people today as it did in her time.

Resources

Books

Frye, Bob. *Best Hikers Near Pittsburgh.* Guilford, Connecticut: The Globe Press, 2009.

Greater Pittsburgh Convention & Visitors Bureau. *Official Visitors Guide Pittsburgh.* Pittsburgh, Pennsylvania: VisitPittsburgh, 2013.

Oberlin, Loriamm Hoff, Jean Phillips, and Evan M. Pattack. *Insiders' Guide Pittsburgh.* Helena, Montana: Falcon Publishing, 2000.

Websites

Ed Blazina. "Pittsburgh making a splash with refreshed Point State Park fountain." *Pittsburgh Post-Gazette.* http://www.post-gazette.com/hp_mobile/2013/06/07/Pittsburgh-making-a-splash-with-refreshed-Point-State-Park-fountain/stories/201306070182#ixzz352ivzpeH (accessed June 18, 2014).

Greater Pittsburgh Convention & Visitors Bureau. *Visit Pittsburgh.* http://www.visitpittsburgh.com/about-pittsburgh (accessed July 12, 2014).

Kimberly Powell. *10 Things to Love About Pittsburgh.* About.com Pittsburgh. http://pittsburgh.about.com/od/about_pittsburgh/tp/things_to_love.htm (accessed July 7, 2014).

Korean War Memorial. http://www.donnan.com/koreanmem.htm (accessed June 13, 2014).

J. Michael Krivyanski. Pittsburgh Neighborhoods Examiner. *Pittsburgh Area Public Art: Mythic Source and Piazza Lavoro.* http://www.examiner.com/article/pittsburgh-area-public-art-mythic-source-and-piazza-lavoro (accessed June 13, 2014).

Law Enforcement Memorial. City of Pittsburgh. http://pittsburghpa.gov/police/memorial (accessed June 13, 2014).

Livability. Top 10 Best Downtowns. http://livability.com/top-10/downtowns/top-10-best-downtowns/2015/pennsylvania/pittsburgh (accessed March 4, 2015).

Muller, Edward K. *Downtown Pittsburgh, Renaissance and Renewal.* http://upress.pitt.edu/htmlSourceFiles/pdfs/9780822942825exr.pdf (accessed July 12, 2014).

National Park Service. *Flight 93 National Memorial.* http://www.nps.gov/flni/index.htm (accessed July 3, 2014).

Pittsburgh, Pa—The Liberty Avenue Musicians. http://www.simonsculpture.com/public-art/pittsburgh,pa-the-liberty-avenue-musicians/ (accessed June 13, 2014).

Pittsburgh Water Limo. http://pittsburghwaterlimo.com (accessed June 17, 2014).

Popular Pittsburgh. *Information on Everything Pittsburgh.* http://www.popularpittsburgh.com/pittsburgh-info/pittsburgh-culture/creche.aspx (accessed June 17, 2014).

Rachel Carson Homestead. http://rachel_carson_homestead.myupsite.com (accessed July 3, 2014).

Senator John Heinz History Center. www.heinzhistorycenter.org (accessed July 4, 2014).

Sostek, Ann. "Mr. Rogers Takes Rightful Place at Riverside Tribute." *Pittsburgh Post-Gazette,* November 6, 2009. http://www.post-gazette.com/local/city/2009/11/06/Mr-Rogers-takes-rightful-place-at-riverside-tribute/stories/200911060261#ixzz34Zoj8llQ (accessed June 13, 2014).

Station Square Landmarks Entertainment. http://www.stationsquare.com (accessed June 16, 2014).

The National Aviary. http://www.aviary.org/about-us (accessed July 2, 2014).

The Port of Pittsburgh. http://www.ops.fhwa.dot.gov/freight/Memphis/appendix_materials/mccarville.ppt (accessed July 7, 2014).

Torsten Ove. "Southwestern Pennsylvania World War II Memorial Dedicated." *Pittsburgh Post-Gazette.* http://www.post-gazette.com/local/region/2013/12/06/Southwestern-Pennsylvania-World-War-II-Memorial-dedicated/stories/201312060175 (accessed June 30, 2014).

Venture Outdoors. *Paddle at the Point.* http://www.paddleatthepoint.com (accessed June 17, 2014).

Western Pennsylvania Conservancy. *TreeVitalize Pittsburgh.* http://waterlandlife.org/216 (accessed June 16, 2014).

WTAE Pittsburgh Action News. *Just How Many Bridges Are There In Pittsburgh?* http://www.wtae.com/Just-How-Many-Bridges-Are-There-In-Pittsburgh/7685514#ixzz34LYqbgWT (accessed June 10, 2014).